The Twentieth-Century English Novel

Garland Reference Library of the Humanities (Vol. 56)

The Twentieth-Century English Novel
An Annotated Bibliography of General Criticism

A. F. Cassis

Garland Publishing, Inc., New York & London

1977

Library of Congress Cataloging in Publication Data

Cassis, A   F
    The twentieth-century English novel.

    (Garland reference library of the humanities ; v. 56)
    Includes indexes.
    1. English fiction--20th century--History and
criticism--Bibliography. I. Title.
Z2014.F5C35 [PR881]   016.823'9'109   76-24735
ISBN 0-8240-9942-7

Printed in the United States of America

Contents

Preface

The need for a comprehensive bibliography of general criticism of the English novel of the twentieth century has impressed me since the late sixties. With the increasing interest in, and study of, twentieth-century writers at universities, especially in North America, and the consequent ever-increasing volume of criticism, it became apparent to me that a comprehensive annotated bibliography of general criticism was needed, not only as a speedy reference for the student and the scholar, or as an indication of those areas of research that have been neglected or "overworked," but also as a means to facilitate the task of any serious student in charting the various eddies and currents of the twentieth-century novel, tracing changes in technique and narration, re-examining and re-evaluating, after becoming aware of what has been said or thought on the subject.

There have been numerous bibliographies of individual novelists, and bibliographies of general criticism of the English novel of the twentieth century may be in the offing, or even in press; but perhaps the only other one presently in print—apart from the occasional checklist appended to book-length studies of the novel—is to be found in the pertinent sections of *The New Cambridge Bibliography of English Literature*, Vol. IV. Current checklists, annual and semi-annual, sometimes annotated, are also to be found in several periodicals, mostly post-1950 and concerned with contemporary criticism.

This volume is an attempt to compile and annotate a comprehensive bibliography of *general* criticism on the *English* novel of the twentieth century, as distinct from criticism on the American novel or the novel as written in various parts of the Commonwealth other than England. Furthermore, only critical works on the English novel as a literary genre are included, and studies on "pulp," "pop," or "popular" fiction, science fiction and the short story are excluded. (The rather arbitrary exclusion of

vii

PREFACE

these categories is not meant to cast any doubt on their value, but is necessary as a process of elimination to reduce the present volume to a reasonable size.)

Because the bibliography deals with criticism written from 1900 to 1972 on the English novel of the twentieth century, general studies that deal with novelists who had been writing in the latter part of the nineteenth century, but many of whose works appear in the twentieth, are included, e.g., J. Conrad and H. James—the latter not only because he was naturalized as a British subject in 1915, but also for his importance in the development of the novel. The critical studies listed are of a general nature; studies confined to individual writers are generally excluded. Critical works, whether books, chapters of books, articles or dissertations that deal with more than one novelist are included, as are selected works dealing with the art and technique of the twentieth-century novel and pertinent review articles. The cutoff date for critical studies is the end of 1972.

Entries are listed alphabetically by author. In the case of books, first editions and revised editions, if any, are mentioned. Some attempt has been made to give both English and American publishers when available. Reprints in the late sixties and early seventies are also mentioned to indicate their availability today. In the case of articles in periodicals, the titles of article and periodical, date and page numbers are always given. Generally speaking, the volume number is also included except where I have been unable to check the original periodical and had to rely on inter-library-loan photocopies. Anonymous articles are listed by title. In the case of dissertations and theses, the university and date of presentation are given, and if published, title, publisher and date are also listed. These are doctoral dissertations unless otherwise indicated. In most cases, annotations are descriptive rather than critical; i.e., they indicate content and attempt to give the central thesis or purpose of the work, and the novelists considered in the study. There are, however, some twenty-five titles asterisked to indicate that they are not presently available to me for examination. For the convenience of the student and scholar, two indexes are appended: one for novelists mentioned or discussed in the works cited, and the other containing references to thirty-eight selected topics and themes.

In an attempt to ensure comprehensiveness, I consulted the basic bibliographies of English literature listed below.

PREFACE

Abstracts of English Studies. 1958-

Annual Bibliography of English Language and Literature. 1920-

Annual Index to The Times. 1900-

Bibliographic Index: A Cumulative Bibliography of Bibliographies. 1937-

British National Bibliography. 1950-

Canadian Periodical Index. 1938-

Canadian Theses.

Comprehensive Dissertation Index.

Cumulative Book Index. 1928-

Dissertation Abstracts. 1938-

Doctoral Dissertations Accepted by American Universities. 1933-1955. Continued as *Index to American Doctoral Dissertations.* 1955-

Essay and General Literature Index. 1900-

Howard-Hill, T. H. *Bibliography of British Literary Bibliographies* (1969).

Index to Theses Accepted for Higher Degrees in the Universities of Great Britain and Ireland. 1950-

International Index to Periodicals. 1907-

McNamee, Lawrence F. *Dissertations in English and American Literature: Theses Accepted by American, British and German Universities, 1865-1964.* Supplement I (1969).

Modern Language Association Bibliography. 1919-

New Cambridge Bibliography of English Literature, Vol. IV.

New York Times Index. 1900-

Readers' Guide to Periodical Literature. 1900-

Subject Index to Periodicals; 1915-1961. Continued as *British Humanities Index.*

Year's Work in English Studies. 1919-

It has, however, become apparent to me since I started work on the bibliography in the Winter of 1972 that the comprehensiveness I envisaged at the beginning is virtually impossible. Undoubtedly, there are titles—I hope not too many—that have been missed or overlooked. Moreover, many of the 4000 or so titles which I dismissed as irrelevant or marginal might well have been included by another researcher; conversely, several of the 2800 or so titles which I included might have been dismissed on the same grounds

ix

PREFACE

by somebody else. As for errors, I can only beg the reader's indulgence and plead that in a work of such magnitude, errors, though undesirable, are perhaps inevitable. I am almost certain that some errors will be found, and I shall be grateful if they are brought to my attention.

Many have helped in the preparation of this volume. I am particularly grateful to Dr. D. Mueller for his help in translation and for reading the manuscript, Dr. E. H. Mikhail for advice and encouragement, Dr. B. F. Tyson for suggestions relating to the second Index, and my colleagues in the Departments of History and Modern Languages; to the University Library, especially the Inter-Library Loan Service; and to the Library at Trinity College, Dublin. I am also indebted to The University of Lethbridge for sabbatical leave in 1972/73 which got this study underway, and to the University Research Committee for a grant that enabled me to avail myself of the valuable services of Mrs. S. Buswell as a student assistant for three months in the summer of 1975. I also wish to thank Miss R. Ramtej, Miss D. Phillips and Miss B. Oleksy for the care and patience with which they typed the manuscript.

The University of Lethbridge   *A. F. Cassis*
Lethbridge, Alberta
August 1976

MASTER LIST AND TABLE OF ABBREVIATIONS

ABR	American Benedictine Review
Accent	Accent: A Quarterly of New Literature (Urbana, Illinois)
ACQR	American Catholic Quarterly Review (Philadelphia)
Adam	Adam: International Review
Adelphi	Adelphi (London)
Akzente	Akzente
ALB	Almanacco Letterario Bompiani
AM	American Mercury (New York)
America	America: A Catholic Review of the Week (New York)
AmR	American Review
Anglia	Anglia: Zeitschrift für Englische Philologie (Munchen)
AQ	American Quarterly (Philadelphia)
AR	Antioch Review
Archiv	Archiv für das Studium der Neuren Sprachen und Literaturen
ArQ	Arizona Quarterly
AS	American Speech
ASch	American Scholar
AsF	Asiatic Fiction
AsR	Asian Review (London). Also Asiatic Review (1914-1952)
Athenaeum	Athenaeum (London)
AtM	Atlantic Monthly (Massachusetts)
Audit	Audit (University of Buffalo)
AUMLA	Journal of the Australasian Universities Language and Literature Association
Author	Author (London)
AUR	Aberdeen University Review
BA	Books Abroad
BaratR	Barat Review
BBN	British Book News (London)
Bharat Jyoti	Bharat Jyoti (Bombay)
BJA	British Journal of Aesthetics (London)
BJEdS	British Journal of Educational Studies
BJES	British Journal of English Studies
BLM	Bonniers Litterära Magasin

BM	Blackwood's Magazine (Edinburgh)
Bookman	Bookman (London)
Bookman	Bookman (New York)
Books	Books (National Book League, London)
BoT	Books on Trial (Chicago). Superseded by Critic: A Catholic Review of Books and the Arts, 1957.
Broteria	Broteria: Revista de Sciencias Naturaes (Lisbon)
BSUF	Ball State University Forum
BuR	Bucknell Review
CAL	Colorado Academic Library
CalR	Calcutta Review
CasMF	Cassell's Magazine of Fiction (London)
CathW	Catholic World (Now New Catholic World)
CE	College English
CEA	CEA Critic
CentR	The Centennail Review (Michigan State University)
Century	Century (New York)
CF	Canadian Forum: A Monthly Journal of Literature and Public Affairs (Toronto)
CH	Current History (New York)
ChrC	The Christian Century (Chicago)
ChrS	Christian Scholar (New York)
Cithara	Cithara: Essays on the Judeo-Christian Tradition (St. Bonaventure, New York)
CJ	The Classical Journal (Milwaukee, Wisconsin)
CL	Česká Literatura
CLit	Current Literature (Current Opinion as from 1912)
CLM	Central Literary Magazine (Birmingham)
CLS	Comparative Literature Studies (University of Illinois)
CM	Canadian Magazine
CMF	Časopis pro Moderní Filologii
CML	Calendar of Modern Letters (London)
CO	Current Opinion. Supersedes Current Literature.
ColQ	Colorado Quarterly
Commentary	Commentary (New York)
Commonweal	Commonweal (New York)
CompL	Comparative Literature (Eugene, Oregon)

ConL	Contemporary Literature (supersedes Wisconsin Studies in Contemporary Literature)
ConLS	Contemporary Literary Scholarship
ContempR	Contemporary Review (London)
CorM	The Cornhill Magazine (London)
Correspondant	Correspondant (Paris)
CQR	Church Quarterly Review
CR	Century Review
Cresset	Cresset (Valparaiso, Indiana)
Crit	Critique: Studies in Modern Fiction (Minneapolis, Minnesota)
Criterion	Criterion: A Quarterly Review (London)
Critic	Critic: A Catholic Review of Books and the Arts, 1957 (Chicago). Supersedes Books on Trial.
Criticism	Criticism (Wayne State University, Detroit)
CritQ	Critical Quarterly
CritS	Critical Survey (University of Manchester)
Crossbow	Crossbow (London)
CSMWM	Christian Science Monitor Weekly Magazine
Culture	Culture: Revue Trimestrielle, sciences religieuses et sciences profanes au Canada (Montreal)
Daedalus	Daedalus: Proceedings of the American Academy of Arts and Sciences
Delo	Delo za zdravje (Ljubljana)
DESB	Delta Epsilon Sigma Bulletin (Alton, Illinois)
DeutR	Deutsche Rundschau
DHLR	The D. H. Lawrence Review (University of Arkansas)
Dial	Dial (Chicago)
Dialog	Dialog: A Journal of Theology (Minneapolis, Minnesota)
Discourse	Discourse: A Review of the Liberal Arts (Concordia College, Moorhead, Minnesota)
DM	Dublin Magazine (Formerly The Dubliner)
DN	Delaware Notes
DR	Dalhousie Review
DU	Der Deutschunterricht
DubR	Dublin Review (London)
DWB	Dietsche Warande en Belfort
EA	Etudes Anglaises

E&S	Essays and Studies by Members of the English Association
Economist	The Economist (London)
EDH	Essays by Divers Hands (Transactions of the Royal Society of Literature)
EdR	Edinburgh Review
EIC	Essays in Criticism (Oxford)
EigoS	Eigo Seinen [The Rising Generation] (Tokyo)
EJ	English Journal
ELLS	English Literature and Language (Tokyo)
ELT	English Literature in Transition (1880-1920). Supersedes English Fiction in Transition.
Encounter	Encounter (London)
English	English (London)
EngR	English Record
EngRev	English Review
EngW	Englishwoman
Envoy	Envoy: A Review of Literature and Art (Dublin)
ER	Ecclesiastical Review
Erziehung	Erziehung (Leipzig)
ES	English Studies
Esprit	Esprit
Esquire	Esquire (New York)
Ethics	Ethics
EUQ	Emory University Quarterly
Europe	Europe
EvR	Evergreen Review (New York)
ExpT	Expository Times (Aberdeen)
Extrapolation	Extrapolation (Wooster, Ohio)
FECR	Franciscan Education Conference Report (Herman, Pennsylvania)
FL	France Libre
FN	Filologičeskie Nauki
Folio	Folio: Papers on Foreign Languages and Literature
ForumN	Forum (New York)
ForumS	Forum (Houston)
ForumZ	Forum (Zaghreb)
FP	Filološki Pregled (Belgrade)

FQ	Friends' Quarterly (London)
FR	Fortnightly Review (London)
Freeman	Freeman (New York)
GBM	Golden Book Magazine (New York)
Genre	Genre (University of Illinois at Chicago Circle)
Gids	De Gids
GMHC	General Magazine and Historical Chronicle (Philadelphia)
GR	Georgia Review (Athens, Georgia)
GradJ	Graduate Journal
GradSE	Graduate Student of English
Gral	Du Gral (Ravensburg)
GRM	Germanisch-romanische Monatsschrift
Guardian	Guardian (Manchester)
Harper's	Harper's Magazine (New York)
Helicon	Helicon (London)
HJ	Hibbert Journal (London)
HM	Hommes et Mondes (Paris).Revue des Hommes et des Mondes as from 1946.
Hochland	Hochland (München)
Holiday	Holiday (Philadelphia)
Horizon	Horizon (New York)
HR	Holborn Review (London)
HudR	Hudson Review (New York)
Humanist	Humanist (London)
Humanitas	Humanitas (Brescia)
IER	Irish Ecclesiastical Record
IJES	Indian Journal of English Studies
IL	Innostrannaja Literatura (Moscow)
ILN	Illustrated London News
IM	Irish Monthly (Dublin)
Independent	Independent (New York)
Indice	Indice (Madrid)
IntBR	International Book Review (New York and London)
IntJE	International Journal of Ethics (Chicago)
IntL	International Literature (Moscow, 1931-1945). Superseded by Soviet Literature.
IntLA	International Literary Annual

JA	Jahrbuch fur Amerikastudien
JAAC	Journal of Aesthetic and Art Criticism
JAP	Journal of Abnormal Psychology (Chicago)
JAU	Journal of the Annamalai University
JE	Journal of Education (London)
JGE	Journal of General Education
JP	Journal of Philosophy
JPC	Journal of Popular Culture (Bowling Green University)
JSA	Journal of the Society of Arts
KanQ	Kansas Quarterly
KanS	Kano Studies (Ahmadu Bello University, Northern Nigeria)
Kolokon	Kolokon
KR	Kenyon Review
LA	Living Age (Boston)
LabM	Labour Monthly (London)
L&I	Literature and Ideology (Montreal)
L&L	Life and Letters (London)
L&P	Literature and Psychology (Fairleigh Dickinson University)
Lang&S	Language and Style
LanM	Les Langues Modernes
LAssoc	Library Association (London)
LB	Leuvense Bijdragen
LCrit	Literary Criterion (University of Mysore, India)
LDIBR	Literary Digest International Book Review (New York)
LDig	Literary Digest
LG	Literaturnaja Gazeta (Moscow)
LHZ	Literarischer Handweiser Zunächst für alle Katholiken Deutscher Zunge
LibA	Library Assistant (London)
LIBR	Literary International Book Review
Libraries	Libraries (Chicago)
Life	Life (Chicago)
Listener	The Listener (London)
Liter	Die Literatur: Monatsschrift für Literaturfreunde (Berlin & Stuttgart)
LitR	Literary Review (Fairleigh Dickinson University)

LivL	Livres et Lectures: Revue Bibliographique (Paris)
LJ	Library Journal
LL	Langue et Littérature
LM	London Magazine
LMer	London Mercury
LonA	London Aphrodite
LQR	London Quarterly Review
LR	Library Review
LTBM	Levende Talen, Berichten en Mededeelingen
Mainstream	Mainstream (New York)
MarQ	Maryland Quarterly
MCQ	Melbourne Critical Quarterly
MCR	Melbourne Critical Review
Meanjin	Meanjin Quarterly (University of Melbourne)
MerF	Mercure de France (Paris)
MFS	Modern Fiction Studies
Midway	Midway (Chicago)
ML&PSP	Manchester Literary and Philosophical Society. Proceedings.
MLN	Modern Language Notes (John Hopkins University)
MLQ	Modern Language Quarterly
MLR	Modern Language Review (London)
MM	Mariner's Mirror (London)
ModA	Modern Age (Chicago)
ModR	Modern Review
Mois	Mois
Month	Month (London)
Mosaic	Mosaic: A Journal for the Comparative Study of Literature and Ideas
MQ	Midwest Quarterly (Pittsburgh)
MQR	Michigan Quarterly Review
MR	Massachusetts Review (University of Massachusetts)
MSpr	Moderna Språk (Stockholm)
MTA	A Magyar Tudomanyos Akadémia Nyelv-és Irodalomtudomanyi Osztályának Közleményei
NA	New Age (London)
N&A	Nation and Athenaeum

N&Q	Notes and Queries
NAR	North American Review (Cedar Fall, Iowa)
Nation	Nation (New York)
NB	Die Neue Burecherschau (Munchen)
NBl	New Blackfriars. Supersedes Blackfriars.
NC	Nineteenth Century and After (London). Superseded by Twentieth Century.
NCF	Nineteenth Century Fiction
NCrit	New Criterion. Superseded by Criterion.
NDQ	North Dakota Quarterly
Nef	La Nef: Cahier Trimestriel
NER	New English Review (London)
Neuphilolog	Neuphilologus (Groningen)
NEW	New English Weekly (London)
NHQ	New Hungarian Quarterly
Ningen	Ningen (Japan)
NL	Nouvelles Littéraire
NLea	New Leader (New York)
NLit	Neue Literatur (Leipzig)
NLR	New Left Review
NM	Neuphilologische Mitteilungen (Helsinki)
NMonat	Neuphilologische Monatsschrift (Leipzig)
NMQ	New Mexico Quarterly
Norseman	Norseman: A Review of Current Events (London)
Novel	Novel: A Forum on Fiction (Brown University)
NR	National Review (New York)
NRe	Das neue Reich
NRel	Nouvelle Relève (Montreal)
NRep	New Republic (Washington)
NRF	Nouvelle Revue Francaise
NRs	Neue Rundschau
NS	Die Neueren Sprachen
NSoc	New Society
NSta	New Statesman (London)
NVT	Nieuw Vlaams Tijdschrift
NW&D	New Writing and Daylight
NWo	New World

NWW	New World Writing
NY	New Yorker
NYHTBR	New York Herald Tribune Book Review
NYPLR	New York Post Literary Review
NYRB	New York Review of Books
NYTBR	New York Times Book Review
Observer	Observer (London)
OM	Oxford Magazine
OR	Oxford Review
Outlook	Outlook (London)
ParA	Parliamentary Affairs (London)
ParRev	Paris Review
Paunch	Paunch (Buffalo, New York)
Person	Personalist: An International Review of Philosophy (Los Angeles)
Perspective	Perspective: A Magazine of Modern Literature (Washington University)
PhQ	Philosophical Quarterly
Phylon	Phylon (Atlanta, Georgia)
PL	Pamietnik Literacki (Warsaw)
PLL	Papers on Language and Literature (Edwardsville, Illinois)
PMASAL	Papers of the Michigan Academy of Science, Arts and Letters
PMLA	Publications of the Modern Language Association of America
PMLClub	Papers of the Manchester Literary Club
PNW	Penguin New Writing
Pointer	Pointer (Union of Liberal and Progressive Synagogues)
Polemic	Polemic (London)
Ponte	Il Ponte: Revista mensile di politica e letteratura (Florence)
PPR	Philosophy and Phenomenological Research
PQ	Philological Quarterly
PR	Partisan Review
PRev	Parents' Review (London)
PrS	Prairie Schooner (Lincoln, Nebraska)
PS	Pacific Spectator
PSA	Papeles de Son Armadans (Mallorca)

Psychiatry	Psychiatry: Journal for the Study of Interpersonal Processes
PsyR	Psychoanalytic Review (New York)
PubL	Public Libraries (Chicago)
PULC	Princeton University Library Chronicle
QQ	Queen's Quarterly
QR	Quarterly Review (London)
QRL	Quarterly Review of Literature (Princeton)
Ramparts	Ramparts (Menlo Park, California)
RB	Revue Bleue, Littéraire et Politique. Formerly Revue Politique et Littéraire: Revue Bleue.
RDM	Revue des Deux Mondes [Now Nouvelle Revue des Deux Mondes]
Realist	Realist (London)
REL	Review of English Literature (Leeds)
Renascence	Renascence: A Critical Journal of Letters (Milwaukee)
RES	Review of English Studies (London)
RF	Revue de France (Paris)
RG	Revue Germanique (Strasbourg)
RGB	Revue Générale Belge (Brussels)
RGen	Bibliothèque Universelle et Revue de Genève
RGS	Review of General Semantics
RH	Revue Hebdomadaire (Paris)
RLC	Revue de Littérature Comparée
RLM	Revue des Lettres Modernes
RLV	Revue des Langues Vivantes (Brussels)
RMag	Reader Magazine (Indianapolis)
RMS	Renaissance and Modern Studies (University of Nottingham)
RP	Revue de Paris
RQ	Riverside Quarterly (University of Saskatoon)
RUB	Revue de L'Université de Bruxelles
SA	Studi Americana
Salmagundi	Salmagundi (Flushing, New York)
Sammlung	Sammlung
Samtiden	Samtiden: Tidsskrift fur Politik, Litteratur og Samfunnssporsmal (Oslo)

S&SR	Sociology and Social Research (Los Angeles)
SAQ	South Atlantic Quarterly
SAR	South Atlantic Review
SatEP	Saturday Evening Post (Philadelphia)
SatR	Saturday Review (New York)
SchR	Schweizer Rundschau
ScM	Scientific Monthly
Scrutiny	Scrutiny (London)
SEER	Slavonic and East European Review (London)
SELit	Studies in English Literature (English Literary Society of Japan)
SLM	Southern Literary Messenger (Richmond, Virginia)
SMag	Scribner's Magazine [Superseded in 1939 by Scribner's Commentator]
SNNTS	Studies in the Novel (North Texas State University)
SocR	Sociological Review (Manchester)
SoR	Southern Review (Louisiana State University)
Spectator	The Spectator (London)
Speculum	Speculum: A Journal of Mediaeval Studies (Cambridge, Massachusetts)
SR	Sewanee Review
SS	Senior Scholastic
Standpunte	Standpunte (Cape Town, South Africa)
Studies	Studies (Dublin)
SuL	Sprache und Literatur
Sunday Times	Sunday Times
SWR	Southwest Review (Dallas, Texas)
Symposium	Symposium: A Quarterly Journal of Modern Foreign Literature (Syracuse University, New York)
SZ	Stimmen der Zeit
Tat	Die Tat (Leipzig)
TC	Twentieth Century (London)
TCL	Twentieth Century Literature (Los Angeles)
Theology	Theology (London)
Thought	Thought (Fordham University, New York)
Tilskueren	Tilskueren (Copenhagen)
Time	Time (New York)

WU	World Unity (New York)
WVUS	West Virginia University Studies: Philological Papers
WW	Wirkendes Wort
WWork	World's Work (London)
WZUG	Wissenschaftliche Zeitschrift der Ernst Moritz Arndt-Unversität Greifswald
WZUL	Wissenschaftliche Zeitschrift der Karl-Marx-Universität. (Leipzig)
YR	Yale Review
ZAA	Zeitschrift für Anglistik und Amerikanistik (East Berlin)
ZFEU	Zeitschrift für französischen und englischen Unterricht
ZFSL	Zeitschrift für französische Sprache und Literatur
ZNU	Zeitschrift für Neusprachlichen Unterricht (Berlin)
ZRL	Zogadnienia Rodzajow Literackich
ZSL	Poetica: Zeitschrift für Sprach-und-Literaturwissenschaft (Munchen)

1.

Bibliographies and Checklists

1   Adelman, Irving and Rita Dworkin. The Contemporary Novel:
    A Checklist of Critical Literature on the British and Amer-
    ican Novel Since 1945. (Metuchen, New Jersey: Scarecrow
    Press, 1972). [Also includes novelists who wrote before
    1945 but gained recognition or contributed major works after.
    Rather selective with 1968 as a cutoff date. Novelists are
    listed alphabetically. Refers to page numbers in books or
    articles that are relevant to individual novels].

2   Adler, Frederick Henry Herbert and Irma Talmage. American
    and British Novels of Our Day, 1890-1929. (Cleveland, Ohio:
    Cleveland College, Western Reserve University, 1929). [A
    list of novelists and their novels with a one-line review
    on novels written after 1925].

3   Altick, Richard D. and Andrew Wright. Selective Bibliog-
    raphy for the Study of English and American Literature.
    (New York: Macmillan; London: Collier-Macmillan, 1960;
    revised edition, 1963). [A guide to research materials
    with a highly selective list of titles in various fields].

4   Anderson, Eleanor Copenhaver, comp. A List of Novels and
    Stories about Workers. (New York: The Woman's Press,
    1938). [A twelve-page booklet containing some seventy
    titles of novels, some of which are briefly annotated].

5   Anderson, James. British Novels of the Twentieth Century.
    Reader's Guides, 3rd. series, No. 7. (Cambridge: Univer-
    sity Press, 1959 for The National Book League). [A selected
    list of novels "dealing with contemporary life, with a
    small section on 'fantasy and allegory'." The titles, one
    for each author, are annotated].

6   Awad, Ramses, comp. A Bibliography of the English Novel
    after the Second World War, Vol. II. (Doctoral dissertation
    presented to the Faculty of Arts, Ain Shams University,
    Cairo, 1968. Lists novels and their authors].

7   Baker, Ernest A. A Guide to Historical Fiction. (London:
    Routledge, 1914; New York: Burt Franklin, 1969). [Lists
    are arranged by countries and periods. Entries are complete
    with full title--including different title sometimes when
    published in U. S. A.--publisher and date, and descriptive
    annotation].

8   _____ and James Packman. A Guide to the Best Fiction,
    English and American, Including Translations from Foreign
    Languages. (London: Routledge, 1932; New York: Barnes
    and Noble, 1967). [A revised and enlarged edition. Original
    edition 1903; revised 1913. An alphabetical list of the
    most valuable prose fiction in English, with as much "char-
    acterization of the contents, nature and style of each book
    as would go in a few lines of print"].

1

9   Beebe, Maurice. "Modern Fiction Newsletter," Modern Fiction Studies. [A biannual review article from the first appearance of the periodical in 1955 until his last contribution XIV:2 (Summer 1968). Replaced by "Recent Books on Modern Fiction"].

10 _____. "Annual Review Number," Journal of Modern Literature, I:5 (1971), 644-985. [A review of scholarly and critical work in modern literature in 1970].

11 Bell, Inglis F. and Donald Baird. The English Novel, 1578-1956: A Checklist of Twentieth Century Criticisms. (Denver: Allan Swallow, 1958). [A selected checklist of 20th century criticism on individual novels from Lyly's Euphues to G. Greene. Novelists are alphabetically arranged].

12 Bennett, James R. "Style in Twentieth Century British and American Fiction: A Bibliography," West Coast Review, II:3 (Winter 1968), 43-51. [Based on an examination of the Annual Bibliography of English Language and Literature (1925-1956), and the PMLA Annual Bibliography (1946-1965). Regards style as "the texture of writing, with such matters of verbal detail as diction, imagery, syntax, and sound." Contains a "General" section and one on individual novelists, English and American].

13 Besterman, Theodore. Literature: English and American. A Bibliography of Bibliographies. Besterman World Bibliographies. (Totowa, New Jersey: Rowman and Littlefield, 1971). [Lists bibliographies of periods in general and on individual authors].

14 "Bibliography," Literature and Psychology. [Annual and annotated in the fourth issue of each year].

15 Booth, Wayne C. "Bibliography." The Rhetoric of Fiction. (Chicago: University of Chicago Press, 1961), pp. 399-435. [In five parts entitled: General, Technique as Rhetoric, The Author's Objectivity and the 'Second Self,' Artistic Purity, Rhetoric, and the Audience, and Narrative Irony and Unreliable Narrators. Many are annotated. See entry below].

16 Bryer, Jackson R. and Nanneska N. Magee. "The Modern Catholic Novel: A Selected Checklist of Criticism." The Vision Obscured: Perceptions of Some Twentieth-Century Catholic Novelists. Edited by Melvin J. Friedman. (New York: Fordham University Press, 1970), pp. 241-268.

17 Bufkin, E. C. The Twentieth-Century Novel in English: A Checklist. (Athens: University of Georgia Press, 1967). [Lists novelists, English and American, and their works].

18 Carter, Paul J. and George K. Smart. Literature and Society, 1961-1965: A Selective Bibliography. University of Miami

Publications in English and American Literature, IX, 1967.
(Coral Gables, Florida: University of Miami Press, 1967).
[Part I contains 225 entries from books, and Part II 691
entries from periodicals, mostly American. Also includes
a Subject Index].

19 Cary, Norman and Ardoth Casselman. "Bibliography of Religion and Literature," Universitas, I (Fall 1963); Universitas, II (1964), 120-128. [General works and studies on
individual writers].

20 Cotton, Gerald B. and Hilda M. McGill. Fiction Guides.
General: British and American. Readers' Guides Series.
(London: Clive Bingley, 1967).

21 Crook, Arthur. British and Commonwealth Fiction Since 1950.
(London: National Book League, 1966). [A 32-page booklet
listing titles based on "personal choice"].

22 Culpan, Norman. Modern Adult Fiction for School and College
Libraries: A List of Books Published Since 1918, With a
Short List of Critical Works on the Modern Novel, Chosen
and Annotated for the Use of Sixth Forms and other Students.
(London: School Library Association, 1960).

23 _____ and W. J. Messer. Contemporary Adult Fiction,
1945-1956, with a Short List of Critical Works on the Modern
Novel, Chosen and Annotated for the use of Sixth Form and
other Students. (London: School Library Association, 1967).

24 "Current Bibliography," Twentieth Century Literature. [A
regular quarterly feature since 1955 that annotates "articles dealing with the literature and critical problems of
the 20th century"].

25 "Current Literature," English Studies. [An annual survey
since 1935 in two parts: Poetry, Prose and Drama, and
Criticism and Biography].

26 Daiches, David. "Bibliography: Fiction." The Present Age:
After 1920. Introductions to English Literature series.
Edited by Bonamy Dobrée. (London: The Cresset Press, 1958).
Published in U. S. A. as The Present Age in British Literature. (Bloomington: Indiana University Press, 1958), pp.
246-322. [Covers the period from 1914 to the mid-fifties
which he divides into: The Older Generation, The Age of
Experiment, and The 1930s and After. Lists primary sources,
bibliographies, if any, and a selected checklist of biography and criticism on individual novelists. (See below)].

27 Davis, Robert Murray. "An Annotated Checklist for Students
of Allegory in Modern Fiction," Genre, V (1972), 378-384.
[Based on the MLA Bibliography since 1958. Twelve annotated
major items followed by reviews].

3

28 Dawson, Lolita Irene and Marion Davis Hutting. European
War Fiction in English and Personal Narratives; Bibliographies. Useful Reference Series, No. 25. (Boston: F. W.
Faxon, 1921). [Part I is an annotated bibliography of war
fiction in English, and Part II of personal narratives of
the European War. Confined to American bibliographical
sources].

29 Falls, Cyril. War Books: A Critical Guide to the Literature of the Great War. (London: Peter Davies, 1930).
[An annotated list of books on World War I--history, reminiscences, and fiction. Pages 261-303 list and annotate
English war novels].

30 Frampton, Maralee. "Religion and the Modern Novel: A
Selected Bibliography." The Shapeless God: Essays on
Modern Fiction. Edited by Harry J. Mooney and Thomas F.
Staley. (Pittsburgh: University of Pittsburgh Press,
1968), pp. 207-218.

31 Freeman, William. Dictionary of Fictional Characters.
(London: Dent, 1963). Indexed by J. M. F. Leaper 1967
and revised by Fred Urquhart 1973). [Some 20,000 fictitious
characters from approximately 2,000 books by 500 authors.
Gives name of principal character in a family, close relations, name of work, author and original date of appli-
cation].

32 "Gawsworth, John" [T. I. F. Armstrong], ed. Ten Contemporaries: Notes Toward Their Definitive Bibliography. With
a Foreword by Viscount Esher. First Series. (London:
Ernest Benn, 1932). Second Series (London: Joiner and
Steele, 1933). [Bibliographies of primary sources. Included
in the First Series are R. Davies, S. Hudson, and M. S.
Shiel, and in the Second Series H. E. Bates, O. Onions, D.
Richardson, and L. A. G Strong. A three-to-four-page note
precedes each writer].

33 Gerber, Richard. "Appendix: An Annotated List of English
Utopian Fiction, 1901-1951." Utopian Fantasy: A Study of
English Utopian Fiction Since the End of the Nineteenth
Century. (London: Routledge and Kegan Paul, 1955; The
Folcroft Press, 1969), pp. 143-159. [This is followed by a
two-page list of books and articles "concerned with the
principles of Utopian creation" and/or a series of Utopias].

34 Goetsch, Paul and Heinz Kosok. "Literatur zum modernen
englischen Roman: Eine ausgewählte Bibliographie." Der
moderne englische Roman: Interpretationen. Edited by Horst
Oppel. (Berlin: Erich Schmidt Verlag, 1965), pp. 417-432.
Revised edition 1971.

35 Hall, James. "Selected Bibliography: Recent Criticism."
The Lunatic Giant in the Drawing Room: The British and

4

American Novel Since 1930. (Bloomington: Indiana University Press, 1968), pp. 227-337. [Lists books and articles
of the "last dozen years or so on individual writers since
the latest critical works containing a good bibliography"].

36   Hill Winnifred. _The Overseas Empire in Fiction: An Annotated Bibliography._ (London: Oxford University Press,
1930). [Lists novels dealing with various aspects of the
overseas British Empire. Arranged alphabetically according
to country].

37   Jones, Claude E. "Modern Books dealing with the Novel in
English: A Checklist," _Bulletin of Bibliography,_ XXII
(September 1957), 85-87.

38   Kennedy, Arthur G. and Donald B. Sands. _A Concise Bibliography for Students of English._ [Stanford, California:
Stanford University Press, 1963). [An enlarged and revised
edition of 1954. Originally published 1940. Gives, under
fourteen categories, a well-rounded reading list. Pages
51-83, "Prose," list references for English and American
novels].

39   Kerr, Elizabeth Margaret. _Bibliography of the Sequence
Novel._ (Minneapolis: University of Minnesota Press; London:
Oxford University Press, 1950). [Pages 11-39 give a bibliography of the sequence novel in England and America. See
below].

40   Killam, G. D. "Bibliography." _Africa in English Fiction
1874-1939._ (Ibadan: Ibadan University Press, 1968), pp.
175-197. [Novels devoted to Tropical Africa].

41   Kunitz, Stanley J. and H. Haycraft. _Twentieth Century Authors: A Biographical Dictionary of Modern Literature._ (New
York: H. W. Wilson, 1942). [Biographical information on
writers of this century whose books are familiar to readers
of English].

42   _____ and Vineta Colby. First Supplement. (New York:
H. W. Wilson, 1955).

43   Le Claire, Lucien. _A General Analytical Bibliography of the
Regional Novelists of the British Isles, 1800-1950._ Collection D'Histoire et de Littérature Étrangères. (Paris:
Société D'Édition "Les Belles Lettres," 1954). [A companion
piece to _Le Roman regionaliste dans les Iles Britanniques
1800-1950._ A comprehensive table of novelists from 1800 to
1950. Entries of novelists are chronologically arranged and
contain brief biographical notes. The various editions of
the novels are listed in most cases, and, whenever possible,
the scene of the novel].

44   Lewis, Arthur O., Jr. "The Anti-Utopian Novel: Preliminary

Notes and Checklist," Extrapolation, II (May 1961), 27-32.
[A checklist of anti-utopias with brief annotations].

45 Lingenfelter, Mary Rebecca, comp. Vocations in Fiction:
An Annotated Bibliography. (Chicago: American Library
Association, 1938). [Contains 463 novels representing 102
occupations. Gives author, title, date, publisher and price
and a two-to-three-page annotation describing the vocational
rather than the literary significance].

46 Maes-Jelinek, Hena. "Selected Bibliography." Criticism of
Society in the English Novel Between the Wars. Bibliothèque
de la Faculté de Philosophie et Lettres de L'Université de
Liège. (Paris: Société d'Éditions "Les Belles Lettres,"
1970), pp. 529-547. [The first section, pp. 529-536, lists
works of novelists, and the second section lists critical
works: general, pp. 536-539, and on individual authors,
pp. 539-545].

47 May, Derwent, comp. British and Commonwealth Novels of the
Sixties. (London: National Book League, 1970). [Lists
author, title and publisher].

48 Muir, Edwin. "Bibliography: Fiction." The Present Age,
from 1914. (London: The Cresset Press, 1939), pp. 222-268.
[Lists primary sources].

49 Peterson, C. T. "The English Novel--A Short Bibliography,"
Graduate Student of English, I (Spring 1958), 17-21. [Some
twenty descriptive annotations of book-form studies of the
English novel].

50 Pohle, Helen L. "New Literary Forms for a New Age. A Contribution to Bibliography." Bulletin of Bibliography and
Dramatic Index, XV (May-August 1935), 133-135.

51 Rabinovitz, Rubin. "Bibliography." The Reaction Against
Experiment in the English Novel, 1950-1960. (New York and
London: Columbia University Press, 1967), pp. 174-223.
[Lists the works of K. Amis, A. Wilson, and C. P. Snow,
followed by a selected list of general critical works].

52 Rhodes, Dennis E. and Anna E. C. Simoni. Dictionary of
Anonymous and Pseudonymous English Literature, Vol. III:
1900-1950. [Edinburgh and London: Oliver and Boyd, 1956).

53 Richardson, Kenneth R., ed. and R. Clive Willis, assoc. ed.
Twentieth Century Writing: A Reader's Guide to Contemporary
Literature. (London and New York: Newnes Books, 1969).
[A guide to the principal writings of some 1200 authors].

54 Rouse, H. Blair. "A Selective and Critical Bibliography of
Studies in Prose Fiction," Journal of English and Germanic
Philology, XLVIII (April 1949), 259-284; XLIX (July 1950),
358-387; L (July 1951), 376-407; LI (July 1952), 364-392.

55 Souvage, Jacques. An Introduction to the Study of the Novel. With a Foreword by W. Schrickx. (Gent: E. Story-Scienta P. V. B. A., 1965). [Part II, pp. 101-254 is a "systematic bibliography for the study of the novel," American, Continental, and English].

56 Stallman, Robert Wooster. "A Selected Bibliography of Criticism of Fiction." Critiques and Essays on Modern Fiction: 1920-1951. Edited by John W. Aldridge. Foreword by Mark Schorer. (New York: The Ronald Press, 1952), pp. 553-610. [General works and studies on individual novelists].

57 Stevenson, Lionel. "Bibliography." The English Novel: A Panorama. (Boston: Houghton-Mifflin, 1960; London: Constable, 1961), pp. 495-517. [A checklist for each of the seventeen chapters that examine the rise of the novel from the pastoral and picaresque in the 15th century to the post-1915 exploration of "the Psyche"].

58 Stevick, Philip. "Selected Bibliography." The Theory of the Novel. (New York: The Free Press; London: Collier-Macmillan, 1967), pp. 407-429. [some 350 items limited to works in English, that give "theoretical insights." Annotations descriptive but often evaluative].

59 Temple, Ruth Z. and Martin Tucker. Twentieth Century British Literature: A Reference Guide and Bibliography. (New York: F. Ungar, 1968). [Part I, pp. 1-118, is a "reference guide to the books about British books" of the 20th century. Pages 90-102 list and annotate histories of the novel and books on "Theory and Special Studies." Part II, pp. 119-256, lists 20th century authors alphabetically, their works, and bibliographies, if any].

60 Tucker, Martin. "Selected Reading List of Modern African Literature through 1966." Africa in Modern Literature: A Survey of Contemporary Writing in English. (New York: F. Ungar, 1967), pp. 263-311. [See below].

61 Ullrich, Kurt. Who Wrote About Whom: A Bibliography of Books on Contemporary British Authors. (Berlin: Arthur Collignon, 1932). [Some 540 items each of which includes number of pages, year of publication, price, and publishing firm in U. K. and/or U. S. A. Sometimes includes table of contents].

62 Vinson, James, ed. Contemporary Novelists. With a Preface by Walter Allen. (London: St. James Press; New York: St. Martin's Press, 1972). [See below].

63 Wagenknecht, Edward. "Selected Bibliography with Annotations," and "Supplementary Bibliography." Cavalcade of the English Novel. (New York: H. Holt; London: Oxford University Press, 1943), pp. 577-619, 620-661. [On individual

novelists].

64 Ward, A. C. Longman Companion to Twentieth Century Literature. (Harlow: Longman, 1970). [Entries are arranged
alphabetically according to authors--mainly English, Scottish and American--are cross-referenced, and contain biographical and bibliographical information. Also includes
articles on literary categories and literary terms].

65 Watson, George, ed. The Concise Cambridge Bibliography of
English Literature. (Cambridge: University Press, 1958;
revised ed. 1965). [Pages 203-249 deal with 1900 to 1950
and are subdivided into Bibliographies, Literary History
and Criticism, Anthologies and Periodicals, and Individual
Authors].

66 Weinstock, Donald Jay. The Boer War in the Novel in English,
1884-1966: A Descriptive and Critical Bibliography. [Doc-
toral dissertation presented to the University of California,
Los Angeles, 1968].

67 Wheeler, Harold L. Contemporary Novels and Novelists: A
List of References to Biographical and Critical Material.
Bulletin of the School of Mines and Metallurgy, Vol. XII.
(Rolla, Missouri: University of Missouri, 1921). [Refer-
ences provided from a list of 35 critical books and several
periodicals for selected 19th and 20th century novels, English and American, to meet the "needs of students . . .
pursuing course English 421 'The Contemporary Novel'"].

2.
Criticism: Books

68 Adam, G. F. Three Contemporary Anglo-Welsh Novelists: Jack
Jones, Rhys Davies, and Hilda Vaughan. (Bern: A. Francke
A. G., 1948). [The three writers represent three different
aspects of regionalism in the contemporary English novel with
a Welsh background. Also discussed are problems relating
to the regional novel].

69 Adcock, A. St. John. Gods of Modern Grub Street: Impressions of Contemporary Authors. (London: Sampson Low,
Marston; New York: Stokes, 1923). [Semi-biographical and
critical reviews of leading contemporary writers which include A. Bennett, J. D. Beresford, J. Galsworthy, A. S. M.
Hutchinson, S. Kaye-Smith, C. Mackenzie, S. Maugham, M. Sinclair, F. Swinnerton, and H. G. Wells].

70 _____. The Glory that was Grub Street: Impressions
of Contemporary Authors. (London: Sampson Low, Marston;
New York: Stokes, 1928; Books for Libraries, 1969). [Crit-
ical observations on the tone and temper of literature in
the 20th century. Includes A. Huxley, S. Jameson, G. K.
Chesterton, and "R. West"].

71 Aiken, Conrad. A Reviewer's ABC: Collected Criticism of
Conrad Aiken from 1916 to the Present. With an Introduction by Rufus A. Blanshard. (New York: Meridian Books,
1958; London: W. H. Allen, 1961). [Includes reviews of
works by A. Bennett, J. Galsworthy, D. H. Lawrence, W. Lewis,
G. Moore, and V. Woolf].

72 Albérès, René-Marill. Histoire du roman moderne. (Paris:
Éditions Albin Michel, 1962). [Explores the various paths
taken by the modern European Novel. Emphasis on the French
novel].

73 _____. Métamorphoses du roman. (Paris: Éditions
Albin Michel, 1966). [Considers the "mutations" of the
novel between 1920 to the present and attributes the basic
changes in structure and technique to changes in the function of the novel from being an "exposé" or "récit" to the
novel as quest or "énigme". Includes studies of A. Huxley,
L. Durrell, J. Joyce, and V. Woolf].

74 Aldington, Richard. Selected Critical Writings, 1928-1960.
Edited by Alister Kershaw with a Preface by Harry T. Moore.
(Carbondale & Edwardsville: Southern Illinois University
Press; London & Amsterdam: Feffer & Simons, 1970). [In-
cludes essays on A. Huxley, W. Lewis, S. Maugham, L. Durrell,
and D. H. Lawrence].

75 Aldridge, John W. Time to Murder and Create: The Contem-
porary Novel in Crisis. (New York: David McKay, 1966).
[A collection of essays mainly concerned with the American
novel. The last section, "The Brief, Stale Anger of the
English," deals with the contemporary English novel of C.
Wilson, P. O'Connor, and A. Sillitoe].

9

76 _____, ed. Critiques and Essays on Modern Fiction: 1920-1951. Representing the Achievement of Modern American and British Critics. With a Foreword by Mark Schorer. (New York: The Ronald Press, 1952). [Part One, on the technique of fiction, includes essays by P. Lubbock, A. Tate, J. Frank, and M. Schorer. Part Two, a collection of studies in the "Method of Meaning," includes essays on J. Joyce and J. Conrad. Part Three, "The Mode of the Novelist," includes essays on J. Conrad, D. H. Lawrence, A. Huxley, J. Joyce, E. M. Forster, V. Woolf, and G. Greene. Also contains a 50-page selected bibliography of criticism, both general and on individual authors].

77 Aler, J[ean] M[atthieu] M[arie]. Een Ruiker asfodelen, Beschouwing over moderne romankunst. (Purmerend: J. Muusses, 1956). [A 51-page booklet on modern views on the art of the novel].

78 Allen, Arthur B[ruce]. A Tale that is Told: A Pageant of English Literature, 1900-1950. (London: Barrie and Rockliff, 1960). [A "historical record" giving a bird's-eye view of English Letters, sometimes through a series of extracts. Pages 13-113 deal with the novelists of the period, and give brief outlines of each novelist's life and works].

79 Allen, Hervey. "History and the Novel." The Craft of Novel Writing. Edited by A. S. Burack. (Boston: The Writer, Inc., 1948), pp. 139-148. Reprinted from American Mercury, CLXXIII (February 1944), 119-121. [See entry under Periodicals].

80 Allen, Walter [Ernest], ed. Writers on Writing. (London: Phoenix House, 1948). Published in U. S. A. as The Writer on his Art. (New York: Whittlesey House, 1949). [Writers' notes upon their trade as distinct from the criticism of critics. Part Two, pp. 117-255, deals with the novel with chapters devoted to its various aspects, ranging from shape and structure to style].

81 _____. Reading a Novel. (London: Phoenix House; Denver: Alan Swallow, 1949. Revised Edition, 1956). [Introduces the reader to the world of the novel by discussing the fundamental principles of novel writing. Chapter VIII discusses novels by G. Greene, V. Woolf, C. P. Snow, J. Cary, K. Amis, and I. Murdoch].

82 _____. The English Novel: A Short Critical History. (London: Phoenix House, 1954; New York: E. P. Dutton, 1955; Penguin Books, 1958). [Stops with D. H. Lawrence, V. Woolf, and J. Joyce].

83 _____. The Novel Today. (London: Longmans Green, 1955). (For The British Council and the National Book League). [Makes a study of the English novel between 1950

and 1955, concentrating on A. Powell, C. P. Snow, L. P. Hartley, A. Wilson, N. Dennis, J. Wain, and K. Amis].

84 _____. Tradition and Dream: The English and American Novel from the Twenties to Our Time. (London: Phoenix House, 1964). Published in U. S. A. as The Modern Novel in Britain and the United States. (New York: E. P. Dutton, 1964). [A sequel to The English Novel. Equally divided between the English and American novel in the twenties, the thirties, and the war and postwar periods. The introduction brings out the basic differences between the English and American novel].

85 _____. [Tradition and Innovation in Prose Literature]. Tradition and Innovation in Contemporary Literature. The International P. E. N. Conference, October 1964, Budapest. (Budapest: Corvina Press, 1964), pp. 90-94. [Contends that the English novel does not rely on innovation in the sense of new technical methods of expression as an "important continuing tradition itself," but renews itself by "going back to its own past and seeing what its own past has to offer for the present time "].

86 _____. The Novelist as Innovator. Introduction by Walter Allen. (London: British Broadcasting Corporation, 1965). [A series of talks first broadcast on the BBC Third Programme. Six authors--S. Richardson, L. Sterne, C. Dickens, Mrs. Gaskell, H. James and J. Conrad--are discussed, each by a different critic. Special attention is given to innovation, both technical and in the sense of the introduction to the novel of new raw material].

87 Allott, Miriam, ed. Novelists on the Novel. (London: Routledge and Kegan Paul; New York: Doubleday, 1959). [Excerpts from novelists from Fielding to E. M. Forster classified under three headings: The Nature of Prose Fiction, The Genesis of a Novel, and The Craft of Fiction. An Introduction by the editor precedes each section].

88 Allsop, Kenneth. The Angry Decade: A Survey of the Cultural Revolt of the Nineteen-Fifties. (London: Peter Owen; New York: British Book Centre, 1958). [Surveys writers of the fifties--K. Amis, J. Wain, T. Hinde, J. Braine, J. P. Donleavy, I. Murdoch, J. Osborne, N. Dennis, and C. Wilson, examining the origin of their social and intellectual attitudes, and the reception of their books].

89 Ames, Van Meter. "Religious Fiction." Faith of the Free. Edited by Winifred Ernest Garrison. (Chicago & New York: Willett, Clark, 1940), pp. 110-122. [Defines religious fiction rather broadly as any fiction concerned with the "individual, the person, the self," and one which contributes to a transcendence of the "animal organism with its physical environment" to a society of "sympathy and under-

standing." Brief references to H. James, D. H. Lawrence, and V. Woolf among others].

90 _____. "Enjoying the Novel." Enjoyment of the Arts. Edited by Max Schoen. (New York: Philosophical Library, 1944), pp. 214-238. ["The adventure beyond adventure to be enjoyed in the novel" is not that it is a pastime, but "an inspiration that must carry over into what Conrad called 'the hazardous enterprise of living'." J. Conrad, H. James, H. G. Wells, and J. Joyce among others].

91 Amorós, Andrés. Introducción a la novela contemporánea. (Salamanca: Ediciones Anaya, S. A., 1966). [Discusses the different kinds of novels; e.g. 'Catholic', 'political', from the end of the 19th century. V. Woolf, C. Morgan, D. H. Lawrence, and J. Joyce among others].

92 Anderson, David. The Tragic Protest: A Christian Study of Some Modern Literature. (London: SCM Press, 1969; Richmond, Virginia: John Knox Press, 1970). [Mostly concerned with Existentialism. Ch. III examines the work of J. Wain, K. Amis, and J. Braine].

93 Andreach, Robert J. The Slain and Resurrected God: Conrad, Ford and the Christian Myth. (New York: New York University Press; London: University of London Press, 1970). [Studies the similarity between the two novelists' imaginative worlds, and their focus on the heroine as "agent" or "mediatrix" whose reality circumscribes the hero until he begins the quest to discover himself, thus parallelling the role of the Virgin Mary in the Redemption and as Mediatrix].

94 Arns, Karl. Grundriss der Geschichte der Engl. Literatur, von 1832 bis zur Gegenwart. (Paderborn: Ferdinand Schouigh, 1941). [A history of English literature from 1832 to the present. Pages 123-177 survey and classify the novel into Edwardian, Georgian, Psychoanalytic, Stream of consciousness, Postwar, Regional, Scottish, and Adventure].

95 Aspects de la littérature anglaise, de 1918 a 1940. (Algers, 1944). [A special number of the French monthly Fontaine (#27-40) on interwar poetry and prose. Includes translations of essays on J. Joyce, H. James, V. Woolf, D. H. Lawrence, E. M. Forster, and A. Huxley. The Introduction by E. M. Forster describes the cultural and social background of the period. Also includes "Panorama du Roman" by E. Bowen (see separate entry)].

96 Astaldi, Maria Luisa. Nuove letture inglesi. (Firenze: Sansoni, 1958). [Brief articles on English writers from Chaucer to G. Greene. D. Garnett, V. Woolf, D. H. Lawrence, G. Orwell, A. Huxley, E. Bowen, and G. Greene are among the novelists included].

12

97 Auerbach, Erich. Mimesis: The Representation of Reality
in Western Literature. (Princeton, New Jersey: Princeton
University Press, 1953). [Ch. XX, "The Brown Stocking",
is an introduction to the technique of the modern novel
through V. Woolf's To The Lighthouse].

98 Aufseeser, Gretel. Jüdische Gestalten im modernen englischen Roman. (Zurich: Buchdruckerei Müller, Werder, 1940).
[Originally a doctoral dissertation presented to the University of Zurich. A study of the treatment of Jewish characters, Judaism and Jewish problems in the modern English
novel].

99 Axthelm, Peter M. The Modern Confessional Novel. (New
Haven & London: Yale University Press, 1967). [A study
of those novels which present an affected, unbalanced hero,
who at some point in his life suffers from internal chaos,
becomes increasingly intellectual, examines "his past as
well as his innermost thoughts in an effort to achieve some
form of perception," and who finally makes his "confession"
by utilising the technique of the "double" and irony. Ch.
III examines A. Koestler and W. Golding from this viewpoint].

100 Babbage, Stuart Barton. The Mark of Cain: Studies in Literature and Theology. (London: The Paternoster Press;
Grand Rapids, Michigan: Wm. B. Erdman's, 1966). [Contends
that the themes of guilt and purgation as depicted in modern
literature, and especially modern fiction, may be accurate
but are incomplete, for they offer man only one half of the
picture: they do not offer redemption. H. G. Wells, the
"Angry Young Men," W. Golding, G. Greene, E. Waugh, G. Orwell,
and D. H. Lawrence among others].

101 Bailey, James Osler. Pilgrims Through Time and Space:
Trends and Patterns in Scientific and Utopian Fiction. (New
York: Angus Books, 1947). Reprinted, with a Foreword by
Thomas D. Clareson. (Westport, Connecticut: Greenwood Press,
1972). [The intellectual and literary history of the development of science fiction from its origins in the 17th and
18th centuries, including utopias and imaginary voyages, to
World War II. Emphasis on the period between 1870 and 1915,
the generation of J. Verne and H. G. Wells, with reference
to A. Huxley. Also contains a bibliography of scientific
romances].

102 Baker, Denys Val, ed. Writers of Today. (London: Sidgwick
and Jackson, 1946). [A collection of twelve essays on contemporary writers by different contributors. Included are
essays on A. Huxley, G. Greene, J. Joyce, E. Sitwell, J. B.
Priestley, A. Koestler, D. Sayers, and E. M. Forster].

103 _____, ed. Writers of Today. (London: Sidgwick and
Jackson, 1948). [A collection of twelve essays on contemporary writers by different contributors. Included are essays on S. Maugham, V. Woolf, J. C. Powys, E. Waugh, and
H. E. Bates].

13

104 Baker, Ernest A. History of the English Novel. Vols. IX
and X. (London: H. F. & G. Witherby, 1938-39; New York:
Barnes and Noble, 1967). [Vol. IX, The Day Before Yester-
day, deals with G. Moore and H. James among others. Vol.
X, Yesterday, deals with J. Conrad, R. Kipling, K. Mansfield,
S. Butler, G. K. Chesterton, A. Bennett, J. Galsworthy, and
D. H. Lawrence. See below under L. Stevenson for Vol. XI].

105 Bareiss, Dieter. Die Vierpersonenkonstellation im Roman:
Strukturuntersuchungen zur Personenführung Dargestellt an
N. Hawthorne's "The Blithedale Romance," G. Eliot's "Daniel
Deronda," H. James' "The Golden Bowl," and D. H. Lawrence's
"Women in Love." (Bern: Herbert Lang, 1969). [A study of
the structural design created by the centrality of the four-
character pattern].

106 Bascom, Lelia. Contemporary Novel: Guided Club Study.
Bulletin of the University of Wisconsin, Serial No. 1432.
General Series No. 1208. (Madison, Wisconsin: University
of Wisconsin, 1927). [A guide to individual English and
American novels. Selects novels by J. Conrad, H. G. Wells,
J. Galsworthy, A. Bennett, A. D. Sedgwick, H. Walpole, F.
Swinnerton, E. M. Forster, and S. Kaye-Smith. Each study
consists of a brief note on the life of the novelist, sug-
gestions for the study, and references in approximately four
pages].

107 Batho, Edith and Bonamy Dobrée. The Victorians and After:
1830-1914. With a chapter on the Economic Background by
Guy Chapman. (London: The Cresset Press; New York: R.
McBride, 1938; rev. ed. 1948). [Vol. IV of the series "Introductions to English Literature." Pages 76-103 review
fiction between 1830 and 1914, and show the emergence of
the novel as the "most important art form . . . read for
spiritual nourishment." Includes H. James, H. G. Wells,
J. Conrad, and E. M. Forster. Pages 273-328 list the works
of individual novelists and include several critical refer-
ences].

108 *Bati, Laszlo, and Istvan K. Nagy, eds. Az angol irodalom
a huszaduk szazadban. 2 Vols. (Budapest: Gondolat, 1970).
[English Literature in the 20th Century].

109 Bayley, John. The Characters of Love: A Study in the Literature of Personality. (London: Constable, 1960). [Exam-
ines the treatment of love in Troilus and Cressida, Othello,
and H. James' The Golden Bowl. Contains frequent references
to J. Joyce and D. H. Lawrence among others. Also asserts
the independent existence of characters as "other people"
and that their creators should love them as such].

110 Beach, Joseph Warren. The Twentieth Century Novel: Studies
in Technique. (New York: The Century; London: D. Appleton,
1932). [A study in the evolution of the realistic technique
in English and American fiction].

14

111 _____. English Literature of the Nineteenth Century
and the Early Twentieth Century: 1798 to the First World
War. (New York: Oxford University Press, 1950). [A historical survey. Pages 240-248 deal with the pre-World War
I novel].

112 Bedient, Calvin. Architects of the Self: George Eliot,
D. H. Lawrence, and E. M. Forster. (Berkeley: University
of California Press, 1972). [Chooses the three novelists
as a "digest, a colloquium on the question of what the human
being is and ought to be--of what it should mean to be alive
and human," and in whose novels the major ideals of human
character, whether they be christian and ascetic, or pagan
and mystical, or Greek and individualistic are clustered.
Shows how opposed are G. Eliot and D. H. Lawrence, and how
E. M. Forster achieves something of a median position].

113 Beebe, Maurice. Ivory Towers and Sacred Founts: The Artist
as Hero in Fiction from Goethe to Joyce. (New York: New
York University Press, 1964). [Traces the development of
the "portrait-of-the-artist" novel from the late 18th century to the early 20th century, and discusses "the artistic temperament, the creative process, and the relationship
of the artist to society." The discussion of major works
within the tradition includes works by J. Joyce and H. James
among others].

114 Beja, Morris. Epiphany in the Modern Novel. (Seattle:
University of Washington Press; London: Peter Owen, 1971).
[Originally a Doctoral Dissertation presented to Cornell
University, 1963. Examines the tradition of "Epiphany",
the context in which modern authors use the term, and the
role it plays in the novels of J. Joyce and V. Woolf among
others].

115 Bell, Clive. Old Friends: Personal Recollections. (London:
Chatto & Windus, 1956). ["Modest appreciations mingled with
small talk." Included is a chapter on V. Woolf and an article, "Bloomsbury," reprinted from The Twentieth Century].

116 Bell, Quentin. Bloomsbury. (London: Widenfeld and Nicholson, 1968). [A history of the group before, during and
after World War I, bringing out its special character, as
well as the major trends of thought and pattern of social
behaviour in the first quarter of the century].

117 Bellamy, William. The Novels of Wells, Bennett and Galsworthy:
1890-1910. (London: Routledge & Kegan Paul; New York:
Barnes & Noble, 1971). [A study of the three novelists both
as fin de siècle writers and Edwardians, examining the tran-
sition].

118 Bellow, Saul. "Where Do We go From Here: The Future of
Fiction." To The Young Writer: Hopwood Lectures, Second

15

Series. Edited by A. L. Bader. (Ann Arbor: University of Michigan Press, 1965), pp. 136-147. Reprinted from The Michigan Quarterly Review, I (1962), 27-33. [Emphasises the need in the novel for "new ideas about human kind . . . discovered and not invented," ideas which should be seen "in flesh and blood" and not merely asserted].

119 Benedikz, B[enedikt] S., ed. On the Novel: A Present for Walter Allen on His 60th Birthday. (London: J. M. Dent, 1971). [A collection of essays to demonstrate "not only the infinite variety of the novel, but also the length of its roots, the lively present state of its health and the auguries for its future." Included are essays on V. Woolf, M. Lowry, J. Cary, J. Joyce, S. Baring-Gould, and W. Golding].

120 Bennett, E. Arnold. The Author's Craft. (New York: George H. Doran, 1914). [On the function of observation in writing, the attributes required for the writing of novels and plays, and the relation between the artist and the Public].

121 _____. Books and Persons: Being Comments on a Past Epoch: 1908-1911. (London: Chatto & Windus; New York: George H. Doran, 1917). [A collection of a series of weekly articles to the New Age written between 1908 and 1911 under the pseudonym of Jacob Tousan. Valuable as comments by a contemporary. Included are notes on H. G. Wells and J. Galsworthy, and general comments on fiction].

122 Benseler, Frank, ed. Festschrift zum achtzigsten Geburtstag von George Lukács. (Neuwied and Berlin: Hermann Luchterhand Verlag, 1965). [Includes two essays, one by Jack Lindsay, "Time in Modern Literature," and one by Georg Steiner "A Note on Literature and Post-History." See separate entries].

123 Benson, E. F. As We Are: A Modern Revue. (London and New York: Longmans, Green, 1932). [On the changes which the War had brought in the form of fictional narrative--except perhaps when he reviews the literary scene, especially the novelists, in Ch. XII, "Grub Street," where he is concerned with the increase in sex literature].

124 Benson, Frederick R. Writers in Arms: The Literary Impact of the Spanish Civil War. Foreword by Salvador de Madariaga. New York University Studies in Comparative Literature No. 1. (New York: New York University Press, 1967; London: University of London Press, 1968). [Surveys and evaluates European and American Spanish Civil War literature, especially novels, written under the impact of the struggle, examining their treatment and interpretation of the economic, political, and religious aspects of the conflict. A. Koestler and G. Orwell, among other Euro-American writers, are discussed at length].

16

125 Bentley, Eric Russell, ed. The Importance of 'Scrutiny':
Selections from 'Scrutiny': A Quarterly Review, 1932-1948.
(New York: George W. Stewart, 1948; New York University
Press, 1964). [Selections include essays on E. M. Forster,
J. Joyce, D. H. Lawrence, and V. Woolf].

126 Bentley, Phyllis Eleanor. The English Regional Novel. (London: Allen & Unwin, 1941). [Considers C. Brontë, G. Eliot,
T. Hardy and A. Bennett, and their minor contemporaries, as
representatives of the "Golden Age" of the English regional
novel--1840 to 1940--to bring out its characteristics, and
its renaissance in 1930 by W. Greenwood, J. L. Hodson, M. S.
Jameson, W. Holtby, J. B. Priestley, and L. Cooper. Discusses its merits and defects, and estimates its significance in
English national culture].

127 _____. Some Observations on the Art of Narrative.
(London: Home & Van Thal, 1946; New York and London: Macmillan, 1947). [Examines the uses, limitations and power of
three major aspects of narrative art: description, scene,
and summary].

128 Beresford, John Davys. "Experiment in the Novel." Tradition and Experiment in Present-Day Literature. Addresses
delivered at the City Literary Institute. (London and New
York: Oxford University Press, 1929), pp. 23-53. [Confines
his survey to realist fiction, and examines experiments by
H. G. Wells, D. H. Lawrence, G. Moore, D. Richardson, and
J. Joyce, and attributes them to different conceptions of
reality].

129 Bergonzi, Bernard. Heroes' Twilight: A Study of the Literature of the Great War. (London: Constable, 1965; New
York: Coward-McCann, 1966). [A literary analysis and assessment of World War I literature. Ch. IX examines War novels by R. H. Mottram, F. M. Ford, R. Aldington, H. M. Tomlinson, and F. Manning].

130 _____, ed. The Twentieth Century: History of Literature in the English Language. (London: Barrie & Jenkins,
1970). [This critical survey compiled from essays by different critics includes essays on J. Joyce and D. H. Lawrence,
one on the novel in the twenties by M. Bradbury, and "Aspects
of the Novel 1930-1960" by Stephen Wall. See individual
entries].

131 _____. The Situation of the Novel. (London: Macmillan, 1970; Pittsburgh: University of Pittsburgh Press, 1971).
[Regards the novel as a product of a particular phase of
history and culture and simply as a "complex but essentially
self-contained form." Questions the present state of English
fiction, its future, and the cultural attitudes implicit in
recent English fiction, and contrasts it with the American
"comic-apocalyptic school." E. Waugh, A. Powell, C. P. Snow,

17

A. Wilson, and K. Amis].

132 Berneri, Marie Louise. Journey Through Utopia. (London: Routledge & Kegan Paul, 1950; Boston: Beacon Press, 1951). [A description and assessment of the most important Utopian writings since Plato by means of lengthy excerpts linked together to show the development of Utopian thought and its place in the history of social conditions and ideas. Included are H. G. Wells and A. Huxley].

133 Berthoff, Warner. "Fortunes of the Novel: Muriel Spark and Iris Murdoch." Fiction and Events: Essays in Criticism and Literary History. (New York: E. P. Dutton, 1971), pp. 118-154. Reprinted from The Massachusetts Review, VIII (1967), 301-332. [See entry under Periodicals].

134 Bethell, S[amuel] L[eslie]. The Literary Outlook. (London: The Sheldon Press; New York: Macmillan, 1943). [A "religious" approach that takes for granted the degenerate and disordered state of modern literature in a discussion of the "Lowbrows," "Middlebrows," and "Highbrows." Brief references to S. Maugham, D. H. Lawrence, and V. Woolf].

135 Bishop, J[ohn] P[eale]. The Collected Essays. Edited with an Introduction by Edmund Wilson. (New York & London: Charles Scribner's Sons, 1948). [Includes previously published essays on J. Joyce, "Finnegan's Wake," and D. H. Lawrence, "The Distrust of Ideas"].

136 Blackmur, R. P. Anni Mirabiles, 1921-1925: Reason in the Madness of Letters. (Washington: The Library of Congress, 1956). [Four lectures presented under the auspices of the Gertrude Clarke Whittal Poetry and Literature Fund discussing the "new" modes of expression and technique in the literature of the twenties. J. Joyce and E. M. Forster among others].

137 Blanchot, Maurice. Le Livre à venir. (Paris: Gallimard, 1959). Also as Der Gesang der Sirenen: Essays zur modernen Literatur. (Munchen: C. Hauser, 1962). [A collection of essays, mostly on French Literature, reprinted, with slight revisions, from Nouvelle Revue Française. Includes essays on V. Woolf and H. James].

138 Bland, D. S. "Endangering the Reader's Neck: Background Description in the Novel." Critical Approaches to Fiction. Edited by Shiv K. Kumar and Keith F. McKean. (New York: McGraw-Hill, 1968), pp. 229-249. Repr. from Criticism, III (Spring 1961), 121-139. [See entry under Periodicals].

139 Bloomfield, Morton W., ed. The Interpretation of Narrative: Theory and Practice. (Cambridge, Massachusetts: Harvard University Press, 1970). [A collection of essays by different critics on selected works from Beowulf to V. Woolf, fo-

cusing on the narrative principle. Included are essays on
works by H. James, J. Conrad, and V. Woolf].

140 Bloomfield, Paul. Imaginary Worlds or The Evolution of
Utopia. (London: Hamish Hamilton, 1932). [Included in
the survey are H. G. Wells (ch. XII) and A. Huxley (ch. XV)].

141 Blotner, Joseph L[eo]. The Political Novel. (New York:
Doubleday, 1955). [Ch. I describes the nature, importance
and characteristics of the political novel. The remaining
five chapters consider some 82 English, American, and Continental novels. Included are novels by H. James, J. Conrad,
E. M. Forster, A. Huxley, G. Orwell, S. Maugham, and J. Cary].

142 Blumenthal, Margrete. Zur Technik des englischen Gegenwarts-
romans. (Leipzig: Verlag von Bernard Tauchnitz, 1935; Johnson Reprint Corporation, 1966). [A study of technique in
the novels of J. Joyce, A. Huxley, D. H. Lawrence, D. Richardson, and V. Woolf].

143 Bogan, Louise. Selected Criticism: Prose, Poetry. (New
York: The Noonday Press; London: Peter Owen, 1955). [In-
cluded in the works reprinted from The New Yorker and other
periodicals, are essays on H. James, J. Joyce, and V. Woolf].

144 Boileau, Horace Tippin. Italy in the Post-Victorian Novel.
(Philadelphia, 1931). [A doctoral dissertation presented to
the University of Pennsylvania and privately printed. A
chronological examination of the increasing number of novels
written upon Italy, or which make use of it to any extent
for background, setting, atmosphere, and material, or as a
romantic, seductive land of escape and charm. R. Garnett,
H. Ward, G. Gissing,"M. Corelli," H. Caine, M. Hewlett, J.
Conrad, J. Galsworthy, G.W. Deeping, R. Bagot,C. Mackenzie,
R. Hichens, F. B. Young, B. B. Stern, A. Huxley, M. Baring,
E. M. Forster, E. Bowen, and D. H. Lawrence].

145 Booth, Bradford A. "The Novel." Contemporary Literary Scholarship: A Critical Review. Edited by Lewis Leary for The
Committee on Literary-Scholarship and The Teaching of English of the National Council of Teachers of English. (New
York: Appleton-Century-Crofts, 1958),pp. 259-288. [See
entry under Periodicals].

146 Booth, Wayne C[layson]. The Rhetoric of Fiction. (Chicago:
University of Chicago Press, 1961). [Though the first two
parts are pragmatic in the sense that they give the rhetorical devices available to the writer, the book promotes the
basic idea that a novel is a product of art and craft, not
simply a reflection of reality as P. Rahv and W. J. Harvey
would have it, or "Technique" as M. Schorer and J. Aldridge
contend].

147 _____. "Types of Narration." Approaches to the Novel.

Edited by Robert Scholes (Scranton, Pennsylvania: Chandler, 1961). Reprinted from The Rhetoric of Fiction. (Chicago: University of Chicago Press, 1961), Pt. I, ch. 6, pp. 149-168. [On "point of view" and the various ways of handling narration].

148 Borinski, Ludwig. Meister des modernen englischen Romans: Dickens, Galsworthy, H. G. Wells, Joseph Conrad, Virginia Woolf, Aldous Huxley, Graham Greene, George Orwell. (Heidelberg: Quelle & Meyer, 1963). [A detailed critical analysis of specific works by the above mentioned novelists].

149 _____. "Wells, Huxley und die Utopie." Literatur-Kultur-Gesellschaft in England und Amerika: Aspekte und Forschungsbeiträge. Friedrich Schubel zum 60. Geburtstag. Edited by Gerhard Müller-Schwefe and Konrad Tuzinsky. (Frankfurt: Verlag Moritz Diesterweg, 1966). [On the characteristics of 20th century Utopia as distinct from particular reforms of the 19th, and the impact of the war on it].

150 _____, and Gerd Krause. Die Utopie in der modernen englischen Literatur. Die Neueren Sprachen. Beiheft 2. (Frankfurt Am Main: Verlag Moritz Diesterweg, n. d.) [Contains two separate essays, the first on Anti-Utopia by Borinski and the second on the Cultural crises in Utopias of A. Huxley by G. Krause].

151 Bowen, Elizabeth. English Novelists. Britain in Pictures Series. (London: William Collins, 1942). [An illustrated brief survey of novelists from J. Lyly to V. Woolf, highlighting their contributions and the tendency of the English novel towards "living character, likely and lively plot," human relationships, and the provision of pleasure and entertainment].

152 _____. "Panorama du roman." Aspects de la littérature anglaise, de 1918 à 1940. (Translated by Pierre Ponti). (Alger, 1944), pp. 33-44. [A survey of the novel between the two World Wars. Divides the pre-1930 novelists into three groups: those who had established their reputations before World War I (A. Bennett, H. G. Wells, and S. Maugham), those who began to write during the war (J. Joyce, V. Woolf, D. Richardson, and D. H. Lawrence), and the sceptical and disillusioned generation that grew up during the war (A. Huxley, R. Macaulay, K. Mansfield, and C. Dane). Also notices the influence of the second group, and the emergence of the novelists of the thirties--C. Isherwood, E. Waugh, and G. Greene].

153 _____. "Notes on writing a Novel." Orion. Vol. II. Edited by R. Lehmann, D. K. Roberts, C. D. Lewis and E. Muir. (London: Nicholson & Watson, 1945), pp. 18-30. Reprinted in Collected Impressions. (New York: Alfred A. Knopf, 1950), pp. 249-263; Perspectives in Fiction. Edited by J. L. Cal-

derwood and H. E. Toliver. (New York & London: Oxford University Press, 1968), pp. 217-231. [Observations on the literary aspects of plot, character, scene, dialogue, angle, and the "relevance" of material included in the novel].

154 _____. "Out of a Book." Orion. Vol. III. Edited by C. D. Lewis, D. K. Roberts, and R. Lehmann. (London: Nicholson & Watson, 1946), pp. 10-14. Reprinted in Collected Impressions (New York: Alfred A. Knopf, 1950), pp. 246-249. [Questions whether there is such a thing as "creative writing," whether it is not simply an "enforced return," an addiction, to facts and fiction rooted "in a compost of forgotten books"].

155 _____. Collected Impressions. (New York: Alfred A. Knopf, 1950). [Includes reviews of V. Woolf, I. Compton-Burnett, E. M. Forster, J. Conrad, and D. H. Lawrence, and "Notes on Writing a Novel" and "Out of a Book"].

156 _____. "The Writer's Peculiar World." Highlights of Modern Literature: A Permanent Collection of Memorable Essays from 'The New York Times Book Review'. Edited by Francis Brown. (New York: The New American Library, 1954), pp. 32-36. Reprinted from The New York Times Book Review (24 Sep. 1950), 3, 40. [See entry under Periodicals].

157 _____. "The Search for a Story to Tell." Highlights of Modern Literature: A Permanent Collection of Memorable Essays from 'The New York Times Book Review'. Edited by Francis Brown. (New York: The New American Library, 1954), pp. 30-32. Reprinted from The New York Times Book Review (14 Dec. 1952), 1. [See entry under Periodicals].

158 _____. "English Fiction at Mid-Century." Arts at Mid-Century. Edited by Robert Richman. (New York: Horizon Press, 1954), pp. 209-213. Reprinted from The New Republic, CXXIX (21 Sep. 1953), 15-16. [See entry under Periodicals].

159 _____. "Rx for a Story worth Telling." Opinions and Perspectives from 'The New York Times Book Review'. Edited by Francis Brown. (Boston: Houghton and Mifflin, 1964), pp. 230-235. Reprinted from The New York Times Book Review (31 Aug. 1958), 1, 13. [See entry under Periodicals].

160 _____. Afterthought : Pieces About Writing. (London: Longmans, Green, 1962). Published in U. S. A. as Seven Writers: Memories of a Dublin Childhood and Afterthoughts, Pieces on Writing (New York: Alfred A. Knopf, 1962). [A collection of previously published Prefaces, reviews of V. Woolf, R. Lehmann, and E. M. Forster, radio broadcasts, and reflections which include an excerpt from Why Do I Write?].

161 Bowen, Elizabeth, Graham Greene and V. S. Pritchett. 'Why Do I Write?' An Exchange of Views between Authors. With a Preface by V. S. Pritchett. (London: Percival Marshall,

21

1948; The Folcroft Press, 1969). [An exchange of letters between the three novelists discussing the writer's independence from the State and "disloyalty" to any set creed, and his obligation to tell the truth as he sees it].

162 Bowen, John. "Speaking of Books: The Novel as . . ." The Best of 'Speaking of Books' from 'The New York Times Book Review'. Edited, with an Introduction by E. F. Brown. (New York: Holt, Rinehart and Winston, 1969), pp. 231-234. Reprinted from The New York Times Book Review (May 23, 1965), 2. [See entry under Periodicals].

163 Bowling, Lawrence Edward. "What is the Stream of Consciousness Technique?" Critical Approaches to Fiction. Edited by Shiv K. Kumar and Keith F. McKean. (New York: McGraw-Hill, 1968), pp. 349-367. Reprinted from P M L A, LXV:4 (June, 1950), 333-345. [See entry under Periodicals].

164 Bradbury, Malcolm. What Is a Novel? (London: Edward Arnold, 1969). [An informative booklet on the basic constituent elements of the novel, its nature, and contemporary significance].

165 _____. The Social Context of Modern English Literature. (New York: Schocken Books; Oxford: Blackwell, 1971). [A study of the cultural background--"the middle ground between literary study, sociology, and intellectual history"--of English literature from 1870 to the present. A. Bennett, J. Conrad, F. M. Ford, D. H. Lawrence, W. Lewis, V. Woolf, J. Joyce, and E. M. Forster].

166 _____. "The Novel in the 1920's." The Twentieth Century: The Sphere History of Literature in the English Language, Vol. 7. Edited by Bernard Bergonzi. (London: The Cresset Press, 1970), pp. 180-219. [Regards the decade as the time when the "real assimilation of modernism into tradition" occurs, and discusses the impact on the novelist of the "deepening distrust" of the age both of "history and progressivism," the "discovery of technique," and the "drift of style and structure" toward "the ironic and parodic." E. M. Forster, V. Woolf, F. M. Ford, W. Lewis, A. Huxley, and E. Waugh].

167 _____. "The Novel." The Twentieth-Century Mind: History, Ideas, and Literature in Britain. Edited By C. B. Cox and A. E. Dyson, Vol. III, 1945-1965. (London and New York: Oxford University Press, 1972). [In five sections: Sec. 1 (pp. 319-329) discusses in general terms the impact of the war in altering theme and emphasis in the Western novel, making its style and temper hard to characterize even though "the implications and complications of the modernist view" are still with us; Sec. 2 (pp. 329-347) deals with the English novel since the war, its situation and achievements; Sections 3, 4, 5 (pp. 347-383) deal with the novel in Amer-

ica, France and other European countries].

168   Brass, Herta. <u>Der Wandel in der Auffassung des Menschen im</u>
       <u>englischen Roman vom 18. zum 20. Jahrhundert.</u> (Lippstadt/
       Westf., 1931). [Originally a doctoral dissertation presen-
       ted to the University of Tübingen. A brief survey of the
       concept of man in the English novel from the 18th to the
       20th century. Pages 19-29 deal with D. H. Lawrence, J. Gals-
       worthy, J. Joyce, M. Sinclair, D. Richardson, R. Macaulay,
       and A. Huxley].

169   Braybrooke, Patrick. <u>Novelists: We Are Seven.</u> (London:
       C. W. Daniel; Philadelphia: J. B. Lippincott, 1926). [An
       attempt to give the "essence" of seven leading novelists of
       the day: T. Thurston, M. Sinclair, G. Frankau, H. Walpole,
       W. B. Maxwell,"I. Hay," and "R. West"].

170   _____. <u>Peeps at the Mighty.</u> (London: Drane; New York:
       Lippincott, 1927). [A collection of nine essays on literary
       figures, including two on H. G. Wells, and one on each of
       G. K. Chesterton and A. Bennett].

171   _____. <u>Some Goddesses of the Pen, Studies of Eight</u>
       <u>Women Authors.</u> (London: Daniel, 1927; Philadelphia: Lip-
       pincott, 1928; Books for Libraries Press, 1966). [The study
       picks on some salient features of each of the eight women
       authors: S. Kaye-Smith, R. Macaulay, E. M. Dell, Baroness
       Orczy, Mrs. F. Sidgwick, C. Stockley, Mrs. H. de la Pasture,
       and Mrs. Baillie-Reynolds].

172   _____. <u>Philosophies in Modern Fiction.</u> (London: C.
       W. Daniel, 1929). [An attempt to show the outlook embodied
       in the novels of twelve contemporary writers, five of whom
       are discussed in <u>Novelists: We are Seven.</u> The remaining
       seven are J. M. Barrie, H. Belloc, A. Bennett, G. K. Chester-
       ton, T. Hardy, R. Kipling, and H. G. Wells].

173   _____. <u>Some Catholic Novelists: Their Art</u>
       <u>and Outlook.</u> (London: Burns Oates & Washbourne; Milwaukee:
       Bruce, 1931). [Literary criticism and appreciation, with
       special reference to the religious message discerned in the
       writings of G. K. Chesterton, H. Belloc,"J. Ayscough," R. H.
       Benson, P. Gibbs, S. Kaye-Smith, and K. Tynan].

174   Breit, Harvey. <u>The Writer Observed.</u> (Cleveland: World Pub-
       lishing, 1956; London: Alvin Redman, 1957). [Interviews
       with English and American writers mainly. English novelists
       interviewed are: E. Waugh, E. M. Forster, H. Green, E. Bowen,
       A. Huxley, S. Maugham, J. Cary, C. Woodham-Smith, A. Koestler,
       H. MacInnes, J. B. Priestley, C. Isherwood, and C. S. Fores-
       ter].

175   Brewster, Dorothy and Angus Burrell. <u>Dead Reckonings in</u>
       <u>Fiction.</u> (London & New York: Longmans, Green, 1924).

[Makes some attempt to deal with problems connected with evaluation and a "critical point of view". Discusses works by H. James, J. Conrad, M. Sinclair, and D. H. Lawrence among others].

176 _____. Adventure or Experience: Four Essays on Certain Writers and Readers of Novels. (New York: Columbia University Press; London: Oxford University Press, 1930). [Asserts that critical values are tentative, for the reading of fiction is a personal adventure or experience. Discusses works by S. Maugham, A. Bennett, V. Woolf and others].

177 _____. Modern Fiction. (New York: Columbia University Press; London: Oxford University Press, 1934). [Discusses briefly the reader's relation to fiction. Chs. II-VII and IX are revised versions of chapters in Dead Reckonings in Fiction and Adventure or Experience. Includes studies of J. Joyce, A. Huxley, and "proletarian fiction"].

178 _____. "A Pursuit of Values in Fiction." Essays of Three Decades. Edited by Arno L. Bader and Carlton F. Wells. (New York and London: Harper, 1939), pp. 417-430. Also in Modern English Readings. Edited by R. S. Loomis and D. L. Clark. (New York: Farrar, 1934), pp. 123-131. [Advocates personal analyses of novels rather than the application of arbitrary dogmas of criticism to suggest the values of fiction as "a statement of our own confusedly realized experience . . . a dream of what we should like to be . . . an outlet for moods . . . an excuse for self-pity, a device for evasion"].

179 British Writers and Their Work: No. 3. General Editor, T. O. Beachcroft. Editor of the American Edition, J. W. Robinson. (Lincoln: University of Nebraska Press, 1963). [Studies on V. Woolf, E. M. forster, and K. Mansfield, originally published separately (London: Longmans, Green, 1960, 1962, 1963) for the British Council and the National Book League].

180 British Writers and Their Work: No. 10. General Editor, T. O. Beachcroft. Editor of the American Edition, J. W. Robinson. (Lincoln: University of Nebraska Press, 1966). [Studies on H. James, J. Conrad, and D. H. Lawrence, originally published separately (London: Longmans, Green, 1956, 1957, and 1960) for the British Council and the National Book League].

181 Brockway, James. Waar Zijn de Angry Young Men Gebleven? En andere Stukken. (Amsterdam: Uitgeverij Contact, 1965). [A collection of previously published review articles in Dutch magazines and periodicals. Includes four on I. Murdoch, two on each of M. Spark, W. Golding and A. Sillitoe, and one on each of L. Durrell, J. Bowen, C. Wilson, K. Waterhouse, B. Brophy, "The Angry Young Men," S. Barstow, D. Sto-

rey, C. Isherwood, and A. Wilson].

182 Broes, Arthur T., et al. Lectures on Modern Novelists. Carnegie Series in English, 7. (Pittsburgh: Carnegie Institute of Technology, 1963). [Lectures include one on "The
Two Worlds of W. Golding" (pp. 1-15) and another on "The
Vision of H. James" (pp. 55-57)].

183 Brome, Vincent. Six Studies in Quarrelling. (London: The
Cresset Press, 1958). [Excerpts from letters, pamphlets,
books, and documents, with necessary background information,
to provide a record of the literary quarrels between G. B.
Shaw, H. G. Wells, H. A. Jones, H. Belloc, G. K. Chesterton,
and Dr. Coulton].

184 _____. Four Realist Novelists: Arthur Morrison, Edwin
Pugh, Richard Whiteing, William Pett Ridge. (London: Longmans, Green, 1965). [Maintains that though the four novelists had exceptional and individual skills in evoking the
London scene and London characters, and presenting the East
End from the inside, they do not give a representative picture of it, that the English School of Realists' photographic representation of events lacked depth].

185 *Bronzwaer, W. J. M. Vormen van imitatie. Opstellen over
Engelse en Amerikaanse Literatuur. (Amsterdam: Ayhrnsrum-
Polak & Van Gennep, 1969).

186 Brook, Donald. Writer's Gallery: Biographical Sketches of
Britain's Greatest Writers, and their Views on Reconstruction.
(London: Rockliff, 1944). [Writers are alphabetically ar-
ranged and some of them omitted owing to the wartime circum-
stances. G. A. Birmingham, V. Brittain, A. J. Cronin, W. Deep-
ing, G. Frankau, N. Jacob, S. Jameson, S. Kaye-Smith, C.
Mackenzie, W. S. Maugham, J. C. Powys, J. B. Priestley, F.
Swinnerton, H. G. Wells, and F. B. Young].

187 Brooks, Cleanth. The Writer and His Community: The Twenty-
First W. P. Ker Memorial Lecture Delivered in the University
of Glasgow, 15 Oct. 1965. (Glasgow: Jackson, 1968). Reprinted in A Shaping Joy: Studies in the Writer's Craft.
(New York: Harcourt; London: Methuen, 1971), pp. 17-37.
[On the importance of the community, and the alienation of
the writer].

188 _____. A Shaping Joy: Studies in the Writer's Craft.
(New York: Harcourt; London: Methuen, 1971). [Includes
among the collection of essays written and published over
the previous ten years, "The Writer and His Community," pp.
17-37, a study of J. Joyce's Ulysses, pp. 66-87, and "The
Role of Close Analysis" in the criticism of fiction, pp. 143-
166].

189 Brooks, Van Wyck, ed. Writers at Work: The 'Paris Review'

Interviews. With an Introduction by the Editor. Second
Series. (London: Secker & Warburg; New York: The Viking
Press, 1963). [Included in the profiles of contemporary
authors are A. Huxley, H. Green, and L. Durrell].

190 Brophy, Brigid. Don't Never Forget: Collected Views and
Reviews. (London: Jonathan Cape, 1966; New York: Holt,
Rinehart, 1967). [Included are reviews on novels by E. Waugh,
I. Compton-Burnett, and K. Amis--pp. 156-158, 167-171, 217-
223--and review articles on critical works on V. Woolf and
H. James--pp. 182-186, 203-209--written in 1963 and 1964,
and published in The New Statesman, London Magazine, and
The Sunday Times].

191 Brower, R[euben] A[rthur]. The Fields of Light: An Experiment in Critical Reading. (New York: Oxford University
Press, 1951). [Introduces and discusses a number of "de-
signs"--imagery, metaphor, irony, sound and symbol--in selected poetry, three novels and a play. Mrs. Dalloway and
A Passage to India are two of the novels].

192 _____, ed. Twentieth-Century Literature in Retrospect.
Harvard English Studies, 2. (Cambridge, Massachusetts:
Harvard University Press, 1971). [A collection of works by
different critics which includes essays on J. Joyce's The
Dubliners, and I. Murdoch's "London Novels," also F. Kermode's
"The English Novel, circa 1907"].

193 Brown, Curtis. Contacts. (London: Cassell; New York: Harper, 1935). [An account of his contacts with eminent people
of his day, often in the form of autobiographical reminiscences. D. H. Lawrence, H. G. Wells, J. Galsworthy, C. Dane,
and others].

194 Brown, E[dward] K[illoran]. Rhythm in the Novel. (Toronto:
University of Toronto Press, 1950; London: Oxford University
Press, 1951). [The Alexander Lectures delivered at the University of Toronto, 1950. A study of the kinds of rhythm,
"reflection with variation," in the words of E. M. Forster,
in four lectures. The first lecture discusses the simple
combinations of "word and phrase, sequences of incident and
groupings of character," the second, a more complex combination: "the growth of a symbol as it accretes meaning from
a succession of contexts." The third discusses interweaving
themes, and the fourth examines the various combinations in
E. M. Forster's novels. References to H. James, V. Woolf,
and A. Huxley].

195 Brown, [Ernest] Francis, ed. Highlights of Modern Literature: A Permanent Collection of Memorable Essays from 'The
New York Times Book Review'. (New York: The New American
Library, 1954). [A collection which includes articles on
writers and writing by E. Bowen, A. Pryce-Jones, J. Cary,
and E. Janeway. See individual entries].

196   , ed. Opinions and Perspectives from 'The New
York Times Book Review'. (Boston: Houghton MIfflin, 1964).
[A collection which includes articles on contemporary wri-
ters and on authors' experience by K. Amis, E. Bowen, E.
Janeway, V. S. Pritchett, and S. Spender. See individual
entries].

197   , ed. The Best of 'Speaking of Books' from 'The
New York Times Book Review'. With an Introduction. (New
York: Holt, Rinehart and Winston, 1969). [A collection
which includes articles on the writing experience by A. Bur-
gess and A. Waugh, and on aspects of novel writing by B.
Glanville and J. Bowen. See individual entries].

198   Brumm, Ursula. "Symbolism and the Novel." The Partisan
Review Anthology. Edited by William Phillips and Philip
Rahv. (New York: Holt, 1962), pp. 221-230. Also in Critical Approaches to Fiction. Edited by Shiv K. Kumar and
Keith F. McKean. (New York: McGraw-Hill, 1968), pp. 367-
381. Repr. from The Partisan Review, XXV:3 (Summer 1958),
329-342. [See entry under Periodicals].

199   Buckler, William E., ed. Novels in the Making. (Boston:
Houghton Mifflin, 1961). [A collection of selected Prefaces
by J. Conrad, H. James, A. Bennett, and D. H. Lawrence, and
E. Bowen's "Notes on Writing a Novel"].

200   Bullett, Gerald. Modern English Fiction: A Personal View.
(London: Herbert Jenkins, 1926). [Selects for the study,
H. G. Wells, A. Bennett, J. Galsworthy, J. Conrad, and E. M.
Forster as the major writers, the bulk of whose work has
been done in the present century, and considers the work of
J. Joyce, V. Woolf, and D. H. Lawrence under the general
heading of "Eccentricities"].

201   Burack, A[braham] S[aul], ed. The Craft of Novel Writing.
(Boston: The Writer, Inc., 1948). [A collection of articles from The Writer, providing instruction, inspiration and
entertainment on the technical aspects of novel writing.
Includes "Time and the Novel" by L. Krey, pp. 129-139, and
"History and the Novel" by H. Allen, pp. 139-149. See individual entries].

202   Burdett, Osbert. "Tendencies in Recent English Literature."
The New World Order. Essays arranged and edited by F. S.
Marvin. (London: Oxford University Press, 1932), pp. 57-79.
[Originally a lecture delivered August 1931, surveying the
tendencies of poetry, drama, and the novel in the twenties,
and predicting further change].

203   Burgess, Anthony. The Novel Today. Bibliographical Series
of Supplements to British Book News. (London: Longmans,
Green, 1963). [A survey of the contemporary scene. The five-
page introduction expresses the idea that the British novel

is no longer merely produced in Britain, that it is "idle
to search for dominant themes" in the contemporary British
novel].

204 _____. The Novel Now: A Student's Guide to Contemporary Fiction. (London: Faber & Faber, 1967). Published in U. S. A. as: The Novel Now: A Guide to Contemporary Fiction. (New York: W. W. Norton, 1967). [The
Guide concentrates on the forties and fifties, and examines
the variety of themes and techniques of the English novel,
and the achievements of each major novelist].

205 _____. Urgent Copy: Literary Studies. (London: Jonathan Cape; New York: W. W. Norton, 1968). [A collection of
reviews and review articles previously published. Includes
reviews of works by G. Greene, E. Waugh, J. Joyce, W. Lewis,
A. Koestler, and E. Bowen].

206 _____. "Speaking of Books: The Seventeenth Novel."
The Best of 'Speaking of Books' from 'The New York Times Book
Review'. Edited with an Introduction by E. F. Brown. (New
York: Holt, Rinehart and Winston, 1969), pp. 85-89. Re-
printed from The New York Times Book Review (21 August 1966),
pp. 2, 14. [See entry under Periodicals].

207 Burgum, Edwin Berry. The Novel and the World's Dilemma.
(New York & London: Oxford University Press, 1947). [A
collection of essays, some of which are reprinted from peri-
odicals, inquiring into the philosophy of the novel and its
present plight, with special reference to the American novel.
Included are essays on J. Joyce reprinted from the Virginia
Quarterly Review, and one on A. Huxley and V. Woolf from the
Antioch Review].

208 Calder, Jenni. Chronicles of Conscience: A Study of George
Orwell and Arthur Koestler. (London: Secker & Warburg, 1968;
University of Pittsburgh Press, 1969). [Explores the similarities and differences of the two writers in the way they
reflected and reacted to the political life of their time].

209 Calder-Marshall, Arthur. "Fiction Today." The Arts To-day.
Edited by Geoffrey Grigson. (London: The Bodley Head, 1935),
pp. 113-149. [Insists on the novelist's need "to perfect a
prose, each word of which is essential," and to face "the
world in which he lives and understand the nature of its
problems," and considers J. Joyce, D. H. Lawrence, and W.
Lewis as "formative influences" on younger novelists. Also
surveys briefly A. Huxley, V. Woolf, T. P. Powys, J. Hanley,
G. Greene, and C. Isherwood as writers deserving "mention,"
and other leading contemporary American and German novelists].

210 Calderwood, James L. & Harold E. Toliver, eds. Perspectives
in Fiction. (New York, London & Toronto: Oxford University
Press, 1968). [A collection of twenty-six reprinted essays
and extracts by different writers on recurrent topics and

problems ranging from the Nature and Method of Fiction, to Plot, Structure and Character].

211 Calverton, Victor Francis. Sex Expression in Literature. With an Introduction by Harry Elmer Barnes. (New York: Boni & Liveright, 1926). [Discusses sex attitudes and relates sex expression in literature to its social origin. Ch. X, pp. 268-309, discusses 20th century sex release in literature. References to J. Joyce, D. H. Lawrence, H. G. Wells, and A. Huxley].

212 Campos, Christopher. The View of France from Arnold to Bloomsbury. (London: Oxford University Press, 1965). [Originally a doctoral dissertation presented to Gonville and Caius College, Cambridge. Examines the view of France as it is seen through the writings of A. Bennett, H. James, and G. Moore among others].

213 Canby, Henry Seidel. Definitions: Essays in Contemporary Criticism. First Series. (New York: Harcourt, Brace; London: Jonathan Cape, 1922). [A collection of previously published essays and reviews, mostly on American literature. Includes under "Men and their Books," sections on J. Conrad and H. James].

214 _____. Seven Years' Harvest: Notes on Contemporary Literature. (New York: Farrer & Rinehart, 1936; Kennikat Press, 1966). [Essays and reviews from The Saturday Review of Literature, except for one, "Fiction Tells All," written during the depression years, and giving his immediate reactions to ideas and literature. Included are essays on R. Kipling, J. Galsworthy, and D. H. Lawrence].

215 _____, Amy Loveman, William Rose Benet, Christopher Morley, & May Lamberton Becker, eds. Designed for Reading. An anthology drawn from 'The Saturday Review of Literature', 1924-1934. (New York: Macmillan, 1934). [The anthology includes an essay by E. Wharton on modern fiction, pp. 37-42, an editorial on D. H. Lawrence, pp. 167-169, and reviews of critical works on J. Joyce and J. Conrad].

216 Capey, Arthur. "The Post-War English Novel." Literature and Environment: Essays in Reading and Social Studies. Edited by Fred Inglis, with a Foreword by Denys Thompson. (London: Chatto & Windus, 1971), pp. 14-40. [Analyses of selected novels, not necessarily "established classics," but because they are representative of the age and bring into focus contemporary values and attitudes. I. Fleming, N. Shute, H. E. Bates, C. P. Snow, E. Waugh, G. Greene, J. Cary, H. Green, L. P. Hartley, K. Amis, I. Murdoch, W. Golding, J. Braine, A. Sillitoe, L. R. Banks, and E. O'Brien].

217 Carnegie Series in English: No. 7. Lectures on Modern Novelists. (Pittsburgh, Pennsylvania: Carnegie Institute of Technology, 1963). [Includes a lecture on "The Vision of

H. James," one on "The Two Worlds of W. Golding," and another on D. Jones' In Parenthesis].

218 "Carruthers, John." [John Young Thomson Greig]. Scheherazade, or The Future of the English Novel. (London: Kegan Paul, Trench, Trubner; New York: E. P. Dutton, 1927). [A 91-page essay that regards postwar English fiction as falling short because of the spiritual conditions prevailing and the confusing literary and scientific influences].

219 Cary, Joyce. "On the Function of the Novelist." Highlights of Modern Literature: A Permanent Collection of Memorable Essays from the 'New York Times Book Review'. Edited by Francis Brown. (New York: The New American Library, 1954), pp. 53-57. Repr. from The New York Times Book Review (30 October 1949), 1, 52. [See entry under Periodicals].

220 Catholic Profiles, Series I. With an Introduction by Michael de la Bedoyère. (London: Paternoster Publications, 1945). [Short articles reprinted from The Catholic Herald. Includes one on E. Waugh and one on G. Greene].

221 "Caudwell, Christopher." [Christopher St. John Sprigg]. Studies in a Dying Culture. With an Introduction by John Strachey. (London: The Bodley Head, 1938). [Studies of individual writers and themes from a communist viewpoint. Includes studies of D. H. Lawrence and H. G. Wells].

222 Caute, David. The Illusion: An Essay on Politics, Theatre and the Novel. (London: Panther; New York: Harper & Row, 1972). [Discusses the possible relationships of literature to political commitment. Ch. VII examines possibilities in the novel. References to H. James, H. G. Wells, G. Orwell, W. Golding, A. Huxley, and J. Fowles].

223 Cazamian, Louis. "The Method of Discontinuity in Modern Art and Literature." Criticism in the Making. (New York: Macmillan, 1929), pp. 63-80. [Lecture delivered at the Rice Institute, Houston, Texas, in May 1924, on the modern craze for discontinuity and its methods, especially in literature, and the novel in particular, as stimulated by the new psychological realism, and an assessment of its merits and its future].

224 Cazamian, Madeleine L. Le Roman et les idées en Angleterre. (1860-1914). Vol. III. Les doctrines d'action et l'aventure (1880-1914). (Paris: Les Belles Lettres, 1955). [Discusses movements of thought at the turn of the century, the spirit of adventure in the novels of R. L. Stevenson and J. Conrad, the moral and social preoccupation in the novels of G. Meredith, J. Galsworthy, and H. G. Wells, and religion in the novel].

225 Cecchi, Emilio. Scrittori Inglesi e Americani. 2 Vols.

(Milano: G. Carraba, 1935). [Vol. I contains, among others, studies of J. Conrad, H. G. Wells, N. Douglas, and G. K. Chesterton. Vol. II contains, among others, studies of K. Mansfield, V. Woolf, A. Huxley, and D. H. Lawrence].

226 Cecil, Lord David. Poets and Storytellers. (London: Constable; New York: Macmillan, 1949). [Includes an essay, pp. 153-201, on V. Woolf and E. M. Forster].

227 _____. The Fine Art of Reading, and Other Literary Studies. (London: Constable; Indianapolis: Bobbs-Merrill, 1957). [A collection of lectures and talks which include one on J. Conrad and another on the "Forms of English Fiction," pp. 95-110, in which the author emphasises the need for "unity, pattern, harmony," and the creation of an illusion of life in the novel].

228 Chapple, J[ohn] A[lfred] V[ictor]. Documentary and Imaginative Literature, 1880-1920. (London: Blandford Press; New York: Barnes and Noble, 1970). [Attempts to bring out "the many and fascinating ways in which history can be connected with literature." A. Bennett, G. K. Chesterton, J. Conrad, F. M. Ford, E. M. Forster, J. Galsworthy, H. James, J. Joyce, R. Kipling,D. H. Lawrence, W. Lewis, S. Maugham, G. Moore, H. G. Wells, V. Woolf, and others].

229 Charques, R. D. Contemporary Literature and Social Revolution. (London: Martin Secker, 1933; Haskell House, 1966). [Attempts to relate the conditions and characteristics of "post-war" literature, and the apparent trends of poetry and the novel with the social and political tendencies of postwar England. J. Joyce, V. Woolf, D. H. Lawrence, A. Huxley, J. Galsworthy, and E. M. Forster].

230 Chatterjee, Sisir. The Novel as the Modern Epic. (Calcutta: Uttarayan, 1955; The Folcroft Press, 1970). [A 30-page booklet remarking on the absence of both "hero" and "villain" from the modern novel, for the individual is not so much in conflict with others as with social forces changing the modern world].

231 _____. Problems in Modern English Fiction. (Calcutta: Bookland Private Ltd., 1965). [Discusses the disappearance of the story and the hero (see preceding entry), the propagation of ideas, and the emergence and growth of the stream of consciousness technique in the modern novel. H. James, J. Joyce, V. Woolf, J. Conrad, D. H. Lawrence, and A. Huxley].

232 Chattopadhyaya, Sisir. The Technique of the Modern English Novel. (Calcutta: Firma K. L. Mukhopadhyay, 1959). [(N.U.C., C.B.I., and the copy examined reveal "Chattopadhyaya" as author; but the British Museum S. I. entry, and the British Museum Catalogue of Printed Books, and the contents indicate "Chatterjee"). Defines characteristic aspects of modern fiction:

31

the process of turning inward, the new method of characterization, the disappearance of storytelling, and the use of
new language to render the emotional and sensory experience
of man. H. James, J. Conrad, J. Joyce, and V. Woolf].

233   Chesterton, G. K.   "On Philosophy versus Fiction." All Is
      Grist: A Book of Essays. (London: Methuen, 1931; New
      York: Dodd, 1932). Also in G. K. Chesterton. Edited by
      E. V. Knox. (London: Methuen, 1933), pp. 18-24. [On the
      rejection of the religious and the romantic in the modern
      novel and concentration on "the microscopic description of
      . . . aimless appetites"].

234   Chevally, Abel.   Le Roman anglais de notre temps. (London:
      Oxford University Press, 1921). Translated by B. R. Redman
      as The Modern English Novel. (New York: Knopf, 1925).
      [Surveys the rise of the novel until the nineties, and con-
      centrates on those he considers to be the six major contem-
      porary novelists: H. James, J. Joyce, R. Kipling, A. Bennett,
      J. Galsworthy,and J. Conrad, followed by a general study of
      female novelists from G. Eliot to World War I. Chs. X and
      XI discuss the new generation of H. Walpole, O. Onions, C.
      Mackenzie, J. D. Beresford, D. H. Lawrence, and F. Swinner-
      ton, and the postwar novel].

235   Chew, Samuel C[laggett].   The Nineteenth Century and After
      (1789-1939). A Literary History of England (Vol. V). Edi-
      ted by Albert C. Baugh. (New York: Appleton-Century-Crofts;
      London: Routledge & Kegan Paul, 1948). [See: XL. The Mod-
      ern Novel, pp. 1547-1572, also XXXVI. The Novel: Naturalism
      and Romance, pp. 1485-1507].

236   Church, Margaret.   Time and Reality: Studies in Contemporary
      Fiction. (Chapel Hill: The University of North Carolina
      Press, 1963). [A study of the concept of Time as one of the
      central preoccupations of the 20th century novel in France,
      England, America, and Germany. J. Joyce, V. Woolf, and A.
      Huxley among others].

237   Church, Richard.   British Authors. A Twentieth Century Gal-
      lery with 53 Portraits. (London and New York: Longmans,
      Green, 1943; Books for Libraries, 1970). [Miniature word
      pictures of writers pointing out the outstanding qualities
      of each writer and how they are revealed in his work, and
      touching upon the relationship between the writer and his
      background].

238   _____ .   The Growth of the English Novel. (London: Me-
      thuen, 1951). [An historical approach to the novelists who
      have contributed during the past four centuries to the growth
      of the novel. Treatment of contemporary writers, pp. 195-213,
      rather perfunctory].

239   _____ .   Speaking Aloud. (London: Heinemann, 1968).
      [A collection of lectures and talks. Includes "How the Nov-

elist works," pp. 168-204, the Giff Edmonds Memorial Lecture, 7 June 1962, repr. in Essays by Divers Hands, XXXIII (1965), 56-69, and "The Central English Flavour," pp. 13-33 (on H. E. Bates and C. P. Snow)].

240   Churchill, R[eginald] C[harles]. "The Comedy of Ideas: Crosscurrents in the Fiction and Drama of the Twentieth Century." The Pelican Guide to English Literature, Vol. 7. The Modern Age. Edited by Boris Ford. (London: Cassell; Baltimore: Penguin, 1961), pp. 221-230. [On the interchange of techniques and practices between the novel and drama of H. James and G. B. Shaw, and the predominance of the Dickensian tradition of the comedy of ideas in G. B. Shaw, G. K. Chesterton, A. Huxley, and G. Orwell].

241   Clarke, D[avid] Waldo. Modern English Writers. The Essential English Library Series. (London and New York: Longmans, Green, 1947). [A study of writers whose works show "both tradition and experiment," and intended mainly for foreign students. J. Conrad, R. Kipling, A. Bennett, J. Galsworthy, D. H. Lawrence, H. G. Wells, S. Maugham, and J. B. Priestley among others].

242   _____. Writers of Today. The Essential English Library Series. (London and New York: Longmans, Green, 1956). [Examines the literary scene and makes separate studies of J. Joyce, V. Woolf, A. Huxley, C. Morgan, and G. Greene].

243   Clarke, Ignatius Frederick. Voices Prophesying War 1763-1984. (London: Oxford University Press, 1966). [An account of the origin and development of imaginary wars which display various European attitudes to war itself. H. G. Wells, A. Huxley, and G. Orwell among others].

244   Coates, J[ohn] B[ourne]. Ten Modern Prophets. (London: Frederick Muller, 1944). [An outline of the views of ten "thinkers," none of them a specialist on world problems. A. Huxley, D. H. Lawrence, and H. G. Wells among others].

245   Cohn, Dorrit. "Psycho-Analysis: A Means for Rendering Consciousness in Fiction." Probleme des Erzählens in der Weltliteratur: Festschrift für Käte Hamburger zum 75. Geburtstag. Edited by Fritz Martini. (Stuttgart: Ernst Klett Verlag, 1971), pp. 291-303. [Explores the use of similes, "psychoanalogies," in portraying the inner world of fictional characters, either as a complement to, or on occasion, instead of, the interior monologue and the narrated monologue (Erlebte Rede). References to H. James and V. Woolf among others.

246   Cohn, Ruby. "Joyce and Beckett, Irish Cosmopolitan." Proceedings of the IVth Congress of the International Comparative Literature Association, Fribourg, 1964. Edited by Francois Jost. (The Hague & Paris: Mouton, 1966), Vol. I, pp. 109-113. [On their cosmopolitan culture and linguistic

command].

247 Collings, Arthur Simons. English Literature of the Twentieth Century. (London: University Tutorial Press, 1951). Fourth edition, with a postscript on the nineteen-fifties by Frank Whitehead. (London: University Tutorial Press, 1960). [A survey of major writers and tendencies. Chs. X-XVIII consider major individual English novelists: A. Bennett, H. G. Wells, J. Galsworthy, J. Conrad, E. M. Forster, D. H. Lawrence, J. Joyce, V. Woolf, A. Huxley, J. C. Powys, G. Greene, and E. Bowen. Ch. IX, pp. 132-155, is a survey of the novel from 1900 to 1950].

248 Collins, Joseph M. D. The Doctor Looks at Literature: Psychological Studies of Life and Letters. (New York: George H. Doran; London: Allen & Unwin, 1923; Kennikat Press, 1972). [Examines the relationship between psychology and fiction, and makes separate studies of J. Joyce, D. Richardson and D. H. Lawrence among others, and the "literary ladies of London," S. Benson, V. Woolf, K. Mansfield, and "R. West"].

249 Collins, Norman. The Facts of Fiction. (London: Gollancz, 1932; New York: E. P. Dutton, 1933; The Folcroft Press, 1969). [A personal impression of novels from Richardson to J. Joyce, aimed at the general reader. H. James, D. H. Lawrence, G. Moore are examined separately. A. Bennett, H. G. Wells, J. Galsworthy, and J. B. Priestley are grouped under "The Regular Army," pp. 258-276, and J. Joyce and V. Woolf considered in the last chapter].

250 Colmer, John, ed. Approaches to the Novel. (Adelaide: Rigby, 1966; London & Edinburgh: Oliver & Boyd, 1967). [Papers read at a seminar on the study of the novel in the University of Adelaide, August 1965. The first chapter, "Form and Design in the novel" by the Editor, discusses how to give an illusion of real life and retain unity, pattern and harmony. The volume also includes individual studies of H. James and E. Waugh].

251 Colum, Mary M. "The Modern Mode in Literature." The Writer and his Craft. Foreword by Roy W. Cowden. (Ann Arbor: University of Michigan Press, 1954), pp. 158-173. [The 1943 Hopwood Lecture. Suggests that the writer adopt a broad and deep realism that "takes into account the positive as well as the negative aspects of human character," and recover some of the human worth that would free fiction from the "clinical atmosphere"].

252 Combs, George Hamilton. These Amazing Moderns. (St. Louis: The Bethany Press, 1933). [A series of twelve "lectures" on individual writers--among them H. G. Wells, A. Huxley and R. Kipling--given by a minister on "church nights" to an audience which included a "few . . . professional students"].

253 Comfort, Alexander. The Novel and Our Time. (London: Phoenix House; Denver: Alan Swallow, 1948; Folcroft Library Editions, 1970). [Discusses critical and technical problems arising out of the novel in its present setting in an "asocial" society].

254 Connolly, Cyril. The Condemned Playground, Essays: 1927-1944. (London: Routledge & Sons, 1945; New York: Macmillan, 1946). [A series of articles and reviews (previously published) on the literary scene of the thirties. Pages 90-118 deal with the novel].

255 _____. Enemies of Promise. (London: Routledge & Sons, 1938; Boston: Little, Brown, 1939; rev. ed. New York: Macmillan, 1948; London: Routledge & Kegan Paul, 1949). [An inquiry into the nature of contemporary prose style and modern literary tendencies. Part three is autobiographical].

256 _____, ed. The Golden Horizon. With an Introduction by the Editor. (London: Weidenfeld & Nicholson, 1953). [Reprints from Horizon during the war years, but avoids well known essays and translations of essays. Includes essays on J. Joyce, V. Woolf, and H. James].

257 _____. Previous Convictions. (London: Hamish Hamilton; New York: Harper and Row, 1963). [A collection of essays on places of interest he had visited, and on literary figures. Part III is devoted to essays on contemporary writers. Included are three on J. Joyce, two on D. H. Lawrence, and one on each of H. James and G. Orwell].

258 Conrad, Joseph. Joseph Conrad on Fiction. Edited by Walter F. Wright. Regents Critics Series. (Lincoln: University of Nebraska Press, 1964). [Includes excerpts from his Letters, Essays on several books and authors, and his notes and Prefaces from Almayer's Folly (1895) to The Shorter Tales (1924)].

259 Cook, Albert. The Meaning of Fiction. (Detroit: Wayne State University Press, 1960). [An "inductive" approach in order to see the meaning of fiction by focusing on the contents of individual novels, for a novel "presents the results of a cognitive act." Includes H. James, D. H. Lawrence, J. Joyce, and J. Conrad].

260 Cooper, Frederic T. Some English Storytellers: A Book of the Younger Novelists. (New York: Henry Holt; London: Grant Richards, 1912; Books for Libraries, 1968). [Studies of individual novelists, some of which were published in whole, or in part, previously. J. Conrad, M. Hewlett, E. Phillpotts, R. Kipling, J. Galsworthy, A. Bennett, A. Hope, M. Sinclair, A. Ollivant, R. Hichens, "Frank Danby," and Mrs. J. Frankau].

261 Cooper, William. "The Technique of the Novel." The Author and the Public: Problems of Communication. The P. E. N.

Congress, July 1956, London. Edited, with an Introduction by
C. V. Wedgewood. (London: Hutchinson, 1957), pp. 161-165.
[Suggests that the re-introduction of narrative has replaced
the "experimental technique" that had reached its peak in the
thirties, and given new life to the present novel; nevertheless, a recognition of the limitation it imposes on the angle
of vision is necessary for novelists to "know when to think
about throwing it off"].

262 _____. [Tradition and Innovation in Prose Literature].
Tradition and Innovation in Contemporary Literature. (The
International P. E. N. Conference, October 1964, Budapest.
(Budapest: Corvina Press, 1964), pp. 61-68. [Contends that
"communication," "tradition," and "innovation" are words
loaded with "positive value judgments," and condemns writers,
especially novelists, who resort to the anti-novel in the
name of innovation, and "liberated themselves from the tyranny
of time," and consequently, from the coherence and order of
narrative and changing human character].

263 Cornillon, Susan Kappelman, ed. Images of Women in Fiction:
Feminist Perspectives. (Bowling Green, Ohio: Bowling Green
University Popular Press, 1972). [A collection of 23 essays
by different writers illustrating "new directions" for women
in reading and understanding fiction. Essays are grouped
under four main headings: "Woman as Heroine" discussing traditional women, "The Invisible Woman" investigating the role
women are forced to play, "The Woman as Hero" investigating
fiction which deals with women as "whole people," and "Feminist Aesthetics"--portions of the creed and manifesto of
women. J. Joyce, H. James, V. Woolf, and D. H. Lawrence among
others].

264 Cornwell, Ethel F. The "Still Point": Theme and Variations
in the Writings of T. S. Eliot, Coleridge, Yeats, Henry James,
Virginia Woolf, and D. H. Lawrence. (New Brunswick, New
Jersey: Rutgers University Press, 1962). [Discusses the
concept of union with an outside spiritual center, and emphasises "idea" rather than "image"].

265 Courtney, Janet E[lizabeth]. The Women of My Time. (London:
Lovat Dickson, 1934). [Ch. X, pp. 213-247, discusses women's
reactions to the war, relying mainly on what the author re-
members or has heard, and how writers like K. Mansfield, R.
Macaulay, V. Woolf and E. Sitwell found in art a way of es-
cape--"tragic, ironical, dreamy, poetical"--from a world that
had crashed around them].

266 Coveny, Peter. Poor Monkey: The Child in Literature. (London: Rockliff, 1957; rev. and repr. as The Image of Childhood.
With an Introduction by F. R. Leavis. Baltimore: Penguin
Books, 1967). [A study of childhood as it appears in English
and American literature written for adults, in the 19th and
20th centuries. H. James, J. Joyce, V. Woolf, and D. H. Law-
rence].

267 Cowley, Malcolm, ed. Writers at Work: 'The Paris Review'
Interviews. With an Introduction by Malcolm Cowley. (London:
Secker & Warburg; New York: Viking Press, 1958). [A series
of interviews with sixteen writers where the creative process
and the craft of writing is discussed. The script is approved
by those interviewed. Included are E. M. Forster, J. Cary,
and A. Wilson].

268 Cox, C[harles] B[rian]. The Free Spirit: A Study of Liberal
Humanism in the Novels of George Eliot, Henry James, E. M.
Forster, Virginia Woolf, and Angus Wilson. (London and New
York: Oxford University Press, 1963). [Besides focusing on
one aspect of each novelist, the book concludes with a study
of the modern novel].

269 _____ and A. E. Dyson, eds. The Twentieth-Century Mind.
History, Ideas and Literature in Britain, 3 vols. (London
and New York: Oxford University Press, 1972). [Vol. 1 1900-
1918 contains an essay on the novel by Alan Friedman, pp. 414-
447; Vol. 2, 1918-1945, "The English Novel" by G. S. Fraser,
pp. 373-417; Vol. 3, 1945-65, "The Novel" by M. Bradbury, pp.
319-383. See individual entries].

270 Craig, Alec. The Banned Books of England. With a Foreword
by E. M. Forster. (London: Allen & Unwin, 1937). Repr. as
The Banned Books of England and Other Countries. A Study of
the Conception of Literary Obscenity. (London: Allen & Unwin, 1962). [Explains the law of Obscene Libel and how it
works, illustrating from the Montalk case, The Well of Loneliness and Ulysses].

271 _____. Above All Liberties. (London: George Allen &
Unwin, 1942). [A sequel to The Banned Books for a wider class
of readers. A historical method of presentation in which the
problem is set against the background of English literary and
social changes].

272 Cronin, Anthony. A Question of Modernity. (London: Secker
& Warburg, 1966). [Revised versions of previously published
writings. Includes a study of modernity in Ch. 1, an interesting analysis of the modern novel in Ch.IV, studies of J.
Joyce and S. Beckett, Chs. V & VI, and a review in Ch. VIII
of the "real issues" in the forties].

273 Cross, Wilbur L[ucius]. The Modern English Novel: An Address Before the American Academy of Art and Letters. (New
Haven: Yale University Press; London: Oxford University
Press, 1928). [Contends that though they may consider the
earlier generation of novelists to be inadequate, modern novelists learn a great deal from them. V. Woolf, H. G. Wells,
H. James, and J. Joyce among others].

274 _____. Four Contemporary Novelists. (New York & London:
Macmillan, 1930; AMS Press, 1971). [A study of J. Conrad,

37

A. Bennett, J. Galsworthy, and H. G. Wells].

275 Crothers, George D[unlap], ed. Invitation to Learning: English and American Novels. (New York & London: Basic Books, 1966). [Transcripts of radio programmes on the C. B. S., 1950-54. Symposia on English and American novels. J. Galsworthy, D. H. Lawrence, and J. Joyce among others].

276 Crowley, Rev. Cornelius P[atrick] J[oseph], C.S.B. The Human Image in Modern British Fiction. (Toronto: The Radio League of St. Michael, 1962). [Transcript of five talks broadcast for the Trans-Canada Catholic Hour on the C. B. C. C. Williams, G. Greene, C. P. Snow, W. Golding, and M. Spark].

277 Cruse, Amy. After the Victorians. (London: George Allen & Unwin; Chester Springs, Pennsylvania: Dufour Editions, 1938). [This sequel to the Victorians and their Books stops with 1914].

278 Cunliffe, J[ohn] W[illiam]. English Literature During the Last Half-Century. (New York: Macmillan, 1919; rev. and enlarged, London & New York: Macmillan, 1923; Books for Libraries Press, 1971). [Separate studies of individual writers with the exception of the last three chapters. J. Conrad, H. G. Wells, J. Galsworthy, and A. Bennett. Ch. XVI, pp. 304-333, surveys the "new" novelists].

279 _____. English Literature in the Twentieth Century. (New York: Macmillan, 1933; Books for Libraries Press, 1967). [Contains separate studies on each of J. Conrad, H. G. Wells, J. Galsworthy, and A. Bennett. Also surveys in Ch. X, pp. 201-259 the achievements of the "Georgian" novelists, D. H. Lawrence, J. Joyce, H. Walpole, G. Cannan, C. Mackenzie, A. Huxley, and V. Woolf].

280 Dahlberg, Edward & Herbert Read. Truth Is More Sacred: A Critical Exchange on Modern Literature. (London: Routledge & Kegan Paul; New York: Noonday Press, 1961). [The exchange, in the form of letters, focuses on J. Joyce, D. H. Lawrence, H. James, R. Graves, and T. S. Eliot].

281 Daiches, David. The Novel and the Modern World. (Chicago: University of Chicago Press; Cambridge: University Press, 1939; rev. ed. 1960). [A study of the novel in the first thirty years of the century. Discusses ways in which novelists responded to certain features of civilization, and the changing attitudes and techniques that resulted from new views about the nature of time and consciousness. J. Conrad, J. Joyce, D. H. Lawrence, and V. Woolf].

282 _____. "Problems for Modern Novelists." 'Accent' Anthology. Selections from Accent, a Quarterly Review of New Literature, 1940-1945. Edited by Kerber Quinn and Charles Shattuck. (New York: Harcourt Brace, 1946). Repr. from

Accent, III (Spring-Summer 1943), 144-151, 231-239. [See entry under periodicals].

283 _____. "The Nature of Fiction." A Study of Literature: For Readers and Critics. (London & Edinburg: Oliver & Boyd, 1956; New York: Philosophical Library, 1957). [Discusses the "rhetorical" and "aesthetic" intentions and the idea of symbolism in fiction].

284 _____. "The Criticism of Fiction: Some Second Thougts." Literary Essays. (London and Edinburgh: Oliver and Boyd, 1956; New York: Philosophical Library, 1957, and reprinted London and Edinburgh: Oliver and Boyd; University of Chicago Press, 1967), pp. 180-191. [Lecture delivered at the University of Rochester, New York in 1950. Maintains that there are "more types of artfulness at work in fiction than are dreamed of," and that the most fruitful criticism "classifies and explains" the reactions of the "qualified" reader with reference to their causes in the work, and not by determining whether a novel conforms to an ideal definition. H. James, J. Joyce, A. Huxley, and others].

285 _____. The Present Age: After 1920. Introductions to English Literature Series: Edited by Bonamy Dobrée. (London: The Cresset Press, 1958). Published in U. S. A. as The Present Age in British Literature. (Bloomington: Indiana University Press, 1958). [A summary of trends, influences and developments that sees "modern" writers against the background of the period as a whole. Pages 85-119 survey fiction. Also contains a bibliography of the works of each writer and selected criticism on each].

286 "Dataller, Roger." [Arthur Archibald Eaglestone]. The Plain Man and the Novel. Discussion Books Series. (London: Thomas Nelson, 1940; repr. under the name Arthur Archibald Eagleston by The Kennikat Press, 1970). [Discusses the concern of the "plain man" for story, validity of character, the decline of the hero, and, in general, for the absence of fiction that will square with his own experience].

287 Davies, [Daniel] Horton. A Mirror of the Ministry in Modern Novels. (New York: Oxford University Press, 1959; Books for Libraries, 1970). [Examines how the Ministry, with its various types of Preachers, Evangelists, Interpreters of the Faith in crisis, Spiritual Directors, Missionaries, and Community Leaders, is present in the modern English and American novel in spite of pride of place being given to "lay" characters. Also inquires into how good religious fiction can be identified and how adequately novelists have depicted the Ministry. G. Greene, S. Maugham, and A. J. Cronin].

288 Davies, Hugh Sykes. Browning and the Modern Novel. The St. John's College Lecture, 1961-62, delivered at the University of Hull, 16 February 1962. (Hull: University of Hull Pub-

lications, 1962; The Folcroft Press, 1969). [Considers Browning's contribution to the modern novel as the inner monologue and soliloquy which have now taken their place beside narrative and dialogue in depicting "incidents in the development of a soul"].

289 Davies, [William] Robertson. A Voice from the Attic. (New York: Alfred A. Knopf; Toronto: McClelland & Stewart, 1960). [General comments on "some aspects of the world of books today, by no means always seriously," including A. Bennett, J. Cary, E. Waugh, A. Huxley, and on sex in the modern novel].

290 Davis, E[dward], comp. Readings in Modern Fiction. (Cape Town: Simondium Publishers, 1964). [A discussion of individual works by 19th and 20th century novelists. Included are novels by J. Conrad, H. James, J. Joyce, D. H. Lawrence, and V. Woolf].

291 Davis, Robert Gorham. "At the Heart of the Story is Man." Highlights of Modern Literature: A Permanent Collection of Memorable Essays from 'The New York Times Book Review'. Edited by Francis Brown. (New York: The New American Library, 1954), pp. 57-62. Repr. from The New York Times Book Review (28 December 1952), 1. [See entry under Periodicals].

292 Davis, Robert Murray, ed. The Novel: Modern Essays in Criticism. (Englewood Cliffs, New Jersey: Prentice-Hall, 1969). [A collection of twenty reprinted essays mainly by critics rather than novelists, which are historically important for the study of fiction, and which focus on concepts of fictional form and technique. Contributors are H. James, R. Scholes, N. Frye, M. Shroder, R. Freedman, M. Schorer, W. Hardy, P. Rahv, W. J. Harvey, N. Friedman, W. C. Booth, E. M. Forster, W. O'Grady, P. Stevick, E. Muir, J. H. Raleigh, L. Lutwack, S. Marcus, J. Wain, and L. Fiedler. See individual entries].

293 Day, Martin S[teele]. History of English Literature: 1837 to the Present. (Garden City, New York: Doubleday, 1964). [Ch. XI, pp. 367-423, examines the fiction of the 20th century].

294 *Debaene, Luc. De Universiteit in de hedendaagse engelse roma (Antwerp: 1964).

295 Delattre, Floris. Le Roman psychologique de Virginia Woolf. (Paris: J. Vrin, 1932. [Ch. I, "Le Roman Féminin en Angleterre," pp. 6-44, surveys English female novelists from 1837 to 1930].

296 Dell, Floyd. Looking at Life. (New York: Alfred A. Knopf; London: Duckworth, 1924). [A collection of essays which includes one on each of G. Moore, G. K. Chesterton, and H. G. Wells].

297 De Voto, Bernard [Augustine]. The World of Fiction. (New York: Houghton & Mifflin, 1950). ["An analysis of the relationship between the person who writes a novel and the person who reads it"].

298 Dipple, Elizabeth. Plot. The Critical Idiom Series, No. 12. General Editor, John D. Jump. (London: Methuen, 1970). [Traces the changing attitude to plot, from Aristotle to E. Wharton's dismissal of it, and examines the various methods by which the idea of plot has been "expanded" in modern criticism].

299 Dobrée, Bonamy. The Lamp and the Lute: Studies in Six Modern Authors. (Oxford: Clarendon Press, 1929). 2nd edition, enlarged and subtitled: Studies in Seven Authors. (London: Frank Cass, 1964). [Includes studies of E. M. Forster, D. H. Lawrence, and L.Durrell].

300 _____. The Unacknowledged Legislator: Conversations on Literature and Politics in a Warden's Post, 1941. P. E. N. Books. (London: Allen and Unwin, 1942). [A 43-page booklet mainly concerned with the scope of the novel, its function and subject matter].

301 Dolezel, Lubomir. "The Typology of the Narrator: Point of View in Viction." To Honor Roman Jacobson: Essays on the Occasion of His Seventieth Birthday, 11 October 1966. (The Hague: Mouton, 1967). [Describes types of narration and devises a new scheme for their classification].

302 Drescher, Horst W., ed. Englische Literatur der Gegenwart in Einzeldarstellungen. With an Introduction by the Editor. (Stuttgart: Alfred Kröner Verlag, 1970). [Includes an essay on each of E. Waugh, C. P. Snow, A. Powell, D. Lessing, A. Wilson, J. Wain, K. Amis, J. Braine, K. Waterhouse, A. Sillitoe, D. Storey, P. H. Newby, L. Durrell, I. Murdoch, W. Golding, and M. Spark. Each essay is followed by a brief biography of the novelist, a list of primary sources, and a selected checklist of criticism. The 20-page Introduction surveys contemporary literature and traces postwar trends in the novel, drama and poetry].

303 Drew, Elizabeth A. The Modern Novel: Some Aspects of Contemporary Fiction. (New York: Harcourt, Brace; London: Jonathan Cape, 1926; The Kennikat Press, 1967). [A study which focuses on J. Galsworthy, H. G. Wells, A. Bennett, and J. Conrad, but which also evolves criteria for the evaluation of novels, and examines the impact of psychology, increased attention to sex in fiction, and "feminine" fiction].

304 _____. "The Novel." The Enjoyment of Literature. (New York: W. W. Norton; Cambridge: University Press, 1935). [Illustrates from works by H. James, A. Bennett, V. Woolf, and J. Conrad among others, the unique interest and essence

41

of the novel, the pleasure proper to it, and the novelist's
problem of how to make the reader "hear, and feel and see as
he has done himself"].

305 _____. The Novel: A Modern Guide to Fifteen English
Masterpieces. (New York: Dell Publishing, 1963). [Included
are J. Conrad's Lord Jim, D. H. Lawrence's Women in Love, H.
James' The Portrait of a Lady, J. Joyce's Portrait of the
Artist, and V. Woolf's To the Lighthouse].

306 Drummond, Andrew L. The Churches in English Fiction. A Literary and Historical Study, from the Regency to the Present
Time, of British and American Fiction. (Leicester: Edgar
Backus, 1950). [The study stops with the efflorescence of
the High Church Movement in the work of C. Mackenzie, pp.
102-104, and of Roman Catholicism in the writing of Mrs. H.
Ward, pp. 138-140].

307 Dujardin, Édouard. Le Monologue intérieur: son apparition,
ses origines, sa place dans l'oeuvre de James Joyce. (Paris:
Albert Messein, 1931). [A study of the interior monologue:
attempts to define it and distinguish it from other monologues
--the psychological, the dramatic, the "intime"].

308 Dupont, Victor. L'Utopie et le roman utopique dans la littérature anglaise. (Paris et Toulouse: Librairie M. Didier,
1941). [Originally a dissertation presented to Université
de Lyons. A historical approach that examines Utopia up to,
and including, A. Huxley and H. G. Wells].

309 Dyson, A[nthony] E[dward]. The Crazy Fabric: Essays in Irony.
(London: Macmillan; New York: St. Martin's Press, 1965).
[Studies written over a number of years examining the personal
mood and tone of different prose writers concerned with irony
from Swift to Orwell. Included are A. Huxley, E. Waugh, and
G. Orwell].

310 "Eagle, Solomon." [Sir J. Collings Squire]. Books in General.
(London: Heinemann; New York: Alfred A. Knopf, 1919). [Se-
lections from a series of weekly contributions to the New
Statesman. Includes notes on J. Galsworthy ("Depressed Phil-
anthropist"), H. James, H. G. Wells (Utopias), and J. Joyce].

311 Eagleton, Terence. Exiles and Emigres: Studies in Modern
Literature. (London: Chatto & Windus; New York: Schocken
Books, 1970). [A series of critical explorations around the
problems raised by the "emigré" theme in 20th century liter-
ature, especially fiction, written by the exile or the alien.
J. Conrad, E. Waugh, G. Greene, G. Orwell, and D. H. Lawrence].

312 Earnshaw, H[erbert] G[eoffrey]. Modern Writers: A Guide to
Twentieth-Century Literature in the English Language. (Edinburgh and London: W. & R. Chambers, 1968). [Attempts to
give a general view of English and American writing by selecting some sixty writers whose work is historically important.

42

Introduces the general reader to each writer by giving a
brief account of the author's life, major works, and signif-
icant characteristics. Includes H. James, J. Conrad, H. G.
Wells, A. Bennett, J. Galsworthy, H. Belloc, G. K. Chesterton,
D. H. Lawrence, J. Joyce, E. M. Forster, V. Woolf, A. Huxley,
E. Waugh, J. B. Priestley, S. Maugham, G. Greene, G. Orwell,
S. Beckett, W. Golding, L. Durrell, and P. Larkin].

313   Eastman, Richard M. A Guide to the Novel. (San Francisco:
       Chandler Publishing Company, 1965). [A guide meant for the
       general reader. Part I provides the "critical vocabulary"
       by analysing the constituent elements of the novel: plot,
       characterisation, narrative manner, and idea; Part II, pp.
       89-165, is a brief history of the novel from its beginnings
       to 1950; and Part III gives an alphabetical list of novelists
       --French, English, and American--with brief introductions and
       selected works].

314   Eastwood, W[ilfred] and J[ohn] T[hompson] Good. Signposts:
       A Guide to Modern English Literature. (Cambridge: Univer-
       sity Press, 1960. For the National Book League). [Contains
       an 18-page survey of general trends in verse, drama, novel,
       prose, and war literature since 1900, followed by lists of
       selected works in each of these categories].

315   Edel, Léon. The Psychological Novel, 1900-1950. (Philadel-
       phia: J. B. Lippincott; London: Hart-Davis, 1955). Rev.
       and reprinted as The Modern Psychological Novel. (New York:
       Grove Press, 1959). Rev. and enlarged with new introduction
       by the author. (New York: Grosset and Dunlop, 1964). [A
       study of the flow of mental experience and psychological
       techniques in the novel. J. Joyce, H. James, and M. Proust].

316   _____ & Gordon N. Ray. Henry James and H. G. Wells: A
       Record of Their Friendship, Their Debate on the Art of Fiction,
       and Their Quarrel. (Urbana: University of Illinois Press;
       London: Rupert Hart Davies, 1958). [The introduction traces
       three separate phases in the relationship, and the debate
       highlights two attitudes to the novel: one that regards it
       as art-form, and the other as social message].

317   Edgar, Pelham. The Art of the Novel: from 1700 to the Pres-
       ent Time. (New York: Macmillan, 1933; Russell and Russell,
       1966). [The study is divided into two parts: Part I, chs. I
       and II, discusses the "essentials" of fiction, and Part II
       interprets different works to ascertain the main drift of
       fiction. Chs. XVII-XX discuss 20th century English and Amer-
       ican novelists to estimate current tendencies. H. James, J.
       Conrad, J. Galsworthy, H. G. Wells, A. Bennett, G. Moore, S.
       Maugham, N. Douglas, A. Huxley, W. Lewis, J. Joyce, D. Rich-
       ardson, V. Woolf, and D. H. Lawrence among others].

318   Electorowicz, Leszek. Zwierciadlo w okruchach: Szkice o
       powiesci amerykanskiej i angielskiej. (Warsaw: Panstwowy

Instytut Wydawniczy, 1966). [A collection of essays, in Polish, on English and American novels and novelists. Included are essays on H. James' method, J. Joyce's Ulysses, "The Angry Young Men," H. G. Wells, D. H. Lawrence, and G. Greene's allegorical thrillers].

319   Eliot, T. S. After Strange Gods: A Primer of Modern Heresy. (London: Faber & Faber, 1934). [The Page-Barbour Lectures at the University of Virginia, 1933. The first lecture reformulates "Tradition" and reconciles thought and feeling with the implication of absolute values. The second lecture illustrates these reflections by some application to modern English literature and shows the "crippling effect" of not having been brought up in an environment of a living and central tradition. (Illustrates from K. Mansfield, J. Joyce, and D. H. Lawrence among others). The third lecture considers the "alarming importance" of personality, and the intrusion of the "diabole." Illustrates from T. Hardy and D. H. Lawrence].

320   Elliot, Robert Carl. The Shape of Utopia: Studies in a Literary Genre. (Chicago & London: University of Chicago Press, 1970). [Includes interpretive studies of individual utopias, and genre studies of the mode itself. A. Huxley and H. G. Wells among others].

321   Elliott, George P. "The Novelist as Meddler." Conversions: Literature and the Modernist Deviation. (New York: E. P. Dutton, 1971), pp. 94-112; also in Critical Approaches to Fiction. Edited by Shiv K. Kumar and Keith F. McKean. (New York: McGraw-Hill, 1968), pp. 333-349. Reprinted from The Virginia Quarterly Review, XL (Winter 1964), 96-113. [See entry under Periodicals].

322   Ellis, G[eoffrey] U[ther]. Twilight on Parnassus: A Survey of Post-War Fiction and Pre-War Criticism. (London: Michael Joseph; Toronto: Saunders, 1939). [Surveys the 19th century in Chs. I-VII, and the change in mood, and the conditions and trends of the twenties in Chs. VIII & IX; also discusses A. Huxley and D. H. Lawrence in Chs. X-XII, and surveys the changes and innovations of J. Joyce, V. Woolf, E. M. Forster, and W. Lewis in Ch. XIII. Ch. XIV deals with A. Bennett, H. G. Wells, and E. Waugh].

323   Ellis, [Henry] Havelock. From Marlowe to Shaw: The Studies, 1876-1936, in English Literature of Havelock Ellis. Edited, with a Foreword, by John Gawsworth, with a Prefatory letter from Thomas Hardy. (London: Williams and Norgate, 1950; Folcroft Library Editions, 1971). [Includes essays on H. G. Wells, J. Conrad, and G. Moore].

324   Ellmann, Richard, ed. Edwardians and Late Victorians. English Institute Essays, 1959. (New York & London: Columbia University Press, 1960). [Includes an essay on H. G. Wells as novelist, and another by the editor, "The Two Faces of

Edward," pp. 188-211, which surveys the first ten years of
the century. J. Joyce, H. James, H. G. Wells, J. Galsworthy,
J. Conrad, and others].

325 Ellmann, Richard & Charles Feidelson, Jr., eds. The Modern
Tradition: Backgrounds of Modern Literature. (New York:
Oxford University Press, 1965). [An exploratory attempt to
represent, by direct quotations, the various factors one is
obliged to take into account when considering "Modernism."
Quotations are,generally speaking, from writers, artists,
philosophers, and scientists, thematically arranged under
nine blanket titles: Symbolism, Realism, Nature, Cultural
History, The Unconcscious, Myth, Self-consciousness, Existence, and Faith].

326 Elmen, Paul. "Twice-Blessed Enamel Flowers: Reality in Contemporary Fiction." The Climate of Faith in Modern Literature. Edited by Nathan A. Scott, Jr. (New York: Seabury
Press, 1964), pp. 84-102. [Maintains that the factual world
as revealed by the choisistes, or even in the novel of compassion, will always remain absurd unless accompanied by some
"perspective into the Beyond" that involves a "recognition of
sources and destiny." Brief references to J. Joyce and G.
Greene].

327 Elwin, Malcolm. Old Gods Falling. (London: Collins; New
York: Macmillan, 1939). [Though mainly a study of England
and the literature of the nineties, it includes a chapter on
each of A. Bennett and J. Galsworthy].

328 Engel, Claire-Eliane. Profils anglais. Romanciers de guerre.
(Neuchâtel. Editions de la Baconnière, 1946). [Includes
separate studies of C. Morgan, A. Huxley, R. Lehmann,"Anne
Bridge"(Mary D. O'Malley), and R. Warner, and "Nouvelles Formes
et Nouveau Themes," an essay showing the break with the form
of the pre-war novel and the new interest in war topics and
the fantastic].

329 Engelberg, Edward. The Unknown Distance: From Consciousness
to Conscience: Goethe to Camus. (Cambridge, Massachusetts:
Harvard University Press, 1972). [Discusses in Ch. VI, pp.
144-185, the rebelliousness against an overbearing conscience
in M. Arnold, H. James, and J. Conrad].

330 Enright, Dennis Joseph. "To the Lighthouse or to India?"
The Apothecary's Shop: Essays on Literature. (London: Secker
& Warburg, 1957), pp. 168-187. [Examines V. Woolf's and E.
M. Forster's "scrupulous concern for sincerity in personal
relationships" and shows how V. Woolf's "inner world" in To
The Lighthouse opens into, and is linked to "the larger world
outside" in A Passage to India].

331 _____. Conspirators and Poets. (London: Chatto & Windus; Chester Springs, Pennsylvania: Dufour Editions, 1966).

45

[A collection of essays and reviews that includes studies of
C. P. Snow and L. Durrell].

332 Ervine, St. John G. Some Impressions of My Elders. (London:
Allen and Unwin; New York: Macmillan, 1922). [A revised
version of a series of articles published in The North Amer-
ican Review, 1920-1921, under the same title. Includes A.
Bennett, G. K. Chesterton, J. Galsworthy, G. Moore, and H.
G. Wells among others].

333 Evans, Sir Benjamin Ifor. Literature and Science. (London:
Allen & Unwin, 1954). [Examines the position and function
of the artist in modern scientific society, the relationship
between literature and science, and attempts to interpret the
new humanism in contemporary civilization. Chs. XIV-XX, pp.
81-114, deal with the 20th century].

334 _____. English Literature Between the Wars. (London:
Methuen, 1948; Folcroft Press, 1969). [Includes, besides the
survey of the general background, the literary scene, and the
influence of the war on the writer, studies of E. M. Forster,
J. Joyce, D. H. Lawrence, V. Woolf, and the "younger generation" of writers emerging in the thirties].

335 Fairley, Barker. "The Modern Consciousness in English Literature." Essays and Studies by Members of the English Association, Vol. IX. Collected by W. Ker. (Oxford: Clarendon Press, 1924). [Examines the psychological origin of literary innovation, and describes the Freudian concept of the
unconscious as an "attempt on the part of science to keep up
with artistic divination"].

336 Fehr, Bernhard. Die englische Literatur des 19. und 20.
Jahrhunderts: Mit einer Einführung in die englische Früh-
romantik. (Berlin-Neubabelsberg: Akademische Verlagsgesel-
lschaft Athenaion M. B. H., 1923). [A history of literature
in the 19th and eary 20th centuries. Chs. XXXIX-XLVI, pp.
366-427, deal with the novel from 1880 onwards. H. G. Wells,
A. Bennett, J. Galsworthy, and J. Conrad].

337 _____. Englische Prosa von 1880 bis zur Gegenwart.
(Leipzig & Berlin: Verlag und Druck von B. G. Teubner, 1927).
[Pages 1-56 discuss the changes which took place in all areas
of English society, and the new forms of expression and style
invented to cope with new ideas. The rest of the book is
comprised of excerpts from the works of writers from M. Arnold
to J. Joyce to illustrate the changes].

338 _____. Die englische Literatur der Gegenwart und die
Kulturfragen unserer Zeit. (Leipzig: Verlag von Bernhard
Tauchnitz, 1930). [Considers the literature of the time--
poetry, drama, and especially the novel--as an expression of
the cultural problems of the period, and the writers' search
of their own consciousness, their attempt to grasp reality

through themselves, as perhaps the one activity left them
after repudiating the past and being dissatisfied with postwar realism. A. Bennett, H. G. Wells, J. Galsworthy, S.
Kaye-Smith, H. Walpole, J. B. Priestley, R. Macaulay, H. M.
Tomlinson, K. Mansfield, D. H. Lawrence, M. Sinclair, D. Richardson, V. Woolf, J. Joyce, and A. Huxley].

339   . Das England von Heute: Kulturprobleme, Denk-
formen, Schrifttum. (Leipzig: Verlag von Bernhard Tauchnitz, 1932). [Discusses the problems of contemporary civilization and culture, and the art forms utilized by the Elite
and the Masses. H. G. Wells, P. C. Wren, P. Gibbs, G. Frankau, and M. Kennedy].

340   . Die englische Literatur der heutigen Stunde als
Ausdruck der Zeitwende und der englischen Kulturgemeinschaft.
(Leipzig: Verlag von Bernhard Tauchnitz, 1934). [Examines
the literature of the hour--the early thirties--especially
the novel and biography, as an expression of the changes in
the English cultural community, ranging from the uninhibition
of youth, its attack on the system and hopes for the future,
to the growing cult of the senses and the art of the stream
of consciousness. S. Jameson, L. Golding, J. B. Priestley,
P. G. Woodhouse, E. Waugh, A. Waugh, J. Hanley, G. Greene,
H. Nicolson, H. Walpole, S. Benson, R. Lehmann, V. Woolf, T.
F. Powys and others].

341   . Von Englands Geistigen Bestanden. Ausgewahlte
Anfsatze. (Frauenfeld: Verlag Huber & Co. Aktiengesell-
schaft, 1944). [A re-issue of separate papers collected un-
der blanket headings like "The Modern English Novel,"--T.
Hardy, J. Conrad, G. Moore and G. K. Chesterton--"The New
World"--J. Joyce (2 essays), V. Woolf, and D. L. Sayers--and
"Leben, Sprache und Stil" which includes "Substitutionary
Narration and Description" reprinted from English Studies,
XX:3 (June 1938)].

342 Feldman, Gene & Max Gartenberg, eds. The Beat Generation and
the Angry Young Men. (New York: The Citadel Press, 1958).
Published in Britain as Protest. (London: The Souvenir Press,
1959). [A selection from the writings of "The Beat Generation" of the United States, and the group that came to be
known as "The Angry Young Men" in England. The Introduction,
pp. 9-21, distinguishes between the two groups].

343 Feliz, Jozef, ed. O svetovom romane: Sbornik studii. (Brat-
islava: Vydavatel'skvo slovenskej Akademie Vied, 1967). [A
collection of essays by different writers. Includes studies
on "the novel to V. Woolf," J. Joyce, and A. Sillitoe].

344 Fiedler, Leslie. "Class War in British Literature." NO! In
Thunder: Essays on Myth and Literature. (Boston: Beacon
Press, 1960; London: Eyre & Spottiswoode, 1963), pp. 189-208.
Reprinted from Esquire, XLIX (Apr. 1958), 79-81. [See entry

under Periodicals].

345   Fisch, Harold. The Dual Image: The Figure of the Jew in English and American Literature. (London: Lincolns-Prager, 1959). Rev. and enlarged. (London: World Jewish Library, 1971). [A broad survey of the subject of the Jew in English and American Literature. Examines in "Liberals and Reactionaries" in Ch. IV, the 20th Century attempt to "humanise" the Jew, and strip him of the "mythological" outline given him by E. M. Forster, J. Galsworthy, J. Joyce, and G. Greene's treatment of the "Devil-Jew"].

346   Fleishman, Avrom. The English Historical Novel: Walter Scott to Virginia Woolf. (Baltimore and London: The John Hopkins Press, 1971). [Though mainly concerned with the historical novel of the 19th century, Ch. I attempts a "theory of historical fiction," and Ch. VIII, pp. 208-259, discusses J. Conrad and V. Woolf].

347   Fletcher, John. New Directions in Literature: Critical Approaches to a Contemporary Phenomenon. (London: Calder and Boyars, 1968). [Mainly concerned with the new literature in France, especially the novel, which he attempts to place in "the greater European context." S. Beckett, V. Woolf, and I. Compton-Burnett included].

348   Follett, Wilson. The Modern Novel: A Study of the Purpose and Meaning of Fiction. (New York: Alfred A. Knopf, 1918; rev. ed. 1923). [A treatise on the aesthetics of fiction, which includes a "Contemporary Survey," xi-xxiv].

349   _____. "Design in the Novel." Modern Reader: Essays on Present-day Life and Culture. Edited by Walter Lippmann and Allan Nevins. (Boston and New York: D. C. Heath, 1936), pp. 548-562. [A reprint of Ch. IX, pp. 235-262, of The Modern Novel: A Study of the Purpose and Meaning of Fiction. (New York: Alfred S. Knopf, 1918)].

350   _____ and Helen T. Follett. Some Modern Novelists: Appreciations and Estimates. (New York: Holt, 1918; London: Allen & Unwin, 1919: Books for Libraries Press, 1967). [The appreciations and estimates of novelists, mostly English, include H. James, W. de Morgan, E. Phillpotts, A. Bennett, H. G. Wells, J. Galsworthy, J. Conrad, and a survey of the "younger generation"].

351   Ford, Boris, ed. The Pelican Guide to English Literature. Vol. 7: The Modern Age. (London: Cassell; Baltimore: Penguin, 1961). [A collection of essays by independent contributors that gives a survey of the literature of the twentieth century--the novel, poetry and drama--and its social context, with separate studies of H. James, J. Conrad, E. M. Forster, V. Woolf, L. H. Myers, D. H. Lawrence, and J. Joyce among others. Also includes general studies of the novel by R. C. Churchill, Graham Martin and Gilbert Phelps. See separate

entries for general studies].

352 Ford, Ford Maddox. Thus to Revisit: Some Reminiscences.
(London: Chapman & Hall; New York: Dutton, 1921). [On the
English literary scene before World War I. H. James. W. H.
Hudson, and J. Conrad, among others].

353 _____. The English Novel: From the Earliest Days to
the Death of Joseph Conrad. (Philadelphia: Lippincott,
1929; London: Constable, 1930). [A short historical survey
written for American students, which underlines the haphazard, individualistic manner of English novelists until the
technical achievements of H. James and J. Conrad].

354 _____. Return to Yesterday. (London: Victor
Gollancz, 1931). [Reminiscences of H. James, J. Conrad, and
S. Crane between 1894 and 1914, and especially of his collab-
oration with J. Conrad, pp. 190-207].

355 _____. Portraits from Life: Memories and Criticisms.
(Chicago: Regnery; Boston & New York: Houghton Mifflin,
1937). Published in Britain as Mightier than the Sword.
(London: Allen & Unwin, 1938). [Separate studies of indiv-
idual writers including H. James, W. H. Hudson, J. Conrad,
D. H. Lawrence, H. G. Wells, and J. Galsworthy].

356 Forster, E[dward] M[organ]. Aspects of the Novel. (London:
Edward Arnold; New York: Harcourt, Brace, 1927). [The Clark
Lectures delivered at Trinity College, Cambridge, 1927. The
"aspects" discussed are seven: Story, People, Plot, Fantasy,
Prophesy, Pattern and Rhythm].

357 _____. Abinger Harvest. (London: Edward Arnold; New
York: Harcourt, Brace, 1936). [A reprint of some 80 articles, essays, reviews, and poems. Includes "The Early Novels
of V. Woolf," pp. 104-113, and a "Note on J. Conrad," pp.
134-139]·

358 Foster, Jeanette H. Sex Variant Women in Literature: A Historical and Quantitative Survey. (New York: Vantage Press,
1956; London: Frederick Muller, 1958). [Treats of women
conscious of passion for their own sex, with or without overt
expression, and those attached obsessively to other women
over a long period of time and at a mature age. The survey
covers Sappho to post-World War II in French, German, and
English literatures. Chs. IX and X treat the topic in English fiction].

359 Foster, J[oseph] R[eginald]. Modern Christian Literature.
(London: Burns & Oates, 1963). [An expository rather than
a critical examination of imaginative literature that interprets life in Christian terms, in England and America, and
six European countries. H. Belloc, M. Baring, E. Waugh, G.
K. Chesterton, C. Williams, B. Marshall, G. Greene, W. Gold-

ing, and M. Spark].

360 Fox, Ralph. The Novel and the People. (London: Lawrence
& Wishart; New York: International Publishers, 1937). [A
marxist approach that examines the position of the English
novel, the crisis of ideas that has destroyed its foundations
and led to its intellectual bankruptcy, and tries to predict
its future].

361 Fraser, George Sutherland. The Modern Writer and His World.
(London: Derek Verschoyle, 1953; New York: Criterion, 1955.
Rev. ed. London: Deutsch; New York: Praeger, 1964). [A
study of the background of ideas behind "modernism" in English literature, and of the main innovating figures in the
novel, drama, poetry, and criticism. Pt. II, pp. 73-191, is
a study of the novel up to the fifties].

362 _____. "Cultural Nationalism in the Recent English Novel." The Cry of Home: Cultural Nationalism and the Modern
Writer. Edited, with a Preface and an Introduction, by H.
Ernest Lewald. (Knoxville: The University of Tennessee Press
1972), pp. 22-38. [Examines how postwar novelists reflect
the passing of the "rigid hierarchy" of the traditional pattern of English life. J. Wain, K. Amis, J. Braine, A. Wilson,
A. Powell, E. Waugh, and C. P. Snow].

363 _____. "The English Novel." The Twentieth-Century Mind:
History, Ideas, and Literature in Britain, Vol. 2, 1918-1945.
Edited by C. B. Cox and A. E. Dyson. (London and New York:
Oxford University Press, 1972), pp. 373-417. [Though mainly
intended as background reading, the essay focuses on five
major novelists--J. Joyce, D. H. Lawrence, E. M. Forster, V.
Woolf, F. M. Ford--the emergence of the anti-hero, the rise
of the "Menippean Satire" of A. Huxley, E. Waugh, W. Lewis,
and others, and the "accessible . . . artists and craftsmen"
of the 1930's and early 1940's--C. Isherwood, G. Greene, and
others--who were interested in the element of story].

364 Freedman, Ralph. "Nature and Forms of the Lyrical Novel."
The Novel: Modern Essays in Criticism. Edited by Robert
Murray Davis. (Englewood Cliffs, New Jersey: Prentice-Hall,
1969), pp. 59-73. Repr. from The Lyrical Novel: Studies in
Herman Hesse, André Gide, and Virginia Woolf. (Princeton,
New Jersey: Princeton University Press, 1963; London: Oxford University Press, 1963), pp. 1-17. [Shows how the genre
of the lyrical novel has emerged from an attempt "to combine
man and world in strangely inward, yet aesthetically objective form," and isolates its "purely lyrical qualities before
turning to their more involved juxtapositions with other narrative forms"].

365 Freeman, John. The Moderns: Essays in Literary Criticism.
(London: Robert Scott, Roxburghe House, 1916; New York:
Thomas Y. Crowell, 1917; Books for Libraries Press, 1968).

[Includes essays on H. G. Wells, H. James, and J. Conrad].

366 _____. English Portraits and Essays. (London: Hodder and Stoughton, 1924). [A collection of nine essays previously published. Includes one essay on each of G. K. Chesterton, M. Hewlett, and C. Mackenzie].

367 _____. Literature and Locality: The Literary Topography of Britain and Ireland. (London: Cassell, 1963). [A guide to the localities with which some 350 writers have topographical associations. The arrangement of localities follows the chronology of a writer's life. The writers associated with each locality are entered in the Index].

368 Freund, Philip. How to Become a Literary Critic. (New York: The Beechhurst Press, 1947). Revised and published as The Art of Reading the Novel. (New York: Collier Books, 1965). [Examines various aspects of technique--point of view, time, characterization, etc. Illustrates from works by J. Conrad, D. H. Lawrence, and A. Koestler].

369 Fricker, Robert. Der moderne englische Roman. (Göttingen: Vandenhoeck & Ruprecht, 1958. Rev. ed. 1966). [Considers novelists from S. Butler to W. Golding separately. Each study examines the principal novels in chronological order, and discusses the general characteristics of the author. Twenty-one 20th century English novelists are considered].

370 _____. "Das Kathedralenmotiv in der modernen englischen Dichtung." Festschrift Rudolf Stamm, zu seinem sechzigsten Geburtstag. Edited by Eduard Kolb and Jorg Hasler. (Bern and München: Francke Verlag, 1969). [Examines the cathedral as motif in selected novels and dramas of the 20th century. Pages 235-238 examine novels by D. H. Lawrence and W. Golding].

371 Friedman, Alan. The Turn of the Novel. (New York: Oxford University Press, 1966). [Originally a doctoral dissertation presented to the University of California at Berkeley, 1965. Studies the development of the novel in the early 20th century, emphasising the widespread and deliberate shift from the traditional premise of closed experience to the open form resulting not only from an interest in technique, but also from a new vision of experience. J. Conrad, E. M. Forster, and D. H. Lawrence].

372 _____. "The Novel." The Twentieth-Century Mind: History, Ideas and Literature in Britain, Vol. I, 1900-1918. Edited by C. B. Cox and A. E. Dyson. (London and New York: Oxford University Press, 1972), pp. 414-447. [Examines individual novels by H. James, H. G. Wells, A. Bennett, J. Conrad, and early works of E. M. Forster, D. H. Lawrence, and J. Joyce to clarify the impact of the new "unbalanced concentration in the self" on the novelist's treatment of "the in-

ner dimension of character," the departure from objective
realism to a dream world "more responsive to the distortions
of personal awareness," and the modifications in the rendering of Time].

373 Friedman, Maurice. To Deny Our Nothingness: Contemporary
     Images of Man. (London: Victor Gollancz, 1967). [Examines
     the various images of modern man as socialist, mystic, saint,
     gnostic, pragmatist, existentialist, and absurd, as depicted
     by 20th century American and European writers. Included are
     A. Koestler, A. Huxley, G. Greene, and S. Beckett].

374 Friedman, Melvin J[ack]. Stream of Consciousness: A Study
     in Literary Method. (New Haven: Yale University Press,
     1955). [Originally a doctoral dissertation presented to Yale
     University, 1954. Defines the stream of consciousness in
     Ch. I and moves from general considerations of the stream of
     consciousness in the novel, psychology and music, to specific
     studies of E. Dujardin, D. Richardson, V. Woolf, J. Joyce,
     and later imitators].

375 _____, ed. The Vision Obscured: Perceptions of Some
     Twentieth-Century Catholic Novelists. (New York: Fordham
     University Press, 1970). [A collection of essays by differ-
     ent writers which includes one on each of E. Waugh, M. Spark,
     and G. Greene].

376 _____, & John B. Vickery. The Shaken Realist: Essays
     in Modern Literature in Honor of Frederick J. Hoffman. (Bos-
     ton: Louisiana State University Press, 1970). [Includes an
     essay on V. Woolf, pp. 100-127, and another on A. Burgess,
     pp. 300-311].

377 Frierson, William. The English Novel in Transition: 1885-
     1940. (Norman: University of Oklahoma Press, 1942). [At-
     tributes the transition of the English novel to the impact
     of French Naturalism, the "explosion" of the English novel
     by the Russians who revealed its enormous potentialities, and
     the general influence of the War in precipitating freedom of
     thought, expression and experiment. Also maintains that be-
     tween 1926 and 1929 "new urges, new experiments were ended
     and writers harked back to the ideas and forms" that had pre-
     vailed earlier].

378 Frye, Northrop. Anatomy of Criticism: Four Essays. (Prince-
     ton, New Jersey: Princeton University Press, 1957). [Four
     essays of pure critical theory centred round "myth," "symbol,"
     "ritual" and "archetype," the substance of four public lec-
     tures delivered at Princeton 1954, and which are revised ver-
     sions of separately published articles. Three of the essays
     deliberately omit specific criticism, and the 4th essay,
     "Rhetorical Criticism: Theory of Genres," includes "The Four
     Forms of Prose Fiction" reprinted from The Hudson Review, II:4
     (Winter 1950), 582-595. References to H. James and V. Woolf.

(See entry under Periodicals)].

379 _____. The Modern Century. (Toronto: Oxford University Press, 1967). [The Whidden Lectures delivered at McMaster University, 1967. The first, "City of the End of Things," discusses the malaise and alienation created by progress in the 20th century, and the outline of the world the contemporary imagination has drawn up. The second "Improved Binoculars" describes the active role the arts, especially literature, have taken in focusing the contemporary imagination. The third lecture, "Claire de lune Intellectual," describes the way in which creative arts are absorbed into society through education].

380 Fuller, Edmund. Books with Men Behind Them. (New York: Random House, 1962). [Contends that a novel is not a "container" of its author's vision, but is a novelist's "ordered, rational and balanced" vision of life. Discusses English and American writers whose works verge on fantasies and the combination of science and religion. Included are C. P. Snow, C. S. Lewis, C. Williams, and J. R. R. Tolkien].

381 Galsworthy, John. The Creation of Character in Literature. (Oxford: Clarendon Press, 1931). Repr. in The Bookman, LXXIII:6 (Aug. 1931), 561-569, and Candelabra: Selected Essays and Addresses. (London: Heinemann, 1932; New York: Scribners, 1933), pp. 291-311. [See entry under Periodicals].

382 _____. "Faith of a Novelist." Candelabra: Selected Essays and Addresses. (London: Heinemann, 1930; New York: Charles Scribner's Sons, 1933), pp. 235-246. [Describes the task of the novelist as a depiction of a section of life, as he sees it, "in due relation to the whole of life without fear or favour"].

383 Gardiner, Fr. Harold C. Norms for the Novel. (New York: The America Press, 1953; rev. ed., New York: Hanover House, 1960). [Questions whether the norms of morality have any place in the novelist's art and the objectives it is designed to achieve. Though he believes that the novel is more than a sociological tract dressed up, it is the WHAT in a novel-- morally and artistically--that counts more, and not "how" it is handled or treated].

384 _____. In All Conscience: Reflections on Books and Culture. (New York: Hanover House, 1959). [A collection of reviews from America which include G. Greene and E. Waugh, pp. 89-102].

385 Garnett, Edward. Friday Nights: Literary Criticisms and Appreciations. (London: Jonathan Cape, 1929). [Includes appreciations of J. Conrad and D. H. Lawrence (pp. 73-87 and 117-128) and "Some Remarks on American and English Fiction" reprinted from The Atlantic Monthly, CXIV (December 1914), 747-756. (See separate entry under Periodicals)].

386   Garrett, J. C. Utopias in Literature since the Romantic Per-
      iod. (Christchurch, New Zealand: University of Canterbury,
      1968). [The Macmillan Brown Lectures 1967. The first lec-
      ture discusses romantic utopias and experiments in the early 19th
      century, the second deals with utopias and anti-utopias in
      the closing years of the Victorian period, and the third with
      the problems and dilemmas of 20th century utopia, outlining
      the general dominant characteristics of Utopian dreams and
      their recurrent hesitations and contradictions].

387   Garrett, Peter K. Scene and Symbol from George Eliot to
      James Joyce: Studies in Changing Fictional Modes. Yale
      Studies in English, Vol. 172. (New Haven & London: Yale
      University Press, 1969). [Originally a doctoral dissertation
      at Yale University. Examines a "cross-section" of the in-
      creasing impulse toward "a fully autonomous symbolic mode
      which dominates the actuality of the given" in representa-
      tive works by G. Eliot, G. Flaubert, H. James, J. Conrad,
      D. H. Lawrence, and J. Joyce].

388   Garzilli, Enrico. Circles Without Center: Paths to the
      Discovery and Creation of Self in Modern Literature. (Cam-
      bridge, Massachusetts: Harvard University Press, 1972).
      [Examines the various avenues of exploration in the search
      for identity and the self, and the meaning of "anti-heroes."
      S. Beckett and J. Joyce among others].

389   Gaskin, D. Bruce, ed. From 'Lord Jim' to 'Billy Liar': An
      Introduction to the English Novel in the 20th Century. (Lon-
      don & Harlow: Longmans, Green 1969). The Heritage of Lit-
      erature Series. [The "Introduction" is based on selected
      extracts from J. Conrad, H. G. Wells and A. Bennett to J.
      Braine, A. Sillitoe and K. Waterhouse, with a one-to-two page
      prefatory note on each novelist].

390   Gass, William H. Fiction and the Figures of Life. (New York:
      Knopf, 1970). [Collected reviews and essays. Part I is
      concerned with the art of fiction in general, and Part II
      with American writers. Parts III and IV are book reviews and
      essays. Included in Part I are "Philosophy and the Form of
      Fiction,"(see next entry) and "The Medium of Fiction," "The
      Concept of Character in Fiction," and "In Terms of the Toe-
      nail"].

391   _____. "Philosophy and the Form of Fiction." The Phil-
      osopher-Critic. Edited by Robert Scholes. (Tulsa, Oklahoma:
      The University of Tulsa, 1970), pp. 50-66. [Discusses the
      relation of the writer to his work, and the use of philosoph-
      ical ideas in the construction of fictional works. Also
      maintains that philosophy and fiction often make "most acri-
      monious companions," for the latter must "show or exhibit"
      its world, and to do this, the novelist must "actually make
      something . . . and present us with a world that is philo-
      sophically adequate"].

54

392 Gawsworth, John, ed. (Terence Ian Lytton Armstrong). Ten Contemporaries: Notes Toward Their Definitive Bibliography. 1st Series. With a Foreword by Viscount Esher. (London: Ernest Benn, 1932). 2nd Series. (London: Joiner & Steele, 1933). [Bibliographies of his contemporaries' works. Among those included in the 1st series are R. Davies, "S. Hudson" and M. P. Shiel, and in the 2nd series, H. E. Bates, S. Benson, T. Burke, J. Collier, O. Onions, D. Richardson, and L. A. G. Strong. A three-to-four page note precedes each writer].

393 George, W[alter] L[ionel]. A Novelist on Novels. (London: Collins, 1918). Published in U. S. A. as Literary Chapters. (Boston: Little, Brown, 1918; Kennikat Press, 1970). [A general review of the novel and the status of the novelist in England in the first two decades of the 20th century. A. Bennett, J. Conrad, J. Galsworthy, H. G. Wells, H. Walpole, J. D. Beresford, G. Cannan, E. M. Forster, and D. H. Lawrence].

394 Gerber, Richard. Utopian Fantasy. A Study of English Utopian Fiction Since the End of the Nineteenth Century. (London: Routledge & Kegan Paul, 1955; Folcroft Press, 1969). [Originally an M. Litt. thesis, Queen's College, Cambridge, 1955. Examines, thematically, the great number of Utopian forecasts, many of which are "subliterary," in order to delineate the essentials of modern Utopian fantasy in English fiction, which he contends is "the outcome of a comprehensive Utopian imagination and view of life." Also considers "socially constructive utopias," and various kinds of "imaginary commonwealths and fantastical countries." Marginal concern with special literary devices. Includes an annotated list of English Utopian Fantasies, 1901-1951, in the Appendix].

395 Gerould, Gordon Hall. The Patterns of English and American Fiction: A History. (Boston: Little, Brown, 1942; Russell and Russell, 1966). [A history of fiction from its earliest experiments in the 16th century to the thirties "in terms of the patterns of thought and design to which stories have been accommodated from century to century." Chs. XXI and XXII cover English and American fiction in the 20th century].

396 _____. How to Read Fiction. (Princeton: Princeton University Press; London: Oxford University Press, 1937; Russell and Russell, 1969). [Introduces the reader to the art of reading fiction and the principles of criticism in prose fiction].

397 Gerould, Katherine Fullerton. "British Novelists, Ltd." Modes and Morals. (New York: Scribner's, 1920), pp. 218-253. Reprinted from The Yale Review, VII (October 1917), 161-185. [See entry under Periodicals].

398 Gill, Richard. Happy Rural Seat: The English Country House and the Literary Imagination. (New Haven and London: Yale

University Press, 1972). [Originally a doctoral dissertation presented to Columbia University, 1966. Examines the function of the traditional country house as a "recurring motif" in works by H. James, H. G. Wells, E. M. Forster, J. Galsworthy, F. M. Ford, G. B. Shaw, A. Huxley, V. Sackville-West, D. H. Lawrence, E. Waugh, C. Isherwood, W. B. Yeats, and E. Bowen].

399 Gillam, D[ouglas] J[ohn]. Le Moi et l'univers: quelques aspects du roman psychologique contemporain en Angleterre. (Neuchatel: E. Richeme, 1939). [Discusses the novel as the most vigorous reaction to Victorianism. K. Mansfield, D. H. Lawrence, D. Richardson, V. Woolf, and J. Joyce, pp. 5-23].

400 Gillet, Louis. Esquisses anglaises. (Paris: Firmin-Didot et Cie., 1930). [A collection of essays which includes two on Galsworthy (The Forsyte Saga and The Silver Spoon), and one on each of H. G. Wells, J. Conrad, A. Bennett, K. Mansfield, J. Joyce, and V. Woolf among others].

401 Gillett, Eric W[alkey]. Books and Writers. (Singapore: Malaya Publishing House, 1930). [Selections from weekly "discursive papers" written for The Straights Times, Malaya. Included are "Strange Reading" (J. Joyce), "The Happy Warrior" (C. E. Montague), "Bennett de Luxe," "Woman to Women" (V. Woolf), and "Mr. C. Mackenzie on Gallipoli"].

402 Gillie, Christopher. Character in English Literature. (London: Chatto & Windus; New York: Barnes & Noble, 1965). [The study covers a wide range of subjects from Everyman to Women in Love, and attempts to show that the art of characterisation arises from the confrontation of human experience with that which is "alien." "From this confrontation issues growth and identity, and the two combine to form character." Also maintains that "characterisation comes into its own only with the novel . . ." Ch. X makes a study of J. Joyce's Dedalus and D. H. Lawrence's Birkin (Women in Love)].

403 Gindin, James. Postwar British Fiction: New Accents and Attitudes. (Berkeley & Los Angeles: University of California Press; London: Cambridge University Press, 1962). [Describes the attitudes of English postwar novelists, and what they reveal about present society, by surveying novels of A. Sillitoe, K. Amis, D. Lessing, D. Storey, P. Larkin, K. Waterhouse, I. Murdoch, W. Golding, and "The Current Fads"-- C. P. Snow, L. Durrell, and C. Wilson. Also attempts a discussion of existentialism and literature in Ch. XIV].

404 _____. Recent British Fiction. ['Well Beyond Anger']. Suggestions toward Some Views of Modern Fiction. Approaches to the Study of Twentieth Century Literature. Proceedings of the Conference in the Study of Twentieth-Century Literature. Edited by Carl Hartman, second series. (East Lansing, Mich-

igan: Michigan State University, 1962), pp. 67-82. [An address describing the continued interest among writers like C. P. Snow, A. Wilson, A. Sillitoe, I. Murdoch, K. Amis, and J. Wain in the traditional "state of England" question, followed by discussion].

405   . Harvest of a Quiet Eye: The Novel of Compassion. (Bloomington & London: Indiana University Press, 1971). [Examines 19th and 20th century novelists, English and American, whose works can be explained in full, or in part, in the terms "fiction of compassion." H. James, A. Bennett, V. Woolf, E. M. Forster, D. H. Lawrence, J. Joyce, J. Cary, and A. Wilson among others].

406   Glanville, Brian. "The Sporting Novel." The Best of 'Speaking of Books' from 'The New Times Book Review'. Edited, with an Introduction by E. F. Brown. (New York: Holt, Rinehart and Winston, 1969), pp. 226-231. Reprinted from The New York Times Book Review (18 July 1965), 2, 18. [See entry under Periodicals].

407   Glicksberg, Charles I[rving]. Literature and Religion: A Study in Conflict. (Dallas: Southern Methodist University Press, 1960). [A collection of Essays on Poetry, Drama and Fiction which emphasise the search for meaning and the religious revival in modern literature. Pt. IV, "The World of Fiction," pp. 169-225, includes a modified version of "Fiction and Philosophy," reprinted from Arizona Quarterly, XIII (Autumn 1957), 5-17, and "The God of Fiction," reprinted from Colorado Quarterly, VII (Autumn 1958), 207-220. See separate entries under Periodicals].

408   . The Self in Modern Literature. (University Park, Pennsylvania: The Pennsylvania State University Press, 1963). [Traces in chronological sequence the "slow and erratic shift in sensibility" from the 19th to the 20th century, as applied to the imaginative delineation of the "process of psychological disintegration" or the breakdown of the ego in both fiction and drama. A. Huxley, G. Orwell, L. Durrell, and S. Beckett, among others.

409   . Modern Literature and the Death of God. (The Hague: Martinus Nijhoff, 1966). [A collection of essays, some of which have been published previously, dealing with the loss of Faith and the Search for God in modern literature. Includes "Eros and the Death of God," reprinted from Western Humanities Review, XIII:4 (Autumn 1959), 357-368, and "To be or Not to Be: The Literature of Suicide," reprinted from Queen's Quarterly, LXVII:3 (Autumn 1960), 384-395, pp. 36-57 and 88-100. See separate entries under Periodicals].

410   . Modern Literary Perspectivism. (Dallas: Southern Methodist University Press, 1970). [Examines different angles of vision through which writers view the world at

present, what they take for granted, what they revolt against, what ideal of commitment they recommend and how they justify their art, i.e., how writers interpret the ongoing human quest for meaning. Part I shows how perspectivism functions in the context of modern European literature; Part II appraises Chernyshevski and Brecht, the perspectives they assert, the Utopian obsession as set forth, positively and negatively, in the writings of H. G. Wells, A. Huxley and B. F. Spinner. References to G. Orwell and D. H. Lawrence].

411 _____. The Sexual Revolution in Modern English Literature. (The Hague: Martinus Nijhoff, 1973). [A study of the evolution of the post Victorian sex-ethic as it functions in the novels of T. Hardy, H. G. Wells, J. Joyce, D. H. Lawrence and A. Huxley, and the new sexual morality from the thirties to the present as treated in the novels of E. Waugh, I. Murdoch, and C. Wilson].

412 Goetsch, Paul. Die Romankonzeption in England 1880-1910. Anglistische Forschungen Heft 94. (Heidelberg: Carl Winter Universitätsverlag, 1967). [Parts I and II deal with the relation between art and reality in Criticism, and the theory and practice of leading English novelists between 1880 and 1910; Part III gives the change from the Victorian to the modern concept of the novel as mirrored in criticism, as well as the change in the concept of reality. H. G. Wells, A. Bennett, H. James, and J. Conrad among others].

413 Goldberg, Gerald Jay, and Nancy Marmer Goldberg, eds. The Modern Critical Spectrum. (Englewood Cliffs, New Jersey: Prentice-Hall, 1962). [A collection of essays by different contributors on the uses of: formal analysis, the socio-cultural milieu, tradition, biography, humanism, scholarship, psychology and myth. Includes a reprint of M. Schorer's "Technique as Discovery," The Hudson Review, I:1 (Spring 1948), 67-87, and "Fiction and Civilization" from D. Daiches' The Novel and the Modern World. (Chicago: University of Chicago Press, 1939), pp. 70-83 and 109-116 respectively].

414 Goldberg, M.A. "Chronology, Character, and the Human Condition: A Re-appraisal of the Modern Novel." Critical Approaches to Fiction. Edited by Shiv K. Kumar and Keith F. McKean. (New York: McGraw-Hill, 1968), pp. 13-25. Repr. from Criticism, V (Winter 1963), 1-12. [See entry under Periodicals].

415 Goldknopf, David. The Life of the Novel. (Chicago & London: The University of Chicago Press, 1972). [A collection of nine essays, several previously published, on various aspects of the novel from D. Defoe to J. Conrad. Included are "The Confessional Increment: A New Look at the I-Narrator," pp. 25-42, "What Plot Means in the Novel," pp. 100-125, and "Realism in the Novel," pp. 177-199. See separate entries under Periodicals].

416 Goldring, Douglas. *Reputations: Essays in Criticism*. (London: Chapman & Hall; New York: Seltzer, 1920). [Includes an essay on three Georgian novelists--C. Mackenzie, H. Walpole, and G. Cannan--and one on each of D. H. Lawrence, H. G. Wells, and A. Bennett].

417 Gomes, Eugênio. *O Romancista e o Ventriloquo* (Os Cadernos de Cultura). (Rio de Janeiro: Ministerio da Educaçao E Saude, (Servico de Documentaçao), 1952). [Essays on English and American Novelists. Includes an essay on each of C. Dane, D. H. Lawrence, J. Joyce, and two on H. James].

418 _____. *A neve e o girassol*. (Sao Paulo: Conselho Estadual de Cultura, 1967). [A collection of essays on English writers from Shakespeare to C. Day Lewis. Includes essays on H. James, H. G. Wells, J. Joyce, and E. Waugh].

419 Goodheart, Eugene. *The Cult of the Ego: The Self in Modern Literature*. (Chicago & London: The University of Chicago Press, 1968). [Discusses writers who are concerned with the emancipation of the spirit by means of advancing the claims of the self and extending its boundaries. Included are J. Joyce and D. H. Lawrence].

420 Goodman, Theodore. *The Techniques of Fiction: An Analysis of Creative Writing*. (New York: Liveright Publishing Corporation, 1955). [Analyses and examines seven component parts of fiction--the word, imagery, character, pattern, emotion, idea and conflict--which make fiction different from drama, biography or history. Illustrates from both English and American novelists].

421 Gordon, Caroline. *How to Read a Novel*. (New York: The Viking Press; London: Macmillan, 1957). [Insights into the author's craft and the "essential nature of fiction," for the general reader; i.e., tries to answer the questions, "What is a Novel?" and "How should it be read?"].

422 Gottwald, Johannes. *Die Erzählformen der Romane von Aldous Huxley und David Herbert Lawrence*. (Munich: Ludwig-Maximilians-Universität, 1964). [Originally a doctoral dissertation that discusses narrative form in the novels of D. H. Lawrence and A. Huxley].

423 Gould, Gerald. *The English Novel of Today*. (London: John Castle, 1924; New York: MacVeagh, 1925; Books for Libraries Press, 1971). [Traces tendencies, estimates influences, and hazards a prophecy or two on the future of the novel. Confines himself to the contemporary scene, utilizing authors and novels for their value as types and indications of trends. M. Baring, R. Firbank, E. M. Forster, D. Garnett, A. S. M. Hutchinson, A. Huxley, J. Joyce, S. Kaye-Smith, D. H. Lawrence, C. Mackenzie, K. Mansfield, E. Mordaunt, L. H. Myers, T. F. Powys, M. Sinclair, H. Walpole, "R. West," H. G. Wells and others].

424　Grabo, C[arl] H[enry]. The Technique of the Novel. (New
　　York: Scribner's, 1928). [Reveals "the manipulation of the
　　strings" in narrative from the view-point of the writer of
　　stories. Uses H. James' analytical point of view to examine
　　a large number of novels for various narrative principles
　　and devices. Introduces 20th century novels as from p. 230].

425　Graef, Hilda. Modern Gloom and Christian Hope. (Chicago:
　　Henry Regnery, 1959). [A brief study of modern thought and
　　literature intended solely "as a criticism of contemporary
　　pessimism" from the Christian point of view. Included are
　　C. Wilson and G. Greene].

426　Gray, James. On Second Thoughts. (Minneapolis: University
　　of Minnesota Press; London: Oxford University Press, 1946).
　　[A collection of reviews, previously published, about his
　　contemporaries. Included are A. Bennett, J. Galsworthy, H.
　　G. Wells, A. Huxley, P. Bentley, A. Koestler, W. Holtby,
　　and V. Brittain].

427　Grebstein, Sheldon Norman, ed. Perspectives in Contemporary
　　Criticism: A Collection of Recent Essays by American, Eng-
　　lish and European Literary Critics. (New York: Harper and
　　Row, 1968). [This collection is representative of the his-
　　torical, formalist, sociocultural, psychological, and myth-
　　opoeic approaches and types of criticism currently dominant.
　　Included are reprints of "The English Novel and the Three
　　Kinds of Time," by J. H. Raleigh, "Telling and Showing" by
　　W. C. Booth, "Composition and Fate in the Short Novel," by
　　H. Nemerov, and "The Fiction of Anti-Utopia," by I. Howe.
　　See separate entries under periodicals].

428　Green, Martin [Burgess]. A Mirror for Anglo-Saxons: A Dis-
　　covery of America, A Rediscovery of England. (London: Long-
　　mans, Green; New York: Harper, 1960). [A collection of art-
　　icles previously published giving insights, views and opin-
　　ions on English and American cultures and attitudes. Includes
　　"British Decency," reprinted from The Kenyon Review, XXI:4
　　(Autumn 1959), 505-532. See separate entry under Periodicals].

429　Greenberger, Allen J[ay]. The British Image of India: A
　　Study in the Literature of Imperialism 1880-1960. (London:
　　Oxford University Press, 1969). [Examines the images of
　　India, Burma and Ceylon as projected by some forty-five or
　　so English writers of novels and potboilers, and maintains
　　that the images were more often than not determined by what
　　happened in England, and the West generally, rather than by
　　the Indian reality. H. E. Bates, F. W. Bain, E. M. Forster,
　　R. Godden, D. Kincaid, R. Kipling. J. Masters, L. H. Myers,
　　E. Thompson, and others].

430　Greenblatt, Stephen Jay. Three Modern Satirists: Waugh,
　　Orwell, and Huxley. (New Haven & London: Yale University
　　Press, 1965). [Makes a separate study of each satirist, his

vision, interest, prejudice, temperament, style and tone, and notices how widely different they are in each because of their dissimilar world views and "peculiar visions of the source of man's folly and evil"].

431 Greene, Graham. Collected Essays. (London: The Bodley Head, 1969). [Part II, "Novels and Novelists" includes four review articles on H. James, reviews of works by D. Richardson, F. M. Ford, and J. Conrad, and reviews of works on J. Conrad, G. K. Chesterton, A. Bennett and R. Kipling].

432 Greenebaum, Elizabeth. "The Post-Realistic Novel." Prefaces to Fiction: A Discussion of Great Modern Novels, by Robert Morss Lovett. (Chicago: Rockwell, 1931; Books for Libraries Press, 1968), pp. 113-127. [This is Ch.VIII of the volume. The previous seven were written by R. M. Lovett and examine representative novels from six nations. "The Post Realistic Novel" examines the modern realists' abandonment of the search for objective truth as a result of the recent findings in anthropology, sociology, history, and the physical sciences].

433 Gregor, Ian, & Brian Nicholas. The Moral and the Story. (London: Faber & Faber; New York: British Book Service, 1962). [Examines the reciprocally influencing relationship between art and morality, also the moral judgment passed on a novel. Considers the theme in which a woman's guilt or innocence is presumed, and discusses, among other novels, G. Moore's Esther Waters, G. Greene's The End of the Affair and D. H. Lawrence's Lady Chatterley's Lover].

434 Gregory, Horace Victor. The Shield of Achilles: Essays on Beliefs in Poetry. (New York: Harcourt, Brace, 1944). [A collection of critical essays which include one on each of G. Moore, D. H. Lawrence, and V. Woolf].

435 _____. "Mutations of Belief in the Contemporary Novel." Spiritual Problems in Contemporary Literature: A Series of Addresses and Discussions. Edited by Stanley Romaine Hopper. (New York and London: Harper, 1952). [Suggests that the various conditions of "imaginative being" are not continuous and do not proceed from one another in a straight line, but are a series of "intersecting spirals." J. Joyce, J. Conrad, E. Waugh, and G. Greene among others].

436 _____. The Dying Gladiators and Other Essays. (New York: Grove Press; London: Evergreen Books, 1961). [A collection of six essays on W. Lewis, H. G. Wells, G. Moore, "W. Bryher," J. Joyce, and S. Beckett previously published in books and periodicals].

437 Guedalla, Philip. Men of Letters. Collected Essays, Vol. I. (London: Hodder and Stoughton, 1927). [The volume includes an essay on each of H. James, R. Kipling, H. G. Wells, A.

Bennett, J. Conrad, J. Galsworthy, C. Mackenzie, and G. K. Chesterton].

438 Guerra, Alfonso Rangel. _Imagen de la novela_. (Monterrey: Universidad de Nuevo Leon, 1964). [Surveys the various developments of the novel in the nineteenth and twentieth centuries--Ch. VII deals with D. H. Lawrence and J. Joyce among others].

439 Günther, Margarete. _Der englische Kriegsroman und das englische Kriegsdrama 1919 bis 1930_. Neue Deutsche Forschungen. Band 59. (Berlin: Junker und Dünnhaupt Verlag, 1936). [A historical survey examining the impact of World War I on the English novel and drama, and tracing the development of the war novel to its peak in 1929 and 1930].

440 *Gupta, P. _Studies and Sketches_. (Agra: Modern Book Depot, 1941).

441 Hagopian, John V. & Martin Dolch, eds. _Insight II. Analyses of Modern British Literature_. (Frankfurt am Main: Hirschgraben-Verlag, 1965). [Analyses by various critics of selected 20th century works, arranged alphabetically according to author, from J. Conrad and J. Joyce to A. Wilson].

442 Haines, Helen E[lizabeth]. _What's In a Novel_. (New York: Columbia University Press; London: Oxford University Press, 1942). [A study of the novel that attempts to show what is in it by discussing some of its significant manifestations in order to "strengthen confidence in its potentialities," and refute "the stigma of triviality" that rests upon contemporary fiction. The changes in the form of the novel are traced not by critical analysis, but "by specific factual indication of substance and purpose and effect"].

443 Hall, James [Winford]. _The Tragic Comedians: Seven Modern British Novelists_. (Bloomington, Indiana: Indiana University Press; Toronto: Copp, Clarke, 1963). [A study of E. M. Forster, A. Huxley, E. Waugh, H. Green, J. Cary, L. P. Hartley, and A. Powell with one chapter on each novelist, which attempts to "see over-all directions through the progress of main dramatic conflicts . . . and through tone." An introductory chapter discusses the vein of comedy in the modern British novel as a personal "improvisation to meet sudden changes," and a concluding chapter reviews how the tradition works].

444 _____. _The Lunatic Giant in the Drawing Room: The British and American Novel Since 1930_. (Bloomington and London: Indiana University Press, 1968). [A companion piece to _The Tragic Comedians_ which includes studies of E. Bowen, G. Greene, and I. Murdoch].

445 Hallen, Oskar van der. _Spiritualistiche Epiek: Beschouwin-

62

gen over den Katholieken Roman 1920-1940. (Antwerp: Uit-
geversmij. N. V. Standaard-Boekhandel, 1944). [A general
survey of the European Catholic novel with brief references
to C. Mackenzie, M. Baring, and G. K. Chesterton among oth-
ers].

446 Hamill, Elizabeth. These Modern Writers: An Introduction
for Modern Readers. (Melbourne: Georgian House, 1946).
[An elementary work that introduces D. H. Lawrence, A. Huxley, K. Mansfield, V. Woolf, J. Joyce, and E. M. Forster
among others, to the general reader].

447 Hamilton, Clayton. Materials and Methods of Fiction. (New
York: Doubleday, 1908; London: Grant Richards, 1909).
Revised and enlarged as A Manual of the Art of Fiction. Pre-
pared for the use of schools and colleges; with an Introduction by Brander Matthews. (New York: Doubleday; London: Allen & Unwin, 1918). Revised and reprinted as The
Art of Fiction: A Formulation of 16 Fundamental Principles.
Foreword by Booth Tarkington. Introduction by Brander Matthews. Supplementary suggestions and Laboratory Notes by
Burges Johnson. (New York: Doubleday, 1939). [Treats
various aspects of fiction: the purpose of the novel, narrative plot, character setting, point of view. Distinguishes between realism and romance, and discusses the art of
the short story].

448 Hampshire, Stuart. Modern Writers and Other Essays. (London: Chatto & Windus, 1969). [A collection of previously
published essays and reviews emphasising "divergence" or
"controlling distortions" that mark an individual style.
Included are "The Letters of J. Joyce," reprinted from The
New Statesman, and "V. Woolf," "E. M. Forster," and "H.
James," reprinted from The New York Times Book Review].

449 Handy, William. "Toward a Formalist Criticism of Fiction."
The Novel: Modern Essays in Criticism. Edited by Robert
Murray Davis. (Englewood Cliffs, New Jersey: Prentice-Hall,
1969), pp. 94-102. Reprinted from Texas Studies in Literature and Language, III (Spring 1961), 81-88. [See entry
under Periodicals].

450 Hansen, Agnes Camilla. Twentieth Century Forces in European
Fiction. (Chicago: American Library Association, 1934).
[Surveys briefly the history of the modern novel since the
18th century, and discusses 20th century phenomena--social
and economic forces, political and historical concepts,
psychological theories--as reflected by 20th century fic-
tion].

451 Hardy, Barbara. The Appropriate Form: An Essay on the Novel. (London: The Athlone Press, 1964). [Discusses the
variety of narrative forms, i.e., the various combinations
of story, moral view or criticism of life embodied in the
story, and the "truthful realization" or imitation of life ,

through a study of Tolstoy's Anna Karenina and selected
English novelists including H. James, E. M. Forster, and
D. H. Lawrence].

452 Hardy, John Edward. Man in the Modern Novel. (Seattle &
London: University of Washington Press, 1964). [Discusses
the recurrent thematic concerns of the 20th century American and English novel: the theme of self, the effort to
know it and the quest for identity. J. Conrad, E. M. Forster, D. H. Lawrence, J. Joyce, V. Woolf, and E. Waugh among others].

453 Harper, Howard M., Jr. and Charles Edge, eds. The Classic
British Novel. (Athens: University of Georgia Press, 1972).
[A collection of essays by different writers on selected
novels, from Tom Jones to Mrs. Dalloway, but generally concerned in some way with the artist's creative vision and
the "ways in which that vision has shaped his work." Included are essays on works by J. Conrad, J. Joyce, D. H.
Lawrence, and V. Woolf].

454 Harris, Frank. Contemporary Portraits. Third Series. (London: Grant Richards; New York: Brentano, 1920). [Includes
H. G. Wells, J. Galsworthy, and G. K. Chesterton. This is
the third of four volumes published between 1915 and 1924].

455 Harris, Wendell V. "Style and the Twentieth Century Novel."
Critical Approaches to Fiction. Edited by Shiv K. Kumar
and Keith F. McKean. (New York: McGraw-Hill, 1968), pp.
131-147. Reprinted from Western Humanities Review, XVIII
(Spring 1964), 127-140. [See entry under Periodicals].

456 Harrison, John R[aymond]. The Reactionaries: Yeats, Lewis,
Pound, Eliot, Lawrence. A Study of the Anti-Democratic In-
telligentsia. With an Introduction by William Empson. (London: Gollancz, 1966; New York: Schoeken Books, 1967).
[Examines their social, political and artistic principles
to determine WHY they held such sympathetic views on fascism].

457 Hartley, L. P. "The Technique of the Novel." The Author
and the Public: Problems of Communication. (The P. E. N.
Congress held in London, July 1956). Edited, with an Introduction by C. V. Wedgwood. (London: Hutchinson, 1957),
pp. 165-175. An enlarged version of the original address
given to the Association, on March 11, 1951, at the Alliance Hall, Westminster. Reprinted as "The Novelist's Responsibility," English, XIII (1961), 172-177; also as "De
la responsabilité du romancier," Adam, 294-296 (1961), 15-
21. Reprinted in Essays and Studies, XV (1962), 88-100;
and in Essays by Divers Hands, XXXIV (1966), 74-89. [See
entry under Periodicals].

458 _____. The Novelist's Responsibility. (London: Hamish Hamilton; New York: Hillary House, 1967). [A collec-

64

tion of essays and papers which include "The Novelist's Responsibility," and "The Novelist and His Material." (See separate entries under Periodicals)].

459   Hartman, Geoffrey H. "The Heroics of Realism." Beyond Formalism: Literary Essays, 1958-1970. (London & New York: Yale University Press, 1970), pp. 61-71. Reprinted from The Yale Review, LIII (Autumn 1963), 26-35. [See entry under Periodicals].

460   Hartt, Julian N. The Lost Image of Man. (Baton Rouge: Louisiana State University Press, 1963). [Discusses what modern writers say about the "human condition" as a "disclosure of a human reality," and contends that they have negated an "image of man." J. Joyce, L. Durrell, A. Koestler, and G. Greene among others].

461   Harvey, W[illiam] J[ohn]. Character and the Novel. (London: Chatto & Windus; Ithaca, New York: Cornell University Press, 1965). [On the art of the novel. Adopts the attitude of the "mimesis" school that regards art as imitative of nature, and judges its adequacy insofar as it reflects experience. Also examines the controversy between mimetic and autonomical theories of the novel].

462   _____. "Character and the Context of Things." The Novel: Modern Essays in Criticism. Edited by Robert Murray Davis. (Englewood Cliffs, New Jersey: Prentice-Hall, 1969), pp. 126-140. Reprinted from Essays in Criticism, XIII (January 1963), 50-66; reprinted as Chapter II of Character and the Novel. [See entries above and under Periodicals].

463   Hassan, Ihab H. "The Anti-Hero in Modern British and American Fiction." Proceedings of the Second Congress of the International Comparative Literature Association. Edited by Werner P. Friederich. (Chapel Hill: University of Carolina Press, 1959; Johnson Reprint, 1970), pp. 309-323. [Maintains that the modern hero, unlike the "Noble Actor" or traditional protagonist, reverts to the "motive of alienation," lacks "faith in efficient action," is passive and appears in the "guise of a victim" who is defeated on terms not of his own choosing, all of which splits the reader's identification between his character and his predicament. Also points out the reemergence of the anti-hero through satire in the English novel and through violence in the American. J. Joyce, J. Conrad, H. James, A. Huxley, E. Waugh, G. Orwell, and G. Greene among others].

464   Hayman, Ronald, ed. "Le Roman anglais d'après-guerre." La Littérature anglaise d'après-guerre. (Paris: Lettres Modernes, 1955), pp. 81-112. Reprinted from Revue de Lettres Modernes, 111 (1954), 17-48. [See entry under Periodicals].

465   Heddle, Enid Moodie. Modern English Literature. Quest:

A Series of Discussion Pamphlets. (Melbourne & London:
F. W. Cheshire Pty., 1947). [A reading guide drawing attention to significant literary figures that have emerged
in England and America during the previous fifty years, and
to forms and trends in poetry, drama, and the novel].

466 Heiney, Donald W. Contemporary Literature. (New York:
Barron's Educational Series, 1954). [Traces two basic 20th
century tendencies: the continuation of the realistic naturalistic movement of the 19th century and the 20th century
reaction against it as reflected in the repudiation of external objectivity. Also traces the growth of the literature of ideas--Faith, Liberalism, and Existentialism. A.
Bennett, J. Galsworthy, E. M. Forster, D. H. Lawrence, C.
Isherwood, J. Conrad, V. Woolf, K. Mansfield, J. Joyce, A.
Huxley, E. Waugh, G. K. Chesterton, H. G. Wells, G. Orwell,
A. Koestler and other American and European writers].

467 Hellmann, Günter. Ideen und Kräfte in der englischen Nach-
kriegsjugend nach literarischen Selbstzeugnissen. Sprache
und Kultur der germanischen und romanischen Völker. (Breslau: Buchdruckerei Paul Plischke, 1939). [A study of the
ideals and forces shaping post-World War I youth as expressed in the literature of the times. W. Lewis, D. H. Lawrence, and A. Waugh among others].

468 Henderson, Philip. The Novel Today. Studies in Contemporary Attitudes. (London: The Bodley Head, 1936). [A Marxist approach choosing several outstanding English, American,
and European novelists and discussing how they attempt to
solve the problem of living. Regards the novel as a form
of social activity rather than an isolated art form obeying
its own laws, and divides novels into entertainments and
criticisms of life. D. H. Lawrence, J. Joyce, V. Woolf,
E. M. Forster, W. Lewis, J. Galsworthy, H. G. Wells, A. Huxley, S. Jameson, A. Brown, and J. Sommerfield].

469 Heppenstall, [John] Rayner. The Fourfold Tradition: Notes
on the French and English Literatures, with some ethnolog-
ical and historical asides. (London: Barrie and Rockliff;
Norfolk, Connecticut: New Directions, 1961). [The study
is divided into three parts: I. 1400-1900, II. 1900-1950,
and III. After 1950. Parts II and III are concerned mainly
with French and English novelists. J. Joyce. D. H. Lawrence, V. Woolf, K. Amis, J. Wain, and A. Bennett].

470 Herbert, James. Modern English Novelists. (Tokyo: Kenkyusha, 1960; The Folcroft Press, 1970). [A collection of
separate essays, one on each of E. M. Forster, V. Woolf,
A. Huxley, E. Waugh, G. Greene, J. Cary, H. Green, C. P.
Snow, W. Golding, L. Durrell, and the "Younger Novelists"
of the fifties].

471 Herbrüggen, Hubertus Schulte. Utopie und Anti-Utopie: Von

der Strukturanalyse zur Strukturtypologie. (Bochum-Langendreer: Verlag Heinrich Poppinghaus, 1960). [Discusses the term "Utopie," its course in history using More's Utopia as starting point, and the change in form in English Utopian writing that comes with Orwell's 1984].

472 Hewitt, Douglas. The Approach to Fiction: Good and Bad Readings of Novels. (London: Longman, 1972). [Examines several ways in which readers' responses to novels are "controlled, both by what happens in the book and by what conventions exist," with the "metaphor model" in mind; i.e., considering the relationship between a novel and life to be "akin to that between the two parts of a metaphor." Examines three 19th century novels. References to J. Conrad, J. Joyce, H. James, D. H. Lawrence, and V. Woolf among others].

473 Hibbard, G[eorge] R[ichard], ed. Renaissance and Modern Essays. (New York: Barnes & Noble; London: Routledge & Kegan Paul, 1966). [A collection of essays presented to Vivian de Sola Pinto on his 70th birthday. Includes two essays on D. H. Lawrence, one on E. M. Forster and D. H. Lawrence, and one on each of H. James, and A. Sillitoe].

474 Hicks, William Charles Reginald. The School in English and German Fiction. (London: The Soncino Press, 1933). [Analyses and assesses the "reality" which the novel has and which is denied to the manual or official report, in shedding light on the school as an institution, and the way the Public or Day School acts as a formative influence in both England and Germany. A. Bennett, H. A. Vachell, H. Neubolt, C. Mackenzie, H. Walpole, A. Waugh, A. Lunn, and H. G. Wells].

475 Hildick, [Edmund] Wallace. Word for Word: A Study of Authors' Alterations with Exercises. (London: Faber & Faber, 1965). [Examines changes made by D. H. Lawrence, H. James, and V. Woolf among others, and their significance. Maintains that changes are made for "tidying up," for greater accuracy or clarity of expression, and for ideological resons].

476 _____. Thirteen Types of Narrative. (London: Macmillan, 1968). [A technical approach to narrative, with a wide range of illustrations from the English novel, and analytic and creative exercises for each of the thirteen types of narrative].

477 Hillegas, Mark R[obert]. The Future as Nightmare: H. G. Wells and the Anti-Utopians. (New York: Oxford University Press, 1967). [Examines the influence of H. G. Wells' fiction, especially his science fiction, which seems to project a future far worse than the present, on E. M. Forster's "The Machine Stops," A. Huxley's Brave New World, G. Orwell's 1984 and C. S. Lewis' Out of the Silent Planet].

478 _____. Shadows of the Imagination: The Fantasies of
C. S. Lewis, J. R. R. Tolkien, and Charles Williams. With
a Preface by Harry T. Moore. (Carbondale & Edwardsville:
Southern Illinois University Press; London & Amsterdam:
Feffer & Simons, 1969). [A collection of essays by differ-
ent writers on the three novelists].

479 Hind, C[harles] L[ewis]. Authors and I. (New York & London: The Bodley Head, 1921). [Reactions to certain English and American authors and to phases of art, originally
published in The Christian Science Monitor. H. Belloc, A.
Bennett, G. K. Chesterton, J. Conrad, H. James, G. Moore,
H. Walpole, H. G. Wells, and E. Wharton].

480 Hoare, Dorothy M[ackenzie]. Some Studies in The Modern Novel. (London: Chatto & Windus, 1938; Litchfield, Connecticut: Prospect Press, 1940). [Lectures originally delivered in the English Faculty at Cambridge, parts of which
have been published in New Adelphi, The Cambridge Review,
and Everyman. Includes H. James, V. Woolf, E. M. Forster,
D. H. Lawrence, J. Conrad, G. Moore, and J. Joyce].

481 Hoffman, Frederick J[ohn]. Freudianism and the Literary
Mind. (Baton Rouge, Louisiana: Louisiana State University
Press, 1945; London: Calder, 1959). [Originally a doctoral dissertation presented to Ohio State University, 1943.
An exposition and an appraisal of Freudian psychology as it
relates to modern literature: English, American, and German. J. Joyce and D. H. Lawrence among others].

482 _____. "Mortality and Modern Literature." The Mean-
ing of Death. Edited by Herman Feifel. (New York: McGraw-
Hill, 1959). pp. 133-156. A revised version of "Grace,
Violence and Self: Death and Modern Literature," Virginia
Quarterly Review, XXXIV (Summer 1958), 439-454. Further
revised and reprinted as "Introduction" to The Mortal No:
Death and the Modern Imagination." [See entries under Per-
iodicals and below].

483 _____. The Mortal No: Death and the Modern Imagination. (Princeton, New Jersey: Princeton University Press,
1964). [A portion of the volume, as the author indicates,
is reprinted from previously published articles dealing with
the themes of the three parts of the book: Grace, Violence,
and the Self. Chapter XII explores the personal forms of
"improvisation in self-definition, and the metaphors and
habits of creative invention" in D. H. Lawrence and J. Joyce].

484 _____, Charles Allen, and Carolyn F. Ulrich.
The Little Magazine: A History and a Bibliography. (London: Oxford University Press, 1946; Princeton: Princeton
University Press, 1947). [Examines the little magazines as
a source of information about 20th century writing, especially the second and third decades, their relationship in
the formulation of modern ideologies, experimental liter-

ature, the proletarian development of the thirties, and
their contribution to modern criticism.   Also includes an
annotated bibliography, chronologically arranged, but grouped alphabetically within each year].

485   Hogarth, Basil.   The Technique of Novel Writing: A Practical Guide for New Authors.   (London: The Bodley Head,
1934).   [Indicates and analyses the component elements and
technical processes of the modern novel].

486   Hoggart, Richard.   Speaking To Each Other: Essays, 2 Vols.
(New York: Oxford University Press; London: Chatto & Windus, 1970).   [Only Vol. 2 deals with literature.   The essays,
mostly reprints, and written over the previous ten years,
include one on each of G. Greene, D. H. Lawrence, and G.
Orwell].

487   Holloway, [Christopher] John.   "Tank in the Stalls: Notes
on the 'School of Anger'."   The Beat Generation and the
Angry Young Men.   Edited by Gene Feldman and Max Gartenberg.
(New York: The Citadel Press, 1958), pp. 364-373.   Published in England as Protest.   (London: Souvenir Press, 1959).
Reprinted from The Hudson Review, X:3 (Autumn 1957), 424-
429; also reprinted in The Charted Mirror: Literary and
Critical Essays.   (London: Routledge & Kegan Paul, 1960),
pp. 137-145.   [See entry under Periodicals].

488   _____.   The Charted Mirror: Literary and Critical Essays.   (London: Routledge & Kegan Paul, 1960; New York:
Horizon Press, 1962).   [Includes "Tank in the Stalls"--see
above--and an essay on W. Lewis].

489   _____.   "The Literary Scene."   The Pelican Guide to
English Literature, Vol. 7, The Modern Age.   Edited by Boris
Ford.   [London: Cassell; Baltimore and Harmondsworth: Penguin, 1961), pp. 51-103.   [A survey from the turn of the
century to the end of the fifties that considers the assimilation of major continental influences in poetry and the
novel, and the increasing independence from those influences at the end of the period].

490   Honeywell, J. Arthur.   "Plot in the Modern Novel."   Critical Approaches to Fiction.   Edited by Shiv K. Kumar and
Keith F. McKean.   (New York: McGraw-Hill, 1968), pp. 45-57.
[Maintains that the 20th century novelists' rejection of
plot as a construction of logical or rational sequences of
events operating in time,for a structuring of events to present a coherent "world" or vision of reality, "a movement
from appearance to reality," is also partially responsible
for the concept of the anti-hero, and the "new" methods of
narration.   J. Joyce and F. M. Ford].

491   Honig, Edwin.   Dark Conceit: The Making of Allegory.   (London: Faber & Faber; Evanston, Illinois: Northwestern Univ-

ersity Press, 1959). [Explores the methods and ideas that
go into the making of allegory, estimates "biases that obscure the subject," surveys the changing concept of allegory, the "typical constructs of allegorical narration," and
examines three major verbal modes of allegorical fiction,
as well as ideals in allegory, epic, satire, and the pastoral. H. James, D. H. Lawrence, and J. Joyce among others].

492 Hoops, Reinald. Der Einfluss der Psychoanalyse auf die englische Literatur. Anglistische Forschungen, Heft 77.
(Heidelberg: Carl Winters Universitätsbuchhandlung, 1934).
[Examines how deeply psychoanalysis has penetrated 20th
century critical writings, drama, and especially the novel,
with which most of the work is concerned. Contends that
discoveries in psychology may have helped novelists to explore the subconscious, but have not inspired this exploration. M. Sinclair, D. H. Lawrence, J. D. Beresford, H.
Walpole, S. Maugham, J. Joyce, V. Woolf, K. Mansfield, D.
Richardson, R. Macaulay, "R. West," G. B. Stern, and A. Hux-
ley].

493 Horst, Karl August. Das Spectrum des modernen Romans: Eine
Untersuchung. (Munich: Verlag C. H. Beck, 1960). [An
investigation into the constituent elements of the modern
novel with reference to the English, French and German novel].

494 Hortmann, Wilhelm. Englische Literatur im 20. Jahrhundert.
(Dalp Taschenbücher, 379G). (Bern: A. Francke A. G. Verlag,
1965). [A history of English literature in the 20th century, decade by decade, until 1960].

495 Hoskins, Katharine Bail. Today the Struggle: Literature
and Politics in England during the Spanish Civil War. (Austin and London: University of Texas Press, 1969). [Orig-
inally a doctoral dissertation presented to Columbia University, 1965. A study of English writers who, during the
Spanish Civil War, dedicated their literary talents to the
propagation of certain social and political ideas, and the
change that occured in their attitudes. E. Waugh, G. Greene,
W. Lewis, A. Huxley, A. Koestler, G. Orwell, and R. Warner].

496 Hough, Graham. Image and Experience: Studies in a Literary Revolution. (London: Gerald Duckworth, 1960; Lincoln:
University of Nebraska Press, 1964). [The studies fall into
three parts: the first deals with poetry, the second compares the artistic creeds of the 19th and 20th centuries
(D. H. Lawrence), and the third discusses G. Moore's attempts
to redirect the English novel, and J. Conrad as a transitional writer].

497 _____. "Morality and the Novel." The Dream and the
Task: Literature and Morals in the Culture of Today. (London: Gerald Duckworth, 1963; New York: Norton, 1964), pp.
42-57. Reprinted from The Listener, LXIX:1779 (2 May 1963),
747-748. [See entry under Periodicals].

498 _____. "The Novel and History." An Essay on Criticism. (London: Gerald Duckworth; New York: Norton, 1966). Reprinted with "Mimesis I," pp. 42-44, in The Critical Quarterly, VIII (1966), 136-145. [Discusses the relation of the novel to reality, and contends that good novels do not deny the fact that "history is the field in which the novel operates," but the novel may retain an "authentic spiritual freedom" which may transcend both history and society].

499 Howe, Irving. Politics and the Novel. (New York: Horizon Press, 1957; London: Stevens, 1961). [A collection of essays previously published. Examines the relationship between literature and ideas, and discusses 19th and 20th century English, American and Continental novels subjected to the pressures of politics and political ideology. J. Conrad, H. James, A. Koestler, and G. Orwell among others].

500 _____. A World More Attractive: A View of Modern Literature and Politics. (New York: Horizon Press, 1963). [Includes "Mass Society and Post-Modern Fiction," pp. 77-98, and "The Fiction of Anti-Utopia," pp. 216-227, reprinted from The Partisan Review, XXVI:3 (Summer 1959), 420-436, and The New Republic, CXLVI (23 April 1962), 12-16. (See entries under Periodicals)].

501 _____, ed. Literary Modernism. Introduction by the Editor. (Greenwich, Connecticut: Fawcett Publications, 1967). [A collection of essays by different writers on various aspects of modernism. Includes a later version of "The Culture of Modernism" by the editor as an Introduction entitled "The Idea of The Modern," L. Trilling's "On The Modern Element in Literature," (see entries under Periodicals), and S. Spender's "Moderns and Contemporaries," reprinted from The Struggle of the Modern].

502 _____. Decline of the New. (New York: Harcourt, Brace & World, 1970; London: Gollancz, 1971). [A collection of essays all bearing upon the central problem of literary modernism. Included are: "The Culture of Modernism," "The Fiction of Anti-Utopia," and "Mass Society and Post-Modern Fiction." Also includes studies of H. James and G. Orwell].

503 Howe, Susanne. Novels of Empire. (New York: Columbia University Press; London: Oxford University Press, 1949). [Surveys some 200 English, French and German novels as a "running commentary on the ineptitudes and heroism of expansion" and its "limitless inconsistency and confusion." Chooses works from the twentieth century and the second half of the nineteenth that deal with India, Africa, Australia and New Zealand].

504 Hoyt, Charles Alva, ed. Minor British Novelists. Preface by Harry T. Moore. (Carbondale & Edwardsville: Southern Illinois University Press; London and Amsterdam: Feffer

& Simons, 1967). [Separate essays by different writers on novelists of the 19th and 20th centuries. Included among the "minor" writers are A. Machen, C. Williams, and R. Macaulay].

505 Hudson, Derek, ed. English Critical Essays: Twentieth Century. (Second Series). With an Introduction. (London: Oxford University Press, 1958). [A sequel to English Critical Essays: Twentieth Century, selected and introduced by Phyllis M. Jones. The collection of essays consists of works published or written after 1933, and includes C. Morgan's "Creative Imagination," F. R. Leavis' "Henry James's The Europeans," N. Nicholson's "A. Bennett," and J. Lehmann's "V. Woolf"].

506 Hugo, Howard E[ppens]. Aspects of Fiction: A Handbook. (Boston & Toronto: Little, Brown, 1962). [Excerpts from English, American and Continental novelists and writers, chronologically arranged, ranging from Fielding to Alain Robbe-Grillet and dealing with as many "aspects of the novel as could be conveniently touched upon"].

507 Humphrey, Robert. Stream of Consciousness in the Modern Novel. (Berkeley & Los Angeles: University of California Press, 1954). [Originally a doctoral dissertation entitled Creating Consciousness: A Study in Novelistic Techniques, Northwestern University, 1950. An analysis of the technique in an attempt to clarify the literary term, and an interpretation and evaluation of novels by J. Joyce, V. Woolf, and D. Richardson].

508 Hunter, Jim, ed. The Modern Novel in English: Studied in Extracts. (London: Faber & Faber, 1966). [Extracts from novels, arranged in chronological order and preceded by a summary of each novelist's main work and distinctive literary characteristics. Notes include recommendations for further reading].

509 Hyman, Stanley Edgar. "Some Trends in the Novel." The Promised End: Essays and Reviews, 1942-1962. (Cleveland: World Publications, 1963; Books for Libraries Press, 1972), pp. 342-356. Reprinted from College English, XX:1 (October 1958), 1-9. [See entry under Periodicals].

510 Hynes, Samuel. The Edwardian Turn of Mind. (Princeton, New Jersey: Princeton University Press; London: Oxford University Press, 1968). [Deals with the intellectual climate of England in the years before World War I. A. Bennett, E. M. Forster, J. Galsworthy, H. James, J. Joyce. H. G. Wells, and D. H. Lawrence].

511 _____, ed. The Author's Craft and Other Critical Writings of Arnold Bennett. (Lincoln: University of Nebraska Press, 1968). [A collection of A. Bennett's critical writings reprinted from periodicals. Part I gives his views on the state of the novel, the public and the craft of wri-

ting, and Part II gives his views on his contemporaries:
H. James, G. Moore, E. Phillpotts, H. G. Wells, J. Galsworthy, J. Joyce, V. Woolf and others. Also includes a
reprint of the first version of V. Woolf's "Mr. Bennett
and Mrs. Brown"].

512 _____. Edwardian Occasions: Essays on English Wri-
ting in the Early Twentieth Century. (London: Routledge
& Kegan Paul, 1972). [A collection of essays on V. Woolf,
J. Conrad, F. M. Ford, G. K. Chesterton, E. M. Forster,
and M. Hewlett reprinted from The Times Literary Supplement,
Novel, Commonweal, The Sewanee Review, and The Yale Review].

513 Inge, William Ralph, ed. The Post Victorians. (London:
Nicholson & Watson, 1933). [A collection of essays by different critics. Includes one on each of A. Bennett, J. Conrad, J. Galsworthy, D. H. Lawrence, and G. Moore].

514 Isaacs, Jacob. "England." Contemporary Movements in European Literature. Edited by William Rose and J. Isaacs.
(London: Routledge, 1928), pp. 1-30. [Distinguishes between the "literature of direction and the literature of
permanence," and makes the novel his chief concern with poetry and criticism in this order of importance. Discusses
the influences of S. Butler, Frazer, Freud, the Russians
and the war in "fixing the mental background." J. Joyce,
D. H. Lawrence, V. Woolf and W. Lewis among others. The
rest of the volume discusses contemporary literature in
France, Germany, Spain, Italy, Russia, Scandinavia and Czech-
oslovakia].

515 _____. An Assessment of Twentieth-Century Literature.
Six lectures delivered on the B. B. C. Third Programme.
(London: Secker and Warburg, 1951). [The lectures, delivered in September and October 1950, give a comprehensive
survey from a literary historian's perspective. The first
lecture sets out "the pattern" of the half-century's progress in literature, and the 2nd, 3rd and 4th show, among
other things, the emergence of the novel as the dominant
form of literature. The third lecture is devoted, almost
entirely, to the stream-of-consciousness].

516 Ivasheva, V. Anglijskij roman poslednego desjatiletya.
(Moscow: Sovetskij Pisatel', 1962). [Examines the basic
tendencies in the development of the English novel of the
fifties and the "imperialist reaction" against realism and
modernism. C. P. Snow, G. Greene, K. Amis, J. Wain, J.
Braine, J. Aldridge, D. Stewart, B. Davidson, and J. Lind-
say].

517 _____. Angliiskaya literatura XX V. (Moscow: Pros-
veshchenie, 1967). [A survey of twentieth century English
literature, from a Marxist viewpoint. The first part examines the twenties and thirties separately, traces the

growth of modernism and realism, the emergence of the socialist novel, and includes a section on war literature.
Part two examines the postwar literature of despndency,
confession, existentialism, and the rise of the proletarian
novel. Major novelists are examined separately].

518 _____. Angliiskie Dialogi: Etiudy o Sovremennykh
Pisateliakh. (Moscow: Sovetskij pisatel', 1971). [A "study"
of twelve contemporary writers and novelists--S. Chaplin.
N. Lewis, D. Stewart, B. Davidson, C. P. Snow, P.H. Johnson,
W. Cooper, G. Greene, W. Golding, I. Murdoch, J. Wain, A.
Sillitoe, J. Lindsay, and R. Williams--based partly on in-
terviews].

519 Jaloux, Edmond. Au pays du roman. (Paris: Editions R. A.
Correa, 1931). [Studies of English novelists and novels
from T. Hardy to R. Lehmann. Included are H. James, J.
Joyce, M. Baring, C. Dane, K. Mansfield, V. Woolf, A. Huxley, R. Lehmann, and M. Kennedy].

520 James, Henry. The Art of the Novel: Critical Prefaces.
Introduction by R. P. Blackmur. (New York: Scribner's,
1934). [Includes eighteen prefaces to his novels from
Roderick Hudson to The Golden Bowl. These prefaces, in
their entirety, constitute an essay in criticism and a reference on the technical aspects of the art of fiction].

521 _____. Selected Literary Criticism. Edited by Morris
Shapira, prefaced with a note on 'James as Critic' by F. R.
Leavis. (London: Heinemann, 1963; New York: Horizon Press,
1964). [Includes "The Art of Fiction," "The Future of the
Novel," and "The New Novel"].

522 Jameson, [Margaret] Storm. The Georgian Novel and Mr. Robinson. (London: Heinemann; New York: Morrow, 1929). [Also
reprinted in The Bookman, LXIX (July 1929), 449-463. See
entry under Periodicals].

523 _____. The Novel in Contemporary Life. (Boston: The
Writer, Inc., 1938). [Examines the novel in 1937 after the
disappearance of the major figures in the twenties, and contends that the only novelists worth troubling about are
those trying to become more aware of what is happening
around us, and who have not deserted the fiction-reading
public].

524 _____. The Writer's Situation and Other Essays. (London: Macmillan, 1950). [A collection of essays, a few of
which are reprints. Included are "The Form of the Novel,"
"The Novelist Today," and "Literature between the Wars."
See entries under Periodicals].

525 _____. Parthian Words. (London: Collins & Harvill
Press, 1970; New York: Harper, 1971). [The moral auto-

74

biography of a writer as well as an essay in criticism].

526 Janeway, Elizabeth. "What's American and What's British in
the Modern Novel." Highlights of Modern Literature: A
Permanent Collection of Memorable Essays from 'The New York
Times Book Review'. Edited by Francis Brown. (New York:
The New American Library, 1954), pp. 62-68. Reprinted from
The New York Times Book Review, (14 January 1951), 4. [See
entry under Periodicals].

527 _____. "Fiction's Place in a World Awry." Opinions
and Perspectives from 'The New York Times Book Review'.
Edited by Francis Brown. (Boston: Houghton Mifflin, 1964),
pp. 29-34. Reprinted from The New York Times Book Review,
(31 August 1961), pp. 1, 24. [See entry under Periodicals].

528 Jarrasch, Walter. Das Problem der heranwachsenden Jugend
im Spiegel des zeitgenössischen englischen Romans, 1900-
1933. (Leipzig: Noske, 1940). [Doctoral dissertation
presented to Giessen University. A study of the problems
of adolescence as represented in novels by R. Aldington,
J. Conrad, W. Deeping, J. Galsworthy, P. Gibbs, R. Hughes,
J. Joyce, D. H. Lawrence, C. Mackenzie, R. Macaulay, C. E.
Montague, C. Morgan, H. Walpole, and H. G. Wells].

529 Johnson, Pamela Hansford. "Literature." The Baldwin Age.
Edited by John Raymond. (London: Eyre & Spottiswoode,
1960; Chester Springs: Dufour Editions, 1961), pp. 179-189.
[Surveys the literary scene between 1922 and 1937, and shows
how a "great tradition," especially in the novel, was "forced
into retreat," and the various attempts "to replace it utterly . . . by a literature of visual and aural experiment"].

530 Johnson, R[eginald] Brimley. Some Contemporary Novelists:
Women. (London: Leonard Parsons, 1920). [M. Sinclair,
E. Mordaunt, R. Macaulay, S. Kaye-Smith, E. Sidgwick, A.
Reeves, V. Meynell, D. Richardson, V. Woolf, S. Benson, E.
M. Delafield, C. Dane, M. Fulton, and H. Mirrlees].

531 _____. Some Contemporary Novelists: Men. (London:
Leonard Parsons, 1922). [Analyses the chief works of the
"rising" generation of novelists. G. Cannan, H. Walpole,
W. L. George, J. D. Beresford, D. H. Lawrence, C. Mackenzie,
J. C. Snaith, E. M. Forster, J. Buchan, N. Lyons, and F.
Swinnerton].

532 _____. Moral Poison in Modern Fiction. (London: A.
M. Philpot, 1922). [Examines the effect of new theories
of sexual morality, whether assumed or expounded in novels,
and condemns their evil influence].

533 Johnstone, J[ohn] K[eith]. The Bloomsbury Group: A Study
of E. M. Forster, Lytton Strachey, Virginia Woolf, and Their
Circle. (New York: The Noonday Press; London: Secker &
Warburg, 1954). [A study of the literary relationships and

values of the group with insights into the personalities of the writers].

534 Jones, William Sidney Handley. The Priest and the Siren, and other Literary Studies. (London: The Epworth Press, 1953). [A collection of essays reprinted from the London Quarterly Review which includes one on each of G. K. Chesterton, H. G. Wells, A. Bennett, J. Galsworthy, D. H. Lawrence, and A. Huxley ("The Modern Hamlet"). Also discusses the relationship between religion and art in "The Priest and the Siren," pp. 1-12].

535 Kaam, Adrian van, & Kathleen Healy. The Demon and the Dove: Personality Growth Through Literature. (Pittsburgh, Pennsylvania: Duquesne University Press, 1967). [A study that spans the two realms of psychology and literature. Part one, written from a psychologist's viewpoint, discusses the close partnership of literature and psychology in unveiling the depths of human experience. Part two gives a critical analysis of personalities in literature. Included are Marcher in H. James' The Beast and the Jungle and Querry in G. Greene's A Burnt-Out Case].

536 Kahrmann, Bernd. Die idyllische Szene im zeitgenössicshen englischen Roman. Linguistica et Litteraria, 8. (Bad Homburg v.d. H. Berlin. Zurich: Verlag Gehlen, 1969). [A study of the function and use of the "idyllic scene"--defined in Chapter I as escape from, or rejection of reality, when both worlds co-exist, and as a hero's idealisation of reality. I. Murdoch, P. Mortimer, J. Cary, J. Wain, E. Waugh, A. Sillitoe, G. Orwell, J. Braine, W. Golding, D. Storey, and H. James].

537 Kaplan, Harold J. The Passive Voice: An Approach to Modern Fiction. (Athens, Ohio: Ohio University Press, 1966). [Essays on the related topics of the effects of solipsism, moral passivity, and the split consciousness, perspectives of primitive naturalism and variations of the comic mood, all arising from "the crisis of knowledge" in the 20th century and treated by the literary imagination. Included are essays on J. Joyce, D. H. Lawrence, and J. Conrad].

538 Karl, Frederick Robert, & Marvin Magalaner. A Reader's Guide to Great Twentieth Century English Novels. (New York: Noonday Press, 1959; London: Thames & Hudson, 1960). [The Introduction discusses the many forces affecting the shape and content of the 20th century English novel. Includes separate studies of J. Conrad, E. M. Forster, V. Woolf, D. H. Lawrence, J. Joyce, and A. Huxley].

539 _____. A Reader's Guide to the Contemporary English Novel. (New York: Farrar and Strauss, 1962; London: Thames and Hudson, 1963). [Separate studies of S. Beckett, L. Durrell, C. P. Snow, G. Greene, E. Bowen, J. Cary, G.

Orwell, E. Waugh, H. Green, I. Compton-Burnett, and the
"Angry Young Men." Under blanket titles of "The Still Sad
Music of Humanity" and "The Novel as Moral Allegory" are
grouped A. Powell, A. Wilson, N. Dennis, and W. Golding,
I. Murdoch, R. Warner, and P. H. Newby. Chapter I is a
general examination of the characteristics and tendencies
of the "contemporary" English novelists--the writers whose
major development occurred in the thirties].

540 Kashkin, Ivan. Dla chitatelya sovremenikan. Stat'y i iss-
ledovania. (Moscow: Sovetskii Pisatel', 1968). [Essays
and studies on English and American writers. Included are
J. Conrad, G. K. Chesterton, and C. Caudwell].

541 Kateb, George. Utopia and Its Enemies. (New York: The
Free Press of Glencoe; London: Collier-Macmillan, 1963).
[Originally a doctoral dissertation entitled "Anti-Utopianism" presented to Columbia University. Discusses attacks
on government and mechanization as two means needed to achieve three Utopian ends: "perpetual peace, guaranteed abun-
dance, and conditioned virtue." References to A. Huxley,
H. G. Wells, and G. Orwell among others].

542 Kawaguchi, Kyoichi. Gendai Igirisu Shosetsu. (Tokyo:
Kaitaku-Sha, 1959). [A study, in Japanese, of the modern
English novel that discusses selected works by E. M. For-
ster, D. H. Lawrence, S. Beckett, J. Joyce, and W. Golding.
Central focus is on J. Joyce].

543 Kazin, Alfred. The Inmost Leaf: A Selection of Essays.
(New York: Harcourt Brace, 1955). [Essays reprinted from
American periodicals. Included is one on each of J. Joyce,
H. James, and D. H. Lawrence].

544 Kellogg, Gene. The Vital Tradition: The Catholic Novel in
a Period of Convergence. (Chicago: Loyola University Press,
1970). [Originally a doctoral dissertation presented to the
University of Chicago, 1969/70. Examines the rise and decline of the Catholic novel in France, England, and America.
Pages 79-136, "Protestant England," consider G. K. Chesterton, H. Belloc, E. Waugh, and G. Greene].

545 Kennedy, J. M. English Literature. 1880-1905. (London:
Stephen Swift, 1912; Boston, Massachusetts: Maynard, 1913).
[A "literary inquiry" of the period concentrating on major
figures. H. G. Wells, G. Moore, "F. Macleod" (W. Sharp),
and R. Le Gallienne].

546 Kennedy, Margaret. The Outlaws on Parnassus. (London:
The Cresset Press, 1958; New York: Viking Press, 1960).
[On the art of the novel, and a defence of storytelling
against those who refuse to acknowledge it as an art in itself. Illustrates from the English novel at large].

547 Kenner, Hugh. Gnomon: Essays on Contemporary Literature. (New York: McDowell, Obolensky, 1956). [Most of the essays are mainly concerned with poetry. Chapter XI deals with J. Conrad and F. M. Ford, and Chapter XV with W. Lewis].

548 _____. Flaubert, Joyce and Beckett: The Stoic Comedians. (Boston: Beacon Press, 1962; London: Witt, Allen, 1964). [On Flaubert, Joyce and Beckett who carry forward the "novel as Knowing-Machine, lifelike, logical"].

549 Kermode, [John] Frank. Puzzles and Epiphanies: Essays and Reviews, 1958-1961. (London: Routledge & Kegan Paul, 1962). (Included are essays on J. Joyce, E. Waugh, and W. Golding, and reviews of novels by G. Greene, S. Beckett, A. Wilson, and L. Durrell].

550 _____. The Sense of an Ending: Studies in the Theory of Fiction. (New York: Oxford University Press, 1967; London: Oxford University Press, 1968). (The Mary Flexner lectures given at Bryn Maur College, 1965). [The purpose, as he modestly puts it in the Preface, is "to make suggestions, to initiate discussion rather than to settle any of the problems it raises." Investigates the status of fiction, at once "deeply distrusted and yet humanly indispensable," how far one may "cultivate fictional patterns," and the notion that there is a "humanly needed order which we call form"].

551 _____. Continuities. (London: Routledge & Kegan Paul, 1968). [A collection of essays and reviews written and published separately between 1962 and 1967 on the theme of the Modern, Poets, Critics, and Novelists. Included in the latter are D. H. Lawrence, S. Beckett, W. Golding, and M. Spark].

552 _____. Modern Essays. (London: Collins (Fontana Books), 1971). [Includes essays on D. H. Lawrence and M. Spark reprinted from Continuities (see above), and others on S. Beckett, W. Golding and I. Murdoch. Also notices A. Sillitoe and A. Burgess].

553 _____. "The English Novel, circa 1907." Twentieth-Century Literature in Retrospect, Harvard English Studies, 2. Edited by Reuben A. Brower. (Cambridge, Massachusetts: Harvard University Press, 1971), pp. 45-65. [Illustrates the pressure of the times on the popular fiction of E. Glyn, F. Barclay, and W. De Morgan, and examines the growing concern with technical innovation in fiction in its early stages, not just as a refinement, but as a necessary instrument to understand the condition of the world; hence, the association of new techniques with new changed times. H. James, J. Conrad, J. Galsworthy, and G. K. Chesterton].

554 Kerr, Elizabeth Margaret. Bibliography of the Sequence Nov-

el. (Minneapolis: The University of Minnesota Press; London: Oxford University Press, 1950). [Originally a doctoral dissertation presented to the University of Minnesota, 1941/42. Pages 11-39 give a bibliography of the sequence novel in England and America. Also deals with novels in the Romance, Teutonic, and Slavic groups of languages. The Introduction defines the sequence novel as "closely related novels that were originally published as separate, complete novels but that as a series form an artistic whole, unified by structure, and themes that involve more than the recurrence of characters and continuity of action"].

555 Kettle, Arnold. An Introduction to the English Novel, 2 Vols. (London: Hutchinson, 1951, 1953). [Vol. I is to George Eliot. Vol. II concentrates on, and evaluates a selected novel, "of more than casual significance," from each of H. James, S. Butler, T. Hardy, J. Conrad, A. Bennett, H. G. Wells, J. Galsworthy, V. Woolf, D. H. Lawrence, J. Joyce, E. M. Forster, A. Huxley, G. Greene, J. Cary, I. Compton-Burnett, and H. Green in order to build a discussion of the development of the modern English novel].

556 Kiell, Norman. The Adolescent Through Fiction: A Psychological Approach. (New York: International Universities Press; London: Bailey & Swinfen, 1959). [Attempts to show that fiction is a "fruitful field for exploration in the study of adolescent psychology," by setting down "some of the dynamic principles of adolescent development and psychology," with illustrations from contemporary fiction, both English and American. Includes excerpts from A. Bennett, P. Frankau, J. Joyce, D. H. Lawrence, S. Maugham, H. G. Wells, and A. West].

557 Killam, G. D. Africa in English Fiction 1874-1939. (Ibadan: Ibadan University Press, 1968). [Originally a doctoral dissertation entitled The Presentation of Africa between the Sahara and the Union of South Africa in Novels written in English, 1860-1939, University College, London, 1964/65. A "historical" survey of novels devoted to tropical Africa showing a changing regard for Africa from 1874 to 1939. J. Cary, J. Conrad, and W. Holtby].

558 Killinger, John. The Failure of Theology in Modern Literature. (Nashville and New York: Abingdon Press, 1963). [Discusses writings--English, American, and French--that are "related" to the Christian faith. G. Greene, D. H. Lawrence, and A. Huxley among others].

559 Knapp, Ilse. Die Landschaft im modernen englischen Frauenroman. (Borna-Leipzig: Robert Noske, 1935). [A doctoral dissertation presented to the University of Tübingen. Examines technique in the delineation of setting, and the use of landscape from an artistic and ethical viewpoint in works by S. Kaye-Smith, V. Sackville-West, M. Webb, and V. Woolf].

560 Knight, George Wilson. "Lawrence, Joyce and Powys." Neglected Powers: Essays on Nineteenth and Twentieth Century

<u>Literature</u>. (London: Routledge & Kegan Paul; New York: Barnes and Noble, 1971), pp. 142-155. Reprinted from <u>Essays in Criticism</u>, XI:4 (October 1961), 403-417. [See entry under Periodicals].

561 Knight, Grant Cochrane. <u>Superlatives</u>. (New York: Knopf, 1925). [Mainly concerned with the type of hero described in terms of the superlative degree in selected English novels from Defoe to Conrad. Includes separate studies of the central character in H. James' <u>The Turn of the Screw</u>, G. Moore's <u>A Mummer's Wife</u>, and J. Conrad's <u>The Rover</u>].

562 _____. <u>The Novel in English</u>. (New York: Richard R. Smith, 1931). [Studies the development of the novel, English and American, with special reference to its form. Chapter VI, "The Triumph of Realism," considers H. James, G. Moore, J. Conrad, H. G. Wells, J. Galsworthy, and A. Bennett among others. Each chapter is followed by a bibliography].

563 Knüsli, Anna. <u>Die Darstellung des Kindes in der modernen englischen Erzählung</u>. (Affoltern am Albis: J. Weiss, 1943). [Dissertation presented to the University of Zürich. Examines the interest in psychology and the search for new educational objectives in the delineation of the child in modern English narrative. H. Walpole, S. Kaye-Smith, K. Mansfield, J. Joyce, V. Woolf, R. Hughes, D. H. Lawrence, M. Sinclair, A. Huxley, J. D. Beresford, C. Mackenzie, R. Macaulay, H. G. Wells, and J. Hanley].

564 Koestler, Arthur. "The Future of Fiction." <u>The Trial of the Dinosaur and Other Essays</u>. (London: Collins; New York: Macmillan, 1955), pp. 95-101. Reprinted from <u>New Writing and Daylight</u>, VIII:7 (1946), 82-86. [See entry under Periodicals].

565 *Kondo, Ineko. <u>English Novels</u>. (Tokyo: Kenkyusha, 1952).

566 Kostelanetz, Richard, ed. <u>On Contemporary Literature: An Anthology of Critical Essays on the Major Movements and Writers of Contemporary Literature</u>. (New York: Avon Books, 1964; Books for Libraries Press, 1971). [Includes essays on English, American, and European writings with separate essays on each of S. Beckett, A. Burgess, L. Durrell, W. Golding, D. Lessing, I. Murdoch, and M. Spark among others. Also includes L. A. Fiedler's "Class War in British Literature," <u>Esquire</u>, XLIX (April 1958), 79-81. See entry under Periodicals].

567 *Kreemers, Raphael M. J. <u>De Naoorlogsche gewestelijke roman in Engeland</u>. (Brussels, 1935).

568 Krey, Laura. "Time and the Novel." <u>Twentieth Century English</u>. Edited by William S. Knickerbocker. (New York: The Philosophical Library, 1946), pp. 401-416. Reprinted from <u>The Writer</u>, LIV (July 1941), 195-198. [On the novelist's awareness of time].

569 Krieger, Murray. The Tragic Vision: Variations on a Theme
in Literary Interpretation. (New York: Holt, Rinehart &
Winston, 1960; Chicago and London: University of Chicago
Press, 1966). [Examines, among other works, D. H. Lawrence's
Women in Love and J. Conrad's "Heart of Darkness," Lord Jim
and Victory to determine that the "tragic vision" that defies
a rational moral order, is "demoniac," and "casuistical," and
interested in extreme cases, a "distillate" of rebellion, a
"godlessness which . . . purifies itself by rejecting all
palliatives"].

569a Kristensen, Sven Møller, ed. Fremmede Digtere i det 20. år-
hundrede Bind III (København: G. E. C. Gads Forlag, 1968).
[A collection of essays. Includes one on each of E. Waugh,
G. Greene, and S. Beckett by C. A. Bodelsen, Emil Frederiksen
and Einar Tassing].

570 Kronenberger, Louis, ed. Novelists on Novelists: An Anthology. (New York: Doubleday, 1962). [Critical essays on individual English, American, French, and Russian novelists by
novelists. Included is an essay on each of V. Woolf, D. H.
Lawrence, H. James, J. Joyce, and A. Bennett by E. M. Forster,
A. Huxley, G. Greene, H. G. Wells, and S. Maugham respectively].

571 Kulemeyer, Günther. Studien zur Psychologie im neuen englischen Roman: Dorothy Richardson und James Joyce. (Bottrop:
W. Postberg, 1933). [A doctoral dissertation presented to
the Ernst Moritz Arndt University, Greifswald. The 38-page
booklet focuses on content and technique in both writers].

572 Kumar, Shiv K. Bergson and the Stream of Consciousness Novel.
(London: Blackie & Son; Toronto: Ryerson Press, 1962; New
York: New York University Press, 1963). [Originally a doctoral dissertation, Fitzwilliam House, Cambridge, 1955. An
attempt to bring out the parallelism between the notion of
the stream of consciousness in D. Richardson, V. Woolf and
J. Joyce, and the Bergsonian concept of flux].

573 _____, and Keith F. McKean, comps. Critical Approaches
to Fiction. (New York: McGraw-Hill, 1968). [Twenty-six
modern critical essays on plot, character, language, theme,
setting, and technique in the novel and short story, all reprinted with the exception of S. A. Honeywell's essay "Plot
in the Modern Novel." See entries under Periodicals for:
S. Bellow, M. A. Goldberg, W. O'Grady, M. McCarthy, M. Mudrick,
W. V. Harris, D. May, G. Melchiori, D. S. Bland, E. Welty,
M. Schorer, P. Rahv, J. E. Tilford, W. C. Booth, G. P. Eliott,
L. E. Bowling, V. Brumm, and A. H. Wright].

574 Lalou, René. Panorama de la littérature anglaise contemporaine. (Paris: Editions KRA, 1926). [Explains the present
state of literature in the light of the Victorian heritage,
and surveys the diverse tendencies in contemporary literature,
especially the novel. H. G. Wells, J. Joyce, J. Conrad, J.
Galsworthy, A. Bennett, and V. Woolf].

575 Lanoire, Maurice. Les Lorgnettes du roman anglais. Civil-
isations D'Hier et D'Aujourd'hui Series. (Paris: Librarie
Plon, 1959). [A study of the radical change and evolution
of England in the 20th century by means of excerpts from 20th
century English novels interspersed with commentary. The
study is divided into three parts: I. The Edwardian Era,
II. Between the Two Wars: a) reaction against Victorianism,
and b) political and social idealism, and III. Aftermath of
World War II].

576 Larbaud, Valery. Ce Vice impuni, la lecture . . . domaine
anglais. (Paris: Messein, 1925). Revised and enlarged.
(Paris: Librairie Gallimard, 1936). [Introduces English and
American novelists and poets to French readers. Included are
J. Conrad, A. Bennett, H. G. Wells, and J. Joyce].

577 Larrett, William. The English Novel from Thomas Hardy to
Graham Greene. (Frankfurt/Main: Verlag Moritz Diesterweg,
1967). [Surveys briefly the English novel from T. Hardy to
G. Greene, and, in separate studies, focuses on the salient
features of T. Hardy, J. Conrad, E. M. Forster, V. Woolf,
J. Joyce, D. H. Lawrence, and G. Greene as representative of
seven different approaches to the modern novel].

578 Las Vergnas, Raymond. Portraits anglais: G. K. Chesterton,
Hilaire Belloc, Maurice Baring. (Paris: Hachette, 1937).
Translated by C. C. Martindale, S. J., as Chesterton, Belloc,
Baring. (London & New York: Sheed and Ward, 1938). [An
account of their literary work, its style and content, fol-
lowed by an appendix from the translator].

579 _____. "Grande-Bretagne." Les Littératures contemporaines à travers le monde. With a Preface by Roger Caillos.
(Paris: Hachette, 1961), pp. 73-100. [The survey is mostly
concerned with the novel. Compares the state of literature
in 1960 to 1939, and identifies the major tendency in 1960
to be "l'emiettement individualiste." Focuses on W. Sanson,
H. Green, I. Compton-Burnett, and J. Cary, and classifies
others into novelists of: "The Central Tradition"--E. Bowen,
R. Lehmann, N. Balchin, L. P. Hartley--"Humour"--E. Waugh--
"Adventure and Metaphysics"--G. Greene--and "Anger"--K. Amis,
J. Braine, and C. Wilson].

580 Lavers, Annette. L'Usurpateur et le prétendant: Essai: Le
Psychologue dans la littérature contemporaine. (Paris: M. J.
Minard, 1964). [Analyses works containing psychologists as
characters in novels "apres l'exposition des principes qui
les ont inspirées." References to J. Joyce, V. Woolf, G. Orwell, and A. Koestler among others].

581 Lawrence, D. H. Phoenix: The Posthumous Papers of D. H.
Lawrence. Edited, with an Introduction by Edward D. Mc-
Donald. (London: Heinemann; New York: Viking Press 1936).
[Includes "Morality and the Novel" and "Surgery for the Nov-
el, or A Bomb," reprinted from Calendar of Modern Letters,
II (1925), 269-274, and Literary Digest International Book

Review, 1:5 (April 1923), 5-6, 63, (see entry under Periodicals) as well as an essay on J. Galsworthy].

582 _____. Phoenix II: Uncollected, Unpublished and Other
Prose Works. Collected and edited with an Introduction &
Notes by Warren Roberts and Harry T. Moore. (London: Heinemann, 1968). [Includes "The Novel," an essay from Reflections on the Death of a Porcupine, in which he attributes
the decline of the modern novel to the separation of "passionate inspiration" and purpose in the modern novelist].

583 Lawrence, Margaret. The School of Feminity: A Book For
and About Women as They Are Interpreted through Feminine
Writers of Yesterday and Today. (New York: Frederick A.
Stokes, 1936). Published in England as We Write as Women.
(London: M. Joseph, 1937). [Part II, Chs. VII-XIII, looks
into the 20th century postwar scene of feminism, and the
various attitudes to experience in novels by D. Du Maurier,
G. B. Stern, R. Macaulay, S. Jameson, P. Bentley, S. Kaye-
Smith, M. Sinclair, M. Kennedy, "E. M. Delafield," V. Sack-
ville-West, K. Mansfield, C. Dane, and V. Woolf among others].

584 Leary, Lewis, ed. Contemporary Literary Scholarship: A
Critical Review. (New York: Appleton-Century-Crofts, 1958).
[A collection of essays, by different writers, examining
literary scholarship in the various periods and genres of
English literature. Included are Bradford A. Booth's "The
Novel," and Fred B. Millett's "Contemporary British Liter-
ature" (See individual entries)].

585 Leavis, F. R. Towards Standard of Criticism. A Selection
from the Calendar of Modern Letters. (London: Wishart,
1933; The Folcroft Press, 1969). [A reprint of reviews of
individual novels by A. Huxley, M. Kennedy, V. Woolf, M.
Butts, D. Garnett, T. F. Powys, L. P. Hartley, D. H. Lawrence, S. T. Warner, and S. Benson among others].

586 _____. The Great Tradition: George Eliot, Henry James,
Joseph Conrad. (London: Chatto & Windus; New York: George
H. Stewart, 1948. New Edition, 1960). [A reprint of previously published articles in Scrutiny in which he argues
that G. Eliot, H. James, J. Conrad, and J. Austen--he says
very little about her--constitute "the" great tradition of
the English novel].

587 _____. The Common Pursuit. (London: Penguin Books
in Association with Chatto & Windus, 1962). [A collection
of essays previously published in Scrutiny. Includes one
on each of E. M. Forster and H. James, and three on different aspects of D. H. Lawrence].

588 _____. Anna Karenina and Other Essays. (London: Chatto
& Windus, 1967). [Includes two essays on H. James previously
published in Scrutiny, one on J. Conrad from The Sewanee

<u>Review</u>, and another on scholarship and D. H. Lawrence].

589 Leavis, Q. D. <u>Fiction and the Reading Public</u>. (London: Chatto & Windus, 1932). [Examines the history of taste in the past and its significance by its relation to the present, and registers shifts of taste and changes in the cultural background].

590 Lebowitz, Naomi. <u>Humanism and the Absurd in the Modern Novel</u>. (Evanston: Northwestern University Press, 1971). [An attempt to trace two significant and contrasting tones that have remained constant through changes of political and social atmospheres: the humanist and absurdist temperaments. Ch. IV makes a study of E. M. Forster, and Ch. VI, "The 20th Century Novel: Old Wine in New Bottles" compares representative 20th century absurdist novels with those of contemporary writers who, though employing absurdist forms, maintain the humanist tone. H. James and S. Beckett among others].

591 Leclaire, Lucien. <u>Le Roman régionaliste dans les Iles Britanniques (1800-1950)</u>. (Paris: Société d'Edition "Les Belles Lettres," 1954). [A comprehensive study of the regional novel which includes both minor and major novelists, and is divided into three periods: 1800-1830, 1830-1870, and 1870-1950. The study of works, chronologically arranged according to date of publication of relevant work, and the major characteristics of the regional novel in each period are preceded by a brief examination of the background. Owing to its length and its diversity, the last period is subdivided into five sections. Part four defines the genre and its characteristics and the best conditions for its existence].

592 Lehmann, John, ed. <u>The Craft of Letters in England: A Symposium</u>. (London: The Cresset Press, 1956; Boston: Houghton Mifflin, 1957). [A collection of essays by various hands examining the state of contemporary literature, especially postwar literature. Includes "Experiment and the Future of the Novel" by Philip Toynbee, and "Twenty-five Years of the Novel" by Francis Wyndham. (See individual entries)].

593 _____. <u>New Writing in Europe</u>. (London: Allen Lane, Penguin Books, 1940). [Reviews the literature of the thirties, especially poets and prose-writers "who were conscious of great social, political and moral changes going on around them," and who wished to communicate their vision to a wide public. The study, based on a pamphlet <u>New Writing in England</u> (New York, 1939), also shows how the themes and ideals of writing in England were being reached by continental writers. Chapter III concentrates attention on C. Isherwood, E. Upward, and R. Warner. Chapter VIII draws attention to "minor" novelists of the period: A. Calder-Marshall, S. T.

Warner, H. Green, and G. Greene among others].

594 _____. The Open Night. (London: Longmans, Green; New York: Harcourt, Brace, 1952). [A collection of essays, some of which were previously published, on writers who lived in his lifetime. Included are essays on V. Woolf, H. James, J. Conrad, and J. Joyce].

595 Lesser, Simon O. Fiction and the Unconscious. With a Preface by Ernest Jones. (Boston: Beacon Press, 1957; London: Peter Owen, 1960). [A study of the needs that impel us to read fiction, the formal characteristics and subject matter of fiction which enable it to satisfy those needs, and the processes, conscious or unconscious, involved in responding to fiction].

596 Lester, John A., Jr. Journey Through Despair 1880-1914: Transformations in British Literary Culture. (Princeton, New Jersey: Princeton University Press, 1968). [Examines how the years between 1880 and 1914 jarred and shifted "the bearings of man's imaginative life" leaving him bewildered as to how to recover his lost meaning and purpose. Considers J. Joyce, J. Conrad, and D. H. Lawrence among others as providing the characteristic responses to the crisis resulting from the confusion and search for new terms on which the imagination could live].

597 Lever, Katherine. The Novel and the Reader. (London: Methuen; New York: Appleton-Century-Crofts, 1961). [A "handbook" for students that tries to foster a "love" and understanding of novels by explaining the art of the novel and answering five basic questions: What is a novel? A novelist? A reader of novels? A critic of novels? and A student of novels? Illustrations from both English and American novels].

598 Levi, Albert William. Literature, Philosophy and the Imagination. (Bloomington: Indiana University Press, 1962). [Attempts a philosophical justification of the humanities' imagination as that "human faculty from whose active functioning the humanities stem," in much the same way as "understanding" is to Kant the faculty of the mind upon which natural science is founded. Illustrates from the contemporary works of A. Robbe-Grillet and N. Sarraute, with references to J. Joyce and V. Woolf. Also includes a section on A. Huxley and G. Greene].

599 Lewis, Wyndham. Men Without Art. (London: Cassell, 1934). [A defence of satire--identified for all practical purposes with art--illustrating from his own work as a "fictionist deliberately dealing with satire," and from H. James and V. Woolf].

600 _____. The Writer and the Absolute. (London: Methuen,

85

I952). [Cautious against the encroachment of such "Absolutes" as collectivity, the community, and especially after World War II, the political situation, on the writer's creative life and his right to express himself. Discusses three French writers and selects G. Orwell for analysis in Part IV, as the "only" English postwar political writer worthy of attention, and discusses his evaluation of A. Koestler].

601 Leyburn, Ellen Douglas. Satiric Allegory: Mirror of Man. Yale Studies in English, Vol. 130. [New Haven: Yale University Press, 1956). [Examines the propensity of satire towards allegorical forms, and makes a critical survey of English satiric allegory from Swift to A. Huxley and G. Orwell].

602 Liddell, Robert. A Treatise on the Novel. (London: Jonathan Cape, Toronto: Clarke, Irwin, 1947). [Examines several controversial aspects of the novel--range, novelist's values, plot, character, and background--from the standpoint of a critic interested in fictional techniques, and explains its intricacies by observing the "workshop methods" of major novelists. Illustrates from J. Joyce, V. Woolf, J. Galsworthy, H. James, I. Compton-Burnett, and E. M. Forster among others].

603 _____. Some Principles of Fiction. (London: Jonathan Cape, 1953; Bloomington: Indiana University Press, 1954). [A sequel to A Treatise on the Novel treating subject, style, summary, dialogue, and the meaning of various critical terms, and concentrating on the difficulties that attend the writing of fiction].

604 _____. Robert Liddell on the Novel. With an Introduction by Wayne C. Booth. (Chicago: University of Chicago Press, 1969). [A reprint of Treatise on the Novel and Some Principles of Fiction in one volume].

605 Linati, Carlo. Scrittori Anglo-Americani D'Oggi. (Milano: Corticelli, 1932; enlarged edition, 1944). [A collection of essays on contemporary English and American writers. Included are essays on Huxley, W. Lewis, E. M. Forster, R. Aldington and V. Woolf. The enlarged edition includes an additional essay on D. H. Lawrence].

606 Lindsay, Jack. After the Thirties: The Novel in Britain and Its Future. (London: Lawrence & Wishart, 1956). [Part I concentrates on the novelists of the thirties and postwar times showing the achievements--and "regressions"--of the novel. Part II is mainly concerned with the problems of writing, ranging from a study of the origin of art to creativeness].

607 _____. "Time in Modern Literature." Festschrift zum

achtzigsten Geburtstag von George Lukacs. Edited by Frank
Benseler. (Neuwid and Berlin: Herman Luchterhand Verlag,
1965), pp. 491-501. [On George Lukacs' statement that the
modern writer identifies "a subjective human experience with
reality," whereas the realist sets a "significant, specifically modern experience in a wider context." Illustrations from J. Joyce, Proust and V. Woolf].

608 Lodge, David. Language of Fiction: Essays in Criticism
and Verbal Analysis of the English Novel. (London: Routledge and Kegan Paul; New York: Columbia University Press,
1966). [Attempts to justify criticism of novels on the
basis of detailed study of the language novelists use. Part
I discusses uncertainty in modern criticism about the language of prose fiction and the usefulness and limitations
of critical and analytical methods applied to the language
of the novel. Part II includes essays on H. James, H. G.
Wells, and K. Amis from a linguistic standpoint].

609 _____. The Novelist at the Crossroads and Other Essays
on Fiction and Criticism. (London: Routledge and Kegan
Paul; Ithaca: Cornell University Press, 1971). [A collection of critical essays, all but one previously published,
on the fiction of novelists dealing with Catholicism, Modernism and Utopia, and on "the plurality of methods, styles
and approaches of the critic of fiction." Included are
studies of G. Greene, M. Spark, G. K. Chesterton, H. Belloc,
S. Beckett, H. G. Wells, and others].

610 _____, ed. Twentieth Century Literary Criticism: A
Reader. (London: Longman, 1972). [An anthology of critical comment, mostly English and American, emphasising the
varieties of method and approach in 20th century literary
criticism. Articles are chronologically arranged in order
of first publication with an introductory note to each one.
Includes H. James' Preface to The Ambassadors, V. Woolf's
"Modern Fiction," D. H. Lawrence's "Morality in the Novel,"
M. Schorer's "Technique as Discovery," R. Williams' "Realism
and the Contemporary Novel," an excerpt from Aspects of the
Novel, and Chapter III of W. Booth's The Rhetoric of Fiction].

611 Longaker, Mark, and Edwin C. Bolles. Contemporary English
Literature. (New York: Appleton-Century-Crofts, 1953).
[Considers briefly the historical background and time-spirit
of England at the turn of the century and between the wars.
Discusses the fiction of England between 1890 and 1914, and
between 1918 and 1950. Includes all major novelists from
J. Conrad, H. G. Wells, and A. Bennett to G. Greene, R. Lehmann, and G. Orwell. Includes select bibliographies of both
primary and secondary sources].

612 Lovett, Robert M., and Helen Sard Hughes. The History of
the Novel in England. (Boston: Houghton, Mifflin, 1932;
London: George G. Harrap, 1933). [Chapter XIV covers the

Edwardian novelists--S. Butler, J. Galsworthy, A. Bennett, H. G. Wells, and J. Conrad--and Chapter XV the Georgians--E. M. Forster, D. H. Lawrence, M. Sinclair, S. Kaye-Smith, D. Richardson, V. Woolf, and J. Joyce].

613 Lubbock, Percy. The Craft of Fiction. (London: J. Cape; New York: Scribner's, 1921). [An essentially "Jamesian" approach to the basic question of "how a novel is made." Also treats other related questions of the novelist's intention, "manner of his imagination," and choice of subject, illustrating the elements of the "craft" from selected masterpieces].

614 Lukacs, Gyorgy. The Meaning of Contemporary Realism. Translated from the German by John and Necke Mander. (London: Merlin Press, 1963). Published in U. S. A. as Realism in Our Time: Literature and the Class Struggle. With a Preface by George Steiner. (New York: Harper & Row, Publishers, 1964). [A Marxist approach. Discusses the relationship between critical and socialist realism in a socialist society, and contends that the mastery of the great realists does not spring from their technical virtuosity but from the depth of their experiences of reality].

615 Lynd, Robert. Old and New Masters. (London: T. Fisher Unwin; New York: Scribner's, 1919). [A collection of essays and reviews which includes one on G. K. Chesterton and H. Belloc, and one on each of H. James, J. Conrad, and R. Kipling].

616 _____. Books and Authors. (London: Richard Cobden-Sanderson, 1922; New York: Putnam's, 1923). [Includes essays on A. Bennett, J. Conrad, and H. G. Wells].

617 _____. Books and Writers. With a Foreword by Richard Church. (London: J. M. Dent, 1952). [Includes essays on H. James, G. Moore ("Falseness in Literature"), and J. Joyce. In "The Bounds of Decency" he discusses the "increasing absorption of novelists in the 'sexual' life of man"].

618 MacCarthy, Desmond. Portraits. (New York: Putnam, 1931; London: MacGibbon & Kee, 1949). [Includes "portraits" of J. Conrad, H. James, and G. Moore].

619 _____. Criticism. (London & New York: Putnam, 1932; The Folcroft Press, 1969). [Includes essays on A. Huxley, D. H. Lawrence and J. Joyce. The Chapter entitled "Notes on the Novel" makes observations on various aspects of the novel ranging from morality and "real" people to psychoanalysis and "streams of thought" in fiction].

620 _____. Memories. Foreword by Raymond Mortimer and Cyril Connolly. (London: MacGibbon & Kee; New York: Oxford University Press, 1953). [Includes reminiscences of

A. Bennett, H. G. Wells, J. Joyce, and the "Bloomsbury" group].

621 McCarthy, Mary Therese. On the Contrary. (New York: Farrar, Strauss and Cudahy, 1961; London: Heinemann, 1962). [Includes "The Fact in Fiction," and "Characters in Fiction" reprinted from The Partisan Review, XVII (Summer 1960), 438-458 and XVIII:2 (Spring 1961), 171-191. See entries under Periodicals].

622 _____. The Writing on the Wall and Other Literary Essays. (New York: Harcourt, Brace; London: Weidenfeld and Nicolson, 1970). [The volume includes two essays on I. Compton-Burnett, and one on G. Orwell, "The Writing on the Wall." "One Touch of Nature" remarks on the disappearance of nature from prose fiction. See entry under Periodicals].

623 McCormick, John. Catastrophe and Imagination: An Interpretation of the Recent English and American Novel. (London: Longmans, Green, 1957). [Compares the English and American novel using a "national approach" to determine the influence of national modes on the "modern sensibility," and to demonstrate that the American novel is not an "English novel manqué, but a legitimate heir" of a common form, maintaining a "curious and complex relationship with the English novel." Also explores the fallacy of "Genre Criticism" with regard to the novel of manners, and examines naturalism, tradition, the themes of war and politics, and the reliance upon a "mystique" and the return to the "stricter forms" of allegory and satire in the English and American novel. H. James, A. Huxley, V. Woolf, H. G. Wells, E. Waugh, R. Warner, A. Powell, G. Orwell, P. H. Newby, and D. H. Lawrence among others].

624 McCullough, Bruce. Representative British Novelists: Defoe to Conrad. (New York & London: Harper, 1946). [Examines the processes of change in fictional art that have been taking place through a study of representative novels and novelists beginning with Defoe's Moll Flanders and ending with Conrad's Lord Jim. Included are studies of Esther Waters by G. Moore, The Ambassadors by H. James, The Old Wives Tale by A. Bennett, The Forsyte Saga by J. Galsworthy and Lord Jim by Conrad].

625 MacDonald, Margaret. "The Language of Fiction." Perspectives on Fiction. Edited by James L. Calderwood and Harold E. Toliver. (New York and London: Oxford University Press, 1968), pp. 55-70. [Attempts to determine the logical character of the expressions of fiction, how they operate, and how they differ from statements and emotive expressions].

626 Mack, Edward C. Public Schools and British Opinion Since 1860: The Relationship between Contemporary Ideas and the Evolution of an English Institution. (New York: Columbia

University Press, 1941; Greenwood Press, 1971). [A sequel to an earlier volume Public Schools and British Opinion, 1780 to 1860. Attempts what is primarily a history of opinion in regard to public schools through an analysis of prose fiction, history, poetry and pamphlet literature. H. A. Vachell, C. Mackenzie, H. Walpole, J. D. Beresford, H. G. Wells, S. Maugham, A. Lunn, E. F. Benson, A. Waugh, and E. Waugh].

627   Mack, Maynard, & Ian Gregor, eds. Imagined Worlds: Essays on Some English Novels and Novelists in Honour of John Butt. (London: Methuen; New York: Barnes and Noble, 1968). [Part III of the volume considers part of the theory and practice of the 20th century English novel, and includes essays on J. Conrad, H. James, D. H. Lawrence, J. Joyce, E. Waugh, and R. Heppenstall].

628   Mackenzie, Compton. Literature in My Time. (London: Rich & Cowan, 1933). [Chapters XIV to XXIX examine aspects of 20th century literature. Includes essays on J. Conrad, "The Women Novelists," and "Best Sellers," and one essay on J. Galsworthy, A. Bennett, and H. G. Wells].

629   MacLennan, Hugh. "The Future of the Novel as an Art Form." Scotchman's Return, and Other Essays. (Toronto: The Macmillan Company of Canada; New York: Scribner's, 1960; London: Heinemann, 1961), pp. 142-158. [An address given at the Golden Jubilee of the University of Saskatchewan, October 1959. Contends that the future of the novel is assured for "modern life is unable to be static," and also because the novel has developed technically to a point where it can contain "almost any symphony of ideas and feelings a writer wishes to pour into it"].

630   McMullen, Roy. "Since Finnegan's Wake." Art, Affluence and Alienation: The Fine Arts Today. (New York & London: Frederick A. Praeger, 1968). [Suggests "ways of thinking about the novel in general" as a result of the polarity created by the traditional novel and the art novel in England and America].

631   MacShane, Frank, ed. Critical Writings of Ford Madox Ford. (Regents Critics Series). (Lincoln: University of Nebraska Press, 1964). [Selections from previously published works on the novel, novelists, and poetry, and the relation of impressionism to the two genres. Includes sections on J. Conrad, H. James, and letters to J. Galsworthy, H. G. Wells and others].

632   Macy, John [Albert]. The Critical Game. (New York: Boni and Liveright, 1922; The Folcroft Press, 1969). [A collection of essays on English, American and European writers. Includes essays on J. Conrad, H. G. Wells and Utopia, G. Moore, J. Joyce, and D. H. Lawrence].

633 Maes-Jelinek, Hena. Criticism of Society in the English
     Novel Between the Wars. (Bibliothèque de la Faculté de
     Philosophie et Lettres de L'Université de Liège). (Paris:
     Société d'Editions "Les Belles Lettres," 1970). [Discusses
     the impact of philosophy, science and especially the war in
     shaping the personal responses of novelists to the social
     attitudes of the inter-war years. Separate chapters for D.
     H. Lawrence, V. Woolf, W. Lewis, R. Firbank, A. Huxley, W.
     Gerhardie, L. H. Myers, G. Orwell, E. Waugh, C. Isherwood,
     R. Warner, and A. Powell].

634 Mais, Stuart Petre Brodie. "The Modern Novel." From Shake-
     speare to O. Henry: Studies in Literature. (London: Grant
     Richards, 1917; New York: Dodd, Mead, 1918; Books for Lib-
     raries Press, 1968), pp. 136-160. [Surveys a "score or so
     of writers" whom he regards as "representatives" of the mod-
     ern novel as a "new religion, an essential factor in educa-
     tion," and not merely as a"diversion"].

635 _____. Books and Their Writers. (London: Grant Rich-
     ards; New York: Dodd, Mead, 1920). [Part I, "Novelists and
     Novels," includes an essay on each of C. Mackenzie, F. Swin-
     nerton, C. Dane, and D. Richardson].

636 _____. Why We Should Read. (London: Grant Richards;
     New York: Dodd, Mead, 1921). [Part II of the volume, "Some
     Contemporaries," includes essays on each of J. D. Beresford,
     F. M. Ford, E. M. Forster, and S. Kaye-Smith].

637 _____. Some Modern Authors: Essays. (London: Grant
     Richards; New York: Dodd, Mead, 1923). [Part I, "Some Mod-
     ern Novelists," is a study of individual English and Amer-
     ican novelists. Includes G. Cannan, J. Galsworthy, A. S. M.
     Hutchinson, K. Mansfield, S. Maugham, J. C. Snaith, J. M.
     Murry, H. Walpole, and V. Sackville-West].

638 Mallinson, Vernon. Tendances nouvelles de la littérature
     anglais contemporain. Le Roman, la poésie, le théâtre.
     Traduit de l'anglais par M. C. H. (Brussels: Les Editions
     Lumière, 1947). [Surveys the "tendencies" between 1935 and
     1945. Part I examines individual novelists of the decade
     including G. Greene, R. Warner, W. Sanson, H. Green A. Huxley,
     C. Morgan, and V. Woolf, as well as war novels].

639 Mander, John. The Writer and Commitment. (London: Secker
     & Warburg, 1961; Chester Springs, Philadelphia: Dufour Ed-
     itions; New York: British Book Service, 1962). [A critical
     study of "Left" writing over the past thirty years, using
     "commitment"--a term which is vaguely defined--as a yard-
     stick to measure the achievement of G. Orwell and A. Wilson
     among others].

640 Manners, Penelope J. Novels of Today: Extract from Contem-
     porary English Novels. (University of London Press, 1967).

[Extracts are from E. Waugh's Officer and Gentlemen, G.
Greene's The Quiet American, K. Amis' Lucky Jim, J. Wain's
Strike the Father Dead, J. Braine's Room at the Top, A.
Sillitoe's The Loneliness of the Long Distance Runner, W.
Mankowitz' My Old Man's A Dustman, D. Storey's Flight into
Camden, M. Spark's The Ballad of Peckham Rye, A. Wilson's
Anglo-Saxon Attitudes, C. MacInnes' Absolute Beginners, I.
Murdoch's The Sandcastle, W. Golding's Lord of the Flies,
and "J. Wyndham's" The Chrysalids. Each extract is preceded
by a two-page note on the novelist. Also includes a three-
page general introduction].

641   "Mansfield, Katherine." [Kathleen Mansfield Beauchamp].
       Novels and Novelists. Edited by J. Middleton Murry. (Lon-
       don: Constable; New York: Knopf, 1930). [Some 200 brief
       notices and reviews of novels published in The Athenaeum
       from April 1919 to December 1920, and reprinted in chrono-
       logical order].

642   Marble, Annie Russell. A Study of the Modern Novel, British
       and American Since 1900. (New York and London: D. Apple-
       ton, 1928). [Part I surveys all major and minor English
       novelists who published works after 1900, and classifies
       them under the broad titles of "History and Romance," "Fan-
       tasy and Mystery," "Characterisation and Manners," "Revolt
       and Escape," and "Whimsicality and Humor." Each novelist
       is supplied with introductory biographical paragraphs, a
       selective bibliography, references, and in the case of major
       writers, brief critical comments emphasising distinctive
       traits. Part II repeats the same process with the American
       novel].

643   Marinoff, Irene. Neues Lebensgefühl und neue Wertungen im
       englischen Roman der Nachkriegszeit. (Berlin: Emil Eber-
       ing, 1929). [A doctoral dissertation presented to the Univ-
       ersity of Marburg, 1928. Examines new attitudes to life
       and new value judgments in the English postwar novel. A.
       Bennett, J. Galsworthy, P. Gibbs, A. S. M. Hutchinson, J.
       Joyce, R. Macaulay, C. Mackenzie, S. Maugham, G. Moore, S.
       Kaye-Smith, F. Swinnerton, H. Walpole, and H. G. Wells among
       others].

644   _____. Neue Wertungen im englischen Roman: Problem-
       geschichte des englischen Romans im Zwanzigsten Jahrhundert.
       (Leipzig: Verlag von Bernhard Tauchnitz, 1932). [Examines
       new value judgments of life as it is reflected in the Eng-
       lish novel of the 20th century].

645   Markovic, Vida E. Engleski roman XX veka, 2 Vols. (English
       Novel in the 20th Century). (Beograd: Neucna Rnjiga, 1963
       & 1965). [A study of individual novelists. Volume I in-
       cludes H. G. Wells, A. Bennett, J. Galsworthy, H. James, J.
       Conrad, E. M. Forster, D. H. Lawrence, J. Joyce, and V. Woolf.
       Volume II includes A. Huxley, H. Green, I. Compton-Burnett,

G. Greene, E. Waugh, R. Warner, C. Isherwood, R. Lehmann,
E. Bowen, P. H. Johnson, J. Cary, C. P. Snow, A. Wilson,
and I. Murdoch].

646   . The Changing Face: Disintegration of Personality in the Twentieth Century British Novel, 1900-1950.
(Carbondale & Edwardsville: Southern Illinois University
Press; London & Amsterdam: Feffer & Simons, 1970). [Dis-
cusses nine prominent and "complete" characters from J. Conrad, D. H. Lawrence, J. Joyce, V. Woolf, E. Waugh, G. Greene,
R. Lehmann, E. Bowen, and J. Cary, existing "in their own
right in the world of fiction," as representatives of their
author's "full creation of a human figure" and of the "changing conception of human personality"].

647 Martin, E. W. L., ed. The New Spirit. (London: Dennis
Dobson, 1946). [A collection of critical essays which in-
cludes one on each of J. Joyce and D. H. Lawrence by George
Every].

648 Martin, Graham. "Novelists of three Decades: Evelyn Waugh,
Graham Greene, C. P. Snow." The Pelican Guide to English
Literature, Vol. 7. The Modern Age. Edited by Boris Ford.
(London: Cassell; Baltimore: Penguin, 1961-1964), pp. 394-
414. [Evaluates the achievement of each novelist separately
in the light of his limitations as a "minor" novelist].

649 Maschler, Tom. Declaration. (London: MacGibbon & Kee,
1957; Kennikat Press, 1972). [A collection of separate
statements and credos by the "Angry Young Men" defining
their positions in relation to society. Contributors are
D. Lessing, C. Wilson, J. Osborne, J. Wain, K. Tynan, Bill
Hopkins, L. Anderson, and S. Holroyd].

650 Massingham, Harold John. "Modern Realistic Novels." Letters to X. (London: Constable, 1919; Books for Libraries
Press, 1967), pp. 192-199. [A pre-war view that holds the
Wells-Bennett type of fiction responsible for the "younger
generation's" concern with the "immediate, the momentary,"
and whose fiction is characterized by "uniformity," a "photographic tendency," lack of style, and obsessed by observa-
tion].

651 *Matthews, W. K. Jaunaka anglu literatura 1890-1936. (Riga,
1936).

652 Maugham, William Somerset. Essays on Literature. (London:
New English Library in association with Heinemann, 1967).
[Includes "Some Novelists I Have Known" (reminiscences of
H. James, H. G. Wells, and A. Bennett) reprinted from The
Vagrant Mood (London: Heinemann, 1952), and "The Art of
Fiction" reprinted from Ten Novels and their Authors (Lon-
don: Heinemann, 1954), published in U. S. A. as Great Nov-
elists and Their Novels (Philadelphia: Winston, 1948)].

653 Maurois, André. Magiciens et logiciens. (Paris: B. Gras-
set, 1935). Translated from the French and published under
the title Prophets and Poets. (New York: Harper, 1935;
London: Cassell, 1936). Revised and enlarged with addit-
ional essays on V. Woolf and G. Greene, with a Foreword by
Walter Allen, and published under the title Points of View
from Kipling to Graham Greene. (New York: Ungar, 1968;
London: Frederick Muller, 1969). [Separate studies of R.
Kipling, H. G. Wells, G. K. Chesterton, J. Conrad, D. H.
Lawrence, A. Huxley, K. Mansfield, V. Woolf, and G. Greene].

654 May, Derwent. "The Novelist as Moralist and the Moralist
as Critic." Critical Approaches to Literature. Edited by
Shiv K. Kumar and Keith F. McKean. (New York: McGraw-Hill,
1968), pp. 177-185. Reprinted from Essays in Criticism,
X:3 (July 1960), 320-328. [See entry under Periodicals].

655 Mayoux, Jean-Jacques. L'Inconscient et la vie intérieure
dans le roman anglais (1905-1940). Departement Étude des
Civilizations. (Nancy: Centre Européen Universitaire, 1952).
[A series of lectures on individual values and the inner
life which are regarded as a protest against the encroach-
ing material civilisation as seen in the works of E. M. Forster, D. H. Lawrence, V. Woolf, J. Joyce, and A. Huxley].

656 _____. Vivants piliers: Le Roman anglo-saxon et les
symboles. Les Lettres Nouvelles, 6. (Paris: Julliard,
1960). [A collection of essays, previously published, on
English and American writers. Includes essays on H. James,
J. Conrad, J. Joyce, V. Woolf, and S. Beckett].

657 Megroz, Rodolphe Louis. Five Novelist Poets of To-day.
(London: Joiner & Steele, 1933; Books for Libraries, 1969).
[Critical reviews of the prose works of W. De la Mare, L. A.
G. Strong, M. Armstrong, O. Sitwell, and D. H. Lawrence as
manifestations of "the union of poetry and prose," and an
assessment of the novelist poets' contribution to fiction.
Also includes a chronological list of first editions of
their works].

658 _____. Thirty-One Bedside Essays. (Hadleigh, Essex:
Tower Bridge Publications, 1951). [A collection of essays,
previously published, which includes "The Sacred Lunatic"
(H. G. Wells), "Bouncing us into Belief" (see entry under
Periodicals), and "Poets and Novelists" where he surveys
the alliance between poetry and prose which achieves prominence in the twenties and thirties].

659 Melchiori, Giorgio. The Tightrope Walkers: Studies of Mannerism in Modern English Literature. (London: Routledge &
Kegan Paul; New York: Macmillan, 1956). [A collection of
essays dealing with several aspects of English literature
in the 20th century in an attempt to find out the "common
characteristics of the style of an age so full of contra-

94

diction and uncertainty." H. James, J. Joyce, and H. Green
among others. Also includes "The Moment as a Time Unit in
Fiction," reprinted from Essays in Criticism, III:4 (October 1953), 434-446. (See entry under Periodicals)].

660 Mencken, Henry Louis. "Novel." Prejudices (Third Series).
(New York: Knopf, 1922; London: Cape, 1923), pp. 201-212.
[Contends that the novel still "radiates an aroma of effim-
inacy," and that women are better fitted to succeed in realistically representing life than men].

661 Mendilow, A. A. Time and the Novel. With an Introduction
by Professor J. Isaacs. (London: Peter Nevill; New York:
British Book Centre, 1952). [Originally a doctoral dissertation entitled "Time Factors and Values in the Novel," presented to the University of London, 1950. An analytical
study of the numerous and complex devices involved in the
control and deployment of time in the novel, time being the
greatest preoccupation of novelists in the 20th century. J.
Conrad, A. Huxley, H. James, J. Joyce, D. Richardson, and
V. Woolf among others].

662 Mertner, Edgar. "Der Roman der jungen Generation in England."
Sprache und Literatur Englands und Amerikas. "Dritter Band:
Die wissenschaftliche Erschliessung der Prosa." Edited by
Gerhard Müller-Schwefe and Herman Metzger. (Tübingen: Max
Niemeyer Verlag, 1959), pp. 101-124. [Examines the gener-
ation of the "Angry Young Men," not without comparison to
the post-World War I generation, and with special reference
to K. Allsop's The Angry Decade].

663 *Metzger, Joseph. Das Katholische Schrifttum im heutigen
England. (München: Kosel and Pustet, 1937).

664 Meyer, Kurt Robert. Zur Erlebten Rede im englischen Roman
des zwanzigsten Jahrhunderts. Schweizer Anglistische Arb-
eiten. Swiss Studies in English. (Bern: Francke Verlag,
1957). [An investigation of the handling of the interior
monologue in the works of A. Bennett, J. Conrad, E. M. Forster, D. H. Lawrence, D. Richardson, and V. Woolf].

665 Meyerhoff, Hans. Time in Literature. (Berkeley & Los Angeles: University of California Press; London: Cambridge
University Press, 1955). [Examines the function of scientific and literary analyses of time, the concern of literature with the contrast between them, and the philosophical
problem of "correlating the treatment of time in literature
with aspects in experience and nature." Illustrates from
works by A. Huxley, J. Joyce, and V. Woolf among others].

666 Meyers, Jeffrey. Fiction and the Colonial Experience. (To-
towa, New Jersey: Rowman and Littlefield, 1968). [Origin-
ally a doctoral dissertation entitled The Hero in British
Colonial Fiction, University of California, Berkeley, 1967.
An analysis of the "colonial novels" of R. Kipling, E. M.
Forster, J. Conrad, J. Cary, and G. Greene that consider cultural

conflicts and race relations and "offer a valuable humanistic approach to the problems of colonialism" to provide
a "framework" and a "standard" by which the colonial novel
can be measured].

667 Migner, Karl. Theorie des modernen Romans: Eine Einführung.
(Stuttgart: Alfred Kröner Verlag, 1970). [An introduction
to the art of the modern novel. References to J. Joyce and
V. Woolf].

668 Mikhal'skaya, N. P. Puti razvitiya angliiskogo romana 1920-
1930kh Godov. Utrata i poiski Geroya. (Moscow: Vysshaya
Shkola, 1966). [Discusses the loss of, and search for, the
hero in the English novel of the twenties and thirties. J.
Joyce, V. Woolf, D. H. Lawrence, E. M. Forster, R. Aldington, and R. Fox].

669 Miller, James E., ed. Myth and Method: Modern Theories of
Fiction. (Lincoln, Nebraska: University of Nebraska Press,
1960). [Includes essays by H. James, J. Conrad, and E. Bowen
on the art of fiction, selections from the critical writings
of P. Lubbock, R. Humphrey and M. Schorer on technique in
fiction, and excerpts from E. M. Forster, R. Chase, and N.
Frye illustrating the trend of criticism in fiction towards
the quest for myth and archetype].

670 Miller, Karl, ed. Writing in England Today: The Last Fifteen Years. (Harmondsworth: Penguin Books, 1968). [An anthology compiled from novels, reviews, criticism, and drama,
with a sampling of poetry, to illustrate English writing in
the last fifteen years. Also includes a general introduction by the Editor. Excerpts are from novels by K. Amis,
E. Waugh, C. MacInnes, S. Bedford, A. Sillitoe, D. Storey,
W. Golding, P. White, M. Spark, B. Moore, D. Lessing, D.
Jacobson, A. Burgess, B. Brophy, D. Drabble, and others].

671 Millett, Fred B. "Contemporary Literary Scholarship." Contemporary Literary Scholarship: A Critical Review. Edited by Leavis Leary. (New York: Appleton-Century-Crofts,
1958), pp. 187-200. [Surveys literary criticism on the
novel, drama, and poetry from the twenties to the mid-fifties. In the four pages devoted to the novel, he selects
major critical works on J. Conrad, J. Joyce, and D. H. Lawrence, and gives "less space to the criticism" on E. M. Forster, V. Woolf, and A. Huxley].

672 Minning, Ruth. Der Heimatroman des 20. Jahrhunderts in
Süd-England und Wales. (Bleicherode am Herz: Carl Nieft,
Buchdruckerei und Verlag, 1937). [Originally a Ph.D. dissertation presented to Breslau University. The Introduction
defines the subject, its limitations, the use of "regional,"
and gives a brief survey of the English regional novel cul-
minating with Hardy. The study that follows is in two parts:
1) landscape in the regional novel; i.e., the physical setting, nature and man, and 2) the folklore elements of the

region; i.e., custom and tradition and superstition. S. Kaye-Smith, V. Sackville-West, J. C. Powys, E. Phillpotts, J. Trevena, F. T. Jesse, M. Webb, C. Evans, H. Vaughan, and F. B. Young].

673 Moeller, Charles. Littérature du XXe siècle et Christianisme. (S. A. Tournai (Belgium): Casterman, 1953). [A study in four volumes. Vol. I includes an essay on each of A. Huxley and G. Greene, and Vol. II an essay on H. James].

674 _____. "Religion and Literature: An Essay on Ways of Reading." Mansions of the Spirit: Essays in Literature and Religion. Edited by George A. Panichas, with an Introductory Essay by Thomas Merton. (New York: Hawthorne Books, 1967), pp. 59-73. (Essay translated by Melvin Zimmerman). Reprinted from Comparative Literature Studies, II:4 (1965), 323-333. [See entry under Periodicals].

675 Molina Quiros, Gorge. La novela utopica inglesa (Tomas Moro, Swift, Huxley, Orwell). (Colecion 'Vislumbres' No. 9). (Madrid: Prensa Espanola, 1967). [Includes a study of scientific anti-utopia in his consideration of A. Huxley's Brave New World, and political Utopia in his consideration of G. Orwell's 1984].

676 Molnar, Thomas. Utopia: The Perennial Heresy. (New York: Sheed and Ward, 1967). [Discusses the "truth about Utopia and heresy, and the link between them." H. G. Wells, G. Orwell, and A. Huxley among others].

677 Monod, Sylvére. Histoire de la littérature anglaise: de Victoria à Elisabeth II. (Paris: Librairie Armand Colin, 1970). ["Une série de monographies" with brief commentary to place writers in their age and indicate changes. Each author is examined in the genre in which he wrote successfully. Biographical data are incorporated into the study].

678 Monroe, Nellie Elizabeth. The Novel and Society: A Critical Study of the Modern Novel. (Chapel Hill: The University of North Carolina Press, 1941; London: Oxford University Press, 1942). [Asserts that the modern novel cannot survive the "disorder of the age" without a "process of Christian and human values," whereby the novelist can lose his preoccupation with self; i.e., re-orient himself to "human experience in its totality." Discusses the difficulties in six women novelists--Danish, Swedish, three American and one English--"who had the good fortune to inherit standards or to find them . . . or to reach them. . . . " V. Woolf, J. Joyce, D. H. Lawrence, and A. Huxley].

679 Mooney, Harry J., Jr. & Thomas F. Staley, eds. The Shapeless God: Essays on Modern Fiction. (Pittsburgh: University of Pittsburgh Press, 1968). [Includes an essay on each of G. Greene and E. Waugh, and a selected bibliography on religion and the modern novel].

680   Moore, Harry T. Age of the Modern and Other Literary Essays.
      (Carbondale and Edwardsville: Southern Illinois University
      Press; London and Amsterdam: Feffer & Simons, 1971). [A
      collection of essays and reviews previously published, which
      includes reviews of D. Richardson's Pilgrimage and D. H.
      Lawrence's Lady Chatterley's Lover, an essay on D. H. Law-
      rence, and part of a lecture on H. James].

681   Moorman, Charles. Arthurian Triptych: Mythic Materials in
      Charles Williams, C. S. Lewis, and T. S. Eliot. (Berkeley
      and Los Angeles: University of California Press; Cambridge:
      University Press, 1960). [Discusses the use of myth in mod-
      ern literature as a way of bringing "stature, order and mean-
      ing" to a chaotic world, as well as the differences between
      "legend" and "myth," and examines the Arthurian myth as it
      appears in the work of the three writers to ascertain its
      "functional use" in the works of each].

682   Morgan, Charles [Langridge]. Dialogue in Novels and Plays.
      (Aldington, Ashford, Kent: The Hand and Flower Press, 1954).
      [The First Hermon Ould Memorial Lecture. Also published as
      an article in Études Anglaises, VI:2 (May 1953), 97-108.
      See entry under Periodicals].

683   _____. The Writer and His World. Lectures and Essays.
      (London: Macmillan, 1960). [Includes "A Defence of Story-
      Telling," and "Dialogue in Novels and Plays," reprinted from
      The Yale Review, XXIII (June 1934), 771-787 and Études Ang-
      laises, VI:2 (May 1953), 97-108. See entries under Period-
      icals].

684   Morgan, Louise. Writers at Work. (London: Chatto & Windus,
      1951). [Comments by R. Aldington, S. T. Warner, E. Wallace,
      W. Lewis, and S. Maugham among others on their own work.
      Each statement has been revised and approved by the novelist
      before publication].

685   Morris, Robert K. Continuance and Change: The Contemporary
      British Novel Sequence. With a Preface by Harry T. Moore.
      (London & Amsterdam: Feffer & Simons; Carbondale & Edwards-
      ville: Southern Illinois University Press, 1972). [Exam-
      ines two major concepts of time--continuance and change-- in
      six novel sequences written after 1956 by D. Lessing, O. Man-
      ning, L. Durrell, A. Burgess, C. P. Snow, and A. Powell].

686   Morrow, Christine. Le Roman irréaliste dans les littératures
      contemporaines de langues francaise et anglaise. (Toulouse
      & Paris: Librarie Didier, 1941). [Originally a doctoral
      dissertation presented to the University of Toulouse. Exam-
      ines the distinctive features of the "roman irréaliste," its
      precursors, and its manifestation in V. Woolf, C. Morgan,
      and J. Barrie among others].

687   Morton, A. L. The English Utopia. (London: Lawrence &

Wishart, 1952). [A history of English Utopia. Chapter VII, "Yesterday and Tomorrow," considers H. G. Wells, A. Huxley, and G. Orwell].

688   Moseley, Edwin M. Pseudonyms of Christ in the Modern Novel: Motifs and Methods. (Pittsburgh: University of Pittsburgh Press, 1962). [Considers the recurrence of the Christ archetype and accounts for its variations in J. Conrad, D. H. Lawrence, E. M. Forster, and A. Koestler among others].

689 *Motoda, Shuichi. The Method and Philosophy of Modern English and American Literature. (Tokyo: Kaibunsha, 1957).

690   Mottram, Ralph Hale. "Tradition in the Novel." Tradition and Experiment in Present-Day Literature. Addresses delivered at the City Literary Institute. (London: Oxford University Press, 1929), pp. 1-22. [Surveys the English tradition of novel writing--"backbone of personal life, or part-life narrative," life-like character drawing, "convincing dialogue and opposite description," the love interest and the happy ending--and examines how the novels of A. Bennett, J. Galsworthy, H. James, and J. Conrad relate to it].

691   Mudrick, Marvin. On Culture and Literature. (New York: Horizon Press, 1970). [A reprint of essays published between 1955 and 1970. Includes studies of G. Orwell, A. Koestler, and J. Conrad among others, and "Character and Event in Fiction," reprinted from The Yale Review, L (December 1960), 202-218. See entry under Periodicals].

692   Mueller, William R. The Prophetic Voice in Modern Fiction. (New York: Association Press, 1959). [Discusses six modern novels with biblical themes and associations. Includes a study of the theme of "Vocation" in J. Joyce's A Portrait of the Artist, and one on the theme of love in G. Greene's The Heart of the Matter].

693   _____. Celebration of Life: Studies in Modern Fiction. (New York: Sheed and Ward, 1972). [The study is divided into four parts: Man and Vocation, Man and Nature, Man and Other Men, and Man and God. Discusses, among others, J. Joyce's quest for identity and vocation, J. Conrad's search for man's place in the natural order, and the inquiry into man's relationship to other humans in D. H. Lawrence, G. Orwell, and V. Woolf].

694   Muir, Edwin. Transition: Essays on Contemporary Literature. (London: The Hogarth Press; New York: The Viking Press, 1926). [A study of English post-World War I poetry and fiction. Chapter I, "The Zeitgeist," attempts to explain the state of English literature in the early twenties by attributing its literary problems to the "cultural environment" and forces that oppress the age, and especially the influence of scientific theories, urban living and impersonal feelings

99

and continuous changes. Devotes separate chapters to the study of J. Joyce, D. H. Lawrence, V. Woolf, and "S. Hudson," and concludes with a chapter on "Contemporary Fiction"].

695 _____. The Structure of the Novel. (London: The Hogarth Press, 1928; New York: Harcourt, Brace, 1929). [A classification of novels into the "dramatic," "character," and the "chronicle," and a study of the lines along which events move in some novels, as a viable alternative to E. M. Forster's Aspects of the Novel. Argues that plot in the novel is as "necessarily poetic or aesthetic" as any other kind of imaginative creation, for the novel is primarily a "form of art," and plot is an "image of life" and not a record of experience].

696 _____. The Present Age, from 1914. (London: The Cresset Press, 1939; New York: McBride, 1940). [A summary of trends and influences in the period between the two wars in poetry, fiction, general prose, criticism and drama, followed by a bibliography of primary sources].

697 _____. "Natural Man and the Political Man." British Thought, 1947. Introduction by Ivor Brown. (New York: The Gresham Press, 1947), pp. 253-263. [Contends that literature has not initiated but merely reflected the change in the idea of man"from the civilized to the primitive," i.e., the natural man, where the emphasis is on sensation, appetite, impulse, on ideas incompatible with the political aims of man. A. Huxley and D. H. Lawrence among others].

698 _____. Essays on Literature and Society. (London: The Hogarth Press, 1949; enlarged and revised edition, 1965). [The collection includes "The Political View of Literature," a reprint of "The Novel and the Modern World," Horizon, II (November 1940), 246-253, and "The Decline of the Novel," a reprint of "The Status of the Novel," The New Republic, CV (11 August 1941), 193-195. See entries under Periodicals].

699 Muller, Herbert J. Modern Fiction: A Study of Values. (New York & London: Funk & Wagnalls, 1937). [The study is mainly concerned with the novelist's vision of life and the "widespread, often feverish pursuit of values and meanings," which underlies modern fiction. Examines this aspect in representative English, American, and European novelists, and appraises their contributions. G. Moore, A. Bennett, J. Galsworthy, S. Maugham, J. Conrad, D. H. Lawrence, J. Joyce, V. Woolf, and A. Huxley among others].

700 Müller-Schwefe, Gerhard and Herman Metzger, eds. Sprache und Literatur Englands und Amerikas. Dritter Band: Die Wissenschaftliche Exschliessung der Prosa. (Tubingen: Max Niemeyer Verlag, 1959). [A collection of essays gy different writers on the scientific exploration of prose. Includes "Zum Problem der Interpretation und Wertung Zeitgenössischer

Romanliterature" by H. Straumann, and "Der Roman der Jungen Generation in England" by E. Mertner. See separate entries].

701 Murdoch, Iris. "Existentialists and Mystics: A Note on the Novel in the Utilitarian Age." Essays and Poems Presented to Lord David Cecil. Edited by W. W. Robson. (London: Constable, 1970), pp. 169-184. [Examines two prevalent types of recent novels: the "existential" and the "mystical," both showing freedom and virtue, the former as the "assertion of will" and the latter as "understanding, or obedience to the good." Also discusses the "demythologizing of religion," as a great "moral tonic." Brief references to D. H. Lawrence, K. Amis, G. Greene, M. Spark, and W. Golding].

702 Musgrove, S. Anthropological Themes in the Modern Novel. Bulletin No. 35, English Series No. 3. (Auckland: Auckland University College, 1949). [Originally a lecture delivered in 1947. Contends that with the assimilation of anthropology into the consciousness of man, the anthropological novel, now a separate sub-type like the Gothic horror story, will disappear and like Darwinism, will become one of the unspoken presuppositions of normal thought, thus feeding its literary offspring].

703 Muste, John M. Say that We Saw Spain Die: Literary Consequences of the Spanish Civil War. (Seattle & London: University of Washington Press, 1966). [Originally a doctoral dissertation entitled "The Spanish Civil War in the Literature of the United States and Great Britain" presented to the University of Wisconsin, 1960. Shows how the decline of faith in the ideology revealed in the literature of the early months of the war killed the idea that revolutionary doctrine can provide a way to order chaotic experience, and led to the renouncement of political ideologies in the literatures of England and the U. S. References to B. Marshall, J. Lindsay, and G. Orwell, among others].

704 Myers, Walter L. The Later Realism: A Study of Characterization in the British Novel. (Chicago: The University of Chicago Press, 1927; Cambridge: Cambridge University Press, 1927). [A study of the general influences--the literary, the scientific and philosophical, the psychological--on the materials and elements of character portrayal in the English novel from late Victorian times to 1923, in an attempt to define the "new conception of normality in fiction." A. Bennett, C. Dane, J. Galsworthy, H. James, J. Joyce, D. H. Lawrence, D. Richardson, M. Sinclair, H. G. Wells, "R. West" among others].

705 *Nakanishi, Kazuo. English Literature in the 20th Century. (Tokyo: Kenkyuska, 1950).

706 Nandakumar, Prema. The Glory and the Good: Essays on Literature. (London and New York: Asia Publishing House, 1965).

[A collection of twenty-eight essays which include one on
each of V. Woolf, R. Warner, and S. Beckett].

707 Neill, S. Diana. A Short History of the English Novel.
     (London: Jarrolds; New York: Macmillan, 1951). [On orth-
     odox lines: gives short biographies, social background,
     and literary influences. Chs. IX-XII consider the 20th cen-
     tury novel up to 1939].

708 Nélod, Gilles. Panorama du roman historique. (Paris: Ed-
     itions Sodi, 1969). [A chronological survey of the histor-
     ical novel and its related problems in Europe and America.
     Pages 355-357 of Ch. VI and pp. 405-409 of Ch. VII deal with
     novelists of the twentieth century].

709 Nemerov, Howard. "Composition and Fate in the Short Novel."
     Poetry and Fiction: Essays. (New Brunswick, New Jersey:
     Rutgers University Press, 1963), pp. 229-246. [On the "mat-
     erial economy" and "style of composition" of the novella as
     a tradition distinct from the short story and the novel, and
     suggestive of the "tragedies of antiquity." References to
     J. Conrad and D. H. Lawrence].

710 Neri, Nicoletta. "Il romanzo di conversazione." Friend-
     ship's Garland: Essays presented to Mario Praz on His Seven-
     tieth Birthday, Vol. II. Edited by Vittorio Gabrieli. (Roma:
     Edizioni di Storia e Letteratura, 1966), pp. 269-330. [Dis-
     cusses the kind of novel that revolves on conversation which
     does not rise from the action and is not functional in any
     way, but is present in the novel for its own sake. J. Joyce,
     V. Woolf, A. Huxley and others].

711 Neubert, Albrecht. Die Stilformen der 'Erlebte Rede' im
     neueren englischen Roman. (Halle: VEB Max Niemeyer Verlag,
     1957). [Bibliographical and factual information on the char-
     acter of "Erlebte Rede," and its style forms in the English
     novel from J. Austen to J. Joyce. J. Galsworthy, V. Woolf,
     D. Richardson, and J. Joyce among others].

712 Neuschaffer, W. Dostojewskijs Einfluss auf den englischen
     Roman. (Anglistische Forschungen). (Heidelberg: Carl
     Winters Universitätsbuchhandlung, 1935). [Traces the influ-
     ence of Dostoyevsky on the English Novel at the turn of the
     century as in G. Gissing, on the novel enriched by psychology
     as in J. Conrad, H. Walpole and E. Sidgwick, on the "kultur-
     problem" novel of D. H. Lawrence, A. Huxley and B. Nichols,
     and on the experimental novel of V. Woolf, D. Garnett, and
     D. M. Richardson].

713 Newby, P. H. The Novel, 1945-1950. (London: Longmans,
     Green, 1951. For the British Council). [A 41-page survey
     that considers the effect of the war upon the writing of
     fiction, and focuses upon E. Bowen, A. Huxley, G. Orwell,
     E. Waugh, I. Compton-Burnett, H. Green, G. Greene, J. Cary,

and L.P. Hartley].

714   Newquist, Roy, comp. & ed. <u>Counterpoint</u>. (Chicago: R. McNally, 1964; London: Allen & Unwin, 1965). [A collection of some 63 interviews with writers and critics. Included are interviews with M. Edelamn, "G. Fielding," I. Fleming, J. Fowles, P. Frankau, P. H. Johnson, D. Lessing, M. Sharp, C. P. Snow, and M. Stewart].

715   Nicholson, Norman. <u>Man and Literature</u>. (London: S. C. M. Press, 1943). [An inquiry into the assumptions regarding the nature and purpose of Man which underlie much of the writing of the 20th century. Also traces the characteristic attitudes of writers to the "gradual abandoning of the Christian faith and belief in the supernatural." A. Bennett, H. G. Wells, D. H. Lawrence, A. Huxley, J. Joyce, and T. F. Powys among others].

716   Nicolson, Harold. <u>The New Spirit in Literature. . . An Essay</u>. (London: B. B. C., 1931). [A reprint of ten talks on the B. B. C., published in <u>The Listener</u>. See entry under Periodicals].

717   Nin, Anais. <u>Realism and Reality</u>. (No. 6 of "Outcast" Series of Chapbooks). (New York: Alicat Book Shop, 1946). [A ten-page study supporting the "novelist's preoccupation with inner distortions . . . as a truthful mirror of today's drama." Brief references to J. Joyce and D. H. Lawrence].

718   Nojima, Hidekatsu. <u>Exile's Literature: A Study of James Joyce, D. H. Lawrence and T. S. Eliot</u>. (Tokyo: Nan-un-dō, 1963). [Contains separate studies of the three writers. In Japanese].

719   Norman, Sylva, ed. <u>Contemporary Essays: 1933</u>. (London: Matthews & Marrot, 1933). [A collection of essays by different writers on four topics. Includes, under "Books and Authors," an essay on each of D. H. Lawrence and H. James].

720   Nott, Kathleen. <u>The Emperor's Clothes</u>. (London: Heinemann, 1953; Indiana University Press, 1954). [Asserts the "principle of the Unity of Knowledge," and discusses the relations that exist between the growing body of knowledge and the "human mind in its imaginative and creative functions." In the chapters entitled "Lord Peter Views the Soul," and "Augustinian Novelists," C. S. Lewis, D. Sayers, and G. Greene are attacked for their dogmatic orthodoxy].

721   O'Brien, Conor Cruise. <u>Maria Cross: Imaginative Patterns in a Group of Modern Catholic Writers</u>. (New York: Oxford University Press, 1952; London: Chatto & Windus, 1954). [Originally published under the pseudonym of Donat O'Donnell. The 1963 edition published under his name includes an essay on each of G. Greene and E. Waugh].

722 O'Brien, Kate. "The Technique of the Novel." The Author and the Public: Problems of Communication. (The P. E. N. Congress, July 1956, London). Edited, with an Introduction by C. V. Wedgwood. (London: Hutchinson, 1957), pp. 175-179. [Contends that technique is not something to be studied or learnt; for it "is the writer," a personality expressing itself].

723 "O'Connor, Frank" [Michael O'Donovan]. The Mirror in the Roadway: A Study of the Modern Novel. (New York: Knopf, 1956; London: Hamish Hamilton, 1957). [Lectures delivered at Harvard Summer School in 1953 and 1954. Mostly concerned with the English, French and Russian novel as a limited but serious middle-class art, and the curious relationship between truth and imagination. Includes a chapter on H. James as a transitional figure between the classical novel and the modern novel. Part V examines the reaction of D. H. Lawrence, M. Proust, and J. Joyce to the "objective and analytic tradition of European prose," and their impact in directing the novel towards "allegory"].

724 O'Connor, William Van, ed. Forms of Modern Fiction: Essays Collected in Honor of Joseph Warren Beach. (Minneapolis: The University of Minnesota Press, 1948; London: Oxford University Press, 1949). [Twenty-three essays on technique and form, and individual English, French and American novelists, of which nineteen were previously published. Includes M. Schorer's "Technique as Discovery," A. Tate's "Techniques of Fiction," L. Trilling's "Manners, Morals, and the Novel," and C. H. Rickwood's "A Note on Fiction." (See entries under Periodicals). Also includes two essays on J. Joyce, and one on each of D. H. Lawrence, E. M. Forster, A. Huxley, H. James, V. Woolf, and G. Greene].

725 _____. The New University Wits and the End of Modernism. With a Preface by Harry T. Moore. (Carbondale: Southern Illinois University Press, 1963). [A historical and evaluative study of the "new" literature of the fifties as distinct from the modernist movement of the twenties and thirties. P. Larkin, J. Wain, I. Murdoch, K. Amis, D. Storey, J. Braine, and A. Sillitoe].

726 O'Faolain, Sean. The Vanishing Hero: Studies in the Novelists of the Twenties. (London: Eyre & Spottiswoode; Boston: Little, Brown, 1956). [The 1953 Christian Gauss Seminars in Criticism at Princeton University. Contends that "the central assumption of the contemporary novel . . . is the virtual disappearance from fiction of that focal character of the classical novel, the conceptual hero," and his replacement by the "anti-hero" or "the tortured martyr." Includes an essay on A. Huxley and E. Waugh, another on V. Woolf and J. Joyce, and one on each of G. Greene and E. Bowen among others].

727 *Ogawa, Kazuo. Modern English Literature and Intellect. (Tokyo: Kenkyusha, 1952).

728 O'Grady, Walter. "On Plot in Modern Fiction: Hardy, James, Conrad." Critical Approaches to Literature. Edited by Shiv K. Kumar and Keith F. McKean. (New York: McGraw-Hill, 1968), pp. 57-67. Reprinted from Modern Fiction Studies, XI:2 (Summer, 1965), 107-115. [See entry under Periodicals].

729 Oppel, Horst, ed. Der moderne englische Roman: Interpretationen. (Berlin: Erich Schmidt Verlag, 1965). [A collection of seventeen essays by different contributors, each analysing an individual novel. Includes studies of novels by J. Conrad, J. Joyce, D. H. Lawrence, E. M. Forster, V. Woolf, A. Huxley, C. Morgan, G. Greene, J. Cary, E. Waugh, W. Golding, I. Murdoch, A. Wilson, I. Compton-Burnett, and L. Durrell. This is followed by a selected checklist of critical works by Paul Goetsch and Heinz Kosok].

730 Orage, Alfred Richard. Selected Essays and Critical Writings. Edited by H. Read and D. Saurat. (London: Stanley Nott, 1935). ["The Art of Reading" contains some views on A. Bennett, D. H. Lawrence, H. James, R. Kipling, G. K. Chesterton and H. G. Wells; also included is a note on "The End of Fiction," pp. 137-138].

731 Ortega Y Gasset, José. The Dehumanization of Art and Notes on the Novel. Translated by Helene Weyl. (Princeton, New Jersey: Princeton University Press, 1948). [Analyses and recommends the "dehumanizing" element in the novel; i.e., the tendency to get away from the "human element of lived reality"].

732 Orwell, George. The Collected Essays, Journalism and Letters of George Orwell, 4 vols. Edited by Sonia Orwell and Ian Angus. (London: Secker & Warburg; New York: Harcourt, 1968). [Vol. 1 An Age Like This: 1920-1940, includes "In Defence of the Novel" reprinted from New English Weekly (See entry under Periodicals). Vol. II My Country Right or Left, 1940-1943, includes "The Rediscovery of Europe" reprinted from The Listener (See entry under Periodicals). Vol. III As I Please, 1943-1945, includes an essay on each of A. Koestler and P. G. Wodehouse. Vol. IV In Front of Your Nose, 1945-1950, includes "The Prevention of Literature" reprinted from Polemic (See entry under Periodicals)].

733 Overton, Grant. American Nights Entertainment. (New York: Appleton - Doran - Doubleday - Scribner's, 1923). [Includes essays on J. Galsworthy, J. Conrad, and V. Sackville-West].

734 _____. Authors of the Day: Studies in Contemporary Literature. (New York: Doran, 1924; Books for Libraries, 1971). [Includes essays on J. Galsworthy, J. Conrad, V. Sackville-West, H. Walpole, "R. West," A. Bennett, and F. Swinnerton].

735 _____. The Philosophy of Fiction. (New York & London:
D. Appleton, 1928). [Traces principles and offers examples
of practice to the reader of fiction. Part of the work is
devoted to a short history of fiction].

736 Panichas, George A., ed. Mansions of the Spirit: Essays in
Literature and Religion. Introductory essay by Thomas Merton.
(New York: Hawthorn Books, 1967). [A collection of essays
by writers of different religious persuasions concerned with
the relation between literature and religion. Part I deals
with the theory, and Part II with individual writers. Included are studies on D. H. Lawrence, A. Huxley, and J. Masefield].

737 _____. The Politics of Twentieth-Century Novelists.
With a Foreword by John W. Aldridge. (New York: Hawthorn
Books, 1971). [A sequel to Mansions of the Spirit. The col-
lection of critical essays on individual novelists by differ-
ent critics is divided into three parts: English, Continen-
tal, and American. The English novelists discussed are H. G.
Wells, E. M. Forster, D. H. Lawrence, W. Lewis, A. Huxley,
G. Orwell, G. Greene, and C. P. Snow].

738 Parry, Benita. Delusions and Discoveries: Studies on India
in the British Imagination 1880-1930. (London: Allen Lane,
The Penguin Press, 1972). [Originally an M.A. thesis, entitled The Image of India: Some Literary Expressions of the
British Experience in India, University of Birmingham, 1966/67.
Examines what writers saw or discovered in and through India,
how they reordered their ideas and perceptions in fiction,
and how they reacted to the demands for understanding which
India made on their imaginations and intellects. Includes
studies of E. J. Thompson, R. Kipling, and E. M. Forster].

739 Partridge, Eric. Journey to the Edge of Morning: Thoughts
Upon Books, Love, Life. (London: Frederick Muller, 1946;
Books for Libraries Press, 1969). [Chapter I contains an
informal and unacademic series of personal judgments on 20th
century novelists and novels of all ranks].

740 Patt, Gertrud. Der Kampf zwischen Vater und Sohn im englischen Roman des 20. Jahrhunderts. (Munsterer Anglistische
Studien--Zweites Heft). (Emsdetten: Verlagsanstalt Heinr.
& J. Lechte, 1938). [Doctoral dissertation presented to the
University of Muenster, 1938. Surveys briefly the father-
son conflict in the 19th century novel, discusses the basic,
natural and social causes for the conflict, from the standpoint of both father and son, and illustrates how this conflict reveals itself in works by S. Butler, J. Galsworthy,
H. G. Wells, A. Bennett, G. Cannan, H. Walpole, R. Macaulay,
R. Aldington, "N. Bell," M. Mander, and O. Baldwin].

741 Paul, Leslie. "The Writer and the Human Condition." Alternatives to Christian Belief: A Critical Survey of the Contemporary Search for Meaning. (New York: Doubleday, 1967),

pp. 160-183. Revised and reprinted from The Kenyon Review, XXIX:1 (January 1967), 21-38. [See entry under Periodicals].

742   Pearson, Hesketh. Modern Men and Mummers. (London: George Allen & Unwin, 1921). [Includes sketches of F. Harris, H. G. Wells, J. Conrad, and G. K. Chesterton].

743   Pendry, E. D. The New Feminism of English Fiction: A Study in Contemporary Women-Novelists. (Tokyo: Kenkyusha, 1956). [Gives an outline of the social and literary history of women's growing independence until V. Woolf, followed by an attempt to examine common characteristics in the works of women writers as the "basis of a tradition." Selects I. Compton-Burnett, E. Bowen, R. Lehmann, and O. Manning for detailed study].

744   Pérez Gállego, Candido. Literatura y rebeldia en la Inglaterra actual: Los Angeles "Angry Young Men." un movimiento social de los anos cincuenta. (Madrid: Consejo Superior de Investigaciones Cientificas, 1968). [Examines the "social movement" in the literature of the "Angry Young Men" in the fifties. Includes biographical and critical studies of K. Amis, L. Anderson, J. Braine, S. Delaney, W. Hopkins, D. Lessing, I. Murdoch, A. Sillitoe, J. Wain, and C. Wilson].

745   Pérez Minik, Domingo. Introduccion a la novela inglesa actual. (Madred: Ediciones Guardarrama, 1968). [Evaluates and analyses English novels from V. Woolf to the generation of the "Angry Young Men" in their sociological context. Inclues V. Woolf, E. M. Forster, J. Wain, I. Compton-Burnett, H. Green, G. Greene, R. Hughes, J. Cary, A. Wilson, G. Orwell, and L. Durrell].

746   Phelps, G. H., ed. Living Writers. Being Critical Studies Broadcast in the B. B. C. Third Programme. (London: Sylvan Press, 1947). [Twelve critical talks on contemporary writers including G. Greene, C. Isherwood, E. Bowen, W. Lewis, I. Compton-Burnett, E. M. Forster, G. Orwell, A. Huxley, E. Waugh, and T. F. Powys].

747   _____. The Russian Novel in English Fiction. (London: Hutchinson's University Library, 1956). [Traces the reception of the Russian novel in England, and the impact of its novelists, especially Turgenev, on English and American novelists in the 19th and early 20th centuries. Examines Turgenev's influence on H. James in Ch. V, on G. Moore and G. Gissing in Ch. VI, and on A. Bennett, J. Galsworthy, J. Conrad and V. Woolf in Ch. VII. Also surveys English reaction to Tolstoy and Dostoyevsky in Chs. VIII, IX, and X].

748   _____. "The Novel Today." The Pelican Guide to English Literature, Vol. 7: The Modern Age. Edited by Boris Ford. (London: Cassell; Baltimore: Penguin, 1961), pp. 475-495. [A survey that divides novelists into four groups: survivors of the thirties--C. Morgan, R. Warner, C. Isherwood,

A. Huxley, E. Waugh, G. Greene, and W. Lewis--novelists who
achieved maturity and recognition after the war but who may
have written earlier--I. Compton-Burnett, L. P. Hartley,
C. P. Snow, A. Powell, and J. Cary--the "Angry Young Men"
--K. Amis, J. Wain, J. Brain, A. Sillitoe--and those who
belong to no category at all-- L. Durrell and A. Wilson.
Contends that the trend of the post-World War II English
novel is a "turning aside from the mainstream of European
literature, and a tendency to retreat into parochialism"].

749 Phelps, William Lion. The Advance of the English Novel.
     (London: John Murray, 1919). [A history that discusses in
     Chapter I "The Present State of the Novel," realism in, and
     popularity of, the novel in the 20th century. Chapter VIII
     focuses on J. Conrad and J. Galsworthy, and Chapter IX sur-
     veys English contemporary novelists E. Phillpotts, G. Moore,
     H. G. Wells, W. B. Maxwell, A. S. M. Hutchinson, and St. John
     Ervine among others].

750 Pitt, Valerie. The Writer and the Modern World: A Study
     in Literature and Dogma. (London: S. P. C. K., 1966).
     [A Christian criticism on English post-World War II writers
     --few of whom are held to be religious--that discusses the
     religious and theological implications of their writings.
     J. Braine, A. Wilson, R. Hughes, J. Wain, C. P. Snow, M.
     Spark, I. Murdoch, and W. Golding among others].

751 Pocock, Guy N[oel]. Pen and Ink: Twelve Practical Talks
     on the Writing of English Prose. (London: J. M. Dent, 1925).
     [The twelve talks on the many and varied forms of English
     prose are followed by an examination of the art as practised
     by several contemporary writers among whom are R. Kipling,
     J. Conrad, W. H. Hudson, and H. G. Wells].

752 Podhoretz, Norman. "The New Nihilism and the Novel." Do-
     ings and Undoings: The Fifties and After in American Writing.
     (New York: Farrar & Strauss, 1964), pp. 159-178. Reprinted
     from The Partisan Review, XXV:4 (Fall, 1958), 576-590. [See
     entry under Periodicals].

753 Pongs, Hermann. Romanschaffen im Umbruch der Zeit: Eine
     Chronik von 1952 bis 1962. (Tübingen: Verlag der Deusts-
     chen Hochschullehrerzeitung, 1963). [Though it is mainly
     concerned with the German novel in "changing times," the
     "chronicle" includes short studies of J. Joyce, G. Greene,
     J. Conrad, and A. Huxley].

754 Porter, Katherine Anne. The Collected Essays and Occasional
     Writings of Katherine Anne Porter. (New York: Delacorte
     Press, 1970). [Includes discussions of K. Mansfield, V.
     Woolf, E. M. Forster, and D. H. Lawrence's Lady Chatterley's
     Lover].

755 Pound, Ezra. Investigations. (New York: Boni & Liveright,

1920; Books for Libraries Press, 1967). [Includes studies of J. Joyce and H. James].

756 _____. Literary Essays of Ezra Pound. Edited, with an Introduction by T. S. Eliot. (London: Faber, 1960). [Includes three essays on J. Joyce and one on W. Lewis].

757 Prescott, Orville. In My Opinion: An Inquiry into the Contemporary Novel. (New York: Bobbs-Merrill; Toronto: McLellan, 1952; Books for Libraries Press, 1971). [Discusses English and American novelists whose works were published between 1940 and 1951, and who are significant for their "artistic achievement, their influence and the ideas which they champion." G. Orwell, A. Koestler, H. Green, I. Compton-Burnett, E. Bowen, G. Greene, E. Waugh, and J. Cary among others].

758 Price, Martin. "The Other Self: Thoughts about Character in the Novels." Imagined Worlds: Essays on Some English Novels and Novelists in Honour of John Butt. Edited by Maynard Mack and Ian Gregor. (London: Methuen; New York: Barnes & Noble, 1968), pp. 279-299. [On the "analogy of fictional character and our conceptions of the self," the "framing effect" of the novel leading to "ambiguity of figure and ground," and the problem of character in the "symbolist" novel. V. Woolf and D. H. Lawrence among others].

759 Priestley, J. B. "Those Terrible Novelists." I for One. (London: John Lane, 1923; Books for Libraries Press, 1967), pp. 117-123. [Personal impressions of contemporary novelists, whose "omniscient and uncharitable" attitudes, and "motiveless sneering" he rejects].

760 _____. The English Novel. (London: Ernest Benn, 1927; Scholarly Press, 1971). [An account of the English novel from the 18th century to 1925. Makes use of the chronological method in the survey, and estimates novelists "according to their value to us, here and now." Chapter VII deals with the first quarter of the 20th century].

761 _____. Figures in Modern Literature. (London: John Lane; The Bodley Head; New York: Dodd & Mead, 1928; Books for Libraries Press, 1970). [Includes A. Bennett, M. Hewlett, and W. W. Jacobs].

762 _____. "The Newest Novels." Thoughts in the Wilderness. (London: Heinemann; New York: Harper, 1957), pp. 54-59. Reprinted from New Stateman and Nation, XLVII (26 June 1954), 824, 826. [See entry under Periodicals].

763 _____. Literature and Western Man. (London: Heinemann; New York: Harper, 1960). [The survey of European literature from the second half of the 15th century to World

War II, tries to give an account of Western Man "in terms
of the literature he has created. . . " and avoids criticism and critics. Part V is devoted to the 20th century.
References to A. Bennett, E. M. Forster, J. Galsworthy, J.
Joyce, and V. Woolf among others].

764   Pritchett, V. S. The Living Novel. (London: Chatto & Windus, 1946; New York: Reynal & Hitchcock, 1947). Revised
and expanded to include the contents of The Working Novelist.
(London: Chatto & Windus, 1965), and published as The Living Novel and Later Appreciations. (New York: Random House,
1964). [A collection of essays on individual novelists,
English and continental, most of which were published in
The Statesman and Nation. Essays on English novelists are
chronologically arranged according to author. Includes an
essay on each of H. G. Wells, A. Bennett, D. H. Lawrence,
J. Conrad, E. M. Forster, F. M. Ford, J. Galsworthy, A. Powell, L. Durrell, W. Golding, and S. Beckett among others].

765   _____. "The Future of English Fiction." The New Partisan Reader, 1945-1953. Edited by William Phillips and
Philip Rahv. (New York: Harcourt, Brace, 1953), pp. 249-
257. Reprinted from New Writing and Daylight, VIII:7 (1946),
75-79. [See entry under Periodicals].

766   _____. Why Do I Write? An Exchange of Views between
Elizabeth Bowen, Graham Greene and V.S. Pritchett. With a
Preface by V. S. Pritchett (London: Spearman, 1948; The
Folcroft Press, 1969). [See entry under Bowen, Elizabeth].

767   _____. Books in General. (London: Chatto & Windus;
New York: Harcourt, Brace, 1953; Greenwood Press, 1970).
[A collection of essays on English and Continental writers
reprinted from The New Statesman and Nation with the excep-
tion of "The Art of A. Koestler." Includes essays on H.
James, A. Koestler, J. Conrad ("An Emigré"), R. Firbank,
W. W. Jacobs, and W. Lewis ("The Eye-Man")].

768   _____. "In Writing Nothing Fails Like Success." Opinions and Perspectives from 'The New York Times Book Review'.
Edited by Francis Brown. (Boston: Houghton Mifflin, 1964),
pp. 216-222. Reprinted from The New York Times Book Review
(22 January 1961), 1, 38. [See entry under Periodicals].

769   _____. The Working Novelist. (London: Chatto & Windus,
1965). [A collection of Essays on 20th century English and
American novelists. Essays on F. M. Ford, J. Galsworthy,
S. Beckett, L. Durrell, E. M. Forster, W. Golding, A. Powell,
and J. Conrad among others].

770   Proctor, Mortimer R. The English University Novel. (Berkeley & Los Angeles: University of California Press; Cambridge University Press, 1957). [A historical and critical

study of how fictional representation of English university life developed from Chaucer to the mid-forties, from an "initial stage of crudeness and vulgarity, through a middle period in which humour and the doctrines of university reforms were strangely mingled, to the final achievement of a serious and mature statement of the very nature of a university education." Refers to some seventy 20th century works by novelists of all ranks. Also contains a chronologically arranged bibliography of English University Fiction from Fielding to A. Wilson].

771 Pryce-Jones, Alan. "The Novelist in a World Awry." Highlights of Modern Literature: A Permanent Collection of Memorable Essays from 'The New York Times Book Review'. Edited by Francis Brown. (New York: The New American Library, 1954), pp. 49-53. Reprinted from The New York Times Book Review, (10 December 1950), 1, 22. [See entry under Periodicals].

772 _____. "Plagued by the Nature of Truth." Highlights of Modern Literature: A Permanent Collection of Memorable Essays from 'The New York Times Book Review'. Edited by Francis Brown. (New York: The New American Library, 1954), pp. 72-76. Reprinted from The New York Times Book Review, (8 July 1951), 1, 18. [See entry under Periodicals].

773 Putt, S. Gorley. Scholars of the Heart: Essays in Criticism. (London: Faber & Faber, 1962; New York: Hillary House, 1963). [The collection of previously published essays includes one on each of A. Huxley, E. M. Forster, and F. Reid. Part 3, "Professor Emeritus," consists of four essays on H. James' novels].

774 Quennell, Peter. The Singular Preference: Portraits and Essays. (London: Collins, 1952; New York: The Viking Press, 1953; Kennikat Press, 1971). [Includes an essay on each of R. Kipling and H. G. Wells].

775 _____. The Sign of the Fish. (London: Collins; New York: The Viking Press, 1960). [A book of reminiscences, travels, and studies. Discusses the penalties and pains of writing, and includes a chapter, "Stylists," on H. G. Wells and G. Moore. References to J. Joyce, G. Greene, D. H. Lawrence, and A. Huxley].

776 Raban, Jonathan. The Technique of Modern Fiction: Essays in Practical Criticism. (London: Arnold; Notre Dame, Indiana: University of Notre Dame Press, 1968). [Critical discussions on 15 aspects of fictional technique divided equally between narrative, character, and style and language. Each aspect or topic is introduced with some general observations, followed by an extract from post-1945 English and American fiction which is then analysed. Extracts from C. Isherwood, A. Wilson, I. Murdoch, K. Waterhouse, M. Drabble, D. Storey, and G. Orwell included].

777 Rabinovitz, Rubin. _The Reaction Against Experiment in the English Novel, 1950-1960_. (New York & London: Columbia University Press, 1967). [Originally a doctoral dissertation presented to Columbia University, 1966. A survey of the social changes since World War II, followed by a study of K. Amis, A. Wilson, and C. P. Snow. Shows how K. Amis revives the 18th century picaresque tradition, and A. Wilson and C. P. Snow, the traditions of Dickens and Trollope respectively. Contains a bibliography of the writings of each of the novelists and a list of selected general critical works].

778 Rahv, Philip. _Image and Idea, Twenty Essays on Literary Themes_. (London: Weidenfeld and Nicolson, 1949. Revised and enlarged, 1957. Also Norfold, Connecticut: New Directions, 1957). [A collection of essays previously published. Includes two essays on H. James and one on each of V. Woolf and A. Koestler].

779 _____. _The Myth and the Powerhouse: Essays on Literature and Ideas_. (New York: Farrar, Straus and Giroux, 1965). [A collection of essays previously published. Included are: "The Myth and the Powerhouse" reprinted from _The Partisan Review_, XX:6 (November-December, 1953), 635-648; and "Fiction and the Criticism of Fiction" from _The Kenyon Review_, XVIII (Spring 1956), 276-299. See entries under Periodicals].

780 _____. _Literature and the Sixth Sense_. (Boston: Houghton, Mifflin, 1969; London: Faber and Faber, 1970). [A reprint of _Image and Idea_ and essays from _The Myth and the Powerhouse_. (See above). Also includes "The Unfuture of Utopia," reprinted with a postscript 1969, from _The Partisan Review_, XVI:7 (July 1949), in which he discusses G. Orwell's _1984_ and A. Koestler's _Darkness at Noon_ as "documents" of the crisis of socialism representing a "melancholy mid-century genre of lost illusions and Utopia betrayed"].

781 Rajan, B., ed. _The Novelist as Thinker_. Focus Four. (London: Dennis Dobson, 1948). [A symposium discussing the effect of a writer's beliefs on his novels. Included are two essays by D. S. Savage, one on each of A. Huxley and E. Waugh, and two by G. H. Bantock, one on each of C. Isherwood and L. H. Myers].

782 Raleigh, John Henry. _Time, Place, and Idea: Essays on the Novel_. With a Preface by Harry T. Moore. (Carbondale & Edwardsville: Southern Illinois University Press; London & Amsterdam: Feffer & Simons, 1968). [Includes an essay on Henry James, "Victorian Morals and the Modern Novel," pp. 137-163, and "The English Novel and Three Kinds of Time," reprinted from _The Partisan Review_, XXV:2 (Spring 1958), 241-264 and _The Sewanee Review_, LXII (July 1954), 428-440. (See entries under Periodicals)].

783 Rann, Ernest H. The Homeland of English Authors. (London:
     Methuen; New York: Dutton, 1927). [Attempts to describe
     parts of England where some authors have lived and left the
     "mark of their personality either in memories of their pre-
     sence or in their books." H. James, S. Kaye-Smith, E. Phill-
     potts, and A. Bennett among others].

784 Ransom, John Crowe, ed. The Kenyon Critics: Studies in Mod-
     ern Literature from 'The Kenyon Review.' (Cleveland: World
     Publishing, 1951; Kennikat Press, 1967). [A reprint of 33
     essays and book reviews. Includes an essay on each of H.
     James, E. Waugh, and F. M. Ford, and a review of A. Huxley's
     Time Must Have a Stop].

785 Rantavaara, Irma. Virginia Woolf and Bloomsbury. (Helsinki:
     Suomalaisen Tiedeakatemian Toi ituksia. Annales Academiae
     Scientiarum Fennicoe. Sarjasir B. Nide-Tom 82, 1. 1953).
     [An attempt to understand the Bloomsbury Group through a
     study of V. Woolf].

786 Raskin, Jonah. The Mythology of Imperialism: Rudyard Kip-
     ling, Joseph Conrad, E. M. Forster, D. H. Lawrence, and Joyce
     Cary. (New York: Random House, 1971). [Examines "patterns
     of conflict and struggle, space and time" by posing Kipling
     and Conrad, and Forster and Cary as antagonists, and regard-
     ing D. H. Lawrence as a "pioneer voyager in space and time"
     urging a "revolution for life." The book developed from a
     doctoral dissertation entitled "The Mythology of Imperialism:
     A Study of Joseph Conrad and Rudyard Kipling" and presented
     to the University of Manchester, 1967].

787 Ratcliffe, Michael. The Novel Today. (London: Longmans,
     Greene, 1968). Published for The British Council.   [A brief
     survey. Also includes a selected reading list].

788 Rathbun, Robert C. and Martin Steinmann, Jr., eds. From
     Jane Austen to Joseph Conrad: Essays Collected in Memory of
     James T. Hillhouse. (Minneapolis: University of Minnesota
     Press, 1958). [The collection of twenty essays is mainly
     concerned with the 19th century novel. Includes M. Stein-
     mann's "The Old and the New" (see separate entry), an essay
     on S. Butler and Bloomsbury, and another on J. Conrad].

789 Raymond, E. T. Portraits of the New Century: The First Ten
     Years. (London: Ernest Benn; New York: Doubleday, Doran,
     1928). [Brings out the "peculiar individuality" of the Ed-
     wardian Period through "sketches" assembled from previously
     published articles. Of interest in this regard are "Liter-
     ary Swashbucklers and Sentimentalists," and "Henry James and
     Max Beerbohm"].

790 Raymond, John. England's On the Anvil! And Other Essays.
     (London: Collins, 1958). [A collection of 34 essays by a
     literary journalist, most of which had appeared in The New

                                113

Statesman. Includes an essay on each of R. Kipling ("Martha's Son"), H. Belloc ("Beau Sabreur"), G. K. Chesterton ("Jeekay-cee"), S. Maugham ("Carey and Ashenden"), G. Orwell ("The Barrack-Room Lawyer"), and two on J. Buchan].

791 _____. The Doge of Dover and Other Essays. (London: MacGibbon & Kee, 1960). [A collection of essays, or parts of essays, reprinted from The Times Literary Supplement, The New Statesman, and History Today, very often in the form of review articles. Included are "Alive and Kicking" (H. G. Wells), "Salute to a Friendless Girl" ("R. West"), "The Cows of Our Day" (P. H. Johnson), "Meg Eliot Surprised" (A. Wilson), and "The Unclassified Image" (I. Murdoch)].

792 Read, Herbert. "The Modern Novel (Cursory Notes)." Reason and Romanticism: Essays in Literary Criticism. (London: Faber and Faber, 1926; New York: Russell, 1963). [Notes on action, duration, expression, and sense of values in the modern novel, with reference to H. James and J. Joyce].

793 _____ and Edward Dahlberg. Truth is More Sacred: A Critical Exchange in Modern Literature. (London: Routledge & Kegan Paul; New York: Horizon Press, 1961). [Includes one essay on each of H. James, J. Joyce, and D. H. Lawrence].

794 Reade, A. R. Main Currents in Modern Literature. (London: Ivor Nicholson and Watson, 1935). [Sees the unity of the Victorians shattered and a period of analysis rather than synthesis following. Selects typical figures and tries to focus attention on what is most significant in each for the future. Included are R. Kipling, H. G. Wells, J. Masefield, J. Galsworthy, J. Conrad, V. Woolf, and D. H. Lawrence].

795 Reed, Henry. The Novel Since 1939. (London: Longmans, Greene, 1946). Published for The British Council. Reprinted in Since 1939. Vol. II. (London: Phoenix House, 1949), pp. 61-103. [Considers the English novel at the hands of "serious practitioners" during the years of World War II. The survey attempts to place in perspective significant novelists, but also covers minor or emerging writers].

796 Reed, John R. Old School Ties: The Public Schools in British Literature. (Syracuse, New York: Syracuse University Press, 1964). [Originally a doctoral dissertation entitled "Made in England: A Study of the Private Educational System in English Literature" presented to University of Rochester. Indicates the various ways in which E. M. Forster, A. Huxley, G. Greene, A. Powell, H. G. Wells, E. Waugh, H. Walpole and J. Wain utilized certain experiences acquired in the English Public School System in their novels].

797 Rehder, Jessie. The Nature of Fiction. (Chapel Hill: University of North Carolina Extension Library, 1948). [An elementary study outline which includes outlines of novels by

114

R. Hughes, H. James, E. M. Forster, S. Maugham, and E. Waugh].

798   Reichwagen, Wilhelm. Der expressionistische Zug im neuesten englischen Roman: Eine Weltanschaulich-stilkritische Studie. (Greifswald: Verlag Hans Dallmeyer, 1935). [Part I deals with a basic interpretation of the theory of expressionism and the problems of the expressionistic novel. Part II traces the expressionistic element in the world views (Weltanschauung) expressed; i.e. relationship of people and their ideas, and in the form; i.e., the artistic composition and style. Concentrates mainly on D. H. Lawrence with references to R. Aldington and A. Bennett].

799   Reilly, Joseph J. Of Books and Men. (New York: Julian Messner, 1942). [Contains a study of the novels of M. Baring and an appraisal of J. Galsworthy as a novelist].

800   Reilly, Robert J. Romantic Religion: A Study of Barfield, Lewis, Williams and Tolkien. (Athens: University of Georgia Press, 1971). [Originally a doctoral dissertation presented to Michigan State University, 1960-1961. Attempts to reveal, on analysis, the "deliberate and conscious attempt" of these four writers to "defend romanticism by showing it to be religious, and to defend religion by traditionally romantic means"].

801   Reinhardt, Kurt F. Theological Novel of Modern Europe: An Analysis of Masterpieces by Eight Authors. (New York: Frederick Ungar, 1969). [Includes an analysis of a novel by each of G. Greene and E. Waugh].

802   Reiss, Hans S. "Style and Structure in Modern Experimental Fiction." Stil und Formprobleme in der Literatur. Edited by Paul Bockmann. (Heidelberg: Carl Winter Universitäts-verlag, 1959), pp. 419-424. [Lecture delivered at the 7th Congress of the International Federation of Modern Languages and Literatures, August 1957 in Heidelberg and reprinted in German as "Stil und Struktur im modernen europäischen experimentellen Roman," Akzente, V (1958), 202-213. A general discussion of the style, structure and the need for experiment in these areas in the European novel--including England].

803   Rexroth, Kenneth. Assays. Norfolk, Connecticut: New Directions Books, 1961). [A collection of essays and reviews previously published. Includes a review of Henry James and H. G. Wells. Edited and introduced by Leon Edel and Gordon N. Ray, and three reviews of L. Durrell's works].

804   Rickword, C. H. "A Note on Fiction." Towards Standards of Criticism: Selections from the Calendar of Modern Letters, 1925-1927. Chosen with an Introduction by F. R. Leavis. (London: Wishart, 1933; Folcroft Press, 1969), pp. 29-43. Reprinted from The Calendar of Modern Letters, lll (1926-1927), 226-233. [See entry under Periodicals].

805   Rickword, Edgell, ed. <u>Scrutinies</u>, Vol. II. (London: Wish-
       art, 1931). [Includes "Note on the Form of the Novel" by
       Brian Penton, reprinted from <u>London Aphrodite</u>, VI (1929),
       434-444 (see entry under Periodicals), and essays on each of
       A. Huxley, J. Joyce, D. H. Lawrence, W. Lewis, and V. Woolf
       among others].

806   Rillo, Lila E. <u>Katherine Mansfield and Virginia Woolf</u>. Eng-
       lish Pamphlets Series No. 7. (Buenos Aires: Argentine Ass-
       ociation of English Culture, 1944). [A 7-page pamphlet
       pointing out instances of similarities in characterisation,
       setting and scenery, wording, and attitudes between the two
       writers].

807   Rippier, Joseph S. <u>Some Postwar English Novelists</u>. (Frank-
       furt: Verlag Moritz Diesterweg, 1965). [Selects eight auth-
       ors--A. Wilson, W. Golding, I. Murdoch, L. Durrell, K. Amis,
       J. Wain, J. Braine and A. Sillitoe--who have published their
       main works after World War II to indicate various tendencies.
       Discusses novels, and includes a few biographical details
       about each author as well as a list of published works].

808   Roberts, Denys Kilham, ed. <u>Titles to Fame</u>. (London: Thomas
       Nelson, 1937). [Essays by English novelists, each describing
       the inception or composition of a particular novel. H. Wal-
       pole, M. Kennedy, H. M. Tomlinson, D. L. Sayers, A. J. Cronin,
       "E. M. Delafield," R. H. Mottram, E. A. Robertson, E. Raymond,
       and M. Irwin give the "biographies" of their most successful
       books].

809   Robinson, J. W., ed. <u>British Writers and Their Work</u>, No. 3.
       (Lincoln: University of Nebraska Press, 1964). [Essays on
       V. Woolf, E. M. Forster and K. Mansfield by B. Blackstone,
       Rex Warner and Ian A. Gordon originally published separately
       for the British Council].

810   Robson, W. W. <u>Critical Essays</u>. (London: Routledge & Kegan
       Paul, 1966; New York: Barnes & Noble, 1967). [Includes an
       essay on each of H. James, R. Kipling, and D. H. Lawrence].

811   _____. <u>Modern English Literature</u>. (London: Oxford
       University Press, 1970). [A critical account of the works
       of a selection of novelists, poets and dramatists from G. B.
       Shaw to G. Orwell with a 10-page Epilogue on the fifties.
       Chapters II and IV are devoted to the "Edwardian Realists,"
       and to Joyce and Lawrence respectively; sections from Chapter
       I deal with H. G. Wells and G. K. Chesterton; Chapter V deals
       with the Bloomsbury Group, and Chapter VII with the novel-
       ists of the thirties--C. Isherwood, I. Compton-Burnett, L.
       H. Myers, A. Koestler, W. Lewis, E. Waugh, G. Greene, and A.
       Wilson].

812   Rodway, Allan Edwin. <u>Science and Modern Writing</u>. (London
       and New York: Sheed and Ward, 1964). [Surveys the impact

of science on literary criticism and creative literature.
References to H. G. Wells, K. Amis, A. Huxley, J. Joyce, and
the psychological fiction of D. H. Lawrence, J. Joyce, and
V. Woolf].

813   Roger-Henrichsen, Gudmund. England Genskabes 1945-1960.
Koldrigsarenes mennesker, problemer og stil; britiske romaner.
(Copenhagen: J. H. Schultz Forlag, 1961).   [A portrait of
postwar England: the years of the cold war, the people,
their mores, disillusionment and protests, and their several
problems as reflected in the novel, with special reference
to I. Murdoch, D. Lessing and L. Durrell].

814   Rogers, Robert. A Psychoanalytic Study of The Double in
Literature.   (Detroit: Wayne State University Press; Toronto: Copp, Clark, 1970).   [Selects works by Kafka, J. Barth,
J. Conrad and H. James to illustrate the psychological framework of doubling which is "sporadic rather than omnipresent
in literature," and to show that it is a "basic literary process reflecting fundamental tendencies of the human mind and
not just an aberration on the part of a few authors"].

815   Romberg, Bertil. Studies in the Narrative Technique of the
First-Person Novel. Translated into English by Michael Taylor and Harold H. Borland. (Stockholm: Almquist and Wiksell,
1962).   [Part I gives a systematical survey of "the technical
features of narration in the first-person novel." Part II
analyses four novels--2 German, and Clarissa and L. Durrell's
Alexandria Quartet--to show the functioning of the different
devices of this narrative technique.   Appendix, pp. 311-319,
gives a brief historical survey].

816   Rosenbaum, S. P., ed. English Literature and British Philosophy. A collection of essays with an Introduction by the
Editor.   (Chicago and London: University of Chicago Press,
1973).   [The essays, even while displaying the relations
that exist between native philosophy and literature from
Bacon to V. Woolf, are restricted to those in which philosophy affects literature.   Chs. XIV and XV consider D. H.
Lawrence and V. Woolf].

817   Rosenberg, Edgar. From Shylock to Svengali: Jewish Stereotypes in English Fiction. (Stanford, California: Stanford
University Press, 1960; London: Peter Owen, 1961).   [Orig-
inally a doctoral dissertation entitled "Jewish Stereotypes
in English Fiction" presented to Stanford University, 1958.
Analyses two types: the Jewish criminal and the Jewish par-
agon as they appear in the English novel between 1795 and
1895. Also considers G. Greene, E. Waugh, J. Joyce and C.
P. Snow and the "type" they use on pp. 300-305].

818   Rosenfeld, Paul. Men Seen: Twenty-Four Modern Authors.
(New York: Dial Press, 1925; Books for Libraries Press,
1967).   [A miscellany of "men and women, related to each

other in point of time and in medium of expression" but moving in different directions. Included are J. Joyce and D. H. Lawrence].

819 Rosenthal, Erwin Theodor. Das Fragmentarische Universum: Wege und Umwege des modernen Romans. (München: Nymphenburger Verlag buchhandlung, 1970). [Analyses trends in the modern novel of England, Germany and France. Includes a section on J. Joyce's use of language, and one on S. Beckett's narrative manner].

820 Ross, Ernest C. The Development of the English Sea Novel from Defoe to Conrad. (Ann Arbor: Edwards, 1925; Folcroft Press, 1969). [Includes both English and American novelists. W. W. Jacobs and J. Conrad among others].

821 Ross, Harry. Utopias Old and New. (London: Nicholson and Watson, 1938). [Presents some familiar Utopias of the past, together with some of the present, interspersed with a few of the less well-known Utopias for discussion. Utopias chosen are described with some personal views. Includes H. G. Wells and A. Huxley].

822 Ross, Stephen D. Literature and Philosophy: An Analysis of the Philosophical Novel. (New York: Appleton-Century-Crofts, 1969). [Part I explains difficulties encountered in writing a novel of artistic merit and philosophic value, describes methods used to express philosophical convictions "without the characteristic forms of argument," and how the merit of such a work is enhanced. Part II analyses five selected novels by H. Hesse, F. Kafka, F. Dostoyevsky, A. Camus and H. James as being "most susceptible of the combined modes of literary and philosophic analysis"].

823 Rotter, Adolf. Der Arbeiterroman in England seit 1880. Ein Beitrag zur Geschichte des sozialen Romans in England. Schriften der deutschen wissenschaftlichen Gesellschaft in Reichenberg, Heft 7. (Reichenberg: Gebruder Stiepel, 1929). [A study of the development of the novel of the working classes equally divided between the eighties, nineties and the early 20th century. Considers works by R. Kipling, R. Whiteing, H. Brighouse, B. Kennedy, "R. Tressell," J. Welsh, and H. A. Vachell].

824 Rousseaux, André. Littérature du xx siècle. 7 Vols. (Paris: Editions Albin Michel, 1938+). [Studies of English and European writers. Vol. 1 includes an essay on C. Morgan's Sparkenbroke and one on V. Woolf and A. Huxley. Vols. 4 & 5 include an essay on each of G. Greene and S. Beckett respectively. Each of Vols. 6 & 7 includes an essay on V. Woolf].

825 Routh, H. V. Money, Morals and Manners as Revealed in Modern Literature. (London: Ivor Nicholson and Watson, 1935). [The study begins with the early part of the 19th century.

Chs. XII to XVI deal with the turn of the century and the first three decades of the 20th century. H. James, H. G. Wells, and J. Galsworthy among others].

826 _____. English Literature and Ideas in the Twentieth Century: An Enquiry into Present Difficulties and Future Prospects. (London: Methuen, 1946). [Part I covers the tendencies in the three genres in the pre-War period, and discusses the unsettlement in habits and ideas, problems of authorship, and the reading public. Part II considers the impact of the war, analyses the inter-war cultural atmosphere, and discusses the "leading interpreters" of the period, the tendency towards experimentation, and the "reorientation" of the thirties. R. Kipling, J. Conrad, H.G. Wells, A. Bennett, J. Galsworthy, J. Masefield, E. M. Forster, S. Maugham, D. H. Lawrence, J. Joyce, V. Woolf, A. Huxley, J. B. Priestley, and C. Morgan among others].

827 Roz, Firmin. Le Roman anglais contemporain. (Paris: Librairie Hachette, 1912). [Full length studies of five novelists: G. Meredith, T. Hardy, Mrs. H. Ward, R. Kipling, and H. G. Wells].

828 Rubin, Louis D., Jr. The Teller in the Tale. (Seattle and London: University of Washington Press, 1967). [Examines the way in which "the authorial personality telling the story" figures in a novel, its role, and to "what extent does one's experience in reading the novel actively involve the presence of the novelist" in works by H. James and J. Joyce among others].

829 Ruotolo, Lucio P. Six Existential Heroes: The Politics of Faith. (Cambridge, Massachusetts: Harvard University Press, 1973). [Discusses six heroes who are led "beyond self-worship toward a continually expanding vision of self and of world." Included are Clarissa Dalloway (V. Woolf), Rose Wilson (G. Greene), and Ralph (W. Golding)].

830 Russell, Bertrand. Portraits from Memory and Other Essays. (London: George Allen & Unwin; New York: Simon Schuster, 1956). [Includes portraits of H. G. Wells, J. Conrad, and D. H. Lawrence, and an essay on G. Orwell].

831 Russell, Frances Theresa. Touring Utopia: The Dealer of Constructive Humanism. (New York: Dial Press, 1932). [An account of the various manifestations of Utopian literature from earliest times to A. Huxley, and the place occupied by each in literature and thought. Includes R. H. Benson, A. Huxley, and H. G. Wells].

832 Sacks, Wolfgang. Der Anglo-Katholizismus im englischen Nachkriegsroman. (Halle: Buchdruckerei Aug. Klöppel, 1934). [Doctoral dissertation presented to Martin Luther University, Halle, Wittenberg. Traces the rise of Anglo-Catholicism to

the thirties. More emphasis on Anglo-Catholicism than the novel. Examines works by E. F. Benson, "G. A. Birmingham", S. Kaye-Smith, R. Keable, S. Leslie, C. Mackenzie, and E. Raymond among others].

833   Sackville-West, E. Inclinations. (London: Secker and Warburg, 1949). [Contains a chapter on each of H. James and J. Conrad, and another, Ch. VI, on E. Bowen and I. Compton-Burnett].

834   Sadleir, Michael. "Long Novels." Essays of the Year (1929-1930). (London: The Argonaut Press, 1930), pp. 229-252. [Reviews the publishing history of the long novel and its present condition in the light of two recent examples of the genre: J. B. Priestley's The Good Companion and J. C. Powys' Wolf Solent].

835   Sale, Roger, ed. Discussions of the Novel. (Boston: D. C. Heath, 1960). [A collection of "literary" essays beginning with N. Frye's attempt to "define" the novel. Section Two consists of essays that delineate different attitudes towards the history of the novel, and Section Three with the "relationship between the criticism of fiction and the life that fiction represents"].

836   Sandison, Alan. The Wheel of Empire: A Study of the Imperial Idea in Some Late Nineteenth and Early Twentieth Century Fiction. (London: Macmillan; New York: St. Martin's Press, 1967). [Originally a doctoral dissertation entitled "The Imperial Idea in English Fiction: A Study in the Literary Expression of the Idea, with Special Reference to the Works of Kipling, Conrad, and Buchan." (Peterhouse, Cambridge University, 1964)].

837   Sarbu, Aladar. Szocialista Realista Törekvések a modern Angol Regényben. (Budapest: Akadémiai Kiadó, 1967). [Traces the rise of socialist realistic tendencies in the English novel from the years prior to World War I to the contemporary scene. "L. G. Gibbon," M. Heinemann, L. Jones, D. Lambert, J. Lindsay, N. Mitchison, A. Sillitoe, "R. Tressell," E. Upward, J. Wain, R. Williams and others].

838   Savage, D. S. The Withered Branch: Six Studies in the Modern Novel. (London: Eyre & Spottiswoode, 1950; New York: Pellegrini & Cudahy, 1952). [Includes studies of E. M. Forster, V. Woolf, A. Huxley, and J. Joyce].

839   Schelling, Felix E. Appraisements and Asperities: As to Some Contemporary Writers. (Philadelphia & London: J. B. Lippincott, 1922). [Contains two brief notes on J. Conrad and H. James reprinted from The Evening Public Ledger (Philadelphia)].

840   Schirmer, Walter. Der englische Roman der neuesten Zeit.

(Kultur und Sprache, Vol. 1). (Heidelberg: Carl Winters
Universitätsbuchhandlung, 1923). [An 80-page booklet assess-
ing the accomplishments of H. G. Wells, J. Galsworthy, G.
Moore, A. Bennett, and J. Conrad, and remarks on the spiri-
tual freedom, range, and insight of the "New Generation."
Pages 59-77 give a sketch of each novelist and his works].

841 Schleussner, Bruno. Der neopikareske Roman: Pikareske Elemente in der Struktur englischer Romane 1950-1960. (Bonn:
H. Bouvier Verlag, 1969). [Considers the neo-picaresque
tradition in J. Wain's Hurry on Down, K. Amis's Lucky Jim
and K. Waterhouse's Billy Liar, and picaresque features in
the non-picaresque Under the Net by I. Murdoch, Room at the
Top by J. Braine, and Saturday Night and Sunday Morning by
A. Sillitoe, as well as the "basic patterns" of the Spanish
picaresque and English neo-picaresque].

842 Schluter, Kurt. Kuriose Welt im modernen englischen Roman.
Dartestellt an ausgewählten Werken von Evelyn Waugh und Angus
Wilson. (Berlin: Erich Schmidt Verlag, 1969). [Discusses
the creation and development of a "bizarre," strange and odd
world in six novels by E. Waugh and the old representation
of modern spheres of reality in four novels by A. Wilson].

843 Schmucker, Wilhelm G. Die moderne englische Jugend. Eine
Analyse nach Zeugnissen der neueren englischen Literatur.
(Bottrop: Wilh. Postberg, 1936). [Originally a dissertation
presented to the Faculty of Philosophy, Ernst-Moritz-Arndt-
Universität zu Greifswald. A study of modern English youth
based on the plays and novels of the 20th century. Includes
R. Aldington, C. Dane, J. Galsworthy, R. Macaulay, C. Mac-
kenzie, R. H. Mottram, and H. Walpole].

844 Scholes, Robert, ed. Approaches to the Novel. (Scranton,
Pennsylvania: Chandler Publishing, 1961; revised edition,
1966). [A collection of previously published essays and
excerpts from critical works on the novel. Attempts to supply
the general reader--and critic--with various approaches to
the novel by presenting problems and offering "some solutions
appropriate to any study of the novel in any language." Contributors are A. Warner, N. Frye, E. Auerbach, I. Watt, H.
Levin, L. Trilling, M. Schorer, M. Turnell, V. Woolf, N. Sarraute, E. M. Forster, R. S. Crane, P. Lubbock, and W. C.
Booth. See individual entries under Books and Periodicals].

845 _____. The Fabulators. (New York: Oxford University
Press, 1967). [Examines several dimensions of "modern fabulation"--return to story, "black humour" and allegory--and
contends that though it tends away from "the representation
of reality," modern fabulation "returns toward the actual
human life by way of ethically controlled fantasy," and provides "one answer to the great question of where fiction
could go after the realistic novel." L. Durrell, J. Joyce,
and I. Murdoch among others].

846 _____. Elements of Fiction. (London & New York: Oxford University Press, 1968). [Rather elementary and deals
with fundamentals in Part I. This is followed by three short
stories and commentaries in Part II].

847 _____, ed. Some Modern Writers: Essays and Fiction by
Conrad, Dinesen, Lawrence, Orwell, Faulkner, Ellison. (New
York: Oxford University Press, 1971). [Selections from their
critical writings and works of fiction followed by a short
note on each].

848 _____ and Robert Kellogg. The Nature of Narrative.
(London & New York: Oxford University Press, 1966). [A
historical and analytical study of narrative which seems to
endorse N. Frye's view of the concept of "genre," that the
novel is only ONE form of fiction].

849 _____. "The Narrative Tradition." The Novel: Modern
Essays in Criticism. Edited by Robert Murray Davis. (Englewood Cliffs, New Jersey: Prentice-Hall, 1969), pp. 16-27.
Reprinted from The Nature of Narrative. (New York: Oxford
University Press, 1966). [Advocates a broader perspective
for narrative literature than the post-Jamesian "novel-cen-
tered view"].

850 Schorer, Mark, ed. "Foreword: Self and Society." Society
and Self in the Novel: English Institute Essays, 1955.
(New York: Columbia University Press; London: Oxford University Press, 1956), pp. vii-xvi. [Distinguishes two kinds
of novels: the documentary, "written in a spirit of dissent
. . . shows the power of social authority" and the evocative
"reaching towards the condition of poetry, written in a spirit
of alienation."].

851 _____. The Novelist and the Modern World. (Tucson,
Arizona: University of Arizona Press, 1957). [Riecker Memorial Lecture No. 3. The novelist's problem is to "adjudi-
cate, in terms of structure, the claims of social convention
and the claims of individual aspiration," and the measure in
which these two extremes draw farther apart makes the problem
of containing them in a unified work proportionately more
acute].

852 _____. Modern British Fiction: Essays in Criticism.
(New York: Oxford University Press, 1961). [Essays by dif-
ferent writers to evaluate the major works of T. Hardy, J.
Conrad, F. M. Ford, E. M. Forster, D. H. Lawrence, J. Joyce,
V. Woolf. Also includes "Modern Fiction" by V. Woolf and
"Surgery for the Novel--or a Bomb" by D. H. Lawrence. See
separate entries].

853 _____. The World We Imagine: Selected Essays. (New
York: Farrar, Straus and Giroux, 1961; London: Chatto and
Windus, 1969). [Includes "Technique as Discovery," and

"Fiction and the Analogical Matrix" reprinted from The Hudson Review I:1 (Spring 1948), 67-87, and The Kenyon Review, XI:4 (Autumn 1949), 539-560. See entries under Periodicals. Also includes three essays on D. H. Lawrence].

854 *Schrey, Helmut. Didaktik des zeitgenossischen englischen Romans. Versuch auf der Grenze von Literaturkritik und Fachdidaktik. Beitrage zur Fachdidaktik, 10. (Wuppertal: Henn, 1970).

855 Schulze, Sigurd. Die Darstellung der Landbevölkerung im englischen Roman. (Düsseldorf: Verlag G. H. Nolte, 1937). [Originally a dissertation presented to Königsberg University. Traces the representation of the rural population in the English novel, especially the novel of the 19th century. Only two sections, pp. 16-27 and 100-115, discuss E. Phillpots, T. F. Powys, D. H. Lawrence, V. Sackville-West, and S. Kaye-Smith].

856 Scott, Dixon. Men of Letters. With an Introduction by Max Beerbohm. (London & New York: Hodder and Stoughton, 1916). [A collection of essays and literary criticisms published posthumously. Includes essays on each of R. Kipling, H. James, H. G. Wells, G. K. Chesterton, J. Masefield, and C.E. Montague].

857 Scott, Nathan A., Jr. The Climate of Faith in Modern Literature. (New York: Seabury Press, 1964). [A collection of ten essays by different writers on how the genres of poetry, novel and drama formulate Christian ideas that reveal the "rapprochement between art and faith." J. Joyce, G. Greene and W. Golding. See entry under Paul Elmen].

858 _____. The Broken Center: Studies in the Theological Horizon of Modern Literature. (New Haven: Yale University Press, 1966). [An essentially "theological order of discourse and evaluation" of the "negatively theological" character of modern American, English and Continental literature whose basic premise is that the "anchoring center of life is broken and the world is . . . abandoned and adrift." References to V. Woolf, J. Joyce, A. Huxley, and S. Beckett among others].

859 _____. Craters of the Spirit: Studies in the Modern Novel. (Washington, D.C.: Corpus Books, 1968; London and Sydney; Sheed and Ward, 1969). [Chooses eight novelists, among whom are T. Hardy, S. Beckett, and G. Greene, to describe a phase of literature distinguished by the complex notions of quest and exploration performed by the human spirit at a time when the "absence of God moves about . . . with the intimacy of a presence"; hence, the vision of hazard and prospect expressed by each novelist considered, as he "navigates some of the deepest craters of the human spirit"].

860 Scott-James, R[olfe] A[rnold]. Personality in Literature

1913-1931). (London: Martin Secker, 1913; revised and enlarged, London: Martin Secker, 1931; New York: Holt, 1932).
[Includes essays on H. G. Wells, A. Bennett, and G. K. Chesterton. The revised edition includes "1913-1931," a survey
that points out that in spite of the "admiration for novelty"
which followed the war, G. B. Shaw, A. Bennett, and H. G. Wells
still remain as "vital forces of the present" rather than
"honoured relics" of the past].

861 _____. Fifty Years of English Literature. 1900-1950.
With a Postscript--1951 to 1955. (London: Longmans, Green,
1956). [A study that focuses on the novel and poetry. See
Chs. IV, V, VII, XII, XIV and the Postscript for H. G. Wells,
A. Bennett, G. Galsworthy, H. James, J. Conrad, G. Moore,
F. M. Ford, E. M. Forster, N. Douglas, W. H. Hudson, D. H.
Lawrence, J. Joyce, V. Woolf, D. Richardson, C. Isherwood,
G. Greene, J. Cary and others].

862 Seeber, Hans Ulrich. Wandlungen der Form in der literarischen
Utopie: Studien zur Entfaltung des utopischen Romans in England. Göppinger Akademische Beiträge, No. 13. (Göppingen:
Verlag Alfred Kümmerle, 1970). [Discusses the emergence of
the utopian "novel" by analysing and comparing individual
literary utopias from More's "classic satire" to 20th century dystopias. S. Butler, A. Huxley, E. M. Forster and G.
Orwell among others].

863 Servotte, Herman. De verteller in de Engelse roman: Een
studie over romantechniek. With an English Summary. (Has-
selt: Uitgeverij Heideland, 1965). [A Dutch translation
and edition of a doctoral dissertation presented to the University of Leuven in 1962 originally entitled The Narrator in
English Fiction: A Contribution to the Literary History of
the Novel. Analyses two main aspects of narrative: the relation between the narrator and his fictional world, and the
relation between the narrator and his public. Also describes
the changes and interprets and explains the "succession of
these changes" in representative novels by D. Defoe, G. Eliot, H. James, D. H. Lawrence, J. Conrad, and J. Joyce].

864 _____. Literatuur als levenskunst. Essays over hedendaagse Engelse Literatuur. (Antwerpen: De Nederlandsche
Boekhandel, 1966). [A collection of nine essays on present-
day English literature, previously published. Includes an
essay on each of G. Greene, E. Waugh, L. Durrell, and two on
W. Golding. Underlying the essays is the assumption that the
reader's interpretation of the particular situation described
by the novelist is a necessary complement to the meaning of
a novel].

865 Seward, Barbara. The Symbolic Rose. (New York: Columbia
University Press, 1960). [Originally a doctoral dissertation
presented to Columbia University, 1953. Traces the rose symbol from Dante onwards, emphasising its importance and pop-

ularity as a "central expression of current times," especially in W. B. Yeats, T. S. Eliot, and J. Joyce. Ch. V, "The Contemporary Symbol," discusses the use of symbolic roses by V. Woolf, E. M. Forster, E. Bowen, and H. Green to express what they valued most on "the temporal plane," as well as its use by D. H. Lawrence, G. Greene and C. Williams. Ch. VII is devoted to Joyce's use of the rose].

866 Seward, William Ward, Jr. Contrasts in Modern Writers: Some Aspects of British and American Fiction Since Mid-Century. (New York: Frederick Fell, 1963). [A collection of brief essays and book reviews most of which had appeared in The Virginia Pilot or broadcast on the local Radio Station WMTI-FM in the fifties. Part Two, "British Majors and Minors," pp. 33-53, contains some sixteen "pieces" on English, Irish and Australian writers. These include three reviews of works on J. Joyce and D. H. Lawrence, and brief reviews of novels and stories by A. Huxley, J. Cary and R. Lehmann].

867 Shanks, Edward. First Essays on Literature. (London: Collins, 1923). [A collection of essays reprinted from The London Mercury, The New Statesman, and Saturday Westminster Gazette. Includes an essay on H. G. Wells and another "Reflections on the Recent History of the English Novel" reprinted from The London Mercury, IV (June 1921), 173-183. See entry under Periodicals].

868 _____. Second Essays on Literature. (London: Collins, 1927). [A collection of essays reprinted from The London Mercury, Quarterly Review and Illustrated Review. Includes an essay on each of R. Kipling, J. Conrad, and J. Galsworthy].

869 Shapiro, Charles, ed. Twelve Original Essays on Great English Novels. (Detroit: Wayne State University Press, 1960). [Includes an essay on each of D. H. Lawrence's Sons and Lovers, J. Conrad's Victory, J. Joyce's Ulysses and E. M. Forster's A Passage to India].

870 _____, ed. Contemporary British Novelists. Preface by Harry T. Moore. (Carbondale & Edwardsville: Southern Illinois University Press, 1965). [A collection of ten essays by American critics on K. Amis, L. Durrell, W. Golding, D. Lessing, I. Murdoch, A. Powell, A. Sillitoe, C. P. Snow, M. Spark, and A. Wilson. Essays tend, in varying degrees, to show the changes and effects produced by social changes upon current British writing].

871 Sherman, Stuart P. On Contemporary Literature. (New York: Holt, 1917; London: Grant Richards, 1923). [A study of literary themes and topics in ten English, American, French and Irish writers. Separate studies of H. G. Wells, A. Bennett, and H. James among others].

872 _____. My Dear Cornelia. (Boston: The Atlantic Monthly Press, 1924). [Includes a brief discussion on pages 27-

125

57 of H. G. Wells, J. Galsworthy, J. D. Beresford and D. H. Lawrence--among others--and their challenge of the "Idea of Chastity" in their novels].

873 _____. Critical Woodcuts: Essays on Writers and Writing. Illustrated with portraits engraved on wood by Bertrand Zadig. (New York and London: Charles Scribner's Sons, 1926; Kennikat Press, 1967). ["Twenty-six critical impressions" divided into three galleries. D. H. Lawrence (Ch. II) and H. G. Wells (Ch. VIII)].

874 Shroder, Maurice Z. "The Novel as a Genre." The Novel: Modern Essays in Criticism. Edited by Robert Murray Davis. (Englewood Cliffs, New Jersey: Prentice-Hall, 1969), pp. 43-57. Reprinted from The Massachusetts Review, IV (1963), 291-308. [See entry under Periodicals].

875 Shuster, George N. The Catholic Spirit in Modern English Literature. (New York: Macmillan, 1922; Books for Libraries Press, 1967). [A survey of the rise of the Catholic way of living and of looking upon life in England, especially in the 19th century, and how this Catholic Idea was used in literary art. The survey is aimed at the general reader rather than the scholar. R. H. Benson, "J. Ayscough," and G. K. Chesterton among others].

876 Sillitoe, Alan. "Both Sides of the Street." The Writer's Dilemma: Essays first published in the Times Literary Supplement under the heading "Limits of Control." Introduction by Stephen Spender. (London and New York: Oxford University Press, 1961), pp. 68-75. Reprinted from The Times Literary Supplement, 3045 (9 July 1960), 435. [See entry under Periodicals].

877 Simon, Irène. Formes du roman anglais de Dickens à Joyce. (Bibliothéque de la Faculté de Philosophie et Lettres de L'Université de Liège--Fascicule CXVIII). (Liège: Faculté de Philosophie et Lettres, 1949). [A study of form as an expression of the novelist's perception of reality, indicating the respective merits and characteristics of the "forme épique" of Dickens and Thackeray, the "dramatic" form of E. Bronte, G. Eliot, G. Meredith, T. Hardy, H. James and J. Conrad, and the "lyrical" form of D. H. Lawrence, V. Woolf and J. Joyce. Discusses the work of each writer in a separate chapter].

878 _____. Bloomsbury and Its Critics. Langues Vivantes No. 53. (Paris: Marcel Didier, 1957). [Lecture given at the University of Gröningen, 7 May 1957. Discusses the ethos of Bloomsbury, its shaping factors and its implications, and examines what the critics of Bloomsbury had to say about it].

879 Singh, Bhupal. A Survey of Anglo-Indian Fiction. (London: Oxford University Press, 1934). [Surveys 150 years of Anglo-Indian fiction, i.e., novels dealing with India written in

English, specifically of Englishmen in India, of Eurasians or Anglo-Indians. The survey is divided into three periods, the third beginning with the partition of Bengal in 1905 until 1930. R. Kipling, E. M. Forster, and E. Thompson among others].

880 Sitwell, Osbert. "A Note on the Novel." Penny Foolish: A Book of Tirades and Panegyrics. (London: Macmillan, 1935), pp. 298-302. [Examines briefly "detective fiction," and voices his dissatisfaction with the "decadence of the novel of the twenties" which he attributes to the novelists' confusion on what a novel should be, their not being "readable," and of their lack of "design" and "discipline"].

881 _____. "The Modern Novel: Its Cause and Cure." Trio: Dissertations on Some Aspects of National Genius. (London: Macmillan, 1938), pp. 47-93. [One of the Northcliffe Lectures delivered at the University of London, 1937. Enlarges upon the statements made in his "A Note on the Novel." After extolling the virtues of Dickens as a novelist, he suggests two principles for the modern novel which can take advantage of the increased rapidity of the human mind: the "cinematographic" and the "microscopic." Also suggests that the novel "be dreamt more than thought out . . . be a poem"].

882 Slater, John Rothwell. Recent Literature and Religion. (The Ayer Lectures. The Colgate-Rochester Divinity School). (New York and London: Harper, 1938). [An attempt to show how English and American fiction, drama, and poetry since 1900 still reflect, on occasion, "moods of faith in God and man." The second lecture, "Religion in Fiction: The Older Generation," deals with J. Conrad, T. Hardy, J. Galsworthy, H. G. Wells, A. Bennett, G. K. Chesterton and G. B. Shaw. The third lecture, "Religion in novels and dramas of Today," discusses three types: the literature of: "contemplative insight," "religion in practice," and "the lonely struggle of the soul." Brief references made to A. Huxley and H. Walpole].

883 Slawinski, Janusz, ed. W kregu zagadnieu teorii powiesci. (Wroclaw: Zaklad Narodowy Imienia Ossolinskich Wydawnietwo Polskiej Nauk, 1967). [A collection of essays in Polish by different writers on the theory of the novel covering narrative expression, problems of time, the "nouveau roman," and the interior monologue].

884 Sloan, Sam Berkley. The Contemporary Novel in English: An Outline for Study Clubs. (University of Iowa Extension Bulletin, No. 270). (Iowa City: University of Iowa, 1931). [Questions on twelve English and American novels. Each chapter includes one paragraph on the novelist, a list of five or six selected references and two or three pages of questions on a specific novel. Included are G. Moore's Esther Waters, H. G. Wells' Ann Veronica, J. Galsworthy's Beyond, H. Walpole's The Cathedral and S. Kaye-Smith's Green Apple Harvest].

127

885 Slochower, Harry. No Voice is Wholly Lost: Writers and
     Thinkers in War and Peace. (London: Dennis Dobson, 1946).
     [Examines two aspects of alienation in the war epoch: the
     philosophy of freedom or the surrender of absolutes, and the
     adoption of forms of traditional orthodoxy. Also attempts
     a reintegration of the two extremes. A. Huxley, D. H. Law-
     rence, and J. Joyce among others].

886 Slote, Bernice, ed. Literature and Society. A selection
     of papers delivered at the joint meeting of the Midwest Mod-
     ern Language Association and the Central Renaissance Confer-
     ence, 1963. (Lincoln: University of Nebraska Press, 1964).
     [Includes a study of G. Greene by M. Joselyn and another on
     H. James by J. G. Cawelti].

887 Smith, Samuel Stephenson. "The Psychological Novel." Craft
     of the Critic. (New York: Crowell, 1931; Books for Librar-
     ies Press, 1969), pp. 166-205. [Chapter X discusses the con-
     tribution of Stendhal, Dostoyevsky, N. Couperus, H. James,
     M. Proust, and J. Joyce separately].

888 Souvage, Jacques. An Introduction to the Study of the Novel.
     With a Foreword by W. Schrickx. (Gent: E. Story-Scientia
     P. V. B. A., 1965). [Part I, "The Theory of the Novel," is
     a scholarly work that discusses the various problems facing
     the novelist ranging from the language of the novel to nar-
     rative technique and "spatial form," and brings a conspectus
     of 20th century views to bear on them. Part II is a "system-
     atic bibliography for the study of the novel," American, Eng-
     lish and continental].

889 Souviron, José Maria. El principe de este siglo: La Liter-
     atura moderna y el demonio. (Madrid: Ediciones Cultura
     Hispanica, 1967). [Discusses various manifestations of "el
     demonio" in literature from Victor Hugo to the present. Con-
     tains sections on H. James, G. Greene, J. Green, and S. Beck-
     ett].

890 Speirs, John. "Poetry into Novel." Poetry Towards Novel.
     (London: Faber and Faber, 1971), pp. 283-334. [Investigates
     aspects and affinities in Dickens, the Brontes, G. Eliot, H.
     James, J. Conrad, and D. H. Lawrence which relate them to
     poets, and especially the Romantics].

891 Spencer, Sharon. Space, Time and Structure in the Modern
     Novel. (New York: New York University Press, 1971). [Ex-
     amines "Architectonic Novels"--novels that embody "approxi-
     mations of time-space fusions achieved by ingenious struc-
     tural procedures"--as responses by serious writers to the
     new theories of the nature of reality aroused by the specu-
     lations of modern science. V. Woolf and S. Beckett among
     others].

892 Spender, Stephen. The Destructive Element: A Study of Mod-

ern Writers and Beliefs. (London: Jonathan Cape, 1935).
[Examines the relations between modern literature and social
decay to reveal the consciousness in modern literature of a
destructive principle in modern society even when it seems
least apparent. H. James and D. H. Lawrence].

893 _____. The Creative Element: A Study of Vision, Despair and Orthodoxy Among Some Modern Writers. (London: Hamish Hamilton, 1953). [The study identifies three stages in
the development of the major movement in literature over the
past eighty years: a highly developed individual vision,
"anti-vision" and despair, and a return to orthodoxy. E. M.
Forster, D. H. Lawrence, G. Orwell, and E. Waugh among others].

894 _____, ed. The Writer's Dilemma: Essays first Published
in 'Times Literary Supplement' Under the Heading: 'Limits of
Control.' (London: Oxford University Press, 1961). [Ten
answers to the question: What are the limits beyond his own
control that threaten the modern writer? See entries by L.
Durrell, N. Sarraute, W. Golding, and A. Sillitoe under Per-
iodicals].

895 _____. The Struggle of the Modern. (London:
Hamish Hamilton; Berkeley: University of California Press,
1963). [A study of the "relationship of literature to modern life" in an attempt to place the modern movement in art
and literature into some kind of perspective. Part II distinguishes between the modern and contemporary, the former
relying on an "imagistic poetic" prose method--J. Joyce, D.
H. Lawrence, and V. Woolf coupling new techniques and a modern sensibility--and the latter a "realist" one in the tradition of A. Bennett, H. G. Wells, and J. Galsworthy. Rejects present downgrading of the literary experimentalists,
and argues against views held by P. H. Johnson, C. P. Snow
and others].

896 _____. "Is There no more Need to Experiment?" Opinions and Perspectives from 'The New York Times Book Review'.
Edited by Francis Brown. (Boston: Houghton Mifflin, 1964),
pp. 34-41. Reprinted from The New York Times Book Review,
(20 July 1958), 1. [See entry under Periodicals].

897 _____. "Literature." The Great Ideas Today. Edited by
Robert B. Hutchins and Mortimer J. Alder. (Chicago and London: Encyclopaedia Britannica, 1965), pp. 166-211. [A writer's review of the "year's harvest"--1964--of imaginative
writing. Pages 176-193 review English contemporary novelists'
concern with the "historic situation" within which the English find themselves--A. Wilson, D. Storey, J. Braine, C.
Isherwood--and the "academic convention" of W. Golding and
A. Powell].

898 Spicer-Simson, Theodore. Men of Letters of the British Isles.
Portrait Medallions from the Life. With critical essays by

Stuart P. Sherman. Preface by G. F. Hill. (New York: William Edwin Rudge, 1924). [Among the authors portrayed are A. Bennett, J. D. Beresford, G. K. Chesterton, J. Conrad, J. Galsworthy, W. H. Hudson, J. Joyce, H. Walpole, and H. G. Wells].

899   Spiel, Hilde. Der Park und die Wildnis: zur Situation der neueren englischen Literatur. (München: C. H. Beck'sche Verlagsbuchhandlung, 1953). [Contains a survey of the post-World War II English novel, and separate studies of V. Woolf, K. Mansfield, C. Morgan, E. Waugh, A. Huxley, E. Bowen, and I. Compton-Burnett].

900   Squire, J. C. Sunday Mornings. (London: Heinemann, 1930). [A collection of essays reprinted from The Observer. Includes one on H. G. Wells and two on J. Conrad].

901   Stallman, Robert W. The Houses that James Built and Other Literary Studies. (East Lansing, Michigan: The Michigan State University Press, 1961). [Separate essays that attempt an interpretation, in the light of the "New Criticism," of representative works of fiction which include, among others, works by H. James and J. Conrad. Part II reprints a slightly enlarged version of "Fiction and its Critics" from The Kenyon Review, XIX (Spring 1957), 290-299, in which he argues for the infusion of the poetic use of language in prose fiction].

902   Stanton, Robert. An Introduction to Fiction. (New York & London: Holt, Rinehart and Winston, 1965). [A 90-page introduction to the reading and critical study of the novel and short story. Explains principal elements, techniques, types of fiction and critical vocabulary].

903   Stanzel, Franz. Narrative Situations in the Novel: Tom Jones, Moby-Dick, The Ambassadors, Ulysses. Translated by James P. Pusack. (Bloomington and London: Indiana University Press, 1971). [Originally published as Die typischen Erzählsituationen im Roman dargestellt an Tom Jones, Moby Dick, The Ambassadors. (Vienna: Wilhelm Braumüller, Universitäts-verlagsbuchhandlung, 1955). Maintains a "double perspective" in the study of the structurally determinative elements in the novel: the standpoint of the author and that of the reader. Contends that the narrative situation determines structure by the order in which the author or narrator will unfold the fictional world to the reader, and the latter's expectations of a "definite consistency of illusion in the narrative"].

904   Starkie, Enid. From Gautier to Eliot: The Influence of France on English Literature, 1851-1939. (London: Hutchinson, 1960). [A general investigation of the prevalence and extent of the influence. Part I surveys the "haphazard manner" of the influence until World War I, and Part II discusses the influence in Poetry, Fiction, and Drama between the two Wars. Chapter

130

X, "Fiction," discusses the influence of Proust on J. Joyce
and V. Woolf, and mentions briefly the English version of
the "crapule hero" in G. Greene, the interest in children
and youth in H. Walpole, E. Bowen and R. Lehmann, and the
hero as "product of his physical condition" in J. Galsworthy,
C. Mackenzie, and H. Walpole. Also mentions briefly the influence in short story writing].

905   Starr, Meredith. The Future of the Novel. Famous Authors
       on their Methods: A Series of Interviews with Renowned Auth-
       ors. Preamble by W. H. Chesson. (London: Heath Cranton,
       1921; Boston: Small, Maynard, 1922; Kennikat Press, 1970).
       [The interviews had originally appeared in The Pall Mall Ga-
       zette. Includes M. Hewlett, R. Hichens, F. Swinnerton, S.
       Kaye-Smith, A. Waugh, D. Richardson, E. Phillpotts, J. D.
       Beresford, G. Frankau, E. T. Thurston, E. F. Benson, L. Gold-
       ing, H. Walpole and some fifty other writers].

906   Starr, Nathan Comfort. King Arthur Today: The Arthurian
       Legend in English and American Literature, 1901-1953. (Gain-
       esville: University of Florida Press, 1954). [Discusses
       20th century "innovations" which give new "vitality and or-
       iginality" and "fresh strength" to the Arthurian legend which
       is no longer confined to the narrative poem, but is now used
       to good effect in novels and plays. M. Baring, W. Deeping,
       A. Machen, J. Masefield, J. C. Powys, and C. Williams among
       others].

907   Steeves, Harrison Ross. "Prose Fiction." Literary Aims and
       Art. (Newark: Silver, Burdett, 1927), pp. 29-76. [Discusses
       the general aims and methods of narrative fiction--including
       the short story--and defines several of its forms. Brief
       references to J. Conrad, H. James, and A. Burnett].

908   Steinberg, Günter. Erlebte Rede: Ihre Eigenart und ihre
       Formen in neuerer deutscher, französischer und englischer
       Erzählliteratur. (Göppinger Arbeiten zur Germanistik, Nr.
       50/51). (Göppingen: Verlag Alfred Kummerle, 1971). [Orig-
       inally a dissertation entitled "Eigenart und Formen der er-
       lebten Rede" presented to the Faculty of Philosophy, Free
       University of Berlin. The study confines itself to the styl-
       istic and grammatical aspects of the interior monologue in
       German, French and English literature. J. Joyce, V. Woolf,
       J. Conrad, and S. Beckett. Includes a bibliography on the
       topic in Part II].

909   Steiner, George. "A Note on Literature and Post-History."
       Festschrift zum achtzigsten Geburtstag von Georg Lukacs.
       Edited by Frank Benseler. (Neuwid and Berlin: Hermann Luch-
       terhand Verlag, 1965), pp. 502-511. [On utopias and "ele-
       ments in the present that may contain hints of future reality."
       Brief reference to "the diminution of the reality-function
       in the novel" of the two world wars].

131

910   _____. Language and Silence: Essays on Language,
Literature, and the Inhuman. (New York: Atheneum; London:
Faber, 1967). [A collection of pieces, slightly altered
from their first appearances in periodicals or as Prefaces.
Mainly concerned with a "philosophy of language." Includes
two sections on "Lawrence Durrell and the Baroque Novel"
and "Building a Movement," (W. Golding)].

911   Steinmann, Martin, Jr. "The Old Novel and the New." From
Jane Austen to Joseph Conrad: Essays Collected in Memory
of James T. Hillhouse. Edited by Robert C. Rathburn and
Martin Steinmann, Jr. (Minneapolis: University of Minnesota Press, 1958), pp. 286-306. [Attempts to show in his
comparison of the 19th century novel with the 20th century
novel that the disappearance of the author in the latter
does not mean the elimination of the old conventions of
style, structure and point of view, but their replacement
with new conventions].

912   Stevenson, Lionel. The English Novel: A Panorama. (Cambridge, Massachusetts: The Riverside Press, 1960; London:
Constable, 1961). [An inductive approach that examines the
rise of prose fiction from the 15th century to the second
World War. Chapter XVI deals with "M. Corelli," D. Du Maurier, J. Conrad, H. G. Wells, A. Bennett, J. Galsworthy, S.
Maugham, and E. M. Forster, and Chapter XVII with D. H. Lawrence, J. Joyce, V. Woolf, F. M. Ford, C. Morgan, J. C. Powys,
W. Lewis, E. Waugh, G. Greene, J. Cary, and others].

913   _____. The History of the English Novel XI: Yesterday and After. (New York: Barnes & Noble, 1967). [An additional volume in the 10 volume History of the English Novel by Ernest A. Baker. Complements Vol. X (see above) by
including the contemporaries of A. Bennett and J. Galsworthy
--excluded from the previous volume--and brings the history
to the sixties].

914   Stevick, Philip, comp. The Theory of the Novel. (New York:
Free Press; London: Collier-Macmillan, 1967). [A collection of articles, previously published, grouped under "Generic Identity," Narrative Technique, Point of View, Plot,
Style, Character, Time and Place, and Symbol. See entries
for M. Shroder, N. Frye, M. Schorer, W. C. Booth, N. Friedman, P. Stevick, L. Lutwack, D. S. Bland, and V. Brumm under
Periodicals. Also includes excerpts from books by P. Bentley, H. James, E. M. Forster, W. J. Harvey, A. A. Mendilow,
and W. T. Tindall].

915   _____. The Chapter in Fiction: Theories of Narrative
Division. (Syracuse, New York: Syracuse University Press,
1970). [Contends that the imaginative use of chapters al-
ters the vision and import of novels, that the convention
of chapter-making is an object of meticulous craftsmanship,
and that the reader's response is enhanced by recognition

of the chapter as a fact of fiction].

916 Stewart, Douglas. The Ark of God: Studies in Five Modern
     Novelists: James Joyce, Aldous Huxley, Graham Greene, Rose
     Macaulay, Joyce Cary. (London: The Carey Kingsgate Press,
     1961). [W. T. Whitley Lectures for 1960. The five lectures
     are concerned with the "message" these writers have, not
     simply for the world, but the church].

917 Stewart, J. I. M. Eight Modern Writers. (Oxford and New
     York: Oxford University Press, 1963). [This is Vol. 12 of
     the Oxford History of English Literature, edited by B. Dob-
     rée, N. Davis and F. P. Wilson. Includes studies of H.
     James, J. Conrad, R. Kipling, J. Joyce, and D. H. Lawrence.
     Also contains bibliographies of primary and secondary sour-
     ces for each writer].

918 Stonier, G. W. Gog Magog and Other Critical Essays. (Lon-
     don: J. M. Dent, 1933). [Includes an essay on each of D.
     H. Lawrence, W. Lewis, and J. Joyce ("Words! Words!")].

919 Strachey, John. The Strangled Cry: On Orwell, Koestler,
     Chambers, and Pasternak. Edited by Stephen Spender & Mel-
     vin J. Laski. (London: Encounter Pamphlet Series, No. 3,
     1960; London: Bodley Head; New York: W. Sloane Associates,
     1962). [Examines the rejection of politics by those writers].

920 Straumann, Heinrich. "Zum Problem der Interpretation und
     Wertung zeitgenössischer Romanliteratur." Sprache und Lit-
     eratur Englands und Amerikas. Dritter Band: Die Wissen-
     schaftliche Erschliessung der Prosa. (Tübingen: Max Nie-
     meyer Verlag, 1959), pp. 79-100. [A review article on crit-
     ical works dealing with the evaluation and interpretation
     of contemporary novels].

921 Strong, L. A. G. Personal Remarks. (London: Peter Nevill,
     1953). [A collection of critical essays written over twenty
     years. Includes an essay on each of E. Bowen and H. Walpole,
     another on H. James and J. Joyce, and "Notes on Four Con-
     temporary Writers" (C. D. Lewis, R. Church, L. H. Myers, and
     E. M. Forster)].

922 Sühnel, Rudolf and Dieter Riesner, eds. Englische Dichter
     der Moderne: Ihr Leben und Werk. Unter Mitarbeit zahlrei-
     cher. (Berlin: Erich Schmidt Verlag, 1971). [A collection
     of essays by different critics on each of H. James, R. Kip-
     ling, J. Conrad, F. M. Ford, J. Galsworthy, H. G. Wells, W.
     Lewis, J. Joyce, V. Woolf, E. M. Forster, D. H. Lawrence,
     N. Douglas, S. Maugham, D. Sayers, E. Waugh, A. Huxley, G.
     Orwell, C. S. Lewis, A. Wilson, W. Golding, S. Beckett and
     others. Also includes an Introduction, "Eine Betrachtung
     über die englischen Klassiker der Moderne" by R. Sühnel].

923 Surmelian, Leon. Techniques of Fiction Writing: Measure

and Madness. Introduction by Mark Schorer. (New York: Doubleday, 1968). [An analysis of the "multiple means" by which the creative literary impulse behind a work of fiction manages to get itself expressed. References to J. Joyce, V. Woolf, H. James, S. Beckett, J. Conrad, S. Maugham, G. Greene, and A. Huxley among others].

924   Sutherland, William O. S., ed. Six Contemporary Novels: Six Introductory Essays in Modern Fiction. (Austin, Texas: Humanities Research Center, University of Texas, 1962). [A collection of essays--with the exception of the second on B. Pasternak--presented in the Department of English, University of Texas. Each develops a critical statement on an individual novel. Includes essays on each of L. Durrell's Alexandria Quartet, C. P. Snow's The Masters, and S. Beckett's Molloy].

925   Swinnerton, Frank. A London Bookman. (London: Martin Secker, 1928). [Selections from his montly letter to The Bookman (New York) from 1920 to 1927. Includes notes on J. Conrad, A. Huxley, F. M. Ford, D. H. Lawrence and N. Douglas, and The Letters of H. James. Also discusses the V. Woolf/A. Bennett controversy in two articles: "Mrs. Woolf on the Novel" and "Mrs. Woolf Again"].

926   _____. The Georgian Literary Scene. (London: Heinemann, 1935; rev. ed. London: Dent, 1938). [A literary and critical panorama of the age, containing "sketches, portraits and illustrative episodes" of writers. H. James, H. G. Wells, J. Conrad, A. Bennett, G. Moore, J. Galsworthy, S. Maugham, F. M. Ford, R. Macaulay, S. Kaye-Smith, "H. H. Richardson," O. Onions, J. D. Beresford, C. Mackenzie, G. Cannan, H. Walpole, V. Woolf, D. Richardson, E. M. Forster, D. H. Lawrence, J. Joyce, A. Huxley, W. Lewis, D. Garnett, P. G. Wodehouse, J. B. Priestley and other minor novelists, and poets and dramatists].

927   _____. "The Bridge of Ideas: British and American Novelists." Bridging the Atlantic: Anglo-American Fellowship as the Way to World Peace: A Survey from Both Sides. Edited by Sir Philip Hamilton Gibbs. (London: Hutchinson; New York: Doubleday, 1943; Books for Libraries Press, 1970), pp. 78-93. [Surveys the mode and tradition of the English novel, American indebtedness to it until the beginning of this century, the divergent tendencies with Dreiser and Sinclair in the U. S. novel and the "intellectual and intuitional gymnastics of D. Richardson, J. Joyce, V. Woolf," as well as the contrast between the "undeviating drive and punch . . . intensely critical, alert, sophisticated" of American novelists and the "musings upon the general spectacle of life, more often studies of individual characters" of the English].

928   _____. Authors I Never Met. With drawings by Alfred

134

E. Taylor. (London: Frederick Books; Allen and Unwin,
1956). [A collection of five talks on English novelists
broadcast on the B. B. C. third programme. Included are
H. James, J. Conrad, D. H. Lawrence, and N. Douglas. (The
note on N. Douglas was specially written for the publication
of the collection].

929 _____. Background with Chorus: A Footnote to Changes
in English Literary Fashion Between 1901 and 1917. (London: Hutchinson; New York: Farrar, Straus and Cudahy,
1956). [Observations on the novel mostly confined to Chapter II "From Henry James to Gissing," Chapter XV "Four
Young Novelists" (D. H. Lawrence, H. Walpole, C. Mackenzie,
and S. Maugham), and Chapter XVII "Three Older Novelists"
(H. G. Wells, J. Galsworthy, and A. Bennett)].

930 _____. Figures in the Foreground: Literary Reminiscences, 1917-1940. (London: Hutchinson, 1963; New York:
Doubleday, 1964). [Contains, like its predecessor, Background with Chorus: 1900-1917, reminiscences of people acquired as writer, publisher and reviewer].

931 Symons, Julian. "Of Crisis and Dismay: A Study of the Writings in the 'Thirties." Focus One. Edited by B. Rajan
and Andrew Pearce. (London: Dennis Dobson, 1945). [Exam-
ines the reasons which led to the "new vigour" of English
social realism in the poetry and prose of the thirties and
its "unheroic death" by the second World War].

932 _____. Critical Occasions. (London: Hamish Hamilton,
1966). [A collection of articles previously published. Includes two on G. Orwell, and one on each of A. Machen ("Dis-
torting Mirrors"), C. P. Snow ("Of Bureaucratic Man"), E.
Waugh and A. Powell ("A Long Way from Firbank"), and W. Lew-
is].

933 Talbot, Francis X., ed. Fiction by Its Makers. (New York:
The American Press, 1928). [A collection of essays previously published in America in which English, American and
French Catholic Novelists comment on the novel from a Catholic moral viewpoint. Among the contributors are C. Mackenzie and G. K. Chesterton].

934 Tate, Allen. "Techniques of Fiction." Collected Essays.
(Denver, Colorado: Alan Swallow, 1959), pp. 129-146. Re-
printed from Sewanee Review, LII (Spring 1944), 210-225.
[See entry under Periodicals].

935 Temple, Ruth Z. & Martin Tucker, comp. & eds. A Library of
Literary Criticism: Modern British Literature, 3 Vols.
(New York: Frederick Ungar, 1966). [Selected excerpts from
critical works on some 400 English 20th century writers.
Writers are listed alphabetically: Vol. I, A to G, Vol. II,
H to P and Vol. III, Q to Z. Excerpts, chronologically ar-

ranged, describe the qualities of a writer, "define his
status, indicate . . . something of his life and personality, and specify . . . [any] other pursuits." Also includes
a brief bibliography of writers' published works at the end
of each volume. Includes novelists from H. James and J.
Conrad to A. Sillitoe].

936 Tilford, John E., Jr. "Point of View in the Novel." Critical Approaches to Fiction. Edited by Shiv K. Kumar and
Keith F. McKean. (New York: McGraw-Hill, 1968), pp. 305-
315. Reprinted from Emory University Quarterly, XX:2 (Summer 1964), 121-130. [See entry under Periodicals].

937 Tillotson, Kathleen. The Tale and the Teller. (London:
Rupert Hart-Davis, 1959). [Inaugural lecture delivered at
Bedford College, University of London, 29 January 1959.
Advocates a reinstatement of the "teller," the narrative
"I" which has been discarded in the name of objectivity,
and discusses the possibilities of the method, "one of the
more delicate tools of narrative art"].

938 Tillyard, E. M. V. The Epic Strain in the English Novel.
(London: Chatto & Windus; Fair Lawn, New Jersey: Essential Books, 1958). [Contends that the novel is not "a literary kind" but a vague term that denotes "at most a prose
medium, some pretense of action, a minimum length, and a
minimum organisation," but which can "answer to most of the
habits of mind on which the literary kinds can be truly
based." Chooses works from English fiction that "are of or
near the epic kind" and explains his choice. Includes A.
Bennett, J. Conrad, H. James, and J. Joyce].

939 The Times Literary Supplement. Essays and Reviews, 1964,
Vol. 3. (London: Oxford University Press, 1965). [Con-
tains, among other items, reviews of individual novels.
Included are The Spire by W. Golding, How It Is by S. Beckett, Corridors of Power by C. P. Snow, Late Call by A. Wilson, The Valley of Bosses by A. Powell, and The Day the Call
Came by "T. Hinde"].

940 Tindall, William York. Forces in Modern British Literature,
1885-1956. (New York: Knopf, 1947; revised edition, New
York: Vintage Books, 1956). [Examines the meanings and
values of the changes in English literature, and its connec-
tions with French literature and "foreign ideas." Considers
E. M. Forster, A. Huxley, E. Waugh, A. Powell among others
in Chapter IV, G. Moore, A. Bennett, J. Galsworthy among
others in Chapter V, H. James, J. Conrad, D. Richardson, J.
Joyce and V. Woolf in Chapter VII, and G. Greene, D. H. Lawrence and J. Joyce among others in Chapter VIII].

941 _____. The Literary Symbol. (New York: Columbia University Press, 1955). [Determines the function and effect
of the symbol in literary creation, especially the modern

novel of J. Joyce, V. Woolf, and H. Green among others. "Supreme Fictions," pp. 68-102, gives a general treatment of the symbolist novel--"a creative relationship of images, rhythms and tones"--in the 20th century].

942   Toynbee, Philip. "Experiment and the Future of the Novel." The Craft of Letters in England: A Symposium. Edited by John Lehmann. (London: The Cresset Press, 1956; Boston: Houghton, Mifflin, 1957), pp. 60-73. Reprinted from The London Magazine, III:5 (May 1956), 48-56. [See entry under Periodicals].

943   Tradition and Experiment in Present-Day Literature. Addresses delivered at the City Literary Institute by J. D. Beresford, E. Blunden, O. Burdett, A. Dukes, T. S. Eliot, R. H. Mottram, C. K. Munro, E. Sitwell, A. J. A. Symons, "R. West." (London: Oxford University Press, 1929). [Includes "Tradition in the Novel" by R. H. Mottram and "Experiment in the Novel" by J. D. Beresford. See individual entries].

944   Tradition and Innovation in Contemporary Literature: A Round Table Conference of International PEN, Budapest, 16-17 October, 1964. [Deliberations of the Conference on Poetry, Prose Fiction, and Drama. Includes addresses by W. Cooper and W. Allen. See individual entries].

945   Trilling, Lionel. The Liberal Imagination: Essays on Literature and Society. (New York: The Viking Press, 1950; London: Secker and Warburg, 1951). [A collection of essays previously published. Includes an essay on H. James' The Princess Casamassima and one on R. Kipling. Also includes "Manners, Morals, and the Novel," and "Art and Fortune" reprinted from The Kenyon Review, X (1948), 11-27, and The Partisan Review, XV (December 1948), 1271-92. See entries under Periodicals].

946   Troy, William, Selected Essays. Edited, and with an Introduction, by Stanley Edgar Hyman. With a Memoir by Allen Tate. (New Brunswick: Rutgers University Press, 1967). [Includes two essays on each of H. James, J. Joyce, and D. H. Lawrence, and an essay on V. Woolf].

947   Tucker, Martin. Africa in Modern Literature: A Survey of Contemporary Writing in English. (New York: Frederick Ungar, 1967). [Surveys literature about Africa, written in English, in the 20th century by English, American and African writers, with special emphasis on the novel as a medium in which "social realism and commentary play an outstanding part." J. Buchan, J. Cary, E. Waugh, G. Greene, E. Huxley, and A. Burgess among others].

948   Turnell, Martin. Modern Literature and Christian Faith. (London: Darton, Longman & Todd, 1961). [Underlying the "Lauriston Lectures" for 1959 are two conflicting views:

that a writer's system of beliefs may strengthen his creative ability and broaden his range, or it may restrict his vision and stunt his talent. Discusses, in the second of the three lectures, D. H. Lawrence, E. M. Forster, and V. Woolf as delineators of modern man: the man of feeling versus the rational man, and adopts in the third lecture a Christian interpretation of the modern world, illustrating from G. Greene among others].

949 Tuzinski, Konrad. "Kultur--und Gesellschaftskritik im modernen englischen Zukunftsroman." Literatur - Kultur - Gesellschaft in England und America: Aspekte und Forschungsbeiträge. Friedrich Schubel zum 60. Geburtstag. Edited by Gerhard Müller-Schwefe and Konrad Tuzinski. (Frankfurt: Verlag Moritz Diesterweg, 1966), pp. 278-298. [Criticism of culture and society in the modern English anti-utopia. E. M. Forster, C. Haldane, G. Orwell, A. Huxley and others].

950 Tynan, Kenneth. Persona Grata. (London: Allan Wintage, 1953). [An alphabetically arranged portrait gallery in words and pictures of artists and writers. Included are I. Compton-Burnett, E. M. Forster, H. Green, G. Greene, and A. Koestler].

951 *Ueda, Tsutomu. Modern English Writers. (Tokyo: Kenkyusha, 1962).

952 Unterecker, John, ed. Approaches to the Twentieth Century Novel. With Introduction. (New York: Thomas Y. Crowell, 1965). [A collection of six essays by different critics that focus on technique in six 20th century novels. Includes J. Joyce's Portrait of the Artist, D. H. Lawrence's Women in Love and J. Conrad's Nostromo].

953 Urang, Gunnar. Shadows of Heaven; Religion and Fantasy in the Writing of C. S. Lewis, Charles Williams and J. R. R. Tolkien. (Philadelphia: Pilgrim Press, 1971). [Examines how the shape of each writer's belief correlates with "the unique literary qualities of his fiction" and questions whether "the pattern of belief represented" is "adequate to the experience and the developing consciousness of modern man"].

954 "The Uses of Comic Vision." The British Imagination: A Critical Survey from "The Times Literary Supplement." With an Introduction by Arthur Crook. (London: Cassell; New York: Atheneum, 1961), pp. 20-26. Reprinted from The Times Literary Supplement, 3054 (9 September 1960), ix. (Special No.). [See entry under Periodicals].

955 Vancura, Z. Dvadcat' let anglijskogo romana (1945-1964). (Moskva: Vysšaja Škola, 1968). [Twenty years of the English Novel. Translated from Czech into Russian by M. Arnautova and E. Olonova. Examines separately the "chroniclers"

138

of the period, the "Angry Young Men," the anti-colonial novel, the novel of the working classes, and the problems of the historical novel].

956 Van Doren, Carl & Mark Van Doren. American and British Literature Since 1890. (New York: D. Appleton-Century, 1925). Revised edition 1939. [Part Two, Chapter II "Prose Fiction," is an exposition of G. Moore, J. M. Barrie, J. Conrad, H. G. Wells, A. Bennett, J. Galsworthy, S. Maugham, D. H. Lawrence, A. Huxley, K. Mansfield, and V. Woolf].

957 Van Gelder, Robert. Writers and Writing. (New York: Scribner's, 1946). [Interviews with American writers mainly. Includes " H. G. Wells Discusses Himself and His Work," pp. 127-132, and "Mr. Maugham on the Essentials of Writing," pp. 138-142].

958 Van Ghent, Dorothy. The English Novel: Form and Function. (New York: Holt, Rinehart and Winston; London: Clarke, Irwin, 1953). [Studies of eighteen "classical" English novels in their historical sequence from The Pilgrim's Progress to A Portrait of the Artist to "ascertain and place in focus the pattern of each novel as an aesthetic whole." Includes H. James' The Portrait of a Lady, J. Conrad's Lord Jim, D. H. Lawrence's Sons and Lovers, and J. Joyce's A Portrait of the Artist as a Young Man].

959 *Van Kranendonk, A. G. De Engelsche Literatur Sinds 1880. (Amsterdam: Elsevier Uitgeversmaatschappij, 1924).

960 Varela Jácome, Benito. Novelistas del siglo XX. (San Sebastian: Agora, 1962). [Examines briefly aspects of the novel in France, Germany, Italy, Greece, England, and North America. Includes a brief essay on G. Greene as a Catholic novelist, one on the technique of A. Huxley and another on J. Joyce's Ulysses].

961 _____. Renovación de la Novela en el siglo XX. (Barcelona: Ediciónes Destino, 1967). [On the European Novel: Spanish, English, French, German and Italian. Contains a study (pp. 19-41) of the complex determining factors that led to the renewal of the novel in the 20th century, and studies of V. Woolf, J. Joyce, and A. Huxley].

962 Verschoyle, Derek, ed. The English Novelists: A Survey of the Novel by Twenty Contemporary Novelists. (London: Chatto & Windus; New York: Harcourt, Brace, 1936; Folcroft Press, 1969). [Twenty essays by English and American writers assessing important contributions by individual novelists toward the development of the novel from Chaucer to Joyce. Includes essays on each of H. James, S. Butler, J. Joyce, one on T. Hardy and J. Conrad, and another on E. M. Forster and V. Woolf].

963 Vickery, John B., ed. Myth and Literature: Contemporary

Theory and Practice. (Lincoln: University of Nebraska Press, 1966). [A collection of 34 essays to introduce "myth criticism," its theories, methods and problems. Part I deals with the nature of myth; Part II aims at relating generic types of plot, character and theme to similar elements in myth and folktales, and seeks to "evaluate the use of myth in critical theory and practice." The 21 essays in Part III apply myth criticism to individual literary works and authors, including J. Joyce's Finnegan's Wake, V. Woolf's To the Lighthouse, J. Conrad's Nostromo, and the shorter fiction of D. H. Lawrence].

964 Vines, Sherard. Movements in Modern English Poetry and Prose. With an Introductory Note by G. S. Gordon. (London: Oxford University Press; Tokyo: Ohkayama Publishing, 1927). [A map of the English literary world in the first quarter of the century. Ch. III, "Fiction and the Unrest of the Age" attempts to sketch the most significant "movements and cross-currents"--excluding popular fiction--by selecting novelists who are chiefly responsible for them. M. Sinclair, S Kaye-Smith, H. Walpole, A. Bennett, J. Joyce, D. Richardson, V. Woolf, R. Firbank, N. Douglas, A. Huxley, D. H. Lawrence, K. Mansfield, "R. West," E. M. Forster and others].

965 _____. 100 Years of English Literature. (London: Gerald Duckworth, 1950). [A survey of poetry, drama and the novel beginning with "Romantics and Victorians." Ch. XIII deals with The Modern Novel].

966 Vinson, James, ed. Contemporary Novelists. With a Preface by Walter Allen. (London: St. James Press, 1972; New York: St. Martin's Press, 1972). [A comprehensive reference guide for all living novelists writing in English. Each entry consists of a biographical sketch, a bibliography of writings until 1972, a comment by the novelist on his fiction, and a signed critical essay].

967 Viswanatham, Kalive. India in English Fiction. (Waltair: Andhra University Press, 1971). [An interpretative and evaluative study to show the varying attitudes to India as a theme in English fiction in selected novels by W. Scott, F. M. Taylor, R. Kipling, E. M. Forster, F. W. Bain, L. H. Myers and S. Maugham. Novels examined are arranged in chronological order].

968 *Vocadlo, Otakar. Anglicka literatura XX. Stolete (1901-1931). (Prague: Aventinum, 1932).

969 Vowinckel, Ernst. Der englische Roman der neuesten Zeit und Gegenwart. Stilformen und Entwicklungslinien. (Berlin: F. A. Herbig Verlagsbuchhandlung, 1926). [A study of the "Stilformen" and "Entwicklungslinien" or lines of development in the English novel from the Victorians to the early 1920's, including several American writers, and the short

story. E. F. Benson, S. Kaye-Smith, H. G. Wells, S. Butler,
C. Mackenzie, S. Maugham, F. Swinnerton, M. Hewlett, J. D.
Beresford, G. Cannan, D. H. Lawrence, J. Galsworthy, A. Ben-
nett, R. Macaulay, G. Moore, A. Huxley, V. Woolf, H. James,
J. Joyce, D. Richardson, J. Conrad and others].

970 _____. "Der englische Roman." Handbuch der Ausland-
skunde: Englandkunde, Vol. I. (Frankfurt am Main: Diesterweg, 1928), pp. 176-209. [A survey that traces trends
and fashions in the novel from Richardson to Galsworthy].

971 _____. Der englische Roman zwischen den Jahrzehnten
1927-1935. (Berlin: F. A. Herbig Verlagsbuchhandlung,
1936). [A sequel to Der englische Roman der neuesten Zeit
und Gegenwart, analyzing trends and classifying novelists
into neat compartments].

972 Wagenknecht, Edward. Cavalcade of the English Novel. (New
York: Henry Holt; London: Oxford University Press, 1943;
revised edition 1954). [A central concern with "value-
judgments" of the English novel from the fiction of Shakespeare's time to V. Woolf. Chapter XXIII "Towards a New Century" considers G. Gissing, G. Moore and S. Butler; Chapters XXIV-XXVIII J. Conrad, A. Bennett, H. G. Wells, J.
Galsworthy, and D. H. Lawrence; Chapter XXIX examines the
stream of consciousness in D. Richardson, J. Joyce and V.
Woolf. Also includes a substantial annotated bibliography
of individual novelists].

973 Wagner, Hans. Der englische Bildungsroman bis in die Zeit
des Ersten Weltkrieges. Swiss Studies in English, No. 27.
(Bern: Verlag A. Francke Ag., 1951). [Traces the evolution
of the English "Bildungsroman" from early Victorian times
to World War I, and contains a brief survey of its postwar
state. A. Bennett, H. G. Wells, G. Cannan, J. D. Beresford,
C. Mackenzie, S. Maugham, H. Walpole, A. Waugh, D. H. Lawrence, J. Joyce, V. Woolf, M. Sinclair, M. Baring, F. Swinnerton, W. Deeping, C. Morgan, and H. Spring].

974 Wain, John. Essays on Literature and Ideas. (London: Macmillan, 1963; New York: St. Martin's Press, 1966). [In-
cludes "The Conflict of Forms in Contemporary Literature"
reprinted from The Critical Quarterly (see entry under Periodicals), and two essays on G. Orwell].

975 Walcutt, Charles C. Man's Changing Mask: Modes and Methods
of Characterization in Fiction. (Minneapolis: University
of Minnesota Press; London: Oxford University Press, 1966).
[Explores and defines character as an essential component
of fiction, and considers this particular aspect in the modern novel, especially the American novel. Includes H. James,
J. Conrad, L. Durrell, A. Huxley, V. Woolf, J. Joyce, and
S. Beckett].

976 Waldemar, Charles. *Spielarten der Liebe: Erotische Elemente im modernen Roman*. (Flensburg: C. Stephenson-Verlag, 1962). [A study of the various representations of love in the modern European and American novels. Includes D. H. Lawrence, J. Joyce, J. Cary, G. Greene, and E. Waugh].

977 Waldock, A. J. A. "Experiment in the Novel: With Special Reference to James Joyce." *Some Recent Developments in English Literature*. A Series of Sydney University Extension Lectures. (Sydney: University of Sydney Extension Board, 1935), pp. 8-18. [Recognizes briefly three stages in his "summary scheme" of the technical development of the English novel--H. Fielding, H. James, and J. Joyce--and examines Joyce's experiments in *Ulysses* in an attempt to "place" him into perspective with his predecessors].

978 _____. *James, Joyce, and Others*. (London: Williams & Norgate, 1937; Books for Libraries Press, 1967). [Contains an essay on each of J. Joyce and H. James].

979 *Walker, Brenda Mary, comp. *The Angry Young Men: Aspects of Contemporary Literature*. Library Association. Special Subject List. No. 23. (London, 1957).

980 Wall, Stephen. "Aspects of the Novel 1930-1960." *The Twentieth Century: The Sphere History of Literature in the English Language*, Vol. 7. Edited by Bernard Bergonzi. (London: The Cresset Press, 1970), pp. 222-276. [Examines separately the achievements of S. Beckett, G. Greene, E. Waugh, A. Powell, J. Cary, H. Green, I. Compton-Burnett, E. Bowen, A. Wilson, W. Golding, L. Durrell, and I. Murdoch, indicating "some of the qualities" and distinctive contributions of each to the continuance of the novel as "the dominant literary form of the time"].

981 Wallace, A. Doyle and Woodburn O. Ross, eds. *Studies in Honor of John Wilcox*. (Detroit: Wayne State University Press, 1958). [A collection of eighteen essays by members of the Department of English. Includes an essay on J. Galsworthy, one on each of E. M. Forster's *Passage to India* and V. Woolf's *Mrs. Dalloway*, and a checklist of criticism on D. Richardson].

982 Walpole, Hugh. *The English Novel: Some Notes on Its Evolution*. The Rede Lecture, 1925. (Cambridge: University Press, 1925). [Questions whether the novel over the past 100 years has changed its aspects as to be no longer the novel at all].

983 _____, et al. *Tendencies of the Modern Novel*. (London: Allen & Unwin; New York: Peter Smith, 1934). [A collection of eight essays on the state of the novel in England, France, U. S. A., Germany, Spain, Russia, Italy and Scandinavia, all of which had appeared earlier in *The Fortnightly Review*. The essay on the English novel by H. Walpole is

reprinted from <u>The Fortnightly Review</u>, CXL (October 1933), 407-415. See entry under Periodicals].

984 Walsh, Chad. <u>From Utopia to Nightmare</u>. (London: Geoffrey Bles; New York and Evanston: Harper and Row, 1962). [Examines the decline of the Utopian novel and its displacement by "dystopia" or the "inverted novel" through a study of selected 19th and 20th century works. A. Huxley, A. Koestler, E. M. Forster, and G. Orwell among others].

985 Ward, A. C. <u>Twentieth Century Literature, 1901-1960</u>. (London: Methuen, 1964; New York: Barnes & Noble, 1965). [This was originally published as <u>Twentieth Century Literature, 1900-1925: The Age of Interrogation</u>. (London: Methuen, 1928). Enlarged and revised in 1940, 1956, and 1964. Part II examines H. G. Wells, A. Bennett, J. Galsworthy, and J. Conrad in separate studies. Chapter V surveys C. Mackenzie, H. Walpole, S. Maugham, D. H. Lawrence, A. Huxley, J. Joyce and others. Chapter VI, "Women Novelists," surveys the achievement of M. Sinclair, R. Macaulay, V. Woolf, D. Sayers, and I. Murdoch, and Chapter VIII surveys E. Waugh, G. Greene, G. Orwell, J. Cary, J. Wain, A. Wilson, L. Durrell, and others].

986 _____. <u>The Nineteen-Twenties: Literature and Ideas in the Post-War Decade</u>. (London: Methuen, 1930). [A review of literature in the twenties and a "free fantasia on contemporary themes." Considers the "new" fiction and the novelists' concern with time in Chapter III but the main emphasis is on H. G. Wells, A. Bennett, J. Galsworthy and the "Scroungers and Scavengers of Society"--D. H. Lawrence, A. Huxley, and R. Macaulay].

987 Warren, Austin. <u>Rage for Order: Essays in Criticism</u>. (Chicago: University of Chicago Press, 1948). [A collection of essays that postulate an equilibrium between the two contraries of intensity and calm for a successful work. Contains an essay on each of E. M. Forster and H. James].

988 _____. "The Nature of Modes of Fiction." <u>Theory of Literature</u>, by Rene Wellek and Austin Warren. (New York: Harcourt, Brace & World; London: J. Cape; Toronto: Clarke, Irwin, 1949), pp. 212-225. Reprinted in <u>Approaches to the Novel</u>. Edited by Robert Scholes. (Scranton, Pennsylvania: Chandler, 1961), pp. 5-22; <u>Perspectives in Fiction</u>. Edited by James L. Calderwood and Harold E. Toliver. (New York & London: Oxford University Press, 1968), pp. 73-89. [Surveys the fictional "world" of the novelist--plot, characters, narration and setting--and discusses the relationship of narrative fiction to life. Mentions H. James, J. Joyce, J. Conrad, J. Galsworthy, and V. Woolf among others].

989 Waugh, Alec. "A Novelist in Search of Plots that Thicken." <u>Opinions and Perspectives from 'The New York Times Book Re-</u>

143

view'. Edited by Francis Brown. (Boston: Houghton Mifflin, 1964), pp. 314-320. Reprinted from The New York Times Book Review, (24 July 1960), 4. [See entry under Periodicals].

990 _____. "The Novelist as Hero," The Best of 'Speaking of Books' from 'The New York Times Book Review'. Edited, with an Introduction by E. F. Brown. (New York: Holt, Rinehart and Winston, 1969), pp. 89-93. Reprinted from The New York Times Book Review, (20 June 1965), 2. [See entry under Periodicals].

991 Waugh, Arthur. Tradition and Change: Studies in Contemporary Literature. (London: Chapman & Hall, 1919; Books for Libraries Press, 1969). [The studies are divided between Poetry and Prose. Includes several Victorian novelists and H. James, J. Conrad, S. Butler, and J. Galsworthy, and "The New Realism" reprinted from The Fortnightly Review. See entry under Periodicals].

992 Weber, Conrad, G. Studies in the English Outlook in the Period Between the World Wars. With an Introductory Chapter on Periodology. (Bern: A. Francke A.-G, 1945). [Surveys the "forces and facts" responsible for shaping the modern outlook in English writing. References to A. Huxley, D. H. Lawrence, and V. Woolf among others].

993 Webster, Harvey Curtis. After the Trauma: Representative British Novelists Since 1920. (Lexington: The University Press of Kentucky, 1970). [A collection of essays on novelists who have matured during the years that included and followed World War I as distinct from the "older" writers who survived the "trauma but none of them felt it unusual enough to affect their already chosen directions." R. Macaulay, A. Huxley, I. Compton-burnett, E. Waugh, G. Greene, J. Cary, L. P. Hartley, and C. P. Snow].

994 Wedgwood, C. V., ed. The Author and the Public. Problems of Communication. The P. E. N. Congress, July 1956, London. (London: Hutchinson, 1957). [Contains a symposium on "Contemporary Techniques in Fiction" by William Cooper, L. P. Hartley, and K. O'Brien, pp. 161-179. See individual entries].

995 Weinmann, Robert. "New Criticism" und die Entwicklung bürgerlicher Literaturwissenschaft: Geschichte und Kritik neuer Interpretations-methoden. (Halle, Saale: Veb Max Niemeyer Verlag, 1962). [The history and criticism of new methods of interpretation in the study of literature. Part IV reviews the present situation in research, the contributions of H. James and P. Lubbock, and the concept of technique in narrative art].

996 Weintraub, Stanley. The Last Great Cause: The Intellectuals and the Spanish Civil War. (New York: Weybright and Talley, 1968). [Includes a chapter on each of G. Orwell (Homage to

144

Utopia) and A. Koestler (The Adopted Englishman), and another on G. B. Shaw and J. Joyce (The Aloof Olympians)].

997 Welty, Eudora. Place in Fiction. (New York: House of Books, 1957). Also in Critical Approaches to Fiction. Edited by Shiv K. Kumar and Keith F. McKean. (New York: McGraw Hill, 1968), pp. 249-267. Reprinted from The South Atlantic Quarterly, LV:1 (January 1956), 57-72. [See entry under Periodicals].

998 West, Anthony. Principles and Persuasions. (New York: Harcourt, Brace, 1957; London: Eyre & Spottiswoode, 1958). [A collection of essays that had been previously published in The New Yorker in which he tries to remove "the honeysuckle from the persona the writer poses to the public." Contains an essay on each of H. G. Wells, H. Walpole, G. Orwell, G. Greene, and I. Compton-Burnett among others].

999 West, Katharine. Chapter of Governesses: A Study of the Governess in English Fiction 1800-1949. (London: Cohen & West, 1949). [A "portrait-gallery of governesses" chronologically arranged. Examines works by H. James, H. Walpole, J. Conrad, V. Sackville-West, R. Lehmann, "E. M. Delafield," A. Thirkell, E. Taylor, I. Compton-Burnett, M. Baring, and T. H. White among others].

1000 West, Paul. The Growth of the Novel: Eight Radio Talks as Heard on C. B. C. University of the Air. (Toronto: Canadian Broadcasting Corporation, 1959). [Considers the progression of the five periods: The Classical, The Growing Realism of the post Renaissance, The Realistic Novel of the 18th century, The Nineteenth Century, and the "unsurpassed" variety of the twentieth. This last is examined in Chapters VII and VIII: "The Poet's Novel"--M. Proust, J. Joyce and V. Woolf--and "A Fractured Mirror"--E. M. Forster, D. H. Lawrence and G. Orwell among others].

1001 _____. The Modern Novel. (London: Hutchinson, 1963. Second edition in 2 Vols., 1965). [Juxtaposes in Vol. 1, Part II, the English and French novel. Vol. 2 examines the novel in U. S. A., Germany, Russia, and Spain. Shows a central concern with the novelist's effort "to bring psychology back into proportion with manners, and to augment these two with a view of man in the abstract." Emphasises, in his survey of English novelists from J. Galsworthy to D. Storey, the distincitve features of the English novel: its reliance on society and manners, farce, self-parody, use of plain language and the "deletion of metaphysics to the advantage of story"].

1002 _____. The Wine of Absurdity: Essays on Literature and Consolation. (University Park, Pennsylvania: The Pennsylvania State University Press, 1966). [The essays examine aspects of 20th century literary consolation. Each wri-

ter discussed mitigates, in some way for the author, the
absurdity of being human.   Includes D. H. Lawrence and G.
Greene].

1003   "West, Rebecca" [Cicily Isobel Andrews, née Fairfield].
The Strange Necessity: Essays and Reviews. (London: Jona-
than Cape, 1928).   [Includes an essay on each of J. Joyce
(The Strange Necessity), A. Bennett (Uncle Bennett), and
F. M. Ford (Galleous Reach)].

1004   _____. "Non-conformist Assenters and Independent In-
troverts."   The Court and the Castle: Some Treatments of
a Recurrent Theme. (New Haven: Yale University Press,
1957), pp. 203-224.   English edition subtitled The Interaction of Political and Religious Ideas in Imaginative Literature. (London: Macmillan, 1958), pp. 163-178. [Exam-
ines the role of the will of man in salvation, the saving
action of grace and the exploration of the self in H. James,
R. Kipling, J. Conrad, D. Richardson, and D. H. Lawrence
among others].

1005   _____. Ending in Earnest: A Literary Log. (New York:
Doubleday, Doran, 1931; Books for Libraries Press, 1967).
[A collection of contributions to The Bookman during 1929
and 1930 as "Letters from Europe." Includes notes on J.
Galsworthy, V. Woolf, E. Waugh and D. H. Lawrence].

1006   Westland, Peter. Contemporary Literature, 1880-1950. (The
Teach Yourself History of English Literature, Vol. VI).
(London: The English Universities Press, 1950). [Pages
37-83 survey the novel from H. James to J. Cary and enum-
erate its most significant features].

1007   Weyand, Herbert. Der Englische Kriegsroman. Strukturprob-
leme. Bonner Studien zur Englischen Philologie. Heft 18.
(Bonn: Peter Hanstein Verlagsbuchhandlung, 1933). [An examination of the various constituent topical elements of
the war novel and their treatment in novels by R. Aldington,
E. Blunden, G. Cannan, C. Edmonds, F. M. Ford, R. Graves,
J. K. Jerome, S. Kaye-Smith, W. LeQueux, A. Machen, C. Montague, R. M. Mottram, H. M. Tomlinson, H. Walpole, H. G.
Wells, "R. West," and H. Williamson. Also contains an annotated list of the best war books].

1008   Weygandt, Cornelius. A Century of the English Novel. To-
gether with an appreciation of novelists from the heyday of
Scott to the death of Conrad. (London: Brentano; New York:
Appleton, Century, 1925). [Emphasises the prevailing qual-
ity of each novelist. Includes a chapter on each of G.
Moore, J. Conrad, J. Galsworthy, M. Newlett, H. G. Wells,
A. Bennett, and the "Neo-Georgians"].

1009   White, John J. Mythology in the Modern Novel: A Study of
Prefigurative Techniques. (Princeton: Princeton University

146

Press, 1971). [Discusses the role of mythology, problems of interpretation and "patterns of correspondences" established between "subjects and classical prefigurations," mainly in contemporary English, American and German novels. J. Bowen, A. Burgess, A. Huxley, and J. Joyce among others].

1010 Wickes, George. Masters of Modern British Fiction. (New York: Macmillan, 1963). [Traces the course of 20th century English fiction through representative selections, chronologically arranged, illustrating a characteristic style or theme. J. Conrad, H. G. Wells, A. Bennett, J. Galsworthy, N. Douglas, F. M. Ford, J. Joyce, D. H. Lawrence, W. Lewis, E. M. Forster, V. Woolf, K. Mansfield, A. Huxley, G. Orwell, G. Greene, E. Waugh, J. Cary, I. Compton-Burnett, E. Bowen, K. Amis and L. Durrell. These are grouped in periods of two decades roughly, each beginning with an essay by a writers of the period and an average two-page critical introduction to each author].

1011 Wickham, Harvey. The Impuritans: A Glimpse of that New World Whose Pilgrim Fathers are Otto Weinniger, Havelock Ellis, James Branch Cabell, Marcel Proust, James Joyce, H. L. Mencken, D. H. Lawrence, Sherwood Anderson, et id genus omne. (New York: The Dial Press; London: Allen & Unwin, 1929). [Examines in some detail the "new prophets" who tried to free people from the Puritan ethic. Contains in Chapter X "The Cult of the Great," two sections on J. Joyce and D. H. Lawrence, pp. 235-243, and 258-268].

1012 Wild, Friedrich. Die englische Literatur der Gegenwart seit 1870. Drama und Roman. (Wiesbaden: Im Dioskuren Verlag, 1928). [A history of the novel and drama from 1870 to the twenties. Also discusses the various influences--from world events to psychology--which affected the growth of the English novel in that period].

1013 Williams, Harold. Modern English Writers: Being a Study of Imaginative Literature 1890-1914. (London: Sidgwick & Jackson, 1918. Revised Edition, 1925; Kennikat Press, 1970). [Part IV of the study is devoted to the novel. Chapter III surveys the "contemporary" scene of the male Edwardian novelists, and Chapter IV surveys the women novelists].

1014 _____. Outlines of Modern English Literature, 1890-1914. (London: Sidgwick & Jackson, 1920). [Extracts, sometimes rearranged and rewritten, from Modern English Writers. Part Four surveys the novel between 1890 and 1914].

1015 Williams, Raymond. Culture and Society, 1780-1950. (London: Chatto & Windus; New York: Columbia University Press, 1958). ["An account and an interpretation of our response in thought and feeling to the changes in English society since the late 18th century." Includes a chapter on D. H. Lawrence and one on G. Orwell].

1016 _____. The English Novel: From Dickens to Lawrence. (London: Chatto & Windus; New York: Oxford University Press, 1970). [Examines the "substance and meaning of community"--what it is, how it relates to individuals and relationships--as a central decisive bearing in the novel from Dickens to Lawrence. H. G. Wells, H. James, A. Bennett, J. Conrad, J. Joyce, and D. H. Lawrence].

1017 Williams, William Emrys. "Contemporary Fiction: Novel and Short Story." The Craft of Literature. (London: Methuen, 1925; Books for Libraries Press, 1967). [Indicates a few salient features of the 20th century novel, especially its subject matter, its submission to severer limitations than its precursor, and its relationship to the short story].

1018 Williamson, Claude C. H. Writers of Three Centuries, 1789-1914. (London: Grant Richards; Philadelphia: George W. Jacobs, 1920). [Seventy-five essays on English, American and European writers "as personalities under the action of spiritual forces, or as themselves so many forces." Includes essays on H. James, J. Conrad, H. G. Wells, R. H. Benson, R. Kipling, and G. K. Chesterton].

1019 Wilson, Angus. "The Novelist and the Narrator." English Studies Today: Second Series. Lectures and Papers Read at the Fourth Conference of the International Association of University Professors of English held at Lausanne and Berne, August 1959. Edited by G. A. Bonnard. (Berne: Francke Verlag, 1961), pp. 43-50. [Generalises from his own experience on the "schizophrenic process" or the division of personality between "the narrative part of the author and the rest of him," and the advantages and disadvantages of certain well known forms of narration].

1020 Wilson, Colin. The Age of Defeat. (London: Victor Gollancz, 1959). Published in U. S. A. as The Stature of Man. (Boston: Houghton Mifflin, 1959). [Argues that the "vanishing hero" or sense of defeat that underlies much of modern writing cannot be regarded solely as a "literary problem" and explained as such, but is a phenomenon that also needs explaining in terms of the "social crises" of the 20th century. Combines the evidence of sociology and of literature--American, English and European--to show that if the heroes of modern fiction seem "negative," it is because they reflect the world their creators live in. References to D. H. Lawrence, A. Huxley, J. Joyce, J. Cary and G. Greene among others].

1021 _____. "The Existential Temper of the Modern Novel." Christian Faith and the Contemporary Arts. Edited by Finley Eversole. (New York & Nashville: Albingdon Press, 1962), pp. 115-120. [Contends that the modern novel, defined and limited by its "endless interest in fine shades of psychological analysis and in the detailed description of physical actuality," cannot survive without asking questions that lead to a development of values, religious or moral. References to H. G. Wells, J. Joyce and G. Greene among others].

1022 _____. The Strength to Dream: Literature and the Imagination. (London: Victor Gollancz; Boston: Houghton Mifflin, 1962). [Contends that a writer's creative imagination produces a "reality that is consistent with the facts it sees around it"; hence, a study of the imaginations of different writers will reveal how these facts are interpreted, "and, indirectly, something about the nature and implication of the facts." E. Waugh, G. Greene, S. Beckett, H. G. Wells, J. R. R. Tolkien, D. H. Lawrence, and A. Huxley among others].

1023 _____. Eagle and Earwig. (London: John Baker, 1965). [A collection of essays on Literature and Philosophy, Individual Writers, and the Writer and Society written from an existential critic's viewpoint; i.e., rejecting the limits fixed by set and "limited human values" in order to probe "transcendental values" that question the meaning of human existence. Includes studies of J. C. Powys, L. H. Myers, and H. Williamson among others, with frequent references to J. Joyce, A. Huxley, A. Koestler, and D. H. Lawrence. Also includes "The Existential Temper of the Modern Novel." (See separate entry)].

1024 Wilson, Edmund. Classics and Commercials: A Literary Chronicle of the Forties. (New York: Farrar, Strauss, 1950; London: W. H. Allen, 1951). [The selection of literary articles contains one on each of A. Huxley and J. Joyce and two on E. Waugh].

1025 _____. The Wound and the Bow: Seven Studies in Literature. (London: W. H. Allen, Boston: Houghton Mifflin, 1941. Revised edition 1952). [Includes studies of R. Kipling and J. Joyce (The Dream of H. C. Earwicker)].

1026 Wilson, Harris, ed. Arnold Bennett and H. G. Wells: A Record of a Personal and a Literary Friendship. With an Introduction by the Editor. (Urbana, Illinois: University of Illinois Press; London: Rupert Hart-Davis, 1960). [Contains the correspondence between the two novelists which extends from 30 September 1897 to 17 February 1931. Some of the letters included are published for the first time as the Editor points out in the Foreword. The Introduction discusses the circumstances and background which led to the exchange of letters and the friendship, as well as the ideas and activities of the two men].

1027 Wilson, John. The Faith of an Artist. (London: Allen & Unwin, 1962). [Personal statements by writers, musicians, sculptors, painters, and architects over the past few decades.

Includes a statement by G. Greene from Why Do I Write and one by S. Maugham from A Writer's Notebook].

1028 Wingfield-Stratford, Esmé [Cecil]. The Victorian Aftermath 1901-1914. (London: George Routledge, 1933). [This is the third volume of the trilogy, the other two being The Victorian Tragedy and The Victorian Sunset. A Survey that brings out the social and political philosophy of the Edwardian Age. Notices the exposition of psychology through fiction and the general characteristics and accomplishments of J. Galsworthy, G. K. Chesterton, J. Conrad, H. James and H. G. Wells].

1029 Wood, Neal. Communism and British Intellectuals. (London: Victor Gollancz, 1959). [Surveys the impact of communism and its appeal to English intellectuals during the twenties and thirties. References to A. Koestler, G. Orwell, V. Woolf, and H. G. Wells among others].

1030 Woodcock, George. The Writer and Politics. (London: The Porcupine Press, 1948). [A sociological approach to literature and thought that considers society as a conditioning factor in a writer's work and life. G. Orwell, G. Greene, and A. Koestler among others].

1031 Woolf, Virginia. Collected Essays, 4 Vols. (London: The Hogarth Press; Toronto: Clarke, Irwin; New York: Harcourt Brace & World, 1966). [A reprint of the essays published in The Common Reader, The Common Reader: Second Series, The Death of the Moth and Other Essays, The Moment and Other Essays, The Captain's Death Bed and Other Essays, and Granite and Rainbow. Leonard Woolf indicates in his Editorial Note that "the essays in Vols. I and II are mainly literary and critical, those in Vols. III and IV are mainly biographical." Vol. I includes "Mr. Bennett and Mrs. Brown" (see entry under Periodicals), and essays on H. James, J. Conrad, G. Moore, E. M. Forster, and D. H. Lawrence. Vol. II contains the well known "Modern Fiction" in which V. Woolf contrasts the "materialist" novelists' way of depicting life--J. Galsworthy, H. G. Wells, and A. Bennett--with the task of "spiritual" novelists like J. Joyce in conveying "the luminous halo . . . this varying, this unknown and uncircumscribed spirit . . . with as little mixture of the alien and external"].

1032 "The Workaday World that the Novelist Never Enters." The British Imagination: A Critical Survey from 'The Times Literary Supplement'. With an Introduction by Arthur Crook. (London: Cassell; New York: Atheneum, 1961), pp. 13-19. Reprinted from The Times Literary Supplement, 3054 (9 September 1960), vii (Special No.). [See entry under Periodicals].

1033 Wurche, Erich. Die geistige Wandlung der Frau im modernen

englischen Frauenroman. (Greifswald: Buchdruckerei Hans
Adler, 1936). [Doctoral dissertation presented to the University of Greifswald. A study of the emergence of the "new
woman" of the 20th century and the problems she encounters
in her attitude and relation to men and children. S. Kaye-
Smith, M. Sinclair, M. Kennedy, C. Dane, R. Macaulay, V.
Woolf, and D. Richardson].

1034 Wyndham, Francis. "Twenty-Five Years of the Novel." The
Craft of Letters in England. Edited by John Lehmann.
(London: The Cressett Press, 1956; Boston: Houghton Mifflin, 1957). [Surveys English novelists from 1930 to 1956,
and brings out their "artistic isolation," the "prescribed
cycle" to which novelists conform before they are read,
the emergence of young writers since 1940, the importance
of dialogue in modern writing, and the high standard of
novel writing in England. Also suggests that in spite of
the absence "both of giants and brilliant newcomers" in the
fifties, the novel is nowhere more alive than in England].

1035 Yamamoto, Yukio. Gendai Eikiku Sakkaron. (Tokyo: Kiri-
hara Sohten, 1972). [In Japanese. A study of S. Maugham
and G. Greene with an appendix on the prevailing tendencies
in recent English novels].

1036 *Yoshida, Kenichi. Modern English Literature. (Tokyo:
Tarumi-shobo, 1959).

1037 Yuill, W. E. "Tradition and Nightmare--Some Reflections
on the Postwar Novel in England and Germany." Affinities:
Essays in German and English Literature. Dedicated to the
memory of Oswald Wolff (1897-1968). Edited by R. W. Last.
(London: Oswald Wolff, 1971), pp. 154-167. [Contrasts
the "massive English tradition of plain narrative and social
observation" in post-World War II fiction with the German
novel as a vehicle of "recondite philosophies and cultural
analysis, critically symbolic . . . pervaded by a night-
marish sense of fatality "].

1038 Zabel, Morton Dauwen. Craft and Character: Texts, Method
and Vocation in Modern Fiction. (London: Victor Gollancz;
New York: Viking Press, 1957). [A collection of essays,
many revised, which attempt to show the relation between
the novelist and his craft, the relevance of the novelist's
moral personality and intelligence to his work. Contains
a chapter on each of H. James, E. M. Forster, F. M. Ford,
and G. Greene among others, and four on J. Conrad].

1039 Zantieva, Diliara Girecvna. Angliskij roman xx Veka, 1918-
1939. (Moscow: Nauka, 1965). [Contains separate studies
of J. Joyce, V. Woolf, D. H. Lawrence, J. Galsworthy, H.
G. Wells, E. M. Forster, A. Huxley, and R. Aldington].

1040 Zeller, Hildegard. Die Ich-Erzählung im englischen Roman.

Sprache und Kultur der germanischen und romanischen Völker. Band XIV. (Breslau: Priebatsch's Buchhandlung, 1933). [Traces the first person narrative tradition from its epic origins and its beginnings in English literature to its flourish in the 18th century novel, and the continuation of the tradition in the 19th and 20th centuries. Includes H. G. Wells, A. Huxley, W. Gerhardi, A. P. Herbert, G. Dennis, and R. Graves].

1041 Ziolkowski, Theodore. Fictional Transfigurations of Jesus. (Princeton, New Jersey: Princeton University Press, 1972). [Surveys and analyses some twenty European, English, and American novels with a fictional narrative in which the characters and action, irrespective of meaning or theme, are "prefigured to a noticeable extent by figures and events popularly associated with the life of Jesus as it is known from the Gospels." Among the novels considered are G. Greene's The Power and the Glory, and A. Koestler's Darkness at Noon, with references to J. Joyce].

2.

Criticism: Articles

1042 Able, Augustus H. "A Short View of Contemporary Fiction,"
      DN, 21st Series (1948), 19-35. [Paper read before the Lit-
      erary Fellowship, Philadelphia, 5 May 1948. Examines the
      leanness and impoverishment of fiction, both English and
      American, in the late forties. Also maintains that the
      great activity upon the level of commercially stimulated
      writing is due to the strong "popular appetite for fiction."
      P. Toynbee and C. Isherwood among others].

1043 Adams, J. Donald. "Contrasts in British and American Fic-
      tion," EJ, XXVII:4 (Apr. 1938), 287-294. [Argues that dif-
      ferences go beyond theme or locale to national temper, ap-
      petite for novelty, sense of humour, sense of place, vital-
      ity, photographic realism and overstatement].

1044 _____. "Speaking of Books," NYTBR, (10 July 1949), 2.
      [Discusses the views expressed by G. Greene, E. Bowen, and
      V. S. Pritchett on the writer's responsibility in "Why Do
      I Write?" An Exchange of Views between Authors. (London:
      Percival Marshall, 1948)].

1045 _____. "Speaking of Books," NYTBR, (1 Apr. 1951), 2;
      (15 Apr. 1951), 2. [Attributes differences in content and
      manner in the English and American novel to "temperamental
      differences" between the two nations. The first article
      considers the English "love and pride in language," their
      "feeling of character," and "love of place," and the second
      remarks on differences in prose and expression].

1046 _____. "Speaking of Books," NYTBR, (31 Jan. 1954), 2.
      [On the tendency of English writers, especially novelists
      in the 20th century, to attempt a broader "range of literary
      forms" than the Americans. J. Conrad, A. Bennett, S. Maugham,
      J. Galsworthy, D. H. Lawrence, J. B. Priestley, S. Jameson,
      S. Kaye-Smith, C. Mackenzie and others].

1047 _____. "Speaking of Books," NYTBR, (3 Oct. 1954), 2.
      [Reviews the views of H. Nicholson, P. Toynbee, and D. Sayers
      on the present moribund state of the novel].

1048 _____. "Speaking of Books," NYTBR, (5 June 1955), 2.
      [Remarks on the novelist's presentation of character. E. M.
      Forster, J. Galsworthy, and S. Maugham].

1049 _____. "Speaking of Books," NYTBR, (2 Dec. 1956),
      2. [Considers remarks made by E. Bowen on a BBC broadcast
      concerning the matter of Fiction vs. Fact and how the former
      enlarges our experience].

1050 Adams, J. R. "Mysticism's Newest Handmaid," ACQR, XLV:177
      (Jan. 1920), 1-54. [On the English Catholic novel concerned
      with the "mysticism of suffering and the mysticism of God's
      Providence." R. H. Benson and O. K. Parr].

1051   . "The Modern Catholic Novel," ACQR, XLVII (Jan. 1922), 130-135. [Examines the novels of R. H. Benson, Canon Sheehan, "John Ayscough," Dr. Barry and M. Carmichael].

1052 Adcock, A. St. John. "British Authors and the War," Bookman (London), (Dec. 1915), 80-87. [Surveys English authors who have joined the Army since the beginning of World War I. Includes thirteen portraits of authors].

1053   . "Gods of Modern Grub Street," CM, LXI (May 1923), 33-37; LXI (June 1923), 204-207; LXI (Aug. 1923), 329-334; LXI (Sep. 1923), 431-435; LXII (Nov. 1923), 60-64; LXII (Dec. 1923), 149-152. [Separate essays on individual novelists. T. Hardy, R. Kipling, H. G. Wells, A. Bennett, J. Galsworthy, and J. Masefield].

1054   . "What's Wrong with Modern Fiction," Bookman (London), LXXVI (Apr. 1929), 16-17. [A review article on Storm Jameson's The Georgian Novel and Mr. Robinson emphasising her view that Georgian novelists, with but a few exceptions, have lost the art of telling stories].

1055 Addleshaw, S. "Modern Novels and Christian Morals," CQR, CV (Oct. 1927), 79-98. [Maintains that the trend of modern fiction is away from Christianity, and that it gives a view of life "antagonistic to the moral teaching of the church." Illustrates from novels by A. Bennett, J. Joyce, J. Galsworthy, and D. H. Lawrence].

1056 "After the War," NYTBR, (25 Apr. 1915), 164. [Editorial on the views of English writers as they have appeared in the London Book Monthly over the question, "How is the great war now raging likely to influence the permanent way of English literature?" Includes views by A. Bennett, E. Phillpotts, and H. G. Wells].

1057 Albérès, R. M. "Les Littératures européennes en 1963," TR, CLXXXI (1963), 72-90. [Examines the tendencies of literature in Germany, England, Italy, Spain, and France, and concludes that the "picaresque" and not the tragic is best suited to express the complexity of the external world].

1058   . "Renaissance du roman picaresque," RP, LXXV (Feb. 1968), 46-53. [On the new picaresque novel of the fifties and early sixties that replaced the "roman de la condition humaine" in Germany, England and Italy].

1059 Aldington, Richard. "Knowledge and the Novelist," TLS, 1900 (2 July 1938), 448. [A special article discussing the sort of knowledge a novelist possesses or should possess, taking into consideration that the novelist "entertains," i.e., should "interest" as well as "amuse". A. Huxley, J.

Joyce, and D. H. Lawrence. (Editorial on Article on page 449)].

1060 Aldridge, A. O. "Introduction: Shifting Trends in Narrative Criticism," CLS, VI (Sep. 1969), 225-229. [Contends that narrative criticism is paying more attention to the element of storytelling, and is moving beyond the confines of the novel to the epic and related works].

1061 Alexander, William. "Business in Fiction," CorM, LXV:386 (Aug. 1928), 176-185. [On the suitability of business as a theme in literature and why it was neglected so far. A. Bennett and J. Galsworthy among others].

1062 Allen, Hervey. "History and the Novel," AM, CLXXIII (Feb. 1944), 119-121. Reprinted in The Writer, LVII (Oct. 1944), 294-297, and The Craft of Novel Writing. Edited by A. S. Burack. (Boston: The Writer, 1948), pp. 139-148. [Examines history and the historical novel as art forms differing in aim and in kind].

1063 Allen, J. L., et al. "Will the Novel Disappear?" NAR, CLXXV (Sep. 1902), 289-298. [A symposium on J. Verne's view that the novel will disappear in "fifty or a hundred years from now," for it is declining in merit, will not be needed, and is being replaced by newspapers].

1064 Allen, Walter. "The Future of Fiction," NW&D, VIII:7 (1946), 91-94. [Makes "a plea for the free exercise of imagination and invention on the part of the novelist" as distinct from "fidelity to personal experience," the sine qua non of the novel of the thirties].

1065 _____. "The Novelist's Use of People," Listener, LIV: 1388 (6 Oct. 1955), 541-542. [Lifts the ban imposed by L. C. Knights on the discussion of character].

1066 _____. "Speaking of Books," NYTBR, (17 Nov. 1957), 2. [Calls on English fiction to learn the "self-consciousness" that gives the American novel "an extra dimension," so that it can interpret "all the implications of a changed Britain" to its readers].

1067 _____. "The Newest Voice in English Literature is from the Working Class," NYTBR, (20 Dec. 1959), 4. [Discusses the English working class in fiction and the emergence of its contemporary spokesmen, A. Sillitoe and K. Waterhouse].

1068 _____. "And Now the Mid-Atlantic Man," NYTBR, (27 Dec. 1964), 1. [Examines the mid-Atlantic novelists-- novelists equally at home on either side of the Atlantic

155

who know and appreciate both cultures without any sense of sacrificing "national identity." H. James, G. Greene, P. H. Johnson, and K. Amis among others].

1069 _____. "Recent Trends in the English Novel," English, XVIII:100 (Spring 1969), 2-5. [Surveys contemporary novelists, and remarks on the age being unpropitious to the novelist's art. Also predicts that the novel will become "more, not less, tentative and provisional . . . more personal, and the boundaries between fiction and autobiography . . . increasingly blurred"].

1070 Allen, W. Gore. "Evelyn Waugh and Graham Greene," IM, LXXVII (Jan. 1949), 16-22. [Originally a talk broadcast from Radio Eireann in November 1948. Examines the lines on which the two English Catholic novelists are thinking, and emphasises their differences in spite of the common Faith and religious experience they share].

1071 _____. "Rake's Progress of the English Novel," IER, (Dec. 1949), 534-539. [Describes the changes which the theme of love and its treatment underwent in the novel during the twenties and thirties, and the rise of the new regionalism].

1072 Allott, Miriam. "The Temporal Mode: Four Kinds of Fiction," EIC, VIII (1958), 214-216. [Gives tentative definitions to "four types of structure" resulting from "the alterations in sensibility" which took place in the 19th century].

1073 Allsop, Kenneth. "The Anguish of Remembrance," NYTBR, (7 Feb. 1965), 5, 38. [On the recent trend by H. Williamson, R. Hughes, C. P. Snow and E. Waugh to ignore the experiments of the Continent, America, and England's "literary fifties," and backtrack into worked-out country to recreate "a deeply insular English experience"].

1074 Ames, Van Meter. "The Novel: Between Art and Science," KR, V (Winter 1943), 34-48. [Discusses the role of the novelist in a science-ridden world].

1075 Amis, Kingsley. "Laughter's to Be Taken Seriously," NYTBR, (7 July 1957), 1, 13. [On the use of satire in fiction as an attack against vice and folly, and its revival in post-war England in the mode of Fielding rather than the pre-War modes of A. Huxley and E. Waugh].

1076 Anand, Mulk Raj. "English Novels of the 20th Century on India," AsR, (NS) XXXIX (July 1943), 244-257. [The text of a paper delivered 21 Apr. 1943, followed by discussion including comments by E. M. Forster, G. Orwell, and others. The paper examines "significant" novels by R. Kipling, E. M. Forster, F. A.

156

Steel, and E. Thompson, and maintains that English novelists were "maturing a kind of regional tradition of the English novel" in India, and reflecting the "general attitude towards Empire problems of the period"].

1077 Andersch, Alfred. "On the Short List," TLS, 3472 (12 Sep. 1968), 981-982. [Attributes the virtual absence of the contemporary English novel on the continent--with the exception of G. Greene and E. Waugh--to lack of "promotion" due to English understatement, lack of recognition and its non-conformism].

1078 Anderson, R.C. "Naval Warfare in Fiction," MM, LI (Aug. 1965), 243-252. [Examines novels by writers describing naval warfare as they expected it to be within a few years of the time of writing. Mostly 19th century with brief reference to three 20th century novels: The Invasion of 1910 by W. LeQueux, The Great Pacific War by H. C. Baywater, and The Autocracy of Mr. Parham by H. G. Wells].

1079 "Anglo-Indian Fiction," EdR, CCXLII: 494 (Oct. 1925), 324-338. [Maintains, in his review of the characteristics of Anglo-Indian fiction over the previous fifty years until E. M. Forster's Passage to India, that the tradition lives not so much by virtue of its literary qualities as by the "complete and unique picture that it has given of the life in India."].

1080 "Approach to the Novel," TLS, 2682 (26 June 1953), 413. [A leading article that attributes "the stunted growth of many modern novels" to the attitude that novel writing is a "spare-time occupation," and to economic subservience].

1081 ApRoberts, Ruth. "Frank Kermode and the Invented World," Novel, I (Winter 1968), 171-177. [A review article on Frank Kermode's The Sense of an Ending: Studies in the Theory of Fiction. (New York: Oxford University Press, 1967)].

1082 "Are There Any Good Books This Spring," LDig, LXXVII (7 Apr. 1923), 62-72. [Wide ranging comments on the state of the present-day novel followed by lists of books to be published in Spring].

1083 Arland, Marcel. "Sur le roman," NRF, 305 (Feb. 1939), 332-337. [Discusses several of E. M. Forster's statements on the novel and the seeming contradictions of the component requirements in a novel].

1084 Armstrong, Anne. "Farewell to 1932-Novels," SatR, (31 Dec. 1932), 697. [Reviews briefly the novel output for 1932 and lists outstanding novels].

1085 Armstrong, William A. "Recent Trends in English Poetry and

Fiction," <u>NM</u>, LI (Aug. 1950), 132-145. [Surveys the evolution of the novel since World War I].

1086   Armytage, W. H. G. "The Disenchanted Mecanophobes in Twentieth Century England," Extrapolation, IX (1968), 33-60. [Discusses the rejection of "scientific" Utopia by G. K. Chesterton, R. Kipling, E. M. Forster and H. Read, and the views of R. Warner, D. H. Lawrence, A. Huxley, and G. Orwell on Utopia].

1087   Arnold, Aerol. "Why Structure in Fiction: A Note to Social Scientists," <u>AQ</u>, X (Fall 1958), 325-337. [Emphasises the interdependence of structure and meaning, the former being the work of the intellectual poet, the result of the "critical faculty of the creative mind operating on the material"].

1088   Arns, Karl. "Der Moderne Englische Frauenroman," <u>NS</u>, XXXV:3 (1927), 192-196. [Maintains that women writers are more representative of modern trends, and more outspoken on sex. M. Sinclair, R. Wilson, C. Dane, S. Kaye-Smith, N. Mitchison, K. Mansfield, and D. Richardson].

1089   _____. "Der englische Gegenwartsroman in englischer Beleuchtung," <u>ZFEU</u>, XXVII (1928), 199-208, 278-288. [A review article on contemporary English critical works on the novel. Includes G. Gould's The English Novel of Today, G. Bullett's Modern English Fiction, and E. A. Drew's The Modern Novel: Some Aspects of Contemporary Fiction].

1090   _____. "Der katholische Geist in der neuen und neuesten englischen Literatur," NRe, X:1011 (1928), 1028-30. [A brief review of the Catholic spirit in the literature of the first two decades of the 20th century, with special reference to the novel. R. H. Benson, "J. Ayscough," W. Ward, F. M. Crawford, and M. Baring].

1091   _____. "Der Krieg in der englischen Literatur," <u>LHZ</u>, LXV:10 (1929), 742-744. [A brief survey listing novels and plays dealing with World War I].

1092   _____. "Moderne englische Literatur über den Roman," ZFEU, (1930), 421-427. [A review article on "literature about the novel." Includes P. Lubbock's Craft of Fiction, E. M. Forster's Aspects of the Novel, J. Carruther's Scherezade or The Future of the English Novel, E. Muir's The Structure of the Novel, W. L. Myers' The Later Realism, and W. L. Cross' The Modern English Novel].

1093   _____. "Neueste englische Literatur," <u>LHZ</u>, LXVII (1930-31), 86-91. [A survey of poetry, the novel and the short story published in 1929 and the early months of 1930].

1094 _____. "Familien-und Sippenkunde in der neuen englischen Literatur," ZNU, XXXIV (1935), 232-241. [Discusses
families, social background and genealogy in recent English
literature. A. Huxley, V. Woolf and F. M. Ford among others].

1095 _____. "Unsere Meinung: Überblick über die neuere
anglo-jüdische Literatur," NLit, XXXVII (1936), 178-181.
[A survey of recent Anglo-Jewish literature. References to
F. Swinnerton, G. Cannan, I. Cohen, and L. Golding among
others].

1096 * _____. "Die neue Gesellschaft im neuen englischen
Roman," Vilhaven u. Klasings Monatshefte, XL:ii (1926),
584-585.

1097 "Art and Anarchy," TLS, 2798 (14 Oct. 1955), 605; 2800
(28 Oct. 1955), 639. [Leading article discussing Leon Edel's
The Psychological Novel, 1900-1950, followed by a letter to
the Editor by E. R. Punshow].

1098 "The Art of Great Fiction," Nation, XCIV:2447 (23 May 1912),
510-511. [On the attempt of W. De Morgan, A. Bennett and
R. Pryce to bring back into fiction "the fulness of life"
characteristic of Mid-Victorian novels].

1099 Ashley, Robert P. "What Makes a Good Novel?" EJ, LX:5 (May
1971), 596-598, 620. [Suggests a series of eight tests to assess the greatness of a novel. Mentions A. Huxley, G.
Orwell, J. Conrad, J. Joyce, and W. Golding among others].

1100 Asimov, Isaac. "Escape into Reality," Humanist, XVIII:6
(Nov.-Dec. 1957), 326-332. [Discusses the "false-background
literatures" of fantasy, social satire and science fiction.
Includes in the second category Utopian literature as well
as Huxley's Brave New World and Orwell's 1984. Mainly interested in the third category].

1101 Astre, G. A., ed. "Cinéma et roman: eléments d'appréciation,"
RLM, V: 36-38 (Été 1958), 131-324. [Essays by several contributors on "Les Deux Langues," "Problèmes de l'adaptation,"
and "Echanges et convergences." Scattered references to
the English novel with one essay on V. Woolf].

1102 Atkins, John. "Marking Time: A Glance at the Contemporary
English Literary Scene," AR, IX (Sep. 1949), 332-339.
[Observes that the same names that claimed our attention
in the thirties are still the same in the forties, and remarks on the absence of young writers and the difficulties
they face].

1103 "The Autumn Flood: What the Public Reads," TLS, 616 (30
Oct. 1913), 487 - 488. [An estimate of the tendencies of
the novel-reading public and how each "imaginable human

interest" has its "prophet or inquirer among the novelists"].

1104 "Ayscough, John." [F. B. D. Bickerstaffe-Drew]. "A Dog and a Bad Name: Some Notes on the Novel and Its Present Function," ACQR, XXXVIII (Apr. 1913), 291-305. [Reviews briefly the English novel, from a Catholic viewpoint, to justify Catholics' distrust of it, and argues for the recognition of the novel as an effective "medium of promulgation" which should not be left entirely in the hands of non-Catholics, and suggests the usefulness of various types of Catholic novels].

1105 Bailhache, Jean. "Angry Young Men," LanM, 52 (Mar.-Apr. 1958), 143-158. [Examines works by K. Amis, J. Wain, J. Braine, and J. Osborne, the attitudes and tendencies they show in common--"an acute class-consciousness," and "inverted" snobbism, their provincialism and leftist-socialist views--as well as C. Wilson's views in "Beyond the Outsider."].

1106 Baiwir, Albert. "Jeunes Anglais 'en colère'," RUB, XVII (1964), 74-124. [Considers the ideological contents of the novels of the "Angry Young Men," why their writers have adopted a wholly non-conformist attitude that oscillates between discontent and anger, and the various manifestations of this attitude. J. Osborne, K. Amis, J. Wain, I. Murdoch, N. Dennis, "Thomas Hinde", J. Braine, A. Sillitoe, and C. Wilson].

1107 Baker, Denys Val. "The Younger British Writers," Norseman, (Jan.-Feb. 1948), 68-75. [Surveys the young post-World War I poets and novelists of England, Ireland and Wales, and notices the lack of a sense of common purpose, a "disgust with political and material movements," and a "passionate concern for individual values"].

1108 Balakian, Nona. "The Flight from Innocence: England's Newest Literary Generation," BA, XXXIII (1959), 261-270. [Surveys the writings of J. Osborne, I. Murdoch, K. Amis, J. Braine, and J. P. Donleavy, emphasising their "insight into the contemporary scene," and their ability "to distil the philosophical essence of [the] time and to create authentic character"].

1109 _____. "The Prophetic Voice of the Anti-Heroine," SWR, XLVII (Spring 1962), 134-141. [Examines the decline of the "romantic ideal" and the conventionally "desirable and vulnerable" heroine, and her replacement by creatures "devoid of feminine charm, sensibility and passion." Illustrates from American novels but contains references to D. H. Lawrence, S. Maugham, and G. B. Shaw].

160

1110 Balmforth, Ramsden. "'A Challenge to Novelists,' A Reply to Dr. Lyttleton," HJ, XXXVIII:1 (Oct. 1939), 115-123. [Rejects E. Lyttleton's views (see below), and proposes that the novelist or dramatist be "free from the limitations of conventional beliefs and decaying mythologies," and adopt what J. Maritain calls "true Humanism" which finds "the principle of the world in a Spirit greater than man," a "heroic humanism"].

1111 Banzie, Eric de. "When the Novelist Looks at Life," LR, 38 (1936), 260-265. [On the problem of distinguishing between fiction and fact in contemporary novels. R. Whiteing, H. G. Wells, and S. Maugham].

1112 Barclay, Rev. William. "Religion in Contemporary Fiction," ExpT, (Nov. 1939), 76-79. [Surveys briefly three kinds of novels where the keynote is either a revolt against accepted standards and teachings of morality, or despair, or Christianity as a "solution of life." W. Deeping, H. G. Wells, G. Frankau, H. Walpole, and A. S. M. Hutchinson].

1113 Bard, Joseph. "Tradition and Experiment," EDH, XXI (1944), 103-124. [Prefers to use "modern" in the Arnoldian sense meaning a craving for moral and "intellectual deliverance of man," and substitutes experiment for it when referring to 20th century English writers. Also dwells on Bergson's "durée interieure" and Joyce's experiments, and questions what is meant by the "Spirit of the Age"].

1114 Barlow, George. "L'Anti-Utopie moderne," Esprit, 3 (1961), 381-396. [Surveys briefly the methods of Utopia since Thomas More, and the distinctive features of anti-Utopia, expecially its despair, with special emphasis on the anti-Utopias of G. Orwell and A. Huxley in the past thirty years].

1115 Barnes, Hazel E. "Literature and the Politics of the Future," UDQ, V (Spring 1970), 41-64. [Examines literature which "in its response to the contemporary situation seeks to point the way toward a different kind of future." C. S. Lewis and A. Huxley].

1116 Barnes, John. "Politics and the English Novel: Post-War Britain as seen through the eyes of contemporary Novelists in this Country," Crossbow, X (Jan.-Mar. 1967), 36-38. [Describes briefly novelists's attitudes to the "decadence" of England, their frustration with the welfare state, and the "liberal failure" generally. C. P. Snow, H. Williamson, E. Waugh, K. Amis, I. Murdoch, A. Sillitoe, A. Wilson, W. Golding, R. Williams, and J. Cary].

1117 Barr, Donald. "Freud and Fiction," SatR, XXXIX (5 May 1956), 36. [Considers, in a brief note, Freud's contribution to fiction as giving to symbolism a "better excuse than the

occultism on which many British and American writers had
been tying to their symbolic practice at the turn of the
century"].

1118   Barth, J. Robert. "The Value-Functions of the Novel and
        Its Criticism," Renascence, X:1 (Fall 1957), 11-18. Re-
        printed in the Twenty-Fifth Anniversary Issue of Renascence,
        XXV:4 (Summer 1971), 227-234. [Maintains that the critic
        should not concern himself only with the form, structure
        and technique of a novel but also with the writer's "meta-
        physical attitude" to the experience he creates, and "judge
        the premises" of the novelist in "accordance with what he
        himself believes to be true"].

1119   _____. "Theology and Modern Literature," America,
        (11 Feb. 1961), 626-627, 630. [Discusses the relationship
        between theology and modern literature, especially the
        novel as a "vehicle for serious ideas" in recent years].

1120   Barzun, Jacques. "Venus at Large: Sexuality and the Limits
        of Literature," Encounter, XXVI: 3 (Mar. 1966), 24-30.
        [Discusses sexuality as deserving limitless literary ex-
        pression versus detailed description of the sex act. Brief
        references to D. H. Lawrence and J. Joyce].

1121   Bateman, May. "Catholic View in Modern Fiction," CathW,
        CII (Feb. 1916), 577-589; also in FR, CV (Mar. 1916), 526-
        537. [Discusses the "subtlety and directness of view" in
        Catholic writing in the early days of World War I. Ref-
        erences to H. G. Wells, "J. Ayscough," and R. H. Benson].

1122   Bates, H. E. "Novelist's Ear: Conversation in English
        Novels," FR, CXLV (NS) CXXXIX (Mar. 1936), 277-282. [Con-
        siders the question of speech in the novel and the novelist's
        responsibility to record it for it is the "key to the char-
        acter of an age." References to G. Moore and D. H. Lawrence
        among others].

1123   Bateson, F. W. "Contradictory Aspirations of the Novel,"
        Listener, LI: 1314 (6 May 1954), 781. [Discusses the ten-
        dency of the novel qua novel to tell a story and its ten-
        dency to mean something larger than itself as a work of
        art].

1124   Bayley, John. "Two Catholic Novelists," NR, CXXXII (Feb.
        1949), 232-235. [Considers the "novel with a purpose" as
        written by G. Greene and E. Waugh].

1125   _____. "The Novel and the Life Standard," LM, VIII:2
        (Feb. 1961), 60-66. [Examines the "partisan sense" of life
        implied in novel writing as distinct from "the sense of
        vitality or the sense of inclusiveness." E. M. Forster,

162

D. H. Lawrence, and H. James among others].

1126 _____. "The Points of Novels," The Times, (27 Dec.
1962), p. 9. [Calls for the "continuation of social awareness" in the novel. J. R. Ackerley and B. Brophy].

1127 Beach, Joseph Warren. "The English Sentimentalists," NAR,
CCXVI:800 (July 1922), 89-101. [Examines A. S. M. Hutchinson's If Winter Comes and H. Walpole's The Captives to illustrate the characteristics of the English sentimentalists].

1128 _____. "New Intentions in the Novel," NAR, CCXVIII:813
(Aug. 1923), 233-245. [Examines J. Hergesheimer's Java Head
and D. Richardson's Pilgrimage series to describe the "new
spirit" of aestheticism in fiction. References to F.
Swinnerton and J. Conrad among others].

1129 _____. "Proud Words," AtM, CXXXII:4 (Oct. 1923), 511-
515. [On the vocabulary of novelists, expecially their
"mania for indicating emotion by means of adjectives." A.
S. M. Hutchinson, F. Swinnerton, and H. Walpole among others].

1130 _____. "Sawing the Air," AtM, CXXXII (Nov. 1923), 629-
633. [On the mechanical and "suicidal practice" of A. S. M.
Hutchinson, F. Swinnerton and H. Walpole to use superlatives
and repetitions to denote "extremity of feeling"].

1131 _____. "The Novel From James to Joyce," Nation, CXXXII:
3440 (10 June 1931), 634-636. [Examines Joyce's developments
of James' novelistic formulas of restricted viewpoint, plot,
author's self-effacement, and realism].

1132 Beary, Thomas John. "Religion and the Modern Novel," CathW,
CLXVI (Dec. 1947), 203-211. [Examines the post 1940 interest
in some aspect of man's relation with God as revealed in
novels by G. Greene, A. Huxley, E. Waugh, and American novelist H. Sylvester].

1133 Becher, Hubert. "Priestergestalten in der Romanliteratur der
Gegenwart," SZ, CLIII (1953), 345-355. [Examines the priest
as hero in contemporary English, French, and German novels.
G. Greene, B. Marshall, and A. J. Cronin among others].

1134 Beck, Ronald. "Art and Life in the Novel," JAAC, XXXI:1 (Fall
1972), 63-66. [Attributes to the "natural novel myth" the
confusion arising from a failure to distinguish between
"life as inchoate raw subject matter . . . and life as novelistic life," and the tendency of critics to see life and
art in the novel in "dialectical terms, as opposite or antagonistic forces"].

1135 Beck, Warren. "Abstract and Chronicle," CE, XXI:3 (Dec. 1959),
117-126. [Discusses the "controlled" tension between the

concrete and abstract which, he contends, is a condition
of creativity in fiction. Brief references of J. Conrad,
H. James, and E. M. Forster].

1136 Beharriell, Frederick J. "Freud and Literature," QQ, LXV
(Spring 1958), 118-125. [A review article on E. Jones'
The Life and Work of Sigmund Freud in which he attempts a
"kind of poll" of significant English, American, German, and
French writers' attitudes to, and use of, psychoanalysis.
D. H. Lawrence and J. Joyce among others].

1137 Belgion, Montgomery. "British and American Taste," EJ,
XVII:3 (Mar. 1928), 185-193. [Attributes the contrast between the "slow and enduring" fame of a novelist in England
and the "sudden yet fleeting" fame of a novelist in U. S. A.
to the different literary tastes of the two countries.
A. S. M. Hutchinson, B. Marshall, P. Gibbs, E. M. Forster,
M. Kennedy, J. Galsworthy, and V. Woolf among others].

1138 Bellow, Saul. "Where Do We Go from Here: The Future of
Fiction," MQR, I (1962), 27-33. Reprinted in To the Young
Writer: Hopwood Lectures, Second Series. Edited by A. L.
Bader. (Ann Arbor, Michigan: University of Michigan Press,
1965), pp. 136-147. [Emphasises the need in the novel for
"new ideas about humankind . . . discovered and not invented," which should be seen "in flesh and blood" and not
merely asserted].

1139 _____. "The Writer as Moralist," AtM, CCXI (Mar. 1963),
58-62. [Argues that the writer, whether he considers himself a "moralist" or a "purely objective artist," cannot
divorce his moral function from art for he "bears the burden
of priest or teacher." G. Greene, J. Joyce, and A. Koestler
among others].

1140 Bel'Skii, A. "Orealisticheskom romane zapada 1955-1965kh
gadov," Permskii universitet, Perm', CLXXXVIII (1968), 3-
18. [Notes the "epic form" in the social realistic novel of
the Western World, including England in the second postwar
decade. G. Greene and J. Wain among others].

1141 Bennemann, H. "Der II Weltkrieg im englischen Roman," WZUL,
XII (1963), 533-539. [Surveys some 64 World War II novels
by 44 authors to ascertain the ideological position of the
war generation, the concept of the "hero," and attitudes of
German fascism to their own side and to communism].

1142 Bennett, Arnold. "The Novel-Reading Public," NA, IV (4 Feb.
1909), 304; (11 Feb. 1909), 325; (18 Feb. 1909), 347. Reprinted in The Author's Craft and Other Critical Writings of
Arnold Bennett. Edited by Samuel Hynes. (Lincoln: University of Nebraska Press, 1968), pp. 75-86. [Describes, in a

light vein, the characteristics of the Middle Class which forms the backbone of his public, and which rarely, if ever, provides material for the novelist].

1143 _____. "The Story Teller's Craft: II. Writing Novels," EngRev, XIV (June 1913), 349-360. [Considers "sense of beauty," "intensity of vision," and "fineness of mind" as essential attributes to a novelist, and examines "design" and "semblance to life" in novel writing].

1144 _____. "Is the Novel Decaying?" CasMF, (28 Mar. 1923), 47. Reprinted in Things That Have Interested Me. (New York: George H. Doran, 1926), pp. 160-163; also in The Author's Craft and Other Critical Writings of Arnold Bennett. Edited by Samuel Hynes. (Lincoln: University of Nebraska Press, 1968), pp. 87-89. [Contends that the "foundation of good fiction is character-creating, and nothing else"].

1145 _____. "Progress of the Novel," Realist, I (Apr. 1929), 3-11. Reprinted in The Author's Craft and Other Critical Writings of Arnold Bennett. Edited by Samuel Hynes. (Lincoln: University of Nebraska Press, 1968), pp. 90-98. [Classifies novels into three categories characterized by 1) breadth of outlook, 2) destructiveness and constructiveness of criticism implied, and 3) sympathy or antipathy towards individual characters. H. G. Wells, J. Joyce, D. H. Lawrence, R. H. Mottram, J. Galsworthy, V. Woolf, and A. Huxley].

1146 Bensen, Alice R. "Certain Problems of Distancing in the Twentieth Century Novel," LL, 6 (1962), 312-313. [A short note on experiments at which the human being and his actions are distanced: stream of consciousness or expressionistic techniques, isolation of man "from some or most of his non-self from his past," and many distances at once].

1147 Benson, E. F. "Two Types of Modern Fiction," LMer, XVII (Feb. 1928), 418-427. [Discusses "M. Arlen's" The Green Hat and V. Woolf's Mrs. Dalloway as examples of two different types of modern fiction, apparently opposed, but whose "consanguinity" is found in two ruling principles: "the lust for nakedness"--one for the body and the other the soul--and the total "absence of joy" in them].

1148 Bentley, Phyllis. "The Story-Teller in Fiction," Bookman, (London), LXXXI (Oct. 1931), 11-13. [Discusses the "complex use" of the storyteller device. M. Beerbohm, H. James and J. Conrad among others].

1149 _____. "Is the British Novel Dead?" SatR, XIX (28 Jan. 1939), 3-4, 14. [Rejects J. Strechey's statement on the "general decay of English imaginative letters" by citing the achievements of E. Bowen, R. C. Hutchinson, G. Greene,

E. C. Large, G. Jones, R. Warner, L. Cooper, A. Brown and J. Hanley--the generation then rising into literary prominence--as proof that the genre is "robustly alive and kicking"].

1150 _____. "Contemporary British Fiction," EJ, XXVIII:4 (Apr. 1939), 251-261. [Surveys the novel in the thirties and reveals V. Woolf and A. Huxley as the two "innovators and pioneers" dominating the scene in spite of older writers like H. G. Wells and S. Maugham, or the "familiar and respected figures" of H. Walpole and F. B. Young and the controversial C. Morgan. Also groups S. Jameson, R. Bates, J. Hanley, J. L. Hodson, F. Tilsley, and W. Greenwood as novelists with definite social aims, and highlights "consciousness" as the contribution of the novelist to literature in the twenties and thirties].

1151 _____. "'Tell Me a Story': The Art of Narrative," CE, I:2 (Nov. 1939), 118-127. [Remarks on the absence of, and need for, a critical history of the art of narrative, narrative being central to the novel, and examines its various kinds bringing out the use of "panorama" and "scene" in it. S. Jameson, J. Galsworthy, A. Bennett, and V. Woolf].

1152 _____. "The Armistice Period in British Fiction," NYTBR, (31 Aug. 1941), 2, 12. [Discusses English fiction between 1919 and 1939, its variety, the changes it introduced, and its salient features, and concludes that it is an age of "experiment" rather than achievement].

1153 _____. "England in Her Fiction," LJ, LXVI:1 (1 Sep. 1941), 695-699. [Examines diversity, scenery, speech and custom in the English regional novel. A. Bennett, A. J. Cronin, W. Holtby, J. B. Priestley, and H. Walpole among others].

1154 _____. "Telling a Story," SatR, XXIX (21 Dec. 1946), 7-8, 30. [Illustrates the need for a critic to explore "the art of narrative." Also explains scene, description and summary in novel writing].

1155 _____. "The Changing Novel," Listener, XLV:1143 (25 Jan. 1951), 149-150. [Describes the changes in technique, in subject matter, and in aim of the novel today by comparing it to the mid-Victorian "pattern" of the novel].

1156 _____. "Yorkshire and the Novelist," EDH, XXXIII (1965), 145-157. Reprinted in KR, XXX:4 (1968), 509-522. [Examines what Yorkshire offers the novelist--landscape, forms of vigorous and concise dialect speech, contrasts--and the special qualities that characterise the Yorkshire novelist. S. Jameson, L. Walmsley, W. Holtby, J. B. Priestly, L. Cooper, T. Armstrong and others].

1157   Beresford, J. D. "Psycho-Analysis and the Novel," LMer,
       (Feb. 1920), 426-434. [Discusses the applicability of
       psychoanalysis to fiction, and suggests that "properly com-
       prehended and applied," i.e., assimilated and transmuted
       so as to become a personal experience and conviction, and
       not merely utilized deliberately and intellectually, psycho-
       analysis may become "a powerful influence in the novel of
       the future"].

1158   _____. "Successors of Charles Dickens," Nation, (Lon-
       don), XXXIV (29 Dec. 1923), 487-488. [Questions V. Woolf's
       condemnation of H. G. Wells, J. Galsworthy, and A. Bennett
       for their inability to create character in the manner of
       Dickens or Thackeray, and attributes the difference to the
       20th century novelists' "change of attitude and of method"].

1159   _____. "Le Declin de l'influence de la psycho-analyse
       sur le roman anglais," MerF, (1 Sep. 1926), 257-266. [No-
       tices the elimination of the Freudian theme of sexual re-
       pression in the novels between 1918 and 1922, and attributes
       its decline to the critics' hostility to psychoanalysis
       and the reaction of the British reading public to such
       themes as "unhealthy" and "unpleasant," as well as the nov-
       elists' reluctance to run the risk in the face of such op-
       position. D. H. Lawrence, M. Sinclair, D. Richardson, C.
       Dane, "R. West", R. Macaulay, and A. Huxley].

1160   _____. "The Tendency of Recent Fiction," Bookman,
       (London), LXXVIII:464 (May 1930), 107-108. [Contends that
       the novel is moving away from the "classical and romantic
       forms" towards a "sterner . . . more depressing realism"].

1161   Bergonzi, Bernard. "The Novelist and His Subject-Matter:
       Reflections on Henry James and H. G. Wells," Listener, LX:
       1538 (18 Sep. 1958), 426-427. [A review article on L. Edel's
       and G. N. Ray's Henry James and H. G. Wells: A Record of
       Their Friendship, Their Debate on the Art of Fiction, and
       Their Quarrel. (Urbana: University of Illinois Press; Lon-
       don: Hart-Davis, 1958)].

1162   _____. "The Novel no Longer Novel," Listener, LXX:
       1799 (Sep. 1963), 415-416. [Discusses A. Robbe-Grillet's
       reaction against V. Woolf and M. Proust and the "impasse"
       of the modern novel, and maintains that contemporary fic-
       tion merely provides an "identikit" novel, "prefabricated"
       from ready made elements].

1163   _____. "Before 1914: Writers and the Threat of War,"
       CritQ, VI:2 (Summer 1964), 126-134. [Examines the concern
       of some writers with the eruption of violence and impending
       disaster. E. M. Forster, H. G. Wells, "Saki", G. K. Ches-
       terton, and E. Childers among others].

1164 _____. "The New Novel and the Old Book," Listener,
LXXVII:1982 (23 Mar. 1967), 391-392. [Contends that the
novel is not a dead form, and that in spite of the "revolt
against chronology" in the 20th century and the experimental "nouveau roman" of A. Robbe-Grillet and M. Butor, it
cannot "escape from the limitations of lineality and chronology"].

1165 _____. "Character and Liberalism," NBl, L:594 (Nov.
1969), 745-753; L:595 (Dec. 1969), 792-798. [Examines several attitudes to the problem of the "free standing character" in fiction, and whether it is likely to withstand the
"varieties of totalitarianism" in the 20th century].

1166 _____. "Sex and Modern Fiction," NBl, LIII (Apr. 1972),
148-154. [A revised version of a talk given to a conference on human sexuality at the Catholic Advisory Council,
May 1971. Outlines prevalent attitudes to sex, and attributes explorations of human sexuality in the novel to both
the "changed nature and possibilities of the fictional form,
and . . . changes in sexual mores" in the 20th century. J.
Joyce and D. H. Lawrence].

1167 Berlyn, Alfred. "Novel as Rostrum," LA, 277 (19 Apr. 1913),
187-189. Reprinted from The Academy. [Deplores the growing prevalence of the "modern tractate-novel" that became
fashionable with H. G. Wells' Socialist Utopias].

1168 Berthoff, Warner. "Fortunes of the Novel: Muriel Spark
and Iris Murdoch," MR, VIII (1967), 301-332. Reprinted with
an "Afterword" in Fiction and Events: Essays in Criticism
and Literary History. (New York: Dutton, 1971), pp. 118-
154. [A study of M. Spark's The Mandlebaum Gate and I.
Murdoch's The Red and the Green].

1169 Bevan, T. W. "The Profitable Reading of Fiction," HR, (Oct.
1929), 487-496. [Examines how T. Hardy's "The Profitable
Reading of Fiction" (1888), has stood the test of time and
experience by emphasising the "aesthetic profit" of fiction].

1170 Bickerton, Dere. "Modes of Interior Monologue: A Formal
Definition," MLQ, XXVIII (June 1967), 229-239. [Advocates
"formal over-conceptual" definitions and affirms that "inner speech" can only be rendered by one of the four methods
used for rendering spoken speech: direct speech (soliloquy),
indirect speech (omniscient description), free indirect
speech (indirect interior monologue), free direct speech
(direct interior monologue)].

1171 Bicknell, Frank M. "The Yankee in British Fiction," Outlook,
XCVI (19 Nov. 1910), 632-639. [Reviews the delineation of
the "Yankee" by A. Lang, R. Whiteing, E. P. Oppenheim, E.
W. Hornun and others, and lists their errors].

1172 Bird, Stephen B. "Natural Science and the Modern Novel," EngR, XVI (Feb. 1966), 2-6. [Criticises contemporary novelists for considering the knowledge of the universe as irrelevant to their art. L. Durrell, M. McCarthy, and W. Golding].

1173 Blakeston, Oswell. "'Sang-Freud' or The Thought-Stream Novel," Bookman, LXXXVII:517 (Oct. 1934), 36. [Considers J. Joyce and Freud not as having provided "ground plans" for present-day achievement but as having "solidly rounded off" the Victorian era. Also itemises protests against the "thought-stream" novel being "too personal in its appeal" and formless].

1174 Bland, D. S. "Too Many Particulars," ELT, II:1 (1959), 36-38. [Discusses the role and technique of background description in the novel. J. Galsworthy and V. Woolf].

1175 _____. "Endangering the Reader's Neck: Background Description in the Novel," Criticism, III (Spring 1961), 121-139. Reprinted in Critical Approaches to Fiction. Edited by Shiv K. Kumar and Keith F. McKean. (New York: McGraw-Hill, 1968), pp. 229-249. [Examines landscape description in the novel as something that cannot be detached and enjoyed for its own sake or "wished away . . . without damaging its fabric." This is a more elaborate treatment of the same topic in his earlier article "Too Many Particulars," ELT, II:1 (1959), 36-38].

1176 Blanke, Gustav H. "Aristokratie und Gentleman im englischen und amerikanischen Roman des 19. und 20. Jahrhunderts," GRM, XIII (July 1963), 280-306. [Argues that plot and character in the 19th and 20th century novel has thrown into doubt the conventional notion that the "gentleman" is of necessity an "aristocrat" or of high social standing. H. G. Wells, J. Galsworthy, S. Maugham, D. H. Lawrence, and E. Waugh among others].

1177 Blehl, Vincent F. "Look Back at Anger," America, CIII (16 Apr. 1960), 64-65. [A brief and "somewhat tentative" reappraisal of K. Amis, J. Osborne, C. Wilson, J. Wain and J. Braine, showing the "greater promise" of A. Wilson and W. Golding].

1178 Bley, Edgar S. "Identification: A Key to Literature," EJ, XXXIV:1 (Jan. 1945), 26-32. [Analyses the role of the identification process between reader and protagonist, and suggests ways in which its findings may be applied].

1179 Blissett, William. "Wagnerian Fiction in English," Criticism, V (Summer 1963), 239-260. [Illustrates the presence of "Wagnerism" -- incidental or topical references, thematic importance of characters experiencing Wagner's music, deriving techniques of fiction "from Wagner's mythical method

169

or leit motif system" -- in 20th century English and American fiction. V. Woolf, A. Bennett, and E. M. Forster among others].

1180 Bluefarb, Sam. "The Sea--Mirror and Maker of Character in Fiction and Drama," EJ, XLVIII:9 (Dec. 1959), 501-510. [Discusses the role of the sea in shaping and reflecting character, as "symbol of succor and escape," and as antagonist, in Conrad, O'Neill, and Melville].

1181 Bluestone, George. "Time in Film and Fiction," JAAC,XIX: 3 (Spring 1961), 311-315. [Discusses the general theory, especially the "usable distinction" and "comparative abilities" of the two forms to render various types of time].

1182 Blyton, W. J. "Idealism in Recent Fiction," HJ, XXXI:2 (Jan. 1933), 231-242. [Examines the "intuitive sympathetic approach," the new artistic faith that is more interested in what happens to "people's inner selves," their souls, rather than the "outward, the descriptive reported type of realism." A. Huxley, E. Waugh, V. Sackville-West, S. Kaye-Smith, J. D. Beresford, G. Cannan, and H. G. Wells].

1183 Bode, Carl. "The Redbrick Cinderellas," CE, XX:7 (Apr. 1960), 331-337. [Discusses the achievement of J. Osborne, J. Wain, K. Amis, and R. Hoggart, and their contributions to the "Movement"].

1184 Bodelsen, C. A. "Moderne engelske Satirikere," Tilskueren, XLV (Sep. 1928), 180-187. [A study of satire in selected novels by A. Huxley, O. Sitwell, W. Gerhardi, W. Douglas, R. Macaulay, and "E. M. Delafield"].

1185 Bohlen, A. "Lehrer und Schüler im neueren französischen und englischen Schulroman," NS, XLIII (1935), 127-161, 203-218, 239-266. [Considers 20th century novels, both English and French, where teacher and student play significant parts. Includes novels by L. A. G. Strong, A. Waugh, E. Phillpotts, H. Walpole, H. A. Vachell, and H. G. Wells].

1186 Boll, Ernest. "Social Causation in the English Novel of the Armistice Interval," Psychiatry, IX (1946), 309-321. [A study of the influence of contemporary social forces upon the structure and content of realistic novels between 1918 and 1939].

1187 _____. "A Rationale for the Criticism of the Realistic Novel," MLQ, IX (June 1948), 208-215. [Considers five different "sightings that the critic may take . . . to arrive at a fair and comprehensive judgment" of the realistic novel].

1188 Booth, Bradford A. "The Novel Has Attained its Full Dignity,"

LJ, LXXV:4 (15 Feb. 1950), 239-242. [Argues that the novel today not only fulfills its role as entertainer, but also has become a "mature art form" in its position as "expositor-interpreter" and in its "devotion to a new-found artistic idealism"].

1189   _____. "The Novel," ConLS, (1958),   259-288. [A review article on the trends and developments of criticism of the novel in the past 50 years].

1190   Booth, Wayne C. "Distance and Point-of-View: An Essay in Classification," EIC, XL:1 (Jan. 1961), 60-79. Reprinted in Poetique, IV (1970), 511-524. [An early version of Chapter VI, Part One, of The Rhetoric of Fiction. (Chicago: University of Chicago Press, 1961). A tabulation of the various forms the author's voice can take].

1191   _____. "Telling and Showing in Fiction," Midway, IX (1962), 16-29. A reprint of Chapter I of The Rhetoric of Fiction. (Chicago: University of Chicago Press, 1961), pp. 3-23. Also in Perspectives in Contemporary Criticism: A Collection of Recent Essays by American, English, and European Literary Critics. Edited by Sheldon Norman Grebstein. (New York & London: Harper & Row, 1968), pp. 108-120. [Maintains that even though direct and authoritative authorial comment is giving way to "objective," "impersonal," or "dramatic" modes of narration as being superior and artistic, the writer's judgment is always present and evident to those who look for it, for the author simply chooses his disguise; he can never disappear].

1192   _____. "The Rhetoric of Fiction and the Poetics of Fiction," Novel, I:2 (Winter 1968), 105-117. [A reply to various critiques of his book, Rhetoric of Fiction, especially the topic of the "second self" which elicited an extensive response from John Killham].

1193   Borden, Mary. "Personal Experience and the Art of Fiction," EDH, XXIX (1958), 87-96. [Rejects the assumption that personal experience, "broad in scope, rich in variety . . . [is] necessary, or especially valuable or even good for the literary artist," and argues that the "ideal climate of experience" for a writer, particularly a woman writer, is not "rich and varied, but spartan, meagre and restricted"].

1194   Bowen, Elizabeth. "What We Need in Writing," Spectator, CLVII (20 Nov. 1936), 901-902. [Calls for "more normal and disengaged" writers, free from "arbitrary loyalties," with an "unflagging devotion to art" if life is to be examined and the results shown].

1195   _____. "Once Upon a Yesterday," SatR, XXXIII (27 May 1950), 9-10, 36-37. [Discusses the causes which prompt writers to retreat from the present and have recourse "to life in the past," and the "two routes" to it].

1196 _____. "The Writer's Peculiar World," NYTBR,(24 Sep. 1950), 3, 40. Reprinted in Highlights of Modern Literature: A Permanent Collection of Memorable Essays from 'The New York Times Book Review.' Edited by Francis Brown. (New York: The New American Library, 1954), pp. 32-36. [Elaborates on a statement by G. Greene in "Why Do I Write?" (London: Percival Marshall, 1948) on the "disloyalties of the writer" to any fixed standpoint in society].

1197 _____. "The Search for a Story to Tell," NYTBR, (14 Dec. 1952),1. Reprinted in Highlights of Modern Literature: A Permanent Collection of Memorable Essays from 'The New York Times Book Review.' Edited by Francis Brown. (New York: The New American Library, 1954), pp. 30-32. [On the various stages of a writer's search for a subject].

1198 _____. "English Fiction at Mid-Century," NRep, CXXIX (21 Sep. 1953), 15-16. Reprinted in Arts at Mid-Century. Edited by Robert Richman. (New York: Horizon Press, 1954), pp. 209-213. [Arranges, classifies and rates the novel from 1914, notices the "moral drama" and "social drama" novels, and the absence of the political novel and the infrequency of the "ideological" novel at mid-century].

1199 _____. "Truth and Fiction-I. Story, Theme and Situation," Listener, LVI:1439 (25 Oct. 1956), 651-652. [The first of three talks on the novelist's craft. Comments and illustrates three "essentials" of a story: simplicity, general interest, and a good start, two "attributes" of theme, the moral element and its deep submergence, and variants of situation].

1200 _____. "Truth and Fiction-II. People: the Creation of Character," Listener, LVI:1440 (1 Nov. 1956), 704-706. [The second of three talks on the novelist's craft. Comments on the central concern of the novel with people, and illustrates how a novelist introduces and develops his characters by analysis or by dialogue].

1201 _____. "Truth and Fiction-III. Time, Period and Reality," Listener, LVI:1441 (8 Nov. 1956), 751-752. [The last of three talks on the novelist's craft. Comments on time as a "major component" of the novel, and illustrates its uses in creating suspense, the feeling of concern and reality the creation of the actual scene, and of "time as timing," and "time outside the novel"].

1202 _____. "Rx for a Story Worth the Telling," NYTBR, (31 Aug. 1958), 1, 13. Reprinted in Opinions and Perspectives from 'The New York Times Book Review.' Edited by

Francis Brown. (Boston: Houghton Mifflin, 1964), pp. 230-235. [Considers the "essentials" of a story and its different facets in novel writing].

1203 Bowen, John. "One Man's Meat: The Idea of Individual Responsibility," TLS, 2997 (7 Aug. 1959), xii-xiii. (British Books Around the World). [Considers L. Durrell, W. Golding, A. Wilson, and I. Murdoch in terms of a common denominator that marks them off from their predecessors: "their refusal to accept soap values of any kind, and deep concern with man as an individual and his individual acceptance of his responsibilities to God or to other men"].

1204 _____. "Literary Letter from London," NYTBR, (24 Nov. 1963), 66. [Surveys briefly the recent works of I. Murdoch, M. Spark, D. Storey, J. Wain, A. Wilson, and K. Amis].

1205 _____. "Speaking of Books: The Novel As . . . . . . ," NYTBR, (23 May 1965), 2. Reprinted in The Best of 'Speaking of Books' from 'The New York Times Book Review.' Edited with an Introduction by E. F. Brown. (New York: Holt, Rinehart and Winston, 1969), pp. 231-234. [Rejects the approach to novel writing as therapy (self-expressionism), as "eyeglasses," as "tract," as "toy" (an aesthetic object), as "game," as "love-object," and reasserts the importance of the story element].

1206 _____. "Speaking of Books: Out of Experience," NYTBR, (4 Sep. 1966), 2. [Discusses experience as "raw material" for the novelist].

1207 _____. "It's a Pleasure, or Is It?" NYTBR, (24 Sep. 1967), 2. [Discusses the disappearance of "pleasure" in literature and novels in particular, as a result of the growing belief that masterpieces should be "different" and "personal." D. H. Lawrence and J. Joyce].

1208 Bowen, Robert O. "Agonies and Anesthetics," Renascence, X (1958), 144-149. [A review article of "Catholic" novels that deal with death and its "inevitable association with His agony," and Faith as a "happiness pill." M. Dickens and C. Mackenzie among others].

1209 Bowling, Lawrence Edward. "What is the Stream of Consciousness Technique?" PMLA, LXV:4 (June 1950), 333-345. Reprinted in Critical Approaches to Fiction. Edited by Shiv K. Kumar and Keith F. McKean. (New York: McGraw-Hill, 1968), pp. 349-367. [Attributes the general confusion over what the stream of consciousness is, or how it originated, to the failure of critics "to recognize different variations within the stream of consciousness technique," and their inability to distinguish "the technique from another similar method with which it is confused." Examines some definitions

173

against specific examples from Dujardin and D. Richardson, and distinguishes between "stream of consciousness," "interior monologue," and "internal analysis"].

1210 Boyle, Robert. "Literature and Pornography," CathW, CXCIII (Aug. 1961), 295-302. [Considers the duty of society to stamp out pornography, and the risks involved in censorship, especially when great literature is in question. J. Joyce and G. Greene among others].

1211 Boynton, H. W. "Ideas, Sex and the Novel," Dial, LX (13 Apr. 1916), 359-362. [Rejects English current fiction for being a "vehicle for theories . . . arguments . . . garbage of one sort or another" and not an "embodiment, through the interpretation of human character in action . . . of truth." H. James, A. Bennett, and H. G. Wells].

1212 _____. "The 'New Novel' in England," Independent, CX (14 Apr. 1923), 249. [Considers English novels of the 20th century as being "largely experimental or derived" and falling into one or two classes: the "from-Wellsians . . . commentators first and story-tellers second," and the "near-Continentals" who interpret English life "in terms of the French or Russian soul." Also notices the prominence of women novelists].

1213 Brace, Gerald Warner. "The Essential Novel," TQ, VIII:1 (Spring 1965), 28-38. [Considers problems the modern novelist faces--change in the function of the novel, its existence as a self-sustaining work of art, content and technique--and calls for the return of "dramatic tension and emotional commitment in the novel," as well as a commitment to "human value and human purpose" without which the novel exists in a "state of inferiority and eclipse." V. Woolf, J. Joyce, and J. Conrad among others].

1214 _____. "Witness: Theme in Fiction," MR, XI (Winter 1970), 180-185. [Discusses a novelist's handling of theme and the various ways he has to convey it. Brief general references to D. H. Lawrence, J. Conrad, and J. Galsworthy among others].

1215 Bradbury, Malcolm. "The Taste for Anarchy," SatR, XLV (30 June 1962), 10-12, 49. [Examines the present state of civilization, and attributes the present crisis in modern literature, and the "sapless" state of the English novel and poetry, to the loss of the "liberal view" of art as an ideal of "general enlargement," and the artist feeling himself "less at the center of his society and more at its periphery. E. M. Forster and D. H. Lawrence].

1216 _____. "Recent English Novels," CritS, I (Autumn 1963), 138-140. [Reviews A. Sillitoe's The Ragman's Daughter, D.

Storey's Radcliffe, I. Murdoch's The Unicorn, and G. Phelps The Winter People].

1217 _____. "Towards a Poetics of Fiction: 1) An Approach Through Structure," Novel, I (Fall 1967), 45-52. [Justifies a new approach through structure which he defines as a "devised chain of events that presented by narration, conditions the successive choices . . . and constitutes not only an entire narrative but an attitude towards it, . . . the substantive myth that we can derive from the novel without regarding it as something independent of it"].

1218 _____. "Myths and Manners," TLS, 3425 (9 Oct. 1967), 983-984. [Attributes the charge that contemporary English fiction is unambitious and experimental to the way English postwar society has evolved and to people's expectations of what contributes to the worth and interest of fiction].

1219 _____ and Dudley Andres. "The Sugar Beet Generation: A Note to English Intellectual History," TQ, III:4 (1960), 38-47. [On the origins, characteristics and influence of the semi-literary group, The Sugar Beet Generation, that preceded the "Angry Young Men" in England, and the American Beat Generation].

1220 Brady, Charles A. "The British Novel Today," Thought, XXXIV (1959), 518-546. [Surveys the English novel from 1940 and traces the trends of social realism and allegorical romance in K. Amis, J. Wain, A. Powell, C. P. Snow, C. Williams, and C. S. Lewis].

1221 _____. "Catholic Fiction: 2. Lifting Fog?" America, LXV (30 Aug. 1941), 579-580. [Addresses himself to the question why Catholics cannot write good novels. Brief references to G. K. Chesterton, R. H. Benson, H. G. Wells, and A. Huxley].

1222 _____. "A Brief Survey of Catholic Fiction," BoT, XII (Jan.-Feb. 1954), 159-160, 190-191. [Assumes that the Catholic novel is, par excellence, the "novel with a metaphysic." Survey covers England, France, and the U. S. A. in the 20th century. M. Baring, E. Waugh, and G. Greene among others].

1223 Brady, Ignatius, O. F. M., M. A. "Catholic English Literature in the British Isles in the Twentieth Century," FECR, XXII (Dec. 1940), 103-120. [Regards the Catholic Literary renaissance as a development of traditional Christian culture and humanism. Pages 109-112 survey English Catholic novelists and their themes between 1890 and 1940. G. K. Chesterton, "J. Ayscough," C. Mackenzie, S. Kaye-Smith, M. Baring, and E. Dinnis].

1224 Bragg, Melvyn. "Class and the Novel," TLS, 3633 (15 Oct.

1971), 1261-63. [Argues for class in writing to become "more overt," for it is neither "too crude" nor "literary bad taste." V. Woolf, K. Amis, D. H. Lawrence, E. Waugh and others].

1225 * Bragin, R. I. "Nekotorye aspekty angliiskogo anti-kolonial upgo romane," Sbornik nauchnyckh rabot Belorusskago gos, Universiteta, Minsk, II (1967), 70-88.

1226 Braine, John. "The Modern Novelist," JSA, LXVI (June 1968), 565-574. [Paper read to the Society on 7 Feb. 1968 . An appraisal of the English novel in the fifties and early sixties pointing out the change in "its subject matter, and its general tone," and lack of interest in form. W. Cooper, K. Amis, J. Wain, C. Wilson, D. Storey, and A. Sillitoe].

1227 Braybrooke, Neville. "Catholics and the Novel," Blackfriars, (Feb. 1950), 54-64. Reprinted with minor changes in Renascence, V (Autumn 1952), 22-32. [Traces briefly the emergence of the novel in English literature and how the "Catholic Novel" came into being. G. Greene and E. Waugh among others].

1228 Brick, Allen. "The Madman in His Cell: Joyce, Beckett, Nabokov and the Stereotypes," MR, I (Oct. 1959), 40-55. [Discusses these novelists' reaction to their "understanding of the imprisonment of the public mind by mass culture" by creating heroes "who struggle to hold viable illusions" of the world].

1229 Bricknell, Herschel. "The Present State of Fiction," VQR, XXV (Winter 1949), 92-98. [Describes the basic weakness of the present state of the novel and the short story as a leanness of content, especially in character, and not of technique. J. Conrad, H. James, and H. G. Wells among others].

1230 Brickner, Richard P. "Is It Autobiographical," NLea, LV:24 (1972), 20-22. [Maintains that "attitudes" of a novelist rather than specific details of his life constitute the "autobiographical" element in a novel. J. Joyce and F. M. Ford among others].

1231 Bridges, George. "Il romanzo," Ulisse, X (Spring-Summer 1956), 807-813. [Surveys the return to plot, intrigue, violence and mystery in the novels of G. Greene, D. Welch, J. Cary, political fantasy in G. Orwell, and satire and parody in E. Waugh. Confined to post-1945 works].

1232 Brière, Annie. "Où va le roman anglais-américain?" RDM,7 (Apr. 1963), 415-423. [An interview with John Wain discussing his views on the contemporary English novel followed by a shorter section discussing John Aldridge's views].

176

1233 Broieh, Ulrich. "Tradition und Rebellion. Zur Renaissance des pikaresken Romans in der englischen Literatur der Gegenwart,"ZSL, I (1967), 415-429. [Discusses innovations introduced on the picaresque tradition in the contemporary novel of J. Wain, K. Amis, and I. Murdoch].

1234 Brooke-Rose, Christine. "Le Roman expérimental en Angleterre," LanM, LXIII (1969), 158-168. [Discusses the achievement of I. Compton-Burnett, M. Spark, W. Golding, A. Burgess, and R. Heppenstal as "experimental" novelists, meaning by "experimental" not a movement or school but simply individuals "qui font chacun quelque chose de différent, sans theorie"].

1235 Brown, Dennis. "The Integrity of the Novel," KanS, L (1965), 18-23. [Discusses the preoccupation of the English novel with Truth--what is meant by "Integrity"--and its "close connection" with the mainstream of Western thought. J. Joyce and D. H. Lawrence among others].

1236 Brown, E. K. "E. M. Forster and the Contemplative Novel," UTQ, III (Apr. 1934), 349-361. [Argues that the novel need not merely belong to the world of actions, but can also record a man's quest of the "comtemplative ideal." C. Morgan and E. M. Forster].

1237 _____. "Two Formulas for Fiction: Henry James and H. G. Wells," CE, VIII:1 (Oct. 1946), 7-17. [Discusses the charges made by H. G. Wells against the substance and form of the fiction of H. James].

1238 Brown, Hilton. "South India in Present-Day Fiction," AsF, (NS) XXXIV (Jan. 1938), 9-30. [Examines novels and short stories written by Europeans and Indians over the past twenty years on the Hyderabad-Travancor-Mysore area. E. M. Forster and R. Kipling among others].

1239 Brown, Stephen J., S. J. "The Catholic Novelist and His Themes," IM, LXIII (July 1935), 432-444. [Maintains that the Catholic novelist, like any other, can venture on any "ground accessible to literature," but only he can deal with "reality in all its depths and heights;" i.e., with the "supra-human" (the Holy Ghost), and the "infra-human" (the beast in man). Brief references to "J. Ayscough," M. Baring, R. H. Benson, and E. Dinnis].

1240 Browning, Gordon. "Toward a Set of Standards for Everlasting Anti-Utopian Fiction," Cithara, X:1 (Dec. 1970), 18-32. [Discusses Zamiatin's WE, G. Orwell's 1984 and A. Huxley's Brave New World in the light of criteria devised from a definition of Anti-Utopian Fiction, that relies heavily on I. Howe's "The Fiction of Anti-Utopia," NRep, CXLVI (23 Apr. 1962), 13-16].

1241 Brumm, Ursula. "Symbolism and the Novel," PR, XXV:3 (Summer

1958), 329-342. Reprinted in The Partisan Review Anthology.
Edited by William Phillips and Philip Rahv (New York: Holt,
1962), pp. 221-230, and Critical Approaches to Fiction.
Edited by Shiv K. Kumar and Keith F. McKean (New York:
McGraw-Hill, 1968), pp. 367-381. [Discusses the nature and
function of symbol in the novel. Reduces variations of
symbol to "the cause-linked 'realistic' symbol" and the
"transcendent or magic symbol" of the poetic novel. General
references to English and American novels. The article is
translated from the German by Willard R. Trask].

1242 Bryden, Ronald. "British Fiction, 1959-1960," IntLA, III
(1961), 40-53. [A survey pointing out the achievement of
individual novelists through their latest novels, and the
general tendency of novelists to avoid "technical experiment,"
their attempt to evoke a "world," and their "reexamination
and redefinition from the ground up of British Society."
W. Golding, I. Murdoch, A. Wilson, L. Durrell, J. Braine,
A. Sillitoe, K. Amis, J. Wain, A. Powell, C. P. Snow, P.
H. Johnson, and C. MacInnes].

1243 Buchanan, George. "The Novel Proper," TLS,1941 (15 Apr.
1939), 216. [Contends that though the "Novel Proper"
reached its height in Dickens' time and may be ailing at
present, it is "not so much dead as not achieved;" and that
in future, it will concentrate "on relations and great sen-
timents instead of facts and anecdotes," thus returning to
the main tradition. Editorial comment "The Novel in Crisis"
on p. 217. Letter to Editor by John Chitney "Truth and
'Escape' in Modern Literature," (29 Apr. 1939), 249].

1244 Buck, Pearl S. "Fiction and the Front Page," YR, XXV
(Spring 1936), 477-487. [Discusses the attitude novelists
should take to current events and "front page news," and
advises the novelist "to guard as his soul," his detachment
from the times].

1245 Burgess, Anthony. "The Birth of A Best-Seller," Observer,
(7 Oct. 1962), p. 24. [Reviews J. Braine's Life at The Top,
E. Linklater's Husband of Delilah, L. Reid-Banks' An End to
Running, "G. Fielding's" The Birthday King, and H. E. Bates'
A Crown of Wild Myrtle].

1246 _____. "The Corruption of the Exotic," Listener, LXX
(26 Sep. 1963), 465-467. [Discusses the problems and dangers of relying on the exotic and the strange in the subject-
matter of novels].

1247 _____. "A Novelist's Sources are Myth, Language, and
the Here-and-Now," NYTBR, (19 July 1964), 5, 26. [Calls on
novelists to be "less concerned with what they write about
and more concerned with how they write." Suggests the cultivation of the "here-and-now" as a means of "exploring myth

and exploiting language"].

1248 _____. "Powers That Be," Encounter, XXIV:1 (Jan. 1965),
71-76. [A review article on C. P. Snow's Corridors of
Power and A. Wilson's Late Call, describing the "fictional
tradition" in which they write as belonging to the "contemporary novel of the middle way"].

1249 _____. "What Now in the Novel?" Spectator, CCXIV:7135
(26 Mar. 1965), 400. [Voices his dissatisfaction with the
all-out morality and social themes inherited from the novel
of the fifties, and hopes that future novelists will experiment with form and language. K. Amis, W. Golding, E.
Waugh, and C. P. Snow].

1250 _____. "Novels are Made of Words," TLS, 3295 (22 Apr.
1965), 317. [Argues that exactness of the presentation of
real life should "begin on the printed page"].

1251 _____. "Religion and the Arts: 1--The Manicheans,"
TLS, 3340 (3 Mar. 1966), 153-154. [Wants an imaginative
rendering of religious experience--themes like "sainthood,
sin, eschatological sanctions of behaviour"--to provide
more of the novelist's subject matter and be as acceptable
as the experience of the common man. A. Huxley, G. Greene,
W. Golding, and E. Waugh].

1252 _____. "Speaking of Books: The Writer's Purpose,"
NYTBR, (1 May 1966), 2, 43. [Questions whether literature in
general, and the novel in particular, should have a social purpose].

1253 _____. "Speaking of Books: The Seventeenth Novel,"
NYTBR, (21 Aug. 1966), 2, 14. Reprinted in The Best of
'Speaking of Books' from 'The New York Times Book Review.'
Edited, with an Introduction by Francis Brown. (New York:
Holt, Rinehart and Winston, 1969), pp. 85-89. [Maintains
that the novelist resorts to experiment when he is bored
from treading the worn path; i.e., afraid of repeating
himself].

1254 _____. "The Novel in 2000 A. D.," NYTBR, (29 Mar.
1970), 2, 19. [Speculates that the novel of 2000 A. D. will
be very much like a film script characterized by structural
simplification and an augmentation of vocabulary].

1255 _____. "Viewpoint," TLS, 3668 (16 June 1972), 686.
[Calls for the "easy flow of the picaresque" rather than
the novels that "the textbook admires"].

1256 Burns, Wayne. "The Novelist as Revolutionary," ArQ, VII
(1951), 13-27. [On the divergent claims of fictional art
and ideology].

1257 _____. "The Genuine and the Counterfeit: A Study of

Victorian and Modern Fiction," CE, XVIII:3 (Dec. 1956),
143-150. [A controversial essay stating that any novel
must belong to one of two classes: art and counterfeit art.
The former expresses the novelist's "unique vision" and
gives the reader "a symbolic illumination" of the real world,
and the latter expresses "myths" or conventional beliefs
the novelist does not share; hence, the more demanding task
of the modern novelist not to sacrifice his "vision." References to J. Joyce, D. H. Lawrence, G. Orwell, and V. Woolf
among others].

1258   Burt, Struthers. "For a Literary Lend-Lease: Proposing a
        Pool of American and English Literary Secrets," SatR, XXVII
        (4 Nov. 1944), 5-6. [Attributes the superiority of the
        English novel over the American to a "sense of language and
        of atmosphere and of character," but maintains that the
        former presently lacks the fourth essential: subject-
        matter].

1259   Bush, Douglas. "Sex in the Modern Novel," AtM, CCIII:1
        (Jan. 1959), 73-75. Reprinted in Engaged and Disengaged.
        (Harvard University Press, 1966), pp. 42-49. [Questions
        the value of the "surfeit of sex and sensationalism" in
        the modern novel].

1260   Butler, Mrs. "The Morality of the Novel," PRev, (Jan. 1920),
        21-28. [Attempts to find out what the morality of a novel
        consists of, whether the art of the novel is marred by its
        purpose. H. G. Wells, J. Conrad, and J. Galsworthy].

1261   Cabell, James Branch. "A Note on Alcoves," NRep, XXX:384
        (12 Apr. 1922), 4-5. [Regards the form and scope of the
        novel as "fluctuating and indeterminable"].

1262   Callander, T. E. "Novels of 1934," LibA, (Jan. 1935), 16-
        21. [Reviews "long" novels of 1934 by R. Graves, J. Lindsay,
        E. Sackville-West, M. Irwin, E. Shanks, E. Waugh, and R.
        Aldington among others].

1263   Cam, Helen. "Historical Novels--Fact or Fiction?" Listener,
        LXIX:1783 (30 May 1963), 914-915. [Finds value and merit
        in the reading of historical novels not only as a means of
        escape, but also for the interest in history that is aroused].

1264   Cammaerts, Emile. "A Foreign View of Modern English Liter-
        ature," EdR, CCXLIX:507 (Jan. 1929), 93-104. [A survey
        from a Continental viewpoint. Dwells on the association
        of the "real and the fantastic" in a work, and the ability
        to excel in both prose and verse as two features that dis-
        tinguish English writers from their European confrères. W.
        de la Mare, D. Garnett, and H. G. Wells among others].

1265   Campbell, P. G. C. "Sex in Fiction," QQ, XXXV (July-Sep.

1927), 82-93. [Originally an address given to the English
Club at Queen's University. Regards the preponderance of
sex in fiction as constituting a danger to society for it
saps its foundations and tends to lower the "moral tone"
of the reading public].

1266 Canby, Henry Seidel. "Sex in Fiction," Century, CV (Nov.
1922), 98-105. Reprinted in Definitions: Essays in Contemporary Criticism. Second Series. (New York: Harcourt,
Brace, 1924), pp. 81-98. [Distinguishes between stories of
"sex in proportion" and "sex out of proportion," the latter
roughly classified into "behavioristic," "phallic," "neur-
otics," and "stereotyped varieties." A. Huxley, R. Macaulay,
J. Joyce, D. H. Lawrence, and J. Galsworthy among others].

1267 _____. "Fiction Tells All," Harper's, CLXXI (Aug.
1935), 308-315. Reprinted in Seven Years' Harvest: Notes
on Contemporary Literature. (New York: Holt, Rinehart and
Winston, 1936), pp. 118-132. [Brief references to D. H.
Lawrence, J. Joyce, and A. Bennett].

1268 _____. "The Present State of English Literature,"
SatR, XVI (11 Sep. 1937), 8. [General observations on the
present "decadence" of the novel and drama and their attempt
to seek "new channels"].

1269 Cannan, Gilbert. "The New Spirit in the Art of Fiction,"
LDIBR, I:3 (Feb. 1923), 33. [Discusses the growing interest in human life rather than plot, in discovery rather than
invention].

1270 Cannan, Joanna. "The New Trend in Fiction," Bookman (London),
85 (Dec. 1933), 143-144. [Reviews R. Fraser's Tropical
Waters, C. S. Forester's The Gun, H. Talbot's Gentlemen -
The Regiment, N. B. Morrison's The Gowk Storm and general
short stories to indicate the "new virility" characteristic
of the revival of the novel of action].

1271 Carpenter, Thomas P. "Abnormal Psychology in Twentieth
Century Novels," L&P, XVI (Winter 1966), 43-47. [An amended
and updated 1946 Ph.D. dissertation abstract pointing out
the use English and American novelists have made of abnormal psychology, their success, and the values and difficulties inherent in the subject matter. Lists novels by E.
Bowen, V. Brittain, C. Dane, D. Garnett, R. Godden, R.
Hall, C. Isherwood, A. Koestler, R. Lehmann, N. Royde-
Smith, and S. T. Warner among others].

1272 Carter, Henry. "The Penalty of Cleverness," UR, X (Oct.
1918), 368-375. [On the characteristic of cleverness in
G. K. Chesterton, H. G. Wells, and G. B. Shaw].

1273 Cary, Joyce. "On the Function of the Novelist," NYTBR,

(30 Oct. 1949), 1, 52. Reprinted in Highlights of Modern
Literature: A Permanent Collection of Memorable Essays
from 'The New York Times Book Review.' Edited by Francis
Brown. (New York: The New American Library, 1954), pp.
53-57. [Argues that the function of the novelist is to
"make the world contemplate and understand itself," to give
meaning to life by reaching the emotions of the readers].

1274 _____ . "A Novel is a Novel is a Novel," NYTBR, (30
Apr. 1950), 1, 34. Reprinted in Adam, XVIII (Nov.-Dec.1950),
1-3. [Maintains that though definitions for novels may be
necessary, they should be "simple" and no "serious attention" should be paid to them].

1275 Cassidy, John. "America and Innocence: Henry James and
Graham Greene," Blackfriars, XXXVIII:447 (June 1957), 261-
267. [Examines the two writers' attitudes to the American
abroad as a "valid correlative" for innocence in Daisy
Miller and The Quiet American].

1276 Castelli, Alberta. "Scrittori Inglesi Contemporanei di
Fronte al Christianesimo," Humanitas, VII (Feb. 1952),
184-194; VII (Mar. 1952), 307-316. [Discusses T. S. Eliot
J. Joyce, and D. H. Lawrence in the first article, and A. '
Huxley and G. Greene in the second as writers confronted
with Christian issues].

1277 Caudill, Rebecca. "Role of the Novelist in Today's Crisis,"
LJ, LXXXIII (1 Feb. 1958), 351-356. [Attempts an assessment of the role of the novelist in today's asocial world
and gives four reasons why the novel is in difficulty: 1)
variations of form, 2) predominent interest in natural
sciences, 3) novelists not saying anything significant, and
4) its nature as a representation of life and a commentary
on it].

1278 Caute, David. "A Writer's Prospect -- IX," LM, VII (Feb.
1960), 40-46. [Attributes English writers' rejection of
social realist art to a dislike of communist values, the
"empirical tradition," and a suspicion of the "rationalist
or committed, element in writing." Brief references to
English 20th century novelists].

1279 Cazamian, Louis. "Le Temps dans le roman anglais contemporain," EA, III (Oct. 1939), 338-342. [Discusses two notions
of time -- "la durée concrete" in V. Woolf and J. Joyce,
and "temps abstrait" in A. Huxley -- as well as the moral
significance of this preoccupation with time].

1280 _____ . "Dans l'ombre de la guerre," EA, VI (May 1953),
109-116. [A general survey of the English scene -- part of
an additional chapter on the period 1914-1950 in his History
of English Literature -- bringing out the major features of

the age with its great number of talented and brilliant
writers and the relative scarcity of great works and authors].

1281 Cecil, Lord David. "The Author in a Suffering World. War's
      Impact on Our Literature," TLS, 2032 (11 Jan. 1941), 18, 20.
      [Discusses the reasons for the contrast between writers'
      eager response in 1914 and their silence in 1939, and calls
      for a new point of view which can include the experience
      of the war].

1282 Chamberlain, John. "Volition and the Novel," Commonweal,
      XI (20 Nov. 1929), 81-82. [Attributes the paleness of con-
      temporary English and American fiction -- its lack of "human
      significance," or, at best, its "negative significance" --
      to its loss of belief in the human being as a responsible
      moral agent. J. Joyce and V. Woolf among others].

1283 Champigny, Robert. "Implicitness in Narrative Fiction,"
      PMLA, LXXV:5 (Oct. 1970), 988-991. [Argues that causal
      laws are not applicable to fiction, and thereby cannot
      make the implicit explicit in novels].

1284 Champion de Crespigny, Rose. "Ideals in Fiction," NC,
      LXXXIX (Mar. 1921), 437-444. [Questions the validity and
      value of dwelling upon the "purely trivial" and exploring
      the "squalid side of existence," carried out by the post-
      World War I novel].

1285 "The Changing Novel," Nation, CXVI:3021 (30 May 1923), 620.
      [A quick look at the various forms of the novel from Field-
      ing's discursiveness to the "tighter form" of Galsworthy
      and Conrad, from H. G. Wells' "explicit sociologies" to the
      "experimental" novel of J. Joyce and D. Richardson].

1286 Chapman, Robert T. "'Parties . . . Parties . . . Parties':
      Some Images of the 'Gay Twenties'," English, XXI:111 (Autumn
      1972), 93-97. [Examines instances of social gatherings in
      the twenties as merely functional devices in the mechanics
      of plot, and as symbols of "the hollow frivolity of the era
      as of its gaiety." E. Waugh, A. Huxley. W. Lewis, D. H.
      Lawrence, and V. Woolf among others].

1287 "Character and Tendency of Contemporary Fiction," LA, 281
      (16 May 1914), 435-438. Reprinted from The Athenaeum. [In-
      dicates its "seriousness of aim," "tendency to social crit-
      icism," "tentativeness of form," and the "fusion of earlier
      methods" to point out the "transitional" state of the novel.
      H. G. Wells, A. Bennett, J. Galsworthy, H. Walpole, G. Cannan,
      O. Onions, and E. M. Forster].

1288 Charles, Gerda. "Our Literary Anglo-Jewish Cousins," Nation,
      CCVI (8 Apr. 1968), 477-478. [Surveys the "small flood" of
      Jewish novelists and dramatists let loose by B. Glanville's

publication of The Bankrupts. A. Baron and F. Raphael among others].

1289 Chesterton, G. K. "Contemporary Fiction," RMag, IX (Dec. 1906), 78-82. [Remarks on the growth of fiction as a literary form, but excludes "M. Corelli," H. Caine, and H. Ward from its ranks because they use it as a vehicle for "any kind of ideas or any sort of mission" rather than from "the natural impulse of narrative"].

1290 _____. "A Desert Island Library of Recent English Fiction," LIBR, I:2 (Jan. 1923), 8-9. [A review of R. Macaulay's The ·Mystery of Geneva, A. Marshall's Pippin, E. Bramah's Kai Lung's Golden Hours, H. Belloc's The Mercy of Allah, and H. Walpole's The Cathedral].

1291 _____. "The Spirit of the Age in Literature," FR, (NS) CXXVIII (Sep. 1930), 289-298. Reprinted in AS, LXXII (Oct. 1930), 97-103. [Regards the new individualism, the "insociable quality of intellect" and irresponsibility towards "communal ideals" as the new spirit of the age in postwar literature, and looks upon J. Joyce's "verbal eccentricity," D. H. Lawrence's "spirit of syncopation or separatism," "R. West's" "abnormal reaction to the normal," and A. Huxley's pessimism as manifestations of this new spirit].

1292 _____. "The End of the Moderns," Bookman, (America), LXXV (Dec. 1932), 807-811. Also in LMer, XXVII (Jan. 1933), 228-233. [Contends that the revolutionary elements or modernity in the last decade does "not mark the beginning, but the end, of an epoch of revolution." References to D. H. Lawrence and A. Huxley].

1293 _____. "Writers of the Present Reign," ILN, (Silver Jubilee No.), (1935), 59-61. [A brief survey of Georgian writers and writings].

1294 Chevalley, Abel. "Younger English Novelists," LA, 311 (15 Oct. 1921), 139-144. Reprinted from RF, (1 Aug. 1921). [Examines the Russian influence in promoting "incoherence and lack of form" and interest in the "elastic" form of the sequence novel, and the English interest in objectivity, the "point of view" principle, and the subconscious. W. de Morgan, J. D. Beresford, O. Onions, A. Bennett, J. Galsworthy, C. Mackenzie, G. Cannan, D. H. Lawrence, D. Richardson, and C. Dane].

1295 _____. "La Littérature féminine en Angleterre," NL, (30 Mar. 1929), 10. [Surveys the "lesser" known female novelists of the previous decade, pointing out two major characteristics: the psychology of a social morality, and the "croissante" invasion of "l'esprit et . . . la formation historique"].

1296 Cheyney, Lynne. "Joseph Conrad's The Secret Agent and Graham Greene's It's a Battlefield: A Study in Structural Meaning," MFS, XVI:2 (Summer 1970), 117-131. [Discusses the importance and use of structure as a device to communicate meaning in the two novels].

1297 Church, Margaret. "Concepts of Time in Novels of Virginia Woolf and Aldous Huxley." MFS, I:2 (1955), 19-24. Reprinted in Time and Reality: Studies in Contemporary Fiction. (Chapel Hill: University of North Carolina Press, 1963). [Examines two attitudes toward time -- as "duration" and "clock time" in A. Huxley's Those Barren Leaves and Time Must Have a Stop and V. Woolf's Jacob's Room and The Waves].

1298 Church, Richard. "The Poet and the Novel," EDH, XVIII (1940), 1-18; also FR, CL (NS) CXLIV (Nov. 1938), 593-604. [On the poet turning to the novel as the modern form and substitute of the epic poem, and the difficulties the poet encounters in the process].

1299 _____. "How a Novelist Works," EDH, XXXIII (1965), 56-69. [A look, from the inside, on how a novel is made and what factors impede or accelerate the process of work].

1300 Churchill, R. C. "The Rural Novel," Spectator, CLXXI (22 Oct. 1943), 381. [Remarks briefly on the predominantly rural tradition of the English novel and the lack, so far, of an equivalent urban one. References to J. B. Priestley, G. Greene, A. Bennett, and others].

1301 _____. "Literature or Propaganda? A Survey of the Marxist 'thirties," NC, CXXXIV (Nov. 1943), 227-237. [Regards the Marxist achievement in the literature of the thirties as a "by-line." R. Warner, E. Upward, N. Mitchison, and A. Wilson among others].

1302 Clark, Rev. Henry W. "The Diffidence of the Modern Novelist," NWo, (Sep. 1920), 331-337. [Contrasts the modern novelist's photographic "method of portraiture" of character with the "creative" method of the master-novelists].

1303 Cleeve, Brian T. "The Worm as Hero," Studies, XLVII (Spring 1958), 21-29. [Considers the predominence of the hero in modern literature who admits defeat without struggling, and examines the causes that gave rise to such a trend, its history and its effect. J. Joyce, G. Greene, and S. Beckett among others. This is followed by comments from Sean O'Faolain, Peadar O'Donnell, John C. Kelly and a reply from the author].

1304 Clulow, T. I. M. "Some Fiction of 1936," LAssoc, XXX (Jan. 1937), 16-20. [A review of some fifteen novels eclectically chosen among which are S. Smith's Novel on Yellow Paper,

R. Graves' <u>Antigua, Penny, Price</u>, A. Huxley's <u>Eyeless in Gaza</u>, C. S. Forester's <u>The General</u>, R. J. Cruikshank's <u>The Double Quest</u>, "R. West's" <u>The Thinking Reed</u> and C. Morgan's <u>Sparkenbroke</u>].

1305 Cockshut, A. O. J. "Sentimentality in Fiction," <u>TC</u>, CLIX (Apr. 1957), 354-364. [Maintains that sentimentality is always "unconscious, . . . due to a failure to realize that two ideas, or feelings, or artistic purposes, are in conflict," and is a critical term to be used as a word of censure but not of contempt. G. Greene, J. Galsworthy, E. M. Forster and others].

1306 Cody, Richard. "Secret Service Fiction," <u>GradSE</u>, III:4 (1960), 6-12. [On English international "high adventure" and espionage fiction. Mostly confined to I. Fleming and writers of thrillers with brief reference to G. Greene and J. Conrad].

1307 Cohen, J. M. "The Earth is Hungry," <u>Listener</u>, LXXIV (11 Nov. 1965), 753-755. [Mainly confined to poetry, with brief reference to R. Graves' <u>Goodbye to All That</u>, E. Blunden's <u>Undertones of War</u>, and F. M. Ford's <u>Parades End</u>].

1308 Cohen-Portheim, P. "Der englische Roman von heute," <u>NB</u>, 5 Folge (1927), 280-283. [A brief survey of postwar "disillusioned" novelists. N. Douglas, A. Huxley, D. Garnett, D. H. Lawrence, V. Woolf, and J. Joyce among others].

1309 _____. "England's Unseen Change," <u>LA</u>, 339 (Feb. 1931), 626-629. Translated from <u>Literarische Welt</u> (Berlin). [Notices the correspondence between England's literary and political development, and draws the line of great English novelists from Dickens to Joyce].

1310 Cohn, Dorrit. "Narrated Monologue: Definitions of a Fictional Style," <u>CompL</u>, XVIII:2 (Spring 1966), 97-112. [Sketches the history and meaning of <u>erlebte rede</u> as distinct from interior monologue or the rendering of a character's consciousness "in the remembered part of first-person narration," its grammatical structure and the narrative situations in which it is most likely to be used, its connection with the stream of consciousness novel, the relationship between narrator and character and the "lyric and ironic possibilities" of this narrative style. J. Joyce, D. H. Lawrence, V. Woolf and others].

1311 Cohn, Ruby. "The Contemporary English Novel," <u>Perspective</u>, X (1958), 103-105. [An Editorial that discusses several generalizations on the post-World War II English novel but denies it a "genus . . . morphologically distinct from the novel of other generations or countries." P. H. Newby, W. Golding, K. Amis, J. Wain, and A. Powell].

1312 Colby, Elbridge. "The Priest in Fiction," ER, (July 1915), 24-38; (Aug. 1915), 156-169. [Examines the priest character and his role in novels written by Protestant writers in the first paper, and by Catholics in the second. Includes M. Bowen, G. Moore, H. Caine, E. T. Thurston, H. G. Wells, R. Hichens, R. H. Benson, J. Conrad, F. M. Crawford, and H. de la Pasture among others].

1313 Coleman, Rev. A. M. "The Parson in Fiction," CLM, (Jan. 1935), 24-30; (Apr. 1935), 51-58. [Surveys the delineation of the parson from the beginning of the 19th century. The second part of the survey discusses R. H. Benson, H. G. Wells, and S. Kaye-Smith among others].

1314 Coleman, John. "The Facts of Fiction," Spectator, (23 Oct. 1959), 559-560. [A review article on Paul Johnson's Left of Centre, S. Raven's Brother Cain, B. Oliver's The Square Within, and B. W. Aldiss' The Canopy of Time emphasising the "strangling convention" of boring "vulgarised sex," and the "peculiar literary sanction" of resorting to sex to rescue a "wandering plot"].

1315 Collins, R. G. "Divagations on the Novel as Experiment," Mosaic, IV:3 (1971), 1-11. [Contends that since every novel is an "experiment" that seeks at once "form" and release from "fixity," and the "flux of life," the attempt to reach an "aesthetic" of the novel that will explain it and, at the same time, "tie it firmly to its sibling arts," is more difficult and elusive than in other forms of literature. E. M. Forster, D. H. Lawrence, H. James, and J. Joyce among others].

1316 "Colour and Local Colour in the English Novel," TLS, 3154 (10 Aug. 1962), 590. [Special Number: A Language in Common. VII. On the paradox of the English novel: "insular," and yet, often set in other countries and including "experience of the greater part of the world." E. M. Forster, J. Cary, and G. Greene among others].

1317 Colum, Mary M. "Where Realism Ends," Freeman, VIII:85 (26 Sep. 1923), 56-58. [Discusses the two tendencies in literature to study human beings in "relation to a particular region" in the tradition of Hardy and Flaubert, and man "in relation to himself and his own subconsciousness" as in J. Joyce, V. Woolf, and D. Richardson].

1318 _____. "The Changing Novel," SatR, V (1 June 1929), 1070-71. [Examines the impact of external influences--decay of religion, motion pictures, new psychological and scientific discoveries--and internal changes, viz., stream of consciousness and new presentation of reality, on the technique and content of the novel].

187

1319 _____. "How Trivial are Modern Books?" Forum, XC
(Nov. 1933), 265-269. [Emphasises literary innovations
and discoveries as inventions of writers "thoroughly trained
in the part of literature," and that below any development
in contemporary literature is a philosophic idea, and that
powerful innovators are "men of hard intellectual training
and strong intellectual power"].

1320 Colum, Padraic. "Aspects of the Novel," Envoy, (Nov. 1950),
67-73. [Suggests H. James as a model for novelists who
wish to "diminish the externality that is inherent in prose
narrative," and which is liable to become "pedestrian and
commonplace"].

1321 Connolly, Francis X. "Our Orderly Novelists," Commonweal,
XV (9 Dec. 1931), 149-151. [Deplores the use of "orderly
mechanical fiction," -- sheer action or problem novels --
English and American, as a vehicle to project ideas on the
public when it lacks life and great characters. J. Galsworthy, H. G. Wells, and A. Bennett among others].

1322 _____. "Philosophy into Fiction," Commonweal, XXIV
(21 Aug. 1936), 402-403. [On the connection between the
prevailing philosophies and serious and creative art, especially the novel, for the "return to philosophy will be
made through art, particularly the art of fiction" since
one will come to grips with the "universal only through the
particular." Refers to C. Morgan's The Fountain and Sparkenbroke and A. Huxley's Point Counterpoint and Brave New
World].

1323 _____. "The Catholic Writer and Contemporary Culture,"
Thought, XIV (Sep. 1939), 373-383. [Examines the problem
the Catholic writer has to face in adapting himself to the
contemporary milieu without sacrificing his intelligence
or his character. References to A. Huxley, D. H. Lawrence,
E. Waugh, G. K. Chesterton, J. Joyce and others].

1324 _____. "Catholic Fiction: 4. Two Reactions," America,
LXV (13 Sep. 1941), 634-635. [On the "Be Honest School"
whose literature shocks the "world into the meaning of sin
and the need for salvation," and the "Be Prudent School"
whose imagination is "accountable to the higher truths of
philosophy." References to E. Waugh and G. Greene].

1325 "The Contractile Vacuole," TLS, 2,755 (19 Nov. 1954), 739.
[Leading article discussing S. Maugham's Ten Novels and
Their Authors and W. Allen's The English Novel].

1326 Cook, Richard. "Rudyard Kipling and George Orwell," MFS,
VII:2 (Summer 1961), 125-135. [Examines their careers and
works to show their shared attitudes and aversions in spite
of their different political outlooks].

1327   Cooper, Frederick Taber. "The Twentieth Century Novel,"
        Bookman (New York), LXV (Mar. 1927), 42-47. [Discusses
        "tendencies of the hour" in the fiction of writers who have
        "matured within the present century" in both England and
        the U. S. H. James, J. Joyce, A. Huxley, V. Woolf, and
        D. H. Lawrence among others].

1328   Cooper, Lettice. "The New Novelists: An Enquiry," LM, V:11
        (Nov. 1958), 17-21. Postscript, pp. 28-29. [A symposium:
        other contributors are Anthony Quinton, Frank Kermode and
        Maurice Cranston. Remarks on postwar novelists' fear of
        "anything phoney or high falutin" and their "oblique" ap-
        proach to the times with irony, comedy, and farce as weapons.
        Subdivides novelists into a pre-Lucky Jim group -- A. Wilson,
        P. H. Newby, F. King -- and post-Lucky Jim novelists whose
        favourite subjects are class distinction and money and who
        use farce as an "ingredient" like J. Wain, I. Murdoch, J.
        Braine, and W. Cooper].

1329   Cooper, William. "Novel and Anti-Novel," Sunday Times,
        (17 Dec. 1961), 21. [Welcomes the increasing concern in
        the English novel with man, not in isolation, but in society,
        as distinct from its predecessor of the thirties, or the
        "anti-novelist's outright attack on mind"].

1330   Cooperman, Stanley. "The Imperial Posture and the Shrine
        of Darkness: Kipling's The Naulahka and E. M. Forster's
        A Passage to India," ELT, VI:1 (1963), 9-13. [A compara-
        tive study of the two writers' preoccupation with the "res-
        olution of negation"].

1331   Corke, Hilary. "Matters of Opinion," Encounter, VI (Jan.
        1956), 88-91. [Reviews of novels by G. Greene, E. Thompson,
        and P. Forster among others].

1332   Corrigan, Matthew. "The Poet's Intuition of Prose Fiction:
        Pound and Eliot on the Novel," UWR, II:1 (1966), 33-51.
        [Examines their ideas on prose fiction, and how they evolved
        through their critical analyses of certain trends in fic-
        tion and of specific novelists, especially H. James, J.
        Joyce, and D. H. Lawrence].

1333   Coughlan, Robert. "Why Britain: Angry Young Men Boil
        Over," Life, XLIV (26 May 1958), 138-140, 145-148. [Ex-
        amines the social and political causes that gave rise to
        the "Angry Young Men." K. Amis, J. Braine, J. Wain, and
        playwright J. Osborne].

1334   Cournos, John. "The Rebel Mood in Literature," CH, XXXVII
        (Dec. 1932), 308-313. [Contends that disintegration in
        modern Literature "has its source in life." Illustration
        from the European novel generally with brief references
        to A. Bennett, H. G. Wells, and J. Joyce].

1335 _____. "God, Existentialism and the Novel," ASch,
XVIII (Winter 1949), 116-127. [A review article on existential novels emphasising the common elements they share;
viz., concern with serious fundamental issues, responsibility and total absence of romance and propaganda. Includes
G. Greene's The Heart of The Matter, E. Waugh's Brideshead
Revisited, and A. Huxley's Ape and Essence].

1336 "The Course of the English Novel," TLS, 809 (19 July 1917),
337-338. [Maintains that the English novel has made little
progress since J. Austen because the novelist seeks to
interest others and ignores his task--"to discover the
nature of his own interest in life, to know what he knows
about human beings, and to express it in the form of a
story"].

1337 Courtney, Mrs. W. L. "The Younger Novelists," NAR, CXCVIII
(July 1913), 76-86. [A review article of 1913 Spring novels.
Includes G. Cannan's Round the Corner, H. Walpole's Forti-
tude, M. Sinclair's The Combined Maze, and H. Marriott's
The Catfish].

1338 Cox, C. B., Norman St. John-Stevas, Donald Davie, Martin
Jarrett-Kerr, and C. S. Lewis. "Pornography and Obscenity,"
CritQ, III:2 (Summer 1961), 99-122. [A symposium on issues
related to morality and art prompted by the Chatterley
trial. N. St. John-Stevas reviews English censorship laws
to 1961, D. Davie discusses D. H. Lawrence's remark that
"the essential function of art is moral," M. Jarrett-Kerr
explains the Christian viewpoint, and C. S. Lewis comments
on the use of four-letter words as the "vocabulary either
of farce or of vituperation"].

1339 Craft, Robert. "Stravinsky and Some Writers," Harper's,
CCXXXVII (Dec. 1968), 101-108. [Informal exchanges with
Stravinsky, W. H. Auden, E. Waugh, A. Huxley, and C. Isher-
wood].

1340 Craig, David. "The British Working-Class Novel Today,"
ZAA, XI (Jan. 1963), 29-41. [Paper delivered 25 August
1962, in Dresden to teachers of English and American literature. A survey of novels "fully engrossed by the life
of workers" and which reaches the conclusion that only
"whole-hearted socialism" can give rise to a wholly ex-
cellent piece of literature. W. Allen, "R. Tressell," M.
Heinemann, R. Williams, and A. Sillitoe].

1341 Cranston, Maurice. "The Young and the Established," Encounter, VII (Nov. 1956), 81-84. [Reviews novels by J.
Fane, P. Larkin, and W. Lewis].

1342 _____, et al. "The Writer in His Age," LM, IV:5 (May
1957), 38-55. [A symposium. Contributors are M. Cranston,

D. J. Enright, Roy Fuller, W. Golding, P. Larkin, J. Osborne, S. Spender, J. Wain, and C. Wilson].

1343 _____. "The New Novelists: An Enquiry," LM, V:11 (Nov. 1958), 25-28. Postscript, pp. 30-31. [A symposium. Contributors are: A. Quinton, L. Cooper and F. Kermode. Limits the list of significant "novelists under forty" to P. H. Newby, F. King, I. Murdoch, and E. Humphreys. Expresses disappointment at the work of the "Angries" and sees "few signs of life among the young"].

1344 Cross, Wilbur Lucius. "Some Novels of 1920," YR, (NS) X (Jan. 1921), 396-411. [A review of 1920 novels by D. Richardson, C. Dane, D. Golding, H. Johnston, E. L. Masters, V. Woolf, W. L. George, J. Conrad, J. Galsworthy, M. Sinclair, and G. Cannan as a "mirror of the new age," some of which reflect the impact of Freud].

1345 _____. "The New Fiction," YR, (NS) XI:3 (Apr. 1922), 449-466. [Examines the novel in 1921 as it is written by H. Walpole, M. Sinclair, H. Johnston, R. Macaulay as well as American novelists, and traces its evolution from its adherence to Victorian ideals to its new form and substance, especially in its analysis of sex and interest in the "philosophy of the subconscious"].

1346 _____. "Novels of N Dimensions," YR, (NS) XII:3 (Apr. 1923), 477-496. [Examines the new trend in novel writing in H. G. Wells, "R. West," V. Woolf, J. Joyce and others, and observes that characters suffer "a loss of reality" whenever "psychological theory intrudes," that "the new 'psychic synthesis' is more a hope than a fact"].

1347 _____. "The Modern English Novel," SatR, V (15 Sep. 1928), 122-123. [Part of the address delivered to the American Academy of Art and Letters and published in book form by Yale University Press, 1928. Considers how the present day novelists have reshaped the earlier form of the novel. V. Woolf, H. G. Wells, H. James, and J. Joyce among others].

1348 Cruttwell, Patrick. "Makers and Persons," HudR, XII (Winter 1959-1960), 487-507. [Describes four ways in which the maker is an exhibitionist, the "acute distress to the person" such exhibitionism may cause, and the two problems -- "one of method and one of morals" -- it raises for the critic. V. Woolf, J. Conrad, and J. Joyce among others].

1349 Dahl, Liisa. "The Attributive Sentence Structure in the Stream-of-Consciousness-Technique. With Special Reference to the Interior Monologue used by Virginia Woolf, James Joyce and Eugene O'Neill," Neuphilolog, LXVI (1967), 440-454. [Illustrates differences in the usage of the Attribu-

191

tive Sentence structure and its "loose modifiers" by the
literary form each writer emphasised: pure impressionism
in V. Woolf, the combination of impressionism and expressionism in J. Joyce, and expressionism in O'Neill].

1350 Daiches, David. "Problems for Modern Novelists: 1. The
Novel as Symbolic Communication," Accent, III (Spring 1943),
144-151. Reprinted in Accent Anthology. Edited by Kerber
Quinn and Charles Shattuck. (New York: Harcourt, 1946),
pp. 548-559. [Discusses the "adequate machinery" necessary
for the "proper symbolization of character in fiction," the
writer's "point of preliminary contact" with the reader, the
"rhetorical aspect" of fiction, and suggests that fiction
is returning to the "rhetorical tradition" of English fiction away from "the more tenuous envelope in the tradition
of James, Proust and V. Woolf"].

1351 _____. "Problems for Modern Novelists: 2. Plot,
Style, and The Question of Value," Accent, III (Summer 1943),
231-239. Reprinted in Accent Anthology. Edited by Kerber
Quinn and Charles Shattuck. (New York: Harcourt, 1946),
pp. 559-570. [Discusses structure and style as methods of
symbolization, the significance of their relationship and
the way in which the novelist's methods depend on his relation to his readers].

1352 _____. "Sensibility and Technique," KR, V (Autumn
1943), 569-579. [Though mostly concerned with H. James as
a "novelist of sensibility," with references to V. Woolf,
the article distinguishes two schools of novelists: the
traditional and the "modern," the latter relying upon individual sensibility to portray experience and as "guide
to what ideal truth is." Also refutes the widespread notion that the modern novelist is concerned with "the technique of expression merely"].

1353 _____. "The Progress of Criticism--IV. How to Crit-
icise a Novel," Listener, XLVIII:1229 (18 Sep. 1952), 468-
469. [Accepts the tendency of modern criticism of fiction
to discover the "true meaning and vitality of a novel
through an exploration of the author's technique," but does
not belittle or deny the importance and significance of
"background studies." (Letter to the Editor by C. H. Lay
(2 Oct. 1952), 551; reply by D. Daiches (9 Oct. 1952), 590].

1354 _____. "Britons Find It Jolly Good Reading," NYTBR,
(5 Sep. 1954), 1, 14. [States that novelty, strength and
substance are the qualities that make for the popularity of
the American novel in England, that these same are lacking
from its British counterpart which is "predictable and conventional in theme and manner"].

1355 _____. "The Possibilities of Heroism," ASch, XXV

(Winter 1956), 94-106. [Discusses the stature of the hero in the light of the problems posed by new psychological knowledge and whether the hero can achieve "moral stature" in modern fiction. J. Joyce, A. Huxley, G. Greene, E. M. Forster, D. H. Lawrence, and V. Woolf among others].

1356 _____. "The Background of Recent English Literature," Folio, XXII (Winter 1956-57), 52-64. Reprinted as Chapter I, "General Background" in The Present Age After 1920. (London: The Cresset Press, 1958), pp. 1-21. Issued in the U. S. as The Present Age in British Literature. (Bloomington, Indiana: Indiana University Press, 1958). [A literary historian's views on the forces at work on English culture from the 1920's to the present].

1357 _____. "Selection and 'Significance' in the Modern Novel," Midway, IV (1961), 2-13. A reprint of Chapter I of the revised edition of The Novel and the Modern World. (Chicago: University of Chicago Press, 1960), pp. 1-11. [Discusses the "radical redefinition of the nature and function of fiction" as a result of the "breakdown of public agreement about what is significant in experience--the new view of time, and the new view of the nature of consciousness"].

1358 _____. "Time and Sensibility," MLQ, XXV (1964), 26-31. [A review article of M. Church's Time and Reality:Studies in Contemporary Fiction and R. Freedman's The Lyrical Novel: Studies in Hermann Hesse, André Gide, and Virginia Woolf].

1359 _____. "Speaking of Books: Society and the Artist," NYTBR, (28 Nov. 1965), 2. [Argues that the outstanding characteristic of modern literature is the artist "contracting out of the official culture," contrary to the traditional belief of literature being "mimetic in nature and didactic in purpose"].

1360 Dalgish, Doris N. "Some Contemporary Women Novelists," ContempR, CXXVII (Jan. 1925), 79-85. [A survey of contemporary women novelists focusing on the "artistic sincerity and moral and intellectual courage" of R. Macaulay, S. Kaye-Smith, and C. Holme].

1361 Danchin, F. C. "Revue annuelle: le roman anglais et le roman americain," RG, (Apr.-June 1921), 143-178. [Pages 147-172 deal with the English novel followed by C. Cestre on the American, pp. 173-178. Reviews continental editions of English novels by A. Bennett, J. C. Snaith, Mrs. H. Ward, E. F. Benson, J. Conrad, G. Moore, H. G. Wells and others].

1362 _____. "Le Roman anglais," RG, (Apr.-June 1922), 130-159. [A review article divided into four parts. Part 1 reviews A. Chevally's The English Novel, part 2 contains brief comments on the masters (T. Hardy, J. Conrad and R. Kipling), part 3 reviews the works of popular novelists (J.

K. Jerome, J. Oppenheim, E. Phillpotts and others), and part
4 surveys the influence of R. Tagore on English thought].

1363 Dangerfield, George. "English Ebb, American Flow," SatR,
XV (3 Apr. 1937), 3-4, 26, 28. [A comparison between the
English and American novel of the thirties. V. Woolf, A.
Calder-Marshall, S. Maugham, and S. T. Warner among others].

1364 Daniel-Rops. "Une Technique nouvelle: le monologue intérie-
eur," Correspondant, 326 (1931), 281-305. [Discusses Joyce's
use of the monologue, its limitations and merits after a
brief historical survey that traces its origins and growth].

1365 "The Dark Side," Listener, LXVIII:1761 (27 Dec. 1962), 1076.
[Editorial on A. Wilson's "Evil in the English Novel." (See
below)].

1366 Davenport, Guy. "Jungles of the Imagination," NR, XIII (9
Oct. 1962), 273-274. [A review of J. Jones' The Thin Red
Line, W. Golding's The Inheritors and J. Wain's Strike the
Father Dead. Underlines two common elements: the writers
positing "a jungle as symbol of the complexity of the world"
and the "persistent modern dichotomy of energy and its denial"].

1367 Davidson, Donald. "Decorum in the Novel," ModA, IX (Winter
1964-65), 34-48. [On the "pattern of liberation" and licence
resulting from the legal battle in the U. S. over Ulysses
and Lady Chatterley's Lover].

1368 Davis, Elmer. "Short Weight in Long Novels," Bookman (New
York), XLVIII (Feb. 1919), 706-709. [Objects to the "practice of adulterating" new novels with "an admixture of the
incidents and characters" of earlier works in the "novel-
group of the Mackenzie-Bennett type"].

1369 Davis, Oswald H. "The Morality of the Modern Novelist,"
CLM (Apr. 1922), 231-234. [Draws attention to the "persis-
tent ethical questing," and "fanatical zeal" for truth to
vision and the "unflinching candour" which characterizes
English novelists of the 20th century. Mentions G. Moore,
H. G. Wells, R. Kipling, J. Conrad, M. Hewlett, J. Gals-
worthy, M. Sinclair, H. Walpole, J. D. Beresford, and D. H.
Lawrence].

1370 Davis, Robert Gorham. "At the Heart of the Story is Man,"
NYTBR, (28 Dec. 1952), 1. Reprinted in Highlights of
Modern Literature: A Permanent Collection of Memorable
Essays from 'The New York Times Book Review.' Edited by
Francis Brown. (New York: The New American Library, 1954),
pp. 57-62. [Discusses the "stable order of values" of writ-
ers, especially novelists, and notes that "nothing in the
history of the novel gives reason for pessimism about its

future, so long as the freedom and responsibility and dignity of the individual remain primary concerns in our society, and so long as writers know that they themselves have the power to create values"].

1371 _____. "From Fiat to Inquiry: Recent Trends in the Criticism of Fiction," CEA, XXXI:3 (Dec. 1968), 4-6. [Points out the distinction between the different theories rather than their continuity, as well as their premises and implications].

1372 _____. "The Shrinking Garden and New Exits: The Comic-Satiric Novel in the Twentieth Century," KanQ, I:3 (Summer 1969), 5-16. [Describes the evolution of the comic-satiric novel from the novel of ideas of A. Huxley and N. Douglas to the "externalist" novel of E. Waugh and R. Firbank, and to modern absurdist comedy. Contends that these changes "reflect a modification in the sensibility that produces and the audience that enjoys it"].

1373 _____. "Market Depressed and Unstable: Spring Surveys of the the Recent English Novel," PLL, VI:2 (Spring 1970), 211-223. [A review essay on critical works dealing with the contemporary English novel. Includes K. Alsop's The Angry Decade, W. Van O'Connor's The New University Wits and the End of Modernism, R. Rabinowitz' The Reaction Against Experiment in the English Novel, 1950-1960, J. McCormick's Catastrophe and Imagination, J. Gindin's Postwar British Fiction: New Accents and Attitudes, F. R. Karl's A Reader's Guide to the Contemporary English Novel, R. Scholes The Fabulators, R. Kellogg and R. Scholes' The Nature of Narrative, J. Hall's The Lunatic Giant in The Drawing Room: The The British and American Novel Since 1930, and The Tragic Comedians].

1374 Dawson, S. W. "A Personal Report on the Literary Fifties," Audit, I:1 (1960), 12-15. [Observations on the literary set-up of the fifties ranging from the "boom of University writers," especially novelists and reviewers, to the establishment of Departments for American Studies].

1375 Deal, Bordon. "The Future of Fiction," PrS, XXVIII (Fall 1954), 228-233. [Gives reasons why modern fiction no longer attracts an audience, is not trusted as "interpreter of life and truth," and why it has 'ceased to communicate"].

1376 _____. "Storytelling as Symbolism," SWR, LIII (Summer 1968), 293-298. [Asserts the importance of storytelling in the novel and considers the story man's "primary symbol" in whose "movement and development" is embodied the writer's message. Brief reference to W. Golding and J. R. R. Tolkien].

1377 "A Defence of Poor Prose in Great Novels," CO, LXVIII (Apr. 1920), 538-539. [Extracts from V. Woolf's review of L. P.

Smith's Treasury of English Prose in which she contends that most great novelists write the poorest prose].

1378 De Gramont, Elisabeth. "Ecrivains anglais vus de Paris," RH, (18 July 1931), 317-338. [Recollections of English poets and novelists].

1379 Dell, Floyd. "The Difference Between Life and Fiction," NRep, XXX:384 (12 Apr. 1922), 7-8. Reprinted in The Novel of Tomorrow and the Scope of Fiction. (Indianapolis: Bobbs-Merrill, 1922), pp. 39-48. [Maintains that though fiction aims at a "simple pragmatic truth," it gives us life "made emotionally intelligible," not the raw materials of life].

1380 Delteil, Francois. "Romanciers catholiques anglais," LivL, 14 (1948), 293-294; 17 (1948), 433-435. [Separate articles on E. Waugh and G. Greene with bibliographical notes].

1381 Demmig, Charlotte. "Moderne Tendenzen im englischen Frauen-roman," Der Gral, XXVI (1932), 453-459. [Examines modern topics of women novelists of the twentieth century. "R. West," M. Sinclair, M. Borden, V. Woolf, R. Macaulay, S. Kaye-Smith, D. Richardson and others].

1382 "Democracy in English Fiction," LA, 269 (1 Apr. 1911), 3-11. Reprinted from CQR. [On the representation of the life of the different classes in fiction and the growth of profanity and coarseness in recent novels. References to A. Bennett and C. J. C. Hyne].

1383 De Mott, Benjamin. "Dirty Words?" HudR, XIX (Spring 1965), 31-44. [Examines the theme of silence or the deprecation of language in literature, especially I. Murdoch's Under the Net, and J. P. Salinger's fiction. References to J. Conrad, and J. Joyce among others].

1384 De Romain, Yvonne. "L'évolution du roman anglais," RB, LXIX (3 Jan. 1931), 13-20. [Traces the impact of the overthrow of values, both literary and moral, after World War I, on the contents of the English novel].

1385 Desmond, Shaw. "What is a Novel?" Bookman (London), LXXIII (Jan. 1928), 211-213. [Describes the novel as the "world's most important work" that serves as a "link between life and the mind of man," and identifies two kinds of novelists: the "conscious" and the instinctive or "unconscious," mean-ing by the former those who have a "feeling," an understand-ing of a purpose behind life. Also predicts the future of the novel to lie in the direction of the fantastic and the realistic. H. G. Wells, R. Kipling, E. M. Forster, and A. Bennett].

1386 Detweiler, Robert. "Moment of Death in Modern Fiction,"

ConL, XIII (Summer 1972), 267-294. [Analyses the moment of death in modern fiction--its "particular interiority . . . as felt by the die-er and presented from his perspective"-- from the "standpoint of phenomology and structuralism." Illustrates from the death of Joycelin in W. Golding's The Spire and the execution of Rubeshov in A. Koestler's Darkness at Noon among others].

1387 De Voto, Bernard. "English '37: The Novelist and the Reader," SatR, XVI (26 June 1937), 8-9; (3 July 1937), 8-9; (10 July 1937), 8, 14; (17 July 1937), 8; (24 July 1937), 8; (31 July 1937), 8, 13; (7 Aug. 1937), 8, 13; (14 Aug. 1938), 8, 12; (21 Aug. 1937), 8, 14; (28 Aug. 1937), 8; (4 Sep. 1937), 8, 11. [A series of eleven articles on various aspects of the novelist's art--necessity of technique, narration, focal characters, description, information, emotion, and his relations to the reader. Wide-ranging references to both English and American novels].

1388 _____. "Freud's Influence on Literature," SatR, XX (7 Oct. 1939), 10-11. [A brief general account of the widespread influence Freud had on literature, and especially the "literary fashion" of psychoanalytical fiction].

1389 _____. "The Invisible Novelist," PS, IV:1 (Winter 1950), 30-54. Reprinted in The World of Fiction (Boston: Houghton-Mifflin, 1950), pp. 205-229. [On how a novelist relates his fiction "without appearing in his own person"].

1390 _____. "Why Read Dull Novels?" Harper's, CCIV:1221 (Feb. 1952), 65-69. [Argues that shallow fashionable assertions, inept inferior craftsmanship, and trivialising of experience are responsible for the sad state of the novel].

1391 D'Exideuil, Pierre. "Perspectives anglaises," Europe, XIX: 76 (15 Apr. 1929), 564-575. [Surveys the "emancipated," English post-World War I literary scene--excluding Catholic poets and Anglo-Irish writers. Pages 570-575 underline the emergence of the novel as a literary medium which is becoming more analytical and psychologically subtle at the expense of craftsmanship and "character." A. Huxley, V. Woolf, D. Richardson, J. Joyce, D. Garnett, and D. H. Lawrence].

1392 Diakonova, Nina. "Notes on the Evaluation of the Bildungsroman in England," ZAA, XVI (1968), 341-351. [From Roderick Random to The Alexandrian Quartet. Maintains that the bildungsroman in the sense of a narrative concentrating on the "personal problems of a certain individual and on his evolution for an extended period of time, rather than on the peculiarities of his environment" is virtually nonexistent today. E. M. Forster, A. Bennett, S. Maugham, R. Aldington, D. H. Lawrence, D. Richardson, J. Joyce, V. Woolf, J. Galsworthy, K. Amis, G. Greene, and L. Durrell among others].

1393   Dickens, Monica. "The Facts of Fiction," Writer, LXXXI
       (May 1968), 21-24. [Discusses the connection between imag-
       ination and reality, and asserts that "all fiction is fact,
       molded, manipulated and enriched by the author's imagina-
       tion"].

1394   Dickinson, Ruth F. "Contemporary Literature: Lost Without
       God," Cresset, XXX (Jan. 1967), 14-16. [Examines what
       poetry, novel, and drama tell us about man's condition, the
       condition of the church, and "the need for truth and the
       search for God." References to G. Greene and J. Joyce
       among others].

1395   Dobrée, Bonamy. "Novels and Subject Criticism," NR, C
       (Apr. 1933), 561-568. [On the chaos existing in the criti-
       cism of fiction and the proper "business of the critic of
       novels"].

1396   _____. "The Novel: Has It a Function To-Day?" EDH,
       XIII (1934), 57-76. [Discusses what the "business of the
       novel is," raises the question of the position of the nov-
       elist "as part of the organism of society," and suggests
       two realms which the novelist may deal with: "what is
       happening in contemporary minds . . . and to contemporary
       bodies"].

1397   _____. "No Man's Land," SR, LXV:2 (1957), 309-326.
       [A review article on K. Amis's Lucky Jim, J. Wain's Hurry
       on Down, I. Murdoch's Under the Net, C. Wilson's The Out-
       sider, J. Osborne's Look Back in Anger, and G. Scott's auto-
       biography Time and Place as works representative of the new
       criticism--and rejection--of the "phoney" in middleclass
       values, and the old bases of sexual morality and religion].

1398   Donagan, Alan and Martin Steinmann. "Art and Counterfeit
       Art," CE, XX:5 (Feb. 1960), 252-254. [Questions the "status,
       meaning, presupposition, and consequences" of W. Burns'
       thesis in "The Genuine and Counterfeit," CE, XVIII:3 (Dec.
       1956), 143-150, which, they contend, has not been "supported
       or clarified"].

1399   Dooley, David Joseph. "Some Uses and Mutations of the
       Picaresque," DR, XXXVII (Winter 1958), 363-377. [On the
       picaresque tradition in English up to Dickens and its re-
       vival in the twentieth century by H. G. Wells, E. Waugh,
       and J. Wain].

1400   _____. "The Strategy of the Catholic Novelist," CathW,
       CLXXXIX (July 1959), 300-304. [Maintains that the Catholic
       novelist can, like E. Waugh, "shock people" into an aware-
       ness of how "chaotic society is without God," or like G.

Greene, show the "presence of Grace" where it is least ex-
pected].

1401 Dottin, Paul. "La Littérature anglaise en 1931," RF, XII
(1 July 1932), 120-143. [Reviews English literary output in
1931 pointing out "les oeuvres les plus marquantes" in the
different genres. Pages 121-133 deal with the novel and
are subdivided into 1) Novels of war and naturalism, 2)
Adventure and detective stories, 3) Fantasy and the supernatural, 4) the "psychological" novel, and 5) Chronicle
novels].

1402 _____. "La Littérature anglaise en 1932," RF, (15 Sep.
1933), 311-332. [Reviews and classifies the best novels of
1932 into 1) social, 2) "psychological" studies (A. J. Cronin,
S. Jameson, C. Morgan), 3) visions of the future (A. Huxley,
J. B. Priestley), 4) mysteries, 5) the "exotic" 6) historical (H. Walpole), 7) Irish Realism, and 8) Scottish].

1403 _____. "La Littérature anglaise en 1933," RF, (1 June
1934), 522-543. [Reviews and classifies novels of 1933 into
1) Travel (S. Maugham), 2) Escape (J. D. Beresford and H.
Walpole), 3) Historical (M. Borden, R. H. Mottram), 4) Realistic (R. Aldington, A. J. Cronin), 5) Critical of society
(H. G. Wells), 6) sequence or "family" novel (J. D. Beresford, J. C. Powys), and 7) Spiritual (E. F. Benson, J. Green)].

1404 _____. "La Littérature anglaise en 1935," RF, (Aug.
1936), 527-544; (Sep. 1936), 129-146. [Reviews and classifies the novels of 1935 into 1) Novels with a Dickensian
flavour (L. Walmsey, S. Kaye-Smith, M. Baring), 2) Historical novels (J. Lindsay, M. Borden, M. Simpson, C. Oman), 3)
Adventure (J. Masefield, R. H. Mottram), 4) "romans d'antic-
ipations" (J. Connell, T. F. Powys), and 5) Detective stories].

1405 _____. "La Littérature anglaise en 1936: 1. Le roman,"
RF, (15 July 1937), 302-323. [Reviews and classifies the
novels of 1936 into 1) "L'école mystico-realiste" (C. Morgan,
R. Lehmann, C. Houghton), 2) Novels where heroes reshape
the pattern of their lives (R. Croft-Cooke, H. W. Freeman,
M. R. C. Sheriff, S. McKenna, A. Huxley), 3) Novels of "l'au-
tre homme en nous," (L. Sieveking, R. Speaight, E. Phillpotts),
4) The regional novel (W. Holtby, R. Hall, S. Kaye-Smith,
D. Wallace), 5) The social novel, 6) The historical, 7)
Exotic realism, 8) Satirical and humorous, and 9) Detective
stories].

1406 _____. "La Littérature anglaise en 1937: 1. Le roman,"
RF, (15 June 1938), 520-532. [Reviews and classifies the
novels of 1937 into 1) The realism of S. Maugham and the
"realism" of V. Woolf, 2) Social novels, 3) Chronicles of
the times, 4) Explorations of the unconscious, 5) The "roman
exotique," 6) The historical, and 7) Detective stories].

1407 _____. "La Littérature anglaise en 1938: 1. le roman,"
RF, XIX (1 July 1939), 79-93. [Reviews and classifies the
novels of 1938 into novels of 1) The sea, 2) "exotisme im-
périal," 3) present discontent, 4) Middleclass life, 5) complex and disturbed spirits, 6) historical events, and 7) detective stories].

1408 Downing, Francis. "The Art of Fiction," Commonweal, LV (28
Dec. 1951), 297-299. [Asserts that what distinguishes the
artist is not so much his subject but his ability to convert
"the very pulses of the air into revelations." Illustrates
from works by J. Conrad, H. James, and G. Greene].

1409 Drabble, Margaret. "Women Novelists," Books, 375 (Autumn
1968), 87-90. [Examines the problem of language in English
and American women novelists' handling of "gynaecological
literature"--childbirth, breast-feeding, contraception,
abortion, and copulation. Brief references to P. Mortimer,
E. O'Brien, and D. Lessing].

1410 Durrell, Lawrence. "Limits of Control: iii. No Clue to
Living," TLS, 3039 (27 May 1960), 339. Reprinted in The
Writer's Dilemma: Essays first Published in Times Liter-
Supplement Under the Heading: 'Limits of Control'. Edited
by Stephen Spender. (London: Oxford University Press,
1961), pp. 17-25. [Maintains that the artist's concern is
with the pure art of self-penetration, of self-disentangle-
ment, i.e., no clue to living].

1411 Duvall, Ellen. "The New Paganism," AtM, CXXXVI (Nov. 1925),
633-637. [Contends that "modern fiction," in contrast to
the old paganism of the Greeks, is not "constructive," but
simply mirrors the "menacing truth of disintegration and
decay," and is especially interested in depicting man's capacity for concupiscence].

1412 Edel, Leon. "Speaking of Books: Sex and the Novel," NYTBR,
(1 Nov. 1964), 2. [Argues that the sexual "liberation" in
the novel in the first four decades of this century has led
to a "trivial, passionless mechanical attitude toward sex,"
to a kind of "dehumanization of sex" in fiction].

1413 Edelman, Maurice. "The Novel as Metaphor," The Times, (20
Dec. 1962), p. 11. [Asserts that there is no "absolute
formula" for the novel, for within its "amorphous mass" it
can accommodate any "anti-novel" or "no-novel," provided it
conveys to the reader "a microcosm of human experience"].

1414 Edgar, Pelham. "The Drift of Modern Fiction," UTQ, I (1931)
123-139. [Examines the effect upon fiction of the contrasted
efforts of J. Galsworthy and J. Joyce].

1415 "Edwardian," TLS, 3084 (7 Apr. 1961), 217. [Leading article
discussing the use of the term in Edwardians and Late Vic-

torians. Edited by Richard Ellmann. (New York: Columbia University Press and Oxford University Press, 1961)].

1416 "The Edwardian Novel," TLS, 2369 (28 June 1947), 322. [A review that regards Edwardian novelists as "professional writers" without "priggishness," to whom entertainment was a "legitimate activity of the human spirit"].

1417 Edwards, Oliver. "Annals of the Poor," The Times, (16 June 1955), p. 11. [Discusses fiction "from which political consequences may flow," with special reference to A. Morrison and R. Whiteing].

1418 Egan, Maurice Francis. "The Return to the Quiet Novel," Bookman (New York), LIV (Sep. 1921), 17-23. [Discusses the reaction to H. G. Wells and "all the New School," and the return to the "quiet novel" of A. Marshall].

1419 Egri, Peter. "Anger and Form," ZAA, XI (1963), 269-280. [A review article on K. Allsop's The Angry Decade and J. Russell's Anger and After: A Guide to the New British Drama. Pages 270-272 examine special features of the "dissentience of the fifties," with reference to K. Amis, J. Wain, and J. Braine].

1420 "Eight from Britain," SatR, XL (30 Nov. 1957), 15-17, 31-32. [A collection of eight reviews by different reviewers on new works by O. Manning, A. Wilson, S. Jameson, G. B. Stern, M. Baldwin, A. Thirkell, N. Loft, and E. Glyn].

1421 Eliot, T. S. "London Letter: The Novel," Dial, LXXIII (Sep. 1922), 329-331. [Classifies the English contemporary novel into three categories: the old narrative method of the tale, the psychoanalytic type, and "the Dostoyevsky type"].

1422 _____. "Le Roman anglais contemporain," NRF, 28 (1 May 1927), 669-675. [Maintains that the contemporary English novel "est en retard," is devoid of Hawthorne's "moral preoccupation," is inspired and influenced by psychoanalysis, and has lost a great deal in seriousness and depth. D. H. Lawrence, V. Woolf, D. Garnett, and A. Huxley].

1423 Elliot, George P. "A Defense of Fiction," HudR, XVI:1 (Spring 1963), 9-48. [Taking N. Frye's "fourfold division" of fiction as the frame of his essay, he attempts "an ampler way of talking about fiction" than the "constructive" one which the combination of Jamesianism and the New Criticism has generated].

1424 _____. "The Novelist as Meddler," VQR, XL (Winter 1964), 96-113. Reprinted in Conversions: Literature and the Modernist Deviation (New York: Dutton, 1971), pp. 94-112; and in Critical Approaches to Fiction. Edited by Shiv K. Kumar and

Keith F. McKean. (New York: McGraw-Hill, 1968), pp. 333-349. [Discusses ways in which "author-meddling does not damage a novel," and when they can be turned to a novel's advantage, and in section 6, the areas in which the novelist should not interfere. Brief references to D. H. Lawrence and H. James among others].

1425 Ellis, S. M. "The Literature of 1921," FR, CXVII (Jan. 1922), 154-165. [A survey of the literary output which shows biographical and autobiographical works in the forefront. Fiction is briefly surveyed on pp. 163-164].

1426 Ellman, Richard. "Contemporary Directions in Literature," BaratR, III (June-Sep. 1968), 63-68. [Discusses the tendency to explore "those things which are opposite to the traditional realities of society and literature" and the consequent "social irrealism" which has become the subject-matter of literature. References to J. Joyce, V. Woolf, and S. Beckett among others].

1427 Endicott, N. J. "The Novel in England Between the Wars," UTQ, XII (Oct. 1942), 18-31. [Maintains that the temper and experiments of the twenties are best seen in V. Woolf, J. Joyce, D. H. Lawrence, and A. Huxley rather than J. Galsworthy, H. G. Wells, A. Bennett and S. Maugham, and that as a result of the interest in self, the novel has become more abstracted and introspective avoiding social relations, but the swing of the pendulum, coming in the late thirties, has brought a renewed realization that action is interesting and profoundly revealing].

1428 Engel, Claire-Elaine. "L'Exotisme dans la littérature anglaise," RGen, (Dec. 1930), 734-745. [Discusses interest in exotic lands and scenes displayed by writers in the early part of the 20th century. R. Kipling, J. Conrad, E. M. Forster, F. Yeats-Brown and others].

1429 _____. "Einige englische Romanciers von heute," DU, VIII (Jan. 1948), 28. [Examines the new spiritualism and intellectual tendencies resulting from the war in the novels of C. Morgan, G. Greene, and H. Green].

1430 Engelborghs, Maurits. "Engelse beschouwingen over de roman," DWB, CVI (1961), 58-66. ["English views on the novel." Reviews M. Allott's Novelists on the Novel and R. Stang's The Theory of the Novel in England, 1850-1870, and comments on the novel as a literary genre and the "looseness" of the term "novel"].

1431 _____. "Over Karakterstudie in de Engelse Literatuur," DWB, CX:10 (1965), 756-761. [A review article on English studies on character].

1432 _____. "Karakter en intrige in de roman," DWB, CXII
(1967), 133-136. [A review article on C. C. Walcutt's
Man's Changing Mask. Modes and Methods of Characterization
in Fiction].

1433 _____. "Over de vitaliteit van de roman: Voorbeelden
en Symptonen," DWB, CXIII (1968), 614-621. [Argues that
the volume of novels published, paperbacks, popular editions, statistics of sales and critical interest aroused
indicate the "vitality" of the novel, and that it is far
from dead].

1434 _____. "Britise 'Lady Novelists'," DWB, CXIV (1969),
286-292. [Considers recent novels by M. Spark and E. O'Brien
as examples of feminine emancipation, and as daring and
aggressive as anything written by male novelists].

1435 "England's Glut of Fiction," LDig, XLVIII (25 Apr. 1914),
986. [On the overproduction of novels and the shrinkage
of the English reading public. Quotes Mr. W. Heinemann as
reported by the London correspondent of Boston's Transcript].

1436 "English and American Fiction, 1909: A Review and Comparison," AtM, CIV (Nov. 1909), 679-687. [A review article
restricted to novels published in 1909 pointing out "the
solid substratum" of the English novel, great diversifica-
tion and wide range, its interest in the life of the lower
classes and the "local colour" tale of foreign lands. C.
F. Keary, A. N. Lyons, W. Deeping, F. Forbes-Robertson, and
E. Oldmeadow].

1437 "The English and American Novels," Outlook, CXXXI (23 Aug.
1922), 661. [A comparison that admits the superiority of
the English novel owing to its "firmness of texture and
thoroughness of workmanship," and its "orderly, progressive" development].

1438 "The English and American Novel," TLS, 2639 (29 Aug. 1952),
xii. [Estimates the influence of the "Great Simplifiers"--
E. Waugh, C. Isherwood, and E. Hemingway--on both sides of
the Atlantic in delivering the novel from "Mr. Bennett and
Mrs. Brown," and brings out the defects of "assimilation
and intelligence" in the English novel, and those of "style
and moderation" in the American].

1439 "English and American Novels," TLS, 3233 (13 Feb. 1964),
126. [Review article on W. Allen's Tradition and Dream.
(London: Phoenix House, 1964), and C. E. Eisinger's Fiction
of the Forties. (Chicago: University Press, 1964)].

1440 "English and French," TLS, 3039 (27 May 1960), 337. [Lead-
ing article reviewing two issues devoted to the contemporary
novel in England and France by A Review of English Liter-

ature and Yale French Studies].

1441 "English Fiction in War Time," Outlook, CXI (17 Nov. 1915),
652-654. [On the absence of alarm, fear, and disaster in
the novels of J. Galsworthy, G. Parker, H. G. Wells, E.
Phillpotts, M. Hewlett in the Autumn of 1915, and their
interest in "the finer issues of life, the delicate lines
of art" in spite of the war].

1442 "English Literature of Today," EngRev, III (Oct. 1909),
481-494; (Nov. 1909), 655-672. [Considers, in the second
article, H. James, J. Conrad, G. Moore, and perhaps J. Galsworthy, as conscious artists representing the "main-stream
of the current of European literature," and H. G. Wells,
A. Bennett, and R. Kipling as representative of the traditions of the "insularly English novel"].

1443 "The English Novel," Nation, (7 Sep. 1918), 594-595; (28
Sep. 1918), 676-677. [Examines the impact of the "disruptive forces" of the war in creating the "hybrid 'novel-
essay'" of H. G. Wells, and the "individualism and contempt
of form and tradition" characteristic of postwar younger
novelists].

1444 "English Novels of the Year," LA, 332 (15 Jan. 1927), 173.
[A brief record of English novels published in 1926].

1445 "The English Unviversity Novel," TLS, 2921 (21 Feb. 1958),
101. [Leading article discussing M. R. Proctor's The English University Novel].

1446 Epstein, E. L. "The Irrelevant Narrator: A Stylistic Note
on the Place of the Author in Contemporary Technique of the
Novel," Lang&S, II (1969), 92-94. [Discusses J. Joyce's
"isolative method," and the novelist's search for a "convenient niche for Ego in the novel"].

1447 Erickson, R. C. "Sex as the Writer's New Myth," ChrC,
LXXXII (19 May 1965), 641-643. [Contends that the modern
writer's depiction of sex is not reality but the writer's
"disembodied and wishful fantasy" often traceable to the
"romanticized realism" of D. H. Lawrence and a "simplified
Freudianism." Brief references to L. Durrell and D. H.
Lawrence among others].

1448 Evans, B. Ifor. "La Littérature anglaise entre les deux
guerres," RUB, IV (1951/1952), 102-126. [Discusses the
values and "mouvements eminents, differences de gout . . .
valeurs spirituelles" and significant figures of the period.
Included are E. M. Forster, V. Woolf, J. Joyce, "R. West,"
and D. H. Lawrence].

1449 "Experience of a Lifetime," TLS, 2938 (20 June 1958), 345. [Leading article on the contemporary "Roman Fleuve" or "Chronicle Novel" of D. Lessing, A. Powell, L. Durrell, and C. P. Snow].

1450 "Experiment in Prose," TLS, 2842 (17 Aug. 1956), ii. [Special Autumn Number: "Frontiers of Literature." Deplores the general postwar reluctance of novelists to experiment. R. Warner, W. Sansom, C. Isherwood, and P. Toynbee].

1451 "Fact or Fiction?" TLS, 3058 (7 Oct. 1960), 645. [Leading article discussing Miss McCarthy"s "problem": can any novelist who is cut away from the ordinary workaday world write fiction that is true to actual life?].

1452 Fagan, Edward R. "Disjointed Time and the Contemporary Novel," JGE, XXIII:1 (Apr. 1971), 151-160. [Examines English and American "experimental achronic novels" of the sixties that exemplify "displaced time phenomena," and suggests "scientific literary origins" for such experimentation. F. Baker and L. Durrell among others].

1453 Fairbanks, N. David. "The Class Character of the 'Working Class' Fiction in Post-War England," L&I, II (1972), 25-36. [A marxist approach that rejects the works of A. Sillitoe, M. Heinemann, D. Storey, and R. Williams as representative of the working experience, for their criticism of bourgeois relations never goes "beyond the limits the capitalist system sets"].

1454 "Faith and the Writer. Christian Dimensions in Literature," TLS, 3111 (13 Oct. 1961), 696-697. [Surveys the dilemmas the Christian writer faces and the state of Christian literature in Ireland, Spain, Germany, Holland, England, and France. Focuses on T. S. Eliot, G. Greene, E. Waugh, and C. Williams in England].

1455 Farber, Marjorie. "Subjectivity in Modern Fiction," KR, VII (Autumn 1945), 645-652. [Attributes the lack of novels to the absence of a "sense of character . . . of our human identity." Concentrates on Kafka, and on the supernatural, with references to D. H. Lawrence and J. Joyce].

1456 Farrar, John. "Sex Psychology in Modern Fiction," Independent, CXVII:3933 (11 Dec. 1926), 669-670, 691. [Contends that the sex psychology of Ellis, Jung, and Freud has not created "a new set of emotions" in English and American fiction, but has given the novelist "a new approach, and a new jargon," and sanctioned his "intraversion" whereby he "capitalizes his ego, or betrays it." Brief references to J. Joyce and D. H. Lawrence].

1457 _____. "The Race for Immortality," EJ, XVI:3 (Mar. 1927), 171-179. [Examines the "virtues" of certain young writers who have claimed attention lately to assess their chances to be "numbered among the immortals." "M. Arlen," V. Woolf, and A. Huxley among others].

1458 Fecher, Charles A. "Literary Freedom and the Catholic Novelist," CathW, CLXXXIV (Feb. 1957), 340-344. [Reiterates the demand that Catholic writers should enjoy the same freedom as non-Catholic novelists, and that the faith of Catholic novelists far from being a hindrance is a positive asset. References to E. Waugh, G. Greene, and J. Joyce].

1459 Fehr, Bernhard. "Englische Gegenwartskrisen und englische Zeitromane," NRs, III (1935), 161-171. [Examines economic, cultural and intellectual crises as reflected in the novels of the times. J. B. Priestley, R. Davies, W. Greenwood, J. Landsdale, J. Lindsay, and R. Graves].

1460 _____. "Zwei angelsächsische Ideenromane," NRs, IV (1937), 671-675. [An examination of two Anglo-Saxon novels that deal with cultural development: G. Santayana's The Last Puritan and C. Morgan's Sparkenbroke].

1461 _____. "Substitutionary Narration and Description," ES, XX:3 (June 1938), 97-107. Reprinted in Von Englands geistigen Beständen: Ausgewählte Aufsätze. (Frauenfeld: Verlag Huber & Co. Aktiengesellschaft, 1944), pp. 264-281. [Illustrates the stylistic component of different variations of substitutionary narration and description, "Erlebte Darstellung," which have become expressive in modern fiction].

1462 Feilner, Bermann. "Deutsche und englische Kriegsepik," Liter, XXXIX (1937), 711-714. [Compares English and German World War I novels. C. E. Mongague, R. Aldington, R. H. Mottram, C. Morgan, and E. Blunden among others].

1463 Fennell, Desmond. "The Writer and the Church," DubR, CCXLII: 516 (Summer 1968), 99-105. [Discusses what the English Catholic Church would like English Catholic writers to do].

1464 Feuerlicht, Ignace. "Christ Figures in Literature," Person, LXVIII (Autumn 1967), 461-472. [A survey of Christ figures in modern German, French, American, and English literatures. Brief references to J. Conrad, G. Greene, and J. Joyce].

1465 "Fiction and Literature," TLS, 3371 (6 Oct. 1966), 919. [A leading article discussing the rise of thriller-writers and the educational function" of fiction by the literary novel].

1466 Fiedler, Leslie A. "The Novel in the Post-Political World," PR, XXIII:3 (Summer 1956), 358-365. [A review article on two English and two American novels. Includes E. J. Howard's The Long View and I. Murdoch's Flight from the Enchanter].

1467 _____. "Class War in British Literature," Esquire, XLIX (Apr. 1958), 79-91. Reprinted in No! in Thunder, Essays on Myth and Literature. (Boston: Beacon Press, 1960), pp. 189-208; Fiction. Edited by Richard Kostelanetz. (New York: Avon Books, 1964), pp. 64-81; and The Collected Essays of Leslie Fiedler. (New York: Stein and Day, 1971), Vol. 1, pp. 409-429. [On the rise of the "anti-Bloomsbury" group of writers in the fifties. Focuses on novelists K. Amis, J. Wain, and I. Murdoch with their "merciless" and satirical delineation of the "familiar" that seems so "new" in fiction, and their "acceptance of the declassing of experience"].

1468 Field, John C. "The Literary Scene 1968-1970," RLV, (1970), 652-662. [Discusses works which future critical studies are likely to find "significant" and cannot ignore though they may lack the criterion of "quality". Included are novels by K. Amis, M. Spark, and I. Murdoch].

1469 _____. "The Literary Scene: 1968-1970," RLV, XXXVIII (1972), 91-98, 205-211. [A review article in two parts. The first part reviews C. P. Snow's Strangers and Brothers among other novels and poetry of 1970, and the second part reviews L. Durrell's Nunquam, M. Spark's The Driver's Seat, I. Murdoch's A Fairly Honourable Defeat, and E. O'Brien's A Pagan Place among other novels].

1470 Field, Louise Maunsell. "The Modern Hero," ForumN, LI (May 1914), 765-769. [Examines the change that has come over the modern hero as a result of today's "ardent interest in life and living"].

1471 _____. "Religion in the Modern Novel," ForumN, LII (Oct. 1914), 603-608. [Describes four ways in which religion evinces itself in the modern novel: a revolt against tradition, a recognition of "duty" as a result of a broader humanitarianism, a "quickened spirituality," and a vague reaching out for the Infinite or Divine. References to W. Churchill and H. G. Wells among others].

1472 _____. "Social Relations in the Modern Novel," ForumN, LIII (Feb. 1915), 244-250. [Discusses the rapidly changing social organism and its manifestations in some English and American novels. H. G. Wells and M. Sinclair among others].

1473 _____. "The Apotheosis of the Worker in Modern Fiction," Bookman (New York), XLV (Mar. 1917), 89-92. [Examines the glorification of the "inherent remunerative qualities" in work in English and American fiction. J. D. Beresford and

E. Mordaunt among others].

1474 _____ . "A New Orthodoxy in Fiction," Bookman (New York), XLV (Apr. 1917), 175-178. [Examines the movement from the "materialistic to the spiritual" in English and American fiction. H. G. Wells, J. D. Beresford, and A. Blackwood].

1475 _____ . "What's Wrong with the Men?" NAR, CCXXXI (Mar. 1931), 234-240. [Notices the disappearance of the cult of the hero in English and American fiction, with the exception of the detective story].

1476 _____ . What's Wrong with the Women?" NAR, CCXXXII (Sep. 1931), 274-280. [Notices that women in recent novels written by women are "remote from the world of changing ideas," are unaffected by what is around them, and are mere prototypes of their "ousted predecessors"].

1477 _____ . "The Modest Novelists," NAR, CCXXXV (Jan. 1933), 63-69. [Remarks on the all but entire disappearance of the "panacea novel," and its replacement by today's novel that presents conditions as they are, addresses the individual or the group involved, and preaches, "sometimes avowedly, often tacitly, a gospel of futility and despair." P. Bentley, J. Galsworthy, and J. B. Priestley among others].

1478 _____ . "Heroines Back at the Hearth," NAR, CCXXXVI (Aug. 1933), 176-183. [Discusses the rise of the "modern heroine," the job-holding and job-hunting woman and her decline into "unmitigated domesticity" in English and American fiction. H. G. Wells, J. Galsworthy, L. Merrick, C. Mackenzie, and A. S. M. Hutchinson among others].

1479 _____ . "Mothers in Fiction," NAR, CCXXXVII (Mar. 1934), 250-256. [Describes the role of mothers in present day fiction, and their release from the early"death of imbecility" to which they were subjected earlier. H. Walpole, J. D. Beresford, and E. Phillpotts among others].

1480 _____ . "Emancipating the Novel," NAR, CCXL (Sep. 1935), 318-324. [Maintains that the "emancipation from the once inescapable love interest has not merely permitted but impelled the modern novel to go further afield socially, historically, and especially pathologically" than it has done before which led, in turn, to "length, form and style" claiming the same liberty as subject. G. Gissing and J. Joyce among others].

1481 "Fielding, Gabriel." [Alan Gabriel Barnsley] "Four Cheers for the Novelist," Sunday Times, (3 Nov. 1963), 37. [Comments briefly on the growing reading public and its expectations of the "raised function" of the novel that may enable it to occupy, once more, its place "on the slopes of Parnassus"].

1482 _____. "Sex Symbolism and Modern Literature," _Critic_, XXVI (Aug.-Sep. 1967), 18-22. Reprinted in _Aquarius_ (Ireland) formerly _Everyman_, 5 (1972), 44-50. [Maintains that symbolism and the freedom to describe sexual behaviour "when honestly employed" are beneficial in illuminating "sexual guilt," furthering the quest for "essential human dignity," and giving "elegence" to a story. J. Joyce, D. H. Lawrence, G. Greene, M. Spark, and E. Waugh among others].

1483 Figgis, Darrel. "Some Recent Notable Novels," _NC_, LXXIV: 440 (Oct. 1913), 792-802; also in _LA_, 279 (22 Nov. 1913), 458-466. [A review article on novels ·by H. Caine, W. B. Maxwell, O. Onions, A. Bennett, C. E. Montague, A. Blackwood, M. Sinclair, and H. G. Wells].

1484 Finlay, Ida. "New Lamps for Old," _CorM_, (NS) LXVIII:406, (Apr. 1930), 476-482. [Examines the "traditional" novel and the "modern variety" as forms of expression necessitated by the spirit of the present age, and rejects H. Walpole's view that _The Forsyte Saga_ will remain a masterpiece to posterity].

1485 Fleming, Thomas J. "The Novel of the Future," _America_, CXIV (7 Mar. 1966), 654-656. [Surmises that with the death of the sociological and historical traditions, the novel of today and the future will deal "not simply with ideas, but with values, with a vision of life"].

1486 Fletcher, Winston. "Come In, Business Novels," _NSoc_, (19 Aug. 1971), 340-341. [Remarks on the absence of any worthwhile business novels, for the writing of such novels tends to be left to businessmen. D. Jewell, R. Townshend, and R. Fuller].

1487 Flint, F. Cudworth. "Fiction and Form: Remarks on the Novel," _Symposium_, I (Jan. 1930), 84-96. [A review article on Edwin Muir's _The Structure of the Novel_, F. M. Ford's _The English Novel_, G. Overton's _An Hour of the American Novel_, and S. Jameson's _The Georgian Novel and Mr. Robinson_].

1488 _____. "Recent Fiction," _SoR_, II (Spring 1937), 835-855. [A review article of recent novels advocating "some agreement on classificatory terminology." Includes novels by R. C. Hutchinson and S. Kaye-Smith].

1489 "The Flood of Fiction," _LA_, 251 (20 Oct. 1906), 179-184. Reprinted from _The Gentleman's Magazine_. [Discusses the enormous output of fiction, the short life of the popular novel, the dearth of purely literary work, and the tendency of novelists to write about what pleases the public].

1490 Follett, Wilson. "The Dotted Style," Bookman (New York),
XLVII (Aug. 1918), 612-614. [Examines the new style creep-
ing into fiction, characterised by the "disintegration of
the sentence into random scraps of phraseology, strung together without syntax . . . [and] rows of printed dots"].

1491 Ford, Ford Madox. "Thus to Revisit," Dial, LXIX (July 1920),
52-60; LXIX (Aug. 1920), 132-141. [Reminiscences of the
English literary world, especially of J. Conrad and H. James,
at the turn of the century. The second part deals with J.
Conrad and H. G. Wells, and the new form of the novel].

1492 _____. "A Haughty and Proud Generation," YR, (NS) XI
(July 1922), 703-717. [On the generation of N. Douglas,
W. Lewis, D. H. Lawrence, F. Swinnerton, K. Mansfield,
C. Dane, D. Richardson, and J. Joyce, "vigorous and free
in their passions and adventures" as they carry the "complex
world into the consciousness, into the spring of action of
their character -- to render it, not objectively, but from
the inside"].

1493 _____. "The English Novel from the Earliest Days to
the Death of Joseph Conrad," Bookman (New York), LXVIII
(Dec. 1928), 369-375; LXVIII (Jan. 1929), 538-547; LXVIII
(Feb. 1929), 672-682; LXIX (Mar. 1929), 68-79. [Traces the
main lines of the "gradual progress of the English novel, to
the point where it becomes a novel" in four articles. Pages
77-79 of the last article discuss the novel at the turn of
the century].

1494 _____. "Techniques," SoR, I (July 1935), 20-35. [Em-
phasises the importance of technique in writing in general,
and the novel in particular, for the purpose of technique
is "to help the writer to please." H. James, J. Conrad, and
R. Kipling among others].

1495 Forman, R. S. "First Novels of the Year," Bookman (London),
LXXXI (Dec. 1931), 185. [A brief review which selects D.
du Maurier's The Loving Spirit, H. Parkington's Four in
Family, D. W. Wilson's Early Closing, R. B. Brown's Miss
Higgs and Her Silver Flamingo, R. C. Sherriff's The Fort-
night in September, and M. Masterman's Gentlemen's Daughters
as the best six first novels of 1931].

1496 "Forum: The Conference on the Artist-Hero Novel," ELT, V:1
(1962), 27-34. [Comments by Charles J. McCanne, Eric Solomon, Sister Mary Bernetta, Lionel Stevenson, and James G.
Kennedy on the aesthetics of the artist-hero novel, before
1880 and after it, in reply to papers by G. Golding and J.
C. Knoepflmacher. ELT, IV:3 (1961). (See entries under
McCann and Kennedy].

1497 Foster, E. M. "Butterflies and Beetles," L&L, (July 1929),

1-9. [On fantasy in literature, with special reference to R. Firbank and D. Garnett].

1498 Fowles, John. "Notes on Writing a Novel," Harper's, CXXXVII (July 1968), 88-97. [On the process of creating a long work of fiction].

1499 _____. "Is the Novel Dead?" Books, 1 (Autumn 1970), 2-5. [Focuses on the "viability of the novel form as a means of communicating human experience," and singles out "precision of description," "freedom of form and style," and the nature of the reading experience as being peculiar to the novel form].

1500 Fox, R. M. "The Wage-Earner in Literature," NSta, (22 Jan. 1927), 445-446. [Notices the growing awareness of English and American writers, especially novelists, of the wage-earners and their special problems. H. G. Wells and "R. Tressell" among others].

1501 Francis, Sister Mary. "A Note on the Reputation of Narrative," Renascence, XI (1958), 20-23. [Discusses the notion of "plot," its inseparable involvement in the literary structure, and as something we momentarily abstract in our minds].

1502 Frank, Waldo. "The Major Issue," NRep, XXX:384 (12 Apr. 1922), 9-12. [Rejects judgement of a novel on the basis of a given "psychological or documentary measure of fact, truth, reality, and the like," and contends that each contribution should be "gauged by the inner law of its own genesis"].

1503 Fraser, G. S. "The Revival of Romance," EngRev, LXI (July 1935), 23-30. [Argues that the faults of contemporary English fiction -- its "rarefied" atmosphere, its deliberate effect of purposelessness, its "vacuous and formless" character, its lack of "story" and conflict -- can be remedied by a new romantic revival in England. References to A. Huxley and V. Woolf among others].

1504 Fraser, Ronald. "Butor's You: Comments on Michel Butor's 'The Use of the Personal Pronoun in the Novel'," NLR, 37 (May-June 1966), 62-68. [Discusses the author's relation to the characters in his novel and to the novel itself and the various ramifications resulting from the introduction of the "I" narrator].

1505 Frederick, John T. "New Techniques in the Novel," EJ, XXIV:5 (May 1935), 355-363. [Attributes new techniques in the novel in the 20th century to the demands of new materials and the writers' preoccupation with "the problem of how to share experience," and examines two ways in which the novelists' presentation of material may vary: style, and the "relation assumed by the narrator to the material to be presented." J. Joyce and A. Huxley among others].

1506 _____. "Fiction of the Second World War," CE, XVII:4 (Jan. 1956), 197-204. [Reviews some twenty English and American novels written in the decade following the war, and dealing with wartime experiences in the services. Includes N. Monsarrat, A. Barron, and E. Waugh].

1507 Freedman, William. "The Literary Motif: A Definition and Evaluation," Novel, IV:2 (Winter 1971) 123-131. [Analyses, in detail, the factors indispensable to the establishment of the device and how it functions, and examines the literary value of the motif "in the combination of its intellectual and effective appeals"].

1508 Fremantle, Anne. "Vision in the Novels," Commonweal, LXI (25 Feb. 1955), 545-547. [Examines English visionary writing with S. Butler's Erewhon, H. G. Wells' sequence of prophetic books, and R. H. Benson's "vision of man grown cancer" in Lord of the World as the book that most nearly foreshadows A. Huxley's Brave New World and G. Orwell's 1984].

1509 Friedman, Norman. "Forms of the Plot," JGE, VIII (July 1955), 241-253. [Defines and illustrates some fourteen types of plot forms in an attempt to make available "a range of alternative hypotheses to apply to any given plot when trying to analyze its organizations"].

1510 _____. "Point of View in Fiction: The Development of a Critical Concept," PMLA, LXX:5 (Dec. 1955), 1160-84. [Traces the emergence of point-of-view as a critical tool, outlines its basic principles, and discusses "its significance in relation to the problem of artistic technique generally," especially contemporary practice].

1511 _____. "Criticism and the Novel: Hardy, Hemingway, Crane, Woolf, Conrad," AR, XVIII (Fall 1958), 343-370. [Discusses current standard interpretations of The Mayor of Casterbridge, A Farewell to Arms, The Red Badge of Courage, Mrs. Dalloway, and The Nigger of 'The Narcissus,' and shows how each interpretation fails to explain "important facets of its subject," and suggests a remedy].

1512 Frohock, W. M. "The Failing Center: Recent Fiction and the Picaresque Tradition," Novel, III:1 (Fall 1969), 62-69. [Remarks on the changes in meaning in the usage of "picaresque" as a critical term, and questions how well it characterizes the writing it is applied to, especially during the last decade].

1513 Frye, Northrop. "The Four Forms of Prose Fiction," HudR, II:4 (Winter 1950), 582-595. Revised and reprinted in

212

<u>Anatomy of Criticism: Four Essays</u>. (Princeton, New Jersey: Princeton University Press, 1957), pp. 33-52. [Considers the novel as one of four forms of fiction, the other three being the romance, "confession," and "anatomy," but that they inevitably overlap].

1514 _____. "Varieties of Literary Utopias," <u>Daedalus</u>, XCIV (Spring 1965), 323-347. Reprinted in <u>Utopias and Utopian Thought</u>. Edited by Frank E. Manuel. (Boston: Houghton Mifflin, 1966), pp. 24-49. [Discusses Utopia as a "speculative myth" of the "constructive literary imagination" that communicates a "vision" to its readers based on a "social contract," and distinguishes between the pastoral convention or Arcadia and the classical Utopia and satirical Utopia. References to H. G. Wells, S. Butler, A Huxley, and G. Orwell among others].

1515 "The Future of the Novel," <u>ContempR</u>, XCIV:22 (Dec. 1909), 1-3. (Literary Supplement). [Remarks on the present "remarkable level of excellence" of the novel, and calls upon the novelist "to hold the balance" between emotion and intellect].

1516 "The Future of the Novel: Towards a New Classicism," <u>TLS</u>, 2066 (6 Sep. 1941), 444. [A special article predicting the revival of the impulse of pure narrative after the War -- an impulse lacking in most of the "intellectual and experimental fiction of the past generation"— and an interest in pursuing "order and stability . . . a stricter aesthetic discipline"].

1517 Fyvel, T. R. "Problems of the Modern Novelist," <u>Listener</u>, LIII:1364 (21 Apr. 1955), 708-709. [Discusses whether the novel in England and U. S. A. has been able to adjust itself to the new conditions and environment of the postwar Welfare State, and to the Cold War].

1518 _____. "Britain: A Second-Rank Literary Power?" <u>Listener</u>, LXIX:1781 (16 May 1963), 834-835. [Remarks on the absence of young English novelists whom one can name as having "more than British interest"].

1519 Gable, Sister Mariella, O. S. B. "English Prose Satire and the Modern Christian Temper," <u>DESB</u>, V (1960), 87-98. Reprinted as "Prose Satire and the Modern Christian Temper," <u>ABR</u>, XI (1960), 21-34. [Discusses the positive content and values of English prose satire after 1914 "in accord with the Christian ideal" regardless of the religious persuasion of the satirist, and which seem to argue "as with one voice," for the "validity of Christian principles." G. Orwell, A. Huxley, E. Waugh, K. Amis, A. Menen, A. Wilson, and M. Spark].

1520 Gaines, Clarence H. "Some Modern Novels," NAR, CCXXII
(Sep. 1925), 163-167. [Reviews The Polyglots by W. Gerhardi,
The Great Pandolfo by W. J. Locke, Thus Far by J. C. Snaith,
and Young Mrs. Cruse by V. Meynell, and remarks on two
tendencies he discovers: "the tendency to perpetuate and
modernize the older tradition and the tendency to break
away from restraints and to smash the tradition"].

1521 Gallagher, Michael P. "Human Values in Modern Literature,"
Studies, 57 (Summer 1968), 142-152. [Examines the tendency of modern writers to express viewpoints that run counter
to the "conscious" and "liberal, progressive humanist ideals"
of the day, in the direction of despair, loneliness and
futility, which are apparent also in the "anti-human" tendency of Christian writing. G. Greene, W. Golding, J.
Joyce, S. Beckett, and F. Waugh among others].

1522 Galsworthy, John. "The Novelist's Allegory," AtM, CIII
(June 1909), 790-795; also in FR, XCI (June 1909), 1069-77.
[A description in the form of an allegory, of the novelist's
function in bringing "vision to the human eye," and showing
not only the good but the evil as well].

1523 _____. "The Creation of Character in Literature,"
Bookman (New York), LXXIII (Aug. 1931), 561-569. Reprinted
as a booklet (Oxford University Press, 1931); also in Candelabra: Selected Essays and Addresses. (London: Heinemann, 1932; New York: Scribners, 1933), pp. 291-311. [The
Romanes Lecture delivered 21 May 1931. Examines the process of the creation of character in biography, drama and
the novel, emphasising "the creation of individual character as the chief motive and function of the novelist"].

1524 Gardiner, Harold C. "Hollow Men Give Way to Heroes?"
America, XCI (11 Sep. 1954), 568-569. [Though mainly concerned with U. S. fiction, it poses the question whether
the modern novelist's quest for the "common man" reflecting
"the social, political and cultural tensions and struggles"
has blinded him to "the miniscule heroism" of which he is
sometimes capable].

1525 Garnett, David. "Some Tendencies of the Novel: Remarks on
the Novel," Symposium, I (Jan. 1930), 96-105. [Sorts out
three kinds of novels: outpourings of personal and emotional experiences, tracts or sermons garnished with fiction, and imaginative novels, and concludes that imaginative novels are on the decline, and the first and second
kinds on the increase].

1526 _____. "Literature in 1910," NSta, IX (4 May 1935),
628-630. [A survey of the literary scene in 1910 indicating
that poetry and the novel were in a far "more healthy and
productive state" than they are today].

1527 _____. "Some Writers I Have Known: Galsworthy, Forster, Moore, and Wells," TQ, IV (Autumn 1961), 190-202.
[Reminiscences of their personal lives and impressions of
their writings].

1528 Garnett, Edward. "English Novels and English Life," Nation,
LXXXVIII:2281 (18 Mar. 1909), 272-275. [On the achievements of Mrs. H. Ward, J. Galsworthy, Mrs. Mary E. Mann,
A. Bennett, E. M. Forster, and H. G. Wells in portraying
various aspects of English life].

1529 _____. "Some Remarks on American and English Fiction,"
AtM, CXIV (Dec. 1914), 747-756. Reprinted in Friday Night:
Literary Criticisms and Appreciations. (London: Jonathan
Cape; New York: Knopf, 1922), pp. 189-209. [Though a
large part of the article is devoted to American novelists,
a comparison is made between the practices and prospects
of both English and American novelists].

1530 Garvin, Harry R. "The Novel as Structure: an Ontological
Approach," BuR, XX:2 (Fall 1972), 55-94. [". . . an ontological approach to structure in a novel, the creative
processes of novelists, the aesthetic experiences of readers,
and criticism as related to structure." Brief references
to J. Joyce, V. Woolf, D. H. Lawrence, and H. James among
others].

1531 George, W. L. "Form and the Novel," LA, 281 (4 Apr. 1914),
50-51. Reprinted from The Outlook. Also reprinted in
Literary Chapters. (New York: Little, 1918), pp. 104-110;
published in England as A Novelist on Novels. (London:
Collins, 1918), pp. 118-124. [Contends that the novel, in
its "aspiration towards truth . . . breaks up the old form"].

1532 _____. "Do We Despise the Novelist?" Harper's, CXXXVI:
814 (Mar. 1918), 581-590. [Examines the various attitudes
of society and the state of novelists. Reference to H.
James, H. G. Wells, J. Conrad, G. Parker, and J. Galsworthy
among others].

1533 _____. "A Painter's Literature," EngRev, XXX (Mar.
1920), 223-234. [Divides the English novel of the 20th
century into Neo-Victorian, Edwardian, and Neo-Georgian.
Mainly concerned with the last which he describes as a
"painter's literature" because of its deliberate attempt
to avoid the expression of ideas and its reliance on impressions. J. Joyce, W. Lewis, V. Woolf, R. Wilson, D.
Richardson, and M. Sinclair].

1534 Gerard, Albert. "Les Jeunes Hommes furieux," RGB, (Feb.
1960), 21-30. [On the emergence of the term "Angry Young
Men" and the literary revolt of the fifties as an expression of a new social phenomenon. K. Amis, J. Wain, and

J. Braine].

1535 Gerard, Martin. "Is Your Novel Really Necessary?" QRL, I (1960), 46-52. [On the problem of giving "truth its being, of bringing it into existence through the mediums of a fiction which should not be fictitious"].

1536 Gerber, Richard. "The English Island Myth: Remarks on the Englishness of Utopian Fiction," CritQ, I:1 (Spring 1959), 36-43. [Accounts for the change in the satirical and di-dactic Utopian fiction of More, Swift, and Defoe, "crystal-izing around the symbol of the island," and certain of H. G. Wells' works, A. Huxley's Brave New World, and G. Or-well's 1984].

1537 Gerould, Katharine Fullerton. "The Newest Woman," AtM, CIX (May 1912), 606-611. [Objects to heroines like A. Bennett's Hilda Lessways (Clayhanger trilogy) and H. G. Wells' Isabel Rivers (The New Machiavelli) not because they are immoral "but that they are bad biology," i.e., not convincing and misrepresent their prototypes].

1538 _____. "British Novelists, Ltd.," YR, (NS) VII (Oct. 1917), 161-185. Condensed in CO, LXIII (Nov. 1917), 336. [Examines two groups of novelists: those with "individual-ity of style--Wells, Bennett and Galsworthy--and the "syn-dicate" of H. Walpole, J. D. Beresford, C. Mackenzie, G. Cannan, O. Onions, D. H. Lawrence, and W. L. George--the "new realists" who "write alike . . . deal in the same characters, the same backgrounds, and the same situations; and . . . have the same point of view"].

1539 _____. "The War Novels," YR, (NS) VIII (Oct. 1918), 159-181. [A review article dividing war novels into seri-ous social studies, "mystical" reactions, sentimental tales, attempts to document German psychology, and "'yarns' pure and simple". References to H. G. Wells, St. J. Ervine, M. Sinclair, A. Bennett, "R. West" and others].

1540 _____. "'Stream of Consciousness,'" SatR, IV (22 Oct. 1927), 233-235. [Attributes the usage of the "stream of consciousness" as a valuable dramatic method in English fiction to H. James and J. Conrad prior to D. Richardson and J. Joyce, and its fashionable popularity with "minor" novelists to the ease with which it lends itself to the "taste for salacity" and sentiment].

1541 Gersh, Gabriel. "The English Family Novel," SAQ, LVI (Apr. 1957), 207-216. [Considers the effect of Freud's "Oedipus Theory" on the English novelists' conception of the family "as the object of a cult." D. H. Lawrence, V. Woolf, G. Greene, E. Bowen, J. Cary, and L. P. Hartley].

1542 Ghiselin, Brewster. "Automatism, Intention, and Autonomy in the Novelist's Production," Daedalus, XCII (1963), 297-312. [In the shaping of his work, "the novelist must control through intense awareness both the spontaneous and the voluntary processes of his production, conforming every part of his work to the demands of an ultimate subjective authority which overrides the compulsion both of automation and intention"].

1543 Ghose, Hemendra Prasad. "The Future of Fiction," LA, 268 (21 Jan. 1911), 154-159. [Refutes J. Verne's view that the novel will disappear in a hundred years' time to be replaced by the newspaper].

1544 Gibbins, John. "Some Thoughts on the State of the Novel," QR, CCCI (1963), 48-56. [Regards the novel as perhaps the least influential of the Arts, very few novels being "positive in their own right" as a comment on society, and rejects the "spiritual inarticulateness" of novelists, the anti-cult, the lack of form and joy in contemporary fiction, and the "abstraction and wild experimentation indicative of the artist at a loss"].

1545 Gill, Richard. "Imagination of Disaster," SatR, XLVII (5 Sep. 1964), 10-13, 47. [A reappraisal of English and American literature of World War I. R. H. Mottram, F. M. Ford, R. Aldington, and H. M. Tomlinson among others].

1546 Gillett, Eric. "Modern Prose Forms: V. Fiction," FR, (NS) CLII (Sep. 1942), 197-204. [Notices the decline of the novel in his survey of the inter-war period in spite of the "immense technical skill and research" that go to its making. C. Mackenzie, G. Cannan, H. Walpole, D. H. Lawrence, O. Onions, V. Woolf, J. Joyce, J. B. Priestley, A. Huxley, and others. This is the sixth article in a series of seven describing six modern prose forms].

1547 _____. "The English Literary Scene, 1954," EDH (NS) XXX (1960), 130-146. [A brief survey of fiction in the opening pages that concludes that fiction during the past twenty-five years is "in the doldrums"].

1548 Gindin, James J. "The Reassertion of the Personal," TQ, I (Winter 1958), 126-134. [Contends that the tradition of comedy in the British novel revived by A. Wilson, K. Amis, and J. Wain--as distinct from A. Huxley's and E. Waugh's comedy--is not only essential to enable them to present and comment on the "simple and reasonable in social behavior," but also to re-assert the worth, "the value and dignity of the individual" as well as affirm "the existence of value"].

1549 _____. "Comedy in Contemporary British Fiction,"

PMASAL, XLIV (1959), 389-397. [Rejects the "convenient simplification" of "Britain's Angry Young Men," for "no single theme or tone" or "formula for society can characterize the novels of K. Amis, I. Murdoch, A. Wilson and J. Wain," and discusses their common interest in the creation of the comic novel].

1550 _____. "The Fable Begins to Break Down," ConL, VIII (Winter 1967), 1-18. [Rejects the growing importance attached to the fable or myth as an "improvement" over realism in the contemporary novel because the "rigidity" and "perhaps unwanted metaphysical implications" that its form imposes are not satisfactory in treating the problem of alienation, whether it be "an individual's remoteness or defensive enstrangement," which is still central to fiction. Discusses works by I. Murdoch, L. Durrell, D. Storey, A. Wilson and others].

1551 _____. "Well Beyond Laughter: Directions from 'Fifties Comic Fiction," SNNTS, 3 (1971), 357-364. [Discusses the "comic iconoclasm" in novels by K. Amis, A. Sillitoe, I. Murdoch, J. Wain, and A. Wilson as an attempt to satirize "forms of governmental, religious, or institutional truth," as well as the sense of experimentation and violence in the fiction of the fifties].

1552 Glanvill, Brian. "The Anglo-Jewish Writer," Encounter, XIV: 2 (Feb. 1960), 62-64. [Asserts that Anglo-Jewish writers exist but no Anglo-Jewish writing has emerged in Britain, as in the U. S.].

1553 _____. "The Sporting Novel," NYTBR, (18 July 1965), 2, 18. Reprinted in The Best of 'Speaking of Books' from 'The New York Times Book Review'. Edited, with an Introduction by Francis Brown. (New York: Holt, Rinehart, 1969), pp. 226-231. [Discusses English and American attempts at the "Sporting Novel," which, he convincingly argues, can either be "proletarian" like D. Storey's The Sporting Life, or in terms of "myth and fantasy" like B. Malamud's The Natural].

1554 Glass, Bentley. "The Scientist in Contemporary Fiction," ScM, LXXXV (Dec. 1957), 188-193. [On American and English novels that deal with "science as a social force" and those that centre around the personality of the scientist as he grapples with problems thrust upon him by his way of life].

1555 Glicksberg, Charles I. "Proletarian Fiction in England," UTQ, VIII (Oct. 1938), 41-55. [Defines "proletarian fiction" as that which deals with Industrialism in general, or with some aspect of the labour problem, as distinct from "Marxist," i.e., without reference to the political orientation of the author. R. Bates, "L. G. Gibbon," W. Green-

wood, A. J. Cronin, N. Mitchison, Robert Briffaul and three
Irish writers: J. Hanley, L. O'Flaherty, and S. O'Faolain].

1556   _____. "The Problem of Evil in Modern Literature,"
SWR, XXXII (1947), 353-359. [On the swing of the literary
pendulum from political to moral subjects. G. Orwell, A.
Koestler, and A. Huxley].

1557   _____. "Literature and the Moral Issue," PrS, XXVI
(1952), 10-19. [On the "ritual of repudiation" which has
led to the modern "resigned fatalistic despair" in literature, and the need to discern that the "ideals we cherish
are not epiphenomena," but inextricably woven into the
"character of our conduct." Brief references to A. Huxley
and D. H. Lawrence among others].

1558   _____. "Literature and Society," ArQ, VIII (Summer
1952), 128-139. [On the communist "militant aesthetic" of
a writer assuming his political responsibilities, versus
his duty to himself to report the truth of human experience
without distortion, or political bias. Brief references
to A. Comfort, A. Koestler, D. H. Lawrence, and G. Orwell
among others].

1559   _____. "Anti-Utopianism in Modern Literature," SWR,
XXVII (Summer 1952), 221-228. [Discusses the causes which
led to the "virtual death" of the Utopian mentality, and
the emergence of the anti-utopias of A. Huxley, G. Orwell,
and A. Koestler].

1560   _____. "Anti-Communism in Fiction," SAQ, LIII (Oct.
1954), 485-496. [On novels that express disillusionment
with Communism, satirise it, and express its horror. A.
Koestler and G. Orwell among others].

1561   _____. "Fiction and Philosophy," ArQ, XIII (Autumn
1957), 5-17. Modified and reprinted as chapter XIV, "Fiction, Philosophy and Faith," Literature and Religion: A
Study in Conflict. (Dallas: Southern Methodist University
Press, 1960), pp. 169-180. [Maintains that the view of
life implied in a novel is different from the "philosophy
the author introduces forthrightly into the body of the
text;" the former develops from the "internal tensions"
of the novel and the latter is an "alien intrusion . . . a
spurious effort at preaching or propaganda." References to
J. Conrad, A. Huxley, D. H. Lawrence, and S. Maugham among
others].

1562   _____. "The God of Fiction," ColQ, VII (Autumn 1958),
207-220. Combined with "The Religious Revival in Contemporary Literature," WHR, XI (Winter 1957), 65-78, and reprinted
in Literature and Religion: A Study in Conflict. (Dallas:
Southern Methodist University Press, 1960), pp. 181-192.

[Maintains that the modern novelist, bereft of reliance on "the absolute" and the supernatural, by the secular outlook of the age must necessarily contemplate the contradictions and tensions resulting from the rejection of God. References to G. Greene and A. Huxley among others].

1563 _____. "Eros and the Death of God," WHR, XIII:4 (Autumn 1959), 357-368. Reprinted in Modern Literature and the Death of God (The Hague: Martinus Nijhoff, 1966), pp. 36-57. [On the conflict that runs in man between "the cravings of his sexual being and his imperative longing for transcendence." J. Joyce and D. H. Lawrence among others].

1564 _____. "The Literature of the Angry Young Men," ColQ, VIII (Spring 1960), 293-303. [A general account that attributes a large portion of the "group's" ridicule of, and revolt against the "fetishism" of the social order to their working class background].

1565 _____. "To Be or Not To Be: The Literature of Suicide," QQ, LXVII:3 (Autumn 1960), 384-395. [Contends that the "suicidal obsessions" take hold of literature only when the spiritual health of a culture declines. Examines Dostoyevsky and Camus with brief references to V. Woolf, S. Beckett, and G. Greene].

1566 "Gloomy Dean Hits the Novelists," LDig, LXXIX (15 July 1922), 29-30. [Extracts from Dean Inge's attack on Georgian novelists for making fiction a "medium for the scientific study of mental pathology"].

1567 Goddard, Lord. "Novelists and the Law," NER, I (Mar. 1949), 170-175. [Examines the concern of novelists and the perils they encounter when they embark on legal topics without the help of qualified experts. Mostly confined to Dickens and Trollope with references to A. Marshall and S. Weyman].

1568 "Going Deeper," LitR, III:30 (31 Mar. 1923), 3. [Editorial. Accepts W. L. Cross's criticism YR, (NS) XII (Apr. 1923), 477-496, that novels that probe into psychologies of character for motives, neuroses etc. are unsatisfactory, but cautions that novelists may perforce be led to "dip into the subconscious" for vital distinctions in a standardized world].

1569 Goldberg, Gerald Jay. "The Artist-Novel in Transition," ELT, IV:3 (1961), 12-27. [Examines the four principal forms which the artist-hero takes in the 20th century novel: "Bohemian life, isolation, exile, and suicide." W. Lewis, G. Cannan, S. Maugham, J. Joyce, G. Moore, and D. H. Lawrence among others].

1570 _____. "The Search for the Artist in Some Recent British Fiction," SAQ, LXII (Summer 1963), 387-402. [Argues that I. Murdoch's Under the Net, W. Golding's Free Fall, S. Beckett's Trilogy and L. Durrell's Alexandria Quartet reveal a central major theme: the artist-hero's search for an identity based on an "a priori condition of aliena-tion" from external reality, a search that reveals "not only the moment of discovery, but the logbook of the jour-ney as well," i.e. the search constitutes the narrative action and the meaning of the novels].

1571 Goldberg, M. A. "Chronology, Character, and the Human Condition: A Reappraisal of the Modern Novel," Criticism, V (Winter 1963), 1-12. Reprinted in Critical Approaches to Fiction. Edited by Shiv K. Kumar and Keith F. McKean. (New York: McGraw-Hill, 1968), pp. 13-25. [Classifies novels into the old and the new--those concerned with ad-venture, clock-time, and externality, and the mind, dura-tion, the internal respectively--and those concerned with the universal, human experience, the timeless or eternal. Brief references to W. Golding, J. Joyce, and V. Woolf].

1572 Golding, William. "Limits of Control--VI. On the Crest of the Wave," TLS, 3042 (17 June 1960), 387. Reprinted in The Writer's Dilemma: Essays First Published in T. L. S. Under the Heading 'Limits of Control.' (London: Ox-ford University Press, 1961), pp. 42-52. [Examines the present trends in education and the ideals of the culture prevailing, and estimates their impact on the future of the novel].

1573 _____. "The Condition of the Novel: Britain," NLR, XXIX (Jan.-Feb. 1965), 34-35. [An excerpt from his address to the Conference of European Writers at Leningrad, Summer 1963 . Maintains that the novelist does not limit himself to reporting facts but "diagnoses them, and his vocation has the same value as that of the doctor"].

1574 Goldknopf, David. "The Confessional Increment: A New Look at the I-Narrator," JAAC, XXVIII (Fall 1969), 13-21. Re-printed in The Life of the Novel. (Chicago and London: University of Chicago Press, 1972), pp. 25-41. [An examina-tion of some of the problems and expectations created by the I-narrator in fiction].

1575 _____. "What Plot Means in the Novel," AR, XXIX:4 (Winter 1969-70), 483-496. Reprinted in The Life of the Novel. (Chicago and London: University of Chicago Press, 1972), pp. 25-41. [Surveys, in the light of his contention that the study of the structure of the novel is inseparable from the history of ideas, the rise of linear causation, the impact of the deistic vision of the universe on plot in the Victorian age, and linear causation yielding to "si-multaneous causation" or "field-theory" in the 20th century.

221

Brief references to J. Joyce, D. H. Lawrence, and V. Woolf].

1576 _____. "Realism in the Novel," YR, LX (Oct. 1970), 69-84. Reprinted in The Life of the Novel. (Chicago and London: University of Chicago Press, 1972), pp. 177-199. [The alternative to the conception of reality as "hard-rock donné" or as a "projection . . . of the fantasist" is a concept of reality "as a communal formulation" basic to the "new realism" that recognizes "as a fact of contemporary consciousness, the increasing complexity and even instability of that which the serious novelist must try to represent." J. Joyce and D. H. Lawrence].

1577 "Good Luck to Them All," Listener, LXX:1790 (18 July 1963), 82. [Editorial on first novels].

1578 Gordon, Caroline. "Some Readings and Misreadings," SR, LXI (Summer 1953), 384-407. [Contends that the novelist's imagination often operates "within the pattern of Christian symbolism rather than in the pattern of contemporary thought," that novels are based on the "primal plot: the Christian Scheme of Redemption." Examines works by H. James, J. Joyce, G. Greene, and E. Waugh among others].

1579 Gordon, Donald J. "Letteratura ingleze d'oggi," Ponte, III (July 1947), 672-676. Translated by Ada Businelli. [Surveys poetry and fiction today and during World War II. Maintains that of all the novels published during the war, only four perhaps are of any importance: V. Woolf's Between the Acts, R. Warner's The Aerodrome, L. H. Myers' Rajah Amar, and A. Koestler's Darkness at Noon].

1580 Gorp, H. van. "Recente romantheorie," DWB, CXV (1970), 57-65. [A review on recent theories of the novel by German, French, English, and American critics].

1581 Gosling, S. J. "Catholicism and the Modern Novel," DubR, CCVI (Jan. 1940), 115-133. [Examines the main causes of the revolt against reason--the "motif" of the modern novel-- and its attack against the "liberty and integrity of the human soul." References to D. H. Lawrence, J. Joyce, V. Woolf, and E. M. Forster].

1582 Gould, Gerald. "Novels English and American," AtM, CXLII (July 1928), 125-134. [Emphasises the similarity between them, especially in the "dissolution of manner," and "dissoluteness of matter" which have become widespread in both countries].

1583 _____. "Novels of the Year (1932)," Observer, (1 Jan. 1933). [A survey of the year's production of fiction that attempts "to coordinate according to type"].

1584 _____. "Novels of 1933," Observer, (31 Dec. 1933),
[A survey of the year's production of fiction that classifies "with an eye to the topicality of its subject, as well
as to the merits of its method"].

1585 Gourd, Roger. "Jacket Heroes," NSoc, (9 Mar. 1972), 505-
506. [On English and American paperbacks dealing with the
interest in "rockers and hell's angels"].

1586 Graef, Hilda. "Why All This Anger? Is It the Capital Sin
of Modern Writers?" CathW, CLXXXVIII (Nov. 1958), 122-128.
[Anger, the latest "rage" in literary fashions, is viewed
from a Christian viewpoint as a "facile attitude" and a
"pessimistic pose." J. Osborne (Look Back in Anger) and
C. Wilson].

1587 Graham, W. S. "England's Old Young Men," NRep, CXVIII (26
Apr. 1948), 28-31. [A brief analysis of recent poetry and
fiction in Britain which maintains that established writers like E. Bowen, C. Isherwood, E. Waugh, G. Greene, and
A. Koestler have not developed "beyond their earlier magnitude"--with the possible exception of I. Compton-Burnett--
and that the only sign of a "revitalizing principle in
younger writers" is to be found in H. Green, A. Comfort,
and P. H. Newby].

1588 Grandsen, K. W. "Rebels and Timeservers. The Thirties
and Us," TC, CLXI:961 (Mar. 1957), 220-226. [Maintains
that the tone of contemporary writing shows the strain of
the writer's solitary achievement because the existence of
creative opposition which was taken for granted by older
writers has disappeared, for the intellectuals, who ought
to form it, are running behind the establishment's wagon].

1589 _____. "Thoughts on Contemporary Fiction," REL, I:2
(Apr. 1960), 7-17. [Considers the novel as the most "ca-
pacious of literary forms," and as its own worst enemy.
Suggests three categories: 1) novel of sensibility, 2) of
articulation, and 3) the chronicle, and maintains that novelists offer what they think we want to read, not what they
themselves are compelled to discover about life].

1590 Grant, Douglas. "The Novel and Its Critical Terms," EIC,
I:4 (Oct. 1951), 421-429. [Reexamines, reevaluates, and
redefines the accepted terminology in contemporary criticism of fiction. Brief references to I. Compton-Burnett,
V. Woolf, and J. Joyce].

1591 Greacen, Robert. "Social Class in Post-War English Fiction,"
SoR, IV (Winter 1968), 142-151. [Suggests that English
novelists tend to be wary of taking sides, dislike political parties, will not write thesis novels, and prefer to
remain artists to reflect society rather than change it.

Considers I. Compton-Burnett, G. Greene, E. Waugh, G. Orwell, C. P. Snow, A. Powell, J. B. Priestley, K. Amis, A.
Sillitoe, J. Braine, C. MacInnes, and A. Wilson].

1592   "Green, Henry." [Henry Vincent Yorke]. "A Novelist to
His Readers," Listener, XLIV:1132 (9 Nov. 1950), 505-506;
XLV:1150 (15 Mar. 1951), 425, 427. [Discusses the "unspoken communication between novelist and reader in narrative," and maintains that dialogue will be the "mainstay"
of novels for a long time. Also shows how the novelist's
"arrangement of words and the 'placing' of his characters"
in a particular context are the means whereby he can create, in the mind of the reader, "life which is not, and
which is non-representational"].

1593   Green, Martin. "British Decency," KR, XXI:4 (Autumn 1959),
505-532. Reprinted in Mirror for Anglo-Saxons (New York:
Harper, 1960; London: Longmans, Green, 1961), pp. 95-128.
[On four literary figures who embody the idea "of England
and Englishness": D. H. Lawrence, F. R. Leavis, G. Orwell,
and K. Amis].

1594   _____. "Room at the Middle," Commonweal, LXXII (8
Apr. 1960), 38-39. [A brief survey of the recent fiction
of J. Wain, J. Braine, A. Sillitoe, I. Murdoch, K. Amis,
and K. Waterhouse].

1595   _____. "British Comedy and the British Sense of Humour: Shaw, Waugh, and Amis," TQ, IV (Autumn 1961), 217-
227. [Discusses G. B. Shaw, E. Waugh, and K. Amis, "their
distinctions and brilliances" as humorists, and their influence upon the British sense of humour].

1596   Green, Peter. "Aspects of the Historical Novel," EDH, XXXI
(1962), 35-60. [Discusses the revival of the genre in recent years after defining the historical novel as a reaction "of an age, and the people of that age, from external
evidence," when the novelist is not an "active participant"
but an interpreter of a past age relying on sources that
happened to survive into his own lifetime. N. Mitchison,
W. Golding, R. Graves, and A. Koestler among others].

1597   Greenberg, Alvin. "Open-Endedness in the Novel: Toward a
Structure of Values," Paunch, XXX (1967), 67-78. [Reviews
Alan Friedman's position in The Turn of the Novel (New York:
Oxford University Press, 1966) that open-endedness in 20th
century novels is not merely a structural matter but an
"ethical statement in its own right," i.e., not dictated by
"mythic necessity," but by the novelist's view of human experience, and also suggests that it is in the end of the
novel that we come to grips with something, whether we make
or break our relationship with its fictional world. J.

Conrad, J. Joyce, E. M. Forster, J. R. R. Tolkien, S. Beckett and others].

1598 _____. "Breakable Beginnings: The Fall Into Reality in the Modern Novel," TSLL, X (Spring 1968), 133-142. [Deals with the "novel of disintegration: the need to submit to the wholly destructive forces of the physical and social world in juxtaposition to the individual's need for form and value of endurance." S. Beckett, L. F. Celine, S. Bellow, W. Golding and others].

1599 _____. "The Revolt of Objects: The Opposing World in the Modern Novel," CentR, III (Fall (1969), 366-388. [Examines the various manifestations of the "opposing world"--"hostile . . . outside human control," of degrading pettiness, a mere "world of things" blank and meaningless-- and man's relationship with it after his experience and awareness of it. J. Conrad and S. Beckett among others].

1600 Greene, Graham. "Dark Backward: A Footnote," LMer, XXXII (Oct. 1935), 562-565. [On the inability to convey the "passage of time" in novels by A. Calder-Marshall, F. M. Ford, and E. Bowen].

1601 Greenwood, George A. "'This England' in Contemporary Fiction," WWork, XLI (Mar. 1923), 383-388. [Shows how novels by H. G. Wells, A. Bennett, G. Cannan, C. Mackenzie, H. Walpole, R. Macaulay, D. H. Lawrence, C. Dane, S. Kaye-Smith, M. Sinclair, E. F. Benson, A. S. M. Hutchinson, "R. West", G. Frankau, J. D. Beresford, A. Waugh, D. Goldring, E. M. Forster, and others constitute a "priceless legacy" in that they chronicle the economic, social, political, psychical and religious changes in England over the previous two decades].

1602 Grierson, Helen. "Marriage in English Fiction," FR, (NS) CXXIX (Feb. 1931), 251-259. [Surveys the institution of marriage and novelists' attitudes to it from J. Austen to H. Walpole. Includes J. Galsworthy, A. Bennett, H. G. Wells, and H. Walpole].

1603 Grigson, Geoffrey. "Characteristics of the English Novel," Listener, XLIII:1095 (19 Jan. 1950), 117-118. [This is the first of a series of eight talks on C. Dickens, G. Eliot, H. Fielding, T. Hardy, J. Joyce, S. Richardson, and W. Scott. Shows that the "genuine concern" of the English novel with morality is partly due to a people who are "in a narrow way morally occupied and morally anguished." Brief references to H. James, J. Joyce, and G. Greene among others].

1604 Groger, Erika. "Der bürgerliche Atomwissenschaftler im englisch-amerikanischen Roman von 1945 bis zur Gegenwart," ZAA,

XVI (1968), 25-48. [Considers the bourgeois nuclear scientist in English and American novels from 1945 to the present. C. P. Snow, L. P. Hartley, A. Comfort, N. Monsarrat and others].

1605 Gross, Beverley. "Narrative Time and the Open-Ended Novel," Criticism, VIII (Fall 1966), 362-376. [Considers time as a "shaper" of form with an "almost solid presence," and as "central subject" in open-ended novels. M. Proust, J. Joyce, and V. Woolf].

1606 Gross, Harvey. "From Barabas to Bloom: Notes on the Figure of the Jew," WHR, XI (Spring 1957), 149-156. [Discusses the appeal of the Jew as a symbol for the modern writer's own isolation, "his feelings of being an intruder in a hostile world, his being essentially unassimilable"].

1607 Gross, John. "The Jewish Writer in England," Listener, LXVII (12 Apr. 1962), 636. [Remarks on the paucity of English Jewish writers who write on Jewish themes. Brief references to C. Isherwood and A. Koestler].

1608 "Growth of the English Novel," TLS, 1485 (17 July 1930), 581-582. [A leading article reviewing E. A. Baker's History of the English Novel, (Vol. 3), F. M. Ford's The English Novel: From the Earliest Days to the Death of J. Conrad, and C. Dane's Tradition and H. Walpole].

1609 Guerard, A. "Perspectives on the Novel," Daedalus, XCII (1963). [Introduction to the spring issue of Daedalus which is devoted to a symposium "Perspectives on the Novel" where six literary critics--H. Levin, R. Kiely, D. Stevenson, D. Littlejohn, P. Brooks and A. Lytle--discuss "significant groupings and trends in the contemporary novel," and four literary and psychiatric minds--T. Moser, C. Rosenfield, L. Kohlberg and S. O. Lesser--bear on the relative roles of "conscious intention and unconscious creation in the writing of a novel"].

1610 Hackett, Alice P. "Do You Remember. . . ." SatR, (29 Aug. 1964), 109-125. [An annotated list of books that were popular with Americans from 1924 to 1964. Includes English and American novels].

1611 Hackett, Francis. "The Post-Victorians," Bookman (New York) LXXXI (Mar. 1930), 20-26. [On the rejection by G. B. Shaw, H. G. Wells, and A. Bennett of the Victorian tradition].

1612 Hafley, James. "Walter Pater's 'Marius' and the Technique of Modern Fiction," MFS, III:2 (Summer 1957), 99-109. [Discusses the "historical and intrinsic" significance of Pater's Marius The Epicurean as a "link . . . to demonstrate aesthetically and historically the genesis and order of the modern novel"].

1613   Haines, George. "Forms of Imaginative Prose: 1900-1940,"
       SoR, VII:4 (Spring 1942), 755-775. [Suggests two main
       forms of prose, having language predominantly "semantic,"
       i.e. where the novelist presents "his perception using lan-
       guage as a reference," or predominantly "ironic," where the
       novelist presents "his perception using language as an imi-
       tation of reality." D. H. Lawrence, among others, as rep-
       resentative of the former, and J. Joyce of the latter].

1614   Hale, Edward Everett, Jr.   "The New Realists," Independent,
       LXXXIII (30 Aug. 1915), 297-299. [On D. H. Lawrence, J.
       D. Beresford, O. Onions, and H. Walpole, who find "mystery,
       adventure and romance" in "actual life"].

1615   _____. "The Greater English Novelists," Independent,
       LXXXV (31 Jan. 1916), 162. [A. Bennett, H. G. Wells, and
       J. Galsworthy].

1616   Halio, Jay L. "A Sense of the Present," SoR, (NS) II (1966),
       952-966. [A review article on fifteen novels by I. Murdoch,
       E. Bowen, A. Wilson, A. Powell, H. E. Bates, L. P. Hartley,
       A. Burgess, I. Compton-Burnett, F. Tuohy, J. Fowles, J.
       Wain, and A. Sillitoe].

1617   Hall, James Norman. "The Lives that Authors Lead," Bookman
       (New York), LXXVI (Mar. 1933), 219-221. [On the inability
       of modern novelists to present a "recognizable picture of
       life" mainly because their lives have lost touch with real-
       ity. Brief references to J. Conrad and J. Galsworthy].

1618   _____. "The New Pleasures of the Imagination," VQR,
       XLVI (Autumn 1970), 596-612. [On the novel that interlaces
       social comedy with fantasy. Brief references to G. Greene,
       E. Waugh, and A. Huxley].

1619   Hallett, John. "England Adrift," FR, CXXXIV (Sep. 1930),
       354-362. [On the "fashion of indifferences and the cult of
       futility" characteristic of English politics, philosophy and
       literature in 1930. Brief references to H. G. Wells, A.
       Bennett, and A. Huxley].

1620   Haltrecht, Montague. "Some thoughts on the Jewish Novel,"
       Pointer, 7 (Winter 1971), 6. [Examines what may constitute
       a Jewish novel, and attributes the fact that Jewish writing
       is in the mainstream of American culture, and not in the
       mainstream of English culture, to the difference in the re-
       lationship of the Jewish community in each country with the
       wider culture around it].

1621   Hamalian, Leo. "Rebels Without Claws," Nation, CXCII (25
       Feb. 1961), 172-174. [On the "negative stance" of the "hero"
       as depicted in a review of novels by R. Holles, K. Water-
       house, A. Sillitoe, and W. Feinburgh].

227

1622   Hamilton, Cosmo. "Novels and the English Public," NYPLR,
       V (4 Oct.1924), 8. [Surveys briefly the contemporary out-
       put, and concludes that the taste of the English public
       has become "somewhat less discriminating than before the
       war," and is still divided into the "masses and the classes"].

1623   Hamilton, K. M. "Theological Bearings in Modern Litera-
       ture," DR, XXX (1952), 121-130. [An examination of liter-
       ary tendencies from a theological viewpoint].

1624   Handy, William. "Toward a Formalist Criticism of Fiction,"
       TSLL, III (Spring 1961), 81-88. Reprinted in The Novel:
       Modern Essays in Criticism. Edited by Robert Murray Davis.
       (Englewood Cliffs, N. J.: Prentice-Hall, 1969), pp. 94-
       102. [Holds that because "the essential structure of fic-
       tion . . . is basically the same as that of poetry," the
       methods of analyzing poetry can be transferred to fiction:
       thus "form in fiction" becomes an "embodiment of meaning
       . . . not merely a framework of content," thereby empha-
       sising the importance of "technique"].

1625   Hannigan, D. F. "Twentieth Century Novel: A Critical Dia-
       logue," WRev, CLIII (May 1900), 528-531. [Speculations by
       a realist and a novelist on what kind of novel will prevail
       in the future].

1626   Hansl, Eva v. B. "The Child in Modern Literature," Bookman
       (New York), LXI (Mar. 1925), 37-42. [On the new outlook
       on, and treatment of, the child in novels resulting from
       researches in psychology].

1627   Hara, I. "A Trend in the Development of the English Novel,"
       SELit, XIII (1933), 137-146. [In Japanese. A review ar-
       ticle on P. Lubbock's Craft of Fiction and E. M. Forster's
       Aspects of the Novel].

1628   Harding, D. W. "Psychological Processes in the Reading of
       Fiction," BJA, II:2 (Apr. 1962), 133-147. [Views the read-
       ing of a novel as a "process of looking on at a represen-
       tation of imagined events, or rather, of listening to a
       description of them," a process that depends on "imaginative
       or emphatic insight into other living things," an "evalua-
       tion" of them, and the realisation that they are not people
       but personae].

1629   _____. "The Notion of Escape in Fiction and Entertain-
       ment," OR, 4 (Hilary 1967), 23-32. [Suggests three notions
       of escape in fiction: 1) change from one pursuit to another,
       2) regressive pursuits which fall below one's usual stan-
       dards, and 3) the manipulation of effect--pursuing an emo-
       tional state instead of starting from interest in a situa-
       tion, and accepting the emotional state to which exploration
       leads].

1630   Hardwick, Elizabeth. "Reflections on Fiction," NYRB, (13
       Feb. 1969), 12-17. [Reflections on the ebb and flow in the
       popularity of novelists, the aesthetic entity of a novel,
       its length, and the demands it makes on a reader's time.
       Also contrast the orderly sequence of the traditional nov-
       el with the post-Freudian one. References to J. Joyce, J.
       Galsworthy, and I. Compton-Burnett].

1631   Hardy, Barbara. "Towards a Poetics of Fiction: 3) An
       Approach through Narrative," Novel, II:1 (Fall 1968), 5-14.
       [Argues that narrative is not "to be regarded as an aes-
       thetic invention . . . but as a primary act of mind trans-
       ferred to art from life," and that 19th century novels,
       with their multiple plots and variety of narrative forms,
       sometimes "mime the sheer variety of mental narrative" as
       explicitly as the stream of consciousness. S. Beckett,
       J. Joyce, and H. James among others].

1632   Harkness, Bruce. "The Lucky Crowd--Contemporary British
       Fiction," EJ, XLVII:7 (Oct. 1958), 387-397. [A survey of
       the post-World War II English novel with special emphasis
       on "The Angry Young Men" as representatives of new postwar
       attitudes].

1633   Harrington, Michael. "The Political Novel Today," Common-
       weal, LXIII (28 Oct. 1955), 79-82. [On the causation of
       "the transition from proletarian to peasant" in the Euro-
       pean political novel. Considers A. Koestler and G. Orwell
       among others].

1634   Harris, Henry. "The Symbol of Frontier in the Social Al-
       legory of the 'Thirties," ZAA, XIV (1966), 127-140. [Es-
       tablishes the link between the use of the symbol of "fron-
       tier" in the social allegory or moral fable of the thirties
       with traditional allegorical devices, and with "similar
       symbolic preoccupations elsewhere in the literature of the
       period." R. Warner, R. Todd, and E. Upward among others].

1635   Harris, Mrs. L. H. "The Advance of Civilization in Fiction,"
       Independent, LXV (19 Nov. 1908), 1166-72. [A plea for "less
       indecent mental dexterity" in fiction. A. D. Sedgwick, R.
       Hichens, W. de Morgan, and A. Hope among others].

1636   Harris, Robert T. "Plausibility in Fiction," JP, XLIX:1
       (3 Jan. 1952), 5-10. [An analysis pointing out that plausi-
       bility consists of "the subsumption of fictional events
       under . . . laws of human nature and laws of the formation
       of character," and concludes that good fiction reveals "per-
       manent possibilities in the sphere of individual feeling
       and action and social behavior"].

1637   Harris, Wendell V. "Style and the Twentieth Century Novel,"
       WHR, XVIII (Spring 1964), 127-140. Reprinted in Critical

Approaches to Fiction. Edited by Shiv K. Kumar and Keith F. McKean. (New York: McGraw-Hill, 1968), pp. 131-147. [Attributes the abandonment of the "assured" style in the novels of H. James, J. Joyce, V. Woolf, S. Beckett, and H. Green to three major factors: "the failure to attain to the larger vision," i.e., failure to discover a standpoint from which life could be "contemplated in any wholeness," the continuing shift toward the expression of a "private, highly particularized . . . eccentric outlook," and the trend of "unvarnished" realism from the 1890s].

1638   _____. "Molly's 'Yes': The Transvaluation of Sex in Modern Fiction," TSLL, X (1968), 107-118. [Traces the "evolution from the insistence that sexual satisfaction is important for happiness to the use of the sexual act as a symbol of fulfillment, and thence to the confusion of this symbolic representation with complete fulfillment of the human personality" in key works by A. Bennett, J. Galsworthy, S. Maugham, A. Huxley, D. H. Lawrence, L. Durrell, and G. Greene].

1639   Harrison, Tony. "Black and White and Red All Over: The Fiction of Empire," LM, XII (Aug.-Sep. 1972), 90-103. [A review article on E. Grierson's The Imperial Dream. (London: Collins, 1972), and B. Parry's Delusions and Discoveries: Studies on India in the British Imagination 1880-1930. (London: Allen Lane, The Penguin Press, 1972)].

1640   Hartley, L. C. "The Sacred River: Stream of Consciousness: The Evolution of a Method [in Fiction]," SR, XXXIX (Jan.-Mar. 1931), 80-89. [A lucid definition of the stream of consciousness as used by V. Woolf and J. Joyce especially, tracing its genealogy briefly to Richardson, Sterne, G. Eliot, Meredith and H. James' "fusion of author and character"].

1641   Hartley, L. P. "The Future of Fiction," NW&D, VIII:7 (1946), 86-91. [Fourth article in a series of six on the same topic by R. Macaulay, V. S. Pritchett, A. Koestler, W. Allen, and O. Sitwell. Sees the future of the novel as "largely bound up with the future of society," does not foresee a revival of the comic spirit, or romance, or characterization, but an escape from actuality in the historical novel and the detective story].

1642   _____. "The Novelist and His Material," TLS, 2946 (15 Aug. 1958), iv. [Argues that the novelist's material is largely responsible for weakening the belief in free will and the sense of sin, and also responsible for his present difficulties].

1643   _____. "The Novelist's Responsibility," English, XIII (Summer 1961), 172-177. [From an address given to the

230

Association, 11 Mar. 1961, at the Alliance Hall, Westminster. This is an enlarged version of an address originally given to the P. E. N. Congress held in London, July 1956 and entitled "The Technique of the Novel." The Author and the Public: Problems of Communication. Edited by C. V. Wedgwood. (London: Hutchinson, 1957), pp. 165-175. Reprinted in E&S, XV (1962), 88-100; EDH, XXXIV (1966), 74-89; also as "De la responsabilité du romancier," Adam, 294-296, (1961), 15-21. (Translated into French by Germaine Lot and Marguerite de Ruel). Addresses himself to the problem of how a novelist can interpret his age through the "medium of his sensibility" when faced by a public suspicious of excellence and indifferent, if not opposed, to moral responsibility].

1644 Hartman, Geoffrey H. "The Heroics of Realism," YR, LIII (Autumn 1963), 26-35. Reprinted in Beyond Formalism: Literary Essays, 1958-1970. (Yale University Press, 1972), pp. 61-70. [Argues that as the contemporary novel moves "toward a freer human sensibility," it runs the risk of "inducing too quickly a sense of intimacy with person and place;" hence, the need for a "self-generated distancing" whereby the novelist refuses "to know positively" the familiar world he describes and which leads him to adopt the impersonal mode of narration. H. James, J. Joyce, and V. Woolf among others].

1645 Harvey, W. M. "Have You Anything to Declare? Or Angry Young Men: Fact and Fictions," IntLA, I (1958), 47-59. [Concentrates on J. Osborne's plays and on the novels of K. Amis and J. Wain to sort out the "myth" of the Angry Young Man which he attributes to the confusion over "the character of the writer and the nature of his personae"].

1646 _____. "Work in Progress 1: Character and the Context of Things," EIC, XIII:1 (Jan. 1963), 50-66. Reprinted in Character and the Novel. (London: Chatto and Windus, 1965), pp. 30-51, and The Novel: Modern Essays in Criticism. Edited by Robert Murray Davis. (Englewood-Cliffs, N. J.: Prentice-Hall, 1969), pp. 126-140. [Examines the "relation of people to the world of inanimate objects," extolling the novel that reflects experience. V. Woolf and H. James among others].

1647 Harwood, H. C. "Current Fiction," NC, XCVII:578 (Apr. 1925), 569-577. [Surveys contemporary novelists and remarks on the shortage of humorists and female novelists].

1648 _____. "The Novels of Empire," Outlook, LVII (5 June 1926), xxxviii-xlii. (British Empire Supplement). [Remarks on the absence of new schools of writers, especially of a national fiction, in the various countries of the Empire. Refers to R. Kipling and E. M. Forster].

1649 _____. "The Post-War Novel in England," LA, 333 (1
July 1927), 67-69. Reprinted from Outlook, (7 May 1927).
[Dismisses five postwar illusions cherished by writers that
1) the novel is "frank and daring," 2) the modern young
woman is "uniquely potent," 3) the novelist "has substantially changed," 4) the novel attempts to be topical, and
5) the younger generation is better than the old. Brief
references to D. H. Lawrence, J. Galsworthy, and A. Bennett].

1650 _____. "Recent Tendencies in English Fiction," QR,
CCLII (Apr. 1929), 321-338. [A review article on novels
by A. Huxley, D. H. Lawrence, F. Brett Young, E. M. Forster,
F. M. Ford, and V. Woolf, surveying the novelists' "sense
of incongruity with the universe" and their inability to
resolve it, their "frankness, and foulness of language,"
their movement away from "reality" to "private experiences"
as having "external validity" and examining ways in which
fiction might be "saved"].

1651 _____. "New Novels, 1931-32," SatR (London), CLIII
(2 Jan. 1932), 16-17. [Dismisses 1931 as not a good year
for fiction, and predicts better times for 1932 now that
banality and "dirtiness" are diminishing and there is an
"urge toward simple Englishry" among people].

1652 Hasley, Louis. "The Stream-of-Consciousness Method,"
CathW, CXLIV (Nov. 1937), 210-213. [On the origin of the
method, its use and its legitimacy as a literary device;
also discusses two objections raised in connection with
it--sexual immorality and the denial of free will].

1653 Hatcher, Harlan. "The Literary Fourth Dimension," EJ,
XXVII:6 (June 1938), 455-464. [Observations on the "phenomenon toward the occult, folk mysticism, time, religion
and death" in contemporary literature. A. Huxley and J.
B. Priestley among others].

1654 _____. "A Scene of Confusion," CE, IV (Dec. 1942),
153-159. [A survey of the literary scene in England, U.
S. A., and Europe. References to J. Joyce, V. Woolf, J.
Galsworthy, and D. H. Lawrence].

1655 Hauser, Arnold. "The Conceptions of Time in Modern Art
and Science," PR, XXIII:3 (Summer 1956), 320-333. [On the
Bergsonian concept of time in the 20th century].

1656 Hawkins, A. Desmond. "Fiction Chronicle," Criterion, XV:
60 (Apr. 1936), 479-488. [A review article emphasising
the function of the novel in translating "the fundamental
histoire morale contemporaine into terms of manners and
specific performance," even though recent fiction offers
little to support it as a "contemporary serviceable medium."
J. Hargrave, G. Barker, A. Calder-Marshall, D. Richardson,
and others].

1657 _____. "Fiction Chronicle," Criterion, XVI:62 (Oct. 1936), 103-115. [A review article on novels by C. Morgan, L. H. Myers, S. Spender, T. O. Beachcroft and other English novelists, attempting to "'explain'the phenomenon" of C. Morgan and L. H. Myers and their reputation].

1658 _____. "Fiction Chronicle," Criterion, XVII:66 (Oct. 1937), 107-118. [A review article on works by D. Jones, R. Church, T. Collins, and I. Compton-Burnett rejecting the "mass of detail" and "documentary interests" when they become the novelist's primary occupation].

1659 _____. "Fiction Chronicle," Criterion, XVII:68 (Apr. 1938), 500-513. [Reviews current novels by F. Prokosch, T. O. Beachcroft, C. Day Lewis and others rather briefly on pp. 509-513. The rest of the article deals with the short story].

1660 _____. "Fiction Chronicle," Criterion, XVIII:70 (Oct. 1938), 82-95. [A review article on novels by J. Hanley, R. Hughes, J. Lindsay and others, examining the influence of the "common man" on fiction, followed by a survey of the works of E. Bowen].

1661 Hawkins, Ethel Wallace. "The Stream of Consciousness Novel," AtM, CXXXVIII (Sep. 1926), 356-360. [On the psychological fiction of three women writers: D. Richardson, K. Mansfield, and V. Woolf].

1662 Hayman, Ronald. "Le Roman anglais d'après-guerre: III," RLM, III (Apr. 1954), 81-95. Reprinted in La Littérature anglaise d'après-guerre. (Paris: Lettres Modernes, 1955), pp. 81-112. [Maintains that the volume, mediocrity, lack of form and design in the average postwar English novel is minimising and isolating the achievement of the more serious novelists who could have constituted a new "tradition." A. West, A. Koestler, G. Greene, E. Waugh, and A. Wilson].

1663 *Hayward, John. "Nya namm," BLM, XXIII (1954), 280-283.

1664 Hebblethwaite, Peter. "Crosscurrents--VI: How Catholic is the Catholic Novel," TLS, 3413 (27 July 1967), 678-679. [Identifies the Catholic novel by its contents and what it is about. G. Greene, E. Waugh, and M. Spark].

1665 Heilbrun, Carolyn. "The Woman as Hero," TQ, VIII:4 (Winter 1965), 132-141. [On woman as the protagonist or central character of a work, the one who undergoes the major action and whom "men as well as women, may view as an actor in a destiny possible for them." Restricted to works by male authors. H. James, D. H. Lawrence, and E. M. Forster among others].

233

1666   _____. "The Bloomsbury Group," Midway, IX (Autumn
          1968), 71-85. [A reassessment partly prompted by M. Holroyd's
          biography of Lytton Strachey, bringing out the ascendancy
          of reason and its influence on the group].

1667 Henfrey, Norman V. "The Angry Young Men: Les Raisons d'une
      colère," Culture, XXVII (June 1966), 176-194. [Discusses
      the various causes that led to the birth of the "movement"
      in the fifties].

1668 Heppenstall, Rayner. "Outsiders and Others," TC, CLVIII
      (Nov. 1955), 453-459. [Discusses the "literary closed shop"
      of the day where "connections of some kind" are still im-
      portant even though the major innovating writers of the
      20th century were "outsiders" to it. Part of the article
      discusses the Eliot-Leavis controversy over D. H. Lawrence].

1669   _____. "The Need for Experiment," The Times, (13 Dec.
          1962), p. 14. [Elaborates on a statement that English nov-
          elists experiment with "the matter of their novels" but not
          with the "manner," and describes the French "nouveau roman"
          as a "sign of new life" in fiction].

1670 Hernadi, Paul. "Dual Perspective: Free Indirect Discourse
      and Related Techniques," CompL, XXIV:1 (Winter 1972), 32-
      44. [Examines the "complex perspective" or "dual mode of
      vision" resulting from the narrator saying "in propria per-
      sona what one of the characters means". Illustrates from
      Joyce's Portrait of the Artist as a Young Man and other
      works].

1671 Herrick, Robert. "A Feline World," Bookman (New York), LXIX
      (Mar. 1929), 1-6. [On the new women novelists in English
      and American fiction discarding the purely male concerns of
      the older fiction and describing women's "primary interests,
      among themselves, for themselves"].

1672   _____. "Fiction and Ideas, Bookman (New York), LXIX
          (July 1929), 543-548. [A review article on novels by R.
          Hughes, D. Garnett, and H. G. Wells and others emphasising
          the importance of adult ideas in fiction].

1673   _____. "Hermaphrodites," Bookman (New York), LXIX
          (July 1929), 485-489. [On the men who "write like women."
          References to A. Huxley and E. M. Forster].

1674 Hersey, John. "The Novel of Contemporary History," AtM,
      CLXXXIV (Nov. 1949), 80-84. Reprinted in The Writer's Book.
      Edited by Helen Hull. (New York: Barnes & Noble, 1956).
      [On the aims and standards of the novel that deals with con-
      temporary events. Framework and references in the first
      section are American, but sections two and three deal with
      the art].

234

1675 Herzog, Bert. "Bemerkungen zur Katholischen Literatur der Gegenwart," SZ, CLI (Mar. 1952), 420-426. [Remarks on current Catholic literature in German, French and English. Includes G. Greene and E. Waugh].

1676 _____. "Der Utopische Roman," SchR, LX (1961), 1056-64. [General characteristics of anti-utopias. G. Orwell, A. Huxley, and R. Warner among others].

1677 Heslop, Harold. "The Working Class and the Novel," LabM, XII (Nov. 1931), 689-692. [Contends that novels with a "working class milieu" of the "modern school" of Joyce and Lawrence are not "proletarian" because they do not come from the pens of "worker authors," and are not dedicated to the "advance of a social order of society"].

1678 Hibbard, Addison. "The Road to Modernism," SatR, XIX (21 Jan. 1939), 3-4, 16. [Emphasises six general trends in English and American fiction over the past 50 years. J. Joyce, J. Conrad, and D. Richardson among others].

1679 Hicks, Granville. "Gutter--and then What?," ForumN, LXXX:6 (Dec. 1928), 801-810. [Analyses the "modern temper" and its search for reality which led to the "gutter," to "new forms, new styles, even to new vocabularies," but which may also lead to a "fresh affirmation of life" that will help man face the "worst negations of science and history." J. Joyce, D. H. Lawrence, and A. Huxley among others].

1680 _____. "Literature and the War," CE, I:3 (Dec. 1939), 199-207. [Surveys English literary output during the First World War, and after it, and doubts whether the Second World War will duplicate the output, seeing that the present generation of writers is already suffering from the disillusionment wrought by the previous era].

1681 _____. "Literature in this Global War," CE, IV:8 (May 1943), 453-459. [A survey of war novels in England and U. S. A. A. Koestler, J. B. Priestley, and A. Lewis among others].

1682 Hilton, Frank. "Britain's New Class," Encounter, X:2 (Feb. 1959), 59-63. [On the new "intelligent underdogs," the numerous representatives of the British working class, followed by a quick examination of K. Amis's Lucky Jim, J. Osborne's James Porter, and J. Braine's Joe Lampton].

1683 Hinkson, Pamela. "Fiction Trends," FR, CLXXVI (Aug. 1951), 554-561. [A general survey from 1918 to 1950].

1684 Hobman, D. L. "Jew in Gentile Fiction," ContempR, CLVII (Jan. 1940), 97-103. [Examines the Jew as a "stock" figure who rarely comes alive in fiction. References to J. Joyce,

235

D. Richardson, and D. H. Lawrence among others].

1685 Hobsbaum, Philip. "University Life in English Fiction,"
TC, CLXXIII (Summer 1964), 139-147. [Shows how novels in
the late 19th and 20th centuries "provide the fine focus"
to assess facts regarding the role of English Universities.
C. Mackenzie, H. O. Sturgis, R. Lehmann, D. H. Lawrence, K.
Amis, M. Bradbury, K. Walker, C. P. Snow, and P. Larkin
among others].

1686 "Hoff, Harry" [William Cooper]. "Novel and Anti-Novel,"
Sunday Times, (17 Dec. 1961), 21. [See entry above by
William Cooper].

1687 Hoffman, Frederick J. "The Novel and Its Critics," VQR,
XXXIV:2 (Summer 1958), 317-320. [A review article on Caro-
line Gordon's How to Read a Novel (New York: The Viking
Press, 1958)].

1688 _____. "Grace, Violence and Self: Death and Modern
Literature," VQR, XXXIV (Summer 1958), 439-454. Revised
and reprinted as "Introduction" to The Mortal No: Death
and the Modern Imagination (Princeton, N. J.: Princeton
University Press, 1964), pp. 3-19. [Shows how each term--
grace, violence, and self--determines the ways in which
death, as an event, is "invested with image and metaphor,
and that the pattern of life-death-immortality is distinct
in each case." E. M. Forster, D. H. Lawrence, G. Greene
and others].

1689 Hoffmann, Richard. "Proportion and Incident in Joseph Conrad and Arnold Bennet," SR, XXXII (Jan. 1924), 79-92. [Ex-
amines a few of the differences between them illustrating
from Lord Jim and Clayhanger]

1690 Holloway, John. "Tank in the Stalls: Notes on the 'School
of Anger'," HudR, X:3 (Autumn 1957), 424-429. Reprinted in
The Charted Mirror: Literary and Critical Essays. (London:
Routledge & Kegan Paul, 1960), pp. 137-145; also The Beat
Generation And The Angry Young Men. Edited by Gene Feldman
and Max Gartenberg. (New York: The Citadel Press, 1958),
pp. 364-373; in Great Britain as Protest. (London: Souvenir Press, 1959). [Relates the "Angry Young Men" to the
tradition of the English novel by showing that their preoccupations with the "permanent social stresses" that face
"obscure middle-class provincial life" and their methods are
"recurrent" features of the English novel, and had prevailed
before the invasion of continental influences].

1691 Holloway, Owen. "The Novel and the Private Life: the Teller
and the Told," Listener, LI:1301 (4 Feb. 1954), 227-228.
[Asserts that the art of the novel lies in the expression

236

it gives to the "feeling of person." This is the first of four talks].

1692 _____. "Distinction of Persons: The Teller and the Told II," Listener, LI:1302 (11 Feb. 1954), 258-259. [Formulas for the way a reader may be involved in a story].

1693 _____. "The Time of Our Lives: The Teller and the Told III," Listener, LI: 1303 (18 Feb. 1954), 305-306. [Discusses the "specific language of time" in narrative art whereby the "twin impossibility of looking into the future and putting the clock back" are reconciled].

1694 _____. "Let's Pretend: The Teller and the Told IV," Listener, LI:1305 (4 Mar. 1954), 386-387. [Maintains that the medium of narrative art is constituted by the play the novelist makes with the polarity of our relations with the world. In his last talk he discusses how a piece of fiction may be taken as true even though it is made up].

1695 Holroyd, Stuart. "A Writer's Prospect--VIII," LM, VI:1 (Jan. 1959), 51-59. [Discusses the problem of literature and values and suggests a correspondence between the life of man and his use of language].

1696 Holtby, Winifred. "Novels of the Year," Bookman (London), LXXXI (Dec. 1931), 184. [Chooses novels by N. Mitchison, V. Woolf, S. Benson, E. Linklater, and D. Garnett as the the five best novels of 1931].

1697 _____. "Novels of the Year," Bookman (London), LXXXIII (Dec. 1932), 171-172. [A review of 1932 in which she chooses three outstanding novels "each concerned with a problem and a solution." P. Bentley's Inheritance, C. Morgan's The Fountain, and A. Huxley's Brave New World. Also classifies novels into the "romantic," the "historical," the "humorous," and those which examine social institutions].

1698 Holthusen, Hans Egon. "Through German Eyes," Spectator, CLXXXVII (6 July 1951), 28-30. [A brief survey of the contemporary scene from a German viewpoint, which extols the English novel for its "fusion of genuine fiction with solid literary achievement," especially G. Greene, and to a lesser degree, E. Waugh for being "reading material and intellectual Ereignis conjointly"].

1699 Holzhauer, Jean. "The Nun in Literature," Commonweal, LXV (22 Feb. 1957), 527-529. [On the numerous difficulties attending literary interpretations of the nun, and the resulting revelation of her drama, "obliquely and intermittently," in minor English and American writers].

1700 Honan, Park. "Realism, Reality, and the Novel," Novel, II:3

237

(Spring 1969), 197-211. [A symposium on the critical problems suggested by the topic, and an assessment of the present situation with nine English critics: B. Bergonzi, M.
Bradbury, I. Gregor, B. Hardy, F. Kermode, M. Kinkead-Weekes,
D. Lodge, T. Tanner, and P. Turner].

1701 Honig, Edwin. "The 'Ideal' in Symbolic Fictions," NMQ,
XXIII (Summer 1953), 153-168. [Discusses the common ground
shared by satire, allegory, and the pastoral, and examines
the creation of a "hero and a situation whose progress will
show a kind of idyllic surpassing of real-life adversity
within credible naturalistic surroundings" in the pastoral
novels of D. H. Lawrence, E. M. Forster, and J. Conrad].

1702 *"Hope and Despair in the Modern Novel," Annals, LXXXI (Feb.
1970), 24-25.

1703 Hope, Francis. "Faces in the Novel," TC, CLXXIII: 1023
(Autumn 1964), 56-61. [On the way post-World War II English
novelists mirror modern England].

1704 Hough, Graham. "The Novel and the Reader," Listener, LIII:
1350 (13 Jan. 1955), 71-73; LIII:1352 (20 Jan. 1955), 111,
114-115; LIII:1353 (27 Jan. 1955), 146-148; LIII:1354 (3
Feb. 1955), 196-197, 200-201. [A series of four talks on
the B. B. C. Home Service. The first discusses the basic
desires in the common reader which the novel was meant to
satisfy: interest in story and curiosity about people.
The second discusses the tendency of the novel over the last
eighty years to explore "undercurrents of feeling" that are
present but have not surfaced or have not been generally
noticed and discussed. The third talk examines new techniques and the new subject matter: increasing psychological
complexity, the use of time, and the "attempt to represent
directly the inner lives," the thoughts and feelings of
character. The fourth talk surveys the ground gained by the
technical experiments of the last thirty years and attributes the novel's present loss of authority to the novelists' lack of confidence in what would make society "tick,"
and the interest in technique and "subtle and specialised
effects" at the expense of the "normal texture of ordinary
social life." S. Maugham. G. Greene, D. H. Lawrence, V.
Woolf, A. Huxley, J. Joyce, E. M. Forster, and J. Cary among
others].

1705 _____. "Morality and the Novel," Listener, LXIX:1779
(2 May 1963), 747-748. Revised and reprinted in The Dream
and the Task: Literature and Morals in the Culture of Today. (London: Gerald Duckworth, 1963), pp. 42-57. [Argues
that because the reader, following the novelist, passes
moral judgments on characters and situation, the novelist
ought to be a public moralist who, at the same time, should
not put his readers in blinkers].

238

1706 _____ . "Mimesis: The Novel and History," CritQ, VIII (1966), 136-145. [An extract from An Essay in Criticism. (London: Gerald Duckworth; New York: Norton, 1966), pp. 42-44, 111-120. See entry under books].

1707 "How Novelists Draw Their Characters," Bookman (London), (Apr. 1922), 15-17; (May 1922), 83-84; (June 1922), 121-122. [A symposium. Contributors for the April issue are Sir G. Parker, C. Marriott, F. Swinnerton, A. Perrin, A. Marshall, K. Rhodes, J. S. Clouston, E. F. Benson, H. Walpole, and H. de vere Stackpoole; for the May issue: J. D. Beresford, E. Sidgwick, S. Maugham, J. E. Buckrose, and G. Frankau; for the June issue: A. S. M. Hutchinson, W. J. Locke, H. Dudeney, E. T. Thurston, R. Macaulay, and M. Cholmondeley].

1708 "How to Say It," TLS, 3306 (8 July 1965), 579. [Leading article on sex in novels].

1709 Howarth, Herbert. "Impersonal Aphrodite," Mosaic, I:2 (Jan. 1968), 74-86. [Notices the similarity between L. Durell's and D. H. Lawrence's rejection of "lives" for life, and their search for the "elementals," the fire that "creates or ravages" rather than "psychologies," and correlates Lawrence's "ideas of vitalism, of the earth-gods and the archetypal configurations" with the methods of G. Moore, J. Conrad, and F. M. Ford].

1710 Howe, Irving. "The Future of the Novel: The Political Novel (1)," Tomorrow, X (May 1951), 51-58. [On the novel concerned with "political ideas in their impact on human experience or with the political milieu as a setting for experience," in pre-World War I novels. Limited to Dostoyevsky, H. James and J. Conrad, as writers educating the public to the dangers of rebellion].

1711 _____ . "The Future of the Novel: The Political Novel (2)," Tommorrow, X (June 1951), 49-53. [Examines the contrast between early hope and later disillusion in the Russian Revolution that obsesses A. Malraux, I. Silone, A. Koestler, and V. Serge, and points out that the political novel "offers the most lively possibilities" for the future].

1712 _____ . "Mass Society and Post-Modern Fiction," PR, XXVI 3 (Summer 1959), 420-436. Reprinted in Decline of the New. (New York: Harcourt, Brace & World, 1970), pp. 190-207, and Approaches to the Novel. Edited by Robert Scholes (Scranton, Pa.: Chandler Publishing, 1961), pp. 269-287. [Discusses in what way "mass society" affects the content and structure of the novel, and the sense of foreboding that fills novelists as they see a mass society moving toward a "quiet desert of moderation." Considers briefly the "Angry Young Men" and the "Beat Generation"].

1713 _____. "The Fiction of Anti-Utopia," NRep, CLXVI (23
Apr. 1962), 13-16. Reprinted in Decline of the New. (New
York: Harcourt, Brace & World, 1970), pp. 66-74, and Perspectives in Contemporary Criticism: A Collection of Recent Essays by American, English and European Literary Critics. (New York: Harper, 1968), pp. 220-225. [On the "main
intellectual premise shaping anti-utopian fiction" and the
"formal properties" which distinguish it from other forms
of fiction. Included are G. Orwell and A. Huxley].

1714 _____. "The Culture of Modernism," Commentary, XLIV:5
(Nov. 1967), 48-59. Revised and reprinted as "The Idea of
the Modern," Introduction to Literary Modernism. (Greenwich, Conn.: Fawcett Publications, 1967), pp. 11-41; and
Decline of the New. (New York: Harcourt, Brace & World,
1970), pp. 3-33. [On what we call "modern" in literature,
with some elaboration on pp. 57-58 on several traits of
"the modern hero." References to J. Joyce, V. Woolf, and
D. H. Lawrence].

1715 Howe, P. P. "Fiction and Perpetual Life," Athenaeum, (6
June 1919), 422-423. [On the renewed appearances of the
same characters in successive novels by C. Mackenzie, A.
Bennett, and H. Walpole].

1716 _____. "Fiction: Autumn, 1919," FR, CXIII (Jan. 1920),
60-70. [Distinguishes in his review between novels written
during war time "concerned in a spirit of duty"--J. Galsworthy's Saint's Progress, M. Robert's Hearts of Women, G.
Cannan's Time and Eternity--and those written in "a spirit
of relief" after the war--F. Swinnerton's September, C.
Mackenzie's Poor Relations, F. B. Young's Young Physician,
S. Kaye-Smith's Tamarisk Town, C. Dane's Legend, and the
works of V. Woolf].

1717 Hudson, Stephen. "Remarks on the Novel," Symposium, I (Jan.
1930), 82-83. [Extract from his letter to the Editors on
the state of the contemporary novel].

1718 Hughes, Richard. "Fiction Today," The Times (Saturday Review), (21 Mar. 1970), 1. [Maintains that the flight of
readers today from fiction to a "land of actuality and abstract studies" looks like the flight of a doomed "escapist,
frivolous generation" from a reality about human beings
which fiction might compel them to apprehend].

1719 _____. "Of Use and Beauty," Books, 1 (Autumn 1970),
21-24. [Extracts from an address to the American Academy
of Arts and Letters. Cautions mankind against the perils
resulting from neglect of the novel, for besides mysticism,
it remains to most people the "only way of experiencing
the identity of others"].

240

1720 Humphrey, Robert. "'Stream of Consciousness': Technique or Genre?" PQ, XXX:4 (Oct. 1951), 434-437. [Examines the term and its literary implications, and determines that there is no one "stream of consciousness" technique but several, "quite different in their nature, which are used to present stream of consciousness"].

1721 Humphreys, Emyr. "The 'Protestant' Novelist," Spectator, CLXXIX (21 Nov. 1952), 631-632. [Argues for "high serious- ness," creative intelligence and a responsible attitude to life in novelists instead of the "sensibility" which domin- ated the "post-Joyce-Woolf era"].

1722 _____. "A Protestant View of the Modern Novel," Lis- tener, XLIX:1257 (2 Apr. 1953), 557-559. [Discusses prob- lems of form and expression and how a novelist's attitude governs the way he writes in the post-Joyce era].

1723 Hurrell, John D. "Class and Conscience in John Braine and Kingsley Amis," Crit, II (Spring-Summer 1958), 39-52. [At- tempts to show how the crisis of conscience in a man without distinctive class allegiance who is attempting to adjust in a society where the code of conduct is alien, lends itself to treatment as a comedy--K. Amis--or as a tragedy, by a socially involved novelist--J. Braine].

1724 Hutchens, Eleanor N. "Towards a Poetics of Fiction: 5) The Novel as Chronomorph," Novel, V:3 (Spring 1972), 215- 224. [Argues that the novel is "generically chronomorphic," that human time moulds the materials of the novel and gives it proper form. J. Joyce, V. Woolf, and C. P. Snow among others. (For the other four approaches towards a poetics of fiction, see entries under M. Bradbury, D. Lodge, B. Hardy, and R. Scholes)].

1725 Hyman, Stanley Edgar. "Some Trends in the Novel," CE, XX:1 (Oct. 1958), 1-9. Reprinted in The Promised End: Essays and Reviews, 1942-1962. (New York: World Publications, 1963; Books for Libraries Press, 1972), pp. 342-356. [Identifies three trends: 1) a parody of earlier works, 2) "disguises of love," and 3) a growing body of real fiction. Though mostly on U. S. fiction, there are brief references to A. Koestler, G. Orwell, A. Huxley, and the "Angries"].

1726 Hynes, Sam. "The 'Poor Sod' as Hero," Commonweal, LXIV (13 Apr. 1956), 51-53. [Outlines the characteristics of the English postwar school of novelists--J. Wain, P. H. Newby, K. Amis--their similarities of tone, situation, character, and their "comic view of the sensitive soul"].

1727 _____. "The Beat and the Angry," Commonweal, LXVIII (5 Sep. 1958), 559-561. [Discusses why the American "Beat Generation" and the English "Angry Young Men" appeared when

241

they did, and why the movements should "have taken the forms
they did"].

1728 _____ . "The Whole Contention Between Mr. Bennett and
Mrs. Woolf," Novel, I (Fall 1967), 34-44. Reprinted in Edwardian Occasions: Essays on English Writing in the Early
Twentieth Century. (London: Routledge & Kegan Paul, 1972),
pp. 24-39. [Attempts to put V. Woolf's "Mr. Bennett and
Mrs. Brown" in the right perspective by providing the background material for "the whole of their quarrel"].

1729 "The Illusion of Involvement," TLS, 2842 (17 Aug. 1956), iv.
[Special Autumn Number: "Frontiers of Literature." Examines
the qualities and means essential in sustaining the reader's
illusion of involvement].

1730 "Important Authors of the Fall, Speaking for Themselves,"
NYHTBR, XXVII:8 (8 Oct. 1950), 1-26. [Accounts by English
and American writers on "how they work, what they read, how
they play." Included are S. Maugham, E. Bowen, N. Balchin,
J. Cary, and H. Green].

1731 Inge, Dean. "Reticence in Fiction," Bookman (London), (Dec.
1927), 162-163. [Pleads for a return to the "wholesome
traditions of the English novel" because of the present
"mean and sordid view of human nature," and "perverted morality" of the attitude towards marriage which the novel
expresses].

1732 "Insular Fiction," EdR, CCV:429 (Jan. 1907), 192-211. [A
review article on six English novels of 1906 that stresses
the "'all-British' convention in romance"].

1733 Irvine, Peter L. "The 'Witness' Point of View in Fiction,"
SAQ, LXIX (Spring 1970), 217-225. [On the "special effects"
of the device of the witness narrative and its potential for
"tonal shifts and ironic control" in the novel and the dramatic monologue].

1734 Irwin, W. R. "Permanence and Change in The Edwardians and
Told By An Idiot," MFS, II:2 (May 1956), 63-67. [Examines
the different representations and treatments of the two topics by R. Macaulay and V. Sackville-West].

1735 Ivaseva, V. V. "Anglijskij roman pyatidecyutych godov,"
IL, 1 (1958), 211-217. [Reflections on the tendencies of
English postwar fiction, especially in the fifties. J.
Lindsay, A. Wilson, A. Powell, L. P. Hartley, I. Murdoch,
and C. P. Snow].

1736 _____ . "The Struggle Continues: Some Comments on
English Modernist Esthetics," ZAA, VIII (1960), 409-421.
[A translation from Russian by John Mitchell of an article

that had appeared in IL, 5 (May 1959), 180-188. Argues that
in spite of the growth of realistic trends in English novelists of the fifties, there remains a great deal to be done
before speaking of "final victory" owing to the continuous
pressure of "reactionary ideology" and "bourgeois modernist
ethics." J. Galsworthy, J. Joyce, V. Woolf, H. G. Wells, A.
Bennett, C. Wilson, I. Murdoch, J. Lindsay and others].

1737　　　　　　　. "Sovremennyj anglijskij 'rabocij roman' (1958-
1966)," VMU, XXI:4 (1966), 31-51. [Focuses on the English
working class novel by A. Sillitoe, S. Chaplin, S. Barstow,
and R. Williams, with references to K. Waterhouse and D.
Storey].

1738　　　　　　　. "Tri vstrechi s Anglici," VMU, 1 (1967), 80-
87. [An account of three separate opportunities between
1964 and 1966 afforded the writer to meet with C. P. Snow,
P. H. Johnson, G. Greene, A. Sillitoe, A. Wilson, and I.
Murdoch].

1739　　　　　　　. "V debryakh absurdnogo mira," IL, 3 (1969),
203-216. ["In the Maze of the Absurd World." A political
analysis of the literary scene].

1740　　　　　　　. "Realizm -- magistral anglijskoj literatury
poslevoennogo perioda," VMU, 1 (1969), 3-14. [A survey of
the mainstream of English literature in the postwar period].

1741　　　　　　　. "Sovremennyi Anglijskij filosofskij roman,"
IL, 5 (1970), 190-202. ["The Contemporary English Philo-
sophical Novel." C. Wilson, W. Golding, I. Murdoch, and
J. Wain].

1742　　　　　　　. "Sovremennaja Anglijskaja literatura v svete
něenija V. I. Lewina o dvux kul'turax v kařdoj nacionalnoj
kulture," FN, XIII:2 (1970), 3-13. [Examines English novelists and dramatists of the fifties in the light of Lenin's
teachings on bourgeois culture and proletarian literature.
P. H. Johnson, C. P. Snow, W. Golding, I. Murdoch, J. Wain,
K. Amis, and A. Sillitoe among others].

1743　　　　　　　. "Vstrechi v Anglij," LG, (17 June 1970), p. 25.
[An account of her meetings with English novelists as special
literary correspondent to the gazette].

1744　Jacobi, J. B. "The Limitations of Realism in Modern Fiction,"
ACQR, XLVI (Jan. 1921), 55-69. [Condemns the extreme realism pervaded by naturalism of G. Cannan, H. G. Wells, A.
Bennett, and F. Swinnerton for merely dwelling on the "seamy
side of life" without showing the "ideal shining through it,"
and for being "mimics" whose irony is not "corrective," but
'negatively derisive"].

1745   Jacobson, Dan. "Why Read Novels?" Nation, CLXXXIX (14 Nov. 1959), 343-345. [Maintains that the usefulness of the novel in an age of specialization is in being "the recorded know-ledge of the states of consciousness of different men at different times,"and in giving "point and direction to our consciousness, in the very act of enlarging it"].

1746   _____. "Muffled Majesty," TLS, 3426 (26 Oct. 1967), 1007. [Contends that the novel cannot survive without what H. James dismissed as "the mere muffled majesty of irre-sponsible 'authorship'," that the "narrative presence" can be dramatic and self-justifying as any of the Jamesian or Joycean set of conventions that "have utterly exhausted their utility and expressiveness"].

1747   Jacobson, Josephine. "A Catholic Quartet," ChrS, XLVII (Summer 1964), 139-154. [Discusses the manner in which M. Spark and G. Greene -- and U. S. writers J. F. Powers and F. O'Connor -- express their Catholic vision of life].

1748   James, Henry. "The Younger Generation," TLS, 635 (19 Mar. 1914), 133-134; 637 (2 Apr. 1914), 157-158. [Surveys the work of M. Hewlett, J. Galsworthy, A. Bennett in Part I, and H. Walpole, J. Conrad, and G. Cannan in Part II].

1749   Jameson, Storm. "The Georgian Novel and Mr. Robinson," Bookman, LXIX (July 1929), 449-463. Reprinted with the same title in book-form (London: Heinemann, 1929). [Origi-nally a paper read to the Literary Circle of the National Liberal Club, 23 Nov. 1928. Introduces the average middle class reader--Mr. Robinson--to the various qualities of Georgian fiction. A. Bennett, F. M. Ford, and V. Woolf].

1750   _____. "Decline of Fiction," Athenaeum, XLV (3 Aug. 1929), 594-595. [Suggests that contemporary novelists' "compulsion to 'tell the truth'" makes it impossible for the English novel to become the vehicle for a "higher real-ity," and reduces it to a concern with "being, and never with becoming." A Huxley, D. H. Lawrence, A. Bennett, and J. Galsworthy].

1751   _____. "The Future of the Novel," LibA, (Nov. 1930), 212-222. Reprinted as "Autobiography and the Novel," Book-man (New York), LXXII:6 (Feb. 1931), 557-565. [An address delivered at the London School of Economics, 8 Oct. 1930. Foresees a "new departure" from novels of action, characters, ideas or biography to the "stream" of autobiography, which will "swell and broaden and take on all the characteristics of the main stream," for the inner world is still an "untapped source"].

1752   _____. "The Craft of the Novelist," EngRev, LVIII

(1934), 28-43. [" . . . the worth of a novel is its human
worth, and not any fancied aesthetic quality," for the novelist's true function, the justification for his existence,
is to wrestle with life "in all the forms it assumes in his
time" and not merely to "write beautifully or amusingly."
V. Woolf, D. H. Lawrence, and T. F. Powys].

1753 _____. "Literature Between the Wars and the Tyranny
of Things," TLS, 2172 (18 Sep. 1943), 450. Reprinted in
The Writer's Situation and Other Essays (London: Macmillan,
1950), pp. 126-136. [Examines the conditions which produced a relatively poor literature between the wars, and
advocates "a severe effort of detachment "the opposite of
indifference . . . to see . . . and to know, the world of
objects." Editorial comment p. 451 entitled "The Writer
and Society"].

1754 _____. "The Novelist Today," VQR, XXV:4 (Autumn 1949),
562-574. Reprinted in The Writer's Situation and Other Essays. (London: Macmillan, 1950), pp. 62-83. [Discusses
the problems of the novelist in an "ugly" and chaotic world,
and why he writes, and emphasises the novelist's responsibility to his own vision in spite of any demands made on
him].

1755 _____. "British Literature: Survey and Critique,"
SatR, XXXIV:41 (13 Oct. 1951), 24-26, 47. [Remarks on the
absence of great novelists, and the novelists' concentration
on "personal relations" rather than on "man in relation to
society" as a result of the "appalling chaos in the world
itself," thereby not meeting the challenge offered by the
"contemporary human condition." G. Greene, G. Orwell, A.
Huxley, R. Warner, E. Bowen, L. P. Hartley, N. Balchin, I.
Compton-Burnett, and H. Green among others].

1756 _____. "The Writer in Contemporary Society," ASch,
XXXV:1 (Winter 1965-66), 67-77. Expresses concern with the
possible disappearance of the imaginative writer as a result of the "new electronic mediums"].

1757 _____. "Sex and Society: Love's Labour Exposed,"
Spectator, CCXVI:7180 (4 Feb. 1966), 134. [Discusses the
problem of intelligent women novelists writing "sex fiction"
that describes at length their own or their "characters'
erotic needs and activities"].

1758 _____. "Now and Then," Author, 81 (Summer 1970),
59-63. [Advice to new novelists who wish to begin writing
in the seventies after reviewing the radical moral and intellectual changes over the past forty years].

1759 Janeway, Elizabeth. "What's American and What's British in
the Modern Novel," NYTBR, (14 Jan. 1951), 4. Reprinted in

245

Highlights of Modern Literature: A Permanent Collection of Memorable Essays from 'The New York Times Book Review.' Edited by Francis Brown. (New York: The New American Library), pp. 62-68. [An American viewpoint contrasting the "neatness," art and formal accomplishments of the British novel, with its predominant interest in personal relationships with the "artistic incoherence" resulting from compassing too much experience in the American novel, with its interest in society and an external world of meaningful events].

1760 _____. "Fiction's Place in a World Awry," NYTBR, (13 Aug. 1961), 1, 24. Reprinted in Opinions and Perspectives from 'The New York Times Book Review.' Edited by Francis Brown (Boston: Houghton Mifflin, 1964), pp. 29-34. [Maintains that the novel, as central means of communication in our society, has given way to non-fiction because novelists are intimidated by the achievements of the past which they cannot match, and thus have become "entertainers" instead of "discoverers," and because "puzzled people . . . have got too lost to be able to talk with the rest of us at all, by way of the novel"].

1761 Jarab, Josef. "O nekterych prolemech teorie moderniho romanu v anglosaske literarni vede a kitice," CL, XV (1967), 243-269. [In Czech. "On some problems of the theory of the modern novel in Anglo-Saxon literary criticism." Interprets the views of 20th century English and American critics on the two significant literary concepts of "point of view" and "stream of consciousness". Includes abstract in English].

1762 Jeffares, A. Norman. "Some Academic Novels," WascanaR, V (1970), 5-27. [An extensive review of undergraduate life mainly in Oxford, Cambridge and Dublin Universities as depicted in nineteenth and twentieth century novels. J. Joyce, C. Mackenzie, A. Powell, D. Balsdon, R. Lehmann, A. P. Rossiter, D. Sayers, C. P. Snow, K. Amis, J. Wain, "M. Innes," W. Cooper, "G. Fielding," and H. MacInnes].

1763 Jelly, Oliver. "Fiction and Illness," REL, III:1 (Jan. 1962), 80-89. [Examines the influence of sickness in selected novels and the use novelists make of it. A. E. Ellis and J. Braine among others].

1764 Jerrold, Douglas. "The English Novel and the Modern Problem," NC, CXX (Nov. 1936), 595-604. [On two novels by C. Morgan and R. Speaight that face up to the "modern problem . . . of living our own lives in terms of our destiny as immortal souls"].

1765 Jessey, Cornelia. "Creative Fulfilment," Critic, XXII (Oct.-Nov. 1963), 24-31. [The novelist as "a witness who enregisters the most secret stirring of his time" will include

246

not only man's dreams of progress, but also his "interior bankruptcy." Examines works by R. Hughes, J. Joyce, and G. Greene among others].

1766 Joad, C. E. M. "Complaint against Lady Novelists," NSta, XVIII (19 Aug. 1939), 275-276. [Rejects Lady Novelists' views that a novelist--and his characters--should be solely concerned with recording and analysing personal relations].

1767 Johnson, James William. "The Adolescent Hero: A Trend in Modern Fiction," TCL, V:1 (Apr. 1959), 3-11. [On the wide-spread popularity of the "myth" of adolescence--the "in-effable feeling of loss, the disturbing realization of phys-ical entity and isolation, sexual confusion, emotional en-strangement, intellectual detachment"--as one of the basic concerns in American fiction. J. Joyce and V. Woolf among others].

1768 Johnson, Liana M. "La Letteratura inglese," ALB, (1962), 218-233. [Surveys current publications and focuses on G. Greene's A Burnt-out Case, I. Murdoch's A Severed Head, and A. Wilson's The Old Men at the Zoo].

1769 Johnson, Pamela Hansford. "With Prejudice," Windmill, I (1944), 1-10. [Assesses contemporary fiction in the light of the novelist's "understanding . . . of the scope of great art" and "the degree of realisation of the scope of his art," and predicts that the English novel is "at the edge of a re-birth . . . likely . . . to assume an entirely different form, dignity and vitality"].

1770 _____. "The Sick-Room Hush Over the English Novel," Listener, XLII:1072 (11 Aug. 1949), 235-236. [Attributes the limitation and decline of the English novel, especially its dryness of humour, to its technical experiments and ad-vance in the study of "nervous sensations"].

1771 _____. "Three Novelists and the Drawing of Character: C. P. Snow, Joyce Cary, and Ivy Compton-Burnett," E&S, III (1950), 82-99. [Analysis of character as it appears in all three writers].

1772 _____. "The Debate About the Novel," NSta, LVI:1430 (9 Aug. 1958), 172-173. [A rejection of P. Toynbee's view that the novel should remain in the experimental stage of Joyce and Woolf].

1773 _____. "Modern Fiction and the English Understatement," TLS, 2997 (7 Aug. 1959), iii. [Special Supplement. Re-marks on forms of English understatement in E. Waugh, E. M. Forster, J. Galsworthy, C. P. Snow, and forms of reaction to it in J. Osborne and K. Amis].

247

1774 _____ . "If She Writes, Must She Be a Lady?" NYTBR, (31 Dec. 1961), 1, 22. [Considers, not without some humour, what women can bring to the novel which men cannot].

1775 _____ . "The Genealogy of the Novel," NHQ, V:14 (1964), 97-107. [Surveys briefly the "textual experiments" of D. Richardson, J. Joyce, and V. Woolf before examining the "genealogical tree" from which sprang H. Balzac, W. Scott, C. Dickens, F. Dostoyevsky, and M. Proust].

1776 Jones, Howard Mumford. "Fiction, and the Art of Fiction," NYTBR, (28 July 1946), 2, 8. [Demonstrates the inappropriateness of any one definition for the English novel and suggests four essential qualities that make a novel: narrative power, a "sufficient admixture of autobiography transformed by imagination," central characters that move in a "three-dimensional world" and seem to exist beyond the novel, and lastly, the ability "to sum up an epoch"].

1777 Jones, Jack. "Novelists of the Depression--with an Afterword on Established Novelists," LibA, (Mar. 1937), 62-67. [Presents English, American and European writers between 1926 and 1936 who give true, perhaps "crude" pictures of the times, "without trimmings or padding." "R. Tressell" and J. Galsworthy among others].

1778 Jones, Llewellyn. "Psychoanalysis and Creative Literature," EJ, XXIII:6 (June 1934), 443-452. [Examines how the new psychology affects art and the relation of the critic and reader to the artist. Brief reference to D. Richardson and J. Joyce].

1779 Jones, Mervyn. "Poor Old Novel," Author, 82 (Winter 1971), 151-155. [Suggests that a novelist's perception should interpret by "unifying, not by fragmenting," thereby rescuing the contemporary novel which has lost the sense of relationship between "the ultimates and the observed realities," and split into two kinds of "half-novel," the documentary and the novel of sensibility].

1780 Jump, John D. "The Recent British Novel," ML&PSP, CI (1959), 23-38. [Restricted to a study of the novels of writers "who effectively arrived in or after 1939." J. Cary, L. P. Hartley, A. Wilson, and W. Golding].

1781 Kahler, Erich. "The Transformation of Modern Fiction," CompL, VII (Spring 1955), 121-128. [Suggests that the novel is distinguished from other narratives by its "symbolic quality" which pervaded the European and American tradition from the sixteenth century to the end of the nineteenth; but with the expansion of its social and psychic spheres in the twentieth, novelists resorted to "typification or to a mul-

tiplication and intensification of symbols, a construction
and synthesis of manifold symbolic levels," thereby achieving "pliability" of form. Brief references to H. James, J.
Joyce, V. Woolf, and S. Beckett among others].

1782 Kain, Richard M. "Four Ways of Looking at a Novel," SoR,
      (NS) II:2 (Apr. 1966), 464-470. [Reviews four critical
      works on the novel by G. Lukacs, H. Levin, M. Beebe, and R.
      Freedman].

1783 Kalb, B. "Three Comers," SatR, XXXVIII (7 May 1955), 22.
      [On K. Amis, I. Murdoch, and J. Wain].

1784 Kane, W. T. "Some Notes on Fiction," Month, CL:762 (Dec.
      1927), 493-499. [Admits the importance of selection in
      novel writing, describes the methods of both the romantic
      and the realistic portrayals of life, and suggests that the
      "great" novel is a synthesis of both].

1785 Kantra, Robert A. "The Fiction of Orthodox and Apostate
      Satire," KanQ, I:3 (1969), 78-88. [English satirists, fas-
      cinated by the "socialization of religion," agree, in spite
      of their various social and religious allegiances, that such
      a socialization is a "moral wrong" for it "may exist with-
      out religious knowledge and foster goals which vitiate its
      past values." H. Belloc, R. H. Benson, G. K. Chesterton,
      R. Firbank, E. M. Forster, A. Huxley, G. Orwell, E. Waugh,
      H. G. Wells, and others].

1786 Karl, Frederick R. "Pursuit of the Real," Nation, CXCIV
      (21 Apr. 1962), 345-349. [Maintains that contemporary Eng-
      lish, Continental and American novels reflect a "reality
      that balks resolution"; but whereas the American novel is
      concerned with "daily fact" in a "real world of dislocation,"
      the English and Continental seek "an ultimate reality or
      explore a metaphysical universe." All, however, seem to in-
      dicate that the "cultivation of self-responsibility" is
      perhaps the "only hope in a world that has veered out of
      control"].

1787 _____. "Conrad, Ford, and the Novel," Midway, X:2
      (Autumn 1969), 17-34. [On the relationship between the two
      novelists: the interchange of ideas between them, their
      artistic collaboration and their personal relationship].

1788 Karpf, Fritz. "Die Erlebte Rede im Englischen," Anglia,
      LVII (1933), 225-276. [On the form and use of the interi-
      or monologue in English literature. References to R. Mac-
      aulay, J. Galsworthy, A. Bennett, R. H. Benson, and H. G.
      Wells among others].

1789 Katona, Anna. "The Decline of the Modern in Recent British
      Fiction," ZAA, XIII (1965), 35-44. [On the revival of the

eighteenth and nineteenth centuries' social tradition in
the English novel of the fifties and early sixties as distinct from the "moderns" like V. Woolf, J. Joyce et al].

1790   Kawamoto, Shizuko. "Bildungsroman no Pattern," EigoS,
        CXIV:11 (1 Nov. 1968), 724-726. [In Japanese. Examines
        the "Ordeal of Father," "Ordeal of Woman" and the "Ordeal
        of Money" in the bildungsroman from Dickens to Joyce.
        References to H. G. Wells, S. Maugham, and D. H. Lawrence].

1791   Kaye-Smith, Sheila. "The Novelist's Material," SatR, II:
        28 (6 Feb. 1926), 537-538. [Explores the novelist's "spe-
        cial relation to life" whereby he can reach his public
        directly, and the "artistic canons" that discipline this
        personal element. Rejects the modern physiological and
        psychological processes in the novel as "almost an artis-
        tic betrayal," for their place is the novelist's mind not
        his pages].

1792   Kazin, Alfred. "Form and Anti-Form in Contemporary Liter-
        ature," BaratR, IV (June-July 1969), 92-98. [On the re-
        placement of the cult of form in the sixties by what may
        be called "art for my sake"--anti-form. Brief references
        to J. Joyce and D. H. Lawrence].

1793   Kehoe, W. "Fiction: The Trend of a Quarter-Century," SS,
        XLVII (22 Oct. 1945), 23-24. [A general review of the
        fiction of "despondency and disillusionment" of the twenties
        in English and American fiction, and the American novel
        of "extreme social consciousness" of the thirties. A. Hux-
        ley, J. Joyce, and V. Woolf among others].

1794   Kellogg, Gene. "The Catholic Novel in Convergence," Thought,
        XLV (1970), 265-296. [Defines the term "Catholic novel,"
        describes how the movement began, what it achieved, and why
        it has ebbed in France, England, and America].

1795   Kemp, Bernard. "Een studie over romantechniek," DWB, CXI
        (1966), 291-301. [A review article on H. Servotte's De
        Vorteller in de Engelse Roman (Hasselt: Uitgeverij Heidel-
        and, 1965)].

1796   Kennedy, James G. "The Artist-Hero Novel: Comments on a
        Discussion Guide," ELT, V:1 (1962), 32-34. [Reviews brief-
        ly the artist-hero novel before 1880, between 1880 and 1920,
        and after 1920].

1797   _____. "More General than Fiction: The Uses of His-
        tory in the Criticism of Modern Novels," CE, XXVIII:2 (Nov.
        1966), 150-163. [Rejects Aristotle's judgment that "poet-
        ry" surpasses history because its opinions are general,
        and that the world of the novel is imaginary and does not

refer to the perceptible world; also discusses history's
rules of evidence and the novel's rules or conventions,
and shows how modern novelists resort to history for proof
of their sincerity. References to J. Joyce, V. Woolf, and
E. M. Forster among others].

1798   Kenton, Edna. "Menu in Modern Fiction," Bookman (New York),
        XXXII (Nov. 1910), 257-262. [Examines the value of food
        in providing atmosphere, colour, tone and the development
        of character in novels by H. G. Wells, J. Galsworthy, and
        G. K. Chesterton among others].

1799   Kermode, Frank. "The New Novelists: An Enquiry," LM, V:
        11 (Nov. 1958), 21-25. Postscript, pp. 29-30. [Contends
        that modern English novelists have forgotten the "ultimate
        purpose" behind the "experimental" novel; hence, they do
        not "provide the major pleasures"].

1800   _____. "Myth, Reality and Fiction," Listener, LXVIII
        1744 (30 Aug. 1962), 311-313. [A summary of "The House
        of Ficton." See next entry].

1801   _____. "The House of Fiction: Interviews with Seven
        English Novelists," PR, XXX:1 (Spring 1963), 61-82. [In-
        vites I. Murdoch, G. Greene, A. Wilson, I. Compton-Burnett,
        C. P. Snow, J. Wain, and M. Spark to discuss "the house
        of fiction" before getting on to the subject of their own
        books].

1802   _____. "Edifying Symbols," NSta, LXVI (12 July 1963),
        45-46. [A review article on C. C. O'Brien's Maria Cross].

1803   _____. "Novel, History and Type," Novel, I:3 (Spring
        1968), 231-238. [Examines differences between histories
        and novels, but emphasises the affinities between them,
        especially the former's search for "epiphanies in fact,
        arranging minor events around a central incident, unique
        but complying with a type," and the novel's narrative as
        "explanation" behind which is "some element related to the
        human set: some type." Also advocates that the novel in-
        volve more than "structures of research or terminology
        proper to itself." V. Woolf, J. Conrad, and D. H. Lawrence].

1804   _____. "The Structures of Fiction," MLN, LXXXIV (1969),
        891-915. ["The structures of fiction are plural, inacces-
        sible without severe instrumental interference, and possess
        no validity or interest except in union with acts of idio-
        matic interpretation"].

1805   _____. "British Novel Lives," AtM, CCXXX (July 1972),
        85-88. [Denies rumours of the parlous state of English
        fiction, noting recent works by M. Spark, I. Murdoch, W.
        Golding, and K. Amis, and attributes the cause of the ru-

mours to fiscal difficulties in the publishing industry and to generally incompetent reviewers].

1806 Kettle, Arnold. "Poiski Puti: Zamyetki O Sovremennoy Anglijskoj Literature," IL, 8 (Aug. 1961), 182-188. [Reflections on English contemporary novels and drama. K. Amis, J. Braine, and J. Wain among others].

1807 Khatchadourian, Haig. "Some Major Trends in Twentieth Century English Literature," VQ, XXVII (Autumn 1961), 140-149. [A brief general outline of some salient features "as seen in the context of the prevailing historical and cultural conditions"].

1808 Kiely, Robert. "The Craft of Despondency--The Traditional Novelists," Daedalus, XCII (1963), 220-237. [Discusses three mid-century "traditional" novelists--E. Waugh, G. Greene and K. A. Porter--"austere allegorists of a peculiarly modern kind," profoundly influenced by traditional Christian moral concerns, whose novels are characterized by "sheer mastery of language, eccentricity of characterization, precision, and popularity," in spite of a certain joylessness or gloom in them].

1809 "Kill or Cure: Doctors in Fiction," TLS, 3173 (21 Dec. 1962), 989. [Leading article discussing the new interest in the medical novel].

1810 Killam, G. D. "The 'Educated African' Theme in English Fiction about Africa, 1884-1939," Phylon, XXVII (1966), 155-164. [Surveys the persistence of the stereotype of the Educated African as "despised and unsympathetic" in six "little-known" novels by G. A. Henty, C. Hyne (19th century), M. Gaunt, J. C. Grant, C. Gouldsbury, and F. A. M. Webster].

1811 Killam, John. "The 'Second Self' in Novel Criticism," BJA, VI:3 (July 1966), 272-290. [On the ambiguity and confusion created by Dowden's "second self" and Booth's "implied author"].

1812 Kirkwood, M. M. "Value in the Novel Today," UTQ, XII (Apr. 1943), 282-296. [Attempts to refute F. Swinnerton's "Decay of the Novel," (Spectator, CLXIX (10 July 1942), 32) using R. Llewellyn's How Green Was My Valley and E. Hemingway's For Whom the Bell Tolls. The first section is perhaps more valuable as it notes "the chief lines of attack" in connection with the novel's decline and fall; that is, the "humanist," the "communist" and the "literary"].

1813 Kissling, Helmut. "Die Public Schools im englischen Roman," Die Erziehung, X (1934-35), 444-466. [Examines the relation between teacher and student in the English Public School from novels by R. Kipling, J. Galsworthy, H. G. Wells, E.

Phillpotts, M. Baring, H. A. Vachell, H. Walpole, and R. C. Sheriff to show that the Public School is the moral and political breeding ground for all English youth because it is the ideal to which any school aspires].

1814 Kitchin, Laurence. "Imperial Weekend," Listener, LXXIV:1909 (28 Oct. 1965), 662-663, 667. [First of two articles on the role of country houses in 20th century English fiction].

1815 _____. "The Zombies' Lair," Listener, LXXIV:1910 (4 Nov. 1965), 701-702, 704. [Second of two articles on the role of country houses in 20th century English fiction].

1816 _____. "Colliers," Listener, LXXV:1935 (28 Apr. 1966), 618-619. [Examines the mark left by colliers on novels by D. H. Lawrence, S. Chaplin, D. Storey, and S. Middleton].

1817 Klingopoulos, G. D. "The Criticism of Novels," UE, III (June 1955), 85-90. [Calls for a "more pedestrian, yet not necessarily unenjoyable form of demonstration" in the criticism of novels than "summary impressions." Illustrates from J. Conrad's The Secret Agent that what one refers to as "form" and "structure" is a "cumulatively established" response to the poetic movement and repetition of Conrad's prose].

1818 _____. "The Novel in Education," UQ, XIII (May 1959), 255-264. [On the reluctance and slowness of English universities and schools to recognize the worth of the modern novel as a rewarding subject for close study, in spite of the depth and variety of human experience it portrays, and the opportunities it offers "for a continuous deepening of knowledge and a finer understanding of life"].

1819 Kluth, Käthe. "Audiatur et altera pars (Zum englischen Frauenroman der Gegenwart)," WZUG, X (1961), 253-261. [Classifies contemporary women novelists into: 1) Neo traditionalists--I. Compton-Burnett, E. Bowen, R. Lehmann, O. Manning, 2) historical novelists--M. Irwin, M. Reynolds, and H. F. M. Prescott, 3) satirical novelists--R. Macaulay, N. Mitford, 4) "university wits"--I. Murdoch, 5) "social realists"--D. Lessing, 6) "writers of detective works," and 7) novelists who cannot be classified--P. H. Johnson, D. Du Maurier, and M. Spark].

1820 Knapp, Otto. "Das Bild des Menschen im neuen englischen Roman," Hochland, XXX (1933), 532-544. [On the creation of character through a "mosaic of impressions" in the modern English novel. V. Woolf, D. H. Lawrence, A. Huxley, J. Joyce, and M. Baring].

1821 Knight, George Wilson. "Lawrence, Joyce and Powys," EIC,

XI:4 (Oct. 1961), 403-417. Reprinted in Neglected Powers:
Essays on Nineteenth and Twentieth Century Literature.
(London: Routledge and Kegan Paul; New York: Barnes and
Noble, 1971), pp. 142-155. [On the "sexual challenge" and
"anal obsession" in the three writers].

1822 Koestler, Arthur. "The Artist and Politics," SatR, XXV
(31 Jan. 1942), 3-4, 14-15. Reprinted as "Les Trois Ten-
taions du romancier," FL, VIII:46 (15 Aug. 1944), 278-282.
[Comments on the three options of the novelist: 1) total
withdrawal from the entire world, 2) the "fragmentary optic,"
which suffers from ignorance of facts, and 3) the "Puck
Decade" novel where the novelist becomes a reporter, i.e.,
suffers from an obsession of facts, and suggests that a
"true novel lives by the assimilation of facts"].

1823 _____. "The Future of Fiction," NW&D, VIII:7 (1946),
82-86. Reprinted in The Trail of the Dinosaur and Other
Essays. (London: Collins; New York: Macmillan, 1955),
pp. 95-101. [Predicts that the fiction of the period between the 2nd and 3rd World Wars will be dominated by Realism, "the striving to approach the reality of the human condition," Rhythm, "the measure of its artistic economy . . .
implicitness," and Relevance, "the quality which connects
it with the dynamic currents, the essential pattern of the
period"].

1824 _____. "The Novelist Deals with Character," SatR,
XXXII (1 Jan. 1949), 7-8. [Contends that the vividness of
a character in a reader's mind is not of a "visual nature,"
that our mental representation of a fictional character is
largely based on "the process of projective empathy," i.e.,
an "act of self-transcending identification" whereby the
reader "recreates the character out of his own experience,
using the text as a catalyzing agent"; hence, the tendency
in modern literature to give little or no descriptions of
the visual aspects of a character].

1825 Kohler, Dayton. "Time in the Modern Novel," CE, X (Oct.
1948), 15-24. [Explains time as "consciousness," i.e., a
measurement for the nature and duration of time, and examines the use of time in the 20th century novel as history,
as method, as fantasy, as memory and myth, and as symbol.
H. James, A. Bennett, J. Conrad, J. Joyce, V. Woolf, and H.
G. Wells].

1826 Kolb, A. "Randglossen zur heutigen englischen Literatur,"
NRs, XLII (Jan. 1931), 114-123. [Brief random notes on con-
temporary English literary works. J. Joyce, V. Woolf, K.
Mansfield, E. M. Forster, and D. H. Lawrence among others].

1827 Koljević, Svetozac. "Putevi savremenog engleskog romana,"
Delo, VIII:7 (1962), 870-889. [On the tendencies of the

contemporary novel in England, especially the exploration
of social life through the interrelationships of people.
J. Braine and A. Wilson. (Serbo-Croatian)].

1828 Kort, Wesley. "Recent Fiction and Its Religious Implica-
      tions," CLS, III:2 (1966), 223-234. [Discusses fiction's
      religious importance owing to its "alerting influence" on
      traditional faith, and the importance of traditional faith
      to it. References to W. Golding, E. Waugh, and G. Greene
      among others].

1829 Kraft, Quentin G. "Against Realism: Some Thoughts on Fic-
      tion, Story and Reality," CE, XXXI:4 (Jan. 1970), 344-354.
      [Rejects realism -- and romance -- as "ideal[s] employed
      by readers and critics in their effort to account for the
      nature of a novel," and suggests "story" as a norm].

1830 Kreemers, Raph. "Katholieke Engelsche Letterkunde," LB,
      XXIV (1932), 1-29. [A review article on literary criticism,
      especially on the novel, from a Catholic viewpoint].

1831 _____. "De hedendaagse Englesche roman," LB, XXVI
      (1934), 1-33. [A critical study of sources, bibliography
      of general works on the novel, and an alphabetical regis-
      ter of novelists].

1832 _____. "Katholieke Engelsche Letterkunde in 1933,"
      DWB, XXXIV (1934), 42-51, 137-147. [A review of English
      and Irish literary output in 1933].

1833 Kreutz, Irving. "Mr. Bennett and Mrs. Woolf," MFS, VIII:2
      (Summer 1962), 103-115. [Examines Hilda Lessways and Mrs.
      Dalloway to show that the opening pages of both novels are
      "not unlike in intent and accomplishment," and that V.
      Woolf's remarks on Hilda Lessways in "Mr. Bennett and Mrs.
      Brown" result from a deliberate misreading of the novel
      "for her own purposes"].

1834 Krey, Laura. "Time and the Novel," Writer, LIV (July 1941),
      195-198. Reprinted in Twentieth Century English. Edited
      by William S. Knickerbocker. (New York: The Philosophical
      Library, 1946), pp. 401-416; and in The Craft of Fiction.
      Edited by A. S. Burack (Boston: The Writer, 1948), pp.
      129-138. [On the novelist's awareness of time].

1835 Krutch, Joseph Wood. "Modern Love and Modern Fiction,"
      Nation, CXVIII (25 June 1924), 735-736. [States that mod-
      ern fiction is not interested in sex as an illustration of
      moral and social laws but as an individual problem, and re-
      gards fiction as a "record of individual souls in search
      of a successful way of life." D. H. Lawrence and A. Huxley].

1836 _____. "Novelists Know What Philosophers Don't," Nation,

CXLIII (5 Sep. 1936), 277-278. [Replies to F. X. Connolly's "Philosophy into Fiction" (Commonweal, XXIV (21 Aug. 1936), 402-403) and contends "that the average intellectual finds art--and novelists--more convincing than philosophy because it is, quite literally, truer"].

1837 Kumar, Raj. "Obscurity and Modern Fiction," IJES, VIII (1967), 1-9. [Maintains that the attempt to communicate the "incommunicable," to come closer to psychological truth, and the use of symbolism to convey a poetical or mystical apprehension of the universe, account for obscurity in the 20th century novel. G. Orwell, E. Bowen, J. Joyce et al].

1838 Kumar, Shiv K. "Bergsonism and the Stream of Consciousness Novel," LCrit, IV (Winter 1959), 11-21. [Reviews and rejects the psychoanalytical and "post-impressionistic" interpretations of the "stream of consciousness novel," and suggests Bergsonism as the most comprehensive explanation for the "new" novelists' concept of character as a "process of ceaseless becoming." J. Joyce, V. Woolf, and D. Richardson].

1839 _____. "Bergson's Theory of the Novel," MFS, VI (1960), 325-336. Revised and reprinted in MLR, LVI (Apr. 1961), 172-179. [Shows how Bergson's theory, in the light of his "la durée" and "memoire par excellence," is essential to an understanding of "the creative impulse behind the stream of consciousness novel," which hitherto had been treated as a technical innovation. D. Richardson, V. Woolf, and J. Joyce]

1840 Kuna, F. M. "Current Literature 1970. II: New Writing," ES, LII (1971), 473-483. [A review article on the fiction of 1970 emphasising a renewed interest in the novel as a "flexible form which can take care of what is always unique and new: individual experience." A. Sillitoe, J. Wain. H. Davies, H. E. Bates, L. P. Hartley, E. O'Brien, and others].

1841 Kunkle, Francis L. "The Priest as Scapegoat in the Modern Catholic Novel," Ramparts, I (Jan. 1963), 72-78. [Examines the priest figure in a novel by each of G. Greene, F. Mauriac, S. Stolpe, and M. West to explain the "recurrence of the archetype" of the priest as Christ-like scapegoat. Brief references to G. K. Chesterton, B. Marshall, and A. J. Cronin

1842 Kurz, Paul Konrad. "Gestaltwandel des modernen Romans," SZ, CLXXVI (1965), 253-274. [Discusses the characteristics of the modern novel in general. Brief reference to V. Woolf and J. Joyce].

1843 Kvam, Ragnar. "Teddy-Boys og Nietzsche-Boys," Vinduet, XII (1958), 179-187. [A review article on C. Wilson's The Outsider, J. Osborne's Look Back in Anger, K. Amis' Lucky Jim, and J. Brain's Room at the Top].

1844 _____. "Ny engelsk prosa," Samtiden, LXIX (1960),
549-557. [Examines the contrast between the "socially engaged novel" and the aestheticism of the Bloomsbury ideal
in novels by C. Wilson, C. P. Snow, and L. Durrell].

1845 Kwapien, Maria. "The Anti-Utopia as Distinguished from
Its Cognate Literary Genres in Modern British Fiction,"
ZRL, XIV:2 (1972), 37-47. [Discusses the problems connected with a definition of Anti-Utopia -- variety of names
given to it and the difficulty of distinguishing between
it and science-fiction and other literary works -- in an
attempt to fix the boundaries of the genre. H. G. Wells,
A. Huxley, J. O'Neill, E. M. Forster, J. Wyndham, A. Marshall, G. Orwell, and L. P. Hartley among others].

1846 L., J. G. "Novel--What Will it Become?" LA, 231 (30 Nov.
1901), 587-589. Reprinted from The Academy. [Conjectures
on the "new material" and the "new form" of the novel in
the coming years].

1847 "Lady Novelists: Controversy in New Statesman and Nation,"
LA, 357 (Oct. 1939), 188-190. [Mostly taken up by C. E. M.
Joad's reply to M. E. Mitchell and Daphne Nichol, and N.
Mitchison's rebuke].

1848 "The Lady Vanishes, But What's Become of her Daughters?"
TLS, 3054 (9 Sep. 1960), lix. [Special number on "The
British Imagination." On the vanishing presence and influ-
ence of women in English literature in general].

1849 Lambert, J. Wilson. "War Novels," PMLClub, 63 (1939), 245-
257. [Contends that war novels, even though largely ig-
nored by critics, are a greater record of a soldier's life
than poetry. Also explores three themes emerging from them:
futility of war, good fellowship among soldiers, and man's
inhumanity to man. E. Raymond, R. H. Mottram, G. Frankau
and others].

1850 "Lament for the British Novel," SatR, XVIII (18 June 1938),
8. [Editorial focusing on Storm Jameson's The Novel in Contemporary Life].

1851 Larkin, Philip. "The Writer in His Age," LM, IV (May 1957),
46-47. [Contends that "good social and political literature
can exist only if it originates in the imagination" and not
when the intellect thinks it is important].

1852 Laski, Marghanita. "The New Religious Novel," Spectator,
CLXXXVII (5 Oct. 1971), 421. [A brief note disapproving of
the tendency in the modern religious novel to rely on "an
imperfectly explained character of supernatural spiritual
power" that approximates to Christ, with the mysticism that
it symbolises, as a substitute for an intellectual interpretation of faith].

1853   Las Vergnas, Raymond. "Lettres Etrangères: À propos de
        Graham Greene," HM, IX (May 1949), 147-151. [On the renewed
        French interest in English fiction of the forties].

1854   Lawrence, D. H. "Surgery for the Novel, or a Bomb," LDIBR,
        I:5 (Apr. 1923), 5-6, 63. Reprinted in Phoenix. The Post-
        humous Papers of D. H. Lawrence. Edited, with an Introduc-
        tion by Edward D. McDonald. (London: Heinemann, 1936), pp.
        517-521. [Rejects the popular, "purely emotional" novels,
        as well as the high-browed "self-analytical" novels of J.
        Joyce, D. Richardson and M. Proust for the novel of the
        future: the one which can "tackle new proportions without
        using abstractions"].

1855   _____. "Morality and the Novel," CML, II (1925), 269-
        274. Reprinted in GBM, III (Feb. 1926), 248-250, and in
        Phoenix: The Posthumous Papers of D. H. Lawrence. Edited,
        with an Introduction by Edward D. McDonald. (London: Heine-
        mann, 1936), pp. 527-533. [Maintains that the novel reveals
        true morality, the delicate and changing balance that "pre-
        cedes and accompanies a true relatedness" and not "religious"
        or didactic morality].

1856   Layard, G. S. "Courage in the Writing of Fiction," Bookman
        (London), LXV:385 (Oct. 1923), 3-5. [A symposium. Contrib-
        utors include H. G. Wells, A. Bennett, and J. Galsworthy].

1857   Leavis, Q. D. "Lady Novelists and the Lower Orders," Scru-
        tiny, IV:2 (Sep. 1935), 112-132. [A review article on N.
        Mitchison's We Have Been Warned and A. Williams-Ellis' To
        Tell the Truth, critical of their "inadequate" response to
        the quality of working-class life].

1858   Lee, Robin. "The Novel and Modern Society," Standpunte,
        XCIII (1971), 14-24. [Examines the novelists' exposure to
        new social patterns and new media and their sense of crisis
        in fictional forms. Concedes that the "present vitality of
        the novel is in the writing of the Americans"].

1859   Leech, Clifford. "The Theme of Destitution in Twentieth
        Century Literature," IJES, III (1962), 89-105. [On the para-
        dox of denuding man of all things that make life comfortable
        and disguise it--characteristic of much of modern litera-
        ture--and the "urge to find what is left." References to I.
        Compton-Burnett, A. Wilson, M. Spark, G. Greene and others].

1860   Lees, F. N. "Identification and Emotion in the Novel: A
        Feature of the Narrative Method," BJA, IV:2 (Apr. 1964),
        109-114. [On the impact of "free indirect speech" on "iden-
        tification" i.e., the "relationship between reader and what
        is being read," and the emotional effect it can produce].

1861   Legouis, Émile. "La Guerre vue par les écrivains anglais,"

RDM, 33 (15 May 1916), 302-330. [Examines the attitudes of G. B. Shaw, G. K. Chesterton, H. G. Wells, R. Kipling, and J. Galsworthy to the war].

1862   Lehmann, John. "Signposts in English Literature Today," FR, CLXV (NS) CLIX (Apr. 1946), 278-281. [Focuses on the impact of World War II on poetry and the "skepticism" about issues involved, especially with novelists and short story writers].

1863   _____. "A Literary Letter from England," NYTBR, (6 June 1948), 4. [On the lack of experiment and exploration of new territory in postwar literature, especially the novel].

1864   _____. "English Letters in the Doldrums? An Editor's View," TQ, IV (Autumn 1961), 56-63. [A literary editor's personal views on the state of writing in England from 1945 to 1960].

1865   _____. "Radicalism: Then and Now. A Writer's View," Listener, LXVIII:1741 (9 Aug. 1962), 195-197. [Discusses basic differences between the radicalism of writers in the thirties and in the sixties].

1866   Leisi, Ernst. "Der Erzahlstandpunkt in der neueren englischen Prosa," GRM, XXXVII (1956), 40-51. [On the changes in the narrative standpoint in recent English novels. K. Mansfield, E. M. Forster, A. Huxley, E. Bowen, H. James, and J. Galsworthy among others].

1867   Lemon, Lee T. "The Illusion of Life: A Modern Version of an Old Heresy," WHR, XVII (Winter 1963), 65-74. [Contends that the basis of evaluation for a novel is the "total response of the reader to a work" resulting from the novelist's gratification of "our interest in life," and not "technique" or the "illusion of life" suggested. Brief references to J. Joyce, H. James, and D. H. Lawrence].

1868   Leopold, Keith. "Some Problems of Terminology in the Analysis of the Stream of Consciousness Novel," AUMLA, XIII (May 1960), 23-32. [Examines the term "stream of consciousness," lists six methods of representation that may be employed in this type of novel, and points out the "endless confusion" to which two of them--"erlebte rede" and "interior monologue"--give rise].

1869   Lerner, Laurence. "Novels About the Future," Listener, LXVIII:1739 (26 July 1962), 143-144. [Contends that the prophetic novelist cares not about the future but the present, and uses myths about the past to talk about the relations between the past and the present].

259

1870 Lesort, Paul A. "Note sur le roman," Nef, V:40 (Mar. 1948), 7-18. [Considers the traditional classification of novels into regional, psychological, social, etc., as one not of "méthode, mais d'occasion," for the essential criterion in novel criticism is whether one can participate in a character's personal experience or not].

1871 Lesser, Simon O. "Some Unconscious Elements in the Responses to Fiction," L&P, III (1953), 2-5. [Distinguishes three processes: 1) "spectator" reaction when one unconsciously rather than consciously apprehends certain things, 2) "active" reaction, unconscious participation in the story, and 3) "active" reaction, unconsciously composing stories based on what is read, i.e. "analogizing"].

1872 _____. "The Function of Form in Narrative Art," Psychiatry, XVIII (1955), 51-63. [Discerns three main functions in narrative art--to give pleasure, avoid or relieve guilt and anxiety, and facilitate perception--and identifies means for achieving them. Passing reference to J. Joyce and D. H. Lawrence].

1873 _____. "The Attitude of Fiction," MFS, II:2 (May 1956), 47-55. [Examines why the fictional depiction of conflict gives the reader pleasure and satisfaction, and helps "the ego in its own integrative activity"].

1874 Lett, A. B. "The Novelist's mise en scène," PMLClub, 63 (1939), 108-115. [Comments on the amount and methods of description in the novel. Brief references to A. Bennett, H. G. Wells, J. Conrad and others].

1875 Levidova, I. "Ukroshchenie absurda. Zametki ob angliiskom komicheskom romane," VLit, VIII (1970), 121-140. [Notes on the English comic novels of E. Waugh, M. Spark, J. Wain, and K. Waterhouse].

1876 Levin, Harry. "What was Modernism?" MR, I (1 Aug. 1960), 609-630. Reprinted in Varieties of Literary Experience: 18 Eminent Critics Discuss World Literature. Edited by Stanley Burnshaw. (London: Peter Owen, 1963), pp. 307-331. [On the "zeitgeist" shared by artists "vowed to idiosyncracy, practising a divergent medium, formed in a disparate background" in the twenties. Included are V. Woolf, J. Joyce, D. H. Lawrence, and E. M. Forster].

1877 _____. "Janes and Emilies, Or the Novelist as Heroine," SoR, (NS), I:4 (Oct. 1965), 735-753. [Lecture delivered at the University of Minnesota, 1965. On women in fiction. Brief references to V. Woolf and J. Joyce].

1878 _____. "The Unbanning of the Books," AtM, CCXVII:2 (Feb. 1966), 77-81. [Maintains that the new candour in fiction presently allowed by the courts and promoted by

260

publishing firms puts the burden on the reader for more discriminating criticism].

1879   Lewis, Naomi.   "In Spite of Lit.," TC, CLXIV:978 (Aug. 1958), 114-125.   [Examines the delineation and role of women in fiction, and the 20th century interest in "foreground women." H. James, H. Green, I. Compton-Burnett, and H. G. Wells among others].

1880   Lewis, Wyndham.   "The Propagandist in Fiction," CH, XL (Aug. 1934), 567-572.   [Insists on the "detachment" of the novelist "even in the midst of faction," for as a partisan, he will be "exceedingly ineffective"].

1881   _____.   "'Detachment' and the Fictionist," EngRev, LIX (Oct. 1934), 441-452; LIX (Nov. 1934), 564-573.   [Maintains that fiction, as from 1914, has moved away appreciably from the ivory tower of romancing and the "detachment" of H. James and J. Conrad, to a fiction that takes sides between warring factions].

1882   Lewisohn, Ludwig.   "Foreshadowings of the New Novel," Bookman (New York), XLVIII (Sep. 1918), 79-84.   [Discusses the realistic art of contemporary English and American fiction and rules out a postwar reaction in favour of "soothing romance." J. Galsworthy, H. G. Wells, A. Bennett, and J. Conrad among others].

1883   Lind, L. Robert.   "The Crisis in Literature: 1. Literature Today," SR, XLVII (Jan.-Mar. 1939), 35-62.   [An analysis of literature in his day, "causes for its progressive inanition, and the means it will be most likely to take" if it is to recover its position of importance. Most of section one of the article is devoted to the novel. The first of a series of six articles].

1884   _____.   "The Crisis in Literature: III. Literature and Social Consciousness," SR, XLVII (July-Sep. 1939), 345-364.   [Contends that the best literature must have social significance, that a writer cannot escape from the facts of social background and social consciousness, and especially because the writer's place in society is becoming greater.   References to J. Joyce and H. G. Wells].

1885   _____.   "The Crisis in Literature: IV.   The Literature of the Future," SR, XLVII (Oct.-Dec. 1939), 524-551.   [Predicts that the "abstruseness and preciosity of personal cults" in thought and literature will be replaced with a writing actuated by a new social consciousness].

1886   _____.   "The Crisis in Literature: V. Prophecies and Prophets," SR, XLVIII (1940), 66-85.   [A critical examination of writers and books dealing with the literature of the future; also remarks on the absence of any useful guiding principle in them].

1887 _____ . "The Crisis in Literature: VI. Conclusion,"
SR, XLVIII (1940), 198-203. [Concludes his series by affirming the value of moral philosophy as the ideal function of literature whether this moral philosophy is the materialism that gives rise to Marxian Socialism, the rationalism of the New Humanists, or the "Bergsonian institutionism behind much of the work of the stream of consciousness school"].

1888 Lindsay, Jack. "The English Novel," Mainstream, XVI:8 (1963), 53-57. [A review article on George Wickes' Masters of Modern British Fiction (New York: Macmillan, 1963) expressing views on the decline and fall of the novel].

1889 Linn, Bettina. "The Fortunate Generation," YR, (NS) XXXI:3 (Apr. 1942), 555-568. [On the "new" fiction of V. Woolf, J. Joyce and D. H. Lawrence, the changes they introduced, the meaning of their fiction, and how it related to the new conditions as seen through the eyes of a person who grew up with it].

1890 "A Literary Glove-Fight," Spectator, CXXV (4 Dec. 1920), 732-733. [An account of a debate between G. K. Chesterton and H. Walpole on the resolution that "The Modern Novel is a Sign of Social Decay"].

1891 "Literary Perversities of Modern Novelists," Independent, LV (3 Sep. 1903), 2126-27. [An editorial that denounces the modern novelist's practice of selecting "extreme situations where there is some moral sickness," and his "preference for artificially developed types," and calls on him to accept the "challenge" of illustrating "the average life, the commonplace"].

1892 Littlejohn, David. "The Anti-Realists," Daedalus, XCII (Spring 1963), 250-264. Reprinted in Interruptions (New York: Grossman, 1970), pp. 17-33. [On the novel of "fantasy, illogicality and absurdity," the fictional counterpart of "The Theatre of the Absurd" by the third generation of "pure" anti-realists: S. Beckett, J. L. Borges, J. Hawkes and J. Heller, impatient with the old well-made novel. Passing references to A. Durrell and W. Golding as "marginal" anti-realists].

1893 Lodge, David. "The Contemporary Novel, and all that Jazz," LM, (NS) II:5 (Aug. 1962), 73-80. [Examines the increasing jazz-content of recent English fiction, and several American novels. K. Amis, J. Wain, C. MacInnes, and C. P. Snow among others].

1894 _____ . "Le Roman contemporain en Angleterre," TR, 179

(Dec. 1962), 80-92. [Argues that the English contemporary novel aspires to the "social condition" rather than Pater's "musical condition," and is assessed by the freshness, passion and veracity with which it reflects life. Also maintains that the difference between modern and contemporary novelists lies in their use of language. (This is an early abridged version of "The Modern, The Contemporary, and the Importance of being Amis,"--see below--without the analysis of the novels of K. Amis)].

1895 _____. "The Modern, The Contemporary, and the Importance of Being Amis," CritQ, V (Winter 1963), 335-354. Reprinted in Language of Fiction: Essays in Criticism and Verbal Analysis of the English Novel (London: Routledge and Kegan Paul; New York: Columbia University Press, 1966), pp. 243-267. [Advocates "the analysis of language" as the "most precise way" of indicating the distinction between "modern" and "contemporary"--the distinction made by S. Spender--the literary use of language being the "only tangible evidence" whereby novels can be measured "on the same scale." Illustrations from J. Joyce and J. Braine followed by an analysis of K. Amis's novels].

1896 _____. "Anglo-American Attitudes: Decorum in British and American Fiction," Commonweal, LXXIII:3 (1965), 84-87. [Confines his discussion to language, to "the adjustment of style to subject, to the narrator and to the latter's assumed relationship to his audience." Complements R. Chases' The American Novel and Its Tradition in bringing out the basic differences of English and American fiction].

1897 _____. "Waiting for the End: Current Novel Criticism," CritQ, X:182 (Spring-Summer 1968), 184-199. Reprinted in The Novelist at the Crossroads and Other Essays on Fiction and Criticism. (London: Routledge and Kegan Paul, 1971), pp. 37-54. [A review article on critical works on the novel to identify "current trends of thought," and weed out "irrelevant criticism"].

1898 _____. "Towards a Poetics of Fiction: 2) An Approach though Language," Novel, I:2 (Winter 1968), 158-169. Reprinted in The Novelist at the Crossroads and Other Essays on Fiction and Criticism. (London: Routledge and Kegan Paul, 1971), pp. 55-69. [On the primacy of language for both novelist and critic, language being the "only criterion" for what the novelist "is seeing, and how he sees it, and how he means us to see it" and also because all good criticism "is a response to language"].

1899 _____. "The Novelist at the Crossroads," CritQ, XI:2 (Summer 1969), 105-132. Reprinted in The Novelist at the Crossroads and Other Essays on Fiction and Criticism. (London: Routledge and Kegan Paul, 1971), pp. 3-34. [Discusses the "bewildering plurality of styles" and modes displayed by contemporary fiction, and the situation of the English realistic novel, and maintains that the "compromise between fictional and empirical modes" that flourished in the fifties is undecided whether to go in the direction of the "non-fiction novel" or "fabulation"].

1900 _____. "Realism, Allegory and Symbolism: Some Speculation about the Novel," NBl, LI (1970), 361-373. [Contends that a novel is a new synthesis of existing traditions, that its "synthesizing element is realism; and that the break-up of the novelistic synthesis coincides with a distrust or rejection of realism"].

1901 Logé, Marc. "Quelques Romancières anglaises contemporaines," RB, LXIII (21 Nov. 1925), 753-756. [A study of M. Sinclair, S. Jameson, V. Woolf, "R. West," and C. Dane as emancipated, creative impressionist novelists].

1902 _____. "Trois Romanciers anglais contemporains," RB, (3 Sep. 1927), 534-539. [An evaluation of the works of A. Machen, A. Huxley and T. F. Powys, and their diverse talents as novelists].

1903 Long, Richard A. and Iva G. Jones. "Towards a Definition of the 'Decadent Novel'," CE, XXII:4 (Jan. 1961), 245-249. [Defines the "decadent novel" as one of "sensation and paradox," amoral in outlook, marked by "conscious form" where language "becomes an end in itself," and where a "supposed aesthetic activity or quest takes precedence over all the conditions and conventions of the real world." Among the novelists who fall in this category are F. W. Rolfe, R. Firbank, and the pre-1945 E. Waugh].

1904 Loofbourow, John W. "Literary Realism Re-Defined," Thought, XLV (1970), 433-443. [Defines realism as a "dramatization of existential assumption--shared by the artist and his audience." Brief references to J. Joyce, V. Woolf, and D. H. Lawrence].

1905 Lopez, M. "Capitalism and the Novel," LabM, (Sep. 1927), 562-566. [A Marxist view that condemns the contemporary English novel for not reflecting the "great age of social change," or inspiring "gigantic class battles." Brief references to D. H. Lawrence, J. Galsworthy, A. Huxley, and H. G. Wells].

1906 Lorda Alaiz, F. M. "Kingsley Amis y la joven generación de escritores británicos," PSA, (Oct. 1957), 93-97. [Surveys the "New Movement" or "New Elisabethans"--K. Amis, A. Wilson, J. Osborne, W. J. Morgan, G. Scott, C. Wilson, K. Tynan, J. Wain, I. Murdoch, G. Thomas and P. Larkin--and points out the qualities they share: direct use of language, satire, and a revolt against the English literary tradition].

1907   Loreis, Hector-Jan. "De wortels van de nieuwe roman," NVT,
        XIX (1966), 379-408. [On the forerunners of the "Nouveau
        Roman." J. Joyce, V. Woolf, and H. Green among others].

1908   "Love in Modern Novels," LDig, XLVII (6 Dec. 1913), 1115.
        [Quotation from an editorial of the London Times pointing
        out the curiosity of modern novels about love].

1909   Loveman, Amy. "The Plight of the Novelist," SatR, XXXVI
        (12 Dec. 1953), 28. [Maintains that the novelist, "ham-
        pered by his own fears and confusions, and aware of the sur-
        rounding ambiguities, . . . either devotes himself to the
        trivial or bogs down in a work which demands an olympian
        detachment he cannot achieve"; hence, the present leanness
        of fiction].

1910   Lovett, Robert Morss. "A Note on English Realism," NRep,
        XXXIV (21 Mar. 1923), 109-110. [English realism is con-
        cerned "not only with the representation of the actual, but
        also with its interpretation in terms of a meaning or
        purpose beyond itself," and recent novels testify to a change
        in its "form" and not in its "spirit"].

1911   Lowell, Amy. "Casual Reflections on a Few of the Younger
        English Novelists," Bookman (New York), XLIX (Apr. 1919),
        173-181. [Observations on likenesses in novels by G. Can-
        nan, J. D. Beresford, C. Mackenzie, F. Swinnerton and S.
        McKenna--"their reverence for truth, that strange awe of
        fact," the use of London as background for their stories,
        and the bourgeois life described].

1912   Lucas, Herbert. "Of the Element of Tragedy in Catholic Fic-
        tion," Month, CXXVIII (Oct. 1916), 315-323. [On R. H. Ben-
        son's and "J. Ayscough's" use of suffering, calamities and
        disaster--the "elements of tragedy"--not only for the puri-
        fication or elevation of an individual character, but also
        to serve a spiritual or supernatural purpose].

1913   _____. "Of 'God's Plot' in Catholic Fiction," Month,
        CXXVIII (Dec. 1916), 481-492. [The "Ultima Thule" of the
        Catholic novelist as distinct from the "secular" writer is
        the sanctification of human souls; hence, materials at his
        disposal for the construction of a plot and their manifes-
        tation towards that spiritual end are more varied and subtle
        than those of his "secular" counterpart. R. H. Benson and
        W. Ward].

1914   "Lucky Jim and His Pals," Time, LXIX:21 (27 May 1957), 92,
        94. [Considers the trend and "unique temper" given to Eng-
        lish writing in the fifties by K. Amis, J. Braine, J. Wain,
        "T. Hinde," P. Towry, and J. Osborne].

1915   Lukacs, George. "Essay on the Novel," IntL, VIII:5 (May

1936), 68-74. [A Marxist approach that sees the inner development of the novel from the standpoint of class development and class struggle, its history being the artist's
"struggle against conditions in modern bourgeois life,"
its purpose being to reveal the unsuitableness of such a
life for expression. This is followed by a short sketch
of five periods in novel development].

1916 Lutwack, Leonard. "Mixed and Uniform Prose Styles in the
Novel," JAAC, XVIII:3 (Mar. 1960), 350-357. Reprinted in
Perspectives in Fiction. Edited by James L. Calderwood and
Harold E. Toliver. (New York and London: Oxford Univers-
ity Press, 1968), pp. 27-38. [A generic approach that brings
out the distinction between the styles, and some of their
implications in English and American novels. H. James and
J. Joyce among others].

1917 Lynd, Robert. "The Mistake," NSta, XXX (28 Jan. 1928), 488-
489. [Defends novelists against the "spate" of letters
charging them with errors and inaccuracies].

1918 Lyndky, Winifred. "A Survey of Reprint Texts of Twentieth
Century British Novels," CE, XXI (1959), 183-189. [Also
recommends a critical introduction for inexpensive paper-
backs, and notices the growing popularity of J. Conrad.
Includes A. Huxley, D. H. Lawrence, A. Bennett, E. M. Fors-
ter, J. Galsworthy, G. Greene, J. Joyce, S. Maugham, E.
Waugh, E. Bowen, J. Cary, F. M. Ford, N. Douglas, W. H.
Hudson, R. Hughes, G. Orwell, and H. G. Wells].

1919 Lytle, Andrew Nelson. "The Image as Guide to Meaning in
the Historical Novel," SR, LXI (1953), 408-426. Reprinted
in The Hero With the Private Parts. (Baton Rouge: Louisiana State University Press, 1966), pp. 5-20. [On the novelist's use of a historian's field as well as his methods
of investigation, and the resulting confusion].

1920 _____. "Impressionism, the Ego, and the First Person,"
Daedalus, XCII (1963), 281-296. Reprinted as "The Hero
with the Private Parts" in The Hero with the Private Parts:
Essays. (Baton Rouge: Louisiana State University Press, 1966),
pp. 42-60. [On the moral and technical problems which the
impressionist who uses the first person method will have to
face. H. James and L. Durrell].

1921 Lyttleton, Edward. "What is a Good Novel?" ContempR, CXXXIV
(July 1928), 59-66. [Concentrates attention on the claims
made on a novelist because he deals with human character].

1922 _____. "A Challenge to Novelists," HJ, XXXVII:4 (July
1939), 597-608. [Emphasises the importance of the novelist's
attitude to "traditional" religion, and the necessity of God
or a "higher Power" in the writing of fiction because novel-

266

ists can "teach effectively." (See reply by R. Balmforth above)].

1923   MacAfee, H. "Rebuttal by the Novelist," YR, (NS) XIII (Apr. 1924) 531-548. [A review article on English and American novels of 1923 with special reference to "style," character and "new directions" in the writing of fiction. A. Bennett, S. Kaye-Smith, V. Woolf, S. Jameson and others].

1924   _____. "Some Novelists in Mid-Stream," YR, XV (Jan. 1926), 336-352. [Surveys English and American novelists whose "fates" are not "settled" and who can thus startle, surprise and excite their reader. Includes V. Woolf, S. Kaye-Smith, and D. H. Lawrence].

1925   _____. "Ancient and Modern Legends," YR, XVI (Apr. 1927), 535-550. [Surveys English and American novels of recent months and concludes that the general movement of fiction "has been away from rigid realism towards the freer creative forms--away from history and towards legend"].

1926   Macaulay, Rose. "The Novel of the Future," IntBR, II (Mar. 1924), 281. [Maintains that plot and character, "in combination," and imagination and a good prose-style--"a rare commodity"--may help the novel to survive].

1927   _____. "The Future of Fiction," NW&D, VIII:7 (1946), 71-75. [Sees the present position of the novel as tottering owing to its formidable rivals--film, drama, short story, the report of facts, the thriller and autobiography, and asserts that "some new arrival who shall capture minds and set a mode" is needed because the established novelists cannot decide the future of the novel. First article in a series of six on the same topic by V. S. Pritchett, A. Koestler, L. P. Hartley, W. Allen, and O. Sitwell].

1928   McCann, Charles J. "Portraits of the Artist as Young Men: Fact Versus Fiction," ELT, V:1 (1962), 27-29. [Notes the difficulty of the novelist in maintaining his "historical, personal identity" in proper relation to, or "subjection to the fictional world," and questions "the fictional integrity of portraits of the artists as heroes"].

1929   MacCarthy, Desmond. "Le Roman anglais d'après-guerre, 1919-1929," RP, XXXIX (1 May 1932), 129-152. [A study of the changes in form and content of the English novel in the twenties pointing out the absence of change in the pre-war novelists--H. G. Wells, A. Bennett, and G. Moore--and examining the "new novel"--its characteristics, causes for its attraction--of A. Huxley, D. H. Lawrence, J. Joyce, V. Woolf, and D. Garnett].

1930   McCarthy, B. Eugene. "On Reading Fiction," EngR, XXII:2 (Winter 1971), 4-10. [Concerned with the critical process;

i.e., "the reading of a work," and suggests a "critical synthesis" rather than analysis as the process of discovering
in fiction "all the elements and their relationships towards
the whole within a work"].

1931   McCarthy, Mary. "The Fact in Fiction," PR, XXVII (Summer
        1960), 438-458. Reprinted in On the Contrary. (New York:
        Farrar, Straus and Cudahy, 1961; London: Heinemann, 1962),
        pp. 249-270. [Contends that the novel "is disappearing
        from view" because it is "dissolving into its component
        parts: the essay, the travel book, reporting, on the one
        hand, and the 'pure' fiction of the tale, on the other,"
        and that "the real world exists, but we can no longer ima-
        gine it"].

1932   _____. "Characters in Fiction," PR, XXVIII:2 (Mar.-
        Apr. 1961), 171-191. Reprinted in On the Contrary. (New
        York: Farrar, Straus and Cudahy, 1961; London: Heinemann,
        1962), pp. 271-292, and Critical Approaches to Fiction.
        Edited by Shiv K. Kumar and Keith F. McKean. (New York:
        McGraw-Hill, 1968), pp. 79-97. [Mainly concerned with the
        various fictional experiments and techniques of the twentieth
        century, ranging from Joyce's delineation of character
        "from behind the screen of consciousness" and J. Cary's
        "technique of impressions," to the ruling out of the very
        "notion of character" in the French "nouveau roman," and
        suggesting that comedy or "the fixation of comedy" is essen-
        tial to real characterization. J. Joyce, V. Woolf, and J.
        Cary among others].

1933   _____. "Reflections: One Touch of Nature," NY, (24
        Jan. 1970), 39-57. Reprinted in The Writing on the Wall
        and Other Literary Essays. (New York: Harcourt, Brace &
        World; London: Weidenfeld and Nicolson, 1970), pp. 189-213.
        [Remarks on the disappearance of Nature as a "staple ingred-
        ient" from the modern English, American and European novel,
        and examines the "great explosion of Nature into fiction" in
        the 19th century. Refers to J. Joyce and D. H. Lawrence
        among others].

1934   _____. "Exiles, Expatriates and Internal Emigres,"
        Listener, LXXXVI (25 Nov. 1971), 705-708. [Defines the
        three terms, and reviews several English and Russian novel-
        ists who fit into these categories. G. Greene, S. Beckett,
        J. Joyce, and J. Jones among others].

1935   McConkey, James. "The Voice of the Writer," UKCR, XXV (1958)
        83-90. [Distinguishes between "tone" and "voice" the latter
        implying an author's "attitudes, philosophies, and defenses
        against the world" emanating from his conscious and uncon-
        scious self, notes the decline in the power of voice in mod-
        ern fiction, especially in J. Joyce, and questions the worth
        of such impersonality since the writers we admire most have

distinct "voices" which give colour to their people, and interpret experience].

1936 McCormick, John D. "The Rough and Lurid Vision: Henry James, Graham Greene and the International Theme," JA, II (1957), 158-167. [Examines H. James' and G. Greene's treatment of the American abroad, the idea of power and its effects upon human beings, the sexual theme and the idea of "innocence," and contends that G. Greene in The Quiet American reverses the Jamesian situation of "American innocence" confronted with dissolute Europeans].

1937 McDonald, Walter R. "Coincidence in the Novel: A Necessary Technique," CE, XXIX:5 (Feb. 1968), 373-388. [Enlarges the meaning of coincidence to include all "foreign objects a writer must make indigenous to the story," and classifies coincidence as "structural, contributing, philosophical and mundane." H. James and E. M. Forster among others].

1938 McDowell, Frederick P. W. "'The Devious Involutions of Human Character and Emotions': Reflections on Some Recent British Novels," ConL, IV (1963), 339-366. [A review article on novels by R. Hughes, C. Isherwood, A. Sillitoe, J. Wain, J. Braine, D. Lessing, I. Murdoch, A. Wilson, and A. Powell published late 1961 through early 1963].

1939 _____. "Recent British Fiction: Some Established Writers," ConL, XI (1970), 401-431. [A review of British novels by E. Bowen, L. P. Hartley, K. Amis, J. Braine, A. Sillitoe, K. Waterhouse, "T. Hinde," B. Glanville, C. P. Snow, M. Spark, M. Lowry, L. Durrell, A. Powell, P. H. Newby, A. Burgess, I. Murdoch, D. Lessing, and J. Fowles published from the end of 1967 through Autumn 1969. This is the first of a two-part survey].

1940 _____. "Recent British Fiction: New or Lesser-Known Writers," ConL, XI (1970), 540-578. [Reviews novels published from the end of 1967 through Autumn 1969 by some twenty-five novelists who are "beginning to make a reputation either in England or the United States." This is the second of a two-part survey].

1941 _____. "Time of Plenty: Recent British Novels," ConL, XIII (1972), 361-394. [A review article on some forty English novels published late 1969 through 1971. Shows that the novel is in a "process of consolidation rather than the breaking of new paths," and that the chief direction is "toward a modified realism" rather than experiment].

1942 Machen, Arthur. "Farewell to Materialism," AM, XXXVI (Sep. 1935), 43-51. [Condemns grossness or nastiness in the moderns when it becomes the real, and perhaps the only object, of their work].

1943 MacIntyre, Alasdair. "Sociology and the Novel," TLS, 3143
      (27 July 1967), 657-658. [Asserts that though both the
      sociologist and novelist aspire to general truths by way of
      concrete observations, they are neither rivals nor substi-
      tutes; the former has to be detached and anonymous, whereas
      the latter may choose between detachment and subjectivity,
      and has speculative privileges, too].

1944 MacKendrick, Paul. "The Classics and Contemporary English
      Literature," CJ, XLVII (Oct. 1951), 21-28. [Demonstrates
      that facets of the creative genius of classical tradition--
      "perception of form, autocratic feeling, love of the land,
      the importance of personal relations, the sense of the
      artist in exile"--are to be found in mid-twentieth century
      writers. Chooses E. M. Forster and J. Joyce as demonstra-
      ting "the importance of personal relations and the sense of
      the artist in exile"].

1945 Mackenzie, Agnes Mure. "Heroes," NSta, (2 July 1932), 11-12.
      [Remarks on the increasing numbers of unheroic "heroes" in
      novels, and especially in novels of the twenties].

1946 Mackenzie, Sir Compton. "Poetry and the Modern Novel,"
      EngRev, XI (May 1912), 269-279. [Originally an address
      to the Poets' Club, delivered 28 Mar. 1912. Distinguishes
      between the "false realist and the poetic novelist," and
      maintains that the modern novel lives by virtue of the "poet-
      ry which gives it life"].

1947 _____. "Twentieth Century Writers," Spectator, CXCII
      (21 May 1954), 619. [A brief survey].

1948 _____. "Sidelight: Survival of the Novel," Spectator,
      CXCIII (15 Oct. 1954), 468. [Contends that the novel will
      be dead perhaps in fifty years, not because it will be ex-
      hausted as a literary form, but because "it will seem less
      worth fighting for than higher literary forms when the fu-
      ture of literature itself is threatened"].

1949 Macksey, Richard. "The Artist in the Labyrinth: Design or
      Dasein," MLN, LXXVII (1962), 239-256. [Maintains that novel-
      ists who share a common distrust of the classical elements
      of "construction" and character have replaced these with a
      "labyrinth which was to be (their) own prison" -- paradoxi-
      cally, a more "absolute enactment of self in the novel" --
      with the novelist's job becoming "an epistemological prob-
      lem, a question of hyperbolic doubt." J. Joyce, S. Beckett,
      and H. James among others].

1950 Mackworth, Cecily. "Le Roman anglais d'aujourd'hui," Crit,
      XIV:128 (1958), 32-41. [Shows how the "climat psychologique"
      resulting from the emergence of a new reading postwar public
      smoothed the acceptance of the "anti-romantic hero" in the

novels of K. Amis, J. Wain, J. Braine, and C. Wilson --
heroes whose aesthetic value may be debatable but who reflect a world in transition].

1951 MacLaren-Ross, J. "Storytelling and the Screen," TLS, 2946
(15 Aug. 1958), xxviii. [Special Section: "Books in a
Changing World." Examines the possibilities open to writers with a "strong visual sense" or who write "cinematic
prose," and concludes that there is "little danger of the
novel being superseded by the film." G. Greene and E.
Waugh among others].

1952 MacNeice, Louis. "L'Ecrivain britannique et la guerre,"
FL, XI:62 (15 Dec. 1945), 103-109. [Contends that World
War II has determined the direction which English writers
are to take, for it has at once "modified" and "intensified"
English insularity. A. Huxley, G. Greene, and E. Bowen
among others].

1953 _____. "The English Literary Scene Today," NYTBR,
(28 Sep. 1947), 1. [Sees the major characteristic of its
writers as a "return to honesty . . . responsibility,"
and contends that its best novelists, E. Bowen, G. Greene,
J. Cary, and V. S. Pritchett are "honest, straightforward,"
and avoid experiment with language and new subjects].

1954 Macy, John. "Ends and Endings," Bookman (New York), LXIX
(July 1929), 515-517. [On the variety of endings in literature, the ideal ending being "artistically complete and
yet open, leaving laughter or horror to go to some imaginable but uncertain forever." Brief references to D. H.
Lawrence, J. Joyce, and J. Conrad].

1955 Madden, David. "Form and Life in the Novel: Toward a
Freer Approach to An Elastic Genre," JAAC, XXV:3 (Spring
1967), 323-333. [Surveys briefly literary criticism on
form in the novel and argues that the novel as "an elastic
medium," appropriating for itself "characteristics and devices of art media," can never itself be art; form "debili-
tates" its life, and because of its very nature, it moves
away from form, embracing "more, quantitatively, of life
than the structures of art can control"].

1956 Magalaner, Mervin. "Pitfalls in Modern Reading," EJ, XXXVIII
(Jan. 1949), 6-10. [Considers the nature of our modern
chaotic world, psychoanalysis and symbolism responsible for
the obscurity and difficulty of literature today. References
to J. Joyce and E. Bowen].

1957 Magnus, Sir Philip. "A Modern Aspect of the Novel," QR,
CCLXVI:527 (Jan. 1936), 59-72. [Though meant as a review
of P. Edgar's The Art of the Novel from 1700 to the Present
Time (London: Macmillan, 1933), the article concentrates

271

on three characteristics of the post-World War I novel:
its "poetical," almost lyrical qualities, its handling of
"epic themes," and its artistic use of the "fruits of the
new science of psychology"].

1958 Maini, Darshan Singh. "The Political Novel in England: A
Study in Fantasy," ModR, LXXXV (Feb. 1954), 143-145. [Con-
tends that the post-World War I political novel, as a distinct genre, fell back on allegory and fantasy in keeping
with the tradition of Swift and Butler, as an escape from
the harsh reality of the hour, and because they provided
an effective medium for satire. H. G. Wells, A. Huxley,
R. Warner, and G. Orwell].

1959 Malin, Irving. "Sex in Print," AR, XXIV (Fall 1964), 408-
413. [A review article discussing the publication in the
U. S. of Lady Chatterley's Lover, Memoirs of a Woman of
Pleasure, Candy, Jubb, Radcliffe, and Honey for the Bears].

1960 Malkani, M. U. "Experimentation in English Fiction," Bharat
Jyoti (Bombay), (Sep. 1953), p. 4. [Lists "experimental"
novelists of the twentieth century -- excluding H. James,
J. Conrad, J. Joyce, V. Woolf -- followed by brief reviews
of a novel by each of I. Compton-Burnett, G. Greene, E.
Myers, J. Cary, T. Hanlin, and C. P. Snow].

1961 Mallinson, Vernon. "English Literature in Wartime," RLV,
XI (1946), 82-85; XI (1946), 120-123; XI (1946), 214-218;
XI (1946), 286-289. [Surveys the main trends in contemporary writing, especially novels written during war-time,
and focuses on G. Greene, R. Warner, W. Sanson, H. Green,
and F. L. Green].

1962 _____. "Some War-time Fiction," RLV, XII (1946), 198-
201. [Examines the "escapist" novel of entertainment written during the second World War by J. B. Priestley, N. Balchin, G. Kersh, A. Koestler, R. Lehmann, A. Thirkell, and
E. Waugh].

1963 Maloff, Saul. "The Contemporary British Comic Novel," SatR,
XLIV (8 Apr. 1961), 25-26. [Argues that the reader's multiple and contradictory impressions of the contemporary
novel are due to the "perfunctory and incomplete" postwar
revolution of sorts, and the novelists' varied "politics
of culture and society," that contemporary fiction does
not represent a "trend or movement" but a "variety of stances
. . . several modes of maintaining the comic voice and vision" in a changing world. K. Amis, H. E. Bates, M. Spark
and others].

1964 Manning, Olivia. "Notes on the Future of the Novel," TLS,
2946 (15 Aug. 1958), vi. [Special Number: "Books in a
Changing World." Remarks that television and the cinema
far from encouraging the "novel of discussion," may increase

the novel of character and motive, and that the novel, in its present form, is "perfectly adapted to . . . the expression of our bewildered and self-conscious civilization"].

1965 Marcus, Steven. "The Novel Again," PR, XXIX:2 (Spring 1962), 171-195. [Reviews the causes that led to the current state of the novel and insists that the novel should give its readers "an adequate notion of what it is like to be alive today, why we are the way we are, and what might be done to remedy one bad situation." References to J. Joyce, J. Conrad, and W. Golding among others].

1966 Mariella, Sister O. S. B. "Catholic Fiction," CathW, CLII (Dec. 1940), 296-302. [Defines the "Catholic" novel as a "novel of grace, unfolding . . . the magnificent reaches and depths of the life conscious of the indwelling of the Trinity"; but presently, merely describing a Catholicism "permeated by the materialism of the modern age." References to S. Kaye-Smith, C. Mackenzie, J. Joyce and others].

1967 Marinoff, Irene. "'Imagination' and 'Reality' ein Beitrag zur Welt-und Lebensanschauung des englischen Nachkriegsromans," NS, XL (1932), 80-90. [Rejects Victorian and Edwardian views in favour of the postwar attempt to grasp "reality," for the truth about human nature and life, rather than the "travesty of life" revealed in the world of convention and respectability. J. Galsworthy, H. Walpole, C. Dane, H. G. Wells, R. Hughes, P. Ellery, and A. S. M. Hutchinson].

1968 _____. "Das Lebensgefühl im modernen englischen Roman," Anglia, LVI:4 (1932), 440-448. [Surveys the emotional attitude to life in various post-World War I novels, an attitude which does not, however, exclude intellect. J. Galsworthy, H. Walpole, S. Kaye-Smith and others].

1969 Markham, Edwin. "The Decadent Tendency in Current Fiction," CH, XVIII (Aug. 1923), 715-723. [A sweeping condemnation of the current obsession with sex-excesses, "cynical materialism" and decadent psychology in English and American fiction].

1970 Markovic, Vida E. "Engleski roman pre drugog svetskog rata," ForumZ, (May 1965), 125-176. [(Serbo-Croatian). Surveys the pre-World War II novels of G. Greene, E. Waugh, R.Warner and C. Isherwood, focusing on the thirties].

1971 _____. "Character and the Image of Man in Twentieth Century English Novel," FP, VI (1968), 133-140. Reprinted as Introduction to The Changing Face: Disintegration of Personality in the Twentieth Century British Novel, 1900-1950. Preface by Harry T. Moore. (Carbondale & Edwardsville: Southern Illinois University Press; London & Amsterdam: Feffer & Simons, 1970), pp. xv-xxii. [Outlines her investigation of the roles and values of characters in the English novel between 1900-1950 to show the "changing conception of human personality"].

1972 Marriott, J. W. "Some Tendencies of Modern Fiction," ML& PSP, XLII (1916), 157-174. [Asserts that though modern fiction deals with the familiar, it is not realism but reality it seeks; and, as it moves away from "plot" towards "formlessness," it reveals great psychological insight in characterisation, and analyses human action with increasing candour. A. Bennett, G. Cannan, O. Onions, M. Hewlett, "M. Corelli," D. H. Lawrence, C. Mackenzie, H. G. Wells, and J. Galsworthy].

1973 Marshall, Bruce. "The Responsibilities of the Catholic Novelist," Commonweal, L (27 May 1949), 169-171. [Maintains that the Catholic novelist should get "both the meaning and the accidents of the world right." References to G. Greene, and E. Waugh among others].

1974 _____. "Graham Greene and Evelyn Waugh: Grimness and Gaiety and Grace in Our Times," Commonweal, LI (3 Mar. 1950), 551-553. [Refutes the charge that both novelists write "unnecessarily" about ugly or futile people].

1975 Martin, Burns. "The English Novel Since 1900," DR, XV (1935), 213-218. [Surveys subject matter in the novels of the "traditionalists"--H. G. Wells, J. Galsworthy, D. H. Lawrence, C. E. Montague, J. Conrad, E. M. Forster, A. Bennett, V. Sackville-West, and D. Garnett--and those experimenting with the form and material of the novel--D. Richardson, J. Joyce, and V. Woolf].

1976 Martin, E. W. "English Writing and Writers," IER, LXX (Oct. 1948), 902-915. [Surveys the contemporary scene in an attempt to discover "the new creative writers." C. Isherwood, A. Koestler, G. Bullett, H. E. Bates, R. Mason, H. Green, H. Slater, W. Clewes, E. Taylor, F. King, J. Aistrop, D. Val Baker, and J. Gordon].

1977 _____. "English Writing Today and Tomorrow," IER, (Sep. 1949), 242-254. [Pages 242-248 examine briefly novels published during the previous six months by A. Huxley, R. C. Hutchinson, and E. Brown to illustrate "the disagreement which accompanies a failure in true creativeness." Also notices works by P. H. Newby, O. Manning, and A. Comfort].

1978 "Marxism and the Novel," TLS, 2774 (29 Apr. 1955), 209. [Leading article discussing J. Lindsay's The Moment of Choice and the general English lack of enthusiasm for a littérature engagée. Reply by Jack Lindsay, TLS, 2776 (13 May 1955), 53].

1979 Masuno, Syoei. "Junkyo e no michi," EigoS, CXVI (1970),

317-318, 398-400. ["The Road to Martyrdom." In Japanese.
Examines in two parts the involvement of English writers
in the Spanish Civil War. Part I shows the difference between W. H. Auden, S. Spender, C. D. Lewis and L. MacNeice,
and C. Caldwell, R. Fox, J. Cornford and J. Bell, who "lived
what poets sang." Part II is mainly concerned with the
rise of the Bloomsbury group and J. Bell's involvement in
the War].

1980   Matchett, Willoughby. "Dickens and Some Modern Authors,"
        LA, 288 (12 Feb. 1916), 417-424. Reprinted from The Dicken-
        sian. [Examines English novelists with "Dickensy traits":
        P. Ridge, W. W. Jacobs, H. G. Wells, E. T. Thurston, W. de
        Morgan and others].

1981   Mathias, Roland. "The Writer and the Gun," FR, CLXIV (Aug.
        1948), 116-124. [Considers the influence of two World Wars
        in shaping English wirters' attitudes to life, and conse-
        quently, what they chose to write about. Includes S. Maugham,
        C. Isherwood, G. Greene, E. Waugh, and R. Warner among others].

1982   Maurois, André. "New Types of English Fiction," LA, 329
        (17 Apr. 1927), 158-160. Reprinted from NL, (6 Mar. 1926).
        [Discusses new types characterised by the absence of moral
        tendencies, "a sentimental mysticism" arising from scien-
        tific naturalism and moral nihilism, and a sense of the
        comic. E. M. Forster, V. Woolf, M. Baring, and D. Garnett].

1983   _____. "Novels in the First Person," SatR, VIII (22
        Aug. 1931), 70-71. [Rejects outright condemnation of nov-
        els written in the first person as being easy to write,
        irritating to the reader and not revealing the truth, and
        reveals circumstances in which it would be justifiable to
        write in the first person. Brief references to S. Maugham
        and A. Huxley among others].

1984   Mavity, Nancy Barr. "A Word About Realism," Dial, LXVI
        (28 June 1919), 635-637. [On the various distasteful con-
        notations of the term, and its modern development which
        does not disdain "genuine romance" but is opposed to fal-
        sification, and the "subordination of presentation to pro-
        paganda" and vagueness. Brief references to C. Mackenzie
        and J. D. Beresford].

1985   May, Derwent. "The Novelist as Moralist and the Moralist
        as Critic," EIC, X:3 (July 1960), 320-328. Reprinted in
        Critical Approaches to Fiction. Edited by Shiv K. Kumar
        and Keith F. McKean (New York: McGraw-Hill, 1968), pp.
        177-185. [Distinguishes between the creative novelist and
        the "moral" novelist, between the novelist who works towards
        a "development" of the reader's moral attitude by stimula-
        ting desirable responses through symbolic action, and the
        novelist who simply "proposes a change." Also questions

the kind of "moral criticism [that] can be brought against a novel." D. H. Lawrence, H. James, and J. Conrad among others].

1986 Mayerhoff, Hans. "The Time of Life," ForumS, III:9 (1962), 13-17. [On the characteristic modes, or qualities of human time--relativity, duration--and why they are singled out for treatment in modern literature. (These are discussed more fully in Time in Literature. (Berkeley: University of California Press, 1960)].

1987 Mayersberg, Paul. "The Shared Dream. On the Relationship between Fiction and the Cinema," Listener, LXVIII (27 Sep. 1962), 473-475. [Examines the impact of the cinema on technique and content in the novel].

1988 Meath, Gerard O. P. "Catholic Writing," Blackfriars, XXXII (Dec. 1951), 602-609. [Argues from a Catholic viewpoint that there is no conflict between poetic and moral truth in novel writing, that the two forms of truth "direct one another without either submitting its independence." E. Bowen, B. Marshall, E. Waugh, and G. Greene].

1989 Meckier, Jerome. "Looking Back at Anger: The Success of a Collapsing Stance," DR, LII (Spring 1972), 47-58. [Contends that novels like Lucky Jim, Strike the Father Dead, Saturday Night and Sunday Morning, and Room at the Top were written from a stance resulting from a "tension between the need for rage and a growing scepticism about its efficacy"; hence, the novelists' endorsement of their heroes' discontent with society while "realistically questioning the ability of their young heroes to defeat it"].

1990 Megroz, Rodolphe Louis. "Bouncing us into Belief," DM, (Jan.-Mar. 1948), 32-36. Reprinted in Thirty-one Bedside Essays. (Hadleigh, Essex: Tower Bridge Publications, 1951), pp. 31-35. [Discusses the problem of "credibility" and "truth to life" in the novel. J. Conrad and H. James among others].

1991 Meissner, M. "Das Generationsproblem im modernen englischen Roman," Archiv, CLV (Mar. 1929), 27-47. [On the relationship between father and son in the late Victorian and early 20th century novel. S. Butler, J. Galsworthy, A. Bennett, H. Walpole, R. Macaulay, J. D. Beresford, M. Baring, and C. Mackenzie].

1992 Melchiori, Giorgio. "Il Cattolicesimo e il Romanzo in Inghilterra," Ulisse, X (1957), 1056-59. [Focuses on the Catholic element in the novels of E. Waugh and G. Greene].

1993 _____. "The Moment as a Time-Unit in Fiction," EIC, III:4 (Oct. 1953), 434-446. Reprinted in The Tightrope

Walkers: Studies of Mannerism in Modern English Literature. (London: Routledge and Kegan Paul; New York: Macmillan, 1956), pp. 175-188; also Critical Approaches to Fiction. Edited by Shiv K. Kumar and Keith F. McKean (New York: McGraw-Hill, 1968), pp. 217-229. [Discusses the new concept of time which originated in "the heightened awareness of the intensity of the moment and of the momentary experience,"--J. Joyce's "epiphany" and V. Woolf's "moment of being"--and shows the inevitability of "technical experiment" to treat this new element in fiction].

1994 _____. "Tradizione Americana e Romanzo Inglese," SA, I (1955), 55-71. Reprinted in translation as "The English Novelist and the American Tradition (1955)," SR, LXVIII (Summer 1960), 502-515. [Discusses the "fundamental influence" of the American tradition of Hawthorne and Melville on the twentieth century English novel -- the introduction into narrative of the "continued interchange between reality and symbol" which underlies the work of V. Woolf, J. Joyce, H. James, and L. P. Hartley].

1995 Mercer, Peter. "The Culture of Fictions; or The Fiction of Culture?" CritQ, XII:4 (Winter 1970), 291-300. [Argues that the admitted fictionality that all "fictions are displaced myths," i.e., "imaginative structures of physical or psychological events that are not real but possible," gives the myths of literature "their essential imaginative and educational power"].

1996 Mertner, Edgar. "Der Roman der Jungen Generation in England," SuL, III (1959), 101-123. [A study of the novels of "The Angry Young Men" -- K. Amis, J. Braine, and J. Wain -- which ascribes the popularity of their works to the social attitudes indicated by their heroes].

1997 Miller, Karl. "Poets' Novel," Listener, LXI (25 June 1959), 1099-1100. [On fiction that is wrongly poetic, with the force and complexity of lyrics].

1998 Millett, Fred B. "Feminine Fiction," CorM, CLV:926 (Feb. 1937), 225-235. [Surveys English female postwar novelists and classifies them into three categories: 1) those who had established reputations before the war -- E. Sidgwick, R. Macaulay, S. Kaye-Smith, 2) novelists of the "war generation" -- S. Jameson, C. Dane, D. Richardson, and 3) postwar women novelists whose "formative years coincided with the disorienting conflict" -- S. Benson, E. Olivier, V. Sackville-West, N. Mitchison, M. Kennedy, R. Lehmann, and V. Woolf].

1999 Millgate, Michael. "An Uncertain Feeling in England," NRep, CXXXVII (9 Sep. 1957), 16-17. [A sampling of the current "anti-social and bloody-minded individualism . . .

at best a profound personal integrity" of the "Angry Young Men" in verse, drama, and the novel].

2000   . "Contemporary English Fiction: Some Observations," Venture, II (1961), 214-220. [Considers C. P. Snow and the "anti-experimental novel" as representative of the contemporary novel].

2001 Mitchell, Giles. "Feeling and Will in the Modern Novel," DHLR, IV (1971), 183-196. [A review article of A. Freedman's The Turn of the Novel, J. Hall's The Lunatic Giant in the Drawing Room, H. Kaplan's The Passive Voice and R. Rabinovitz' The Reaction Against Experiment in the English Novel, 1950-1960].

2002 "Modern Creative Fiction," Harper's, CXXX (Apr. 1915), 800-802. [Attempts to show how creative fiction from G. Eliot to J. Conrad, appealing to the "sensibility of readers through sympathy as a psychical sense," contrasts with earlier and contemporary fiction, and has Greek Tragedy as its ancient counterpart].

2003 "Modern Fiction," Harper's, CXXIV:742 (Mar. 1912), 638-640. [On the detachment of the 20th century novelist, with special reference to A. Bennett].

2004 "Modern Novels," TLS, 899 (10 Apr. 1919), 189-190. [Surveys the work of H. G. Wells, A. Bennett and J. Galsworthy, and charges them for being "materialists" as opposed to the "spiritual" Joyce; also remarks on the new interest in psychology. (Leading article)].

2005 Moeller, Charles. "Religion et littérature: Esquisse d'une méthode de lecture," CLS, II:4 (1965), 323-333. Reprinted in Mansions of the Spirit: Essays in Literature and Relinion. Edited by George A. Panichas. (New York: Hawthorne Books, 1967), pp. 59-73. [Suggests that "reading the explicit, discovering the deep motivations, and deciphering the religious symbols" are three approaches, "complementary," and yet, "autonomous." References to J. Joyce, G. Greene, D. H. Lawrence and others].

2006 Monkhouse, Allan. "Society and the Novel," AtM, CLVI (Sep. 1935), 369-371. [Discusses the novel as a mirror of changing moral standards].

2007 Monroe, N. Elizabeth. "Contemporary Fiction and Society," SLM, II (June 1940), 363-367. Revised and reprinted as part of Chapter VIII of The Novel and Society: A Critical Study of the Modern Novel. (Chapel Hill: The University of North Carolina Press, 1941). [Maintains that the problem of the novelist who rejects the concept of art for art's sake or the notion of propaganda is how to reconcile his art with the world in which it lives. J. Joyce and V. Woolf among others].

2008   . "Toward Significance in the Novel," CE, II:6
(Mar. 1941), 541-551. Revised and reprinted as Chapter I
of The Novel and Society: A Critical Study of the Modern
Novel. (Chapel Hill: The University of North Carolina
Press, 1941), pp. 3-38. [Contends that present-day novels
lack "artistic seriousness" and that "experiments" have
failed because they have been turned into "ends in themselves" and novelists had no "adequate notion" of form.
V. Woolf, D. H. Lawrence, A. Huxley, and A. Bennett among
others].

2009   . "Freedom of the Novelist," Thought, XIX (Sep.
1944), 455-464. [On "the relation between freedom of experience and the form which experience takes in art; that
is, the problem of the inner form of reality and its aesthetic expression." D. H. Lawrence and H. James among
others].

2010   Montague, C. E. "'Sez 'E' or 'Thinks 'E'," SatR, V (13 Apr.
1929), 880-881. [On several methods of narration employed
by novelists: the born storytellers -- "spellbinders" --
like Dickens, the "free-and-easy plan" of Thackeray, H.
James' "central consciousness," and R. Kipling's and J.
Conrad's variations on it].

2011   Monteiro-Grillo, J. "Tradição e crise no romance inglês
contemporâneo," Broteria, LXVII (1963), 144-164. [Considers
the novel as a useful means of revealing man and the society
he lives in, and not just as mere entertainment. D. H.
Lawrence, A. Huxley, J. Joyce, V. Woolf, G. K. Chesterton,
W. Lewis, G. Orwell, R. Warner, G. Greene, J. Osborne, K.
Amis, and C. Wilson].

2012   Montgomery, Marion. "Three Types of Novelist -- and My
Ideal," Discourse, IX (1966), 359-366. [Suggests three
attitudes of the novelist to the world he creates, analo-
gous to the Three Persons of the Trinity: 1) the preacher
of "some brand of universal salvation" ranging from "sentimental moralists to polished satirists," 2) the Joycean
ideal "like the God of creation . . . invisible, refined
out of existence. . . .," and 3) the "catalyst," Faulkner's
ideal, who will help create "the magic wonder and surprise
and multiplicity"].

2013   Moody, Philippa. "In the Lavatory of the Athenaeum: Post-
War English Novels," MCQ, VI (1963), 83-92. [Discusses the
"mistrust of language" displayed by C. P. Snow and I. Murdoch and their reliance upon "reflective intelligence,"
facts, "solid objects and evasive intellectualism," versus
A. Sillitoe's "racy, energetic, irreverent idiom," and W.
Golding's novels which can be regarded as "explorations into language"].

2014   Morgan, Charles A. "A Defense of Story-Telling," YR, (NS)
        XXIII (June 1934), 771-787. [Defends storytelling against
        "the suspicious contempt" of "discriminating" people and
        upholds it as one of the "supreme activities of the human
        mind"; and though it may entertain, inform or educate, it
        "revitalizes the reader's perception of reality . . . flu-
        idifies his imagination of universals, making him aware
        by intuition of the nature of things"].

2015   _____. "Defense du roman," RP, (15 Mar. 1938), 409-
        425. [Defends the "aesthetic" novel against the charge
        that it is "anti-social" because it does not contribute
        towards, and even retards the amelioration of the human
        condition].

2016   _____. "L'Avenir du roman," NRel, IV:5 (Nov. 1945),
        367-383. [Analyses the causes that led to the "state of
        confusion" into which the novel had fallen in the thirties
        and war years, and predicts that the novel of the future
        will demand discipline, technique, lucidity, and a "péné-
        tration imaginative" if it is to fulfil its function].

2017   _____. "Dialogue in Novels and Plays," EA, VI:2 (May
        1953), 97-108. Also published as a booklet with the same
        title. (Aldington, Ashford, Kent: The Hand and Flower
        Press, 1954). [Discusses dialogue "in its relationship
        to conversation" in both drama and the novel, and puts
        forward the theory that dialogue is not a "report but a
        distillation, a formal means of penetrating to the essence
        of things"].

2018   Morgan, W. John. "Authentic Voices," TC, CLXI (1957), 138-
        144. [Discusses the creation of the "Young Frankensteins"
        of the fifties--the "Angry Young Men"--whose favourite game
        is "spotting the phoney." K. Amis, W. Cooper, and C. Wil-
        son].

2019   Morrison, Sister Kristin. "James's and Lubbock's Differing
        Points of View," NCF, XVI:3 (Dec. 1961), 245-251. [Con-
        tends that their usage of the term "point of view" is not
        identical, that in H. James it refers "primarily to a know-
        er" and in Lubbock to both "knower and sayer"].

2020 * Moser, Fernando de Mello. "Twentieth Century 'University
        Wits'," Revista de Filologie Romanica si Germanica (Bucarest),
        Series III (1963), 55-71.

2021   Mosley, Nicholas. "The Contemporary Novel," Theology, LXVI
        (July 1963), 266-271. [On the "anti-novel," its various
        forms and practices in France, U. S. A., England, and Ger-
        many, and the paradox behind its denial of freedom or re-
        sponsibility or any special significance in human life at
        a time when freedom is most enjoyed in these countries,
        while on a "realistic level it is widely thought that for

the first time man has control over his destiny." Brief
references to L. Durrell, I. Murdoch, and K. Amis].

2022   Moss, Howard. "Notes on Fiction," ConL, VII (Winter-Spring
        1966), 1-11. [Notes on A. Chekhov and H. James mostly,
        with random references to J. Joyce, M. Proust and E. M.
        Forster].

2023   Moss, Mary. "Significant Tendencies in Current Fiction,"
        AtM, XCV (May 1905), 689-700. [Reviews both English and
        American novels "fresh from the press," and concludes that
        genius, "promise and fulfilment" are to be found "across
        the sea." H. James, A. E. W. Mason, R. Kipling, R. Hichens,
        J. C. Snaith, M. Sinclair and others].

2024   Mudrick, Marwin. "Character and Event in Fiction," YR, L
        (Dec. 1960), 202-218. Reprinted in On Culture and Litera-
        ture. (New York: Horizon Press, 1970), pp. 141-159, and
        Critical Approaches to Fiction. Edited by Shiv K. Kumar
        and Keith F. McKean. (New York: McGraw-Hill, 1968), pp.
        97-113. [Discusses the relationship and concludes that
        events and characters are indistinguishable, for "the dis-
        tinctive talent of the writer of fiction is to make events,"
        to emphasise change and development, "the mark of his ma-
        turity (being) to offer, by way of events, a community of
        individual lives in the act of defining themselves"].

2025   Muir, Edwin. "The Assault on Humanism," Freeman, VII
        (27 June 1923), 369-371. [Condemns the "unconscious" as-
        sault against humanism by D. H. Lawrence, G. B. Shaw, H.
        G. Wells, and Sherwood Anderson as an "aberration" that
        springs from a "spirit which is unawakened to the human-
        istic tradition"].

2026   _____. "A Letter from England," SatR, I (4 Apr. 1925),
        647. [Surveys briefly the contemporary novelists and the
        chief novels published in 1925, noting the advance of the
        novel in all directions and the absence of any central
        tendency, its inability to "incarnate 'the modern conscious-
        ness'," and the death of the "sociological-psychological"
        novel].

2027   _____. "Past and Present," AtM, CXL (Dec. 1927), 776-
        781. [Attempts to reassess, after his book of essays,
        Transition, whether there is anything new or important in
        modern literature. Illustrates from T. S. Eliot and J.
        Joyce].

2028   _____. "Time and the Modern Novel," AtM, CLXV:4 (Apr.
        1940), 535-537. [Discusses the impact of the "historical
        sense," and the "disastrously exclusive consciousness of
        time" on the novel in the past twenty years. V. Woolf and
        J. Joyce].

2029 _____. "The Novel and the Modern World," Horizon, II
(Nov. 1940), 246-253. Reprinted as "The Political View of
Literature" in Essays on Literature and Society. (London:
Hogarth Press, 1949). Revised and enlarged (London: The
Hogarth Press; Cambridge, Mass.: Harvard University Press,
1965), pp. 134-142. [A review article on David Daiches'
The Novel and the Modern World. (Cambridge: University
Press; Chicago: University of Chicago Press, 1939)].

2030 _____. "The Status of the Novel," NRep, CV (11 Aug.
1941), 193-195. Reprinted as "The Decline of the Novel"
in Essays on Literature and Society. (London: Hogarth
Press, 1949). Revised and enlarged (London: Hogarth Press;
Cambridge, Mass.: Harvard University Press, 1965), pp.
143-149. [A succinct statement on the "inclusiveness of
the modern novel and the reasons for its inconclusiveness"].

2031 Muller, Herbert J. "Virginia Woolf and Feminine Fiction,"
SatR, (6 Feb. 1937), 3-4, 14. [On the contribution of
women novelists to modern fiction].

2032 _____. "Impressionism in Fiction: Prism vs. Mirror,"
ASch, VII:3 (Summer 1938), 355-367. [On the nature and
characteristics of Impressionism and its adoption in the
novel, not merely as an "incidental means" in the presentation of an argument, but as "an animating principle, a
systematic approach . . . a self-conscious creed." D. H.
Lawrence, D. Richardson, V. Woolf, and J. Joyce among others]

2033 _____. "Exercises in Incongruity," YR, XXIX (Sep.
1939), 97-112. [Argues for "more dissociation" from the
world, a "perspective of incongruity" for critical purposes as K. Burke practises in Attitudes Toward History.
Brief references to J. Joyce, A. Huxley, V. Woolf, H. James,
D. H. Lawrence, and H. G. Wells among others].

2034 Munson, Gorham B. "English Novels -- from an American
Standpoint. Reflections on Ourselves While Reading Swinnerton, Ford, Nichols, Arlen and H. D.," Bookman (New York),
LXVIII (Jan. 1929), 573-575. [Reviews novels by F. Swinnerton, F. M. Ford, R. Nichols, "M. Arlen," and H. D. (Hilda
Doolittle). Standpoint adopted rather scornfully regards
English literature as having become "devitalized," in re-
taliation for the "incredulous and patronizing" English
attitude to American letters].

2035 Murchland, Bernard G. "The Literature of Despair," Commonweal, LXVII (21 Feb. 1958), 527-530. [Contends that contemporary literature of despair -- "human despair" as distinct from "theological despair" -- has positive qualities,
for it protects against intellectual and social forces and
values that make it difficult to live as a free man. Mainly
concerned with Kafka, Rilke, Malraux and Camus, with brief
references to G. Greene and J. Green]

2036 Murdoch, Iris. "The Sublime and the Beautiful Revisited,"
YR, XLIX (Dec. 1959), 247-271. [A treatment of "recent
changes in the portrayal of character in novels as symptoms
of some more general change of consciousness"].

2037 _____. "Against Dryness: A Polemical Sketch," Encounter, XVI (Jan. 1961), 16-20. [Maintains "prose must
recover its former glory, eloquence, and discourse must
return" if present day literature is to turn our attention
from the "dry symbol, the bogus individual, the false whole,
towards the real impenetrable human person"].

2038 Murphy, Dorothy. "Time and the Modern Novel," WR, I (Spring
1958), 30-40. [Discusses English and American modern novelists' awareness of the "immensity of Time" and its "potent
threat" to the values of the individual. V. Woolf and J.
B. Priestley among others].

2039 Murphy, J. Stanley. "Not on All Fours," America, LXVIII
(27 Feb. 1943), 577-578. [Recognizing the moral influence
of art and its "fundamental necessity" to human nature,
he welcomes novelists like G. Greene, R. Speaight and W.
Cather, for they will "unconsciously" reveal the imprint
of Catholicism].

2040 Murry, John Middleton. "The Fashionable Novel," Nation
(London), XXX (17 Dec. 1921), 473-474; XXX (31 Dec. 1921),
529. [A review article on S. McKenna's The Secret Victory
and W. L. George's The Confession of Ursula Trent as "nov-
el(s) of fashion" which are also fashionable, followed by
a letter to the editor by M. Sadleir].

2041 _____. "The Break-up of the Novel," YR, (NS) XII
(Jan. 1923), 288-304. [On the two "subjective" tendencies
in modern fiction: "the presentation of consciousness,"
an extreme subjectivism "without the control of . . . intuitive selection," therefore "incomprehensible" and "formless," and, the presentation of the vivid' moments of a
consciousness by means of a "common ground" -- the story --
between the novelist's perception and ours].

2042 _____. "Modern English Literature," SatR, II:5 (29
Aug. 1925), 77-78. [Considers 1914 as a watershed in modern English literature between the "constellation" of G.
B. Shaw, H. G. Wells, R. Kipling, J. M. Barrie, A. Bennett,
J. Conrad, and J. Galsworthy with their "fundamental op-
timism" and acceptance of society, and the critical questioning, the despair and cynicism of the younger generation
that survived the war].

2043 Mylne, Vivienne. "Changing Attitudes Towards Truth in Fiction," RMS, VII (1963), 53-77. [Surveys ideas about truth
and fiction in the seventeenth and eighteenth centuries,

and discusses the persistence of the preference for truth in modern ficiton, and its results].

2044 _____. "Illusion and the Novel," BJA, VI (1966), 142-151. [Examines how the novelist can or does create illusion, and the nature of its effects on the reader, illusion being the sine qua non for the enjoyment of novels].

2045 _____. "Reading and Re-Reading Novels," BJA, VII (Jan. 1967), 67-75. [Paper read at the Conference of the British Society of Aesthetics, September 1965. On the type of reader who re-reads a novel, the reasons behind it, and in what way a re-reading can differ from a first reading].

2046 Nakahashi, Kazuo. "Literature and Politics in Modern English Literature," Ningen, (April 1949), 24-31. [In Japanese. Discusses the political concerns of writers in the twenties and thirties].

2047 Nakano, Yoshio. "Indeterminism and Modern Literature: A Brief Study of Some Interrelations between Scientific and Literary Thought," SELit, XV (1935), 473-491. [An address originally delivered in Japanese on 25 Nov. 1934 at the Sixth Annual Meeting of the English Literary Society of Japan at the Kyoto Imperial University. Discusses the "indirect, or unconscious" influence or interrelation, and includes the literature of the "stream of consciousness." References to J. Joyce, V. Woolf, and A. Huxley].

2048 Neame, A. J. "Black and Blue -- A Study in the Catholic Novel," European, 2 (Apr. 1953), 26-36. [Discusses -- and disapproves of -- the manner in which G. Greene and E. Waugh convey Catholicism as "an intelligible and coherent Weltanschauung," for their novels are too "confined" in scope, private miseries or idiosyncrasies being "inappropriate to the times"].

2049 Nemerov, Howard. "Composition and Fate in the Short Novel," GradJ, V:2 (Fall 1963), 375-391. Reprinted in Poetry and Fiction: Essays. (New Brunswick, N. J.: Rutgers University Press, 1963), pp. 229-246, and Perspectives in Contemporary Criticism: A Collection of Recent Essays by American, English and European Literary Critics. Edited by Sheldon Norman Grebstein. (New York and London: Harper and Row, 1968), pp. 120-133. [Originally presented as a lecture before the British Institute at Columbia University, 7 Sep. 1956. On the "material economy" and "style of composition" of the novella as a tradition distinct from the short story and the novel, suggestive of the "tragedies of antiquity." References to J. Conrad and D. H. Lawrence].

2050 "The New Long Novel," TLS, 1928 (14 Jan. 1939), 25. [An editorial pointing out the drawbacks of the revival of the long novel. Correspondence by Richard Rumbold, (21 Jan. 1939), 41].

2051 "The New Novelists: An Enquiry," LM, V:11 (1958), 13-31.
[A symposium. Contributors are A. Quinton, L. Cooper, F.
Kermode, and M. Cranston. See individual entries].

2052 Newman, A. Evelyn. "International Note in the Novels of
the Pre-War Years," WU, 7 (Dec. 1930-Jan. 1931), 155-165,
251-264. [Surveys German, French and English novels, noticing the "well-nigh universal depression" that prevailed
among writers in the first two decades of the century.
Included are J. Galsworthy and H. G. Wells].

2053 Nicholas, H. G. "The Political Novel," ParA, XVI (Spring
1963), 213-216. [Comments on the conditions in which the
novel of political ideas flourishes, its value and the
present decline of institutions in the novel. Brief references to G. Orwell, and J. Cary].

2054 Nicholl, Donald. "La Littérature catholique en Angleterre
depuis la guerre," VI, XXV (June 1954), 58-73. [A survey
of English Catholic postwar writings from the novel to
the physical sciences. Includes brief remarks on G. Greene,
E. Waugh, and B. Marshall on pp. 58-62].

2055 Nichols, Robert. "On Method in Fiction," NSta, XXIX:753
(1 Oct. 1927), 779. [On method as "seeing," i.e., clarify-
ing obscure relations. Also prophesies that the novel will
be characterised by brevity which, however, will not exclude depth and width, by a strong hidden structure, by
an apparent simplicity masking a formidable complexity,
by the abolition of every unnecessary detail, and by a
total impression of compact power and grace].

2056 _____. "Novels of Tomorrow," TrP, XVI (29 Sep. 1928),
5. [Predicts the departures from established directions
which the novel will make, especially a rise in the "interpretive" novels of the "fable phantasies" type, revealing
the "transvaluation of values," and which will reach its
"climax about 1940, and penetrate the social body during
the period 1935-1960." Also notices the decline in the
number of purely subjective novels and the death of objective naturalism].

2057 Nicholson, Norman. "Morals and the Modern Novel," Theology, (June 1940), 412-420. [Asserts that the changing attitudes
towards morality in pre-war novelists range from the "a-
morality" of A. Bennett and H. G. Wells to the misunderstan-
ding of D. H. Lawrence's "morality," especially in the individual's choice of action, and the substitution of a
"false set of values" as in C. Morgan].

2058 _____. "The Provincial Tradition," TLS, 2946 (15 Aug.
1958), xix. [Special Section: "Books in a Changing World."
Identifies the Provincial Tradition as the "tradition of

the inside," rooted in common knowledge, shared experience nurtured by the same environment in spite of disagreement, and where A. Bennett, D. H. Lawrence, G. Eliot got their material, as distinct from the so-called "provincial con- temporaries"--P. Larking, K. Amis and J. Wain--who write "of necessity, from the outside"].

2059 _____. "Significant Modern Writers: The Two Worlds in Modern Literature," ExpT, LXXII (Apr. 1961), 197-200. [Discusses the various ways in which modern and contempor- ary writers--English, American and French--have faced the "two most persistent heresies of the Christian era"--mate- rialism and the world of the spirit or non-matter--and re- vealed their different aspects, especially in their novels. Brief references to writers from H. James to G. Greene].

2060 Nicolson, Harold. "The New Spirit in Literature," Listener, VI:142 (30 Sep. 1931), 545-546; 144 (14 Oct. 1931), 632- 633; 145 (21 Oct. 1931), 684-685; 146 (28 Oct. 1931), 737- 738; 147 (4 Nov. 1931), 780-781; 148 (11 Nov. 1931), 823- 824; 149 (18 Nov. 1931), 864; 150 (25 Nov. 1931), 924; 153 (16 Dec. 1931), 1062; 154 (23 Dec. 1931), 1108. Reprinted in book form as The New Spirit in Literature . . . An Essay. (London: B. B. C., 1931). [Attempts to interpret and ex- plain in ten talks the changes and complexities of the post- war period in English literature. Discusses in his first talk the meaning of the "modern spirit in literature" and the "reading habit" in the second. He then devotes a sep- arate talk to each of A. Huxley, S. Butler, H. Walpole, D. H. Lawrence, V. Woolf, E. M. Forster and C. Mackenzie, and J. Joyce. He concludes the survey by asserting that a "new movement" is underway, and "will form its expression" upon a reaction to the writers discussed].

2061 _____. "Is the Novel Dead?" Observer, (29 Aug. 1954), 7. [Contends that the novel is dead because it is not a permanent but an "occasional" form of expression, lacks a "sense of direction" in the unfavourable conditions of the present generation, and has become an "irrelevant" form by attempting to communicate a "state of mind" rather than relying on narration. (See responses by P. Toynbee and A. Pryce-Jones below)].

2062 Nixon, Elizabeth. "Significant Women Novelists of the Twentieth Century," EngW, XXXVI (Nov. 1917), 137-151. [Out- lines briefly four major tendencies in the contemporary novel -- "fulness of detail," interest in character rather than incident, breadth of scope and concern with social problems -- and discusses the contributions of four female novelists: M. Sinclair, E. Sidgwick, E. Mordaunt, and S. Kaye-Smith].

2063 Noon, William T. "Modern Literature and the Sense of Time,"

Thought, XXXIII (1958), 571-603. [On the efforts of the
imagination to explain to itself "its overriding consciousness of history under the aspects of time." References to
J. Joyce and V. Woolf among others].

2064 _____. "God and Man in Twentieth Century Fiction,"
Thought, XXXVII (Spring 1962), 35-56. [A survey of the
achievements of Kafka, D. H. Lawrence, and J. Joyce --
three apostates to the religion they were born in -- and
their thrust in the direction of transcendence].

2065 _____. "Three Young Men in Rebellion," Thought, (Winter 1963), 559-577. [Discusses the autobiographical dis-
closures made by the heroes of S. Butler's The Way of All
Flesh, J. Joyce's A Portrait of the Artist, and U. S. novelist J. D. Salinger's The Catcher in the Rye, what they
rebelled against and what they sought].

2066 Norris, Frank. "The Novel With a 'Purpose'," WWork, IV
(May 1902), 2117-19. [A general statement on the novel
that sets out to "prove" something by "showing" and "telling"].

2067 Nott, Kathleen. "Down with the Anti-Hero," NSoc, I:8 (22
Nov. 1962), 29. [On the cult of the "little man" or the
anti-hero in the novels of the fifties. K. Amis, J. Braine,
J. Wain, A. Sillitoe, and S. Barstow].

2068 "The Novel in Decline?" The Listener, LIII:1364 (21 Apr.
1955), 692. [An editorial discussing the decrease in the
demand for the novel in the light of a publisher's letter
to the editor and T. R. Fyvel's talk printed in the same
issue].

2069 "The Novel in Disintegration," TLS, 2691 (28 Aug. 1953),
xii. [Special Autumn Number: "Thoughts and Some Second
Thoughts upon Some Outstanding Books of the Half-Century.
1900-1950." Attributes the present "disintegration" of
the novel to writers taking all experience, all knowledge
for their province, the reliance on "documentation" and
the "rarified subjectivism" and experiments which led the
novel into blind alleys. Suggests science fiction as the
"clearest portent of the future"].

2070 "The Novel is Not Dead," Economist, CCXXXIV (14 Feb. 1970),
48, 51. [Discusses the sales of English novels, and surveys briefly the top novelists of the fifties and sixties
and their tendency, with perhaps one exception, to "reflect
the commonsense, empirical frame of mind." G. Greene, C.
P. Snow, A. Powell, L. P. Hartley, W. Golding, L. Durrell,
K. Amis, A. Sillitoe, D. Lessing, M. Spark, C. Brooke-
Rose, O. Manning, P. H. Newby and others].

2071 "The Novel of the Future," CO, LVI (Mar. 1914), 211. [Opinions and quotations from Joseph Keating's article in T. P.'s Weekly (London), that the novel of the future will be occupied with the conflict of blood and spirit].

2072 "Novel Thoughts," Listener, LIII:1350 (13 Jan. 1955), 54. [Editorial discussing G. Hough's series of four articles entitled "The Novel and the Reader"].

2073 "Novel Thoughts," Listener, LVI:1439 (25 Oct. 1956), 648. [Editorial discussing E. Bowen's three talks entitled "Truth and Fiction"].

2074 "The Novel Today: Death or Transmutation? (A Symposium)," BA, XXII (Spring 1958), 117-123; XXXII (Summer 1958), 237-242. [Thirteen critics and writers respond to the Editors' letter-statement on possible causes leading to the present state of the novel. Includes A. Huxley's response].

2075 "The Novel Under Fire Again: Human Stories or Tracts for the Times," TLS, 2160 (26 June 1943), 306. [A special article reviewing E. Monroe's The Novel and Society: A Critical Study of the Modern Novel. The reviewer maintains that the "secret of a novel's life" eludes both "the historian and the moral statistician"].

2076 "The Novelist's Alternative," TLS, 905 (22 May 1919), 269. Reprinted as "Novelists and Novel Reading," LA, 301 (28 June 1919), 808-812. [Asserts the novelists has emerged on an equal footing with the poet; and yet "the vulgarity, triviality and commercialism of the bulk of its practitioners" are causes for contempt for the novel].

2077 "The Novelist's Responsibility," TLS, 2888 (5 July 1957), 413. [Leading article discussing L. P. Hartley's paper with the same title at the Aldenburgh Festival, and in which he rejects the anecdote, and emphasises the "twin concepts of the novelist and of the responsible man"].

2078 "Novelists Who Have Succumbed to the Lure of Psychoanalysis, CO, LXIII (Dec. 1917), 413. [On novelists' interest in the field of psychoanalysis with two excerpts from The Saturday Review and New York Evening Post condemning J. Galsworthy and L. Wilkinson for "overstepping the legitimate boundaries of fiction].

2079 "The Novelist's World," TLS, 2897 (6 Sep. 1957), 533. [Leading article discussing the contemporary novelist's unsqueamish awareness of actualities, class-consciousness, "comedy of bad manners," and the danger of "relaxing into the small humours of a grumbling, self-enclosed cosiness"].

2080 "Novels and Novelty," TLS, 3249 (4 June 1964), 483. [Leading article discussing the view expressed by several con-

tributors to the "World Book Fair" issue of the TLS, that
the contemporary English novel is "concerned too exclusive-
ly with refinements of feeling and nuances of manners"].

2081   "Novels Still to be Written," NSta, XIII (5 July 1919), 346-
347. [Maintains that since the "whole school of fiction is
middle-class," the novels that are still to be written
should be about "working people by writers who belong themselves to working-class families"].

2082   "Novels With a Philosophy," EdR, CCIII:415 (Jan. 1906), 64-
84. Reprinted in LA, 248 (24 Mar. 1906), 724-740. [Chooses
H. G. Wells' Kipps, M. Dearmer's The Difficult Way (1905),
M. Sinclair's The Divine Fire and R. Hichen's The Garden of
Allah to illustrate the increasingly didactic trend of the
modern novelist].

2083   O'Brien, Desmond. "Aspects of the Novelist," Bookman (London), LXXXIV (Apr. 1933), 7-8. [Contends that the attitude
of the novelist to pressing questions is "antipodal to the
philosopher," for his is a "poetic perception" and an "intuitive insight." Brief references to J. Joyce and D. H.
Lawrence].

2084   O'Brien, John. "The Novel of Salvation," Cresset, XXXV:3
(Jan. 1972), 12-15. [Argues for the recognition that the
"novel of salvation" has its own theme and structure. Also
describes two ways in which the religious writer can show
the salvation of a character: by pointing out an observable
human basis for the renewal, i.e., "active virtues," and by
suggesting a character's new understanding or vision. E.
Waugh and G. Greene among others].

2085   O'Connor, Frank. "A Matter-of-Fact Problem in the Writing
of the Novel," NYTBR, (12 Dec. 1954), 5. [Analyses the "new
critical temper" of realism that crept into the novel from
J. Austen to the death of the subjective novel. Rather
skeptical of C. P. Snow's attempts to lead the novel from
Joyce to Trollope].

2086   O'Connor, William Van. "Toward a History of Bloomsbury,"
SWR, XL (Winter 1955), 36-52. [A study of the various
sources -- books, articles and memoirs -- that throw light
on the Bloomsbury group in order to separate fact from fic-
tion].

2087   _____. "Two Types of 'Heroes' in Post-War British
Fiction," PMLA, LXXVII (Mar. 1962), 168-174. [Discusses
the rise of the new kind of protagonist in conflict with
society in novels by A. Sillitoe, D. Storey, J. Braine, K.
Amis, J. Wain, I. Murdoch and "T. Hinde," and distinguishes
between the "seedy, ineffectual, comic" Lucky Jim type,
more akin to S. Beckett's Murphy, and the "personal . . .

moral and heavy" conflict that characterises the Joe Lampton type that recalls the "pre-modern Bennett"].

2088 O'Faolain, Sean. "A Plea for a New Kind of Novel," Spectator, CLI:5497 (3 Nov. 1933), 615-616. Revised and enlarged in VQR, X (Apr. 1934), 189-199. [Suggests that the novel move away from photographic reality and the naturalistic method of representing character].

2089 _____. "Novelists See Too Much," Spectator, CLIV:5567 (8 Mar. 1935), 385-386. [Questions whether the tendency of the 20th century novel to insist on detail has limited its achievements].

2090 _____. "The Modern Novel: A Catholic Point of View," VQR, XI (July 1935), 339-351. [Attributes the basic problems of the modern novel to the disappearance of the ethic that informed it, the movement from realism to naturalism which undermined old values, and the modern novelist's self-chosen task to prove that life is evil: hence, the "joyless novel and the novelist's "isolation"].

2091 _____. "It No Longer Matters, or The Death of the English Novel," Criterion, XV:58 (Oct. 1935), 49-56. [Contends that the modern psychological novel which does not adequately replace the older Vanity Fair type of novel, arose from "a condition of world thought" at the end of the 19th century, and tends to lose the "complete and unified entirety" of man unless revived by a "spiritual view of life," by an attempt to make "that flesh become transparent"].

2092 _____. "Pigeon-Holing the Modern Novel," LMer, XXXIII (Dec. 1935), 159-164. [A rough and ready classification of modern English fiction into five major categories: 1) Traditionalist -- a) standpoint novel, and b) individualist novel, 2) Naturalist, 3) Brutalist, 4) Escapist, and 5) Individualist. Prefers the "standpoint" novel].

2093 _____. "The Proletarian Novel," LMer, XXXV (Apr. 1937) 583-589. [Examines briefly alternatives to the "crude mechanism of the communist," that is, man as a social organism "in relation to the nation" or in relation to God, and the "individualist view of man," and claims that the clash between the communist proletarian novel and the existing English one is a clash between "two concepts of reality," or "attitudes to life and creation"].

2094 _____. "Virginia Woolf and James Joyce -- Narcissa and Lucifer," NWW, 10 (1956), 161-175. Reprinted in The Vanishing Hero: Studies in the Novelists of the Twenties. (London Eyre and Spottiswoode, 1956), pp. 191-222; (Boston: Little, Brown, 1956), pp. 170-204. [Contrasts and compares Joyce's "epiphanies" with V. Woolf's "moments of vision," "his meta-

290

physical view of reality with her rather simple viewpoint,"
places both in "the tradition of individualistic revolt
against the order of nature and society," and questions
whether "literature can be in health and vigour without
some form of faith"].

2095 O'Grady, Walter. "On Plot in Modern Fiction: Hardy, James,
      Conrad," MFS, XI:2 (Summer 1965), 107-115. Reprinted in
      Critical Approaches to Fiction. Edited by Shiv K. Kumar
      and Keith F. McKean. (New York: McGraw-Hill, 1968), pp.
      57-67, and The Novel: Modern Essays in Criticism. Edited
      by R. M. Davis. (Englewood Cliffs, N. J.: Prentice-Hall,
      1969), pp. 206-217. [Emphasises the notion that the es-
      sence of plot is change, process rather than object or
      structure -- following E. M. Forster -- and is the result
      of the interrelationship between "an external situation,
      an internal situation, an external event and an internal
      event." Illustrates from Tess of the D'Urbervilles, The
      Ambassadors, and The Secret Agent].

2096 O'Hare, Charles Bernard. "Myth or Plot? A Study in the
      Ways of Narrative," ArQ, XIII (Autumn 1957), 238-250. [Con-
      tends that though there is a distinction between "plot
      method and mythical method," the two are "not completely
      antithetical." J. Joyce and D. H. Lawrence among others].

2097 "On Ugliness in Fiction," EdR, CCVII (Apr. 1908), 440-464;
      reprinted in LA, 257 (23 May 1908), 451-468. [Condemns the
      cult of ugliness in the English novel when it becomes "con-
      genital to the conception of a story," and justifies his
      claim for "the necessity of intervention" by illustrating
      from works by W. B. Maxwell, J. Galsworthy, J. C. Snaith,
      J. Conrad, M. Sinclair and others].

2098 Onimus, Jean. "L'Expression du temps dans le roman contem-
      porain," RLC, XXVIII:3 (July-Sep. 1954), 299-317. [Attri-
      butes recent changes in techniques of narration to novelists'
      consciousness of time, five aspects of which, 1) linear time,
      2) multiple time, 3) open time, 4) "durée in time," and 5)
      the "pénétration" of the past, are discussed in French,
      German, English, and American novels. References to A. Hux-
      ley, V. Woolf, S. Beckett, G. Greene, and J. Joyce].

2099 Orton, William A. "English Literature Since 1914," Athen-
      aeum (18 June 1920), 801-803. [The Prize Essay. Rejects,
      in the brief survey, the novel as the "vehicle of a socio-
      logical or political or personal preoccupation," for it
      must exist "primarily in its own right"].

2100 Orwell, George. "In Defence of the Novel," NEW, X (12 Nov.
      1936), 91-92; (19 Nov. 1936), 111-112. Reprinted in The
      Collected Essays, Journalism and Letters of George Orwell,
      Vol. 1. Edited by Sonia Orwell and Ian Angus. (London:

Secker & Warburg; New York: Harcourt, 1968), pp. 249-255. [Contends that the novel's "lapse in prestige" can be corrected by more honest reviewing and a "grading" system for novels].

2101 _____. "The Rediscovery of Europe," Listener, XXVII: 688 (19 Mar. 1942), 370-372. Reprinted in The Collected Essays, Journalism and Letters of George Orwell. Vol. 2. Edited by Sonia Orwell and Ian Angus. (London: Secker & Warburg; New York: Harcourt, 1968), pp. 197-207. [Attributes the change in spirit, outlook on life, and technique in the works of the latter part of the second decade to the writers' "reestablished contact with Europe" which broke the "cultural circle" in which England had existed for the best part of a century. H. G. Wells, D. H. Lawrence, J. Galsworthy, A. Huxley, and J. Joyce].

2102 _____. "The Prevention of Literature," Polemic, 2 (Jan. 1950), 4-14. Reprinted in The Collected Essays, Journalism and Letters of George Orwell. Vol. 4. In Front of Your Nose. 1945-1950. Edited by Sonia Orwell and Ian Angus. (London: Secker & Warburg; New York: Harcourt, 1968), pp. 59-72. [Voices his concern over attempts to undermine the intellectual liberty of the writer, for prose literature, unlike poetry perhaps, cannot survive in an age of totalitarianism or if liberty of thought perishes].

2103 Osborne, John. "The Writer in His Age," LM, IV (May 1957), 47-49. [One of a series. The function of the writer is to "get over to as many people as possible . . . without compromise and patronage"].

2104 "Outlook for English Fiction," LA, 226 (20 Aug. 1910), 506-509. [A brief survey of the achievements of major novelists leaves the writer with the belief that English fiction is in "a healthy state . . . and technical craftsmanship of the art steadily rising," even though it is concerned with middle class life and feeling, at the expense of both governing and working classes].

2105 "Over the Top With the New Novelists," CO, LXVI (June 1919), 387-388. [Excerpts from contemporary reviews of the "new" fiction of D. Richardson and J. Joyce highlighting its distinctive features].

2106 Overton, Grant. "As to the Novel," Bookman, LXII (Dec. 1925 452-454. [Brief remarks on the progress of the novel of the previous half century: the sacrifice of chronology, the removed narrative method, the decline of the mystery tale, the elimination of external action and the attempt to go deeper into and explain behaviour through the findings of psychoanalysis].

2107 _____. "On Morality and Deceny in Fiction," EJ, (Jan.

1929), 14-23. [Argues that too much time is wasted on arguments about "decency," i.e., current morality, where one should be looking at the "effect of the book on the spirit." References to J. Joyce, G. Moore, and D. H. Lawrence among others].

2108　Pacey, Desmond. "The Future of the Novel," QQ, LIV:1 (Spring 1947), 74-83. [Asserts that in spite of its present "decadent state," the postwar novel in England and America may be "on the threshold of another great forward movement" in the direction of increasing realism--psycholgical, spiritual or social. J. Joyce, V. Woolf, J. Conrad, and R. Warner among others].

2109　Packer, Edwin. "Hearts are Hardening," NSoc, (9 Jan. 1964), 27. [On the current state of the romantic novel].

2110　Palmer, John. "Antic Literature," NC, XCVIII:584 (Oct. 1925), 614-626. [Discusses and condemns A. Huxley's and J. Joyce's interest in "evil and ugliness" for their own sake, "unrelated to any aesthetic or ethical purpose," as one aspect of "the general fidelity to detail, irrespective of general consequences, which is the peculiar quality of modern work"].

2111　Palmer, V. "Distinguished Realities: What Modern Novelists are Seeking," Independent, CXIII (27 Sep. 1924), 197. [On the necessity of "poetry" as the "dynamic and integrating" quality to animate the novel, instead of the "old realism"].

2112　Paris, Bernard J. "Form, Theme, and Imitation in Realistic Fiction," Novel, I:2 (Winter 1968), 140-149. [A critical approach to the criticism of fiction, suggesting that equal emphasis be put on the study of formal and thematic values in fiction and on the central achievement of realistic fiction--"the imitation of social and psychological reality"].

2113　Parrinder, Patrick. "The Look of Sympathy: Communication and Moral Purpose in the Realistic Novel," Novel, V:2 (Winter 1972), 135-147. [Discusses the recurrent theme of the "extension of our sympathies" in the novel: aesthetically and morally as in G. Eliot, as "internal cultivation of the sensibility" as in H. James and V. Woolf, as concern for other fellow men as in G. Moore and A. Bennett, as "cataclysm" and "regeneration" in D. H. Lawrence, until the rejection of the notion of external moral responsibility for "modes of bizarrely limited consciousness" as in J. Joyce and S. Beckett].

2114　Pascal, Roy. "The Autobiographical Novel and the Autobiography," EIC, IX:2 (Apr. 1959), 134-150. [Maintains that the autobiographical novelist does not merely write of himself, but seeks "something general within himself." Both Sons and Lovers and A Portrait of the Artist are used for illustration].

2115   _____. "Tense and Novel," MLR, LVII (1962), 1-11.
        [On the use and meaning of the preterite as a medium of
        fictional narrative following Kate Hamburger's grammatical
        approach to stylistic appreciation in Die Logik der Dichtung.
        (Stuttgart, 1957). Brief references to H. James, L. Dur-
        rell, and J. Cary among others].

2116   "The Passing of Characters," LitR, III:45 (7 July 1923),
        809. [Editorial that compares and contrasts the Victorian
        novelist's concept and creation of character with the psy-
        chological novelists, and concludes that a fiction in which
        "characters yield to the inchoate moods from which character
        is hewn is indeed a shrunken art"].

2117   Paul, David. "Time and the Novelist," PR, XXI:6 (Nov.-Dec.
        1954), 636-649. [Discusses several novelists' solutions
        to the problem of time. E. M. Forster, J. Joyce, V. Woolf,
        and I. Compton-Burnett among others].

2118   Paul, Leslie. "The Angry Young Men Revisited," KR, XXVII:2
        (Spring 1965), 344-352. [Reconsiders the "angry wave" of
        the fifties which has now been pushed into the background,
        and whose writers have now moved themselves into the "ranks
        of the politico-literary establishment itself." K. Amis,
        J. Braine, J. Wain, C. Wilson, and J. Osborne].

2119   _____. "The Writer and the Human Condition," KR, XXIX:
        1 (Jan. 1967), 21-38. Revised and reprinted in Alternatives
        to Christian Belief: A Critical Survey of the Contemporary
        Search for Meaning. (New York: Doubleday, 1967), pp. 160-
        183. [On the judgment of modern writers, especially novel-
        ists, on the present age--"sick without seeming to know how
        to cure itself"--and their documentation of this affliction.
        References to G. Greene, D. H. Lawrence, and S. Beckett
        among others].

2120   Paull, H. M. "Personal Element in Fiction: A Question of
        Technique," NC, LXXX:478 (Dec. 1916), 1253-66. Reprinted
        in LA, 292 (27 Jan. 1917), 215-225. [Surveys the intrusion
        of the author in the English novel, and suggests that much
        would be gained if novelists do not "abuse" this "licence"
        as they have done in the past. Includes the views of A.
        Bennett and H. James on the matter, and refers to their
        practice as well as to H. G. Wells' and J. Conrad's].

2121   Peddie, J. R. "Modern Tendencies in Novel Writing," LA, 301
        (10 May 1919), 353-355. Reprinted from The Glasgow Herald.
        Also reprinted as "Novel as a Work of Art," Arts and Decor-
        ation, XVIII (Dec. 1922), 74-76. [Surmises that future nov-
        elists will look to H. James and J. Conrad for "inspiration,
        after surveying briefly the "modernized picaresque" of H.
        Walpole, H. G. Wells, and C. Mackenzie, and the sense of
        "order and form, restraint and discipline" in J. Galsworthy,
        J. D. Beresford, and F. Swinnerton].

2122 Pender, R. Herdman. "Die moderne englische Literatur: Ein Uberblick," DeutR, CCIII (May 1925), 168-176; (June 1925), 279-286. [A survey of all three genres. H. G. Wells, G. K. Chesterton, J. Galsworthy, G. Moore, J. Conrad, and J. Joyce among others].

2123 Penton, Brian. "Note on the Form of the Novel," LonA, VI (1929), 434-444. Reprinted in Scrutinies. Vol. 2. Collected by Edgell Rickwork. (London: Wishart, 1931), pp. 235-263. [Maintains that form in the novel is not an "external convention" to be taken up but a projection of self, an "outweaving of personal dynamism." J. Joyce, A. Huxley, J. Conrad, and D. H. Lawrence].

2124 "Perspectives on the Novel," Daedalus, XCII:1 (Spring 1963), 197-383. [Issue devoted to a symposium. Two separate but related enquiries: 1) "Significant Groupings and Trends in the Contemporary Novel," and 2) "Intention and Unconscious Creation in the Novel." See entries under A. Guerard, R. Kiely, D. Littlejohn, and A. Lyttle].

2125 Peschmann, Hermann. "The Nonconformists, Angry Young Men, Lucky Jims, and Outsiders," English, XIII:73 (1960), 12-16. [A brief examination of the work of the group commonly classed together as the "movement" of the Angry Young Men, emphasising the divergence between them in order to highlight the common quality they share: their attitude of nonconformity].

2126 Peterson, R. G. "The Genealogy of Sex in Modern Literature," Dialog, V (Winter 1966), 30-37. [Attributes the preponderance of sex in modern literature to its importance as a central aspect of life, its being the only remaining donné which can provide intelligible symbols and "images of great power," and also its being a "new gospel of fulfillment for the individual and the species." Emphasis on English and American fiction. Included are J. Joyce, A. Huxley, and D. H. Lawrence].

2127 Phelps, William Lyon. "Realism and Reality in Fiction," Century, LXXXV (Apr. 1913), 864-868. [On the distinction between them. Brief references to J. Conrad and A. Bennett].

2128 _____. "Advance of the English Novel," Bookman (New York), XLII (Oct. 1915), 128-134; XLIII (May 1916), 297-308; XLIII (June 1916), 404-413. [A series of nine monthly instalments that trace the rise of the English novel from Defoe onwards. No. 10 deals with leading American novelists. The first article deals with the state of the novel at the turn of the century, the eighth with J. Conrad, J. Galsworthy, J. M. Barrie, and M. Sinclair, and the ninth with the author's contemporaries: E. Phillpotts, G. Moore, H. G. Wells, and others].

2129 "Philosophy and Fiction," Nation (London), XXVI (29 Nov. 1919), 297-298. [Attributes the main weakness of modern fiction to the lack of a "vision" of, or attitude to, life, or a faith of some sort].

2130 Pick, John. "London Letter," Renascence, IX (1956), 3-25. [A survey of English Catholic writers. Pages 12-22 are devoted to the novels of G. Greene, E. Waugh, R. Warner, S. Kaye-Smith, and others].

2131 "The Pick of the Basket," TLS, 616 (30 Oct. 1913), 486. [Reviews the "eight most talked of novels of the Autumn season," by H. G. Wells, H. Ward, A. Arnold, J. Galsworthy, C. Mackenzie, W. B. Maxwell, C. E. Montague, and M. Hewlett].

2132 Pineda, Rafael. "Los 'jovenes furiosos' de Inglaterra contra la celebridad," Indice, 136 (Apr. 1960), 10. [An account of an interview with J. Wain in which the novelist discusses his views on other "Angry Young Men," especially C. Wilson].

2133 Pizer, Donald. "Wayne C. Booth's 'The Rhetoric of Fiction ': Five Years After," CE, XXVIII:6 (Mar. 1967), 471-475. [A review article that attempts to place W. C. Booth's book in its literary and cultural setting].

2134 _____. "A Primer of Fictional Aesthetics," CE, XXX:7 (Apr. 1969), 572-580. [A brief account of the growth of interest in the aesthetics of the novel from H. James onwards, and an examination of the major "schools" of fictional aesthetics operative in the mid-sixties].

2135 Plank, Robert. "The Geography of Utopia: Psychological Factors Shaping the Ideal Location," Extrapolation, VI (1965), 39-49. [On the method of displacement in space and in time in "Heterotopia" (the coalescence of science fiction and Utopia), and the fundamental features of a suitable utopic location. This is followed by a study of the "deeper emotional forces" that motivated the choice of More's Isle of Utopia. References to A. Huxley, G. Orwell, and W. Golding among others].

2136 "Plight of the Younger British Novelist," LDig, LXII (30 Aug. 1919), 32. [Quotes extensively from The Saturday Review (London) to emphasise the "unpleasant" prospects of the English novelist whose market is "undersold" to the young American].

2137 Plomer, William. "The Contemporary Novel: Its Subject Matter," LMer, (Oct. 1936), 504-510. [A brief survey of the subject matter of contemporary novelists ranging from stories about warfare to the use of the novel as a "moulder of manners and morals," regional interests, and the abdication of sex to crime. D. H. Lawrence, A. Huxley, W. Holtby, and G. Greene among others].

2138 Plumb, J. H. "Where are the Novels of Yesteryear?" Spectator, CCCXXII:3733 (10 Jan. 1969), 41. [Suggests that good fiction has lost its "position" and "authority" in England, and is on the way out, contrary to its situation and the possibilities open to it in U. S. A. Reply by Martin Seymour-Smith. (See below)].

2139 Podhoretz, Norma. "The New Nihilism and the Novel," PR, XXV:4 (Fall 1958), 576-590. [On the theme of the loss of values and submission to the meaningless which manifests itself partly, in England, in a revolt against specific conditions and the establishment in the postwar decade].

2140 "The Poet and the Novel: Towards a True Popular Art," TLS, 1924 (17 Dec. 1938), 800. [On the desirability of poets becoming novelists. Correspondence by G. Rostrevor Hamilton, 1925 (24 Dec. 1938), 815].

2141 Popkin, Henry. "Jewish Writers in England," Commentary, XXXI (Feb. 1961), 135-141. [Accounts for the comparative absence of Jewish writers until the early fifties, and surveys briefly present day Jewish dramatists and novelists. Included are B. Glanville, D. Jacobson, F. Raphael, and G. Charles].

2142 "Portents of Literature," LA, CCCXLIV (Aug. 1933), 509-518. [Speculations on what the future holds for England, France and Germany through a survey of postwar literature. Pages 512-516 deal with English writers, especially novelists. S. Maugham, D. H. Lawrence, C. Mackenzie, and A. Huxley among others].

2143 Porteous, Gwen. "The Novel and some of its Modern Aspects," FQ, (July 1947), 144-148. [Maintains that the attempt of the novelist to communicate the "feel" of life on the "various planes of experience" at which the individual lives, at one and the same time, accounts for the "new form" of the novel in the 20th century, insofar as character, plot, and narrator are concerned].

2144 Pratt, Annis. "Women and Nature in Modern Fiction," ConL, XIII (1972), 476-490. [Compares attitudes towards nature in the female and male "Bildungsroman" to determine whether "there is a 'myth of the heroine' as descriptive of the development of the human psyche as the 'myth of the hero' hitherto taken as definitive." J. Joyce, M. Sinclair, D. H. Lawrence, and D. Lessing among others].

2145 Praz, Mario. "La Parabola della Esplorazione interiore," Ulisse, X (1956-57), 978-986. [Regards the stream of consciousness novel or "romanzo introspettivo" as a "genre," traces the genealogy of the term, its treatment by critics, and surveys the tradition in fiction in general. H. James, J. Joyce, D. Richardson, J. Conrad, and V. Woolf among others].

2146 "Present Position of Fiction," LA, 264 (26 Mar. 1910), 814-817. Reprinted from The Athenaeum. [Notices the steady increase in the output of fiction, the impact of serialization, the unhealthy influence of cheap magazines on novel writing, and the "spread of penny literature." Ends up shrewdly questioning whether the novel is "preparing for Revolution"].

2147 Price, Martin. "The Novel: Artifice and Experience," YR, LI (Autumn 1961), 152-158. [Surveys three categories of the English novel over the past fifty years, and identifies a movement away from "the vision of man as defined or deformed by his social conditions," and the deliberate return, after World War II, to the realism of "character in its social conditions," as well as the "intransigent, often angry, often amused exploration of feeling." H. James, V. Woolf, J. Conrad, J. Joyce, D. H. Lawrence, C. P. Snow, and J. Cary among others].

2148 _____. "Reason and Its Alternatives: Some Recent Fiction," YR, LVIII (Spring 1969), 464-474. [Reviews novels by C. P. Snow, I. Murdoch, and M. Spark among others].

2149 Price, R. G. G. "Next Step Forward Is Back," AtM, CCXVI (July 1965), 127-128. [A note predicting a change in the direction of modern writing to "the simple, the comfortable, the middle-brow," anything that is not avant-garde].

2150 Priestley, John Boynton. "Modern English Novelists," EJ, XIV (Jan. 1925), 13-21; (Feb. 1925), 89-97; (Apr. 1925), 261-268; (May 1925), 347-355. [A series of four articles, one on each of J. Conrad, H. G. Wells, A. Bennett, and J. Galsworthy].

2151 _____. "The Younger Novelists," EJ, XIV (June 1925), 435-443. [A sequel to "Modern English Novelists." Considers C. Mackenzie, O. Onions, J. D. Beresford, F. Swinnerton, G. Cannan, and H. Walpole as writers young in years and "literary reputations," who have not "fulfilled their early promise" as writers, and that much may be expected from D. H. Lawrence with his "curious sensitiveness," and the combination of this "sensitiveness and sanity" in E. M. Forster].

2152 _____. "In Defence of Kindness," SatR, CXLII (25 Dec. 1926), 802-803. [On the contemptuous attitude of contemporary novelists towards kindness, and their delight in violence, ruthlessness, and egoism].

2153 _____. "Escape and Pursuit: Being a Note on the Novel," ForumN, LXXX (Dec. 1928), 913-919. [Discusses two apparently opposed impulses that take one to fiction: the desire to escape from life, and the desire to pursue or "grapple with life"].

2154 _____. "Some Reflections of a Popular Novelist," E&S, XVIII (1932), 149-159. [A mild attack on "high-brow" novelists rejecting the snobbish sneering attitudes towards "popular novelists"].

2155 _____. "Thoughts in the Wilderness: The Newest Novels," NSta, XLVII (26 June 1954), 824-826. Reprinted in Thoughts in the Wilderness. (London: Heinemann; New York: Harper, 1957), pp. 54-59. [On the "New English Novel" emerging, with its "unreal" world, its "deliberately unheroic" central character, lonely and isolated, and the attitude of uninterestedness in contemporary society it reveals. Discussion (3-24 July 1954), 16, 44, 76, 103].

2156 _____. "Fact or Fiction?" NSta, LXXIII (6 Jan. 1967), 9. [Objects to the "dehumanizing process" of concentrating on facts and ignoring the "essential humanity" of people that is adopted by writers and encouraged by editors].

2157 Prince, Gerald. "Notes Towards a Categorization of Fictional 'narratees'," Genre IV (1971), 100-106. [An investigation of the various manifestations of "narratees"--the "receivers of the narrators' message"--and their functions, in an attempt to determine their usefulness as critical tools in the "general problem of narrative strategy"].

2158 Pritchett, V. S. "Politics and the English Novel," FR, CXLIII (June 1938), 680-685. [Discusses the "new political impulse" and the achievements and prospects of an English political novel, especially since there is little or no political tradition in the English novel].

2159 _____. "The Future of Fiction," NW&D, VIII:7 (1946), 75-79. Reprinted as "The Future of English Fiction," PR, XV (Oct. 1948), 1063-1070; also in The New Partisan Reader, 1945-1953. Edited by William Phillips and Philip Rahv. (New York: Harcourt, Brace, 1953), pp. 249-257. [The second article in a series of six dealing with the topic, by R. Macaulay, A. Koestler, L. P. Hartley, W. Allen, and O. Sitwell. Examines the contemporary scene to reveal the major problem of the modern novelist: he has a "glut of new means, new manners, new styles; he has been poor in material or passive in his use of it," and concludes that the world can no longer be satisfied with the picaresque novel, and the "craving for . . . moral figures [and] . . . moralities, will impose itself . . . upon the novelist"].

2160 _____. "Prospects for the English Novel," NYTBR, (17

Apr. 1949), 1, 21-22. [Examines the impact of World War II and Revolution on novelists, also the current state of novel writing and predicts a revival of the great English tradition. G. Orwell, R. Warner, R. Lehmann, H. Green, G. Greene, and P. H. Newby].

2161 _____. "A Literary Letter from the British Capital," NYTBR, (7 Jan. 1951), 14. [Maintains that the novel written in naturalistic dialogue is far from finished. H. Green and I. Compton-Burnett].

2162 _____. "A Literary Letter from England," NYTBR, (5 Aug. 1951), 4. [Calls for less "'seriousness' in the tough, stark sense of the word--more comedy and more seriousness in ideas" if the condition of the English novel is to be improved].

2163 _____. "An English Letter on Books and Their Authors," NYTBR, (13 Sep. 1953), 18. [Surveys briefly experiment in the English novel and its value, and predicts a boom in war books].

2164 _____. "The Comic Element in the English Novel: 5. The Last Forty Years," Listener, LI:1320 (17 June 1954), 1047-49, 1053. [The 5th in a series (Nos, 1316-1319, 20 May - 10 June 1954) in which he asserts that the comic sensibility lies at the centre of English literature. Notices the emphasis on the "exorbitant," the reliance on unusual vividness in the serious comic realism of J. Joyce, W. Lewis' satirical imitation, R. Firbank's "clichés and catch phrases," E. Waugh's satirical presentation of comic situation in dialogue, H. Green's Congrevian "artificial comedy," I. Compton-Burnett's social irony, J. Cary's Fielding-like comedy arising from the true observation of nature, and A. Powell's "slow-moving" comedy, heavily underlined with comments].

2165 _____. "A Literary Letter from London," NYTBR, (2 Oct. 1955), 10. [Remarks on the contemporary English novel dealing with "high life," and the split between objective and subjective writing. E. Waugh, R. Lehmann, E. Bowen, J. C. Powys, K. Amis, and others].

2166 _____. "These Writers Couldn't Care Less," NYTBR, (28 Apr. 1957), 1, 38-39. [Asserts that self-interested and "uncommitted to the world outside themselves," the "Angry Young Men"--K. Amis, J. Wain, "T. Hinde," P. Towry, and J. Braine--are nevertheless committed to an England "ugly," "sour," "resentful" and "commonplace," and write about it in a "debunking style" free from all associations of bourgeois romance].

2167 _____. "London Literary Letter: A Report on Writers and Writing," NYTBR, (16 Nov. 1958), 56. [Contends that the "new note" in the fifties is the "impulse toward social realism"].

2168 _____. "In Writing Nothing Fails Like Success," NYTBR, (22 Jan. 1961), 1, 38. Reprinted in Opinions and Perspectives from 'The New York Times Book Review'. Edited by Francis Brown. (Boston: Houghton Mifflin, 1964), pp. 216-222. [Discusses C. Connolly's statement that literary success liberates the writer from a hostile environment, and so paves the way to failure, in the light of the experiences of English novelists in the 19th and 20th centuries].

2169 _____. "Saints and Rogues: Talk in the English Novel," Listener, LXVIII (6 Dec. 1962), 957-959. [On the re-emergence of a Puritanic rogue-like picaroon and the revival of the picaresque novel with everyday talk].

2170 "A Problem of Story-Telling," TLS, 2166 (7 Aug. 1943), 375. [Meander's Mirror. Maintains the novelist must conceive his form as imaginative composition, no matter how social or contemporary its subject, i.e., without making it mere reportage].

2171 "Procession of the Novelists: From Dickens to Virginia Woolf," TLS, 1839 (1 May 1937), 322-323. [Reviews, on the occasion of the centenary of Queen Victoria's accession, English novelists of 1837, 1851, 1879, 1897, 1914, and 1937].

2172 Prothero, J. K. "New Novels and Old Plays," LA, 277 (7 June 1913), 636-638. Reprinted from The New Witness. [Indicates briefly that the decline of the novel is due to the "new form" that seeks "to segregate a section of society, label it and draw up its psychology with a mass of morbid detail," and is interested in the "analysis of temperament" rather than romance or adventure].

2173 Pryce-Jones, Alan. "Books in General," NSta, XXXIV (12 July 1947), 33. [Outlines three stages in the evolution of, and attitude to women in the "sophisticated bestseller" of the 20th century through H. de la Pasture's The Lonely Lady of Grosvenor Square, "M. Arlen's" The Green Hat, and E. Waugh's Brideshead Revisited].

2174 _____. "The Novelist in a World Awry," NYTBR, (10 Dec. 1950), 1, 22. Reprinted in Highlights of Modern Literature: A Permanent Collection of Memorable Essays from 'The New York Times Book Review'. Edited by Francis Brown. (New York: The American Library, 1954), pp. 49-53. [Asserts that most writing presently reflects the tone of "slightly soured middle age," for novelists are especially affected by the disappearance of a subject to write about; also an ever-changing world makes it virtually impossible to "focus" in fiction on subjects which "split and come to-

gether and dart away like mercury." The alternatives left
are "silence and sermonizing"].

2175 _____. "The Frightening Pundits of Bloomsbury," Listener, XLV:1148 (1 Mar. 1951), 345-346. [Personal reminiscences and impressions of the creative spirit of the Bloomsbury group in the twenties. Brief references to E. Waugh,
A. Huxley, V. Woolf, and D. H. Lawrence].

2176 _____. "Plagued by the Nature of Truth," NYTBR, (8
July 1951), 1, 18. Reprinted in Highlights of Modern Literature: A Permanent Collection of Memorable Essays from
'The New York Time Book Review'. Edited by Francis Brown.
(New York: The New American Library, 1954), pp. 72-76.
[Maintains that "logically" the novel ought to be dead, but
novelists defy all logic for they write not because they
have a tale to tell but because they are "plagued by the
elusive nature of truth." This is why novels will be written as long as people wish to explore the truth about them-
selves].

2177 _____. "The Cult of Evil," Listener, XLIX:1259 (16
Apr. 1953), 638-639. [On the importance attached to evil
in modern literature, especially the novel].

2178 _____. "The Novelists' Fault," Observer, (12 Sep.
1954), 8. [Responds to H. Nicolson's provocative statement that the novel is dead (see above) and P. Toynbee's
rebuttal (see below). Asserts that what really matters in
novel writing is the "overmastering need to convey an impression," a quality shared by great novelists, and that
the weakness of the modern English novel is in being "much
too unambitious" and unassertive].

2179 _____. "Speaking of Books: The Beautiful People,"
NYTBR, (27 Nov. 1966), 2. [Regards the writer as a "loner"
who may find it harmful to have access to "in-groups."
Brief reference to V. Woolf, J. Joyce, and S. Maugham].

2180 "The Public School in Fiction," Spectator, CXIX (10 Nov.
1917), 516-517. ["A Mere Schoolmaster" defends the Public
School against its misrepresentation in novels by H. Walpole and E. Waugh].

2181 "The Quality of Current Fiction," LA, 278 (16 Aug. 1913),
443-446. Reprinted from The Nation. [A survey of Edwardian novelists, noting their ineffectiveness in analysing
"movements" or "fertilizing the public mind by the ven-
tilation of new ideas," for each novelist is merely painting an aspect of his small field of vision in keeping with
the realistic novel].

2182 "The Question of Sex in Fiction," LA, 289 (20 May 1916),
475-479. Reprinted from The Athanaeum, 4601 (Jan. 1916),

11-12. [Suggests that sexual realism need not be an end in itself, that not everything should be described. Gives two reasons--perhaps odd today--why English novelists should be wary of treating the sexual aspect with absolute freedom: 1) English, unlike French, tends to be crude and blunt, 2) few English novelists have "proper working knowledge of their trade." The article responds to controversy over the publication of D. H. Lawrence's The Rainbow].

2183 Quinton, Anthony. "A Refusal to Look," Listener, LII:1325 (22 July 1954), 138-139. [Rejects the "retrospectiveness," the preoccupation with the past, the "repudiation of ties," and the unrealism about persons and about moral issues that characterise much of the fiction of novelists with established reputations in postwar England. L. P. Hartley, "T. Hinde," E. Waugh, R. Lehmann, K. Amis, J. Wain, H. Charteris and others].

2184 _____. "The Post-Freudian Hero," LM, IV (July 1957), 56-61. [Discusses the "ordinariness . . . adjustment" and "politics" of self-interest of the hero of the fifties in a review article on F. King's The Widow, J. Braine's Room at the Top, R. Longrigg's Switchboard and E. Glyn's The Ram in the Thicket].

2185 _____. "The New Novelists: An Enquiry," LM, V:11 (Nov. 1958), 13-31. [Maintains that postwar novels can "survive" comparison with the twenties, but a reconsideration points out: 1) no great novelists, 2) techniques of current fiction are "resolutely traditional," 3) novelists who began to write in the thirties are silent, 4) the "typical" novels of our time are realistic, and 5) the most impressive novelists writing are late developers].

2186 _____. "Masculine, Feminine and Neuter, or Three Kinds of Contemporary Novel," LM, VII (Apr. 1960), 63-67. [A review article on five novels by M. West, E. J. Howard, J. Braine, W. Camp, and A. Sinclair suggesting a new scheme of classification for the contemporary output of fiction].

2187 Raban, Jonathan. "Criction," LM, X (May 1970), 89-94. [Discusses B. Bergonzi's The Situation in the Novel as a work of "criction,"--criticism as a "fiction-making activity"--which he considers as the major genre in the 20th century].

2188 Rahv, Philip. "The Myth and the Powerhouse," PR, XX:6 (Nov.-Dec. 1953), 635-648. Reprinted in The Myth and the Powerhouse. (New York: Farrar, Straus and Giroux, 1965), pp. 3-21. [On the new craze for myth and "mythic time"--the eternal past of ritual--in the novel].

2189 _____. "Fiction and the Criticism of Fiction," KR, XVIII (Spring 1956), 276-299. Reprinted in The Myth and the Powerhouse. (New York: Farrar, Straus and Giroux,

303

1965), pp. 33-61. The Novel: Modern Essays in Criticism.
Edited by R. M. Davis. (Englewood Cliffs, N. J.: Prentice-Hall, 1969), pp. 104-126, Literature and the Sixth
Sense. (Boston: Houghton, Mifflin, 1969; London: Faber
and Faber, 1970), pp. 222-243, and Critical Approaches to
Fiction. Edited by Shiv K. Kumar and Keith F. McKean.
(New York: McGraw Hill, 1968), pp. 285-305. [Rejects the
recent "infection of the prose sense by poetics" manifested in 1) the search for allegories, symbols and "mythic
patterns in the novel," 2) "identifying style as the 'essential activity' of imaginative prose," and 3) reducing
"the complex structure and contents of the novel to the
sum of technique"].

2190 Rajan, Balchandra. "Bloomsbury and the Academics: The
Literary Situation in England," HudR, II:3 (Autumn 1949),
451-457. [Contends that the dissociation of the universities from contemporary writing has led to the decline of
criticism and literature].

2191 Raleigh, John Henry. "The English Novel and Three Kinds
of Time," SR, LXII (July-Sep. 1954), 428-440. Reprinted
in Time, Place, and Idea: Essays on the Novel. Preface
by Harry T. Moore. (Carbondale and Edwardsville: Sou-
thern Illinois University Press; London and Amsterdam:
Feffer and Simons, 1968), pp. 43-55, The Novel: Modern
Essays in Criticism. Edited by R. M. Davis. (Englewood
Cliffs, N. J.: Prentice-Hall, 1969), pp. 242-253, and
Perspectives in Contemporary Criticism: A Collection of
Recent Essays by American, English, and European Critics.
Edited by Sheldon Norman Grebstein. (New York & London:
Harper & Row, 1968), pp. 42-50. [Traces the change from
"man-social history to ego-universal history in terms of
the differing conceptions and differing metaphors for the
idea of time-history," showing the breakdown of "historical" time with Hardy and James, and the emergence of "cosmic" and "existential" time as the legitimate province of
the novelist in the 20th century].

2192 _____. "Victorian Morals and the Modern Novel," PR,
XXV:2 (Spring 1958), 241-264. Reprinted in Time, Place,
and Idea: Essays on the Novel. Preface by Harry T. Moore.
(Carbondale and Edwardsville: Southern Illinois University
Press; London and Amsterdam: Feffer and Simons, 1968), pp.
137-163. [On the "anarchist-instinctual rebellion against
codes and restrictions and rationality and rules" in the
"Butler-Forster-Lawrence line," antithetical in every re-
spect to the Joycean tradition].

2193 Ramsey, Roger. "The Available and the Unavailable 'I':
Conrad and James," ELT, XIV:2 (1971), 137-145. [Indicates
the similarity of intent between The Turn of the Screw and
Heart of Darkness, the form of each and the differences be-

tween them, and wonders if Conrad "didn't learn his Marlow lesson from the master"].

2194 Randell, Wilfrid L. "Love Scenes in Fiction," LA, 283 (17 Oct. 1914), 162-170. Reprinted from The British Review. [Examines love scenes of "admitted masters"--Carlyle, C. Bronte, C. Dickens, A. Trollope, T. Hardy, H. G. Wells and H. James--to show that the "definite, effective presentation of love" depends on the novelist's absolute sincerity, and his belief in his characters as living human beings].

2195 _____. "Conversation and the Novelist," ForumN, LIII (May 1915), 635-646. [The "exquisite possibilities" in the art of conversation as exploited by classical novelists are contrasted with the "awkward manner" with which such weapons are wielded by H. James and H. G. Wells among the moderns].

2196 Ransom, John Crowe. "The Content of the Novel: Notes Toward a Critique of Fiction," AmR, VII (June 1936), 301-318. [A discussion of seven different practices respecting the content of the novel, which have won acceptance, or are commonly employed but still controversial, in spite of "the restrictions of an Aristotelian aesthetic"].

2197 _____. "Fiction Harvest," SoR, II (Autumn 1936), 399-418. [Reviews of eleven novels among which are A. Browne's Daughter of Albion, A. Huxley's Eyeless in Gaza, C. Morgan's Sparkenbroke, L. H. Myer's Strange Glory, and "R. West's" The Thinking Reed].

2198 Ratcliffe, S. K. "English Intellectuals in War-Time," Century, XCIV (Oct. 1917), 826-833. Condensed in LDig, LV (6 Oct. 1917), 28-29. [Remarks on the attitude of J. Galsworthy, H. Belloc, G. K. Chesterton, and H. G. Wells on the war and the paucity of literary productions in wartime].

2199 Raven, Simon. "Reflections of a Middle-Aged Novelist," Spectator, CCXXII:7335 (24 Jan. 1969), 104. [Maintains that success in novels depends on the portrayal of "competition, effort and achievement," and of "physical, emotional, mental or moral dispute," i.e., the "perception, and the celebration, of human inequalities" whose greatest enemy is current "egalitarian dogma"].

2200 "Reason in Fiction," Nation, CXVII:3042 (24 Oct. 1923), 453-454. [Denies the "authenticity" of the "new fiction" of D. Richardson, V. Woolf and J. Joyce, and especially that "its complete neglect of the human mind brings us nearer to the inner truth of life"].

2201 "Recent Reflections of a Novel-Reader," AtM, CXI:5 (May 1913), 688-700; CXII:5 (Nov. 1913), 688-701; CXIII:4 (Apr. 1914), 490-500; CXIV:4 (Oct. 1914), 530-532; CXV:4 (Apr.

1915), 501-511; CXVI:4 (Oct. 1915), 499-511; CXVII:5 (May 1916), 623-642. [Review articles, each covering thirty or so novels, English and American].

2202 "Recurrent Themes," TLS, 2791 (26 Aug. 1955), 493. [A leading article discussing contemporary novelists' "rigidity" and "narrowness" in relying on "symbolic pattern[s]" in themes like the "Hunt" rather than the "Quest," and like "the Good Old Days"].

2203 Reilly, R. J. "God, Man, and Literature," Thought, XLII (Winter 1967), 561-583. [A new classification of writers into five groups in a descending order, according to the intensity and the degree with which a writer perceives the God-man relationship. Brief references to D. H. Lawrence, G. Greene, and J. Joyce among others].

2204 Reiss, Hans S. "Stil und Struktur in modernen europäischen experimentellen Roman," Akzente, V (1958), 202-213. Originally a lecture delivered at the Seventh Congress of the International Federation of Modern Languages and Literatures, August 1957 in Heidelberg, in English, and reprinted in Stil-und Formprobleme in der Literatur. Edited by Paul Bockmann. (Heidelberg: Carl Winter, Universitätsverlag, 1959), pp. 419-424. [A general discussion of style, structure, and the need for experiment in these areas in the European novel, including England].

2205 "Relation of the Novel to the Present Social Unrest," Bookman (New York), XL (Nov. 1914), 276-303. [Six critics consider Anti-militarism, the Passing of Capitalism, the Feminist Movement, the Aesthetic and Moral Renaissance, Social Disaffection, and the Religious Revolt as portrayed in English and American fiction. H. G. Wells, H. Walpole, C. Mackenzie, J. Galsworthy, F. Harris, "R. Tressel," and A. Morrison among others].

2206 "Remarks on the Novel," Symposium, I (Jan. 1930), 82-114. [Three articles written independently, and grouped together by the editors. See F. C. Flint, "Fiction and Form," and D. Garnett, "Some Tendencies of the Novel"].

2207 Rey, W. H. "The Destiny of Man in the Utopian Novel," Symposium, VI (May 1952), 140-156. [Attempts to show how a new perspective based on the religious view of man as "the image of God and bearer of His promises" creeps into Utopia, and creates a new confidence in mankind stronger than the doubts and fears of our time. Analyses two 1949 novels, G. Orwell's 1984 and E. Juenger's Heliopolis, Rücklick auf eine Stadt with references to A. Huxley's Ape and Essence, (1948)].

2208 Reynolds, J. D. "Some Fiction of 1937," LAssoc, XXXI (Feb. 1938), 40-46. [A general review of the year's output].

2209 Rhode, Eric. "The Artist as Seducer," Listener, LXIX:1779
(2 May 1963), 751, 754. [Argues that the artist should
"seduce" us to a "total fusion" with his work so that we
may derive the "true pleasure of art" which is preliminary
to critical effort. L. Durrell, I. Murdoch, and A. Wilson,
among others].

2210 Richards, Alun. "Place and the Writer," Listener, LXX:1790
(18 July 1963), 89-90. [Emphasises that parochialism, not
regionalism or provincialism, is inimical to the writer].

2211 Richards, D. J. "Four Utopias," SEER, XL (1961), 220-228.
[On the ideological connection between Dostoyevsky's "leg-
end of the Grand Inquisitor," Zamyatin's 'We,' A. Huxley's
Brave New World, and G. Orwell's 1984].

2212 Richards, I. A. "Nineteen Hundred and Now," AtM, CXL:3
(Sep. 1927), 311-317. [On the "contemporary consciousness"
of the first quarter of the century towards the subordination
of thought to feeling away from "hard thinking" as a guide
to life (H. G. Wells), and feelings "too slight and too
shifting" to dictate any consistent view of life, to the
extreme state where feelings are so deep and so powerful
that reason is enslaved to their service (D. H. Lawrence)].

2213 Richardson, Dorothy. "Novels," L&L, LVI (Mar. 1948), 188-
192. [Asserts that the novel is not to be slighted, for
it remains a "tour of the mind of the author" engaged in a
"collaboration whose outcome is immeasurable," and which,
in all its "branching diversities" today, is to be found
in detective fiction].

2214 Riche, James. "Propaganda for Population Control in Bourgeois Novels," L&I, IV (1969), 41-52. [A "leftist" denun-
ciation of "Malthusian assumptions" as providing a popular
outlook in U. S. fiction. References to G. Orwell, A.
Huxley, and A. Burgess].

2215 Rickert, Edith. "Some Straws in Contemporary Literature:
Fiction in England and America," EJ, XII:8 (Oct. 1923),
509-516. [Shows how deliberately D. Richardson and J.
Joyce tore down previous theories of the novel in order to
emphasise "the moving, shifting, growing stream of consciousness" of the single mind, and their influence on the "revolutionary" trend of D. H. Lawrence and other innovators
like C. Dane. Also examines experimentation in the short
story].

2216 Rickword, C. H. "A Note on Fiction," CML, III (1926-27),
226-233. Reprinted in Towards Standards of Criticism.
Edited by F. R. Leavis (London: Wishart, 1933), pp. 29-43,
and Forms of Modern Fiction. Edited by W. Van O'Connor.
(Minneapolis: University of Minnesota Press, 1948), 294-

305. [On "the status of plot and its relation to the other elements of a novel, particularly its relation to character, in solution." References to H. James and J. Joyce].

2217 Rillie, John A. M. "The Sweet Smell of Failure," TC, CLXXII (Spring 1964), 85-99. [On "the changing status of success as reflected in modern literature." E. M. Forster, J. Conrad, J. Joyce, G. Orwell, G. Greene, J. Braine, and C. P. Snow among others].

2218 Ritchie, Lily Munsell (Mary Briarly). "Pathological Realism," LQR, (Apr. 1926), 145-152. [Deplores the obsession of the "ultra" school of writers with abnormality, especially in sex, as realism or verisimilitude to fundamental human experience].

2219 Robbe-Grillet, Alain. "A Fresh Start for Fiction," EvR, I:3 (1957), 97-104. [Contends that radical changes are imperative in the novel, for it is presently in a "state of stagnation"].

2220 _____. "Reflections on Some Aspects of the Traditional Novel," IntLA, I (1958), 114-121. Translated by David Moore. [Discusses the use of such keywords in literary criticism as "character," "story," "form and content," and concludes that they represent a "dead concept" of the novel].

2221 _____. "Old 'Values' and the New Novel. (Nature, Humanism, Tragedy)," LM, VI:2 (Feb. 1959), 32-49. [Denounces the "exclusive description of surfaces as a gratuitous mutilation of the novelist's art," because objects in fiction should have no symbolic function and should not affect humanistic concerns; hence, minimal attention, he argues, should be given to description. Correspondence by Keith Butler, VI:4 (Apr. 1959), 71-72; Jiri Mucha, VI:5 (May 1959), 56-57].

2222 _____. "From Realism to Reality," EvR, X (1966), 50-53, 83. [A reprint of the last chapter of Pour un Nouveau Roman. (Paris: Les Editions de Minuit, 1963). Translated by Richard Howard as For a New Novel. (New York: Grove Press, 1965). [Contends that by faking a description of the visible things in the present world--in itself "entirely futile"--the novelist evokes "the 'reality' hidden behind," i.e., the real world].

2223 Roberts, K. "For Authors Only: Americans in English Novels," SatEP, CCV (24 Sep. 1932), 14-15, 46, 48, 50. [On the unconvincing delineation of American characters in English fiction, resulting from British novelists' erroneous impressions of Americans. Brief references to J. Galsworthy, J. B. Priestley, and A. P. Herbert].

2224 Roditi, Edouard. "Trick Perspectives," VQR, XX (Oct. 1944), 541-554. [Reminiscences of the author's meetings with M. Proust, J. Conrad, H. James, and G. Moore].

2225 Rodway, Allen. "'Life, Time and the "Art" of Fiction'," BJA, VII:4 (1967), 374-384. Reprinted in The Truths of Fiction. (London: Chatto and Windus; Toronto: Clarke, Irwin, 1970), pp. 160-172. [On the problem of manipulating in fiction the simultaneous interaction of two worlds, the fictional and the real, psychological time and serial time, and the value of "alienation techniques" to give "aesthetic detachment" without sacrificing "vital participation" on the part of the reader or audience].

2226 Rogers, Winfield H. "Form in the Art-Novel," Helicon, II (1939), 1-7. [Suggests an approach to the novel which links "form to the impulse from which it arises," i.e., an attempt to give some synthesis to the individual's "inchoate reality," to establish criteria for the art-novel, by which it may be differentiated from the "pastime-novel"].

2227 Roland, Albert. "A Rebirth of Values in Contemporary Fiction," WHR, VI (Winter 1952), 59-69. [Asserts that the reaffirmation of spiritual values in the novels of the forties is evidenced by the adoption of Catholic standards as in G. Greene and E. Waugh, or by the belief in the ability of man, "by reason and will power to lift himself above animal life and achieve communion with the divine," as in A. Huxley, or by the "realisation of the brotherhood of man"].

2228 Rosenthal, T. G. "The Death of Fiction," NSta, LXXV (22 Mar. 1968), 389. [Regards fiction as the "poor relation" in the publishing world not because there are no great novels published, but because fiction is not "fashionable," and reviewing policies that lump together several novels in one review belittle its importance].

2229 Rourke, Constance Mayfield. "The Genius of the Novel," NRep, XXIX (4 Jan. 1922), 149-151. [Brings out the essential features of the "modern" English novel--its "persistent curiosity and explanatory energy" and the thoroughness with which it "seizes upon situations in moments of flux," --by comparing it to drama].

2230 Routh, H. V. "How the Twentieth Century is 'Returning to Nature'," English, V:28 (1945), 110-114. Reprinted as part of Ch. II in Money, Morals and Manners as Revealed in Modern Literature. (London: Ivor Nicholson and Watson, 1935). [Shows how the "tendency" towards a return to Nature is manifested by the vers-librists and the "revolution" in the art of storytelling in the 20th century. S. Maugham, D. H. Lawrence, and J. Joyce].

2231 _____. "The Quest for Currents in Contemporary English Literature," CE, VIII:4 (Jan. 1947), 169-178, and VIII:5 (Feb. 1947), 240-245. Also in EJ, (June 1947), 277-288. [Examines the "essential" problem of contemporary literature--how to "externalize man's permanence in change" --in the writers of the first two decades of the century. Pages 169-172 deal with the novel. Part II deals with writers between 1920 and 1935].

2232 Rovit, Earl H. "The Ambiguous Modern Novel," YR, XLIX (Mar. 1960), 413-424. [On the growing resemblance of modern fiction to poetry as a result of the application of the "reflexive principle" in reading fiction, and the impact of the dislocation of values which led to 1) the shifting narrative viewpoint, 2) the "tonnage of consciousness" the narrator must bear, 3) the new concept of Time, and 4) the decline of the novel as a vehicle of social criticism. J. Joyce, H. James, and K. Amis among others].

2233 Rudd, John. "Poisoning of Youth," EngRev, XLII (Feb. 1926), 216-221. [Protests the lack of novels morally suitable for high school boys in the post-World War I period].

2234 Russen, Ellen. "Stroomingen in de moderne Engelsche Letterkunde," DWB, XXXII (1932), 3-19. [Examines the new tendencies in views and values that resulted from the break with Victorian ideals and values in the novels of the first two decades. J. Conrad, H. G. Wells, A. Bennett, D. H. Lawrence, J. Joyce, A. Huxley, J. Galsworthy, C. Mackenzie, G. K. Chesterton, and others].

2235 "Russian Novelists and English," Nation, C:2591 (25 Feb. 1915), 214. [A brief sketch of the influence of Russian novelists on the ideals and methods of the "newest British schools." C. Mackenzie, W. B. Maxwell, J. D. Beresford, and G. Cannan].

2236 Ruthven, K. K. "The Savage God: Conrad and Lawrence," CritQ, X:2 (1968), 39-55. [Argues that Heart of Darkness and Women in Love illustrate the "savage primitivism," whose enemy is civilization as indicated by Frazer and Freud; hence, they will endure "as authentic records of the savagery of the modern imagination"].

2237 Ryan, A. "The Novel of Today," NC, XCV:568 (June 1924), 843-851. [Contends that novelists are "out of joint" with the times, more interested in novels than the world, and have failed to capture the cultivated reading public, for their novels are "featureless," and difficult to read, even though the novelists are great masters of prose and competent observers].

2238 Saal, Hubert. "There Will Always Be An English Novel," SatR, XLIII (27 Feb. 1960), 22-23. [Reviews five new novels, including one by each of K. Waterhouse and J. Bowen].

2239   Sacks, Sheldon. "Golden Birds and Dying Generation," CLS,
       VI (Sep. 1969), 274-291. [Notes that the tendency of nov-
       elists in the Western World to include in fiction "idio-
       syncratic social, ethical and psychological experiences"
       led to new forms, away from "represented actions" of the
       Fielding and J. Austen kind, to "fantasies . . . designed
       to alter our attitudes and to make us experience new truths
       about the external world." J. Joyce and W. Golding among
       others].

2240   Sackville-West, V. "The Future of the Novel," Bookman (New
       York), LXXII (Dec. 1930), 350-351. [A note on the "cleav-
       age" that may come in fiction between those who want to
       emancipate it "from its factual bondage" and lift it to
       the plane of poetry, and those who confine it to "the de-
       lineation of life as we know it." V. Woolf and J. Gals-
       worthy].

2241   Said, Edward W. "Narrative: Quest for Origins and Dis-
       covery of the Mausoleum," Salmagundi, XII (1970), 63-75.
       [Attempts to depict the "impressive force of narrative as
       it went about the business of its own life from birth to
       end," by discussing classical works of narrative art using
       Hardy's Jude the Obscure as a point of departure from
       "linear narrative." References to J. Conrad and D. H.
       Lawrence among others].

2242   Saintsbury, George. "Technique," Dial, LXXX (Apr. 1926),
       273-278. [Minimises the character and value of technique
       in literature, and prose fiction in particular, because
       not "one of the very great novels of the world . . . sub-
       jects itself to technique"].

2243   Sapir, Edward. "Realism in Prose Fiction," Dial, LXIII
       (22 Nov. 1917), 503-506. [Argues that " . . . the test of
       a truly realistic technique is the relative ease with
       which the reader. . . can be made to live through the exper-
       iences, thoughts, feelings of the characters," and that is
       best done by not attempting "to individualise all the char-
       acters with equal care." Brief reference to J. Conrad and
       A. Bennett].

2244   Sarbu, Aladar. "Szocialista realista torekvesek az angol
       prózaban az októbere forradalom után," MTA, XXV (1968),
       35-38. [In Hungarian. Analyses the socialist realistic
       tendency in English prose fiction after the October revolu-
       tion. "R. Tressell," E. Upward, N. Mitchison, and "L. G.
       Gibbon"].

2245   Sarraute, Nathalie. "Limits of Control--V. Rebels in a
       World of Platitudes," TLS, 3041 (10 June 1960), 371. Re-
       printed in The Writer's Dilemma: Essays. First Published

in T. L. S. Under the Heading: 'Limits of Control'. Edited by Stephen Spender. (London: Oxford University Press, 1961), pp. 35-42. [Discusses, in general terms, the forces against which the writer, essentially a rebel, has to contend].

2246 Sawyer, Ethel R. "Inspiration in War Literature," PubL, (Mar. 1918), 105-112. [Paper read in Portland, Oregon, Sep. 1917). A brief survey of some 32 books--personal narratives, special correspondents' stories, fiction, etc.-- inspired by the war. D. Hankey, "I. Hay," J. Masefield, H. Walpole, and H. G. Wells among others].

2247 Scheer-Schazier, Brigitte. "Medusa in Arcady: Zum Begriff des Idyllischen im modernen englischen Roman," GRM, 21 (1971), 443-453. [On the concept of the "idyllic" in novels by S. Butler, E. M. Forster, and C. Isherwood among others].

2248 Schneider, Daniel J. "Techniques of Cognition in Modern Fiction," JAAC, XXVI:3 (Spring 1968), 317-328. [Reviews some arguments for and against the proposition that literature gives knowledge to reality, and considers briefly the various techniques of fiction over those of the previous century, as different attempts to get at "the integrity of stubborn facts" and actual experience. Examines a novel by each of D. H. Lawrence and J. Joyce].

2249 Scholes, Robert. "Toward a Poetics of Fiction: 4. An Approach Through Genre," Novel, II:2 (Winter 1969), 101-111. [Argues for a generic approach to the teaching and study of fiction to guard against the errors of general "evaluative principles" and "monistic evaluation"].

2250 Schorer, Mark. "The Chronicle of Doubt," VQR, XVIII (Spring 1942), 200-214. [Describes general characteristics of modern British fiction between the two wars to show the impact that the violent transition in civilisation--religious, social, intellectual and domestic--has made on it. H. G. Wells, J. Glasworthy, J. Joyce, A. Huxley, D. H. Lawrence, and V. Woolf].

2251 _____. "Technique as Discovery," HudR, I:1 (Spring 1948), 67-87. Reprinted in The World We Imagine: Selected Essays. (New York: Farrar, Straus and Giroux, 1968; London: Chatto and Windus, 1969), pp. 3-24, Critiques and Essays on Modern Fiction, 1920-1951. Selected by J. W. Aldridge (New York: The Ronal Press, 1952), pp. 9-31, Forms of Modern Fiction. Edited by W. Van O'Connor (University of Minnesota Press, 1948), pp. 2-29, and Critical Approaches to Fiction. Edited by Shiv K. Kumar and Keith F. McKean (New York: McGraw-Hill, 1968), pp. 267-285. [Suggests that the new critical approaches to poetry should be applied to

the novel, technique being the only means for the writer
in "discovering, developing his subject, of conveying its
meaning, and finally, of evaluating it"].

2252 _____. "Fiction and the 'Analogical Matrix'," KR,
XI:4 (Autumn 1949), 539-560. Reprinted in The World We
Imagine: Selected Essays. (New York: Farrar, Straus and
Giroux, 1968; London: Chatto and Windus, 1969), pp. 24-
29, and Critiques and Essays on Modern Fiction, 1920-1951.
Selected by J. W. Aldridge (New York: The Ronald Press,
1952), pp. 83-98. [Though it confines itself to three 19th
century novels for illustration, the essay is central to
a new critical trend for it underlines the importance of
the study of metaphorical language, not only the "special
quality" of style, but also as a means to define and evaluate theme, and reveal the "character" of an imaginative
work].

2253 _____. "The Substance of Fiction," Writer, LXXX (June
1967), 14-18, 52. Reprinted from The Story: A Critical
Anthology. (Englewood Cliffs, N. J.: Prentice-Hall, 1967).
[Maintains that fiction is basically an art about life,
but different from life itself; that it has its own solid-
ity, form, and selectivity, and is determined by its very
nature--telling a story. V. Woolf, I. Compton-Burnett,
and E. M. Forster].

2254 Schuchart, Max. "Achtergronden van de Moderne Britse Roman,"
Gids, CXVI:2 (1953), 140-148. [Surveys the spiritual,
social and political problems that constitute the background
of the modern English novel, especially after World War II].

2255 Schulze, Sigurd. "Der ländliche Mensch im englischen Roman," NS, XLVI (1938), 452-462. [On the portrayal of rural
man in the English novel. S. Kaye-Smith, D. H. Lawrence,
A. G. Street, M. Webb, T. F. Powys, V. Sackville-West, and
others].

2256 Scott, J. D. "Story and Pattern in the Novel," Listener,
LI:1315 (13 May 1954), 833. [Argues against F. W. Bateson's
claim that there is no story without a pattern and E. M.
Forster's view that the novel is less capable of organisation than drama].

2257 _____. "British Novel: Lively As a Cricket," SatR,
XXXVIII (7 May 1955), 21-23, 46. [On the present state
of the English novel as it is written by those "who broke
new grounds" in post-World War II years. E. Waugh, G.
Greene, H. Green, A. Powell, L. P. Hartley, C. P. Snow,
J. Wain, K. Amis, and I. Murdoch].

2258 _____. "Britain's Angry Young Men," SatR, XL (27
July 1957), 8-11. [Discusses the controversial British

313

literary movement at whose centre are K. Amis, J. Wain, J. Braine, and J. Osborne].

2259 Scott-James, R. A. "The Popular Taste," LA, 277 (7 June 1913), 606-613. Reprinted from The British Review. [Examines current popular taste and the corresponding five categories of novels which cater to it: the novel of "incident," of "sentimental absurdities," of sex, of humour and of morality. C. J. Hyne, W. Le Queux, E. T. Thurston, "I. MacLaren," W. W. Jacobs, "M. Corelli," H. Caine, and J. Galsworthy].

2260 _____. "Modern Accents in English Literature," Bookman (New York), LXXIV (Sep. 1931), 24-28. [Surveys the "diversity of effort" and the "many-sided experimenting" of post-World War I literature, including the novel, and remarks on the number of female novelists who "carried off most of the honours"].

2261 _____. "Proletarians in Print," CSMWM, (10 Nov. 1937), 8. [On the emergence of novels "born out of the consciousness of working-class writers" who retain their proletarian identity when they write. J. Hanley, W. Greenwood and others].

2262 _____. "The Changing Novel," Spectator, CXCVII:6685 (10 Aug. 1956), 203. [Contends that the novel does not conform to prescribed patterns, for it is changing its character].

2263 Scott-Kilvert, Ian. "English Fiction 1958-60, (1)," BBN, 247 (Mar. 1961), 163-168. [Reviews the works of established novelists like C. P. Snow, A. Powell, J. Cary, P. H. Johnson and others whose strength lies in "their grasp of a wide range of human experience," and those like L. Durrell, W. Golding, and S. Beckett whose works are distinguished by style or fictional technique].

2264 _____. "English Fiction, 1958-1960, (2)," BBN, 248 (Apr. 1961), 237-244. [Reviews the fiction of the "newcomers" in the fifties--K. Amis, J. Wain, J. Braine and others--and the landmarks of Commonwealth fiction--West Indies, S. Africa and Canada].

2265 _____. "English-Fiction--1961," BBN, 261 (May 1962), 309-314. [Reviews the fiction of 1961 and indicates that those writers who set themselves to portray society as a "complete whole" rather than "in terms of isolated sections" (like the "Angry Young Men") have produced the most distinguished work].

2266 _____. "English Fiction: 1963," BBN, 282 (Feb. 1964), 85-91. [A general review of the scene in English fiction, including novels by writers of the Commonwealth, 1963 being the "year of the middle-aged and younger writers"].

2267   . "English Fiction: 1964," BBN, 298 (June 1965), 383-388. [Reviews the fiction of 1964 indicating that the characteristics of English fiction are now "more noticeably shaped by the tastes and qualifications of the individual author." Includes in his survey short stories, Commonwealth fiction and the historical novel].

2268   . "English Fiction, 1965," BBN, 310 (June 1966), 397-402. [Reviews the fiction of 1965 and notices the "impression of a phase of intermission, a pause for reassessment," and the absence of any one "single figure" dominating the scene. F. Manning, D. Lessing, P. H. Johnson, M. Bradbury, P. H. Newby and others].

2269   . "English Fiction: 1966," BBN, 322 (June 1967), 409-414. [Reviews the fiction of 1966 "indicating the absence of radical innovations" in the novel even while remaining the most "convenient and flexible form" for the expression of ideas and experience. G. Greene, "R. West," A. Powell, "T. Hinde," K. Amis, I. Murdoch and others].

2270   . "English Fiction: 1967," BBN, 331 (Mar. 1968), 165-169. [Reviews the fiction of 1967, and notices that the masterpiece is becoming "a rarer phenomenon," and points out the increasing influence of television and cinema in the mode of writing. C. Isherwood, W. Golding, A. Wilson, M. Drabble and others].

2271   . "English Fiction, 1969-70," BBN, (June 1971), 425-430. [Reviews the fiction of 1969-70, remarking on the "diversity" rather than the "originality or experiment" of the sixties. C. P. Snow, A. Powell, P. H. Johnson, J. Wain, K. Amis, G. Greene, O. Manning and others].

2272 Scrutton, Mary. "Addiction to Fiction," TC, CLIX (Apr. 1956), 363-373. [Examines the reader's fascination with the imaginary world, and how "wish-fulfilment, excitement and completeness" have disappeared from the novels of J. Joyce and V. Woolf].

2273 Sedgwick, Anne Douglas. "The Heart of the Matter," SatR, II:2 (8 Aug. 1925), 21-22. [On the sensitiveness, insight and mastery of summing up the theme of a book in memorable sentences. V. Woolf, M. Kennedy, and H. James].

2274 Seehase, Georg. "Kapitalistische Entfremdung und humanistische Integration: Bemerkungen zum englischen proletarischen Gegenwartsroman," ZAA, XV (1967), 383-400. [Distinguishes, from a Marxist viewpoint, two classes of writers: those who maintain the present "alienation"--E. Waugh, W. Golding and L. Durrell--and those who offer a "humanistic integration"--J. Aldridge, G. Greene and C. P. Snow. Focuses on the English "proletarian" novel of M. Heinemann, J. Lindsay, A. Sillitoe, S. Chaplin and others].

2275 _____. "Abbild des Klassenkampfes: Aspekte der Wertung demokratischer und sozialistischer Literatur in Grossbritannien," ZAA, XVII (1969), 392-405. [A Marxist viewpoint of class struggle in English literature. Brief references to J. Lindsay, H. Smith, D. Lambert, M. Heinemann, C. MacInnes, A. Sillitoe, G. Greene, C. P. Snow, A. Wilson, J. Aldridge and others].

2276 Sehrt, Ernst Th. "Das Bild des Menschen im neuen englischen Roman," Sammlung, VI (1951), 616-631. [On the portrayal of character by V. Woolf, H. James, J. Conrad, D. H. Lawrence, J. Joyce, R. Macaulay, and G. Greene].

2277 Seldes, Gilbert. "Form and the Novel," Bookman (New York), LXX (Oct. 1929), 128-131. [Surveys views on the "form" of the novel by E. Muir, J. Carruthers, V. Woolf, S. Jameson, F. M. Ford, and P. Lubbock, and asserts that there is no one form for the novel since the purpose of each novelist "imposes the pattern"].

2278 Sen, Srichandra. "Religious and Philosophical Ideas in Recent English Fiction," CalR, (July 1937), 71-86; (Aug. 1937), 193-206. [Examines the decline of religion as an institution represented by an orthodox common creed, and its gradual replacement by an "individual quest," mystical in character, as revealed in novels by A. Huxley, D. H. Lawrence, J. D. Beresford, J. Joyce, S. Maugham, H. G. Wells, and T. F. Powys].

2279 _____. "Marriage and Morals in Recent English Fiction," CalR, (Dec. 1937), 327-336. [Surveys the picture of married life, its conditions and their causes, as depicted by H. G. Wells, R. Aldington and D. H. Lawrence, after a four-page introduction to the ideas then prevalent].

2280 _____. "Some Aspects of Recent English Fiction," CalR, (May 1939), 101-110; (June 1939), 235-243. [Examines briefly the "uncertainty of aim," and "general scepticism" and the "series of experimentations" by the "stream of consciousness novelists"--J. Joyce, V. Woolf and D. Richardson--and the novel of ideas by A. Huxley, H. G. Wells, D. H. Lawrence, and C. E. Montague].

2281 _____. "Love and Romance in Recent English Fiction," CalR, (Aug. 1939), 135-143. [On the various ways love manifests itself in works by D. H. Lawrence, A. Waugh, S. Maugham, and A. Huxley].

2282 _____. "Psychological Studies in English Fiction," CalR, (Sep. 1939), 239-251. [Notes instances of "applied

psychology" in the novels of H. G. Wells, D. H. Lawrence,
A. Huxley, S. Maugham, and J. Joyce].

2283 "The Serious Novel," TLS, 3157 (31 Aug. 1962), 657.
[Leading article discussing seriousness, commitment and the future of the novel in the wake of the International Writers'
Conference in Edinburgh].

2284 Sestakov, D. "Anglijskaja kritika ob anglijskom poslevoennom ramone," VMU, XIX:5 (1964), 28-40. [A survey of English criticism on the postwar English novel].

2285 Seymour-Smith, Martin. "A Reply to Professor Plumb," Spectator, CCCXXII:7334 (17 Jan. 1969), 72. [Challenges P.
H. Plumb's rather pessimistic view concerning the novel
(see entry above), and suggests that English novelists
would do well to look in the direction of Spain, and especially Latin America].

2286 Shanks, Edward. "The War and the Novelists," LA, 299 (2
Nov. 1918), 302-305. Reprinted from Land and Water. [Analyses the unfortunate and diverting effect of World War I
on the art of novel-writing. Passing reference to "R.
West," F. Swinnerton, and J. D. Beresford].

2287 _____. "Sweet Bodements," NSta, XII (25 Jan. 1919),
349-351. Reprinted as "Novels About the Future," LA, 300
(8 Mar. 1919), 606-610. [On the novel of the future, i.e.,
the action of which is set in the future, and which "reveals the social order substantially changed, either by
evolution or by a single catastrophe." H. G. Wells and M.
P. Shiel among others].

2288 _____. "London, January 30," Dial, LXVI (22 Feb. 1919),
195-196. [Maintains that though no limit can be set in
principle on the length of novels, novelists tend to write
shorter novels prompted by "reasons quite other than artistic"].

2289 _____. "Reflections on the Recent History of the English Novel," LMer, 4 (1921), 173-183. Reprinted in First
Essays in Literature (London: Collins, 1923), pp. 172-192.
[A review focusing on meanings of realism, "as a means" in
fiction, as "an end in itself," as an impassive recording
of life in the style of H. G. Wells, A. Bennett, J. Galsworthy, or as in the "school" of J. Joyce, V. Woolf, J.
Richardson, and their young contemporaries C. Mackenzie, J.
D. Beresford, and H. Walpole. Also considers J. Conrad as
the "most significant figure in the English novel" but one
who is not "a realist"].

2290 "Shapers of the Modern Novel: A Catalogue of an Exhibition,"
PULC, XI (Spring 1950), 134-141. [A catalogue of selected

first works. Included are works by H. James, J. Conrad, and J. Joyce].

2291 Shapiro, Stephen A. "The Ambivalent Animal: Man in the Contemporary British and American Novel," CentR, XII (1968), 1-22. [Examines how the post-World War II English and American novel developed the "heritage of doubleness" from the previous century--ambivalent attitudes being "almost obligatory in contemporary fiction"--and how it "responded to our unique situation." Included are A. Wilson, J. Wain, A. Powell, D. Lessing, L. Durrell, K. Amis, J. Braine, A. Sillitoe, M. Spark, and D. Storey].

2292 Sharrock, Roger. "What Happened to Modernism?" Kolokon, 2 (Spring 1967), 5-12. [Rejects the generalization that the postwar novel has abandoned the innovations of J. Joyce and V. Woolf for the tradition of Trollope, A. Bennett and J. Galsworthy, and suggests that these innovations in "techniques of narrative economy and symbolic reference have been quietly filtered into the main body of the novel all along the line from J. Cary to the writers of detective stories"].

2293 Sheed, Wilfrid. "Enemies of Catholic Promise," Commonweal, LXXVII (22 Feb. 1963), 560-563. [On the twofold problem of the Catholic novelist: "telling his story right . . . (and) giving the right impression about Catholic doctrine." E. Waugh and G. Greene].

2294 _____. "Pornography and Literary Pleasure," CathW, CXIV (1962), 222-229. [Distinguishes three conditions for literary pleasure, and makes "some clear distinctions concerning both pornography and literature." J. Joyce and D. H. Lawrence].

2295 Sherman, Stuart P. "A Conversation with Cornelia," AtM, CXXXIII:1 (Jan. 1924), 1-19. [On chastity and sexual relations in fiction. Pages 9-16 deal with the 20th century novel in England and America. J. D. Beresford, H. G. Wells, J. Galsworthy, and D. H. Lawrence among others].

2296 Sherwood, Margaret. "Characters in Recent Fiction," AtM, CIX (May 1912), 672-684. [A review article of some twenty-nine English and American novels deploring the "lamentably small" proportion of novels in which one finds "the purely artistic impulse" to study character closely, and to interpret it for its own sake. "M. Corelli," A. Hope, M. Roberts, Mrs. H. Ward, F. L. Barclay, A. Bennett, M. Hewlett, R. Pryce, J. Farnol, F. Hodgson, "L. Malet," R. Hichens, and others].

2297 Shrapnel, Norman. "Novels Loud and Freakish: The Fictional Fifties," The Guardian (21 Dec. 1959), p. 6. [Emphasises the characteristic "waywardness" and unattachment of its novelists, the "odd, the slightly possessed, the off-normal" which constituted the "dominant note" in its early years until the arrival of the "academic misfits and ex-conscript grousers," and C. P. Snow's "documentaries"].

2298   Shroder, Maurice Z. "The Novel as a Genre," MR, IV (1963), 291-308. Reprinted in The Novel: Modern Essays in Criticism. Edited by R. M. Davis (Englewood Cliffs, N. J.: Prentice-Hall, 1969), pp. 43-57. [Studies how the novel grew from the romance "through the ironic attitude and . . . realism," i.e., authorial attitude and point of view, thus showing that though "the realities of genre underlie individual and external variations," genres evolve, and changes in narrative form give rise to new genres. H. James and J. Joyce among others].

2299   "Significance of the Novel," Outlook, LXIV (21 Apr. 1900), 901-903. [Recognizes the present state of the novel as the "literary form of our time" that frankly records "the passion, the emotion, the questioning, and the aspiration of the age"].

2300   Sillitoe, Alan. "Limits of Control IX: Both Sides of the Street," TLS, 3045 (9 July 1960), 435. Reprinted in The Writer's Dilemma: Essays first published in TLS under the heading 'Limits of Control'. Introduction by Stephen Spender. (London and New York: Oxford University Press, 1961), pp. 68-75. [Contends that there is a "gap" to be filled by novelists capable of writing realistically about the "literary underprivileged class," the working class].

2301   _____. "Violence in Art. 1) The Wild Horse," TC, CLXXIII (Winter 1964-65), 90-92. [Refutes the view that violence is the "natural artistic language of the times" for fiction].

2302   Simon, Irène. "English Letters," RLV, XII (1946), 282-289. [Reviews the best in fiction, poetry and the theatre in the preceding six months].

2303   _____. "Bloomsbury and Its Critics," RLV, XXIII (1957), 385-414. Reprinted as a booklet in the Langues Vivantes Series No. 53. (Paris: Marcel Didier. 1957). [Lecture delivered at the University of Groningen, 7 May 1957. Discusses the ethos of Bloomsbury, its shaping factors and its implications, and examines what the critics of Bloomsbury had to say about it].

2304   _____. "Some Recent English Novels," RLV, XXV (1959), 219-230. [Reviews novels by G. Greene, C. Mackenzie, C. P. Snow, D. Lessing, J. Wain and A. Wilson, pointing out that the English novel is "far from dead"].

2305 Sitwell, Osbert. "The Future of Fiction," NW&D, VIII:7
      (1946), 95-97. [Sixth article in a series of six on the
      same topic by R. Macaulay, V. S. Pritchett, A. Koestler,
      L. P. Hartley, and W. Allen. Maintains that ". . . the
      novel is essentially not an art form," and its future de-
      pends on those who "read and write it," but foresees an
      "enormous enriching, widening and deepening of fiction"
      in every direction, if freedom is guaranteed].

2306 "Six-Shilling Shocker," LA, 264 (5 Feb. 1910), 376-378.
      Reprinted from The Saturday Review. [Deplores the degra-
      dation of the "high function of the novelist" by many in-
      competent professors of the art].

2307 Skozodenko, V. A. "Novye variacii na staruju temu," VLit,
      XI:9 (1967), 117-134. ["New variations on an Old Theme."
      Notes on anti-communism in English postwar literature].

2308 Slosson, Preston. "Dictatorship in Modern Fiction," MQ,
      I (1960), 333-341. [Confined to post-World War I novels
      in which "the dictator himself is an artistic creation of
      the author," and to "fictions realistically treated (deal-
      ing with matters) . . . contemporary or . . . in the near
      future." C. Dane, G. Orwell, and H. G. Wells among others].

2309 Smart, Charles Al. "On the Road to Page One," YR, (NS)
      XXXVII:2 (1947), 242-256. [On the "eugenics of fiction"
      with special consideration given to the "earliest hours
      of gestation" and "the moment of conception." Brief ref-
      erences to H. James, A. Huxley, V. Woolf, E. M. Forster,
      and G. Orwell].

2310 Smith, A. "Ethics of Sensational Fiction," WRev, CLXII
      (Aug. 1904), 188-194. [Reviews the constituent elements
      of the sensational novel, its growing popularity, and how
      indicative are "readers' tastes and the direction of their
      interests"].

2311 Smith, Alice A. "Some English Women Novelists," NAR, CCXIV
      (Dec. 1921), 799-808. [On the new English realist women
      novelists and the way they reflect the life of an England
      in transition in their novels. D. Richardson, V. Meynell,
      A. Reeves, C. Dane, M. Sinclair, "E. M. Delafield," S. Ben-
      son, and S. Kaye-Smith].

2312 Smith, F. Harold. "Experience As a Basis for the Novelist,"
      ML&PSP, 64 (1939), 203-217. [Contends that a novelist can
      write successfully only when he brings experience to his
      work. Illustrations from 19th century novelists and W.
      Greenwood, Sir P. Gibbs and C. E. Montague].

2313 Smith, Harrison. "The Literature of Transition," SatR,
      XXIV (26 July 1941), 10. [Notices briefly the change in

the scene of fiction from "bomb-shocked London to the country" and that novelists are the first to record such "social revaluations"].

2314   Smith, Mrs. J. Wells. "Values in Fiction," Libraries, (Oct. 1928), 401-408. [A lecture delivered at the California Library Association, Riverside, 4 April 1928. Gives a working definition of the novel, assesses its usefulness and contends that the revolt of the contemporary English novel of J. Galsworthy, A. Bennett and H. G. Wells against the "preceding order" bears the "stamp of life itself," that the "energetic, indefatigable curiosity" of the novel is also seen in the novels of D. Richardson and V. Woolf].

2315   Smith, Nelson J., III. "The Dynamics of Fictional Worlds," WHR, XXII (1968), 35-46. [Discusses the reality of the fictional world and the analysis of world views and philosophies on which it depends. References to L. Durrell, K. Amis, and J. Joyce among others].

2316   Smith, William James. "The Indestructible Hero," Commonweal, LXVIII (9 May 1958), 147-149. [A re-examination of the concept of the hero in the current novel, relying heavily on S. O'Faolain's The Vanishing Hero: Studies in the Novelists of the Twenties (London: Eyre and Spottiswoode; Boston: Little, Brown and Company, 1956)].

2317   Snow, C. P. "Storytellers for the Atomic Age," NYTBR, (30 Jan. 1955), 1, 28. [Maintains that the "devitalizing effect" of science on novel writing has resulted in the "novel of sensibility" which polarized the novel as Art and the "popular" novel until 1945; but contemporary writers' awareness of the aesthetic cul-de-sac of "sensibility" and the necessity of relating men to their environment augurs well for the novel].

2318   _____. "The English Realistic Novel, 1957," MSpr, LI (1957), 265-270. [Regards the change of direction in the English postwar "realistic" novels of P. H. Johnson, E. Humphreys, F. King, K. Amis, J. Wain, J. Braine from the "aesthetic" novels of J. Joyce, V. Woolf and D. Richardson, not merely as "counter revolution," but as a new interest in the "individual condition" as well as "the social condition"].

2319   _____. "Challenge to the Intellect," TLS, 2946 (15 Aug. 1958), iii. [Special Section: "Books in a changing world." Contends that the contemporary novelist's challenge is not to surrender his intelligence in the face of scientific achievement, and that the novel need not become alienated from the intellectual life of the time].

2320   _____. "Science, Politics, and the Novelist: or, The Fish and the Net," KR, XXIII (Winter 1961), 1-17. Analyses shortcomings in modern "verbal-aesthetic" criticism which does not recognise the novel as an international art, the "writer-critic confluence" in adopting the stream of consciousness method resulting in the restricted range of the novel, and the exclusion of the themes of science and politics from it].

2321 "Some Aspects of the Modern Novel," LA, 234 (6 Sep. 1902), 577-592. Reprinted from CQR. [General comments on the variety and extent of topics embraced by the modern novel, the "moral mischief" wrought by female novelists, and the "gratuitous and offensive profanity" of popular writers].

2322 "Some Facts About Fiction," TLS, 616 (30 Oct. 1913), 483. Reprinted in LA, 280 (7 Feb. 1914), 373-377. [Considers the impact of "cheapness of production" on the output of novels, and surveys the "successes of the year" and the fate of the short-lived modern novel that fails].

2323 "Some New Novels," BM, CLXXXII (Dec. 1907), 773-781 [A review article deploring the "monotonous uniformity of length" of the "deleterious" fiction that has "disgraced the first decade" of the twentieth century. M. Hewlett, W. De Morgan and others].

2324 "Some of the Authors of 1951, Speaking for Themselves," NYHTBR, (7 Oct. 1951), 1-29. [H. M. Tomlinson, A. Koestler, H. Parkington, and N. Collins among others, speak of how they work and play].

2325 Sonnenfeld, Albert. "Twentieth Century Gothic: Reflections on the Catholic Novel," SoR, (NS) I:2 (Apr. 1965), 388-405. [Considers the nature of the novel in England, Germany and France where it is "a reaction to disorder and the threat of imminent chaos" rather than "celebrative" as in Italy or Spain. G. K. Chesterton, E. Waugh, and G. Greene among others].

2326 Soule, G. "Aesthetic and Moral Renaissance," Bookman (New York), XL (Nov. 1914), 290-295. [Considers the relation of the novel to the aesthetic and moral renaissance by examing J. Galsworthy's The Dark Flower, H. G. Wells' The Passionate Friends, and R. Rolland's Jean Christophe].

2327 Southern, Terry. "Dark Laughter in the Towers," Nation, CXC (23 Apr. 1960), 348-350. [Considers briefly the elements of humour in "primitive existentialist" American fiction and the "acute sense of the absurd" in English fiction of the fifties. K. Amis, J. Wain, K. Waterhouse, and "T. Hinde"].

2328 Speaight, Robert. "Littérature anglaise: écrivains catholiques," TP, (1945), 3. [Reviews the contribution of

English Catholic writers to literature with special emphasis on G. Greene and E. Waugh].

2329 Spearman, Diana. "The Social Influence of Fiction," NSoc, (6 July 1972), 6-8. [Deduces, from some 416 answers to a questionnaire, that the novel still exercises "an influence wide enough to be called social"].

2330 Spence, Lewis. "Novelists and Nonsense," LR, 48 (1938), 362-368. [Maintains that "caste-practice with its bag of tricks" is subversive of the individual ability of novelists, and is the curse of the English novel in this century].

2331 Spencer, John. "A Note on the 'Steady Monologuy of the Interiors'," REL, VI (Apr. 1965), 32-41. [On the characteristic linguistic features adopted by experimental writers, especially Joyce, to express what he called "the unspoken, unacted thoughts of people in the way they occur"].

2332 Spender, Stephen. "Modern Writers in the World of Necessity," PR, XII (Summer 1945), 352-360. [Upholds the view that though the "inner world of personality" is the most important reality the writer knows, it must be "related to the outer world." Brief references to D. H. Lawrence and E. M. Forster among others].

2333 _____. "Life of Literature," PR, XVI (Jan. 1949), 55-66; XVI (Feb. 1949), 182-192. [Reminiscences and sketches of the "Bloomsbury Group" and their contemporaries in postwar years].

2334 _____. "Movements and Influences in English Literature, 1927-1952," BA, XXVII (Winter 1953), 5-32. [Maintains that the previous twenty-five years constitute a reaction from the "principles of the modernist movement," a steady movement away from "individual sensibility as the centre of creative experience in writing, to a periphery of society, or some source of spiritual authority." Study confined to poetry and the novel. Included are J. Joyce, D. H. Lawrence, W. Lewis, A. Huxley, E. M. Forster, and V. Woolf among others].

2335 _____. "A Literary Letter from London," NYTBR, (10 Jan. 1954), 14. [On the new English "provincialism of intellectual life" as a revolt against "Frenchified culture," and "suave" centres like Oxford, Cambridge and London. J. Wain, H. Charteris, and L. P. Hartley].

2336 _____. "Speaking of Books," NYTBR, (13 Jan. 1957), 2. [Notices how writers are conditioned "like vintages," by the decade in which they matured, and the need to discover "a contemporary attitude in order to write about things

which are outside the present time." Brief references to
G. Orwell and D. H. Lawrence among others].

2337   _____. "When the Angry Young Men Grow Older," NYTBR,
(20 July 1958), 1, 12. [Focuses mainly on J. Osborne but
discusses also the chances that he and K. Amis and J. Wain
"will continue their protest when their anger is spent"].

2338   _____. "London Letter: Anglo-Saxon Attitudes," PR,
XXV:1 (Winter 1958), 110-116. [On the attitudes of the
"Angry Young Men"].

2339   _____. "Is There No More Need to Experiment?" NYTBR,
(20 July 1958), 1. Reprinted in Opinions and Perspectives
from 'The New York Times Book Review'. Edited by Francis
Brown (Boston: Houghton Mifflin, 1964), pp. 34-41. [Looks
back on the fifties as a "fragmentary" decade, with a diversity of attitudes, "lacking in a common direction or
tendency" especially in the novel, in spite of the "catchy"
and handy phrase, "Angry Young Men." A. Sillitoe, K. Amis,
A. Wilson, J. Wain, D. Lessing, C. MacInnes, W. Golding,
and I. Murdoch].

2340   _____. "Writers and Politics," PR, XXXIV:3 (Summer
1967), 359-381. [A review article that brings out in the
opening five pages the literary ethos of the "1910 generation" of novelists--V. Woolf, E. M. Forster, and D. H. Law-
rence--who, though sympathetic to anti-Fascism, were "hor-
rified at the idea of literature being compromised by politics"].

2341   Spivack, Charlotte. "The Estranged Hero of Modern Literature," NDQ, XXIX (1961), 13-19. [On the "implicit metaphysical assumptions" that unite the "strange, seemingly
misbegotten figures who occupy central roles" in contemporary literature. J. Conrad, J. P. Sartre, T. Mann, Dostoyevsky, Kafka and others].

2342   Spivak, Gayatri Chakravorty. "Thoughts on the Principle
of Allegory," Genre, V (1972), 327-352. [Contends that the
"great age of allegory" is only a "historic manifestation
of the allegoric tendency within literary discourse" and
modern fiction, and that allegory, like "point of view,"
should be regarded as "one of the global terms of the rhetoric of fiction"].

2343   Spolton, L. "The Secondary School in Post-War Fiction,"
BJES, XI (May 1963), 125-141. [Surveys the proliferation
of novels in postwar England with the kind of background
in which the school--whether grammar, public or preparatory-
is not merely "an interlude but forms the major or sole
part." W. Allen, J. D. Beresford, E. Waugh, C. P. Snow,
C. Mackenzie, G. F. Hughes, A. Powell, W. Cooper, E. R.

Braithwaite, H. Macallister, K. Amis, G. Hanley, M. Spark, A. Burgess, A. Sillitoe, and J. Barlow among others].

2344 "Spring Books, 1963: Facts and Fiction," Economist, CCVII (6 Apr. 1963), 49-50. [Discusses the value of the contemporary novel--English and American--as a means for providing us with insight into, and moral guidelines for, the political, social and metaphysical reality. Brief references to G. Greene, W. Golding, E. Waugh, M. Spark, and I. Murdoch among others].

2345 Srinivasa Iyengar, K. R. "India in Anglo-American Fiction," TSL, III (1958), 107-116. [On novels with Indian locale by Kipling, E. M. Forster, E. Thompson, H. E. Bates, and J. Masters among others].

2346 Stafford, Jean. "The Psychological Novel," KR, X (Spring 1948), 214-227. [Originally a paper read at the Bard College Conference on the Novel. Objects to the use of "psychological" to label and identify novels associated with the methods of Proust, Joyce and Woolf, and suggests that "a psychological novel is the same thing as a novel"].

2347 Stallman, Robert. "Fiction and Its Critics: A Reply to Mr. Rahv," KR, XIX (Spring 1957), 290-299. Reprinted, with a few additions, in The Houses that James Built and Other Literary Studies (East Lansing, Michigan: The Michigan State University Press, 1961), pp. 232-252. [Rejects Mr. P. Rahv's statement that the "prose sense" must not be infected by "poetics" ("Fiction and the Criticism of Fiction," KR, XVIII (Spring 1956), 276-299), and argues for the infusion of the poetic use of language in prose fiction].

2348 Stanford, Derek. "Thoughts on Contemporary Literature," ContempR, CXCI (Apr. 1957), 234-238. [Examines the poetry, literary criticism and novel of English writers of the "matter-of-fact, unheroic school," influenced by "logical or critical positivism," and the "clear-cut contribution" and features of the Wain-Amis novel].

2349 _____. "Report from London: Literature in England: The Present Position," WesR, XXI (Spring 1957), 293-306. [Includes a review of the features of the "new movement novel" of K. Amis, J. Wain, as well as the achievement of individual novelists like J. Pietrkiewicz, "G. Fielding," I. English, and M. Spark].

2350 _____. "Beatniks and Angry Young Men," Meanjin, XVII (Dec. 1958), 413-419. [Brings out the difference between the two groups, and concentrates on the salient characteristics of the English group, especially J. Osborne, C. Wilson, and J. Braine].

2351 _____. "In Britain, Cautious Coexistence," Commonweal, LXVII (7 Mar. 1958), 583-586. [Examines the political and cultural factors behind the decline in political activity among intellectuals, and especially poets and novelists over the previous twenty years. K. Amis, G. Orwell, and A. Koestler].

2352 _____. "Violence in the Modern Novel," Critic, XXII (Aug.-Sep. 1963), 32-36. [Maintains that violence in modern fiction bears a direct relationship to isolation and results from the "non-conforming sensibility" of the outsider and nihilism in sexual and religious matters. A. Huxley, W. Golding, C. Wilson, and A. Sillitoe among others].

2353 Stanford, Raney. "The Return of Trickster: When a Not-a-Hero is a Hero," JPC, I (1967), 228-242. [The reoccurrence of the "trickster-rogue and culture hero" of primitive myth--the "underground man"--in contemporary literature is to "affirm (the) human spirit" and protest society's attempts "to dehumanize man's life"; hence, the characteristics of "alienation, loneliness, hatred of self . . . and . . . a desire for significant love outside of the unstable . . . self" of the anti-hero. G. Orwell and A. Sillitoe among others].

2354 Stanton, Robert. "The Plot-Tone Confict: A New Key to the Novel," CE, XXIX:8 (May 1968), 602-607. [Regards the plot-tone conflict in a novel as indicative of a novelist being of two minds, i.e., having parallel views or values which manifest their "antagonism in a fluctuating tension rather than in a head-on collision"].

2355 Stawell, F. Melian. "Time, Imagination and the Modern Novelist," NC, CVII:656 (Feb. 1930), 274-284. [Contends that the imaginative writer seizes the "vital moments" in experience when "our whole past character, acting in the Present, flings itself forward to meet the Future"; hence, the preoccupation of the modern novelist with "the sense of this full-charged stream." Illustrations from V. Woolf, M. Proust and some of the classics].

2356 Stedmond, John. "What Is a Novel?" Culture, XVIII (Dec. 1957), 367-370. [Illustrates the "complexity of narrative fiction" and the inability of literary criticism to find a "final category" for what may be termed "the novel" by examining definitions from H. Kenner, M. Turnell, D. Grant, A. Kettle, E. Muir, N. Frye, P. Lubbock, E. M. Forster, and H. Read].

2357 Stegner, Wallace. "Is the Novel Done For?" Harper's, CLXXXVI (Dec. 1942), 76-83. [Examines the studies of fiction in 1942 and concludes that the novel in America--and Britain, too--is in a "blind alley," faced either with "metamorphis or extinction," after the encroachment of non-fiction on it. References to J. Joyce, V. Woolf, and A. Huxley among others].

2358 _____. "Fiction: A Lens on Life," SatR, XXXIII:16 (22 Apr. 1950), 9-10, 32-34. [Distinguishes between "serious fiction and the writer of escape entertainment," the former reflecting experience instead of escaping it, stimulating instead of deadening. H. James and J. Conrad among others].

2359 Steinberg, Erwin R. "The Stream-of-Consciousness Novelist: An Inquiry into the Relation of Consciousness and Language," RGS, XVII:4 (Summer 1960), 423-439. [Reviews the history and nature of consciousness to present the view that a stream-of-consciousness novelist "can at best simulate the psychological stream of consciousness." Brief references to V. Woolf and A. Huxley].

2360 Steiner, George. "Last Stop for Mrs. Brown," NY, (12 July 1969), 83-91. [Discusses the "antithetical" achievements and status of two contemporary novelists: C. P. Snow and N. Mosley].

2361 Stéphane, Nelly. "Romans anglais," Europe, 417-418 (1964), 282-288. [Discusses several works by W. Cooper, K. Amis, C. P. Snow and A. Wilson as being representative of the "richesse" and vitality of the English contemporary novel that describes and criticises with great insight, but masks its author's involvement under the guise of humour].

2362 Stephen, Sir Herbert. "Novelists and Recent History," LA, 283 (28 Nov. 1914), 537-542. Reprinted from CorM. [Notices historical inaccuracies and distortion of facts concerning events that had occurred within living memory, in novels by A. Bennett, W. de Morgan, and H. Walpole].

2363 Stephenson, Nathaniel. "Coming thing in Fiction," WT, IX (Aug. 1905), 885-889. [Makes a study of M. Hewlett's The Forest Lovers and concludes that "relentless thinking"-- the coming thing in fiction--is the most hopeful sign of the times].

2364 Stern, Madeline B. "Counterclockwise: Flux of Time in Literature," SR, XLIV (July-Sep. 1936), 338-365. [Discusses the relationship between the concepts of Time in literature and philosophy, and examines the "subjectivity of Time," and Time as "perpetual perishing" in literature. H. G. Wells, V. Woolf and others].

2365 Sternlicht, Sanford. "Two Views of the Builder in Graham Greene's A Burnt-Out Case and William Golding's The Spire," CalR, (NS) 1 (Mar. 1970), 401-404. [Discusses "building" as a religious act and service for man--for his spirit in The Spire and for his body in A Burnt-Out Case].

2366   Stevenson, W. B. "Fiction in 1942," LibA, XXXVI (Jan.-Feb. 1943), 9-15. [A review of English and American novels and short stories pointing out the impact of the war on novelists. H. B. Creswell, N. Shute, N. Balchin, and J. B. Priestly among others].

2367   _____. "Fiction in 1943," LibA, (Jan. 1944), 3-8. [A review of English and American novels and short stories. H. MacInnes, G. Greene, P. Toynbee, A. Koestler, R. Warner, and S. Jameson among others].

2368   Stevick, Philip. "The Limits of Anti-Utopia," Criticism, VI (1964), 233-245. [On the "absence of finality," i.e., a completely realized anti-Utopia and the imaginative impossibility of writing one. G. Orwell, A. Huxley, E. M. Forster and others].

2369   _____. "The Theory of Fictional Chapters," WHR, XX (1966), 231-241. [Part one of the essay argues the point that chapters exist in a novel to make narrative intelligible when it exceeds the "limits of aesthetic understanding," and to enable it to contain "all the truth it will bear." Part two illustrates this from 18th century English fiction and G. Eliot].

2370   _____. "Fictional Chapters and Open Ends," JGE, XVII:4 (Jan. 1966), 261-272. [Argues that the "open end" is a "formal shock" to the reader when he expects a chapter to end, and can be one of the richest "rhetorical possibilities" open to the novelist. H. James, J. Joyce, and E. Waugh among others].

2371   _____. "Novel and Anatomy: Notes Towards an Amplification of Frye," Criticism, X (1968), 153-165. [A discussion of N. Frye's fourth category "anatomy," bringing out the "genre's" freedom from the compulsions of: the "time sequence," the shaping of "manners and morals into a vision which patently corresponds to social and moral experience," and the "chronicling of the growth of personality"; hence, its capacity to use "language in ways radically different from its use in the novel"].

2372   Stewart, D. H. "Contemporary Novel Criticism: A Complaint," QQ, LXVIII:3 (Autumn 1961), 441-455. [Surveys the "New Criticism" that regards art as "autonomous," and focuses on form, "word, style, technique as inseparable from expressed content," and rejects it on the ground that it is "overspecialized and hieratic," and detrimental to "the improvement of public taste and the dissemination of culture"]

2373 Stewart, George R. "The Novelists Take Over Poetry," SatR, XXIII (16 Feb. 1941), 3-4, 18-19. [Examines the new techniques which the novel used after it displaced poetry in 1920 as the major literary genre].

2374 "Stirbt der Roman in England?" Liter, XXXIX (1936), 67-68. ["Is the novel in England dying?" Suggests it is not, that it is merely undergoing change].

2375 Stockum, Th. C. Van. "De Figuur van de Amerikaanse 'tante' in dera vreemde in de Anglo-Amerikaanse letterkunde," LTBM, 219 (1963), 225-232. ["The Figure of the American 'Aunt' away from home in Anglo-American Literature". D. H. Lawrence and M. Allingham].

2376 Stokes, Fraser. "Current British Fiction," EngR, XVI (Feb. 1966), 7-12. [Paper presented at the Annual Conference of the New York State English Council in Buffalo, 1 May 1965. Surveys English fiction after 1958, noticing the change "toward American tone, style and setting," and the range of topics. K. Amis, J. Braine, J. Fowles, W. Golding, M. Drabble, and others].

2377 Stonier, G. W. "Books in General: Edwardian Novelists," NSta, XLIII (5 Jan. 1952), 16-17. [Recommends the novels of A. Leverson and R. Horniman to be included among the "quiet revival" that has been undertaken lately among Edwardian novelists].

2378 Stopp, Frederick J. "Der katholische Roman im heutigen England: Graham Greene and Evelyn Waugh," SZ, CLIII (Mar. 1954), 428-443. [Compares subject matter, technique and background in both novelists].

2379 Strandberg, Victor. "The Crisis of Belief in Modern Literature," EJ, LIII:7 (Oct. 1964), 475-483, 544. [Attributes man's present widespread despair of human stature and dignity, the "hell that is the composite creation of our greatest masters," to Darwinism and Freudianism, and considers some basic responses to this crisis by writers over the previous century. J. Conrad, W. Golding, J. Joyce, and A. Huxley among others].

2380 Straus, Ralph. "This Age in Fiction," Bookman (London), LXXXIII (Oct. 1932), 7-8. [A novelist-reviewer's bird's-eye view of postwar fiction that sees nothing in it "startlingly new or likely to receive attention from the literary historian of the future," and notices the "distinctive" quality of the experiment of Ulysses, the impact of Freud, and war-books].

2381 "Stream of Consciousness," SatR, VIII (9 Jan. 1932), 445. [Reviews Edouard Dujardin's Le Monologue intérieur, in which he claims to have been the first to use the "unspoken monologue"].

2382　Strong, L. A. G. "James Joyce and the New Fiction," AM, XXXV (Aug. 1935), 433-437. [Examines structure and the use of language in the "new fiction," i.e., the experimental, and the demand it makes on the reader's consciousness. Illustrates from J. Joyce's works].

2383　Struve, Gleb. "Monologue intérieur: The Origins of the Formula and the First Statement of its Possibilities," PMLA, LXIX (Dec. 1954), 1101-11. [Attributes the coinage and first usage of the literary formula to the little known Russian literary critic Nikolay Gavrilovich Chernyshevsky (1828-1883) and later to Tolstoy, before E. Dujardin and J. Joyce].

2384　Stuart, Robert Lee. "The Writer-in Waiting," ChrC, LXXXII (19 May 1965), 647-648. [Maintains that the "contemporary writer . . . is committed more to . . . (the) wait than to the quest," or to the pretence that value exists where it does not. Brief references to W. Golding and J. Conrad among others].

2385　Sudrann, Jean. "The Necessary Illusion: A Letter from London," AR, XVIII (Summer 1958), 236-244. [The letter brings home to the American public that an awareness of England's present attempt to creat a new identity--as distinct from making generalizations about British postwar attitudes--is necessary, for this "unflagging belief in man's creative potential lies at the very centre of the contemporary British novel." E. Taylor, K. Amis, N. Dennis, and others].

2386　Sullivan, Walter. "'Where Have All the Flowers Gone?' Part II: The Novel in the Gnostic Twilight," SR, LXXVIII:4 (Oct.-Dec. 1970), 654-664. [A review article on recent English and American novels discussing the deterioration of the "notions of community and the realities of . . . relationship," and their detrimental influence on the novelist's craft and vision. G. Greene and E. Bowen among others].

2387　Sundaram, P. S. "The Problem of Evil in Modern English Fiction," JAU, XXI (1957), 83-138. [A course of three lectures delivered at the Annamalai University. Surveys the presentation of evil and its influence on English fiction up to the end of the 19th century, and examines evil resulting from human actions--"unmerited suffering, and that which causes suffering"--in H. James, J. Conrad, H. G. Wells, C. Holmes, and G. Greene].

2388　"The Sunday Times Guide to the Modern Movement in the Arts. 2. Literature: Men who changed the Nature of Twentieth

Century Writing," Sunday Times, (14 May 1967), 54-55. [The
second of a six-part series on Architecture, Films, Music,
Drama, Literature, and Modern Art. The guide for the general reader attempts to explain several outstanding features
of 20th century poetry and fiction, summarizes outside influences, gives brief accounts of key figures, and explains
catchwords in 20th century literature].

2389   Suzuki, Kenzo. "Nonconformist us Bungaku," EigoS, CXVI
       (1 Mar. 1970), 124-125. ["Non-Conformist Literature." In
       Japanese. On the tradition of modern British novels to be
       anti-traditional, and the agony of being a "working class"
       novelist. A. Sillitoe, G. Orwell, and D. H. Lawrence].

2390   Swift, Benjamin. "The Decay of the Novel," Critic, XLII
       (Jan. 1903), 59-61; XLII (Feb. 1903), 149-160. [Examines
       tendencies of the day in publishing, the causes of the "ex-
       traordinary quantity of contemporary fiction," the degra-
       dation of taste, the "deplorable" customs of literary per-
       iodicals, and the "immoral book" or novel. The second ar-
       ticle includes responses from R. Whiteing, H. G. Wells,
       T. Hardy, J. K. Jerome, E. Phillpotts, E. F. Benson, W. Le
       Queux, and W. L. Courtney].

2391   Swiggart, Peter. "Mr. Booth's Quarrel with Fiction," SR,
       LXXI (1963), 142-159. [A review article on Wayne Booth's
       Rhetoric of Fiction. Rejects Booth's basic concept of fic-
       tional rhetoric and the arbitrary criticism and polemics
       it encourages, and points out that Booth's quarrel is not
       so much with standard interpretations of the function of
       post-Jamesian techniques of narration, but "with writers
       and critics who have refused to impose rigid moral criteria
       upon the writing of fiction"].

2392   Swinnerton, Frank. "The Art of the Novel," NWo, (Dec. 1919),
       3-8. Reprinted in Bookman (New York), L (Jan. 1920), 411-
       417. [Makes a distinction between the "art" and the "craft"
       of novel writing, art being a "bridling of imagination, of
       infinite talent," distinguished by the quality of "origin-
       ality"].

2393   _____. "The Novel of Convention," Adelphi, I (June
       1923), 61-62. [A brief note on the novelist's art as the
       creation of a "living thing" rather than a destruction of
       a convention of writing].

2394   _____. "A Note on the English Novel," Bookman (New
       York), LX (Dec. 1924), 398-403. [Surveys the two charac-
       teristic traits of the English novel--"scrupulous render-
       ing of incidents," and the "comic spirit,"--and attributes
       the decadence of the novel in his day to the current absence
       of the comic spirit, psychology, and the conscious imita-
       tion of the French and the Russian novel].

331

2395 _____. "Younger Generation," SatR, IV (10 Dec. 1927), 421-422. [Deplores the change which came over the literary life in postwar years, when young writers gave way to "eccentricity, pretentious silliness, insincerity and the humour of the latrine," and experimented with form in obedience to "esthetic theory," but were creatively sterile, merely producing a series of "self-portraits, self-studies, self-defences"].

2396 _____. "Variations of Form in the Novel," E&S, XXIII (1937), 79-92. [Surveys the variations since the days of Richardson, stressing the developments and absence of "violent changes" until the 20th century, and contends that the present variety of technical experiment indicates, among other things, a "readiness to adopt the scientific method of trial and error"].

2397 _____. "The Decay of the Novel," Spectator, CLXIX (10 July 1942), 32. [Attributes the "temporary eclipse" in the novel to the current war and the pre-war death of the tragic novel, the comedy arising from the "surfaces of urban society," the ingenious examination of the subconscious, and the lack of creative talent].

2398 _____. "Eclipse of the Novel," SatR, XXXIX (24 Mar. 1956), 13-14, 42-45. Revised and reprinted in ContempR, CLXXXIX:1086 (June 1956), 333-338. [Maintains that the naturalistic, the pseudo-autobiographical and the ideal of "destructive egotism" in novel writing are worn out, and that the "poetic tragedy in prose," such as Hardy and Meredith wrote still remains. H. G. Wells, A. Bennett, and J. Galsworthy].

2399 Symon, J. D. "The Novel under Commerce," EngRev, XXV (Nov. 1917), 411-422. [Argues that the "commercially imposed limits of space" are responsible for the "ephemeral quality" of recent English fiction in spite of the "sound material, the capable and even artistic handling." M. Sinclair, H. G. Wells, R. Kipling and others].

2400 Symons, Julian. "Politics and the Novel," TC, CLXX (Winter 1962), 147-154. [A review article of I. Howe's Politics and the Novel examining several novelists' preoccupation with political themes and the impact of politics on them. J. Conrad, H. James, A. Koestler, G. Orwell, R. Hughes, and A. Wilson].

2401 "Symposium of Novelists," LA, 319 (17 Nov. 1923), 335-336. [H. G. Wells, J. Galsworthy, W. J. Locke, W. de Morgan, and E. P. Oppenheim respond to the question of whether a novelist works out the plot of his novel in his mind before he puts pen to paper, or whether he lets it develop as the characters develop].

2402   Talbert, E. L. "The Modern Novel and the Response of the
        Reader," JAP, 26 (Jan. 1932), 409-414. [Observations on
        the ability of the modern novel to reflect contemporary
        life, on the "composite structure of its varying units,"
        and on the reasons prompting the "response pattern" of the
        reader].

2403   Tate, Allen. "Techniques of Fiction," SR, LII (Spring 1944),
        210-225. Reprinted in The Hovering Fly (Cummington, Mass.:
        The Cummington Press, 1948), pp. 35-51, The Man of Letters
        in the Modern World: Selected Essays, 1928-55. (New York:
        Meridian Books, 1955), pp. 78-93, Collected Essays. (Den-
        ver: Alan Swallow, 1959), pp. 129-146, Forms of Modern
        Fiction. Edited by W. Van O'Connor. (University of Min-
        nesota Press, 1948), pp. 30-45, and Critiques and Essays
        on Modern Fiction, 1920-51. Edited by John W. Aldridge.
        (New York: The Ronald Press, 1952), pp. 31-42. [Rejects
        the approach of Percy Lubbock, E. M. Forster and Edwin Muir
        and suggests that "completeness of presentation" in the art
        of fiction can only be achieved when "the action is not
        stated from the point of view of the author . . . [but]
        rendered in terms of situation and scene"].

2404   _____. "The Post of Observation in Fiction," MarQ, II
        (Mar. 1944), 61-64. [Discusses the question of "form" and
        Henry James' "post of observation," or "central intelligence"
        which he regards as the distinctive feature of the modern
        novel].

2405   Taylor, Rachel Annand. "The Post-War English Novel," SocR,
        XX:3 (July 1928), 177-196. [Paper read at a meeting of the
        Sociological Society on 22 May 1928. Surveys the novelists
        of postwar England and their achievements, and notices the
        impact of the war on the general decline of the novel, its
        new psychological content and its interest in experimenting
        with new forms].

2406   Taylor, W. D. "University Novelists," AUR, (Nov. 1930),
        12-25. [Examines the novels of A. M. Mackenzie, L. Storm
        (Mrs. Clark), N. Shepherd, and E. Linklater, between 1923
        and 1929, which are set in Deeside, Aberdeen, or the Uni-
        versity itself].

2407   Temple, D. C. "Public School in Fiction," JE, LIX (Apr.
        1927), 250-252. [Surveys briefly the subject of public
        school life in fiction and the tendency towards the "per-
        sonal" novel. B. Nichols, A. Waugh, E. F. Benson, H. Wal-
        pole, and C. Dane].

2408   "Theory of Heroes and Some Recent Novels," Bookman, (New
        York), XXXIII (Apr. 1911), 191-196. [Examines a new defin-
        ition of the hero or heroine as "a unit of measurement" in
        novels by A. Bennett and D. H. Lawrence among others].

2409 *Thialet, Georges. "Le Roman nouveau en Angleterre," Sang Nouveau (Charleroi, Belgique), (Aug. 1932).

2410 Thiébault, Marcel. "Romans anglais," RP, I (Apr. 1933), 697-720. [A review article on the translation into French of novels by M. Baring, A. Huxley, C. Dane, D. H. Lawrence, and J. Galsworthy].

2411 Tilby, A. Wyatt. "The Post-War Novel," EdR, CCXXXVIII (July 1923), 139-147. [A review article that focuses on two novels by each of R. Macaulay, "R. West," R. Keable and M. Sadleir].

2412 Tilford, John E., Jr. "Some Changes in the Technique of the Novel," EUQ, IX (1953), 167-174. [A revised version of a paper read at the Georgia Writers' Conference, Emory at Oxford, June 1952. Discusses five important changes which distinguish early novels from those of today: the matter of fact versus fiction, the presence of the author within the pages of the novel, point of view, "the way the meaning is put in novels," and "symbolic values" given the various elements of the novel].

2413 _____. "Point of View in the Novel," EUQ, XX:2 (Summer 1964), 121-130. Reprinted in Critical Approaches to Fiction. Edited by Shiv K. Kumar and Keith F. McKean. (New York: McGraw-Hill, 1968), pp. 305-315. [Discusses variations on two basic ways of story telling: "from the inside," that is, making one of the characters do it, or "from the out-side, as a more-or-less omniscient author." Illustrations from English and American novels. Included are S. Butler, H. James, J. Joyce, J. Conrad, and L. Durrell].

2414 Tillyard, E. M. V. "The Novel as Literary Kind," E&S, IX (1956), 73-86. [Discusses the term "novel," its imprecision, its inclusiveness, its convenience as a label, and how the muddle about the nature of prose fiction arose].

2415 TLS. "Sounding the Sixties," 3309 (29 July 1965), 623-624. [Special Issue. A survey of the English literary scene].

2416 Tindall, William York. "Many-Levelled Fiction: Virginia Woolf to Ross Lockridge," CE, X:2 (Nov. 1948), 65-71. [Ex-amines the many-levelled novel in works by V. Woolf, R. Lockridge, and M. Cowley].

2417 _____. "The Symbolic Novel," A. D., III (1952), 56-68. [Discusses J. Conrad's Heart of Darkness, H. Green's Party Going, and J. Joyce's Portrait of the Artist as ex-amples of the "poetic," and "many-levelled" novel presenting reality in the least discursive manner].

2418 _____. "The Criticism of Fiction," TQ, I:1 (1958), 101-

111. [On the difficulty arising from the criticism of isolated elements in the novel, especially the symbolist novel].

2419   Tinker, Chancey Brewster. "The Fall of the Curtain," YR, XI (Oct. 1921), 130-138. [On the "fixed" general rule of modern novels not to "suggest any finalities," that there be no "end," in contrast to the Victorian formula].

2420   "Today's Spirit in Novel and Play: Debate Between John Drinkwater and Hugh Walpole," LDig, LXXI (31 Dec. 1921), 25-26. [Extracts from the debate on whether the novel or the drama more "accurately reflects the spirit of the age"].

2421   Todd, Olivier. "Jeunes gens en colère?" TM, (1959), 895-910. [A review article on Declaration. Edited by T. Maschler. (London: MacGibbon & Kee, 1957)].

2422   Todd, William. "The Ethical Functions of the Novel," Ethics, LXXV:3 (Apr. 1965), 201-206. [On the relationship between normative ethics and the writing of novels].

2423   Tomlinson, H. M. "Problems of a Novelist," SatR, X:43 (12 May 1934), 685-686. [Calls for "good writing" in a novel and an "austere regard in solitude for the honor of a tradition" instead of the current trusting to intuition, instincts, and "deference of the mob"].

2424   Tomlinson, T. B. "Literature and History--the Novel," MCQ, IV (1961), 93-101. [Argues for literature and history as the "keystone of courses in the humanities," also that literary criticism may "'grow into' a concern for sociology and history" without losing its identity as a discipline, especially in the novel, and comments on the historian's use of such material. Focuses on the English nineteenth century novel, and C. P. Snow and D. H. Lawrence for illustration].

2425   _____. "Recent Criticism of the Novel," MCQ, XI (1968), 106-120. [A review article on what may be termed in novel criticism the "metaphysical or aesthetic" bent (F. Kermod, L. Lerner, and M. Krieger), and the "empiricists" or those interested in techniques and kinds and genres (A. Friedman, D. Lodge, I. Gregor, and B. Nichols). Also rejects the "abstracting symbolist metaphysical approach to novels"].

2426   Tonkin, Humphrey. "Utopias: Notes on a Pattern of Thought," CentR, XIV (Fall 1970), 385-395. [On the danger of Utopian Idealism, its "lack of flexibility and the overpowering demands it puts upon the individual to sacrifice himself to the interests of social order." H. G. Wells, A. Huxley, and G. Orwell among others].

2427   Torchiana, Donald T. "Victorian and Modern Fiction: A Rejoinder," CE, XX (Dec. 1958), 140-143. [Rebuts W. Burns' contention ("The Genuine and the Counterfeit," CE, XVII (Dec. 1956), 143-150) that "vision" is the "sine qua non of genuine fiction"].

2428   Toynbee, Philip. "The Decline and Future of the English Novel," PNW, 23 (1945), 127-139. [Attributes the decline of the novel as written by the generation of the thirties-- C. Isherwood, G. Greene, R. Hughes, H. Green, R. Warner, and E. Waugh--to the "overweening influence of contemporary events, and the vastly enlarged scope of the novelists' territory," and sees the solution in the novelist concentrating on the "particular," on "detail"].

2429   _____. "The English Literary Scene," NRep, CXV (2 Dec. 1946), 728-730. [Surveys the scene in 1946 and emphasises the "quiescence" in this "period of retrenchment and deliberation." Singles out novels by E. M. Forster, G. Greene, E. Waugh, and E. Bowen].

2430   _____. "The Defence Brief," Observer, (5 Sep. 1954), 8. [A reply to H. Nicolson's contention that the novel is dead (see above). Refutes the three contentions that the novel is "impermanent and unnecessary," that its scope and function require a period of "social tranquility," and lastly, that the interior monologue has rendered it obscure].

2431   _____. "A Writer's Prospect--1. Experiment and the Future of the Novel," LM, III:5 (May 1956), 48-56. Reprinted in The Craft of Letters in England: A Symposium. Edited by John Lehmann. (London: The Cresset Press, 1956; Boston: Houghton Mifflin, 1957), pp. 60-73. [Makes the subtle distinction between the "concerned" novelist and the "engaged" one, and points out the inevitability of the modern novelist to write about the human condition in spite of his growing isolation, as he struggles "in a collapsed tradition, uncertain of his intractable medium and uncertain of his constantly changing material." A Bennett, J. Joyce, V. Woolf, K. Amis, and C. Mortimer among others].

2432   Trilling, Lionel. "Manners, Morals, and the Novel," KR, X (1948), 11-27. Reprinted in The Liberal Imagination: Essays on Literature and Society. (New York: Viking Press, 1950; London: Secker & Warburg, 1951), pp. 199-216. [Propounds the view of the novel as a "quest for reality" and an "effective agent of the moral imagination," useful in involving the reader in scrutinizing appearance and reality and teaching him the "extent of human variety." Mainly concerned with the American scene with brief references to H. James, D. H. Lawrence, and E. M. Forster].

2433   _____. "Art and Fortune," PR, XV (Dec. 1948), 1271-92. Reprinted in The Liberal Imagination: Essays on Literature and Society. (New York: Viking Press, 1950; London: Secker and Warburg, 1951), pp. 247-272. [Rejects the view that the novel is dead and discusses the "defining conditions" under which it may live, and the particular circumstances of its own nature and action under which it may best succeed].

2434 _____. "On the Modern Element in Modern Literature," PR, XXVIII:1 (Jan.-Feb. 1961), 9-35. An expanded version of a lecture delivered at Vanderbilt Universtiy, Spring 1960, and later in that year at Boston College. Reprinted in Literary Modernism. Edited, with an Introduction by Irving Howe. (Greenwich, Conn.: Fawcett Publication, 1967), pp. 59-83. Reprinted as "On the Teaching of Modern Literature" in Beyond Culture: Essays on Literature and Learning (New York: Viking Press, 1961; London: Secker & Warburg, 1966), pp. 3-31. [Discusses his experiences on first introducing a course that brings out a frequent theme in modern literature: "disenchantment of our culture with itself" or the bitter hostility of modern literature to civilization].

2435 "Trilogies," NYTBR, (16 May 1915), 188. [Editorial on the popularising of the three-volume novel by J. D. Beresford, A. Bennett, and O. Onions].

2436 Troughton, Marion. "Parsons in English Literature," ContempR, CLXXXVII (Jan. 1955), 39-43. [A brief survey of clergymen in the English novel. Includes H. Walpole, E. Raymond, and V. Brittain].

2437 Tucker, Eva. "The Painter in the Novel," Studio, CLXXIV:894 (Nov. 1967), 186-187. [Maintains that the advantage of "immediacy" which the painter possesses by virtue of his art prompts a novelist to explore the "methods of work and the psychology of the painter." Illustrates from novels by V. Woolf, S. Beckett, J. Cary, and A. Huxley].

2438 Turnell, Martin. "The Religious Novel," Commonweal, LV (26 Oct. 1951), 55-57. [Discusses the effect of the religious element on the sensibility of G. Bernanos, F. Mauriac, G. Greene, and E. Waugh].

2439 Turner, W. J. "Music in Novels," NSta, (3 Sep. 1921), 595. [Comments on the awareness of music and musicians in novels by A. Bennett, "H. H. Richardson," and E. Sidgwick].

2440 "Twelve Months' Fiction," LA, 235 (13 Dec. 1902), 698-701. Reprinted from The Academy. [Reviews briefly a dozen or so "popular" novels and places them in order of merit. Also reviews briefly nine "artistic" novels, the best of the year in technique, in emotional power, and in the "achievement of beauty." A. Bennett, R. M. Gilchrist, "J. O. Hobbes," H. James, H. G. Wells and others].

2441   "Twenty-Five Years," TLS, 1735 (2 May 1935), 277-278. [A
        leading article reviewing the English literary scene during
        the 25 years of the reign of King George V].

2442   "Two Views of Fiction," TLS, (7 Nov. 1958), 641. [Leading
        article on views on "The Future of the Novel" expounded by
        A. Quinton, F. Kermode, M. Cranston and L. Cooper in the
        Autumn Reading Number of the London Magazine, and French
        critics in Esprit].

2443   Tynan, Kenneth. "Men of Anger," Holiday, XXIII (Apr. 1958),
        92-93. [Surveys the writings of the "new malcontents" of
        the fifties--J. Osborne, C. Wilson, K. Amis, J. Braine, N.
        Dennis and A. Wilson--unequal in talent, but united by their
        hatred for "the establishment," their "outraged boredom,"
        and the belief that art is an "influence on life," not a
        refuge from it].

2444   "The Uncomfortable Novel," TLS, 1891 (30 Aug. 1938), 295.
        [On the "paradox of an unusual beauty of form devoted to
        the expression of a definitely depressing content," espe-
        cially by women novelists].

2445   "Uncommitted Talents," TLS, 2639 (29 Aug. 1952), iii. [Sup-
        plement. Surveys the varied talents of the "uncommitted
        generation" of novelists in the confusing decade following
        the second World War. A. Comfort, A. Wilson, W. Casper,
        P. H. Newby, O. Manning and others].

2446   "Unconvincing Liars," TLS, 2466 (6 May 1949), 297; 2467 (13
        May 1949), 313. [A leading article on the "average" novel
        since the end of the war, and a letter to the editor by
        John Brophy refuting the "worst misrepresentations" of the
        article].

2447   "Unpleasant Fiction," Bookman (London), LXVIII (Apr. 1925),
        6-15. [A symposium on "sex" novels and on whether fiction
        should tell "the whole truth." M. Sinclair, W. B. Maxwell,
        F. E. M. Young, H. A. Vachell, B. K. Seymour, F. Swinnerton,
        R. Macaulay, W. L. George, V. Rickard, N. Tom-Gallon, J. D.
        Beresford, C. de Crespigny, H. B. L. Webb, E. Raymond, and
        M. Sadleir].

2448   "The Uses of Comic Vision: A Concealed Social Point in
        Playing for Laughs," TLS, 3054 (9 Sep. 1960), ix. [Special
        Number on the British Imagination. On the use of humour by
        English novelists over the previous half-century as a "nat-
        ural situation." H. G. Wells, A. Huxley, A. Powell, K.
        Amis, and A. Sillitoe].

2449   Uzzell, Thomas H. "Modern Innovation," CE, VII:2 (Nov. 1945),
        59-65. [Argues that the new subject matter of the novel--
        realism, psychological, physical and biological--and the

338

novelist's objectivity, are the distinguishing characteristics of the modern novel, rather than its "technical devices"].

2450 _____. "Novels Old and New," LitR, (11 Aug. 1923),
902. [A Letter to the Editor refuting two allegations made
in "The Passing of Characters," LitR, III:45 (7 July 1923),
809, 1) that there is less "story" and more of the "rhap-
sodical, episodic and psychological" in the so-called psychoanalytical novel, and 2) that character has disappeared
from the novel].

2451 _____. "The Novel that Says Something," EJ, XLVII:5
(May 1958), 255-258. [Makes a plea for the moral responsibility of the novelist and the novel with a purpose. Mentions A. Huxley, G. Orwell, and N. Shute as he surveys the
American scene].

2452 Vachell, Horace Annesley. "Technique of Novels and Plays,"
EDH, XVI (1938), 43-60. [Suggests a "rule of thumb" for
evaluating novels, depending on the allocation of marks for
style, story, originality, imagination, credibility, characterisation, right balance of narrator and dialogue, wit
and humour, cumulative tension, and general charm].

2453 Vančura, Zdeněk. "Ztracená generace anglického románu,"
CMF, XLIX (1967), 1-10. [Focuses on the "lost generation"
of English novelist--J. D. Beresford, G. Cannan, H. Walpole,
O. Onions, F. B. Young, F. Swinnerton, and C. Mackenzie--
who is neither classified as Edwardian nor Georgian, and is
lost between the pre-1910 generation and the postwar "giants"].

2454 Van Kranendonk, A. G. "Notes on Methods of Narration in
some English Novels," ES, IV (Feb. 1922), 1-10. [A brief
examination of the merits and limitations of three current
methods of narration: "the direct or epic, the autobiographical and the documentary," advocating experiments in
new narrative techniques to accompany the change in the
"character" of fiction. J. Joyce, H. James, and J. Conrad].

2455 Vaxrusev, V. S. "Progressinivnyk istoričeskij roman v sov-
remennoj anglijskoj literature," FN, VI:1 (1963), 41-52.
["The progressive historical novel in contemporary English
Literature." Mostly confined to the "socially progressive"
novel of the thirties by "L. G. Gibbon," N. Mitchison, and
J. Lindsay].

2456 Vidan, Ivo. "Modifikacije modernog romana," ForumZ, (1966),
269-280. [The article is divided into three sections, each
concerned with changes and modifications in the 20th century
novel. The first part examines briefly J. Joyce's and A.
Sillitoe's usage of the incident of falling in their novels;
the second examines the three generations of novelists--J.

Conrad, J. Joyce, and S. Beckett--and the third discusses the narrator and the open-ended form of the novel of L. Durrell and others].

2457 Viebrock, Helmut. "Sprachstil und Sprachspiel. (Das Motiv 'Bildergalerie' und seine Funktion im englischen Roman)," NS, (1955), 193-207. [On the power of language to depict the motif of "painting" and its function in C. Dickens' Bleak House, G. Meredith's The Egoist, J. Galsworthy's The Forsyte Saga, and C. Morgan's The Fountain].

2458 Vince, Charles. "Art and Time," LMer, (Oct. 1920), 716-721. [Deplores the acute sense of time and decay in the modern novel for it ignores the "supreme privilege of art, which is that it may end where it likes," and loses "the power through art, to escape for a little out of time." Brief references to C. Mackenzie and A. Bennett among others].

2459 Vincent, C. J. "Dilemma in Modern Literature," QQ, LXIX:3 (Autumn 1962), 428-441. [Surveys the growth of the rift between reason and intuition, hope and despair, peace and uncertainty and fear, from the 18th century to the late thirties. E. M. Forster and A. Huxley among others].

2460 Vincent, Melvin J. "Fiction Mirrors the War," S&SR, XXX (Nov. 1945), 101-111. [Reviews some fifty war novels written in or after 1943 by English, American and other writers, from the vantage points of locale or scene of action, and of principal theme. N. Shute, C. Dale, J. B. Priestley, R. D. Henriques, V. Brittain and others].

2461 Vonalt, Larry P. "Of Time and Literature," SR, LXXVII:1 (Winter 1969), 164-170. [A review article on A. Burgess' The Novel Now: A Guide to Contemporary Fiction, L. D. Rubin' The Curious Death of the Novel: Essays in American Literature, and F. Kermode's The Sense of an Ending: Studies in the Theory of Fiction].

2462 Voorhees, Richard J. "The New Comedy," CF, XXXVII (May 1957) 37-39. [Examines J. Wain and K. Amis as "humorists of the first rank"].

2463 Vowinkel, E. "Umwelt und seelicher Lebensraum in der englischen Erzählungskunst der Gegenwart," NMonat, III (1932), 274-286. [On the physical world and spiritual dimensions in contemporary English. H. Walpole, A. Huxley, and S. Jameson].

2464 _____. "Die neue positive Wendung im englischen Roman der Gegenwart," NMonat, IV (1933), 300-310. [A survey of the contemporary novel that reveals a new turn toward a positive attitude after postwar disillusionment].

2465 _____. "Desillusion und Lebensbejahung. Aus der englisch-amerikanischen Erzählungskungst der jünsten Zeit,"
NMonat, V (1934), 540-552. [Maintains that disillusionment
in narrative art can be seen in novels that explore society--
A. Huxley, O. Sitwell--or in those distrustful of values--
H. Vaughan, S. Jameson, S. Maugham, C. Lloyd-Jones--and
"lebensbejahung," in novels that show surface allegiance to
a positive and constructive attitude--S. Lewis, J. B. Priest-
ley--or spiritual dimensions--H. Walpole, R. Davies--or show
man in harmony with his environment--M. Steen, R. H. Mottram].

2466 _____. "Der neue Weg des englischen Romans," NMonat,
VIII (1937), 62-72. [Illustrates, from novels of the early
thirties, the preponderance of realism in A. J. Cronin, G.
Blake, L. Bromfield, the psychological element in S. McKenna,
E. Bowen, G. Bullet, "R. West," and the harmony between man
and his environment in H. Vaughan, W. Townsend, and M. Sharp].

2467 W., G. O. "Oxford Novels New and Old," OM, (26 Nov. 1915),
109-111. [Contrasts novels which represent Oxford life by
H. V. Dickinson, C. Mackenzie, J. Palmer, I. Brown, and M.
T. H. Sadleir with older ones written in the nineteenth cen-
tury].

2468 Wagner, Geoffrey. "The Writer in the Welfare State," Commonweal, LXV (12 Oct. 1956), 49-50. [Discusses C. P. Snow's
re-introduction of "old-fashioned values in the contemporary
novel"].

2469 _____. "Wyndham Lewis and James Joyce: A Study in
Controversy," SAQ, LVI (Jan. 1957), 57-66. [Describes the
manner in which W. Lewis satirized J. Joyce, and the latter's
response].

2470 _____. "Sociology and Fiction," TC, CLXVII (Feb. 1960),
108-114. [On the distinction between the "literary" poetic
novel and the "non-fiction" novel which threatens to restrict
the aesthetic sensibilities, and which is evaluated on the
basis of sociological relevance].

2471 _____. "John Bull's Other Empire," ModA, VIII (1964),
284-290. [On the distortion of "British Colonialism," the
"concepts popularized about it," and the stereotypes resulting from fictive literature. J. Conrad, E. M. Forster, J.
Cary, and G. Orwell].

2472 _____. "The Novel of Empire," EIC, XX:2 (Apr. 1970),
229-242. [Examines the commercial background, moral values
and attitudes to Whitehall in works by R. Kipling, J. Conrad,
E. M. Forster, J. Cary, and G. Orwell].

2473 Waidson, H. M. "Der moderne Roman in England und Deutsch-
land: Eine Orientierung," WW, VII (1957), 152-159. [A sur-

341

vey of the English novel from J. Joyce and V. Woolf to the present].

2474 Wain, John. "The Man in the Blue Suit Belt," SatR, XXXIX (1 Dec. 1956), 15-17. [Describes how London plays a central part in the life of every English man of letters and how his prospects are conditioned by the responses of its editors. Also describes the typical "life cycle" of successful writers and "Young Hopefuls"].

2475 _____. "London Letter," HudR, XV (Summer 1960), 253-260. [On the literary-intellectual scene, especially F. F. Leavis' attack on C. P. Snow. Refers briefly to English novels as "tailor-made suits . . . well made, unobtrusive, in good taste and likely to wear adequately"].

2476 _____. "The Conflict of Forms in Contemporary English Literature (II)," CritQ, IV:2 (Summer 1962), 101-119. Reprinted in Essays, Literature and Ideas. (London: Macmillan, 1963), pp. 1-56. [The second part of a long article which attempts to define the position of contemporary literary forms in relation to their evolution. Part 2 focuses on the contemporary novel as a "form in evident decline" after having lost popular support and being supplanted by mass communication].

2477 _____. "Fiction and Fact," NYTBR, (24 Jan. 1965), 2. [Expresses the view that the predominance of the documentary or "eye-witness report" is a blemish in the contemporary novel, and detracts from the novelist's vision and his imagination].

2478 Walcutt, Charles Child. "Fear Motifs in the Literature Between Wars," SAQ, XLVI (Apr. 1947), 227-238. [On the changing pattern of attitudes toward war that "begins with guilt" after World War I, "turns into fear, and purges itself in confrontation" with World War II. Mainly concerned with poetry, but contains brief references to A. Huxley and H. G. Wells].

2479 Waley, Arthur. "The Quartette," NSta, XXVI (2 Jan. 1926), 356-357. [Indicates that good fiction depends on a balance of its four component parts: narrative of events, dialogue, psychology, and authorial comment].

2480 Walker, Kenneth. "The Role of the Writer in the Present World Crisis," HJ, LII:4 (July 1954), 375-380. [Contends that writers and artists have "not discharged their responsibilities" in the quest for truth, and deplores the fact that novelists have directed their attention "solely to the lower levels of the human mind"].

2481 Walpole, Hugh. "Women Novelists. Another Point of View," SatR, CXXXIII (18 Mar. 1922), 279-290. Revised and reprinted

as "Some Younger English Novelists," Bookman (New York),
LXI (May 1925), 267-270. [Examines the new women's movement
in fiction, women's concerns with the art and technique of
the novel, their attitude to their own sex, and failure in
portraying male character, and the "feminine softness and
looseness" which makes many of their novels "dim and faint."
R. Macaulay, R. Wilson, C. Dane, V. Woolf, V. Sackville-
West, and D. Richardson].

2482   _____. "Critic and Novelist," Bookman (New York),
LXIII (Apr. 1926), 140-145. [An imaginary conversation between critic and novelist in which each speaks of his art
and its problems].

2483   _____. "An Apology for Novel-Writing," CorM, LXVIII:
408 (June 1930), 656-661. [Defends the "traditional" novel
against the charge that it is "completely and irrevocably
dead"].

2484   _____. "Recent English Fiction," Spectator, CXLVI:5355
(14 Feb. 1931), 230. [Personal views on novels of 1930 by
A. Bennett, "H. H. Richardson," J. B. Priestley and A. P.
Herbert commending the "return to sanity, cheerfulness and
generous full-handed creation"].

2485   _____. "Tendencies of the Modern Novel," FR, (NS)
CXXXIV, (Oct. 1933), 407-415. Reprinted in Tendencies of
the Modern Novel. (London: George Allen & Unwin, 1934),
pp. 13-31. [Discusses the influence of D. H. Lawrence, V.
Woolf and A. Huxley on the writing of fiction, and their
experiments in narrations and the creation of character.
This is the first of a series by different writers on tendencies in the modern novel in France, America, Germany,
Spain, Russia, Italy and Scandinavia].

2486   _____. "The Novel of Ideas," LA, 354 (May 1938), 267-
268. Reprinted from The Listener. [Opposes the notion that
"new and arresting ideas" in a novel are more important than
character].

2487   _____. "Families in Fiction," Listener, (19 May 1937),
992-993. Reprinted in LA, 354 (Aug. 1938), 544-547. [On
"sequels" or series of novels that describe the fortunes of
a family in the 19th and 20th centuries. G. B. Stern and
J. Galsworthy among others].

2488   _____. "English Domestic Fiction: Its Influence
Abroad," TLS, 2014 (7 Sep. 1940), 445. [Reviews the English
novel of family life, from Richardson to H. James, J. Galsworthy, H. G. Wells, A. Bennett and E. M. Forster, and discusses its popularity on the Continent].

2489   Walsh, Chad. "Attitudes Toward Science in the Modern 'Inverted Utopia'," Extrapolation, II (1961), 23-26. Original-

ly presented at the Meeting of General Topics 7: Literature
and Science, MLA Meetings, 1960. [Attributes the suspicion
of science in 20th century anti-Utopias to the belief that
science strengthens the "power of evil or misguided men,"
and contributes to make us "forget our roots in the good
earth." A. Huxley, G. Orwell, C. S. Lewis, E. Waugh, and
E. M. Forster's short stories].

2490　Ward, Christopher. "The Futilitarians," Independent, CXVI
(27 Mar. 1926), 351-352. [Emphasises the tendencies and
deficiencies common in modern novels of the previous decade
and which he groups under the general headings of "formlessness," lack of significant content, absence of great character, excessive "philanthropism" and a "lack of courage and
spontaneous gaiety"].

2491　Ward, J. A. "Dining with the Novelists," Person, XLV (1964),
399-411. [On the uses of dining as a "complex and meaningful" experience in the works of English novelists. Included
are H. James, E. Waugh, and J. Joyce].

2492　Wardle, Irving. "Sur le'roman-vérité'," TR, CCXXX (1967),
121-124. Originally in English. Translated by Claude Elsen.
Copyright Opera-Mundi--Observer. [Argues that the crisis
of the English novel is its ceasing to be a vehicle of moral
criticism, the exceptions being W. McIlvanney's Remedy is
None and N. Dennis' A House in Order, that novelists pursue
the method of reporting, are afraid of general ideas and
strong emotions, refuse to judge, and are reluctant to take
risks on the emotional level].

2493　Warnke, F. J. "Some Recent Novels: A Variety of Worlds,"
YR, L (Spring 1961), 627-633. [A review article on novels
by K. Amis, G. Greene, M. Spark, and I. Murdoch].

2494　Warren, C. H. "Literature since the War: England," Outlook,
LIX:1527 (7 May 1927), 523-524. [A brief survey deploring
the absence of talented and creative younger writers].

2495　Watson, Cresap S. "Contemporary Literature," CEA, XIX:8
(Nov. 1957), 1, 4-5. [Though basically an attempt to justify the teaching of contemporary literature at University,
the article outlines the various influences on contemporary
literature in general and its "striking departures and distinctive features"].

2496　Watson, E. H. Lacon. "The Modern Novel and Its Public,"
Dial, L (1 Mar. 1911), 150-152. [On the length of the modern novel, the public's reaction, and author-publisher re-
lationships].

2497　_____. "The Modern English Novel: Some Tendencies,"
Dial, LV (1 Oct. 1913), 251-252. [On the increased length

of novels, the decay of the love interest and gradual extinction of the happy ending, and the self-imposed specialization of novelists in "a certain locality, subject, or even type of character"].

2498 Waugh, Alec. "The Neo-Georgians," FR, CXXI (NS) CXV (Jan. 1924), 126-137. [Considers the "profound and disturbing" impact of peace on the neo-Georgians, especially the poets. Brief references to A. Huxley and J. Joyce].

2499 _____. "The Post-War Novel," Independent, CXIII:3878 (27 Sep. 1924), 194-195. [Summarizes the achievement of G. Cannan and H. Walpole, remarks on the predominance of women writers, and suggests reasons for the death of the "chronicle novel" and its replacement by the "straightforward novel . . . the subject, introspective novel," and the "Aldous Huxley novel"].

2500 _____. "A Novelist Tells of His Search for Plots that Thicken," NYTBR, (24 July 1960), 4. Reprinted in Opinions and Perspectives from 'The New York Time Book Review'. Edited by E. Francis Brown. (Boston: Houghton Mifflin, 1964), pp. 314-320. [Narrates his experiences as he searches for "a theme, a setting, a twist of narrative that will give coherence to the stories" he weaves out of the day-to-day experiences of living].

2501 _____. "The Novelists as Hero," NYTBR, (20 June 1965), 2. Reprinted in The Best of 'Speaking of Books' from 'The New York Times Book Review'. Edited, with an Introduction by E. Francis Brown. (New York: Holt, Rinehart & Winston, 1969), pp. 89-93. [On the novelist's "three-pronged problem"--acquiring the material for his novels, attaining peace of mind in which to write them, and creating human beings who will fit the pattern created by these two demands].

2502 _____. "Speaking of Books: The Future, Fifty Years Ago," NYTBR, (30 July, 1967), 2, 30. [Compares novelists and their conditions today with those of fifty years ago].

2503 _____ and Stephen Spender. "Have English Writers Marked Time? A Conspectus of Prose and Poetry During Six Years of War," SatR, XXIX (5 Jan. 1946), 3-5, 29-30. [A. Waugh explains why the quantity of English wartime novels diminished and S. Spender sketches the achievement of poetry].

2504 Waugh, Arthur. "The New Realism," FR, CV (May 1916), 849-858; LA, 289 (10 June 1916), 677-685. [On the "new realism of the emotions," a new movement in English fiction whose interest "is not the material convenience or inconvenience of life, but the spiritual achievement of man, and his ultimate realization of his soul's responsibilities." G. Cannan, H. G. Wells, C. Mackenzie, and H. Walpole].

2505   Weaver, Robert. "England's Angry Young Men--Mystics, Pro-
       vincials and Radicals," QQ, LXV (Summer 1958), 183-194. [An
       analysis of the achievements of the group, their frustrations
       and reasons for their anger. The group is divided into:
       "Mystics"--C. Wilson, S. Holroyd, Bill Hopkins--"Provincials"
       --K. Amis, J. Wain, J. Braine--and "Radicals"--J. Osborne,
       K. Tynan, L. Anderson].

2506   Weber, Eugen. "The Anti-Utopia of the Twentieth Century,"
       SAQ, LVIII:3 (Summer 1959), 440-447. [On the anti-Utopian
       novel which uses familiar Utopian conventions to express
       a mood of dread and despair occasioned by the results or
       the implications of utopian dreams].

2507   Wegwitz, Paul. "Englische Romane," Tat, XIX (1927), 677-
       690. [A consideration of several English novels including
       one by each of J. Galsworthy and J. Conrad].

2508   Weible, Gladys. "The Novel Today in England and American,"
       CAL, VIII (Summer/Autumn 1972), 9-14. [Examines the "search
       for identity" in contemporary English and American novels
       with the assumption that it is no longer possible to read
       contemporary writing "with the literary standards of the
       past in our minds" after the "revolution in consciousness"
       which followed the second World War. M. Bragg, M. Drabble,
       and I. Murdoch among others. Also includes a list of Eng-
       lish and American novelists whose published writing appeared
       since 1945].

2509   Weidle, Wladimir. "La Jeune Littérature anglaise," Mois,
       (Feb. 1938), 172-182. [A French view of the English lit-
       erary scene, especially in the twenties and early thirties,
       focusing on the new "sensibility" and modes of thought intro-
       duced by writers like V. Woolf, D. Garnett, J. Joyce, W.
       Lewis, E. M. Forster, D. H. Lawrence, and T. F. Powys among
       others].

2510   Weightman, J. G. "Soft Centres," NC, (Nov. 1950), 331-338.
       [Compares C. P. Snow's The Light and the Dark, E. Waugh's
       Brideshead Revisited, A. Huxley's Time Must Have a Stop,
       S. Maugham's The Razor's Edge, and C. Morgan's Sparkenbroke
       to G. Greene's The Power and the Glory, and shows how un-
       reality at the core of the first five novels, that "central
       softness," disqualifies them from the category of serious
       literature].

2511   Weinmann, Robert. "Die Literatur der Angry Young Men. Ein
       Beitrag zur Deutung englischen Gegenwartsliteratur," ZAA,
       VII (1959), 117-189. [Attempts a study of the literature
       of "The Angry Young Men" by analysing the political, social
       and educational background of postwar England, discussing
       the message and problems aroused by two of Osborne's plays,
       three of K. Amis' novels, and J. Braine's Room at the Top.

Also identifies six major characteristics of the literature of these writers].

2512 _____ . "Erzählerstandpunkt und Point of View. Zur Geschichte und Ästhetik der Perspektive im englischen Roman," ZAA, X (1962), 369-416. [A comprehensive study of point of view and narrator's standpoint discussing the aesthetic foundation and history of "perspective" in the English novel].

2513 Weinkauf, Mary S. "Edenic Motifs in Utopian Fiction," Extrapolation, XI (Dec. 1969), 15-22. [Examines the motifs of "purity, harmony, peace, love, beauty and elevation of man above his present limitations" in Utopias in order to emphasise the ideal nature of their imaginary societies].

2514 _____ . "The God Figure in Dystopian Fiction," RQ, IV (1971), 266-271. [On the "God-surrogates" in Dystopian novels by G. Orwell, A. Huxley, and L. P. Hartley among others].

2515 Weir, J. L. "Pen and Sword: Some Soldier-Authors and Their Books," N&Q, CLXXIV (25 June 1938), 452-455. [Notes on "soldiers by profession, writers by natural talent." P. C. Wren, C. McNeile (Sapper), J. Grant, and G. W. Whyte-Melville].

2516 Wellings, Arthur. "In Defence of Young Novelists," Bookman (London), (Nov. 1931), 102-103. [Defends the outspokenness and experiments of younger novelists on the grounds that these writers are in harmony with the spirit of the age and reflect their times].

2517 "The Wells and Bennett Novel," TLS, (23 Aug. 1928), 597-598. [A leading article comparing the two novelists and showing in what ways they enlarge one's sensibilities].

2518 "H. G. Wells Heads a Revolt Against the ¦Weary Giant'," CLit, LII (Jan. 1912), 97-98. [Excerpts from H. G. Wells' "The Contemporary Novel" FR, LXXXIX:539 (Nov. 1911), 860-873), interspersed with comments, giving the substance of Wells' article].

2519 Wells, H. G. "The Contemporary Novel," FR, LXXXIX:539 (Nov. 1911), 860-873. Reprinted in AtM, CIX:1 (Jan. 1912), 1-11, and Social Forces in England and America. (New York: Harper, 1914), pp. 173-198. [Rejects the type of novel which is a "harmless opiate" with a "definite length and definite form," upholds the novel as a "powerful instrument of moral suggestion," as the "only medium" that can reflect the times, and advocates absolute freedom for the novelist in his "choice of topic and incident, and . . . method of treatment." Brief references to J. Conrad, J. Galsworhty, and A. Bennett].

2520 Wells, James M. "The Artist in the English Novel, 1850-1919," WVUS, IV (1943-1944), 77-80. [Surveys the literary conception of the artist in works by M. Roberts and S. Maugham among others].

2521 Welsh, Paul. "Hypotheses, Plausibility, and Fiction," PPR, LXII (Jan. 1953), 102-107. [A discussion of Robert T. Harris's ("Plausibility in Fiction," JP, XLIV (3 Jan. 1952), 5-10) raising the question of what a reader will accept as a significant matter in fiction instead of this plausibility].

2522 Welty, Eudora. "Place in Fiction," SAQ, LV:1 (Jan. 1956), 57-72. Reprinted as a booklet with the same title (New York: House of Books, 1957), and in Critical Approaches to Fiction. Edited by Shiv K. Kumar and Keith F. McKean. (New York: McGraw-Hill, 1968), pp. 249-267. [Argues that sense of place in novel writing is as essential as a "logical mind," and emphasises the importance of place not only as a "plausible abode" for the novel's "world of feeling" but also for its effect on theme and in making character real].

2523 West, Paul. "The Nature of Fiction," EIC, XIII:1 (Jan. 1963) 95-100. [Notes on Art, Fiction, the Novel, and "No-Novel." Asserts individual consciousness to be the "last stage of truth-to-life" beyond which the novel becomes a symbolist poem; hence, his rejection of the anti-novel and his call for the return of form, structure and the narrator to the novel].

2524 _____. "Perpetuating the Obsolete," Commonweal, LXXXVII (17 Nov. 1967), 203-205. [Resents the low-keyed tone and the "homespun" quality of the contemporary English novel and its concern and interest in social matters].

2525 "West, Rebecca." [Cicily Isobel Fairfield] "The Novel of Ideas," NRep, V (20 Nov. 1915), 3-5. (Supplement). [A review article of H. G. Wells' The Research Magnificent underlining the importance and the place of ideas in a novel].

2526 Wexler, Alexanda. Der Abgeschnittene Kopf," DeutR, LXXXVIII (1962), 50-55. ["The Severed Head." Examines different aspects of the "sickness of the times" as depicted in novels by D. H. Lawrence, I. Murdoch, S. Delaney, A. Sillitoe, C. Wilson, and G. Greene].

2527 Weygandt, Cornelius. "The Lies About Life in Modern Letters, GMHC, XLIV (1942), 259-267. [Reviews the quality of life presented by major dramatists and novelists over the previous thirty years].

2528 Wharton, Edith. "The Criticism of Fiction," TLS, 643 (14 May 1914), 229-230. Reprinted in LA, 282 (25 July 1914),

204-211, and in TLS, 2607 (18 Jan. 1952), 52-53. [Agrees with H. James that the criticism of fiction is "practically non-existent" in England and America, discusses the reasons for its non-existence, and argues that the development of professional criticism will help novelists master form and technique, and that it will have something to say to the novelist].

2529 _____. "Character and Situation in the Novel," SMag, LXXVIII:4 (Oct. 1925), 394-399. [Contends that real genious combines both character and situation in the novel].

2530 _____. "Visibility in Fiction," L&L, II (Apr. 1929), 263-272. Also in YR, XVIII (Spring 1929), 480-488. Condensed in LDig, CI (13 Apr. 1929), 28. [Discusses "life-likeness" of characters in a novel, or what makes for visibility in character drawing--that "rarest (gift) in the novelist's endowment." Illustrates from a wide range of novelists, English, American and Continental].

2531 _____. "Tendencies in Modern Fiction," SatR, X (27 Jan. 1934), 433-434. Reprinted in Designed for Reading: An Anthology Drawn from 'The Saturday Review of Literature'. Edited by H. S. Canby and others. (New York: Macmillan, 1934), pp. 37-42, and in Saturday Review Treasury. Selected by John Haverstick, with an Introduction by Joseph Wood Krutch. (New York: Simon & Schuster, 1957), pp. 39-43. [Contends that modern English and American fiction has rejected the past, form in structure, and the drawing of character; hence, its tendency toward "the amorphous and the agglutinative" where younger novelists try to give substance to their creations by "exaggerated physical realism, and . . . singularities of dialect and slang"].

2532 _____. "Permanent Values in Fiction," SatR, X (7 Apr. 1934), 603-604. Reprinted in Writing for Love or for Money, 35 Essays Reprinted from 'The Saturday Review of Literature'. Edited by N. Cousins (London: Longmans, 1949), 52-57. [Maintains that the modern novelist, unhampered by restrictions in his search for new "forms," tends to forget the lasting qualities of fiction: creation of characters and "relating their individual case to the general human problem"].

2533 "What Is a Novel? Symposium," Bookman (New York), XLII (Feb. 1916), 652-667. Condensed in CO, LX (Mar. 1916), 198-199. [Among the 27 contributors are Robert W. Chambers, W. L. George, A. Hope, E. P. Oppenheim, and H. Walpole].

2534 "What Is a Novel" TLS, 2932 (9 May 1958), 255. [A leading article pointing out that that novelist's invention "within a framework of the possibilities of actual life," and its being a "process of groping . . . of moral discovery," distinguishes the novel from other prose works].

2535 Wheaton, L. "All's Love, Yet All's Law," CathW, CXV (Apr. 1922), 10-21. [Considers the realistic novel of the 19th and early 20th centuries from a Catholic viewpoint. H. G. Wells, A. Bennett, J. Galsworthy, and C. Mackenzie among others].

2536 "Where Does Fiction Stand To-Day?" LDig, LXXII (4 May 1922), 31. [Replies by R. Macaulay, M. Sinclair, and G. Saintsbury to Miss Cecily Hamilton's charge that "the novel is played out"].

2537 "Which Man, in Which Novel?" TLS, 3402 (11 May 1967), 400. [A review article on R. A. Donovan's The Shaping Vision (Cornell University Press & Oxford University Press, 1967), H. R. Steeves' Before Jane Austen (London: Allen & Unwin), D. Spearman's The Novel and Society (London: Routledge & Kegan Paul), A. Freedman's The Turn of the Novel (Oxford University Press), C. C. Walcutt's Man's Changing Mask (University of Minnesota Press & Oxford University Press), and L. Lerner's The Truthtellers (London: Chatto & Windus)].

2538 White, John J. "Myths and Pattern in the Modern Novel," Mosaic, II:3 (Spring 1969), 42-55. [Rejects the hypothesis that mythological correspondences in modern novels are simply used to give "shape to events, to structure the plot," and argues that the parallels achieve their main dramatic effect because of the specific order in which they are presented. J. Joyce and A. Burgess among others].

2539 Whiting, B. J. "Historical Novels, 1948-1949," Speculum, XXV (Jan. 1950), 104-122. [A review of some 14 novels, including one by each of N. Mitchison, E. M. Almedingen, and S. T. Warner].

2540 _____. "Historical Novels, 1949-1950," Speculum, XXVI (Apr. 1951), 337-367. [A review of some 27 novels, among which are works by E. Linklater, O. Lancaster, N. Balchin, and R. Graves].

2541 "Why Not War Writers? A Manifesto," Horizon, (Oct. 1941), 236-239. [The manifesto is signed on behalf of younger writers by A. Calder-Marshall, C. Connolly, B. Dobrée, T. Harrison, A. Koestler, A. Lewis, G. Orwell, and S. Spender, and proposes the formation of an official group of war writers, and encourages the international exchange of writers].

2542 "Why Novelists Write Badly," SatR, X (2 June 1934), 724. [An editorial attributing the inferior style of contemporary novels to the influence of journalism and the strain upon language resulting from experiment in fiction].

2543 Wilcock, J. Rodolfo. "Il monologo interiore: Note sull' evoluzione del romanzo," TPr, IV (1959), 208-213. [Maintains that narrative and style constitute technique in fiction, and distinguishes three methods in the "stream of consciousness": the interior monologue--direct as in Molly Bloom's last monologue, and indirect as in the opening page of Mrs. Dalloway--the description of the "flusso del pensiero" as in D. Richardson's Pilgrimage, and the soliloquy as in Faulkner's As I Lay Dying. Also examines variations by G. Greene, E. Bowen, H. Green, and A. Wilson].

2544   Wilkinson, Clennell. "Back to All That," LMer, XXII (Oct. 1930), 439-446. [Confines his review of war books to the category of "personal reminiscences"].

2545   Willey, Frederick. "The Novel and the Natural Man," MQR, VII (Spring 1968), 104-113. [Surveys the novel's preference for a reality discovered through the senses--"spontaneous feeling"--rather than reality through the process of analytical reason, from Cervantes to Camus. H. James and D. H. Lawrence among others].

2546   William-Ellis, A. "Modern Novels," NSta, XXVI (31 Oct. 1925), 76-78. Reprinted in LA, 327 (12 Dec. 1925), 582-585. [Comments on the "queer form of narrative" depicting the consciousness of one person, and which is utilized by D. Richardson, J. Joyce, and V. Woolf].

2547   Williams, Orlo. "Recent Fiction Chronicle," NCrit, XI (Oct. 1931), 86-95. [Deplores the recent absence of any important English novels, and reviews works by A. J. Cronin, S. Kaye-Smith, V. Sackville-West, and D. Garnett].

2548   Williams, Raymond. "Realism and the Contemporary Novel," PR, XXVI:2 (Spring 1959), 200-213. Reprinted as Chapter VII in The Long Revolution. (London: Chatto & Windus; New York: Columbia University Press; Toronto: Clarke Irwin, 1961). [On the existing variations in "realism" as a descriptive term, and on what have now become separate absolutes: the division of the "realist" novel into the social novel and the personal, and the "new realism" as a "continual achievement of balance" between the individual and society. J. Joyce, G. Greene, V. Woolf, W. Golding, A. Huxley, C. P. Snow, E. M. Forster, A. Wilson and others].

2549   _____. "Affluence after Anger," Nation, CCIII (19 Dec. 1966), 676-677. [Compares and contrasts the thirties and fifties to determine what happened to the issues of the fifties and what caused the "dispersion" of its cultural generation].

2550   Williams, S. T. "Aspects of the Modern Novel," TRev, VIII (Apr. 1923), 245-256. [On the persistence of the Victorian novel in the form, interests and ethics of the "modern" novels of R. Macaulay, A. Marshall, Sir H. Johnston, J.

Galsworthy, and H. Walpole, as distinct from the novels of "unrestrained revolt" of D. H. Lawrence and F. Swinnerton].

2551 Williams, W. E. "Can Literature Survive? The Novel and the Cinema," Listener, (21 Aug. 1935), 330-332. [Considers the "possible rivalry" between novel and cinema, and admits that though the cinema may usurp the kind of fiction that depends upon plot, it cannot conquer "one territory of the novel . . . the annotation of human experience"].

2552 Williamson, Henry. "Reality in War Literature," LMer, XIX (Jan. 1929), 295-304. [A record of personal impressions of war books which includes works by W. Ewart, R. H. Mottram, F. M. Ford, G. Duhamel, and E. Blunden].

2553 Willy, Margaret. "What Do They Read? Twentieth Century English Literature in Europe Today," English, XV:88 (Spring 1965), 128-133. [Considers the popularity of 20th century English writers in several European countries].

2554 Wilson, Angus. "Broken Promise," Listener, (12 Apr. 1951), 575-576. [Examines the weaknesses and failure of the "younger generation" of novelists between 1912 and 1922 before the arrival of the new "highbrow literature." H. Walpole, G. Cannan, C. Mackenzie, J. D. Beresford, and S. Kaye-Smith].

2555 _____. "The Future of the English Novel," Listener, LI:1313 (29 Apr. 1954), 746. [Unsigned commentary. On the decline of the entertainment element in serious fiction and its relation to social structure].

2556 _____. "The Art of Fiction XX," ParRev, 17 (1958), 88-105. [An interview by Michael Millgate in which A. Wilson discusses his method of writing, his works and views on others writers].

2557 _____. "Mood of the Month--III," LM, V:4 (Apr. 1958), 40-44. [Discusses the status of the writer and the function of the novel in a status society].

2558 _____. "Diversity and Depth," TLS, 2946 (15 Aug. 1958), viii. [Special section: "Books in a Changing World." Notes the emphasis on the social framework and the restoration of the formal framework of plot and narrative in the postwar English novel as a "temporary rejection of over-exploited devices still rich in promise," and perhaps as indicative of the interest in the "adult" element that combines depth of vision with breadth].

2559 _____. "Evil in the English Novel," Listener, LXVIII: 1761 (27 Dec. 1962), 15-16; LXIX:1762 (3 Jan. 1963), 15-16; LXIX:1763 (10 Jan. 1963), 63-65; LXIX:1764 (17 Jan. 1963), 115-117. Reprinted with minor revisions in KR, XXIX:2 (Mar.

1967), 167-194. [A series of four talks on the B. B. C. Third Programme subtitled "Richardson and Jane Austen," "From George Eliot to Virginia Woolf," "Outside the Central Tradition," and "Evil and the Novelist Today." Surveys the various forms which the shift from abstract evil to right and wrong has taken in the English novel from Richardson to the present, and contends that the removal of the transcendent element from evil emphasises society, sex and morality; hence, a "continental sense of good and evil transcendent" is imperative if the traditional novel is to break its "provincial, encaging shape." H. James, E. M. Forster, J. Conrad, J. C. Powys, G. Greene, W. Woolf, I. Compton-Burnett, W. Golding, and others. Letters to the Editor in the same issues by B. Vincent, W. L. Fryer, L. M. Gough, N. Ronald, E. M. Merry, B. Dobrée, E. Jones, and H. H. Harvey. Correspondence answered by A. Wilson, LXIX:1765 (24 Jan. 1963), 169].

2560 _____. "The Condition of the Novel: Britain," NLR, XXIX (Jan.-Feb. 1965), 35-36. [An excerpt from his address to the Conference of European Writers at Leningrad, Summer 1963. Reject the restricted choice between Russian "socialist realism" and the "nouveau roman" of Robbe-Grillet, and outlines the "variety of forms" which the English contemporary novel enjoys].

2561 _____. "The Artist as Your Enemy is Your Only Friend," SoR, II:2 (1966), 101-114. [Originally a lecture delivered at the Writers' Week during the 1966 Adelaide Festival of Arts. Argues that the "deep division" between the artist and his audience has always existed, but our consciousness of it, which has become apparent since the 19th century is harmful to the advance of art. J. Joyce and V. Woolf among others].

2562 * _____. "Is the Novel a Doomed Art Form?" ELLS, VI (1969), 1-31.

2563 Wilson, Colin. "The Writer and Publicity," Encounter, XIII: 5 (Nov. 1959), 8-13. [Argues that what the writer requires is less consciousness of the press and a greater awareness of human necessities].

2564 Wilson, James Southall. "Four English Novels," VQR, IX (Apr. 1933), 316-320. [Notices in his review a novel by each of D. Garnett, H. G. Wells, S. Maugham, and J. Galsworthy, and mentions the "diversity of method . . . characteristic of the changing novel in the twentieth century"].

2565 _____. "The Changing Novel," VQR, X (Jan. 1934), 42-52. [Observes a disintegration of the novel at the beginning of the 20th century, with the shift from the objective and the matter of fact to the subjective, subtle and experimental, which has given rise to such variety in novels that no one modern novel, unlike the works of the 19th century, can be called representative of its era].

2566 _____. "Time and Virginia Woolf," VQR, XVIII:2 (1942), 267-276. [Deals with time and human consciousness as the novel's dimensions, pointing out Virginia Woolf's concept of Time, and two disruptive influences on the novel: the fulfilment of all the established conventions, and the discrediting, by the Russian novel, of the Victorian version of life. Notes also the novelist's attempt to reach the reader by the poet's method of sense impressions].

2567 Wispelaere, Paul de. "Zijn romanpersonages van vlees en bloed?" Gids, CXXIX:4 (1966), 61-63. [A critical review of W. J. Harvey's Character and the Novel, especially of his attitude towards the "mimesis" school of art].

2568 _____. "De doad van de verteller in de roman," Gids, CXXIX:6 (1966), 191-194. [A review article on H. Servotte's De Verteller in de Engelse roman: Ein studie over roman techniek].

2569 _____. "Zijn romanpersonages van vlees en bloed?" Gids CXXIX:7-8 (1966), 311-313. [This is the second article occasioned by W. J. Harvey's Character and the Novel. Considers the autonomical theory of the novel].

2570 Wolf, Howard R. "British Fathers and Sons, 1773-1913: From Filial Submissiveness to Creativity," PsyR, LII:2 (1965), 53-70. [Charts the pattern of growing consciousness of self on the part of the son in his "role as liberator" from paternal authority, leading to full awareness and revolt. Deals with the early years of the 20th century, and includes E. Gosse, S. Butler, and D. H. Lawrence].

2571 Wolfe, B. "Angry at What?" Nation, CLXXXVII (1 Nov. 1958), 316, 318-322. [Discusses the "anger" and the "London-modulated" complaints of J. Osborne and P. O'Connor as well as the "Fresco-bopped" Beats].

2572 Wolfe, Humbert. "The Limits of Obscenity," SatR, VIII (7 May 1932), 709-710. [Maintains that D. H. Lawrence, J. Joyce, and A. Huxley have attained, each in his own way, the limits of obscenity in their reaction against Victorian prudery and sentimentalism].

2573 Wolle, Francis. "Novels of Two World Wars," WHR, V (Summer 1951), 279-296. [Includes novels by R. Aldington, F. Manning, and H. M. Tomlinson but the main concern is with the American war novel].

2574 Woodbridge, Elisabeth. "The Novelist's Choice," AtM, CX:4

(Oct. 1912), 481-491. [Discusses the choice of the autobiography as a literary form and its possibilities. H.
James and W. de Morgan among others].

2575 Woodcock, George. "Mexico and the English Novelist," WesR,
XXI (Autumn 1956), 21-32. [Argues that the "curiously-
exaggerated" description of Mexico in novels by D. H. Lawrence, A. Huxley and G. Greene is an "imposition over the
true map," of each author's personal hopes and fears, a
projection of a state of mind which he dreads most].

2576 _____. "Utopias in Negative," SR, LXIV (1956), 81-97.
[Contends that the lack of movement implicit in Utopian
society, where every social problem is solved, and "society
is frozen into a crystalline permanence," has caused the
literary form itself to disappear, and anti-Utopian novels
to be written "by men who have looked closely at the reality
which congeals out of the fantasies of the past, and who
have rejected what they see"].

2577 Woolf, Virginia. "Mr. Bennett and Mrs. Brown," LitR, IV
(17 Nov. 1923), 253-254; Nation (London), XXXIV (1 Dec.
1923), 342-343; LA, 320 (2 Feb. 1924), 229-232. Revised
and enlarged as a paper and read to the Heretics, Cambridge,
18 May 1924, and reprinted as "Character in Fiction," Criterion, II:8 (July 1924), 409-430. Also as Mr. Bennett
and Mrs. Brown. (London: The Hogarth Press, 1924). Reprinted in The Captain's Bed and Other Essays. Editorial
Note by Leonard Woolf. (London: The Hogarth Press, 1950),
pp. 90-112, and in Collected Essays , Vol. 1. (London:
The Hogarth Press, 1966), pp. 319-338. [Rejects the "Edwardian convention" of creating character--H. G. Wells, A.
Bennett, and J. Galsworthy--for the new "Georgian" one,
after giving an account of the difficulties which beset
the Georgian novelist].

2578 _____. "The Niece of An Earl," L&L, (Oct. 1928), 356-
361. Reprinted in Collected Essays, Vol. 1. (London: The
Hogarth Press, 1966), pp. 219-224. [Describes the influence
of class distinction and social rank on fiction and the nov-
elist].

2579 Woolfolk, William. "Towards a New Kind of Novel," NYTBR,
(15 Jan. 1967), 2. [Contends that to restore the novel to
its "former breadth of vision," novelists must cease to be
"word-specialists" and make the novel "part of the world
and intelligible to the minds of ordinary men"].

2580 "The Workaday World that the Novelist Never Enters," TLS,
3054 (9 Sep. 1960), vii. [Special Number on The British
Imagination. Examines the fictional achievements of C. P.
Snow, A. Powell, I. Compton-Burnett, W. Golding, L. P. Hartley and their preoccupation with social distinction, child-

hood and fantasy, and sees the fusion of the "crime novel" and the "novel proper" in G. Greene and the realism of A. Wilson as guides towards future development in England].

2581   Wright, Andrew H.   "Irony and Fiction," JAAC, XII:1 (Sep. 1953), 111-118.   Reprinted in Critical Approaches to Fiction. Edited by Shiv K. Kumar and Keith F. McKean.   (New York: McGraw-Hill, 1968), pp. 381-392.   [A broad look at irony: surveys and justifies its application to a world view, its relationship to others modes and, in the latter part of the paper, applies it to fiction].

2582   Wylie, Elinor.   "Symbols in Literature," EJ, XVII:6 (June 1928), 442-445.   [On the use of allegory in novels.   Brief reference to T. F. Powys, D. Garnett, and S. T. Warner].

2583   Wylie, I. A. R.   "Twilight Among the Authors," Century, CXV (Dec. 1927), 143-148.   [Deplores the "rotten state of fiction"--English and American--and attributes its decline to experiment in "technique," the craze for realism and Freudianism].

2584   Yamoto, Sadamiki.   "Shosetsu Gijitsu-ron no Keifu," EigoS, CXIV:2 (1 Feb. 1968), 80-81.   [In Japanese.   A brief historical survey of critical works on technique in fiction. Includes works by H. James, P. Lubbock, J. M. Murry, E. Muir, E. M. Forster, R. B. West, and R. W. Stallman].

2585   Yarros, Victor S.   "Ethics in Modern Fiction," IntJE, (Oct. 1918), 39-47.   [Refutes H. G. Wells' claim for the novel as an instrument of social and moral reform, but concedes "certain social services" it can render without violating the demand for "unity, economy and form"].

2586   Yevish, Irving A.   "The Faculty Novel," GR, XXV (1971), 41-50.   [A survey of the central topics and preoccupations of the new "sub-genre" in English and American fiction.   A. Wilson, C. P. Snow, K. Amis, and M. Bradbury among others].

2587   *Yoshida, Kenichi.   "Modern English Literature," Albion (Japan), I (1949).

2588   "Young English and American Writers," LDig, LXIII (15 Nov. 1919), 30-31.   [Statement by Cannan: "We [young novelists] are a group because fundamentally we feel the same way about things, and are trying to express them a good deal in the same way"].

2589   Young, Francis Brett.   "Confessions of a Novelist," YR, XVIII (Spring 1929), 523-538.   [Discusses the novelist's two-fold responsibility, his duty towards his art and his duty towards his reader].

2590 Zavaradeh, Mas'ud. "Anti-intellectual Intellectualism in the Post-War British Novel: In England and Germany," BSUF, XII:4 (1971), 68-73. [Traces the roots of the new "anti-modernism" of J. Wain, K. Amis, and J. Braine, the "cultured philistinism and anti-intellectual approach to life," and the underlying "anti-values" in their novels].

2591 Zimpel, Lloyd. "The Damnation is Real: Aspects of the New Anti-Hero," UKCR, XXXII (1965), 91-100. [Disagrees with O'Faolain's contention that the hero has vanished from fiction, and maintains he has changed into the man who embodies popular views as they are commonly expressed. Defines the new style anti-hero as one who embodies values not popularly expressed, as distinct from "unpopular" and usually critical views. Illustrates mainly from Cervantes, Ellison's The Invisible Man, J. Wain's Hurry on Down, Smollett's Roderick Random, Le Sagi's Gil Blas, and S. Bellow's Adventures of Augie Marsh].

2592 Zmigrodzka, M. "Problem narratora w teorii powiésa xix i xx Wiekn," PL, LIV (1963), 417-488. [A survey, in Polish, of the problems of the narrator and the theory of the novel in the nineteenth and twentieth centuries].

2593 Zucker, A. E. "The Genealogical Novel, A New Genre," PMLA, XLIII (1928), 551-560. [On the establishment of the genealogical novel by S. Butler and E. Talon, the novel which is a "panorama of several generations," the fortunes of whose characters are presented in detail "as each moves in turn through the picture." Discusses its imitation in England, America and Germany. R. Macaulay and J. Galsworthy among others].

2594 Zucker, W. "Die englische Krise in Roman," NRs, XLIII (1932), 126-132. [Discusses the crisis in theme and form in the novel. J. B. Priestley, V. Sackville-West, and J. C. Powys].

3.

Dissertations and Theses

2595 Adams, Ralph E. The Industrial Novel in England, 1832-1951. (University of Illinois, 1965).

2596 Alcorn, John Marshall. Hardy to Lawrence: A Study in Naturism. (New York University, 1966).

2597 Anantha, Murthy V. R. Politics and Fiction in the 1930s: Studies in Christopher Isherwood and Edward Upward. (University of Birmingham, 1966/67).

2598 Anderton, E. A. Utopian Ideas and Their Effects in English Fiction, 1890-1955. (M.A. Thesis, King's College, University of London, 1957/58).

2599 Aufseeser, Gretel. Jüdische Gestalten im modernem englischen Roman. (University of Zürich, 1940. Published. Zürich: Buchdruckerei Müller, Werder, 1940).

2600 Ausmus, Martin Russey. Some Forms of the Sequence Novel in British Fiction. (University of Oklahoma, 1969).

2601 Awad, Ramses. A Bibliography of the English Novel after the Second World War. (Faculty of Arts, Ain Shams University, Cairo, 1968).

2602 Bache, William B. The Functions of Characters in Fiction. (Pennsylvania State University, 1951/52).

2603 Barnes, R. C. Childhood and Adolescence in Twentieth-Century Fiction in English. (University of Liverpool 1964/65).

2604 Batchelor, J. B. Fantasy in English Prose Fiction Between 1890 and 1914. (University of Cambridge, 1968/69).

2605 Bazzanella, Dominic John. The Mad Narrator in Contemporary Fiction. (Northwestern University, 1970).

2606 Bedient, Calvin Bernard. The Fate of the Self: Self and Society in the Novels of George Eliot, D. H. Lawrence, and E. M. Forster. (University of Washington, 1964). Revised and published as Architects of the Self: George Eliot, D. H. Lawrence, and E. M. Forster. (Berkeley: University of California Press, 1972).

2607 Beebe, Maurice L. The Alienation of the Artist: A Study of Portraits by Henry James, Marcel Proust, and James Joyce. (Cornell University, 1952/53). Revised and published as Ivory Towers and Sacred Founts: The Artist as Hero in Fiction from Goethe to Joyce. (New York: New York University Press, 1964).

2608 Beja, Morris. Evanescent Moments: The Epiphany in the Modern Novel. (Cornell University, 1963). Published as Epiphany in the Modern Novel. (London: Peter Owen; Seattle:

University of Washington Press, 1971).

2609   Bennemann, Heinrich. Der zweite Weltkrieg in englischen
       Roman. (University of Leipzig, 1963).

2610   Bennett, Ernest Eugene. The Image of the Christian Clergy-
       man in Modern Fiction and Drama. (Vanderbilt University
       Divinity School, 1970).

2611   Benson, Frederick R. Writers in Arms: A Comparative Study
       of the Impact of the Spanish Civil War on the Liberal Nov-
       elist. (New York University, 1965/66). Published as Wri-
       ters in Arms: The Literary Impact of the Spanish Civil War.
       Foreword by Salvador de Madariaga. New York University
       Studies in Comparative Literature, No. 1 (New York: New
       York University Press, 1967; London: University of London
       Press, 1968).

2612   Bersani, Leo. Point of View in Fiction: Studies of Nar-
       rative Techniques. (Harvard University, 1957/58).

2613   Bilder, John Raban. The Minor Tradition in English Prose
       Fiction: The Novel of Ideas. (University of Pennsylvania,
       1964).

2614   Blackburn, A. L. The Picaresque Novel: A Literary Idea,
       1554-1954. (Fitzwilliam House, Cambridge, 1962/63).

2615   Bleich, David. Utopia: The Psychology of a Cultural Fan-
       tasy. (New York University, 1968).

2616   Boileau, Horace T. Italy in the Post-Victorian Novel. Un-
       iversity of Pennsylvania, 1931). Privately printed (Phila-
       delphia, 1931).

2617   Bokhari, Z. A. A Study of Anglo-India in Fiction. (Gerton,
       Cambridge, 1964/65).

2618   Bowling, Lawrence E. Dramatizing the Mind: A Study of the
       "Stream of Consciousness Technique." (University of Iowa,
       1945/46).

2619   Brass, Herta. Der Wandel in der Auffassung des Menschen im
       englischen Roman von 18. zum 20. Jahrhundert. (University
       of Tübingen, 1931. Published. Lippstadt/Westf., 1931).

2620   Brennan, Neil Francis. The Aesthetic Tradition in the Eng-
       lish Comic Novel. (University of Illinois, 1959).

2621   Browning, William Gordon. Anti-Utopian Fiction: Definition
       and Standards for Evaluation. (Louisiana State University,
       1966).

2622 Buckstead, Richard Chris. H. G. Wells, Arnold Bennett, John Galsworthy: Three Novelists in Revolt Against the Middle Class. (State University of Iowa, 1960).

2623 Burrows, Carolyn. The Faces of Chronos: Temporal Innovations in the Technique of the Novel. (University of Pennsylvania, 1968).

2624 Campos, C. L. France in English Literature, 1864-1930. (Gonville and Caius College, Cambridge, 1962/63). Published as The View of France from Arnold to Bloomsbury. (London: Oxford University Press, 1965).

2625 Carens, James Francis. Evelyn Waugh: His Satire, His Ideas of Order, and His Relation to Other Modern English Satirical Novelists. (Columbia University, 1958/59).

2626 Chattopadhyay, S. The Technique of the Modern English Novel. (Queen Mary College, 1956/57. Published. Calcutta: Firma K. L. Muckhopadhyay, 1959).

2627 Choudhury, A. F. S. I. The Enemy Territory--A Study of Joseph Conrad, E. M. Forster and D. H. Lawrence in Relation to their Portrayal of Evil. (University of Leicester, 1968/69).

2628 Clark, J. R. A. Realism in English Fiction, 1880-1910. (M.A. Thesis, Queen Mary College, 1954).

2629 Clark, Jeanne Gabriel. London in English Literature, 1880-1955. (Columbia University, 1957).

2630 Collins, Harold Reeves. His Image in Ebony: The African in British Fiction During the Age of Imperialism. (Columbia University, 1951).

2631 Collins, Robert George. Four Critical Interpretations in the Modern Novel. (University of Denver, 1961).

2632 Conn, Edwin Harry. The Impact of Madame Bovary on the English Novel, 1857-1915. (Columbia University, 1952).

2633 Cottrell, Beckman Waldron. Conversation Piece: Four Twentieth Century English Dialogue Novelists. (Columbia University, 1956).

2634 Cunningham, Laurence Springer. The Image of the Priest in Contemporary Anglo-American Fiction. (Florida State University, 1969).

2635 Curzon, Gordon A. Paradise Sought: A Study of the Religious Motivation in Representative British and American Literary Utopias, 1850-1950. (University of California, Riverside, 1969).

2636 Cwiakala, J. Some English and Polish Women Novelists of the Inter-War Period, 1918-1939. (B. Litt. Thesis, University of Oxford, 1969/70).

2637 Daragahi, H. Portrait of the Outsider in the Post-War English Novel. (M.A. Thesis, University of Nottingham, 1969/70).

2638 Davies, P. A. The Major Georgian Novelists and Their Approach to Fiction. (M.A. Thesis, Bangor, Wales, 1965/66).

2639 Davis, John Wesley Ford. A Theory of the Novel: Its Generic Impulse and Controlling Principle. (Stanford University, 1971).

2640 Davis, Robert Murray. The Externalist Method in the Novels of Ronald Firbank, Carl Van Vechten, and Evelyn Waugh. (University of Wisconsin, 1963/64).

2641 Debo, Elizabeth Lea. The Narrative in Henry James, Joseph Conrad and Ford Madox Ford. (University of Nebraska, 1971).

2642 DeMaria, Robert. From Bulwer-Lytton to George Orwell: The Utopian Novel in England 1870-1950. (Columbia University, 1959).

2643 De Nitto, Dennis. Modern Literary Primitivism in the Writings of D. H. Lawrence and Other British Novelists. (Columbia University, 1967).

2644 DeVitis, Angelo A. The Religious Theme in the Novels of Rex Warner, Evelyn Waugh, and Graham Greene. (University of Wisconsin, 1953/54).

2645 Doner, Dean Benton. The Burdening of Narrative. (State University of Iowa, 1953).

2646 Dooley, David Joseph. The Impact of Satire on Fiction: Studies In Norman Douglas, Sinclair Lewis, A. Huxley, E. Waugh and George Orwell. (State University of Iowa, 1955).

2647 Dowie, William John, Jr., S. J. Religious Fiction in a Profane Time: Charles Williams, C. S. Lewis, and J. R. R. Tolkien. (Brandeis University, 1970).

2648 Dulai, Surjit Singh. The White Man's Burden in Anglo-Indian Fiction. (Michigan State University, 1965).

2649 Duncan, Iris Jane Autry. The Theme of the Artist's Isolation in Works by Three Modern British Novelists. (University of Oklahoma, 1965).

2650 Dupont, V. L'Utopie et le roman utopique dans la littérature anglaise. (Université de Lyons, 1940. Published. Paris et Toulouse: Librarie M. Didier, 1941).

361

2651 Eade, D. C. Contemporary Novelists: A Study of Some Themes in the Work of Stan Barstow, John Braine, David Storey and Keith Waterhouse. (M. Phil. Thesis, University of Leeds, 1968/69).

2652 Eberly, Ralph Stevens. Joyce Cary: Theme of Freedom and a Companion with James Joyce and Graham Greene. (University of Michigan, 1970).

2653 El-Ayouty, Mohammed Yassin. Studies in the Development of the English Novel in the Late Nineteenth and Early Twentieth Centuries with Special Reference to Tragic Themes and Treatment. (Queen's College, Belfast, 1950).

2654 Espey, David Baldwin. The Imperial Protagonist: Hero and Anti-Hero in Fiction of the Late British Empire. (University of Michigan, 1971).

2655 Feigenbaum, Lawrence H. War, As Viewed by the Post War Novelists of World Wars I and II. (New York University, 1950/51).

2656 Fernberg, Babeth Grace. Treatment of Jewish Character in the Twentieth Century Novel (1900-1940) in France, Germany, England and United States. (Stanford University, 1943/44).

2657 Freedman, Richard. The Conflict of the Generations in English Autobiographical Fiction. (Cornell University, 1967).

2658 Friedman, Alan Howard. The Turn of the Novel: Changes in the Pattern of English Fiction Since 1890 in Hardy, Conrad, Forster and Lawrence. (University of California, Berkeley, 1964. Published. New York: Oxford University Press, 1966).

2659 Friedman, Melvin J. Stream of Consciousness and the Modern Novel. (Yale University, 1953/54). Published as Stream of Consciousness: A Study in Literary Method. (New Haven: Yale University Press, 1955).

2660 Garrett, Peter K. Scene and Symbol: Changing Mode in the English Novel from George Eliot to Joyce. (Yale University, 1967). Published as Scene and Symbol from George Eliot to James Joyce: Studies in Changing Fiction Modes. Yale Studies in English, Vol. 172. (New Haven & London: Yale University Press, 1969).

2661 Gerber, R. E. H. Utopian Fantasy: A Study of English Utopian Fiction Since the End of the Nineteenth Century. (M. Litt. Thesis, Queen's College, Cambridge, 1955. Published. London: Routledge & Kegan Paul, 1955).

2662 Gill, Richard. The English Country House in Modern Fiction: Archetype of Community. (Columbia University, 1966). Pub-

362

lished as Happy Rural Seat: The English Country House and the Literary Imagination. (New Haven and London: Yale University Press, 1972).

2663 Gillen, Francis Xavier. The Relationship of Rhetorical Control to Meaning in the Novels of Henry James, Virginia Woolf, and E. M. Forster. (Fordham University, 1969).

2664 Gingrich, Patricia Carol Lynn. The Writer as Hero: A Changing Ideal in the British Novel from 1832 to 1914. (Wayne State University, 1969).

2665 Goewey, Herbert J. The Apology for Death and the Rejection of Extended Life in Nineteenth Century and Twentieth Century British Visionary Fiction. (Wayne State University, 1969).

2666 Goldberg, Gerald Jay. The Artist as Hero in British Fiction 1890-1930. (University of Minnesota, 1958).

2667 Goldfarb, Richard Laurence. Arnold Bennett and James Joyce on Art of Fiction: Realism and Symbolism in Modern English Theories of the Novel. (Northwestern University, 1969).

2668 Grahame, Robert M. A Study of the Cross-Section Novel Written in English Since 1915. (University of Minnesota, 1949).

2669 Greenberg, Alvin David. The Novel of Disintegration: A Study of the World View in Contemporary Fiction. (University of Washington, 1964).

2670 Greicus, M. S. The English Novel and the 1914-1918 War. (University of Edinburgh, 1959/60).

2671 Gross, Beverley Adrienne. Open-Ended Forms in the Modern Novel. (University of Chicago, 1966/67).

2672 Gunn, Drewey Wayne. The American and British Author in Mexico, 1911-1941. (University of North Carolina at Chapel Hill, 1968).

2673 Günther, Margarete. Der englische Kriegsroman und das englische Kriegsdrama 1919-1930. (Muenster University, 1936. Published. Berlin: Junker und Dünnhaupt Verlag, 1936).

2674 Gurcke, G. Die Französin im Spiegel des modernen englischen und amerikanischen Romans. (Greifswald, 1934).

2675 Haddow, E. T. The Novel of English Country Life, 1900-1939. (M. A. Thesis, King's College, London, 1956/57).

2676 Hammond, Dorothy Branson. The Image of Africa in British Literature of the Twentieth Century. (Columbia University, 1963).

2677 Hand, Nancy W. The Anatomy of a Genre: The Modern Novelette in English. (Kent State University, 1971).

2678 Harms, William A. Impressionism as a Literary Style. (Indiana University, 1971).

2679 Harris, Eugenie. The Novel as Critique of the Novel. (University of New York, 1970)

2680 Hasan, R. A Linguistic Study of Contrasting Features in the Style of Two Contemporary English Prose Writers, William Golding and Angus Wilson. (Edinburgh University, 1964).

2681 Hawkes, Carol A. Anglo-Indian Fiction: A Conflict of Cultures as Seen by the Novelists. (Columbia University, 1951/52).

2682 Heagarty, Mary Alice. Aesthetic Distance in the Techniques of the Novel. (University of Illinois, 1964).

2683 Helgeson, James Endre. A Study of the Use of Social Conventions in Certain 19th and Early 20th Century English and American Novels. (Indiana University, 1969/70).

2684 Heywood, C. The Influence of the French Realists on English Novelists and Their Critics 1880-1915. (B. Litt. Thesis, New College, Oxford, 1956/57).

2685 Hill, Olive Mary. The English Novel of Rural Life Since 1900. (M. A. Thesis, McGill University, 1933).

2686 Hillebrand, A. Kirchliche Bewegungen Englands im Spiegel der modernen Romanliteratur. (Münster, 1940).

2687 Hoag, Gerald Bryan. Henry James and the Formalist Criticism of the Novel in English in the Twentieth Century. (Tulane University, 1965).

2688 Hofer, E. H. A New Use of Symbolism in English Fiction, Particularly as Illustrated in the Works of Henry James, Dorothy Richardson, Virginia Woolf and Katherine Mansfield. (B. Litt. Thesis, Lincoln College, Oxford, 1952).

2689 Hoffmann, Anastasia C. Outer and Inner Perspectives in the Impressionist Novels of Crane, Conrad and Ford. (University of Wisconsin, 1967/68).

2690 Hoffman, Frederick J. Freudianism: A Study of Influences and Reactions, Especially as Revealed in the Fiction of James Joyce, D. H. Lawrence, Sherwood Anderson and Waldo Frank. (Ohio State University 1943). Revised and published as Freudianism and the Literary Mind. (Baton Rouge, Louisiana: Louisiana State University Press, 1945).

2691 Holmes, C. P. H. The Structure of the Modern Novel. (M.A. Thesis, University of Toronto, 1933).

2692 Honeywell, J. Arthur. An Inquiry Into the Nature of Plot in the Twentieth Century Novel. (University of Chicago, 1963/64).

2693 Hoskins, Katharine Bail. Today the Struggle: A Study of Literature and Politics in England during the Spanish Civil War. (Columbia University, 1965. Published. Austin and London: University of Texas Press, 1969).

2694 Hoskins, Robert B. The Symbol of the Severed Head in Twentieth Century British and American Fiction. (University of Kentucky, 1972).

2695 Howden, K. The Combatant Hero Figure in Novels of the 1914-1918 War. (M.A. Thesis, University of Leeds, 1958/59).

2696 Humphrey, Robert Clay. Creating Consciousness: A Study in Novelistic Techniques. (Northwestern University, 1950). Published as Stream of Consciousness in the Modern Novel. (Berkeley & Los Angeles: University of California Press, 1954).

2697 Hurley, Clinton F., Jr. A Method of Structural Analysis of the Novel. (The University of New Mexico, 1961).

2698 Intrater, Roseline. The Attrition of the Self in Some Contemporary Novels. (Case Western Reserve University, 1970).

2699 Jackson, Ralph H. The Club and the Cave. (Columbia University, 1971).

2700 Jarrasch, Walter. Das Problem der heranwachsenden Jugend im Spiegel des Zeitgenoessischen englischen Romans, 1900-1933. (Giessen University, 1939. Published. Leipzig: Noske, 1940).

2701 Johannsen, Karin. Wiederkehrende Elemente in der Motivik und Form englischer Kunstlerromane. (University of Kiel, 1965).

2702 Johnsen, William Arnold. Toward a Redefinition of the Modern. (University of Illinois at Urbana-Champaign, 1970).

2703 Johnson, Dale Springer. The Development of the non-formalistic Modern English Novel and its Relation to D. H. Lawrence's 'Sons and Lovers'. (University of Michigan, 1968).

2704 Johnston, Walter Eugene. Character and Rhetoric in Prose Fiction. (Cornell University, 1970).

2705   Jones, Robert L. A World of Words: The Function of Style
       in Prose Fiction. (University of North Carolina, 1971).

2706   Jyoti, D. D. Mystical and 'Transcendental' Elements in some
       Modern English and American Writers in relation to Indian
       Thought: R. W. Emerson, H. D. Thoreau, E. M. Forster, T. S.
       Eliot, A. Huxley. (King's College, University of London,
       1956).

2707   Kaplan, Sydney Janet. The Feminine Consciousness in the
       Novels of Five Twentieth Century British Women. (Univer-
       sity of California, Los Angeles, 1971).

2708   Kellogg, Gene. The Catholic Novel in a Period of Convergence
       (University of Chicago, 1969). Published as The Vital Tra-
       dition: The Catholic Novel in a Period of Convergence.
       (Chicago: Loyola University Press, 1970)

2709   Kelly, Robert G. The Premises of Disorganization: A Study
       of Literary Form in Ezra Pound, T. S. Eliot, James Joyce,
       and Dorothy Richardson. (Stanford University, 1951/52).

2710   Kennard, Jean Elizabeth. Towards a Novel of the Absurd:
       A Study of the Relationship between the Concept of the
       Absurd as Defined in the Works of Sartre and Camus and Ideas
       and Form in the Fiction of Joseph Barth, Samuel Beckett,
       Nigel Dennis, Joseph Heller, and James Purdy. (University
       of California, Berkeley, 1968).

2711   Kerr, Elizabeth M. The Sequence Novel: Fictional Method
       of a Scientific Age. (University of Minnesota, 1949).
       Published as Bibliography of the Sequence Novel. (Minne-
       apolis: University of Minnesota Press; London: Oxford
       University Press, 1950).

2712   Killam, G. D. The Presentation of Africa between the Sahara
       and the Union of South Africa in Novels Written in English,
       1860-1939. (University College, London, 1964/65). Pub-
       lished as Africa in English Fiction 1874-1939. (Ibadan:
       Ibadan University Press, 1968).

2713   Kirkpatrick, Larry James. Elizabeth Bowen and Company: A
       Comparative Essay in Literary Judgment. (Duke University,
       1965).

2714   Knapp, Ilse. Die Landschaft im modernen englischen Frauen-
       roman. (University of Tübingen, 1935. Published. Leipzig:
       Noske, 1935).

2715   Knight, A. Moral Values and the Tradition in the English
       Novel from 1880 to the Present Day. (University of Leices-
       ter, 1962/63).

366

2716 Kulemeyer, Gunther. Studien zur Psychologie im neuen eng-
      lischen Roman: Dorothy Richardson und James Joyce. (Ernst
      Moritz Arndt University, Greifswald, 1933. Published. Bot-
      trop: W. Postberg, 1933).

2717 Kumar, S. K. Bergson and the Stream of Consciousness Novel.
      (Fitzwilliam House, Cambridge, 1955. Published. London:
      Blackie & Son; Toronto: Ryerson Press, 1962; New York:
      New York University Press, 1963).

2718 Kwan, Terry A. C. A Study of Techniques of Narration in
      Selected Works of Fiction in the Period 1890-1915. (M. Phil.
      Thesis, University of Leeds, 1968/69).

2719 La Chance, Paul Richard. Man and Religion in the Novels of
      William Golding and Graham Greene. (Kent State University,
      1970).

2720 Langbaum, Anna B. Some English Novels (1855-1917) That Deal
      with the Crimean War. (University of Illinois, 1947/48).

2721 Leaska, Mitchell Alexander. The Rhetoric of Multiple Points
      of View in Selected Contemporary Novels. (New York Univer-
      sity, 1968).

2722 Lethcoe, Ronald James. Narrated Speech and Consciousness.
      (University of Wisconsin, 1969).

2723 Lindblad, William Edward. English Public School Controversy
      in Fiction: 1899-1939. (University of Illinois, 1962).

2724 Lockwood, Bernard. Four Contemporary British Working-Class
      Novelists: A Thematic and Critical Approach to the Fiction
      of Raymond Williams, John Braine, David Storey and Allan
      Sillitoe. (University of Wisconsin, 1966).

2725 Lodge, D. J. Catholic Fiction Since the Oxford Movement:
      Its Literary Form and Religious Content. (M.A. Thesis,
      University College, London, 1958/59).

2726 Lyngstad, Sverre. Time in the Modern British Novel: Con-
      rad, Woolf, Joyce and Huxley. (New York University, 1959/
      60).

2727 MacKenzie, M. F. Elements of Melodrama in the Modern Novel.
      (B. Litt., St. Catherine's College, Oxford, 1961/62).

2728 McLevie, Elaine Marianne. The Hero in the Post World War
      II Novel: Some Differences of Concept in the Works of Eng-
      lish and American Novelists. (Michigan State University,
      1970).

2729 McMahon, T. B. Studies in the Form of the Novel. (B. Litt.
      Thesis, St. Catherine's, Oxford, 1957/58).

2730 McWilliams, D. Some Formal Problems of First World War Fiction, 1914-1922. (M.A. Thesis, University of Kent, 1966/67).

2731 Mangold, Sigrid. Der Kuenstler im Viktorianischen und Edwardianischen Roman. (Heidelberg University, 1959).

2732 Marinoff, Irene. Neues Lebensgefühl und neue Wertungen im englischen Roman der Nachkriegszeit. (University of Marburg, 1929. Published. Berlin: Emil Ebering, 1929).

2733 May, K. M. Symbolism in Some Novels Published between 1915 and 1927. (M.A. Thesis, London [external]).

2734 Mayne, I. The Sociology of Modern Catholic Fiction. (M.A. Thesis, London [external] 1956/57).

2735 Mellen, Joan. Morality in the Novel: A Study of Five English Novelists: Henry Fielding, Jane Austen, George Eliot, Joseph Conrad and D. H. Lawrence. (City University of New York, 1968).

2736 Mendilow, A. A. Time Factors and Values in the Novel. (University of London, 1950). Published as Time and The Novel. (London: Peter Nevill; New York: British Book Centre, 1952).

2737 Merivale, Patricia. The Pan Motif in Modern English Literature. (Harvard University, 1962/63).

2738 Metzger, J. Katholisches Schrifttum im heutigen England. (University of Bonn, 1935. Published. München: Kosel and Pustet, 1937).

2739 Meyers, Carolyn H. Psychotechnology in Fiction about Imaginary Societies 1923-1962. (University of Kentucky, 1965).

2740 Meyers, Jeffrey. The Hero in British Colonial Fiction. (University of California, Berkeley, 1967). Published as Fiction and the Colonail Experience. (Totowa, New Jersey: Rowman and Littlefield, 1968).

2741 Meyers, Walter L. Certain Changes in the Characterization of the British Realistic Novel Since the Victorian Age. (University of Chicago, 1924). Published as The Later Realism: A Study of Characterization in the British Novel. (Chicago: University of Chicago Press; Cambridge, University Press, 1927).

2742 Milbourne, Kathleen E. The Stream of Consciousness in Recent English Fiction by Women. (M.A. Thesis, McGill University, 1934).

2743 Minning, Ruth. Der Heimatroman des 20. Jahrhunderts in

Sud-England un Wales. (Breslau University, 1937. Published. Bleicherode am Herz: Carl Hieft, 1937).

2744 Monk, D. E. A Study of Selected Novels by James and Conrad as Evinced in their Literary Theory and as Exemplified in Three Selected Novels by Each of Them. (M.A. Thesis, University of Manchester, 1959/60).

2745 Morris, Ann Roberson. A Study of Rhythm in the Novel. (Florida State University, 1961).

2746 Muellenbrock, Heinz J. Literatur und Zeitgeschichte in England zwischen dem Ende des 19. Jahrhunderts und dem Ausbruch des ersten Weltkrieges. (University of Hamburg, 1967).

2747 Müller, Elma. Das subjektive Hervortreten des Dichters im neueren englischen Roman. (University of Hamburg, 1915).

2748 Muste, John Martin. The Spanish Civil War in the Literature of the United States and Great Britain. (University of Wisconsin, 1960). Published as Say That We Saw Spain Die: Literary Consequences of the Spanish Civil War. (Seattle & London: University of Washington Press, 1966).

2749 Myrbo, Calvin Leonard. An Analysis of the Character of the Clergyman in Novels for Adolescents. (University of Minnesota, 1964).

2750 Nash, Cristopher Weston. A Modern Bestiary: Representative Animal Motifs in the Encounter Between Nature and Culture in the English, American, French and Italian Novel, 1900-1950. (New York University, 1970).

2751 New, W. H. The Problems of "Growing-Up" treated in Selected English, American and Commonwealth Novels, 1908-1959. (University of Leeds, 1965/66).

2752 Norburn, E. R. English War Novels of the Second World War. (M.A. Thesis, Newcastle-Upon-Tyne, 1964/65).

2753 Novelli, Martin A. Witness to the Times: The War Novels of Ford Madox and Evelyn Waugh. (Temple University, 1971).

2754 O'Grady, Walter Anthony. Political Contexts in the Novels of Graham Greene and Joyce Cary. (University of Toronto, 1971).

2755 Oldsey, Bernard Stanley. Aspects of Combat in the Novel, 1900-1950. (Pennsylvania State University, 1955/56).

2756 Oliver, Marjorie. The Influences of French Naturalism on English Fiction. (M.A. Thesis, University of Chicago, 1913).

2757 Osborne, Marianne Muse. The Hero and Heroine in the British 'Bildungsroman': 'David Copperfield' and 'A Portrait of the Artist as a Young Man', 'Jane Eyre' and 'The Rainbow'. (Tulane University, 1971).

2758 Ottervik, Eric V. The Multiple-Novel in Contemporary British Fiction. (University of Pittsburgh, 1966).

2759 Parrill, Anna Sue. The Theme of Revolution in the English Novel from Disraeli to Conrad. (University of Tennessee, 1965).

2760 Parry, B. The Image of India: Some Literary Expressions of the British Experience in India. (M.A. Thesis, University of Birmingham, 1966/67). Revised and published as Delusions and Discoveries: Studies on India in the British Imagination. (London: Allen Lane, The Penguin Press, 1972).

2761 Patt, Gertrud. Der Kampf zwischen Vater und Sohn in englischen Roman des 20. Jahrhunderts. (University of Muenster, 1938. Published. Emsdetten: Verlagsanstalt Heinr. & J. Lechte, 1938).

2762 Penman, M. E. Moments of Apperception in the Modern Novel: A Study of Henry James, Virginia Woolf, E. M. Forster and James Joyce related to Psychiatric and Philosophic Developments in the Late Nineteenth and Early Twentieth Centuries. (University College, London, 1965/66).

2763 Phillips, Kenneth Allan. A Study of the Catholic Attitudes in the Novels of Graham Greene and Evelyn Waugh. (M.A. Thesis, University of New Brunswick, 1967).

2764 Procter, Margaret Ruth. The Use of Spokesman Characters in the Fiction of E. M. Forster and D. H. Lawrence. (University of Toronto, 1969).

2765 Quinke, Ilse. Das Auftreten der subjectiven Indirekten Rede im englischen Roman. (University of Köln, 1937).

2766 Quinonez, Sister Roza A. The Concept of Man in Representative Dystopian Novels. (University of Michigan, 1969).

2767 Rabinovitz, Rubin. The Reaction Against Experiment: A Study of the English Novel, 1950-1960. (Columbia University, 1966). Published as The Reaction Against Experiment in the English Novel, 1950-1960. (New York & London: Columbia University Press, 1967).

2768 Rachman, S. Presentation of Character by Selected Authors of the English Novel, 1870-1940. (University of Leeds, 1965/66).

2769 Rahman, K. Race Relations in English Fiction between 1919 and 1939. (University of Birmingham, 1962/63).

2770 Raina, M. L. The Use of the Symbol by English Novelists
1900-1930, with particular reference to E. M. Forster, D.
H. Lawrence, and Virginia Woolf. (University of Manchester,
1964/65).

2771 Raskin, J. S. The Mythology of Imperialism: A Study of
Joseph Conrad and Rudyard Kipling. (University of Manches-
ter, 1966/67). Enlarged and published as The Mythology of
Imperialism: Rudyard Kipling, Joseph Conrad, E. M. Fors-
ter, D. H. Lawrence, and Joyce Cary. (New York: Random
House, 1971).

2772 Reddick, Bryan DeWitt. Tone in Dramatic Narrative. (University of California, Davis, 1969).

2773 Reilly, Robert James. Romantic Religion in the Work of
Owen Barfield, C. S. Lewis, Charles Williams and J. R. R.
Tolkien. (Michigan State University, 1960/61). Published
as Romantic Religion: A Study of Barfield, Lewis, Williams
and Tolkien. (Athens: University of Georgia Press, 1971).

2774 Rubin, David George. Music in the Modern Novel. (Columbia
University, 1953).

2775 Rubin, Donald Stuart. The Recusant Myth in Modern Fiction.
(University of Toronto, 1968).

2776 Russell, Mariann Barbara. The Idea of the City of God.
(Columbia University, 1965).

2777 Ryan, J. S. Modern English Myth-Makers: An Examination
of the Imaginative Writings of Charles Williams, C. S. Lewis,
and J. R. R. Tolkien. (University of Cambridge, 1967/68).

2778 Saagpakk, Paul Friidrich. Psychopathological Elements in
British Novels from 1890 to 1930. (Columbia University,
1966).

2779 Sack, F. L. Die Psychoanalyse im modernem englischen Roman.
(University of Zurich, 1930).

2780 Sacks, Wolfgang. Der Anglo-Katholizismus im englischen
Nachkriegsroman. (University of Halle, 1934. Published.
Halle: Buchdruckerei Ang. Kloppel, 1934).

2781 Samaan, A. B. The Novel of Utopianism and Prophecy, from
Lytton, 1871, to Orwell, 1949, with special reference to
its reception. (Birkbeck College, London, 1962/63).

2782 St. John, William E. The Conception of the Novel as Presented by the Leading English and American Novelists Since
1800. (University of Southern California, 1936).

371

2783 Sanders, Joseph L. Fantasy in the Twentieth Century British Novel. (Indiana University, 1972).

2784 Sandison, A. G. The Imperial Idea in English Fiction: A Study in the Literary Expression of the Idea, with special reference to the works of Kipling, Conrad, and Buchan. (Peterhouse, Cambridge, 1963/64). Published as The Wheel of Empire: A Study of the Imperial Idea in Some Late Nineteenth and Early Twentieth Century Fiction. (London: Macmillan; New York: St. Martin's Press, 1967).

2785 Scherbacher, Wolfgang. Der Kuenstler im modernen englischen Roman, 1916-1936. (University of Tübingen, 1954).

2786 Schirmer, Ute. Die Englische Heimat unter den Auswirkungen des Ersten Weltkrieges im Lichte des Romans. (University of Berlin, 1954).

2787 Schmerl, Rudolf Benjamin. Reason's Dream: Anti-Totalitarian Themes and Techniques of Fantasy. (University of Michigan, 1960).

2788 Seaver, Richard W. Le Monologue intérieur dans le roman moderne. (University of Paris, 1954).

2789 Seltzer, Alvin Jay. Chaos in the Novel--The Novel in Chaos. (Pennsylvania State University, 1970).

2790 Seward, Barbara. The Symbolic Rose. (Colorado University, 1952/53. Published. New York: Columbia University Press, 1960).

2791 Shah, S. A. The Empire in the Writings of Kipling, Forster and Orwell. (University of Edinburgh, 1967/68).

2792 Shapiro, Stephen Alan. The Ambivalent Animal: Man in the Contemporary British and American Novel. (University of Washington, 1965).

2793 Sharma, J. K. Technical Innovation in the English Novel, 1900-1940. (M. A. Thesis, University of Leicester, 1969/70).

2794 Sherwin, Jane King. The Literary Epiphany in some Early Fiction of Flaubert, Conrad, Proust and Joyce. (University of Michigan, 1962).

2795 Siemens, Reynold Gerrard. One Role of the Woman in the Artist's Development in certain British-Artist-Hero Novels of the Nineteenth Century and early Twentieth. (University of Wisconsin, 1966).

2796 Simon, Carol T. A Comparative Study of Adolescents in Different Stages of the same Culture as Projected in English and American Novels of the 18th, 19th and 20th Centuries.

(New York University, 1966/67).

2797 Sitzler, Dorothea. Studien zur Problematik von Chaos und
      Erloesung im englischen Roman der Gegenwart. (Mainz Univ-
      ersity, 1955).

2798 Smith, Thomas Francis. Contemporary Criticism of the Novel:
      The Four Basic Approaches. (University of Pittsburgh, 1962).

2799 Solomon, Albert Joseph. James Joyce and George Moore: A
      Study of a Literary Relationship. (Pennsylvania State
      University, 1969).

2800 Spann, Ekkehard. 'Problemkinder' in der englischen Erzahl-
      kunst der Gegenwart. Greene, A. Wilson, Wain, Amis, Murdoch,
      Golding, Braine, Sillitoe. (University of Tübingen, 1970).

2801 Speirs, James Gordon. The Background to the Political Phil-
      osophy of Conrad and Lawrence. (University of Toronto,
      1970).

2802 Spooner, D. E. J. The Response of Some British and Amer-
      ican Writers to the Spanish Civil War. (University of
      Bristol, 1967/68).

2803 Stanford, Raney Baynes. The Tradition of Heroism and the
      Modern Novel. (Columbia University, 1965).

2804 Starr, Nathan C. The Sea in the English Novel from Defoe
      to Melville. (Harvard University, 1928).

2805 Steinberg, Ervin Ray. The Stream of Consciousness Technique
      in James Joyce's "Ulysses". (New York University, 1956).

2806 Stevens, Arthur Wilber. George Orwell and Contemporary
      British Fiction of Burma: The Problem of 'Place'. (Univ-
      ersity of Washington, 1957).

2807 Stinson, John Jerome. The Uses of the Grotesque and other
      Modes of Distortion: Philosophy and Implication in the
      Novels of Iris Murdoch, William Golding, Anthony Burgess,
      and J. P. Donleavy. (New York University, 1971).

2808 Stolterfoth, Jessy. London im neuen englischen Roman.
      Studien zum literarischen Bild einer Stadtlandschaft. Un-
      iversity of Tübingen, 1947).

2809 Stubbs, P. J. A. A Comparative Study of the Fiction of Iris
      Murdoch and Muriel Spark. (M. Phil. Thesis, University
      College, London, 1968/69).

2810 Summers, Marcia Perry. The Use of Subordinate Characters
      as Dramatized Narrators in Twentieth Century Novels. (Un-
      iversity of Illinois, 1969).

2811 Swarthout, Glendon F. The Creative Crisis. (Michigan State University, 1955).

2812 Taylor, Chet H. The Aware Man: Studies in Self-Awareness in the Contemporary Novel. (University of Oregon, 1971).

2813 Taylor, Hawley C., Jr. The Philosophical Novel. (University of Washington, 1969).

2814 Trowbridge, Clinton W. The Twentieth Century British Supernatural Novel. (University of Florida, 1958).

2815 Tucker, Martin. A Survey of the Representative Modern Novel in English about Africa. (New York University, 1963). Published as Africa in Modern Literature: A Survey of Contemporary Writing in English. (New York: Frederick Ungar, 1967).

2816 Unwin, G. H. Structural Studies in Modern Fiction. (M.A. Thesis, University of Toronto, 1928).

2817 Valencia, Willa Ferree. The Picaresque Tradition in the Contemporary English and American Novel. (University of Illinois, 1968).

2818 Wagner, Robert Dean. The Last Illusion: Examples of the Spiritual Life in Modern Literature. (Columbia University).

2819 Walters, Dorothy Jeanne. The Theme of Destructive Innocence in the Modern Novel: Greene, James, Cary, Forster. (University of Oklahoma, 1960).

2820 Ward, Laura A. The Sea in English Fiction from 1918 to 1930. (University of Pennsylvania, 1931).

2821 Webb, Igor Michael. Sense and Sensibility: A Study of the Influence of English Aesthetics from Ruskin to Roger Fry on Ford Madox Ford and Virginia Woolf. (Stanford University, 1971).

2822 Weingart, Seymour Leonard. The Form and Meaning of the Impressionistic Novel. (University of California, Davis, 1964).

2823 Weinstock, Donald Jay. The Boer War in the Novel in English, 1884-1966: A Descriptive and Critical Bibliography. (University of California, Los Angeles, 1968).

2824 Weir, T. J. G. English Historical Novels on the First Century A. D. as Reflecting the Trends of Religious Thought during the Nineteenth and Twentieth Centuries. (University of Edinburgh, 1957/58).

2825 Wight, Marjorie. An Analysis of Selected British Novelists

Between 1945 and 1966 and Their Critics. (University of Southern California, 1968).

2826 Williams, D. M. The Presentation of Character in the Anglo-Welsh Novel: A Study of Techniques and Influences. (M.A. Thesis, University of Wales, 1958/59).

2827 Wilson, George Robert. The Quest Romance in Contemporary Fiction. (Florida State University, 1968).

2828 Wilson, Harris W. The Edwardian Society Novel. (University of Illinois, 1953/54).

2829 Wright, Marjorie Evelyn. The Cosmic Kingdom of Myth: a Study in the Myth-Philosophy of Charles Williams, C. S. Lewis and J. R. R. Tolkien. (University of Illinois, 1959/60).

2830 Wurche, Erich. Die geistige Wandlung der Frau im modernen englischen Frauenroman. (University of Greifswald, 1936. Published. Greifswald: Buchdruckerei Hans Adler, 1936).

2831 Yevish, Irving A. The Education of the Literary Artist in Modern Novels of College and University Life. (Columbia University, 1965).

2832 Zubaida, S. D. Attitudes to Society as Reflected in the English Literature of the 1930s and 1950s. (M.A. Thesis, University of Leicester, 1964/65).

Index (1)

Novelists

INDEX

(1) Novelists

ALDINGTON, Richard
129, 528, 605, 668, 684, 740, 798, 843, 1007, 1039, 1262,
1392, 1403, 1462, 1545, 2279, 2573.

ALDISS, Brian W[ilson]
1314.

ALLEN, Walter [Ernest]
1340, 2343.

ALMEDINGEN, E. M.
2539.

AMIS, Kingsley
81, 83, 88, 92, 131, 190, 196, 216, 302, 362, 403, 404, 441,
469, 516, 579, 608, 640, 670, 701, 725, 744, 748, 777, 807,
812, 841, 870, 1010, 1068, 1075, 1105, 1106, 1108, 1116,
1177, 1183, 1220, 1224, 1233, 1242, 1249, 1311, 1333, 1392,
1397, 1419, 1467, 1468, 1519, 1534, 1548, 1549, 1551, 1591,
1593-1595, 1645, 1682, 1685, 1723, 1726, 1742, 1762, 1773,
1783, 1805, 1806, 1893-1895, 1906, 1914, 1939, 1950, 1963,
1989, 1996, 2011, 2018, 2021, 2058, 2067, 2070, 2087, 2118,
2165, 2166, 2183, 2232, 2257, 2258, 2264, 2269, 2271, 2291,
2315, 2318, 2327, 2337, 2339, 2343, 2348, 2349, 2351, 2361,
2376, 2385, 2431, 2443, 2448, 2462, 2493, 2505, 2511, 2586,
2590, 2800.

"ARLEN, Michael" [Dikran Kouyoumdjian]
1147, 1457, 2034, 2173.

ARMSTRONG, Thomas
1156.

"AYSCOUGH, John" [Francis Browning Drew BICKERSTAFFE-DREW]
173, 875, 1051, 1090, 1104, 1121, 1223, 1239, 1912.

BAIN, Francis William
429, 967.

BALCHIN, Nigel
579, 1730, 1755, 1962, 2366, 2540.

BANKS, L. R.
[See Reid Banks, Lynne]

BARCLAY, Florence Louisa
553, 2296.

BARING, Maurice
144, 359, 423, 445, 519, 578, 799, 906, 973, 999, 1090, 1222,
1223, 1239, 1404, 1813, 1820, 1982, 1991, 2410.

BARING-GOULD, Sabine
119.

BARKER , George Granville
1656.

BARLOW, James
2343.

BARON, Alexander
1288, 1506.

BARRIE, James M[atthew]
686, 956, 2042, 2128.

BARSTOW, Stan
1737, 2067, 2651.

BATES, H[erbert] E[rnest]
103, 216, 239, 392, 429, 441, 611, 1245, 1840, 1963, 1976,
2345.

BATES, Ralph
1150, 1555.

BECKETT, Samuel
246, 272, 312, 347, 373, 388, 408, 436, 539, 542, 548, 549,
551, 552, 566, 569(a), 590, 609, 656, 706, 764, 769, 819,
824, 858, 859, 889, 891, 908, 922-924, 939, 975, 980, 1022,
1228, 1303, 1426, 1521, 1565, 1570, 1597-1599, 1631, 1637,
1781, 1892, 1934, 1949, 2087, 2098, 2113, 2119, 2263, 2437,
2456, 2710.

"BELL, Neil" [Stephen Southwold]
740.

BELLOC, Hilaire
172, 173, 183, 312, 359, 479, 544, 578, 609, 790, 1290, 1785,
2198.

BENNETT, Arnold
69, 71, 104, 106, 117, 120, 121, 165, 170, 172, 176, 199,
200, 212, 228, 234, 241, 247, 249, 260, 278, 279, 289, 303,
304, 312, 317, 327, 332, 336, 338, 350, 372, 389, 401, 405,
412, 416, 426, 431, 437, 466, 469, 474, 505, 510, 511, 513,
534, 555, 556, 562, 570, 574, 576, 612, 616, 620, 624, 628,
643, 645, 652, 664, 690, 699, 704, 715, 730, 734, 747, 761,
763, 764, 783, 798, 826, 840, 860, 861, 871, 882, 895, 898,
912, 913, 925, 926, 929, 938, 940, 956, 964, 969, 972, 973,
985, 986, 1003, 1008, 1010, 1016, 1026, 1031, 1046, 1053,

1055, 1056, 1061, 1098, 1142-1145, 1151, 1153, 1158, 1179,
1211, 1267, 1287, 1294, 1300, 1321, 1334, 1361, 1382, 1385,
1392, 1442, 1483, 1528, 1537-1539, 1601, 1602, 1611, 1615,
1619, 1638, 1649, 1715, 1736, 1744, 1748-1750, 1788, 1825,
1833, 1856, 1874, 1882, 1918, 1923, 1972, 1975, 1991, 2003,
2004, 2008, 2042, 2057, 2058, 2113, 2120, 2127, 2150, 2234,
2243, 2289, 2292, 2296, 2314, 2362, 2398, 2408, 2431, 2435,
2439, 2440, 2458, 2484, 2488, 2517, 2519, 2535, 2577, 2622.

BENSON, E[dward] F[rederick]
626, 832, 905, 969, 1361, 1403, 1601, 1707, 2390, 2407.

BENSON R[obert] H[ugh]
173, 831, 875, 1018, 1050, 1051, 1090, 1121, 1221, 1239,
1312, 1313, 1508, 1785, 1788, 1912, 1913.

BENSON, Stella
340, 392, 530, 585, 1696, 1998, 2311.

BENTLEY, Phyllis
426, 583, 914, 1148-1156, 1477, 1697.

BERESFORD, J[ohn] D[avys]
69, 128, 234, 393, 492, 531, 563, 626, 636, 872, 898, 905,
926, 969, 973, 1157-1160, 1182, 1294, 1369, 1403, 1473, 1474,
1479, 1538, 1601, 1614, 1707, 1911, 1984, 1991, 2121, 2151,
2235, 2278, 2286, 2289, 2295, 2343, 2435, 2447, 2453, 2554.

"BIRMINGHAM, G. A." [James Owen Hannay]
186, 832.

BLACKWOOD, Algernon
1474, 1483.

BLUNDEN, Edmund
1007, 1307, 1462, 2552.

BORDEN, Mary
1381, 1403, 1404.

BOWEN, Elizabeth
96, 144, 151-161, 174, 196, 197, 205, 247, 398, 441, 444,
539, 579, 611, 645, 646, 713, 726, 743, 746, 757, 833, 865,
899, 904, 980, 1009, 1010, 1044, 1049, 1149, 1194-1202,
1271, 1541, 1587, 1600, 1616, 1660, 1730, 1755, 1819, 1847,
1866, 1918, 1939, 1952, 1953, 1956, 1988, 2073, 2165, 2386,
2429, 2466, 2543.

BOWEN, John
1203-1207, 2238.

BRADBURY, Malcolm
164-167, 1215-1219, 1685, 2268, 2586.

BRAGG, Melvyn
    2508.

BRAINE, John
    88, 92, 216, 302, 362, 389, 516, 536, 579, 640, 725, 744,
    748, 750, 807, 841, 897, 1105, 1106, 1108, 1177, 1226, 1242,
    1245,1328, 1333, 1419, 1534, 1591, 1594, 1682, 1723, 1763,
    1806, 1827, 1895, 1914, 1938, 1939, 1950, 1989, 1996, 2067,
    2087, 2118, 2166, 2184, 2186, 2217, 2258, 2264, 2291, 2318,
    2350, 2376, 2443, 2505, 2511, 2590, 2651, 2724, 2800.

BRIGHOUSE, Harold
    823.

BRITTAIN, Vera [Mary]
    186, 426, 1271, 2436, 2460.

BROPHY, Brigid
    190, 670.

BROWN, A.
    468, 1149.

"BRYHER" [Annie Winifred Ellerman]
    436.

BUCHAN, John
    531, 611, 790, 836, 947, 2784.

BURGESS, Anthony
    203-206, 376, 566, 670, 685, 947, 1009, 1234, 1245-1257,
    1616, 1939, 2214, 2343, 2538, 2807.

BURKE, Thomas
    392.

BUTLER, Samuel
    104, 369, 514, 555, 612, 740, 788, 862, 962', 969, 972, 991,
    1508, 1514, 1991, 2060, 2065, 2192, 2247, 2413, 2570.

CAINE, Hall
    144, 1312, 1483, 2259.

CALDER-MARSHALL, Arthur
    593, 1363, 1600, 1656.

CANNAN, Gilbert
    279, 393, 531, 637, 740, 926, 969, 973, 1007, 1095, 1182,
    1287, 1294, 1337, 1344, 1538, 1546, 1569, 1601, 1716, 1744,
    1748, 1911, 1972, 2151, 2235, 2453, 2499, 2504, 2554.

CARY, Joyce
    81, 119, 141, 174, 195, 216, 219, 267, 289, 405, 441, 443,
    470, 536, 539, 555, 557, 579, 611, 645, 646, 666, 713, 729,

745, 748, 757, 786, 861, 866, 912, 916, 947, 976, 980, 985,
993, 1010, 1020, 1116, 1231, 1316, 1541, 1704, 1730, 1771,
1780, 1918, 1932, 1953, 1960, 2053, 2147, 2164, 2263, 2292,
2437, 2471, 2472, 2652, 2771, 2819.

CHAPLIN, Sid[ney]
518, 1737, 1816, 2274.

CHARTERIS, Hugo
2183, 2335.

CHESTERTON, G[ilbert] K[eith]
70, 104, 170, 172, 173, 183, 225, 233, 240, 296, 312, 332,
341, 359, 366, 431, 437, 441, 445, 454, 466, 512, 534, 540,
544, 553, 578, 609, 653, 730, 742, 790, 811, 856, 860, 875,
882, 898, 933, 1018, 1028, 1086, 1163, 1221, 1272, 1289-1293,
1323, 1785, 1798, 1841, 1861, 1890, 2011, 2122, 2198, 2234,
2325.

CHILDERS, Erskine
1163.

CHOLMONDELEY, Mary
1707.

CHURCH, Richard
1298, 1299, 1658.

COLLIER, John
392.

COLLINS, Norman
2324.

COMFORT, Alex[ander]
1558, 1587, 1604, 2445.

COMPTON-BURNETT, Ivy
155, 190, 347, 539, 555, 579, 602, 622, 645, 713, 729, 743,
745, 746, 748, 757, 811, 833, 899, 950, 980, 993, 998, 999,
1010, 1234, 1587, 1590, 1591, 1616, 1630, 1658, 1755, 1771,
1801, 1819, 1859, 1879, 1960, 2117, 2161, 2164, 2253, 2559,
2580.

CONRAD, Joseph
76, 86, 90, 104, 106, 107, 139, 141, 144, 148, 155, 165, 175,
179, 199, 200, 213, 215, 224, 225, 227, 228, 231, 232, 234,
241, 247, 258, 259, 260, 274, 278, 279, 281, 290, 303-305,
310, 312, 317, 323, 324, 329, 336, 341, 346, 350-355, 357,
365, 368, 371, 372, 385, 387, 389, 393, 400, 412, 415, 431,
435, 437, 441, 452, 453, 463, 466, 472, 479, 480, 496, 499,
512, 513, 528, 537, 538, 540, 547, 553, 555, 557, 561, 562,
569, 574, 576, 577, 586, 588, 594, 596, 612, 615, 616, 618,
624, 627, 628, 631, 632, 645, 646, 653, 656, 661, 664, 666,

671, 688, 690, 691, 699, 709, 712, 728, 729, 733, 734, 742,
747, 749, 751, 753, 764, 767, 769, 786, 788, 794, 814, 820,
826, 830, 833, 836, 839, 840, 852, 863, 868, 869, 877, 882,
890, 898, 900, 901, 907, 908, 912, 917, 922, 923, 925, 926,
938, 940, 952, 956, 958, 962, 963, 969, 975, 985, 988, 991,
999, 1004, 1008, 1010, 1018, 1028, 1031, 1038, 1046, 1099,
1128, 1135, 1148, 1180, 1213, 1214, 1229, 1260, 1285, 1296,
1306, 1312, 1344, 1348, 1361, 1362, 1369, 1383, 1408, 1428,
1464, 1491, 1494, 1511, 1532, 1540, 1561, 1597, 1599, 1617,
1678, 1689, 1701, 1709, 1710, 1748, 1787, 1803, 1817, 1825,
1874, 1881, 1882, 1954, 1960, 1965, 1975, 1985, 1990, 2010,
2042, 2049, 2095, 2097, 2108, 2120, 2122, 2123, 2127, 2128,
2145, 2147, 2150, 2193, 2217, 2224, 2234, 2236, 2241, 2243, 2276,
2289, 2290, 2341, 2358, 2379, 2384, 2387, 2400, 2413, 2417,
2454, 2456, 2471, 2472, 2507, 2519, 2559, 2627, 2641, 2658,
2689, 2726, 2735, 2740, 2759, 2771, 2784, 2794.

COOPER, Lettice
126, 1149, 1156, 1328.

COOPER, William
518, 1328, 1762, 2018, 2343, 2361.

COPPARD, A[lfred] E[dgar]
611.

"CORELLI, Marie" [Mary Mackay]
144, 912, 1792, 2259, 2296.

CRAWFORD, Marion Francis
1090, 1312.

CRESWELL, Harry Bulkeley
2366.

CROFT-COOKE, Rupert
1405.

CRONIN, A[rchibald] J[oseph]
186, 287, 808, 1133, 1153, 1402, 1403, 1555, 1841, 2466,
2547.

"DANBY, Frank" [Mrs. Julia Frankau]
260.

"DANE, Clemence" [Winifred Ashton]
152, 193, 417, 519, 530, 583, 635, 704, 843, 1033, 1159,
1271, 1294, 1344, 1492, 1601, 1608, 1716, 1901, 1967, 1998,
2215, 2308, 2311, 2407, 2410, 2481.

DAVIES, Rhys
392, 1459, 2465.

DEEPING, George Warwick
144, 186, 528, 906, 973, 1112, 1436.

"DE LAFIELD, E. M." [Ednee Elizabeth Monica de la Pasture]
583, 808, 999, 2311.

DE LA MARE, Walter
1264.

DELANEY, Shelagh
744, 2526.

DE LA PASTURE, Mrs. Henry
171, 1184, 1312, 2173.

DE MORGAN, William
350, 553, 1098, 1294, 1635, 1980, 2323, 2362, 2401, 2574.

DENNIS, Geoffrey
1040.

DENNIS, Nigel
83, 88, 539, 1106, 2385, 2443, 2492, 2710.

DONLEAVY, J[ames] P[atrick]
88, 1108, 2807.

DOUGLAS, Norman
225, 317, 611, 861, 922, 925, 928, 964, 1010, 1184, 1308,
1372, 1492, 1918, 2646.

DRABBLE, Margaret
670, 776, 1409, 2270, 2376, 2508.

DU MAURIER, Daphne
583, 912, 1495, 1819.

DURRELL, Laurence
73, 74, 189, 299, 302, 312, 331, 403, 408, 441, 460, 470,
539, 549, 566, 685, 729, 745, 748, 764, 769, 803, 807, 813,
815, 845, 864, 870, 894, 910, 924, 975, 980, 985, 1010, 1172,
1203, 1242, 1392, 1410, 1447, 1449, 1452, 1469, 1550, 1570,
1638, 1892, 1920, 1939, 2021, 2070, 2115, 2209, 2263, 2274,
2291, 2315, 2413, 2456.

EDELMAN, Maurice
714.

ERVINE, St. John
1539.

FANE, J.
1341.

FARNOL, Jeffrey
    2296.

"FIELDING, Gabriel" [Alan Gabriel Barnsley]
    714, 1245, 1481, 1482, 1762, 2349.

FIRBANK, Ronald
    423, 633, 767, 964, 1372, 1497, 1785, 1903, 2164, 2640.

FLEMING, Ian
    216, 714.

FORD, Ford Maddox [Hueffer]
    129, 165, 166, 228, 352-356, 363, 398, 431, 490, 512, 547,
    611, 636, 764, 769, 784, 852, 861, 912, 922, 925, 926, 1003,
    1007, 1010, 1038, 1094, 1230, 1307, 1491-1494, 1545, 1600,
    1608, 1650, 1709, 1749, 1787, 1918, 2034, 2277, 2552, 2641,
    2689, 2821.

FORESTER, Cecil Scott
    174, 1270, 1304.

FORSTER, Edward Morgan
    76, 95, 102, 106, 107, 112, 125, 136, 141, 144, 155, 160,
    165, 166, 174, 179, 191, 194, 200, 228, 229, 247, 267, 268,
    299, 312, 322, 330, 345, 351, 356, 357, 363, 371, 372, 393,
    398, 405, 423, 429, 441, 443, 446, 448, 451, 452, 466, 468,
    470, 473, 477, 480, 510, 512, 531, 533, 538, 542, 555, 570,
    577, 587, 590, 602, 605, 611, 612, 636, 645, 655, 664, 666,
    668, 671, 688, 724, 729, 737, 738, 745, 746, 754, 763, 764,
    769, 773, 786, 796, 797, 809, 826, 838, 844, 852, 861, 862,
    865, 869, 879, 893, 912, 914, 921, 922, 926, 940, 948-950,
    962, 964, 967, 981, 984, 987, 1000, 1010, 1031, 1038, 1039,
    1048, 1076, 1079, 1083, 1086, 1125, 1135, 1137, 1163, 1179,
    1215, 1236, 1238, 1287, 1305, 1315, 1316, 1330, 1355, 1385,
    1392, 1428, 1448, 1528, 1581, 1597, 1601, 1648, 1650, 1665,
    1673, 1688, 1701, 1704, 1773, 1785, 1797, 1826, 1845, 1866,
    1876, 1918, 1937, 1944, 1975, 1982, 2022, 2060, 2117, 2151,
    2192, 2217, 2247, 2253, 2256, 2309, 2332, 2334, 2340, 2345,
    2368, 2429, 2432, 2459, 2471, 2488, 2489, 2509, 2548, 2559,
    2584, 2606, 2627, 2658, 2663, 2706, 2762, 2764, 2770, 2771,
    2791, 2819.

FOWLES, John
    222, 714, 1616, 1939, 2376.

FRANKAU, Gilbert
    169, 339, 905, 1112, 1601, 1707, 1849.

FRANKAU, Mrs. Joan [Bennett]
    260.

FRANKAU, Pamela
    556, 714.

FRASER, Ronald
    1270.

FREEMAN, Harold Webber
    1405.

GALSWORTHY, John
    69, 71, 104, 106, 117, 121, 144, 148, 193, 200, 214, 224,
    228, 229, 234, 241, 247, 249, 260, 275, 278, 279, 303, 310,
    312, 317, 324, 327, 332, 336, 338, 345, 350, 355, 381, 382,
    393, 398, 426, 437, 441, 454, 466, 468, 510, 511, 513, 528,
    534, 553, 555, 562, 574, 602, 612, 624, 628, 631, 637, 643,
    645, 690, 699, 704, 711, 733, 734, 740, 747, 749, 763, 764,
    769, 794, 799, 825, 826, 840, 843, 861, 868, 872, 882, 884,
    895, 898, 904, 912, 913, 922, 926, 929, 940, 956, 972, 981,
    985, 986, 988, 991, 1005, 1008, 1010, 1031, 1039, 1046, 1048,
    1053, 1055, 1061, 1137, 1145, 1151, 1158, 1174, 1176, 1214,
    1260, 1266, 1285, 1287, 1294, 1305, 1321, 1344, 1369, 1392,
    1414, 1427, 1441, 1477, 1478, 1484, 1522, 1523, 1528, 1532,
    1538, 1602, 1615, 1617, 1630, 1638, 1649, 1654, 1716, 1736,
    1748, 1750, 1773, 1777, 1788, 1798, 1813, 1856, 1861, 1866,
    1882, 1905, 1918, 1967, 1968, 1972, 1975, 1991, 2004, 2042,
    2052, 2078, 2097, 2101, 2121, 2122, 2128, 2131, 2150, 2198,
    2205, 2223, 2234, 2240, 2250, 2259, 2289, 2292, 2295, 2314,
    2326, 2398, 2401, 2410, 2457, 2487, 2488, 2507, 2519, 2535,
    2550, 2564, 2577, 2593, 2622.

GARNETT, David
    96, 144, 423, 585, 712, 926, 1264, 1308, 1391, 1422, 1497,
    1525-1527, 1672, 1696, 1929, 1975, 1982, 2509, 2547, 2564,
    2583.

GEORGE, W[alter] L[ionel]
    531, 1344, 1531, 1532, 1538, 2040, 2447, 2533.

GERHARDI, William
    633, 1040, 1184, 1520.

"GIBBON, Lewis Grassic" [James Leslie Mitchell]
    837, 1555, 2244, 2455.

GIBBS, Philip
    173, 339, 528, 643, 1137, 2312.

GISSING, George
    712, 747, 929, 972, 1480.

GLANVILLE, Brian
    1288, 1552, 1553, 1939, 2141

GLYN, Elinor
    553, 1420, 2184.

GODDEN, Rumer
429, 1271.

GOLDING, William
99, 100, 119, 182, 216, 217, 222, 276, 302, 312, 340, 359,
369, 370, 403, 470, 518, 536, 539, 542, 549, 551, 552, 566,
670, 701, 729, 750, 764, 769, 807, 829, 857, 864, 870, 894,
897, 905, 910, 922, 939, 980, 1095, 1099, 1116, 1172, 1177,
1203, 1234, 1242, 1249, 1251, 1311, 1342, 1344, 1366, 1376,
1386, 1521, 1570-1573, 1596, 1598, 1741, 1742, 1780, 1805,
1828, 1892, 1965, 2013, 2070, 2135, 2239, 2270, 2274, 2339,
2344, 2352, 2365, 2376, 2379, 2384, 2548, 2559, 2580, 2680,
2800, 2807.

GOLDRING, Douglas
1601.

GRAVES, Robert
1007, 1040, 1262, 1304, 1307, 1459, 1596, 2540.

"GREEN Henry" [Henry Vincent Yorke]
174, 189, 216, 443, 470, 539, 555, 579, 593, 611, 638, 645,
659, 713, 745, 757, 865, 889, 941, 950, 980, 1429, 1587,
1592, 1637, 1730, 1755, 1879, 1907, 1961, 1976, 2160, 2161,
2164, 2257, 2428, 2543.

GREEN, Julian
1403, 2035.

GREENE, Graham
76, 81, 96, 100, 102, 148, 152, 161, 205, 209, 216, 220, 242,
247, 276, 287, 311, 312, 318, 326, 340, 345, 359, 363, 373,
375, 384, 425, 431, 433, 434, 441, 444, 460, 463, 470, 486,
495, 516, 518, 535, 539, 544, 549, 555, 558, 569(a), 570,
577, 579, 593, 598, 609, 611, 638, 640, 645, 646, 648, 653,
666, 673, 679, 692, 701, 713, 720, 721, 724, 726, 729, 737,
745, 746, 748, 753, 757, 775, 796, 801, 811, 817, 824, 829,
857, 859, 861, 864, 865, 886, 889, 904, 912, 916, 923, 940,
947, 948, 950, 960, 976, 980, 985, 993, 998, 1002, 1010,
1020-1022, 1027, 1030, 1035, 1038, 1041, 1044, 1068, 1070,
1077, 1124, 1132, 1133, 1139, 1140, 1149, 1196, 1210, 1222,
1227, 1231, 1251, 1275, 1276, 1296, 1300, 1303, 1305, 1306,
1316, 1324, 1331, 1335, 1355, 1380, 1392, 1394, 1400, 1408,
1429, 1454, 1458, 1464, 1482, 1521, 1541, 1562, 1565, 1578,
1587, 1591, 1600, 1603, 1618, 1638, 1662, 1664, 1675, 1688,
1698, 1704, 1738, 1747, 1765, 1768, 1801, 1808, 1828, 1853,
1859, 1918, 1934, 1936, 1951-1953, 1960, 1961, 1970, 1973,
1981, 1988, 1992, 2005, 2011, 2035, 2039, 2048, 2054, 2059,
2070, 2084, 2098, 2130, 2137, 2160, 2203, 2217, 2227, 2257,
2269, 2271, 2275-2277, 2293, 2304, 2325, 2344, 2365, 2367,
2378, 2386, 2387, 2428, 2429, 2438, 2493, 2510, 2526, 2543,
2548, 2559, 2575, 2580, 2644, 2652, 2763, 2800, 2819.

GREENWOOD, Walter
    126, 1150, 1459, 2261, 2312.

HALL, Radclyffe
    1271.

HANLEY, Gerald
    2343.

HANELY, James
    209, 340, 563, 1149, 1150, 1660, 2261.

HARRIS, Frank
    742, 2205.

HARTLEY, L[eslie] P[oles]
    83, 443, 457, 458, 579, 585, 713, 748, 993, 1116, 1541, 1604,
    1616, 1641-1643, 1735, 1755, 1780, 1840, 1845, 1939, 1994,
    2070, 2183, 2257, 2335, 2514, 2580.

"HAY, I." [John Hay Beith]
    169, 2246.

HEINEMANN, Margot
    837, 1340, 1453, 2274, 2275.

HEPPENSTALL, Rayner
    627, 1234.

HERBERT, Alan Patrick
    1040, 2223, 2484,

HEWLETT, Maurice
    144, 260, 366, 512, 761, 905, 969, 1008, 1369, 1441, 1748,
    1972, 2131, 2296, 2323, 2363.

HICHENS, Robert
    144, 260, 905, 1312, 1635, 2023, 2082, 2296.

"HINDE, Thomas" [Thomas Welles Chitty]
    88, 939, 1106, 1914, 1939, 2087, 2166, 2183, 2327.

"HOBBES, John Oliver" [Pearl Mary Teresa Richards]
    2440.

HODSON, J. L.
    126, 1150.

HOLME, Constance
    1360, 2387.

HOLTBY, Winifred
    126, 426, 557, 1153, 1156, 1405, 1696, 1697.

HOUGHTON, Claude
    1405.

HOWARD, Elizabeth Jane
    1466, 2186.

"HUDSON, Stephen" [Sydney Schiff]
    392, 694.

HUDSON, William Henry
    352, 355, 751, 861, 898, 1918.

HUGHES, Richard
    528, 563, 745, 750, 797, 1073, 1660, 1672, 1718, 1719, 1765,
    1918, 1938, 1967, 2400, 2428.

HUMPHREYS, Emyr [Owen]
    1343, 1721, 1722, 2318.

HUTCHINSON, A[rthur] S[tuart] M[enteth]
    69, 423, 637, 643, 749, 1112, 1127, 1129, 1130, 1137, 1478,
    1601, 1707, 1967.

HUTCHINSON, Ray Croyton
    1149, 1488.

HUXLEY, Aldous
    70, 73, 74, 76, 95, 96, 101, 102, 132, 140-142, 144, 148-150,
    152, 166, 174, 177, 189, 194, 207, 209, 211, 222, 225, 229,
    231, 236, 240, 242-244, 247, 252, 279, 284, 289, 308, 309,
    312, 317, 320, 322, 328, 338, 363, 373, 398, 408, 410, 411,
    422, 423, 426, 430, 441, 443, 446, 463, 466, 468, 470, 477,
    492, 495, 519, 534, 538, 541, 555, 558, 563, 570, 585, 598,
    601, 605, 611, 619, 623, 633, 638, 645, 653, 655, 661, 665,
    671, 673, 675, 676, 678, 687, 697, 699, 710, 712, 713, 715,
    724, 726, 729, 736, 737, 746, 748, 753, 773, 775, 781, 784,
    796, 805, 812, 821, 824, 826, 831, 838, 858, 862, 866, 882,
    885, 899, 916, 922, 923, 925, 926, 940, 947, 949, 956, 960,
    961, 964, 969, 975, 984-986, 992, 993, 1009, 1010, 1022-1024,
    1039, 1040, 1059, 1075, 1086, 1094, 1099, 1100, 1114, 1115,
    1132, 1145, 1159, 1182, 1184, 1221, 1240, 1251, 1266, 1276,
    1279, 1286, 1291, 1292, 1297, 1304, 1322, 1323, 1327, 1335,
    1339, 1355, 1372, 1391, 1402, 1405, 1422, 1427, 1457, 1503,
    1505, 1508, 1514, 1519, 1536, 1546, 1548, 1556, 1557, 1559,
    1561, 1562, 1618, 1619, 1638, 1650, 1653, 1673, 1676, 1679,
    1697, 1704, 1713, 1725, 1750, 1755, 1785, 1793, 1820, 1835,
    1845, 1866, 1902, 1905, 1918, 1929, 1952, 1958, 1983, 2008,
    2011, 2033, 2047, 2074, 2098, 2101, 2110, 2123, 2126, 2135,
    2137, 2142, 2175, 2197, 2207, 2211, 2214, 2227, 2234, 2250,
    2278, 2280-2282, 2309, 2334, 2352, 2357, 2359, 2368, 2379,
    2410, 2426, 2437, 2448, 2451, 2459, 2463, 2465, 2478, 2485,
    2489, 2498, 2510, 2514, 2548, 2572, 2575, 2646, 2706, 2726.

JOHNSON, Pamela Hansford
    518, 645, 714, 791, 895, 1068, 1242, 1738, 1742, 1819, 2263,
    2268, 2271, 2318.

JOHNSTON, H[arry Hamilton]
    1344, 2550.

JONES, David
    217, 1658.

JONES, Gwyn
    1149.

JONES, Jack
    1366, 1934.

JOYCE, James [Augustine Aloysius]
    73, 76, 82, 90, 91, 95, 102, 109, 113, 114, 119, 125, 128,
    130, 135, 136, 142, 143, 152, 165, 188, 192, 200, 205, 207,
    209, 211, 215, 228, 229, 231, 232, 234, 236, 242, 246, 247,
    249, 256, 257, 259, 263, 266, 270, 272, 273, 275, 279-281,
    284, 290, 305, 310, 315, 317-319, 322, 324, 326, 337, 338,
    341, 343, 345, 351, 363, 372, 374, 387, 388, 399-402, 405,
    411, 417-419, 423, 435, 436, 438, 441, 448, 452, 453, 460,
    463, 466, 468, 469, 472, 480, 481, 483, 490-492, 507, 510,
    511, 514, 519, 528, 537, 538, 542, 543, 548, 549, 555, 556,
    560, 563, 570-572, 574, 576, 577, 580, 594, 596, 598, 602,
    607, 611, 612, 617, 619, 620, 627, 632, 643, 646, 647, 655,
    656, 659, 661, 665, 667, 668, 671, 678, 692, 694, 699, 704,
    710, 711, 715, 718, 723, 724, 726, 729, 753, 755, 756, 763,
    775, 792, 793, 805, 811, 812, 817-819, 826, 828, 838, 845,
    852, 857, 858, 861, 863, 865, 866, 869, 877, 885, 887, 895,
    898, 903, 904, 908, 912, 916-918, 922, 923, 926, 927, 938,
    940, 941, 946, 952, 958, 960-964, 969, 972, 973, 975-978,
    985, 988, 996, 1000, 1003, 1009, 1010, 1011, 1016, 1020,
    1021, 1023-1025, 1031, 1041, 1055, 1059, 1099, 1113, 1120,
    1131, 1136, 1139, 1145, 1166, 1173, 1207, 1210, 1213, 1228,
    1230, 1235, 1257, 1266, 1267, 1276, 1279, 1282, 1285, 1291,
    1303, 1308-1310, 1315, 1317, 1323, 1327, 1332, 1334, 1346-
    1349, 1355, 1367, 1383, 1391, 1392, 1394, 1414, 1426, 1427,
    1446, 1448, 1455, 1456, 1458, 1464, 1480, 1482, 1492, 1505,
    1521, 1530, 1533, 1540, 1546, 1563, 1569, 1571, 1575, 1576,
    1578, 1581, 1590, 1597, 1603, 1605, 1613, 1630, 1631, 1637,
    1640, 1644, 1654, 1670, 1677, 1678, 1679, 1684, 1704, 1714,
    1721, 1722, 1724, 1736, 1746, 1762, 1765, 1767, 1772, 1775,
    1778, 1781, 1789, 1790, 1792, 1793, 1797, 1820, 1821, 1825,
    1826, 1837-1839, 1842, 1854, 1867, 1872, 1876, 1877, 1884,
    1889, 1895, 1904, 1907, 1916, 1918, 1929, 1932-1935, 1944,
    1949, 1954, 1956, 1960, 1965, 1966, 1975, 1993, 1994, 2005,
    2007, 2011, 2023, 2027, 2028, 2032, 2033, 2047, 2060, 2063-
    2065, 2083, 2094, 2096, 2098, 2101, 2105, 2107, 2108, 2110,
    2113, 2114, 2117, 2122, 2123, 2126, 2144, 2145, 2164, 2179,
    2200, 2203, 2215, 2217, 2230, 2232, 2234, 2239, 2248, 2250,
    2272, 2276, 2278, 2280, 2282, 2289, 2290, 2292, 2294, 2298,

2315, 2318, 2331, 2334, 2346, 2357, 2370, 2379, 2382, 2383,
2413, 2417, 2431, 2454, 2456, 2469, 2473, 2491, 2498, 2509,
2538, 2546, 2548, 2561, 2572, 2607, 2652, 2660, 2690, 2709,
2716, 2726, 2757, 2762, 2794, 2799, 2805.

KAYE-SMITH, Sheila
    69, 106, 171, 173, 186, 338, 423, 530, 559, 563, 583, 611,
    612, 636, 643, 672, 783, 832, 855, 884, 905, 926, 964, 969,
    1007, 1033, 1046, 1088, 1182, 1223, 1313, 1360, 1381, 1404,
    1405, 1488, 1601, 1716, 1791, 1923, 1924, 1966, 1968, 1998,
    2062, 2130, 2255, 2311, 2547, 2554.

KEABLE, Robert
    832, 2411.

KENNEDY, Margaret
    339, 519, 583, 585, 808, 1033, 1137, 1998, 2273.

KING, Francis [Henry]
    1343, 2184, 2318.

KIPLING, [Joseph] Rudyard
    104, 172, 214, 228, 234, 252, 260, 429, 431, 437, 441, 615,
    653, 666, 730, 738, 751, 774, 786, 794, 810, 823, 826, 836,
    856, 868, 879, 917, 922, 945, 967, 1004, 1018, 1025, 1053,
    1076, 1238, 1326, 1330, 1362, 1369, 1385, 1428, 1442, 1494,
    1648, 1813, 1861, 2010, 2023, 2042, 2345, 2399, 2771, 2784,
    2791.

KOESTLER, Arthur
    99, 102, 124, 174, 205, 208, 368, 426, 460, 466, 495, 499,
    564, 580, 600, 688, 691, 732, 757, 767, 778, 780, 811, 919,
    950, 984, 996, 1023, 1029, 1030, 1041, 1139, 1271, 1386,
    1556, 1558-1560, 1579, 1596, 1607, 1633, 1662, 1681, 1711,
    1725, 1822-1824, 1962, 1976, 2324, 2351, 2367, 2400, 2541.

LANCASTER, Osbert
    2540.

LANG, Andrew
    1171.

LARKIN, Philip [Arthur]
    312, 403, 725, 1341, 1685, 1906, 2058.

LAWRENCE, David Herbert
    71, 74, 76, 82, 89, 91, 95, 96, 100, 105, 109, 112, 125, 128,
    130, 134, 135, 142, 144, 152, 155, 165, 175, 180, 193, 199,
    200, 209, 211, 214, 221, 225, 226, 228, 229, 231, 234, 241,
    244, 247-249, 257, 259, 263, 264, 266, 275, 279-281, 290,
    299, 305, 311, 312, 317-319, 322, 338, 351, 355, 363, 368,
    370-372, 385, 387, 393, 398, 399, 402, 405, 410, 411, 416,
    417, 419, 422, 423, 433, 434, 438, 441, 446, 451-453, 456,
    466-469, 472, 475, 480, 481, 483, 486, 491, 492, 496, 510,

513, 514, 528, 531, 534, 537, 538, 542, 543, 551, 555, 556,
558, 560, 563, 569, 570, 577, 581, 582, 585, 587, 588, 596,
605, 610-612, 619, 623, 627, 632, 633, 645-647, 653, 655,
657, 664, 668, 671, 678, 680, 688, 693, 694, 697, 699, 701,
704, 709, 712, 715, 718, 719, 723, 724, 729, 730, 736, 737,
754, 758, 775, 786, 793, 794, 798, 805, 810-812, 816, 818,
826, 830, 852, 855, 861, 863, 865, 866, 869, 872, 873, 877,
885, 890, 892, 893, 895, 912, 917, 918, 922, 925, 926, 928,
929, 940, 946, 948, 952, 956, 958, 963, 964, 969, 972, 973,
976, 985, 986, 992, 1000, 1002, 1004, 1005, 1010, 1011, 1016,
1020, 1022, 1023, 1031, 1039, 1046, 1055, 1059, 1086, 1109,
1120, 1122, 1125, 1136, 1145, 1159, 1166, 1176, 1207, 1214,
1215, 1224, 1235, 1257, 1266, 1267, 1276, 1286, 1291, 1292,
1294, 1308, 1310, 1315, 1323, 1327, 1332, 1338, 1355, 1367,
1369, 1391, 1392, 1422, 1424, 1427, 1447, 1448, 1455, 1456,
1482, 1492, 1530, 1538, 1541, 1546, 1557, 1558, 1561, 1563,
1569, 1575, 1576, 1581, 1593, 1601, 1613, 1614, 1638, 1649,
1650, 1654, 1665, 1668, 1677, 1679, 1684, 1685, 1688, 1701,
1704, 1714, 1750, 1752, 1790, 1792, 1803, 1816, 1820, 1821,
1826, 1835, 1854, 1855, 1867, 1872, 1876, 1889, 1904, 1905,
1918, 1924, 1933, 1954, 1959, 1972, 1975, 1985, 2005, 2008,
2009, 2011, 2025, 2032, 2033, 2049, 2057, 2058, 2060, 2064,
2083, 2096, 2101, 2107, 2113, 2114, 2123, 2126, 2137, 2142,
2144, 2147, 2151, 2175, 2192, 2203, 2212, 2215, 2230, 2234,
2236, 2241, 2248, 2250, 2255, 2276, 2278-2282, 2294, 2295,
2332, 2334, 2336, 2340, 2375, 2389, 2408, 2410, 2424, 2432,
2485, 2509, 2526, 2545, 2550, 2570, 2572, 2575, 2596, 2606
2627, 2643, 2658, 2690, 2703, 2735, 2757, 2704, 2770, 2771.

LE GALLIENNE, Richard [Thomas]
546.

LEHMANN, Rosamund [Nina]
160, 328, 340, 519, 579, 645, 646, 743, 866, 904, 999, 1271,
1405, 1685, 1762, 1819, 1962, 1998, 2160, 2165, 2183.

LE QUEUX, William [Tufnell]
1007, 1078, 2259, 2390.

LESLIE, [John Randolph] Shane
832.

LESSING, Doris
302, 403, 441, 566, 649, 670, 685, 714, 744, 813, 870, 1409,
1449, 1938, 1939, 2070, 2144, 2268, 2291, 2304, 2339.

LEWIS, Alun
1681.

LEWIS, C[live] S[taples]
380, 477, 478, 681, 720, 800, 922, 953, 1115, 1220, 1338,
2489, 2647, 2773, 2777, 2829.

LEWIS, [Percy] Wyndham
71, 74, 165, 166, 205, 209, 228, 317, 322, 363, 436, 456,
467, 468, 495, 514, 547, 599, 600, 605, 633, 684, 737, 746,
748, 756, 767, 805, 811, 912, 918, 922, 926, 932, 1010, 1286,
1341, 1492, 1533, 2011, 2164, 2334, 2468, 2509.

LINDSAY, Jack
122, 516, 518, 703, 837, 1262, 1404, 1459, 1660, 1735, 1736,
1888, 2274, 2275, 2455.

LINKLATER, Eric [Robert Russell]
1245, 1696, 2406, 2540.

LOCKE, W[illiam] J[ohn]
1520, 1707, 2401.

LOWRY, [Clarence] Malcolm
119, 1939.

MACAULAY, Rose
152, 171, 265, 338, 492, 504, 530, 563, 583, 611, 643, 740,
843, 916, 926, 969, 985, 986, 993, 1033, 1159, 1184, 1266,
1290, 1345, 1360, 1381, 1601, 1707, 1734, 1788, 1819, 1926,
1927, 1991, 1998, 2276, 2411, 2447, 2481, 2536, 2550, 2593.

MCFEE, William
611.

MACHEN, Arthur
504, 906, 932, 1007, 1901.

MACINNES, Colin
640, 670, 1242, 1591, 1893, 2275, 2339.

MCKENNA, Stephen
1405, 2040, 2466.

MACKENZIE [Edward Montague] Compton
69, 144, 186, 234, 279, 306, 366, 401, 423, 437, 445, 474,
531, 563, 611, 626, 628, 635, 643, 832, 843, 904, 926, 929,
933, 969, 973, 985, 1046, 1208, 1223, 1294, 1478, 1538, 1546,
1601, 1685, 1715, 1716, 1762, 1911, 1946-1948, 1966, 1972,
1984, 1991, 2060, 2121, 2131, 2142, 2151, 2205, 2234, 2235,
2289, 2304, 2453, 2458, 2467, 2504, 2535, 2554.

"MACLAREN, Ian" [John Watson]
2259.

"MALET, L." [Mary St. Leger Kingsley]
2296.

MANKOWITZ, Wolf
640.

MANN, Mary E.
    1528.

MANNING, Frederic
    129, 2268, 2573.

MANNING, Olivia
    685, 743, 1420, 1819, 1977, 2070, 2271, 2445.

"MANSFIELD, Katherine" [Kathleen Mansfield Beauchamp]
    104, 152, 179, 225, 248, 265, 319, 338, 400, 423, 441, 446,
    466, 492, 519, 563, 583, 611, 637, 641, 653, 754, 806, 809,
    899, 956, 964, 1010, 1088, 1492, 1661, 1826, 1866, 2688.

MARSHALL, Archibald
    1290, 1418, 1567, 1707, 2550.

MARSHALL, [Claude Cunningham] Bruce
    703, 1133, 1137, 1841, 1973, 1974, 1988, 2054.

MASEFIELD, John
    736, 794, 826, 856, 906, 1053, 1404.

MASTERS, John
    429, 2345.

MAUGHAM, William Somerset
    69, 74, 103, 134, 141, 174, 176, 186, 228, 241, 287, 312,
    317, 441, 492, 556, 570, 611, 626, 637, 652, 684, 699, 790,
    797, 826, 912, 922, 923, 929, 956, 957, 967, 969, 973, 985,
    1027, 1035, 1046, 1048, 1109, 1111, 1150, 1176, 1325, 1363,
    1392, 1561, 1569, 1638, 1704, 1707, 1730, 1790, 1918, 1981,
    1983, 2142, 2179, 2230, 2278, 2281, 2282, 2465, 2510, 2520,
    2564.

MAXWELL, W[illiam] B[abbington]
    169, 949, 1483, 2097, 2131, 2235, 2447.

MENEN, Aubrey
    1519.

MERRICK, Leonard
    1478.

MEYNELL, Viola
    530, 1520, 2311.

MITCHISON, Naomi
    837, 1088, 1301, 1555, 1596, 1696, 1857, 1998, 2244, 2455,
    2539.

MONSARRAT, Nicholas [John Turney]
    1506, 1604.

MONTAGUE, C[harles] E[dward]
611, 856, 1007, 1463, 1483, 1975, 2010, 2131, 2280, 2312.

MOORE, George [Edward]
71, 104, 128, 212, 228, 249, 296, 317, 323, 332, 341, 433,
434, 436, 479, 480, 496, 511, 513, 545, 561, 562, 617, 618,
624, 632, 643, 699, 749, 840, 861, 884, 926, 940, 956, 969,
972, 1031, 1122, 1361, 1369, 1569, 1709, 2107, 2122, 2128,
2224, 2799.

MORDAUNT, Elinor
423, 530, 1473, 2062.

MORGAN, Charles [Langridge]
91, 242, 328, 505, 611, 638, 682, 683, 686, 729, 748, 824,
826, 899, 912, 973, 1150, 1236, 1304, 1322, 1402, 1405, 1429,
1461,1462, 1657, 1697, 1764, 2014-2017, 2197, 2457, 2510.

MORRISON, Arthur
184, 1417, 2205.

MORTIMER, Penelope [Ruth]
536, 1409.

MOSLEY, Nicholas
2021, 2360.

MOTTRAM, R[alph] H[ale]
129, 611, 690, 808, 843, 1007, 1145, 1403, 1404, 1462, 1545,
1849, 2465, 2552.

MUNRO, Hector Hugo "Saki"
1163.

MURDOCH, Iris
81, 88, 133, 192, 216, 302, 403, 404, 411, 444, 518, 536,
539, 552, 566, 645, 701, 725, 729, 744, 750, 776, 791, 807,
813, 841, 845, 870, 980, 985, 1106, 1108, 1116, 1168, 1203,
1204, 1216, 1233, 1242, 1328, 1343, 1397, 1466-1469, 1549-
1551, 1570, 1594, 1616, 1735, 1736, 1738, 1741, 1742, 1768,
1783, 1801, 1805, 1819, 1906, 1938, 1939, 2013, 2021, 2036,
2037, 2087, 2148, 2209, 2257, 2269, 2339, 2344, 2493, 2508,
2526, 2800, 2807, 2809.

MYERS, L[eopold] H[amilton]
351, 423, 429, 633, 781, 811, 921, 967, 1023, 1579, 1657,
2197.

NEWBY, P[ercy] H[oward]
302, 539, 623, 713, 1311, 1328, 1343, 1587, 1726, 1939, 1977,
2070, 2160, 2268, 2445.

NICHOLS, John Beverley
712, 2407.

O'BRIEN, Edna
216, 1409, 1434, 1469, 1840.

O'CONNOR, Philip
75.

OLDMEADOW, Ernest James
1436.

OLLIVANT, Alfred
260.

ONIONS, George Oliver
234, 392, 926, 1287, 1294, 1483, 1538, 1546, 1614, 1972, 2435.

OPPENHEIM, E[dward] Phillips
1171, 1362, 2401.

ORCZY, Baroness Emmuska
171.

ORWELL, George [Eric Blair]
96, 100, 124, 141, 148, 208, 240, 243, 257, 309, 311, 312,
408, 410, 430, 441, 463, 466, 471, 477, 486, 499, 502, 536,
539, 541, 580, 600, 611, 622, 623, 633, 639, 675, 676, 687,
691, 693, 703, 713, 732, 737, 745, 746, 757, 776, 780, 790,
830, 862, 893, 919, 922, 932, 949, 974, 984, 985, 996, 998,
1000, 1010, 1015, 1029, 1030, 1086, 1099, 1100, 1114, 1231,
1240, 1257, 1326, 1508, 1514, 1519, 1536, 1556, 1558-1560,
1591, 1593, 1633, 1676, 1713, 1725, 1785, 1837, 1845, 1918,
1958, 2011, 2053, 2100, 2101, 2135, 2160, 2207, 2211, 2214,
2308, 2309, 2336, 2351, 2353, 2368, 2389, 2400, 2426, 2451,
2471, 2472, 2489, 2514, 2541, 2642, 2646, 2781, 2791, 2806.

PARKER, [Horatio] Gilbert [George]
1441, 1532, 1707.

PHELPS, G.
1216.

PHILLPOTTS, Eden
260, 350, 511, 672, 749, 783, 855, 905, 1056, 1185, 1362,
1405, 1441, 1479, 1813, 2128, 2390.

POWELL, Anthony [Dymoke]
83, 131, 302, 362, 443, 539, 633, 685, 748, 764, 769, 796,
870, 897, 932, 939, 940, 980, 1220, 1242, 1311, 1449, 1591,
1616, 1735, 1762, 1938, 1939, 2070, 2164, 2257, 2263, 2269,
2271, 2291, 2343, 2448, 2580.

POWYS, J[ohn] C[owper]
103, 186, 247, 672, 834, 906, 912, 1023, 1403, 1821, 2165,
2559, 2594.

POWYS, T[heodore] F[rancis]
209, 340, 423, 585, 715, 746, 855, 1404, 1752, 1901, 2255, 2278, 2509, 2582.

PRIESTLEY, J[ohn] B[oynton]
102, 126, 174, 186, 241, 249, 312, 338, 340, 441, 611, 759-763, 826, 834, 926, 1046, 1153, 1156, 1300, 1402, 1546, 1591, 1653, 1681, 1962, 2038, 2150-2157, 2223, 2366, 2460, 2465, 2484, 2594.

PRYCE, Richard
1098.

PUGH, Edwin
184.

RAPHAEL, Frederic [Michael]
1288.

RAVEN, Simon [Arthur Noel]
1314.

RAYMOND, Ernest
808, 832, 1849, 2436, 2447.

REEVES, A.
530, 2311.

REID BANKS, Lynne
216, 1245.

RICHARDSON, Dorothy [Miller]
128, 142, 152, 248, 317, 338, 374, 392, 399, 431, 492, 507, 530, 571, 572, 611, 612, 635, 661, 664, 680, 704, 711, 712, 861, 905, 926, 927, 940, 964, 972, 981, 1004, 1033, 1088, 1159, 1209, 1285, 1294, 1317, 1344, 1381, 1391, 1392, 1492, 1533, 1656, 1661, 1678, 1684, 1775, 1778, 1838, 1839, 1854, 1975, 1998, 2032, 2105, 2145, 2200, 2213, 2215, 2280, 2289, 2311, 2314, 2318, 2481, 2543, 2546, 2688, 2709, 2716.

"RICHARDSON, Henry Handel" [Ethel Florence Lindsay Richardson]
2439, 2484.

RIDGE, William Pett
184, 1980.

ROBERTS, Morley
1716, 2296, 2520.

ROBERTSON E[ileen] Arnot
808

ROSSITER, A. P.
1762.

ROYDE-SMITH, Naomi [Gladys]
1271.

SACKVILLE-WEST, Victoria [Mary]
398, 559, 583, 637, 672, 733, 734, 833, 855, 999, 1182, 1262,
1734, 1975, 1998, 2255, 2481, 2547, 2594.

SADLEIR, Michael [Thomas Harvey]
2411, 2447, 2467.

SANSON, William
579, 638, 1450, 1961.

SAYERS, Dorothy L[eigh]
102, 341, 720, 808, 922, 985, 1047, 1762.

SEDWICK, Anne Douglas
106, 1635.

SEYMOUR, Beatrice Kean
2447.

SHANKS, Edward [Richard Buxton]
1262, 2286-2289.

SHARP, Margery
914, 2466.

SHERIFF, R[obert] C[edric]
1405, 1495, 1813.

SHIEL, M[atthew] P[hipps]
392, 2287.

SHUTE, Nevil [Nevil Shute Norway]
216, 2366, 2451, 2460.

SIDGWICK, Ethel
171, 530, 712, 1707, 1998, 2062, 2439.

SIEVEKING, Lance[lot de giberne]
1405.

SILLITOE, Alan
75, 216, 302, 343, 389, 403, 404, 473, 518, 536, 552, 640,
670, 725, 744, 748, 807, 837, 841, 870, 876, 894, 1067, 1106,
1116, 1216, 1242, 1340, 1453, 1551, 1594, 1616, 1621, 1737,
1738, 1742, 1840, 1938, 1939, 1989, 2013, 2067, 2070, 2087,
2274, 2275, 2291, 2300, 2301, 2339, 2343, 2352, 2353, 2389,
2448, 2526, 2724, 2800.

SINCLAIR, Andrew [Annandale]
2186.

SINCLAIR, May
69, 169, 175, 260, 338, 423, 492, 530, 563, 583, 612, 704,
964, 973, 985, 1033, 1088, 1159, 1337, 1344, 1345, 1369,
1381, 1472, 1483, 1533, 1601, 1901, 2023, 2062, 2082, 2097,
2128, 2144, 2311, 2399, 2447, 2536.

SITWELL, Edith
102, 265.

SITWELL, Osbert
657, 1184, 2305, 2465.

SMITH, Stevie [Florence Margaret]
1304.

SNAITH, J[ohn] C[ollis]
531, 637, 1361, 1520, 2023, 2097.

SNOW, C[harles] P[ercy]
81, 83, 131, 216, 239, 276, 302, 331, 362, 380, 403, 404,
441, 470, 516, 518, 539, 645, 648, 685, 714, 737, 748, 750,
777, 817, 870, 895, 924, 932, 939, 993, 1073, 1116, 1220,
1242, 1248, 1249, 1449, 1469, 1591, 1604, 1685, 1724, 1735,
1738, 1742, 1762, 1771, 1773, 1801, 1893, 1939, 1960, 2013,
2070, 2085, 2147, 2148, 2217, 2257, 2263, 2271, 2274, 2297,
2304, 2317-2320, 2343, 2360, 2361, 2424, 2468, 2475, 2510,
2548, 2580, 2586.

SPARK, Muriel [Sarah]
133, 276, 302, 359, 375, 551, 566, 609, 640, 670, 701, 750,
870, 1168, 1204, 1234, 1434, 1468, 1469, 1482, 1519, 1664,
1747, 1801, 1805, 1819, 1859, 1875, 1939, 1963, 2070, 2148,
2291, 2343, 2344, 2349, 2493, 2809.

SPRING, Howard
973.

STEEL, Flora Annie
1076.

STEEN, Marguerite
2465.

STERN, G[ladys] B[ertha]
144, 492, 583, 1420, 2487.

STEWART, Desmond
516, 518.

STEWART, Mary [Florence Elinor]
714.

STOCKLEY, C.
171.

STOREY, David
  302, 403, 536, 640, 670, 725, 776, 897, 1204, 1216, 1453,
  1550, 1553, 1737, 1816, 2087, 2291, 2651, 2724.

STREET, A[rthur] G[eorge]
  2255.

STRONG, L[eonard] A[lfred] G[eorge]
  392, 611, 657, 921, 1185, 2382.

STURGIS, H[oward] O[vering]
  1685.

SWINNERTON, Frank [Arthur]
  69, 106, 186, 234, 531, 611, 635, 643, 734, 905, 925-930,
  969, 973, 1095, 1128-1130, 1492, 1707, 1716, 1744, 1911,
  2034, 2121, 2151, 2286, 2392-2398, 2447, 2453, 2550.

TAYLOR, Elizabeth
  999, 2385.

THIRKELL, Angela [Margaret]
  999, 1420, 1962.

THOMPSON, Edward [John]
  429, 738, 879, 1076, 1331, 2345.

THURSTON, E[rnest] Temple
  169, 905, 1312, 1707, 1980, 2239.

TOLKIEN, J[ohn] R[onald] R[euel]
  380, 477, 800, 953, 1022, 1376, 1597, 2647, 2773, 2777, 2829.

TOMLINSON, H[enry] M[ajor]
  129, 338, 808, 1007, 1545, 2324, 2423, 2573.

TOYNBEE, [Theodore] Philip
  1042, 1047, 1450, 2367, 2428-2431.

"TRESSELL, Robert" [Robert Noonan]
  823, 837, 1340, 1500, 1777, 2205, 2244.

TUOHY, [John] Francis
  1616.

UPWARD, Edward [Falaise]
  593, 837, 1301, 1634, 2244, 2597.

VACHELL, Horace Annesley
  474, 626, 823, 1185, 1813, 2447.

WAIN, John [Barrington]
  92, 302, 362, 404, 441, 469, 516, 518, 536, 640, 649, 725,

744, 745, 748, 750, 796, 837, 841, 974, 985, 1105, 1106,
1140, 1177, 1183, 1204, 1220, 1232, 1233, 1242, 1311, 1328,
1333, 1342, 1366, 1397, 1399, 1419, 1467, 1534, 1548, 1549,
1551, 1594, 1616, 1645, 1726, 1741, 1742, 1762, 1783, 1801,
1806, 1840, 1875, 1893, 1906, 1914, 1938, 1950, 1989, 1996,
2058, 2067, 2087, 2118, 2132, 2183, 2257, 2264, 2291, 2304,
2318, 2327, 2335, 2337, 2339, 2348, 2349, 2462, 2474-2477,
2505, 2590, 2591, 2800.

WALLACE, Doreen
1405.

WALLACE, Edgar
684.

WALMSLEY, L.
1156, 1404.

WALPOLE, Hugh [Seymour]
106, 169, 234, 338, 340, 393, 423, 474, 479, 492, 531, 563,
611, 626, 637, 643, 712, 734, 740, 796, 808, 882, 884, 898,
904, 905, 964, 973, 982, 983, 985, 998, 999, 1007, 1112,
1127, 1129, 1130, 1150, 1153, 1185, 1287, 1290, 1337, 1345,
1369, 1402, 1403, 1479, 1484, 1538, 1546, 1601, 1602, 1614,
1689, 1707, 1715, 1748, 1813, 1890, 1967, 1968, 1991, 2060,
2121, 2180, 2205, 2246, 2289, 2362, 2407, 2436, 2453, 2463,
2465, 2481-2488, 2499, 2504, 2533, 2550.

WARD, Mrs. Humphrey
144, 306, 1361, 1528, 2130, 2296.

WARNER, Rex [Ernest]
328, 495, 593, 623, 633, 638, 645, 706, 748, 1086, 1301,
1450, 1579, 1634, 1676, 1755, 1958, 1961, 1970, 1981, 2011,
2108, 2130, 2160, 2367, 2428, 2644.

WARNER, Sylvia Townshend
585, 593, 684, 1271, 1363, 2539, 2582.

WATERHOUSE, Keith [Spencer]
302, 389, 403, 776, 841, 1067, 1594, 1621, 1737, 1875, 1939,
2238, 2327, 2651.

WAUGH, Alec [Alexander Raban]
340, 467, 474, 611, 626, 1185, 1601, 2281, 2407, 2498-2503.

WAUGH, Evelyn [Arthur St. John]
100, 103, 131, 152, 166, 174, 190, 205, 216, 220, 250, 289,
302, 309, 311, 312, 322, 340, 359, 362, 363, 375, 384, 398,
411, 418, 430, 435, 443, 452, 463, 466, 470, 495, 536, 539,
544, 549, 569(a), 579, 611, 623, 626, 627, 633, 640, 645,
646, 648, 670, 679, 713, 721, 726, 729, 748, 757, 781, 784,
796, 797, 801, 811, 817, 842, 864, 893, 899, 905, 912, 922,

932, 940, 947, 973, 976, 980, 993, 1005, 1022, 1024, 1070,
1073, 1075, 1077, 1116, 1124, 1132, 1176, 1182, 1222, 1224,
1227, 1231, 1249, 1251, 1262, 1286, 1323,1324, 1335, 1339,
1372, 1380, 1399, 1400, 1438, 1454, 1458, 1482, 1506, 1519,
1521, 1548, 1578, 1591, 1595, 1618, 1662, 1664, 1675,1698,
1773, 1785, 1808, 1828, 1875, 1903, 1918, 1951, 1962, 1970,
1973, 1981, 1988, 1992, 2048, 2054, 2084, 2130, 2164, 2165,
2173, 2175, 2180, 2183, 2227, 2257, 2274, 2293, 2325, 2343,
2344, 2370, 2378, 2428, 2429, 2438, 2489, 2491, 2510, 2625,
2640, 2644, 2646, 2763.

WEBB, Mary [Gladys]
559, 672, 2255.

WELLS, Herbert George
69, 90, 100, 101, 106, 107, 117, 121, 128, 132, 140, 148,
149, 172, 183, 186, 193, 200, 211, 221, 222, 224, 225, 228,
241, 243, 244, 247, 249, 252, 273, 274, 278, 279, 296, 303,
308, 310, 312, 317, 318, 320, 322-324, 332, 336, 338, 339,
350, 355, 365, 372, 389, 393, 398, 400, 410-412, 416, 418,
423, 436, 437, 441, 454, 466, 468, 474, 479, 510, 511, 528,
534, 541, 545, 555, 556, 562, 563, 570, 574, 576, 608, 609,
612, 616, 620, 623, 626, 628, 631, 632, 643, 645, 652, 653,
658, 676, 687, 704, 715, 730, 737, 740, 742, 751, 774, 791,
796, 803, 811, 812, 821, 825, 826, 830, 831, 840, 856, 860,
861, 871-873, 882, 884, 895, 898, 900, 912, 922, 926, 929,
956, 957, 969, 972, 973, 985, 986, 998, 1007, 1008, 1010,
1016, 1018, 1021, 1022, 1026, 1028, 1029, 1031, 1039, 1040,
1053, 1056, 1078, 1111, 1112, 1121, 1145, 1150, 1158, 1163,
1167, 1176, 1182, 1185, 1211, 1221, 1229, 1237, 1260, 1264,
1272, 1285, 1287, 1312, 1313, 1321, 1334, 1346, 1347, 1361,
1369, 1385, 1399, 1403, 1418, 1441, 1442, 1471, 1472, 1474,
1478, 1483, 1491, 1500, 1514, 1528, 1532, 1536-1539, 1601,
1602, 1611, 1615, 1619, 1672, 1736, 1744, 1785, 1788, 1790,
1798, 1825, 1845, 1856, 1861, 1874, 1879, 1882, 1884, 1905,
1918, 1958, 1967, 1972, 2004, 2025, 2033, 2042, 2052, 2057,
2082, 2102, 2120, 2121, 2128, 2131, 2150, 2194, 2195, 2198,
2205, 2212, 2234, 2246, 2250, 2278-2280, 2282, 2287, 2289,
2295, 2308, 2314, 2326, 2364, 2387, 2390, 2398, 2399, 2401,
2426, 2440, 2448, 2478, 2488, 2504, 2518, 2519, 2525, 2535,
2564, 2577, 2585, 2622.

WEST, Anthony
556, 1662.

"WEST, Rebecca" [Cicily Isobel Fairfield]
70, 169, 248, 423, 492, 704, 734, 791, 964, 1003-1005, 1007,
1159, 1291, 1304, 1346, 1381, 1448, 1539, 1601, 1901, 2197,
2269, 2286, 2411, 2466, 2525.

WEYMAN, Stanley [John]
1567.

WHITE, Patrick [Victor Martindale]
670.

WHITE, T[erence] H[anbury]
999.

WHITEING, Richard
184, 823, 1111, 1171, 1417, 2390.

WHYTE-MELVILLE, G. W.
2515.

WILLIAMS, Charles [Walter Stansby]
276, 359, 380, 478, 504, 681, 800, 865, 906, 953, 1220, 1454,
2647, 2773, 2777, 2829.

WILLIAMS, Raymond [Henry]
518, 837, 1116, 1340, 1453, 1737, 2724.

WILLIAMSON, Henry
1007, 1023, 1073, 1116.

WILSON, Angus [Frank Johnstone]
83, 131, 267, 268, 302, 362, 404, 405, 441, 539, 549, 639,
640, 645, 729, 745, 748, 750, 776, 777, 791, 811, 842, 870,
897, 922, 939, 980, 985, 1019, 1116, 1177, 1203, 1204, 1242,
1248, 1301, 1328, 1365, 1420, 1519, 1548-1551, 1591, 1616,
1662, 1738, 1768, 1780, 1827, 1859, 1938, 2209, 2270, 2291,
2304, 2339, 2361, 2400, 2443, 2445, 2543, 2548, 2554-2562,
2580, 2586, 2680, 2800.

WILSON, Colin [Henry]
75, 88, 403, 411, 425, 579, 649, 744, 1105, 1106, 1342, 1397,
1586, 1736, 1741, 1906, 1950, 2011, 2018, 2118, 2132, 2350,
2352, 2443, 2505, 2526, 2563.

WILSON, [Florence] Romer
1088, 1533, 2481.

WODEHOUSE, P[elham] G[renville]
340, 732, 926.

WOODHAM-SMITH, Cecil
174.

WOOLF, Virginia
71, 73, 76, 81, 82, 89, 91, 95-97, 103, 114, 119, 125, 134,
137, 139, 142, 143, 148, 151, 152, 155, 160, 165, 166, 176,
179, 190, 191, 194, 200, 207, 209, 225, 226, 228, 229, 231,
232, 236, 242, 245, 247-249, 256, 263-266, 268, 273, 279,
281, 290, 295, 304, 305, 312, 317, 322, 330, 338, 340, 343,
346, 347, 351, 357, 363, 374, 376, 378, 399-401, 405, 434,
441, 446, 448, 452, 453, 466, 468-470, 472, 475, 480, 492,

505, 507, 511, 512, 514, 519, 530, 533, 538, 555, 559, 563,
570, 572, 574, 577, 580, 583, 585, 594, 598, 599, 602, 605,
607, 610-612, 623, 633, 638, 645, 646, 653, 655, 656, 661,
664, 665, 667, 668, 671, 678, 686, 693, 694, 699, 706, 710-
712, 724, 726, 729, 745, 747, 754, 758, 763, 778, 785, 794,
805, 806, 809, 812, 816, 824, 826, 829, 838, 844, 852, 858,
861, 865, 877, 891, 895, 899, 904, 908, 912, 922, 923, 925-
927, 940, 941, 946, 948, 956, 961-964, 969, 972, 973, 975,
981, 985, 988, 992, 1000, 1005, 1010, 1029, 1031, 1033, 1039,
1094, 1101, 1137, 1145, 1147, 1151, 1158, 1162, 1174, 1179,
1213, 1224, 1257, 1279, 1282, 1286, 1297, 1308, 1310, 1317,
1327, 1346-1350, 1352, 1355, 1363, 1381, 1391, 1392, 1406,
1422, 1426, 1427, 1448, 1456, 1503, 1511, 1530, 1533, 1541,
1546, 1565, 1571, 1575, 1579, 1581, 1590, 1605, 1637, 1640,
1644, 1646, 1650, 1654, 1661, 1696, 1704, 1714, 1716, 1724,
1728, 1736, 1749, 1752, 1767, 1772, 1775, 1781, 1789, 1793,
1797, 1803, 1820, 1825, 1826, 1833, 1838, 1839, 1842, 1876,
1877, 1889, 1901, 1904, 1907, 1923, 1924, 1929, 1932, 1960,
1975, 1982, 1993, 1994, 1998, 2007, 2008, 2011, 2028, 2031-
2033, 2038, 2047, 2060, 2063, 2094, 2098, 2108, 2113, 2117,
2145, 2147, 2175, 2179, 2200, 2240, 2250, 2253, 2272, 2273,
2276, 2277, 2280, 2289, 2292, 2309, 2314, 2318, 2334, 2340,
2346, 2357, 2359, 2364, 2416, 2431, 2437, 2473, 2481, 2485,
2509, 2543, 2546, 2548, 2559, 2561, 2566, 2577, 2578, 2663,
2688, 2726, 2762, 2770, 2821.

WREN, P[ercival] C[hristopher]
339, 2515.

"WYNDHAM, John" [John Benyon Harris]
640, 1845.

YEATS-BROWN, F[rancis] C[harles]
1428.

YOUNG, Francis Brett
144, 186, 611, 672, 1150, 1650, 1716, 2453.

Index (2)

Selected Topics and Themes

INDEX

(2) Selected Topics and Themes

f. "Erlebte Rede"
   245, 664, 711, 908, 1310, 1788.

g. Experiment and Innovation
   26, 51, 73, 85, 86, 128, 262, 322, 377, 777, 896, 942,
   977, 1113, 1212, 1234, 1315, 1319, 1450, 1505, 1669,
   1704, 1772, 1889, 1960, 1975, 2204, 2339, 2382, 2449,
   2456, 2516, 2793.

h. Interior Monologue
   245, 307, 883, 1170, 1364, 2331, 2383, 2543, 2765, 2788.

i. Irony
   15, 309, 1328, 2581.

j. Narrative and Story
   123, 127, 139, 146, 231, 261, 313, 356, 363, 422, 433,
   447, 451, 476, 546, 683, 815, 845, 848, 849, 883, 903,
   907, 914, 937, 938, 1040, 1060, 1123, 1151, 1154, 1191,
   1199, 1202, 1205, 1283, 1376, 1389, 1421, 1461, 1501,
   1631, 1733, 1746, 1860, 1866, 1872, 2096, 2157, 2241,
   2370, 2371, 2454, 2641, 2645, 2718, 2772.

k. Narrators and Storytellers
   15, 226, 260, 301, 415, 683, 863, 937, 1019, 1143, 1148,
   1376, 1446, 1504, 1574, 1670, 1691-1694, 1920, 1951, 1983,
   2010, 2014, 2193, 2317, 2568, 2592, 2605, 2810.

l. Plot and Structure
   105, 153, 210, 298, 313, 356, 371, 415, 490, 602, 695,
   728, 802, 891, 1087, 1217, 1296, 1351, 1509, 1530, 1575,
   1954, 2095, 2096, 2204, 2216, 2354, 2401, 2500, 2671,
   2691, 2692, 2816.

m. Point-of-View
   301, 368, 447, 936, 1190, 1510, 1733, 1761, 2019, 2404,
   2413, 2512, 2612, 2721.

n. Prose Style
   12, 255, 337, 448, 455, 608, 609, 625, 659, 751, 798,
   802, 1129, 1130, 1249, 1250, 1351, 1377, 1490, 1613, 1637,
   1898, 1899, 1916, 2037, 2252, 2542, 2678, 2680, 2705.

o. Rhythm
   194, 356, 2745.

p. Setting
   367, 387, 536, 559, 602, 997, 1174, 1175, 1874, 2210,
   2522, 2660.

q. Stream-of-Consciousness
   94, 163, 231, 340, 374, 507, 515, 572, 1173, 1209, 1349,
   1540, 1640, 1652, 1661, 1720, 1761, 1838, 1839, 1868,
   2004, 2145, 2359, 2381, 2618, 2742, 2805. (See also 27.)

2648, 2706. (See also 9.)

16. THE LITERARY SCENE
    a. Pre-World War I
       352, 489, 596, 929, 1442, 1526, 2453, 2496.

    b. Post-World War I
       334, 489, 696, 926, 1391, 2441.

    c. The Twenties
       334, 484, 489, 529, 694, 696, 926, 1425, 2026, 2441,
       2509.

    d. The Thirties
       242, 254, 334, 484, 489, 529, 696, 926, 1588, 1619,
       1883, 2509, 2549.

    e. The Forties
       242, 272, 489, 600, 1024, 1102, 1587, 1654, 1864, 1944,
       1953, 1976, 1977, 2429.

    f. The Fifties
       489, 600, 1374, 1547, 1588, 1864, 2549.

    g. The Sixties
       1204, 1468, 1469, 1739, 2415, 2475.

17. MODERN AND MODERNISM
       251, 272, 325, 361, 501, 517, 551, 609, 725, 895, 1292,
       1678, 1679, 1714, 1789, 1876, 1895, 2292, 2334, 2434,
       2702.

18. THE MORAL ISSUE
    a. Censorship
       270, 271.

    b. Conscience
       329, 1723.

    c. Evil
       1365, 1556, 2177, 2387, 2559, 2627.

    d. Love
       109, 692, 976, 1071, 1835, 1908, 2194, 2281.

    e. Morality
       383, 411, 433, 497, 532, 654, 825, 1055, 1139, 1249,
       1260, 1369, 1557, 1603, 1705, 1731, 1855, 1985, 2039,
       2057, 2107, 2113, 2192, 2279, 2432, 2550, 2735.

f. Obscenity and Pornography
   1210, 1338, 1382, 1383, 1878, 1942, 2294, 2572.

g. Sex
   123, 211, 289, 303, 358, 411, 532, 617, 872, 1120, 1166,
   1211, 1259, 1265, 1266, 1314, 1345, 1412, 1447, 1456,
   1482, 1563, 1638, 1708, 1757, 1821, 1936, 1959, 2126,
   2182, 2295, 2447.

h. Violence
   1163, 2301, 2352.

19. MYTH AND MYTHOLOGY
    93, 325, 378, 413, 669, 681, 779, 963, 1009, 1247, 1550,
    1869, 1995, 2096, 2188, 2538, 2775, 2829.

20. THE NOVEL: STUDIES AND SURVEYS
    a. Pre-World War I
       94, 107, 117, 234, 277, 324, 372, 510, 512, 553, 575,
       611, 650, 749, 789, 811, 826, 929, 1013, 1028, 1163,
       1291, 1415, 1416, 1436, 1442, 1611, 1732, 2003, 2023,
       2104, 2146, 2181, 2321, 2323, 2377, 2440, 2496, 2497,
       2519, 2577, 2729, 2828.

    b. Inter-War Years
       69, 76, 84, 94, 95, 123, 136, 152, 166, 202, 209, 229,
       322, 334, 338, 340, 363, 416, 423, 517, 524, 575, 593,
       606, 611, 633, 638, 668, 726, 811, 826, 832, 880, 926,
       931, 986, 992, 1034, 1039, 1054, 1071, 1082, 1085, 1107,
       1150, 1152, 1186, 1198, 1286, 1301, 1308, 1327, 1363,
       1401-1407, 1427, 1448, 1459, 1492, 1533, 1546, 1566,
       1649, 1650, 1656-1660, 1749, 1753, 1777, 1882, 1911,
       1929, 1957, 1967, 1968, 1970, 2060, 2136, 2137, 2151,
       2152, 2215, 2237, 2250, 2260, 2278-2282, 2308, 2394,
       2395, 2405, 2411, 2445, 2464, 2465, 2478, 2484, 2485,
       2490, 2494, 2499, 2504, 2507, 2536, 2547, 2554, 2577,
       2583, 2636, 2638, 2729, 2780.

    c. Post-World War II
       6, 76, 84, 88, 131, 158, 167, 203, 204, 216, 302, 403,
       464, 516, 517, 539, 575, 579, 592, 606, 611, 638, 713,
       725, 748, 750, 757, 787, 795, 807, 813, 1034, 1037,
       1042, 1073, 1108, 1116, 1218, 1220, 1226,1229, 1242,
       1311, 1429, 1450, 1452, 1517, 1544, 1549, 1551, 1573,
       1588, 1589, 1591, 1662, 1703, 1735, 1736, 1740, 1742,
       1754, 1780, 1789, 1792, 1827, 1863, 1893, 1894, 1906,
       1909, 1938-1940, 1950, 2013, 2148, 2155, 2162, 2165,
       2183, 2185, 2186, 2227, 2257, 2262-2271, 2291, 2297,
       2302, 2304, 2339, 2343, 2344, 2348, 2349, 2361, 2366,
       2367, 2376, 2385, 2446, 2476, 2477, 2492, 2493, 2558,
       2560, 2590, 2637, 2747.

21. THE NOVEL: A LITERARY CLASSIFICATION
    a. Bildungsroman
       99, 973, 1392, 1790, 2757. (See also 22.a.)

b. Existentialism
   92, 373, 403, 466, 517, 701, 829, 1021, 1335.

c. Humanism
   268, 333, 413, 590, 831, 1110, 2025.

d. Nature and Naturism
   693, 1933, 2144, 2230, 2596, 2643.

e. Nihilism
   1982, 2139.

f. Pessimism and Despair
   425, 893, 1477, 1702, 2035.

g. Philosophy and Fiction
   172, 233, 391, 598, 816, 822, 1023, 1322, 1561, 1741,
   1836, 1887, 2082, 2083, 2129, 2278, 2813.

25. POETS AND POETRY
    657, 658, 850, 881, 890, 1000, 1298, 1946, 1997, 2083,
    2111, 2140, 2232, 2373.

26. POLITICAL AND SOCIAL IDEOLOGIES
    a. Politics
       141, 208, 222, 456, 495, 499, 600, 737, 919, 1030, 1116,
       1256, 1417, 1623, 1710, 1711, 1822, 1958, 2046, 2053,
       2158, 2320, 2340, 2351, 2400, 2597, 2754, 2801.

    b. Socialism and Communism
       221, 517, 837, 1029, 1301, 1560, 1742, 1905, 1915, 1978,
       2093, 2244, 2274, 2275, 2307.

27. PSYCHOLOGY
    a. Consciousness   —
       245, 281, 335, 338, 537, 2041, 2722.

    b. Doppelganger
       99, 814.

    c. Freudianism
       335, 481, 514, 1117, 1136, 1173, 1388, 1456, 2236, 2690.

    d. Personality
       109, 535, 646, 860.

    e. Psychoanalysis
       94, 245, 492, 619, 814, 1157, 1159, 1421, 1568, 1778,
       1956, 2078, 2779.

    f. Psychology: Studies and Influences
       14, 248, 303, 315, 374, 399, 413, 492, 535, 556, 563, 571,
       580, 595, 887, 1097, 1271, 1345, 1346, 1456, 1609, 1628,
       1629, 1704, 2282, 2346, 2762.

g. The Self
112, 372, 388, 408, 419, 452, 758, 850, 1004, 1182,
1455, 1688, 2508, 2698. (See also 5.f., 5.h., and 5.g.)

28. READERS AND THE ART OF READING
81, 176, 177, 191, 227, 286, 313, 396, 421, 446, 472,
576, 589, 595, 597, 730, 863, 1142, 1169, 1178, 1592,
1622, 1704, 1745, 1860, 1867, 1871, 1873, 1930, 1956,
2044, 2045, 2259, 2272, 2402.

29. REALISM AND REALITY
184, 325, 415, 432, 447, 459, 466, 517, 562, 614, 650,
704, 717, 749, 931, 1111, 1160, 1317, 1451, 1576, 1614,
1644, 1700, 1740, 1744, 1786, 1829, 1900, 1904, 1910,
1931, 1984, 1990, 2085, 2088, 2089, 2112, 2113, 2127,
2200, 2218, 2222, 2243, 2289, 2318, 2466, 2477, 2504,
2535, 2548, 2628, 2667, 2684.

30. RELIGION
a. Catholic Novel
16, 173, 220, 375, 445, 544, 609, 663, 721, 875, 933,
1050, 1051, 1090, 1104, 1121, 1124, 1208, 1221-1223,
1227, 1239, 1323, 1324, 1380, 1400, 1458, 1463, 1581,
1664, 1675, 1747, 1749, 1830, 1832, 1912, 1913, 1966,
1973, 1988, 1992, 2048, 2054, 2090, 2130, 2293, 2325,
2378, 2709, 2725, 2734, 2763.

b. Christ Figures
688, 1041, 1464.

c. Christianity
359, 425, 673, 948, 1055, 1276, 1519.

d. Churches and the Ministry
287, 306, 916, 1463, 2686.

e. Faith and Salvation
,325, 435, 466, 857, 948, 1454, 2379.

f. God
409, 693, 859, 1335, 1394, 1562, 1563, 1922, 2064, 2203,
2776.

g. Religious Revival
19, 30, 89, 224, 287, 380, 407, 534, 674, 679, 736, 800,
832, 882, 953, 1018, 1112, 1132, 1251, 1471, 1653, 1785,
1828, 1852, 1922, 2005, 2084, 2278, 2438, 2635, 2644,
2647, 2719, 2818.

h. Theology
100, 558, 750, 801, 858, 1119, 1623. (See also 23.i.)

31. THE RURAL SCENE
398, 885, 1156, 1300, 1814, 1815, 2255, 2313, 2675, 2685.